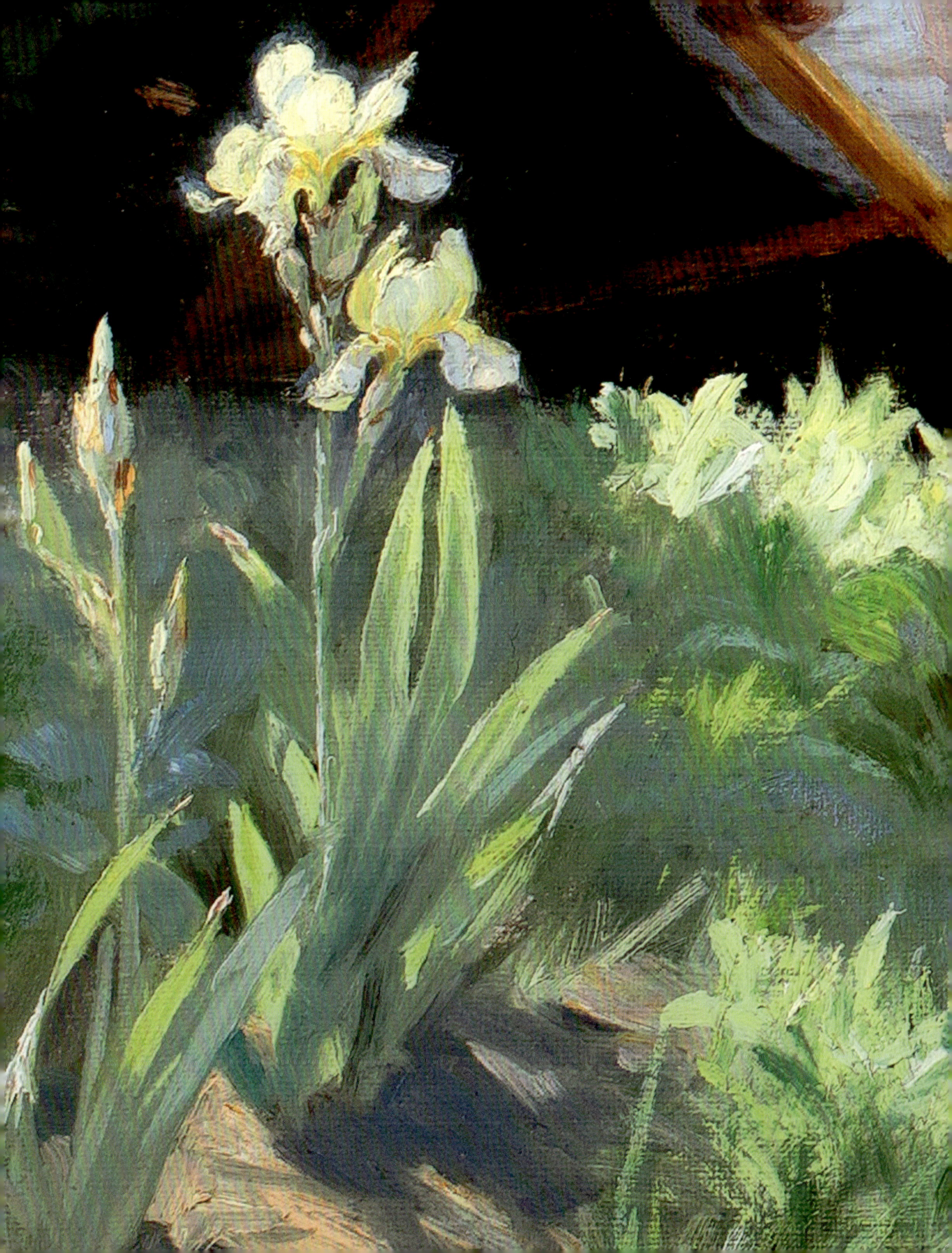

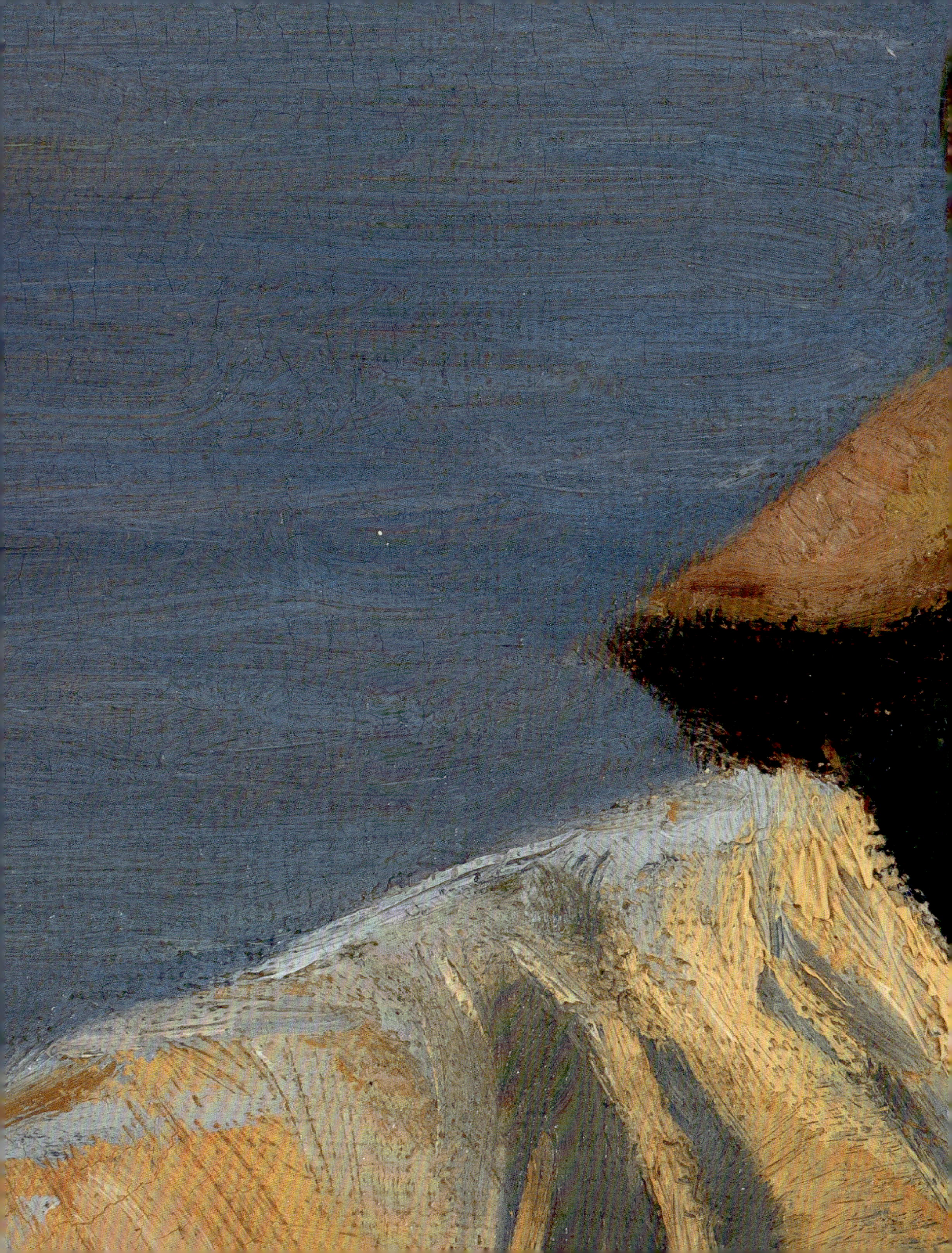

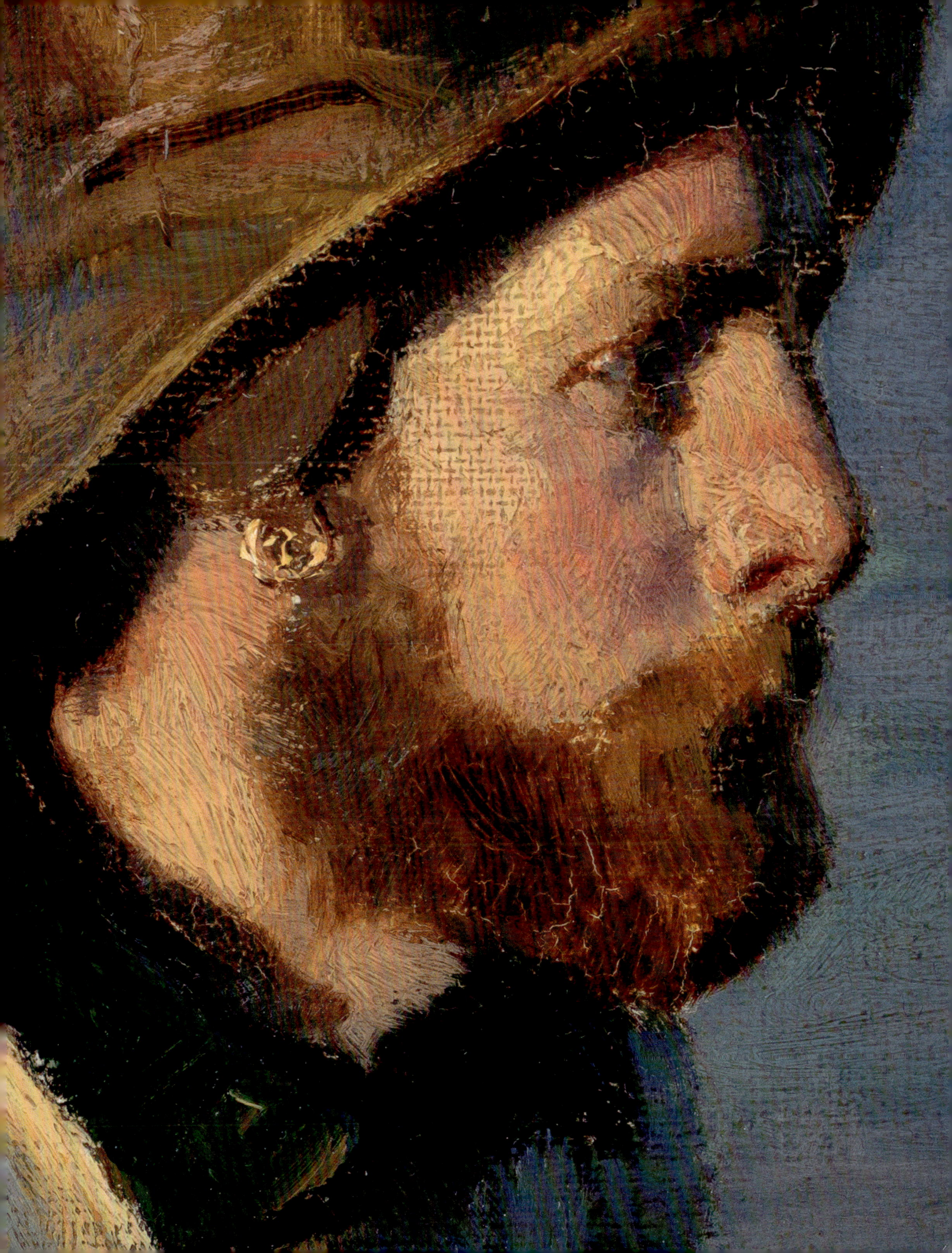

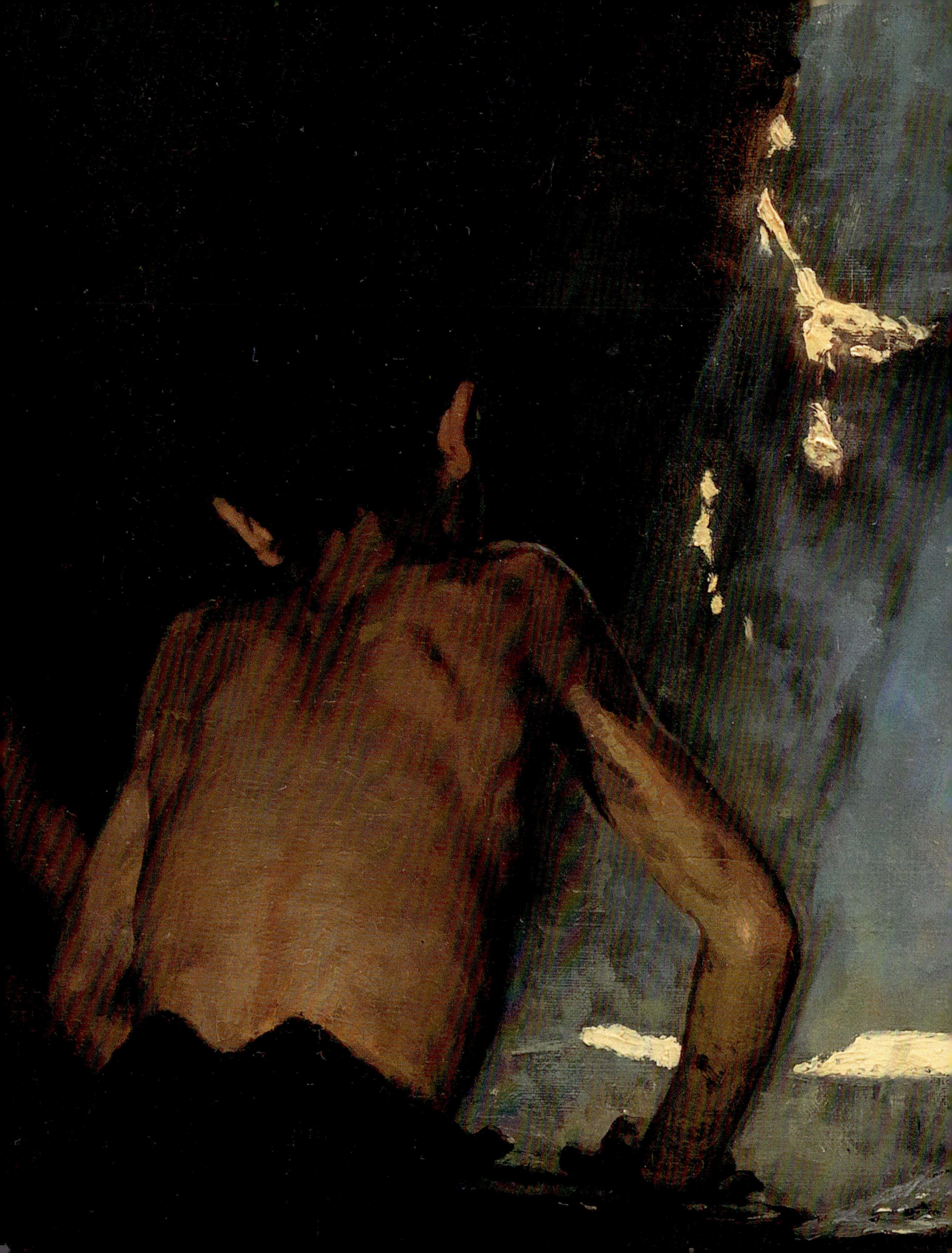

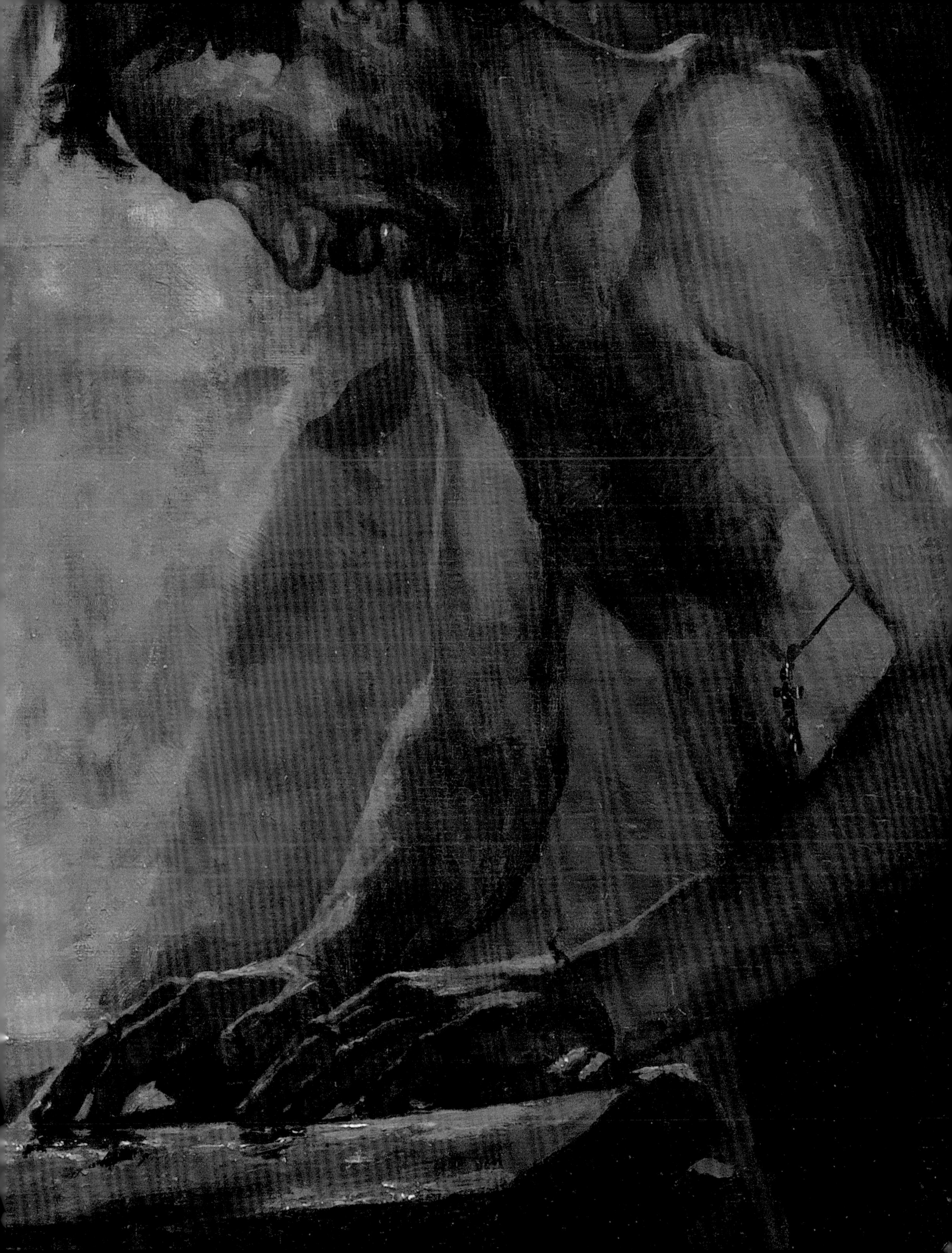

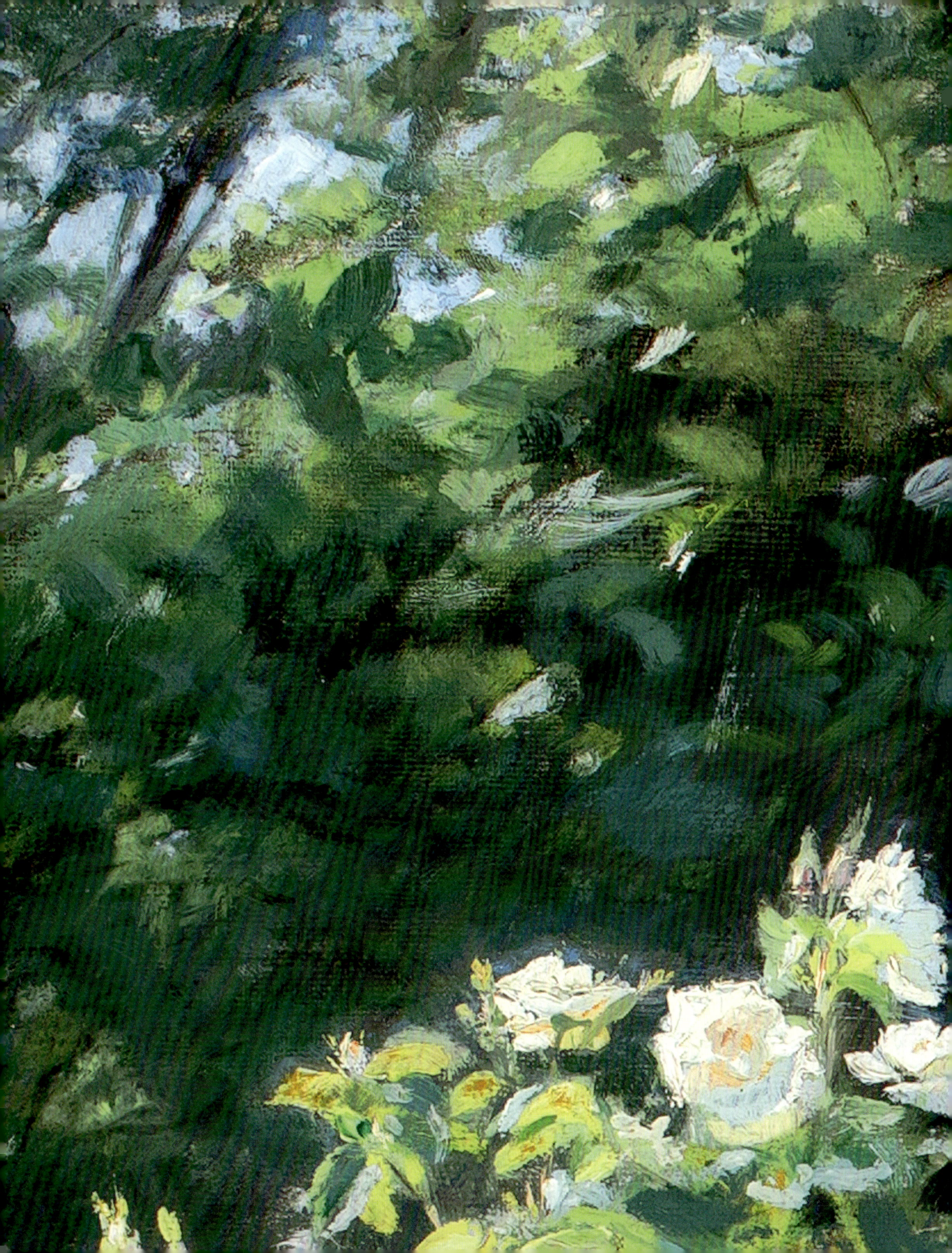

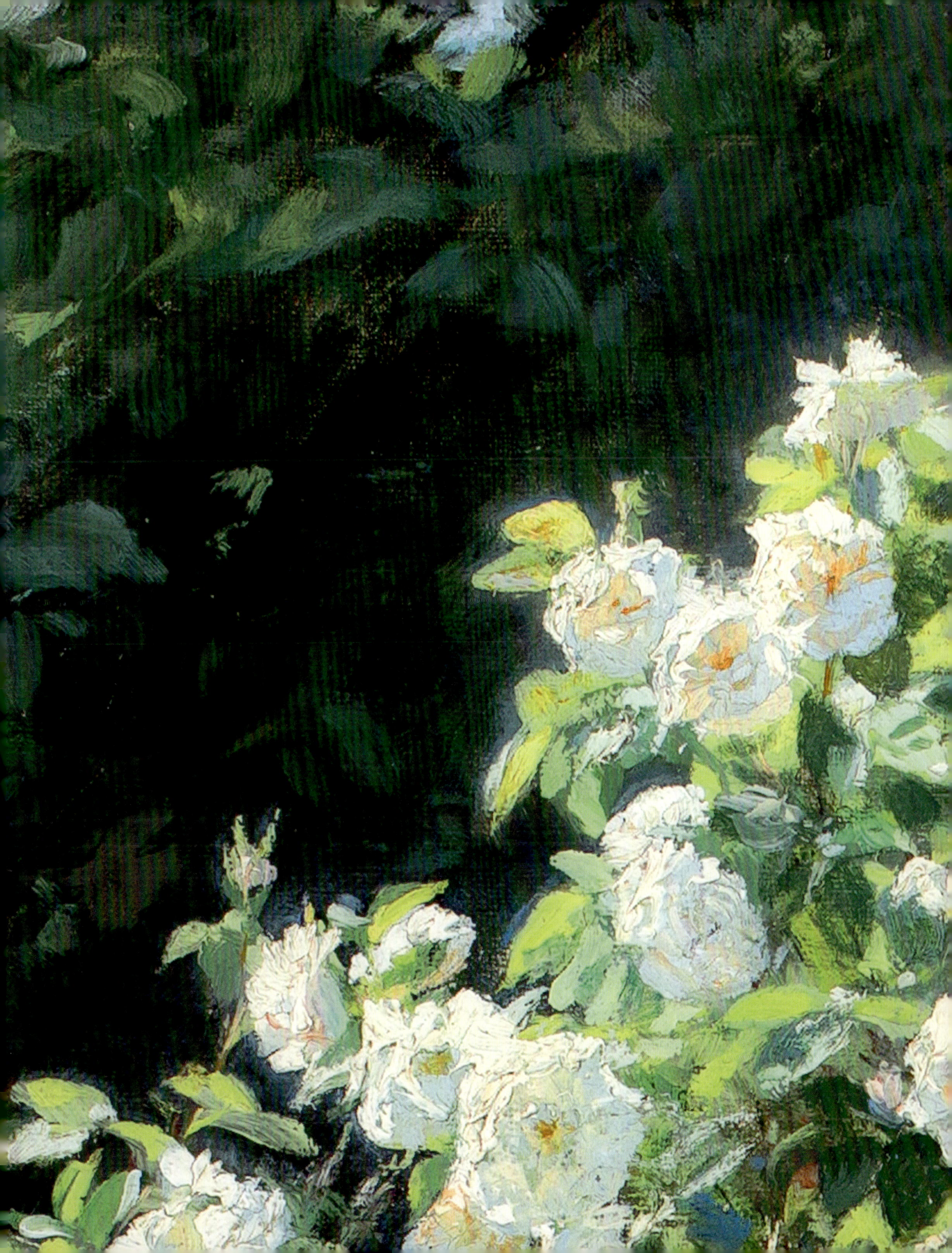

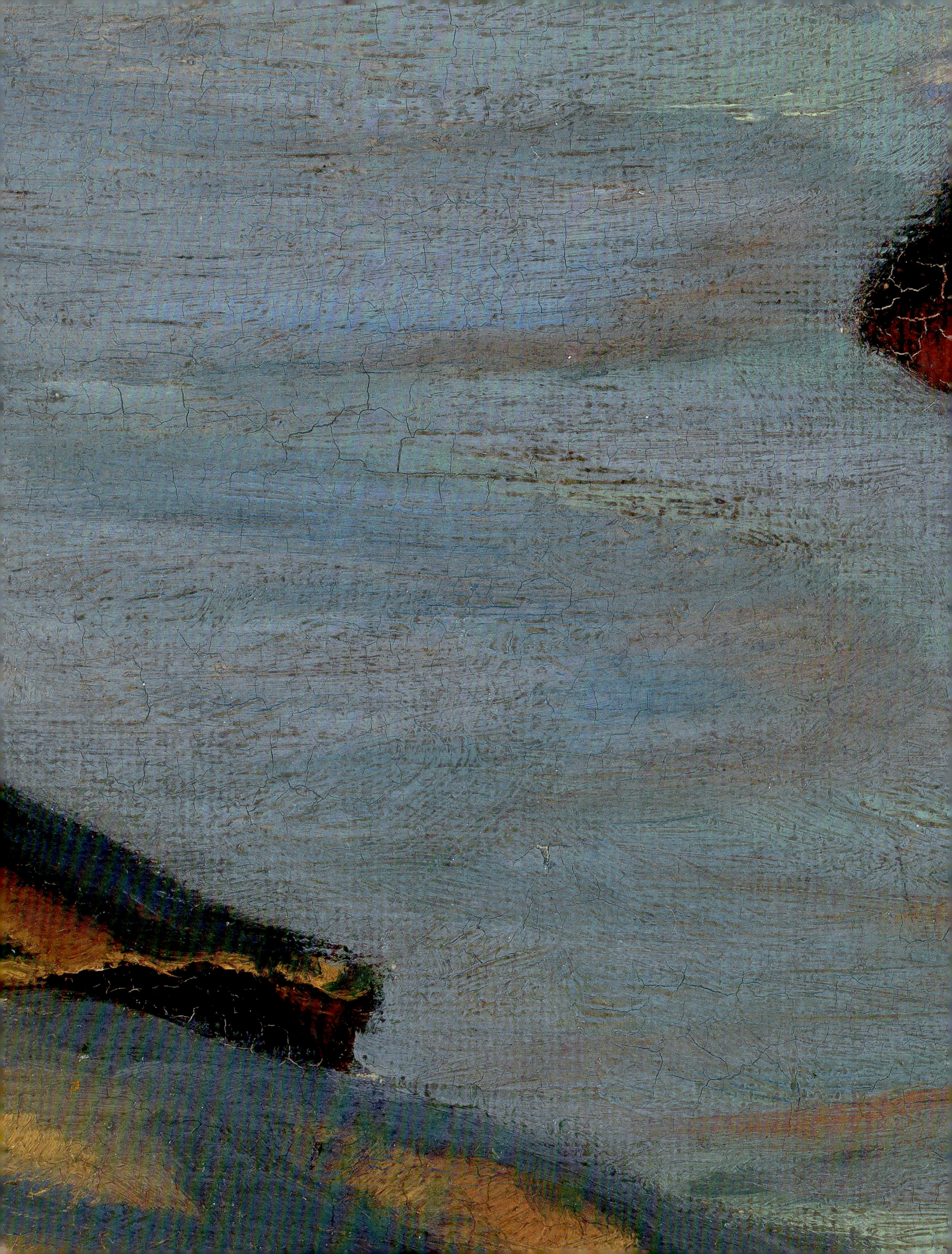

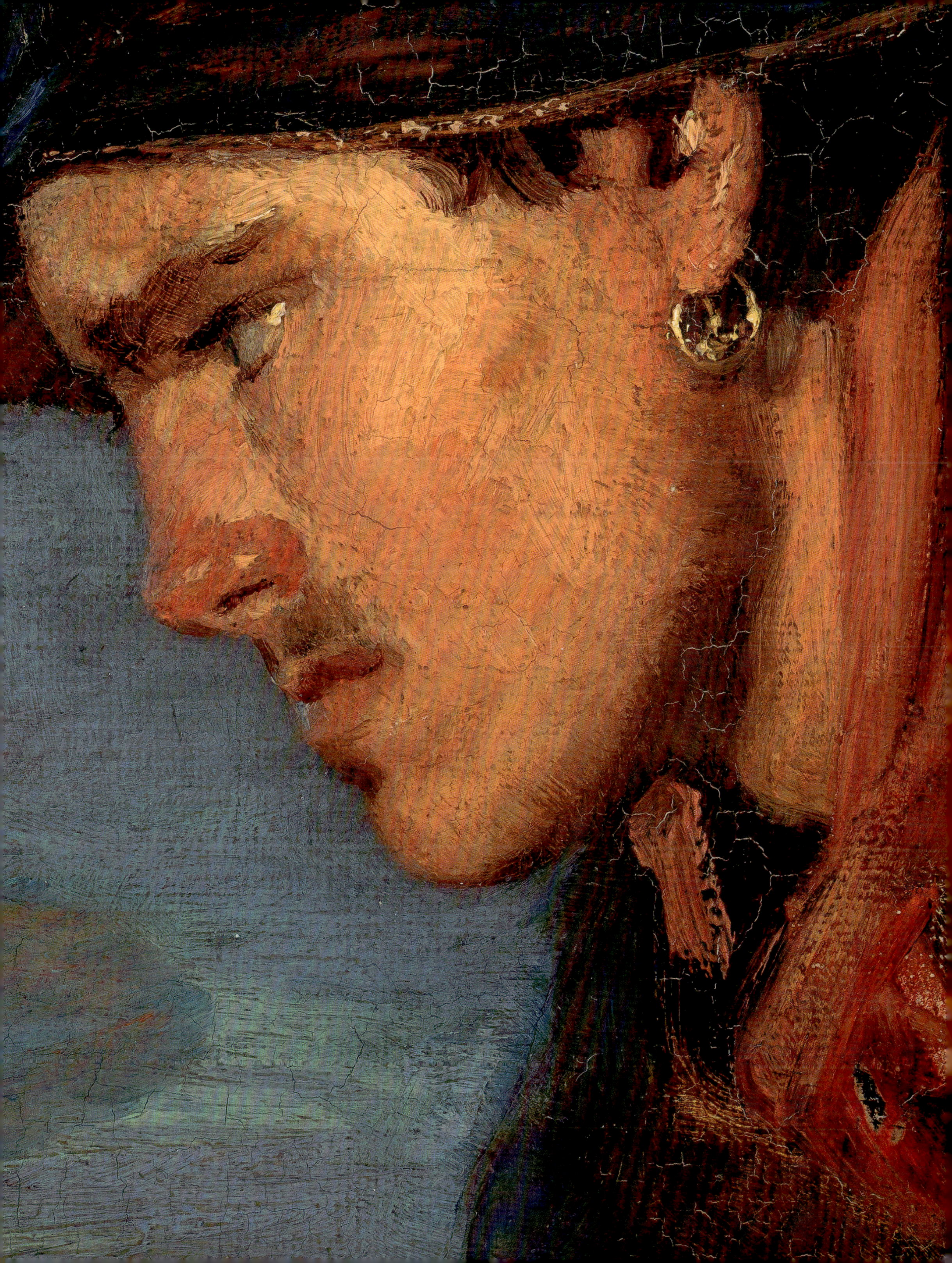

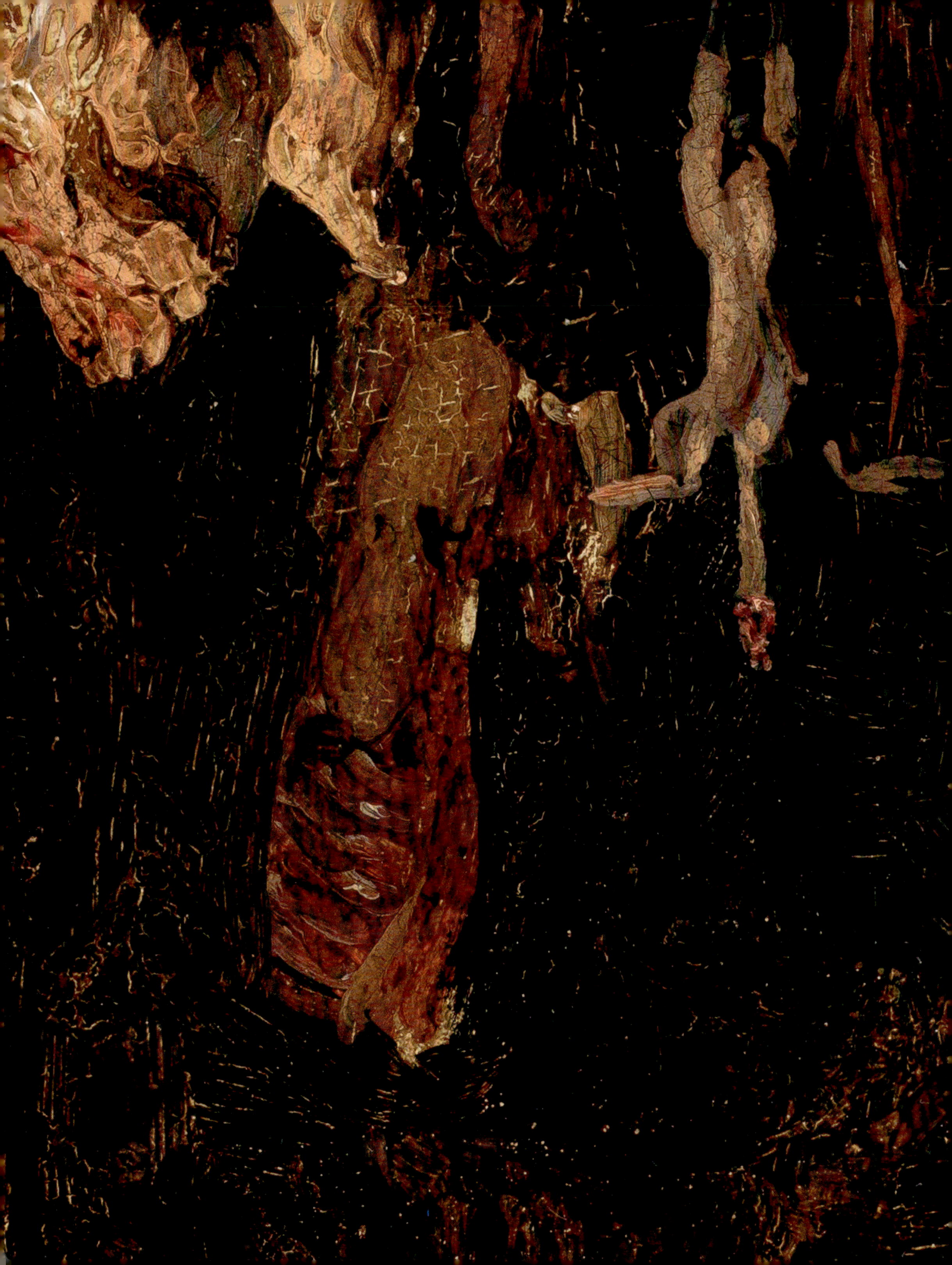

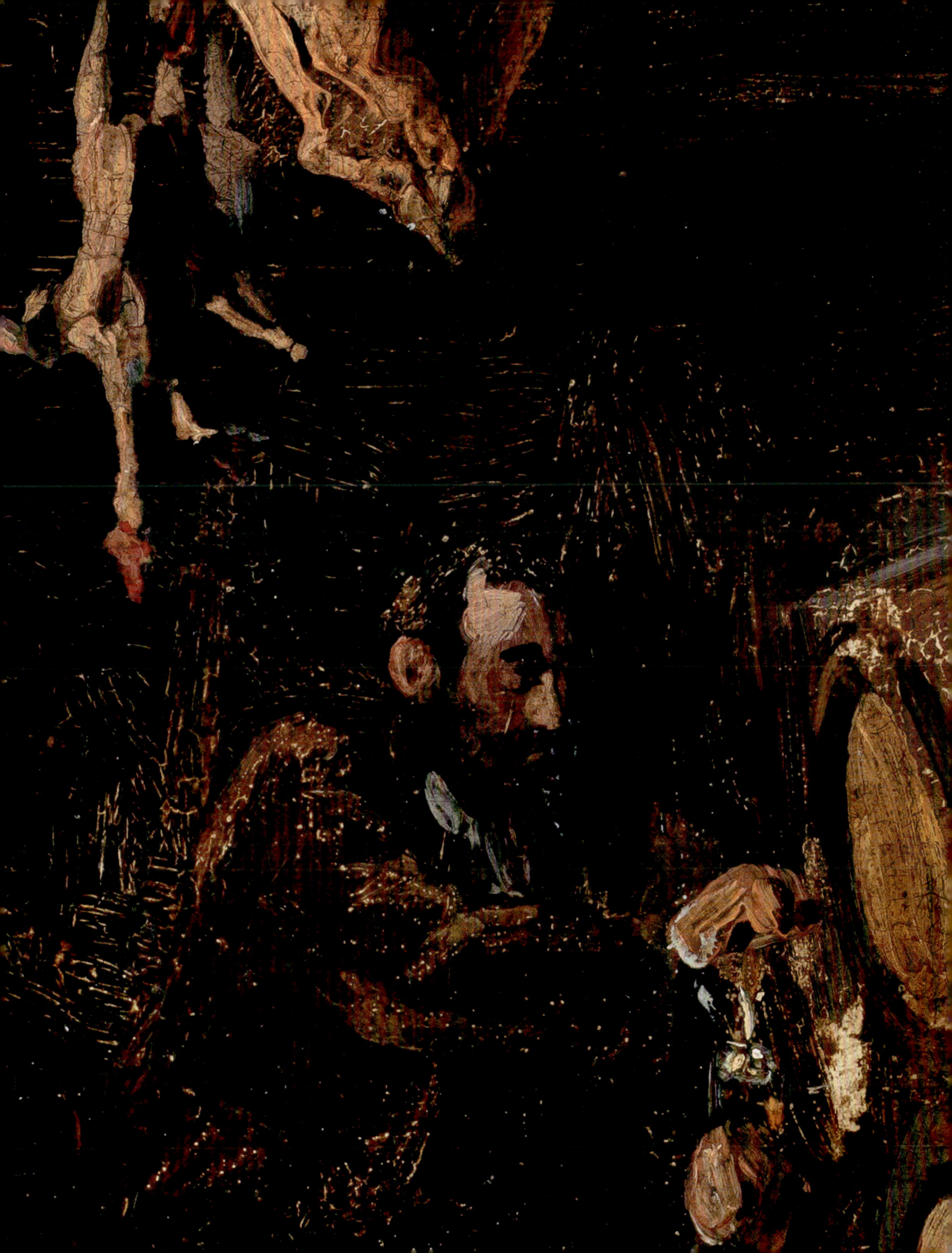

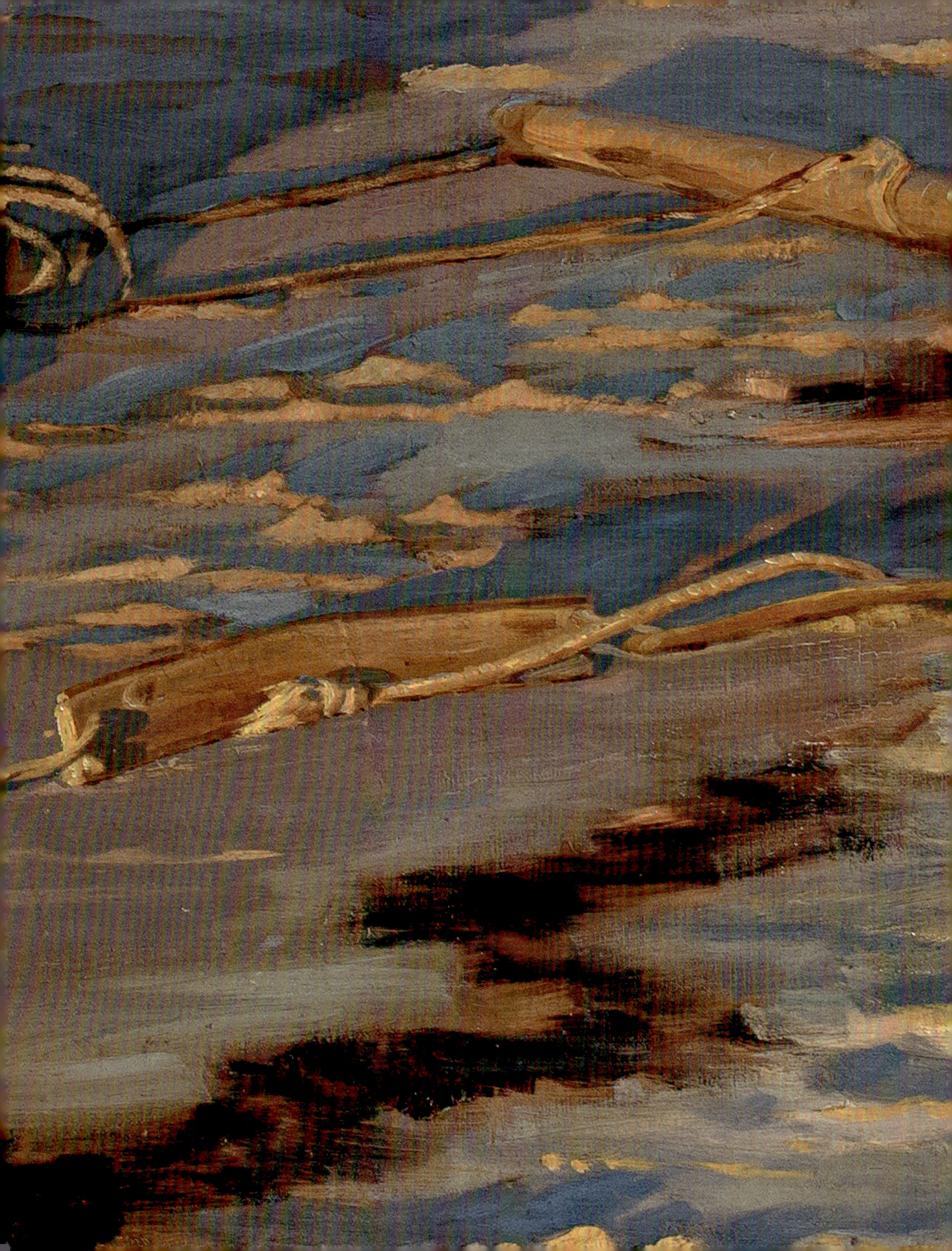

KRØYER and PARIS

French Connections and Nordic Colours

PEDER SEVERIN KRØYER had a wide outlook. While his roots were in Denmark, a little country far to the north of Europe, he travelled extensively throughout his life to gather inspiration, to search for new impressions and not least to meet new people. France in particular would exert a crucial influence on him.

When, in June 2021, the Musée Marmottan Monet in Paris opened the largest exhibition of Krøyer's paintings ever staged in France, it did so to present this truly international Danish artist to French audiences. Now, in 2022, Skagens Kunstmuseer is opening *Krøyer and Paris. French Connections and Nordic Colours* to showcase the French artists and works of art which had the greatest impact on Krøyer's life and work.

France imprinted itself on Krøyer as the most artistically significant destination of all, though he visited several other European countries throughout his life. In Paris, he witnessed and explored the most prominent and internationally oriented art scene of his time. At the Salon, the annual official exhibition of the Académie des Beaux-Arts, he saw works of art hung from floor to ceiling: up to 4,000 works could be gathered in one place there. At first, he was thrilled, then overwhelmed. But later, as one will find in this book, his own works would number among the many exhibits, attracting rich and prestigious accolades on several occasions. Krøyer can compete with the best – then as now.

In Krøyer we find an artist who reached out to like-minded people – to artists with whom he could paint and from whom he could find inspiration. He ventured out into the French provinces where he forged ties with French artists' colonies, and it was here that picked up the method of *plein air* painting which would prove so significant to his work. He avidly absorbed what French artists had to offer, bringing it back to Denmark with him. His shadows grew richer in contrast and his paints thicker, but the distinctive Nordic blue hour remained ethereally dreamlike, the fishermen remained strong and weather-beaten, and the long coastline remained poetic. He retained a Nordic quality in the strokes of his brush.

It is uplifting to see how the deep cultural relations between France and Denmark find expression in the collaboration between the Musée Marmottan Monet and Skagens Kunstmuseer. This time, their collaboration is manifested in yet another unique exhibition and yet another significant research project – both created across national borders.

The exhibition *Krøyer and Paris. French Connections and Nordic Colours* bring an illustrious assemblage of important French works of art to Skagen. They clearly show how Krøyer was able to make his many French impressions his own, translating them into a single brushstroke, a single colour. For that is how it was and is with Krøyer and his art. He comes home again. And he brings the world with him.

Her Majesty Margrethe II
Queen of Denmark

Skagens Kunstmuseer and Musée Marmottan Monet
would like to thank the following for their generous support:

The Danish Agency for Culture and Palaces
The Danish Embassy in Paris
The Danish Ministry of Culture
The Ministry of Foreign Affairs of Denmark
The Augustinus Foundation
The Beckett Foundation
The Knud Højgaard Foundation
The Lemvigh-Müller Foundation
The New Carlsberg Foundation
The Spar Nord Foundation
The Aage og Johanne Louis-Hansen Foundation

Thanks also to the two teams at
Skagens Kunstmuseer and Musée Marmottan Monet
for their exceptional and very diligent work
during the three years of research.

MUSÉE MARMOTTAN MONET
SCIENTIFIC PARTNERSHIP
SKAGENS KUNSTMUSEER

Under the patronage of Her Majesty the Queen Margrethe II of Denmark

Contents

French Connections

In 2019, the Musée Marmottan Monet in Paris and Skagens Kunstmuseer formed a scientific and strategic partnership under the patronage of HM Queen Margrethe II of Denmark. This close collaboration is built around the features we have in common. First and foremost is the history of our two institutions, which were once inhabited dwellings. They are therefore on a domestic scale and bear the marks of their former owners. Secondly, they both host important art collections; one contains the largest accumulation of Monet paintings in the world, while the other possesses a remarkable set of works by Peder Severin Krøyer. As museums for collectors and artists, their mission is to develop and enhance their collections through research and dissemination beyond the borders of their home countries.

Thus it was that in June 2021, the exhibition *The Blue Hour of Peder Severin Krøyer* opened at the Musée Marmottan Monet. This exhibition, the first in France devoted to Krøyer's work, met with huge success. It enabled Parisians to rediscover the art of this major figure of the Northern School who, during his lifetime, had close connections with the French art scene. The relationships he developed with French and other foreign artists have been researched by the two curators of the exhibition, Dominique Lobstein and Mette Harbo Lehmann, and their results will be revealed in the second phase of our partnership.

Opening in the spring of 2022 at Skagens Kunstmuseer, *Krøyer and Paris. French Connections and Nordic Colours* will display Krøyer's works alongside those he became familiar with during his various stays in France between 1877 and 1903. A visitor to the official Salon, he very soon became one of its regular exhibitors, highly praised by critics and the recipient of the jury's awards on several occasions. He formed lasting friendships with artists at the Cernay-la-Ville colony and enjoyed a close working relationship with the representatives of French art with whom he organised a large exhibition in Copenhagen in 1888.

Sympathetic to the Naturalist teaching of Jules Bastien-Lepage, Krøyer was also a witness to Impressionist painting, presenting his own canvases on the same walls as Monet, Renoir, and Sisley at the Galerie Georges Petit in Paris. However, this did not mean he subscribed to the Impressionist movement, and the exhibition will seek to enlarge upon this point by focusing on 10 canvases on an exceptional loan from the Musée Marmottan Monet, among them the masterpiece *Impression, Sunrise*. This picture alone demonstrates the differences and similarities between the Impressionists and Krøyer. Whereas, in this view of Le Havre, Monet works by applying rapid strokes of colour, Krøyer remains loyal to a more traditional technique. However, the subject itself establishes a mysterious harmony between the two painters. In France, the depiction of a sunrise was of minor interest in this period, but for painters of the North it was a major theme. By exhibiting *Impression, Sunrise* in Denmark for the first time, we aim to illustrate the shared sensibilities and the singularities of each of the artists represented here, who were not only contemporaries but sometimes also friends, precursors, or heirs to a new aesthetic.

The book and the exhibition *Krøyer and Paris. French Connections and Nordic Colours* has benefited from the support of many museums in France and abroad, to whom we extend our warmest thanks. We also wish to thank the director of Skagens Kunstmuseer, Lisette Vind Ebbesen, and her team together with the two curators of the exhibitions, Mette Harbo Lehmann and Dominique Lobstein. We are also grateful to the Danish Ministry of Culture and the Ministry of Foreign Affairs of Denmark, the Danish Embassy in Paris, the Danish Agency for Cultural Affairs, and the Carlsberg Foundation, which have all supported us throughout the period of cooperation between our two institutions. Finally, our deep gratitude goes to HM Queen Margrethe II, who has placed these two exhibitions under her patronage.

Érik Desmazières
Member of the Académie des Beaux-Arts
Director of the Musée Marmottan Monet

Nordic Colours

The distance between Skagen and the rest of the world has never been great. It might look that way when perusing a map, but there has always been a lively exchange between Denmark's northernmost town and the wider world that unfolds north, south, east, and west of the headland. For many years, a large part of that exchange was driven by the Skagen Painters, who eagerly set out to find new inspiration and meet other artists, to see new colours and experience new landscapes. The artists took these impressions with them to Skagen, where they all contributed to raising the artistic proficiency of the artists' colony, thereby also helping the small fishing village to evolve. For Skagens Kunstmuseer, continuing this legacy is a crucial part of our mission, and this means maintaining an open dialogue with the world and helping to ensure the exchange of perspectives, experiences, and impressions – in art and in our museums.

This is why it gives us such great pleasure to present the exhibition *Krøyer and Paris. French Connections and Nordic Colours*, which was created in a fruitful collaboration with the Musée Marmottan Monet, and with Krøyer as a marvellous wellspring of inspiration for international exchange. Krøyer travelled extensively throughout his life, with Paris being a favourite destination, and successfully incorporated the many French impulses he encountered into his art, bringing them with him to Skagen.

The exhibition offers a unique opportunity to experience the magnificent and exciting works that Krøyer saw, was inspired by, and commented on during his travels to France. These are works that influenced his choice of subject matter, his colours, and his techniques. He made his first visit to Paris in the spring of 1877 and would return almost every year for the rest of his career. Krøyer became deeply involved in the French art scene as an artist, as a member of various exhibition committees, and through his connections to a wide range of other artists and cultural personalities. Krøyer's French connections were significant and enduring. At the same time, he contributed glimmers of something exotic to the French art scene: the famous 'blue hour' at Skagen, lingering twilight over calm seas by a light sandy beach, with fishermen or white-clad women gazing pensively out while dusk settles over the land. The bright glare of a sunny day with children merrily playing and bathing in the water, or moonlight over the moor at midnight. These Nordic tones formed a melody that won favour with international audiences.

The work on the exhibition marks the conclusion of the academic and strategic collaboration between Skagens Kunstmuseer and the Musée Marmottan Monet. The project has received extensive and crucial support from the Danish Ministry of Culture, the Ministry of Foreign Affairs of Denmark, the Danish Embassy in Paris, the Agency for Culture and Palaces, the Augustinus Foundation, the Beckett Foundation, the Knud Højgaard Foundation, the Lemvigh-Müller Foundation, the New Carlsberg Foundation, the Spar Nord Foundation, and the Aage og Johanne Louis-Hansen Foundation. A special thank you goes to our much-appreciated collaborators at the Musée Marmottan Monet and to HM Queen Margrethe II, who is the patron of this comprehensive and comprehensive project. The combined forces of all these generous contributors have enabled fruitful collaboration in an international perspective, ensuring that we can now – with the exhibition and with this book – enjoy an exquisite slice of the French art scene which for more than two decades inspired and developed Krøyer's art.

Lisette Vind Ebbesen
Director, Skagens Kunstmuseer

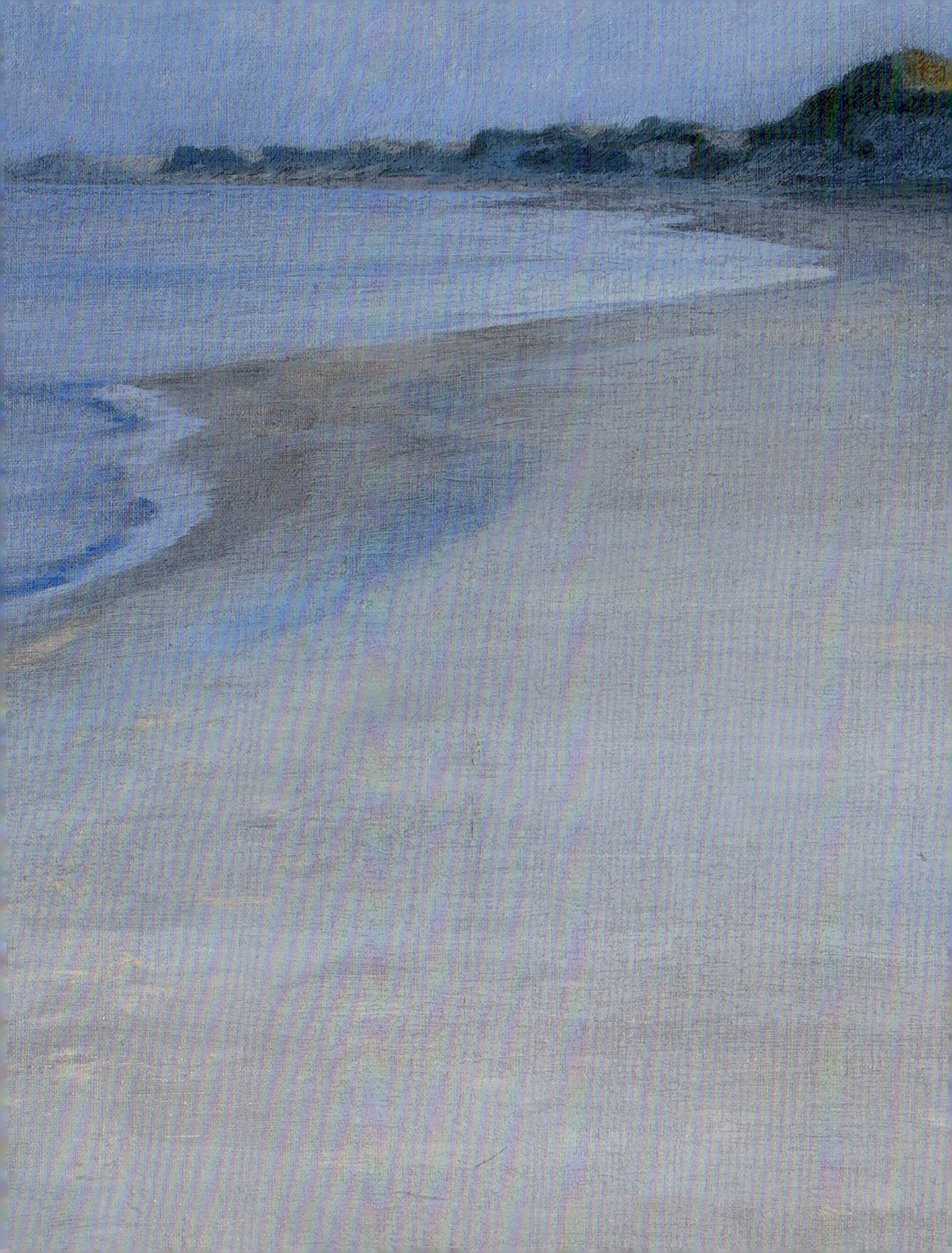

Krøyer and Paris. French Connections and Nordic Colours

Peder Severin Krøyer (1851–1909) was based in Paris for four years, from 1877 to 1881. Here he forged many connections in the flourishing art scene, and in subsequent years he would repeatedly return for briefer stays. His experiences in France proved to be of great significance for his artistic career. It was during this first four-year sojourn abroad that Krøyer developed his Naturalist style of painting. He had trained at Det Kongelige Danske Kunstakademi in Copenhagen from 1864 to 1870, studying under the Golden Age painter Wilhelm Marstrand, who was his professor, while the slightly younger teacher Frederik Vermehren was his main supporter and source of inspiration.

At this point in time, National Romanticism was the predominant style in Denmark, and the nascent Modern Breakthrough in Scandinavia had paved the way for the first artists' colony in Hornbæk, where Krøyer did *plein air* painting during the summers from 1874 to 1876, exhibiting Naturalistic subjects at the academy's annual juried spring exhibitions at Charlottenborg in Copenhagen. Thus, Krøyer's style was still influenced by Danish Golden Age painting when he set out for France in 1877, but his choice of subject matter fell within the scope of the Realism associated with the Modern Breakthrough.

Other researchers have already addressed the topic of Krøyer, France, and international relations, and the catalogue *The Blue Hour of Peder Severin Krøyer* from 2021 by Dominique Lobstein and Mette Harbo Lehmann is a precursor to this book. In 2011–2012, Skagens Kunstmuseer, working in collaboration with Den Hirschsprungske Samling, created the large exhibition project *Krøyer. An International Perspective*, elucidating Krøyer's connections with Paris on a par with his ties to Spain, Italy, England, Norway, and Sweden, primarily in the form of the solid research conducted by Marianne Saabye, the art historian and then director of Den Hirschsprungske Samling. Saabye's research often focuses on direct sources of inspiration – Krøyer sees a painting and then paints his own, drawing direct inspiration from his chosen role model. The approach is beneficial for getting an overview, but in *Krøyer and Paris* we will apply a broader perspective, while also examining a wider art historical development and the differences between Krøyer and his sources of inspiration. Another leading figure within Krøyer research is art critic and art historian Peter Michael Hornung, author of the book *Peder Severin Krøyer*, which was published by Forlaget Palle Fogtdal in 2001. Hornung's book is a biographical treatment of Krøyer's life from cradle to grave and contains a few sections about the artist's stay in Paris. In December 2019, art historian and director of Ribe Kunstmuseum Anne-Mette Villumsen published an article in the online art history journal *Perspective* with the title '"Why do you dance to the tune of the French?" Joakim Skovgaard and the first Danish pupils at the Atelier Bonnat'. The article examines the significance of Danish artists' stays in Paris from the mid-1870s to the early 1890s, when several of them studied under the French artist Léon Bonnat, including Krøyer. Curator at Skagens Kunstmuseer Mette Bøgh Jensen also merits mention for her contribution to Krøyer studies: her comprehensive books *At male sit privatliv. Skagensmalernes selviscenesættelse*, published by Skagens Museum in 2005, and *Brøndums spisesal – til tak for glade dag*, published by Skagens Museum in 2011, take a fresh look at Krøyer and the Skagen Painters. Jensen focuses on how the Skagen Painters' self-awareness as artists and staging of their public personas affected their choice of subject matter and overall artistic endeavours. This also applies to an article in the anthology *Krøyer. An International Perspective* in 2011, addressing inns as meeting places for artists of many nationalities in the international artists' colonies of the period. Not many non-Danish studies are dedicated to Krøyer alone, but several art historians have considered him while addressing broader contexts, including Patricia G. Berman, Frank Claustrat, Vibeke Röstorp, Kerry Greaves, and Thor J. Mednick.[1]

In *Krøyer and Paris. French Connections and Nordic Colours*, we illuminate the artist's relationship with and inspiration from Paris from a range of different angles. It will become apparent that Krøyer had many different sources of inspiration. French contemporary art came to be of great significance for him, but he took a broad outlook in his search for inspiration, looking to different types of artists, various nationalities, and older art, too. Krøyer used his accumulated knowledge to forge his own path – to find his own subject matter and his own distinctive style. Several of the French and Nordic artists mentioned in the following chapters are further described in the texts accompanying individual works, as a number of French and Nordic paintings are shown alongside some of Krøyer's most important pieces. We begin with a review of the Parisian art scene Krøyer entered in 1877, describing how it evolved throughout his career. It can be difficult to discern which French exhibitions were minor, major, very important, or less significant during that period. For example, readers may be unclear on the nature of the Salon, and some confusion reigns about the significance of museums and gallery exhibitions. To clarify matters, this first chapter strives to establish an overview of the period's exhibition setting.

Next comes the whole story of Krøyer's time in Paris and France, covering not only his first four years there, during which he did not return to Denmark, but also his repeated visits over the course of his subsequent career. Accordingly, the main focus is the years 1877 to 1881 and then the following years until around 1900. Krøyer lived until 1909, and while the latter part of his career, after 1900, is also interesting from an art historical perspective, he no longer had a strong connection to or need for Paris at this time. His work underwent a gradual shift in focus, and especially after 1890 it looked far more towards other major foreign art centres such as Berlin, Munich, Vienna, Venice, St Petersburg, London, and Chicago.

1. Among others: Berman, *In Another Light*; Claustrat, *La peinture nordique*; Röstorp, *Le Mythe du retour*; Greaves, 'Pedagogy, Provocation and Paradox'; and Mednick, 'Danish Internationalism'.

The chapter 'Krøyer and the Scandinavian Artists in Paris' looks a little further back in time to understand how a Danish artist was able to make a name for himself in Paris at all. It accounts for a more extensive previous history of Nordic artists in Paris who paved the way for Krøyer and his Nordic motives and colour palettes, as well as explaining how the pioneers' orientation towards France sparked controversy in their native countries.

The French artist Jules Bastien-Lepage is highlighted in the chapter 'Jules Bastien-Lepage and Naturalism'. Bastien-Lepage, with his Naturalist style, was Krøyer's greatest role model. Firmly convinced that originality is crucial to an artist, Krøyer did not copy his style directly, but rather used his knowledge of Bastien-Lepage's manner in his own adaptation of and view of Naturalism.

The Impressionists got their name three years before Krøyer came to Paris, at a time when their artistic movement had been in progress for some years. Because the careers of Krøyer and the French Impressionists overlap slightly in time, many art enthusiasts and several art historians have, somewhat mistakenly, drawn parallels between them up through art history. The chapter 'Impressionism and Naturalism' clarifies who and what the Impressionists were, comparing and contrasting them with Krøyer's Naturalism.

An important event is given special attention in the chapter 'The 1888 French Art Exhibition in Copenhagen'. Numbering more than 600 works, this large exhibition picked up many threads relevant to Krøyer's French connections and also gave rise to new works and newfound acclaim in France. The years and events surrounding the exhibition were of great importance to Krøyer and caused ripples in both Denmark and France. French artists also took part in exhibitions of French art in Vienna, Philadelphia, Melbourne, and Barcelona, but none were as large or prestigious as the Danish instalment.

The final chapter, 'Krøyer's School', caps off the French sojourns and takes us back to Denmark, considering the impact that Krøyer's French connections had on an entire generation of Danish artists who received instruction at his department of Kunstnernes Studieskole over almost two decades – a topic that has not previously received separate attention in academic studies.

The introduction and chapters 2, 3, and 7 were written by Mette Harbo Lehmann, and chapters 1, 4, 5, and 6 by Dominique Lobstein.

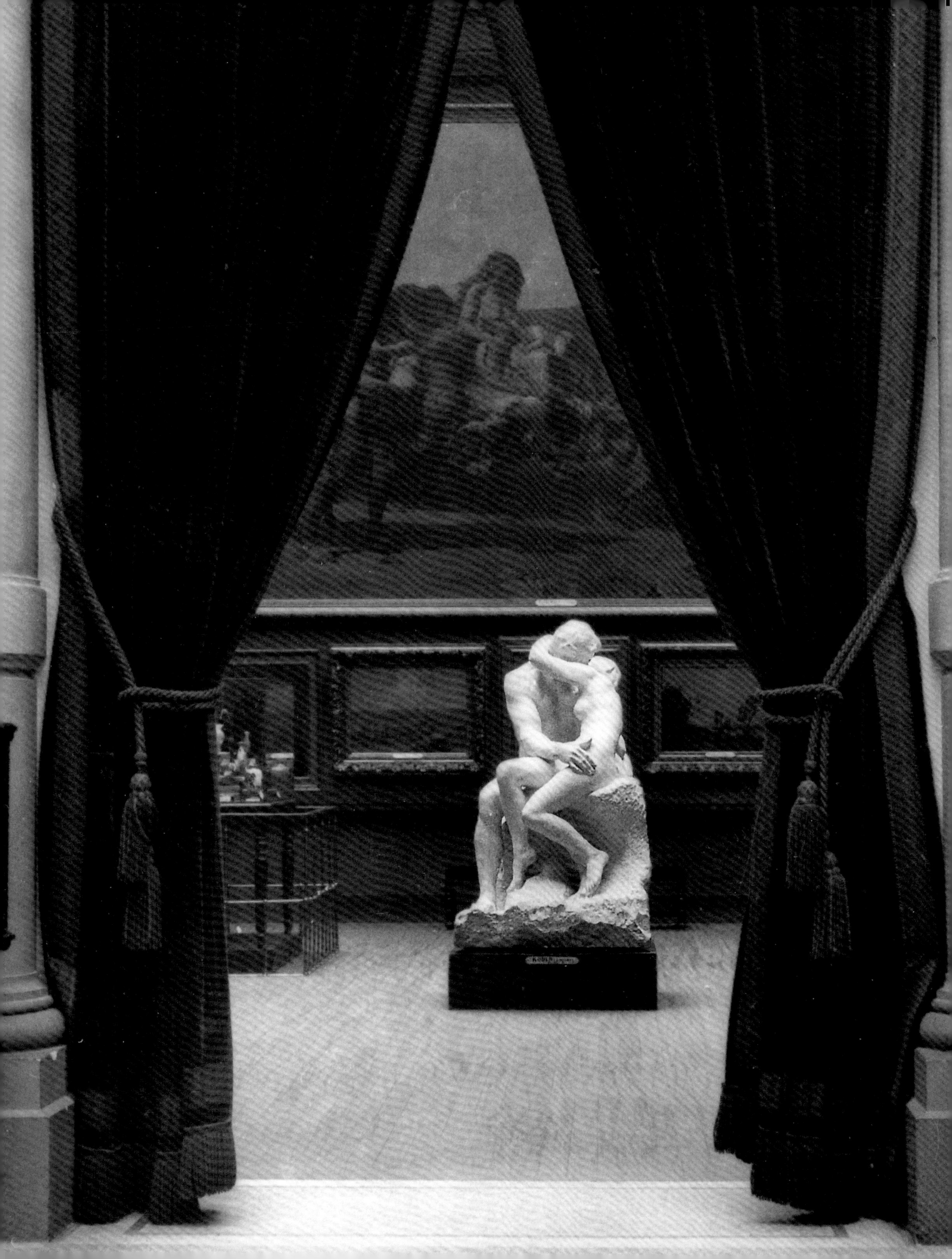

The Paris Art Scene 1870–1910

1

The Parisian art scene before Krøyer, 1817–1877

Art institutions in Paris were supported or controlled by the state and the Académie des Beaux-Arts, which was a distant descendant of an institution created by Louis XIV in 1648; having been abolished during the Revolution, it was revived in 1816. Under the reign of Napoleon III, from 1851 to 1870, these institutions were at their peak, due mainly to three factors, namely training, exhibitions, and museums.[1]

There were many *Écoles des Beaux-Arts* under public supervision – the most important being the one in Paris's rue Bonaparte (ILL. 1), founded in 1817, whose curriculum could lead to the scholarship known as the Prix de Rome and a four-year stay in the Eternal City (ILL. 2). These coexisted with private academies where teaching was often carried out by recognised artists: together, they provided a wide range of training within the French capital.

The presence of artists in both types of establishment offered a stepping stone for students to gain entry to the prestigious annual exhibition known as the 'Salon' or to the Fine Arts exhibitions at World's Fairs, known in France as Expositions Universelles, such as the two held in 1855 and 1867, whose award systems could represent the springboard of a career (ILL. 3). There were many marks of recognition for artists, from a pass with distinction to a gold medal – known as first class – or from the personal medal of honour awarded each year to a painter or sculptor to the Légion d'honneur itself. These accolades enabled artists to establish careers and to see their works exhibited on the fringes of the official event, in the tentative art market that was just beginning to emerge thanks to the appearance and development of new exhibition spaces, in the form of galleries.

Their support from the Ministry of Education meant that the Beaux-Arts had the means to promote artistic activity and, most importantly, possessed a budget enabling them to support and reward artists, and to maintain a modern art museum: the Musée du Luxembourg was the first modern art gallery in the world. From 1818, the state temporarily deposited works there that were the glory of French art (ILL. 4).

But in 1870, after the defeat of Napoleon III and France by Prussia, this useful arrangement soon revealed ten-

1. See, in particular: Vaisse, *La Troisième République*; Thomson, *Art of the Actual*.

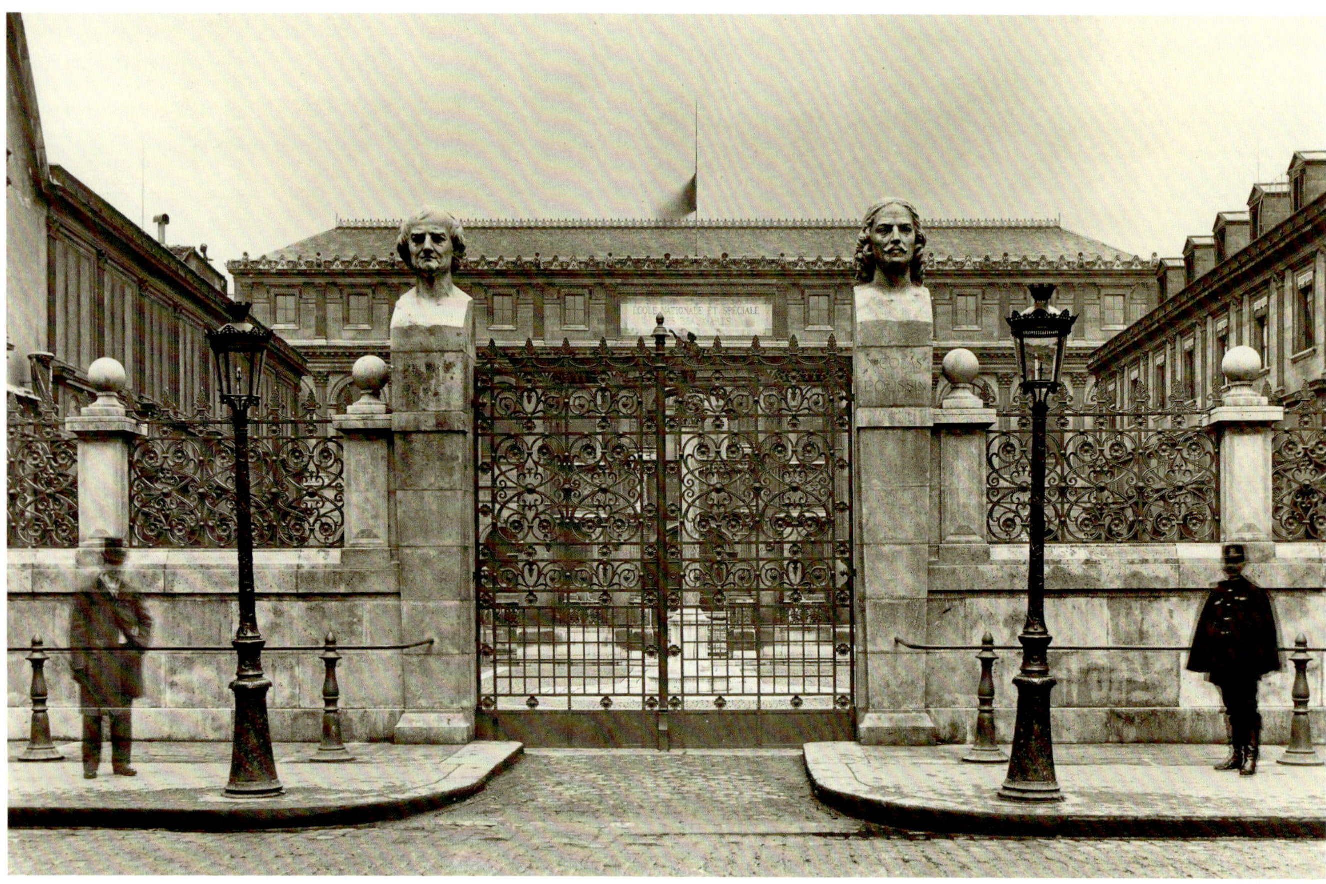

ILL. 1 Adolphe Giraudon: *Façade of the École des Beaux-Arts, 14, rue Bonaparte, Paris*, c. 1900. École nationale supérieure des beaux-arts, Paris. Ph 8675

sions which, until then, had only appeared sporadically. For example, two Salons des Refusés were mounted in 1863 and 1864, and there was an abortive attempt to reform the École des Beaux-Arts in 1863. Relationships between the national administrative system and the Académie (which tended to see itself as a state within the state and, at various times, to play off artists against the administration or *vice versa*) were deteriorating, while an accusing finger was pointed at the administration's role in art training and exhibitions, deeming it anachronistic.

After 1870, therefore, many artists founded their hopes on the new Republican government: it alone seemed capable of restraining the Academicians, whose sole wish seemed to be to maintain tradition and support the status quo. But in 1873, following a royalist majority vote, Marshal Patrice de MacMahon took over as Republican head of state. This military man was a defender of the moral order and remote from the world of art. Until he retired from politics, in 1879, artistic life was dependent on private initiatives which were more concerned with the art market: galleries began to play a more important role and there was increased opposition to the idea of a single Salon. This in turn led to the creation of an independent exhibition, which was subsequently highly publicised, although it was not the first or last. It was the earliest of eight exhibitions described as Impressionist and held between 15 April and 15 May 1874 at 35, Boulevard des Capucines in Paris, in premises vacated by the photographer Nadar. Subsequent exhibitions, organised by young artists in defiance of tradition, took place in 1876 and 1877. The second of these was held between 4 and 30 April at 6, rue Le Peletier, in a five-room apartment situated opposite the Durand-Ruel gallery at number 11 on the same street. It ended before the Danish artist Peder Severin Krøyer could visit it during his first stay in Paris, which began on 10 June. Between this date and his final brief Paris sojourn in June 1903, he would have had intimations of the rapid disintegration of that Beaux-Arts network which had been one of the wonders of France.

Evolution and revolutions of the art scene

Knowing that his stay in Paris would be short lived, and with the help of Danish friends who were already settled in the city, Krøyer wished to benefit from instruction by one of the leading lights in French painting rather than join the École des Beaux-Arts. He therefore presented himself at the renowned studio run by Léon Bonnat near Avenue de Clichy, where several other Danish artists had already spent time, in 1875–1876: Laurits Tuxen, who was to meet Krøyer there in 1877–1878; Theodor Philipsen; and Carl Locher, who would return there in 1878–1879.

This studio was the only one that Krøyer attended, since he had already trained in Copenhagen. He was never interested in the future of the rue Bonaparte school, which in 1870 had been renamed '*École nationale et spéciale des Beaux-Arts*', a name that was retained until 1903. Of all the elements in the Paris artistic landscape, this school was probably the one that changed least. The only major development was that its number of students increased – from 1897 onwards, the École also welcomed women students and it expanded by taking over neighbouring buildings such as the Hôtel de Chimay, on Quai Malaquais, in 1883. It would soon include studios, as well as large rooms intended for posthumous exhibitions

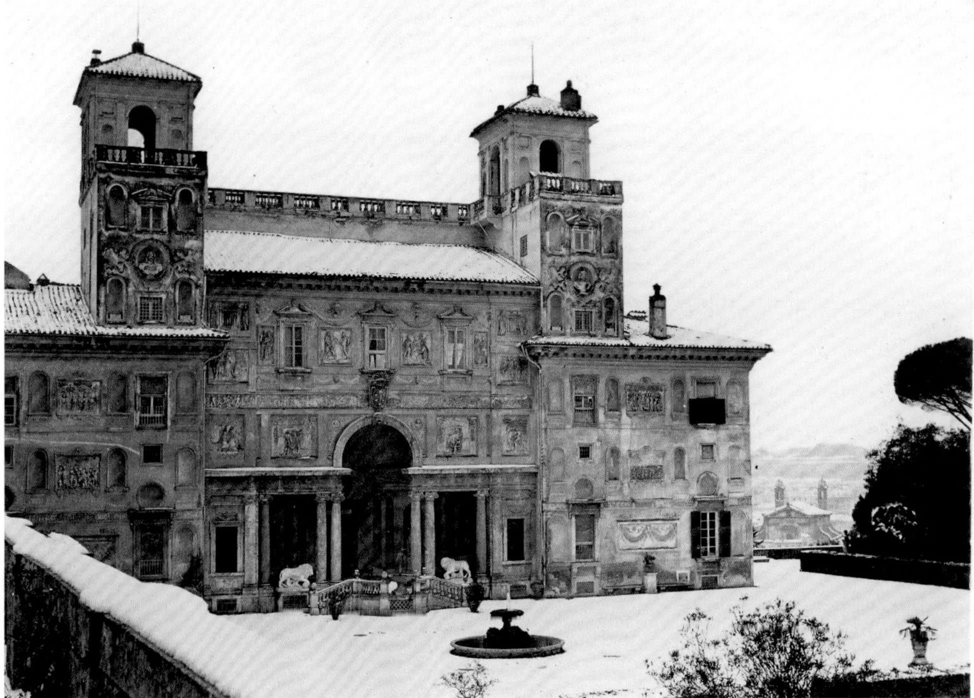

ILL. 2 *View of the Villa Medici, Rome*, 1891. Musée Hébert, Paris. MNEH 1977-4-78

of the work of outstanding artists such as, in March and April 1885, Jules Bastien-Lepage; Krøyer probably visited this exhibition. But he may have been there even before this, to see, for example, the annual exhibition of *Envois de Rome*, which began shortly after his arrival, and ran until 30 June. This was a collection of the compulsory pieces submitted from the Villa Medici by the most recent winners of the Prix de Rome, who would form the future élite of French art.

It was the world of exhibitions that underwent the greatest transformation. Galleries had long been private, for a limited audience, but now they began to experience exponential growth and were soon offering artists an alternative to the Salon. When Krøyer arrived in Paris in June 1877, this was not yet the case, even though the review *La Chronique des arts et de la curiosité*, a supplement of the most important French art magazine, the famous and luxurious *Gazette des Beaux-Arts*, recorded around 10 Paris exhibitions organised for private individuals.

By the time of Krøyer's brief stay in Paris in June 1903, there had been significant changes, and, in addition to the official events, he was able to visit exhibitions devoted to the watercolourist Louis Lessieux at the Trotti gallery, and the painter Georges Manzana, at the Sibelberg gallery.[2] A striking innovation, more prevalent since the 1880s, was that it was not just galleries but many other places that now hosted exhibitions. For example, during those same few days in Paris in 1903, *La Chronique des arts et de la curiosité* suggested that readers should visit no less than seven exhibitions in Paris during the week of 8 to 14 June.[3] These were just a fraction of the nearly 150 Paris exhibitions recorded for that year.

Most of these were one-person exhibitions or brought together a limited number of artists; a significant and steadily increasing share of them were organised on the Salon principle but restricted to one group,[4] or else to a particular theme or technique.[5]

Despite the opportunity offered by all these smaller events, artists still sought public recognition through participation in the official event, with its potential rewards. But between this desire and the reality lay the long-disputed issue of the admissions jury. Despite numerous reforms, this jury was largely in the hands of Academicians who, including teaching among their other roles, tended to favour their own students when it was a question of gaining access to an exhibition whose capacity to accept artworks was not infinite and whose rewards were limited. Each year, therefore, various protests expressed the discontent of those who were excluded. Most of the time, these ended in an attempt at reform that settled nothing and aroused even more discontent. With the departure of MacMahon on 30 January 1879 and the advent of a true Republic the situation changed, and those newly appointed at the Ministry of Education and Fine Arts were able to surround themselves with competent, energetic people. Jules Ferry occupied the ministerial post several times, starting from 4 February 1879, and the day after his appointment he nominated Edmond Turquet as Under-Secretary of State for the Fine Arts.

This decision to appoint a servant of the state who was very familiar with artistic circles, at a time when a spirit

2. The two exhibitions closed on 15 June and 16 June 1903, respectively.
3. The seven recommendations were: *Exposition nationale du Travail (beaux-arts, arts industriels et décoratifs)* at the Salle des fêtes du Globe; the exhibition of the painting *La Revue de Bétheny* by the Russian painter Jean Rosen at the Cercle Militaire; the *Exposition de panneaux pour la décoration de la mairie de Vanves* in the Saint-Jean room of the Hôtel-de-Ville; the *Exposition de peintures coloniales* at the Association syndicale des journalistes coloniaux; and, finally, the *Exposition d'objets d'art et de fontes perdues de M. Adrien A. Hébrard* in his studio.
4. For example, the Société des femmes artistes at the Galerie Georges Petit, or the Société des Agents de la Compagnies P.-L.-M. et des Compagnies de Chemins de fer français.
5. For example, Société des Peintres-enlumineurs-miniaturistes at the Salon Belin, or Peintres et Sculpteurs de Chasse et de Vénerie on the terrace of the Orangerie in the Tuileries Gardens.

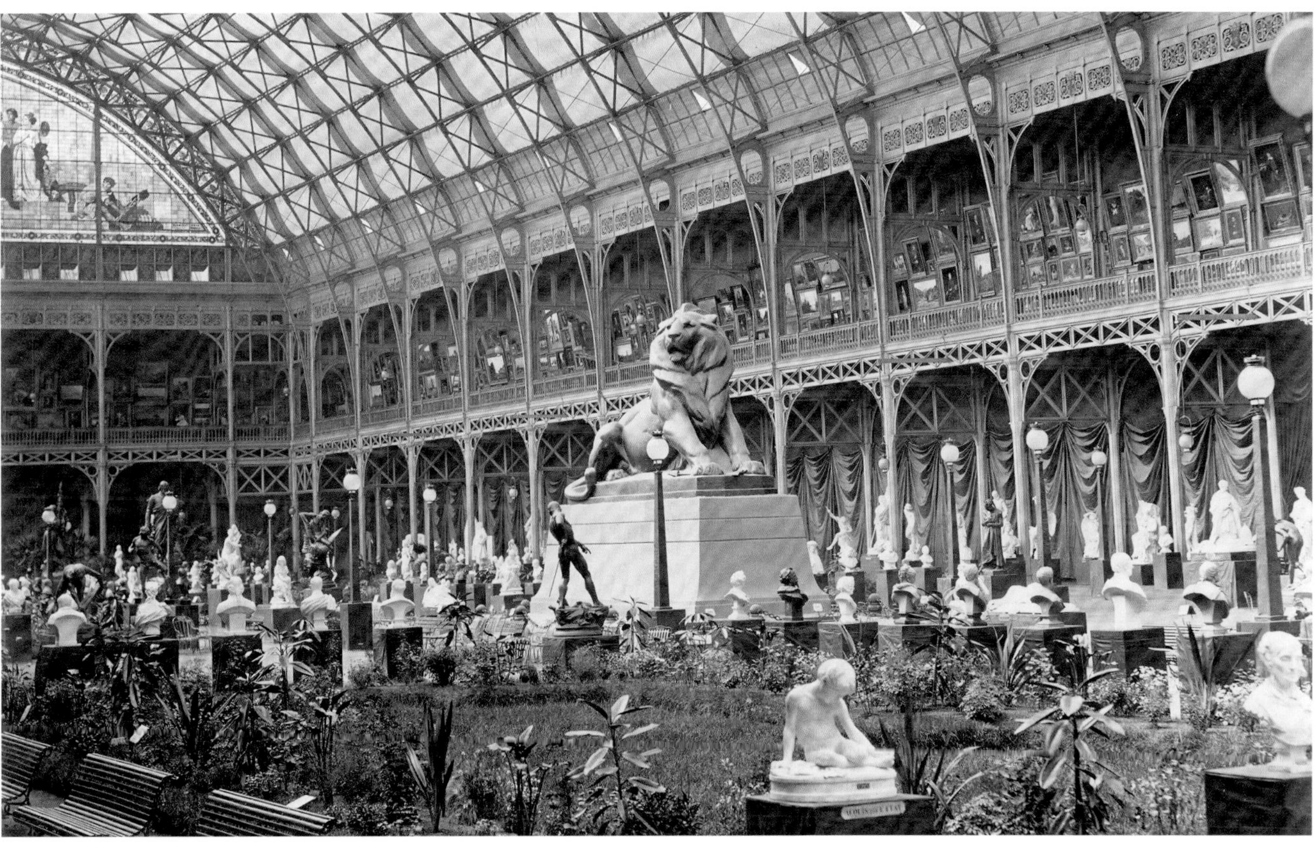

ILL. 3 G. Michelez: *Works exhibited at the annual Salon organised by the Ministère de l'Instruction publique et des Beaux-Arts, on 1 May 1880, at the Palais des Champs-Elysées, à Paris: General view of the garden; Centre*, 1880. Archives Nationales, Paris. F/21/7650/fol. 29

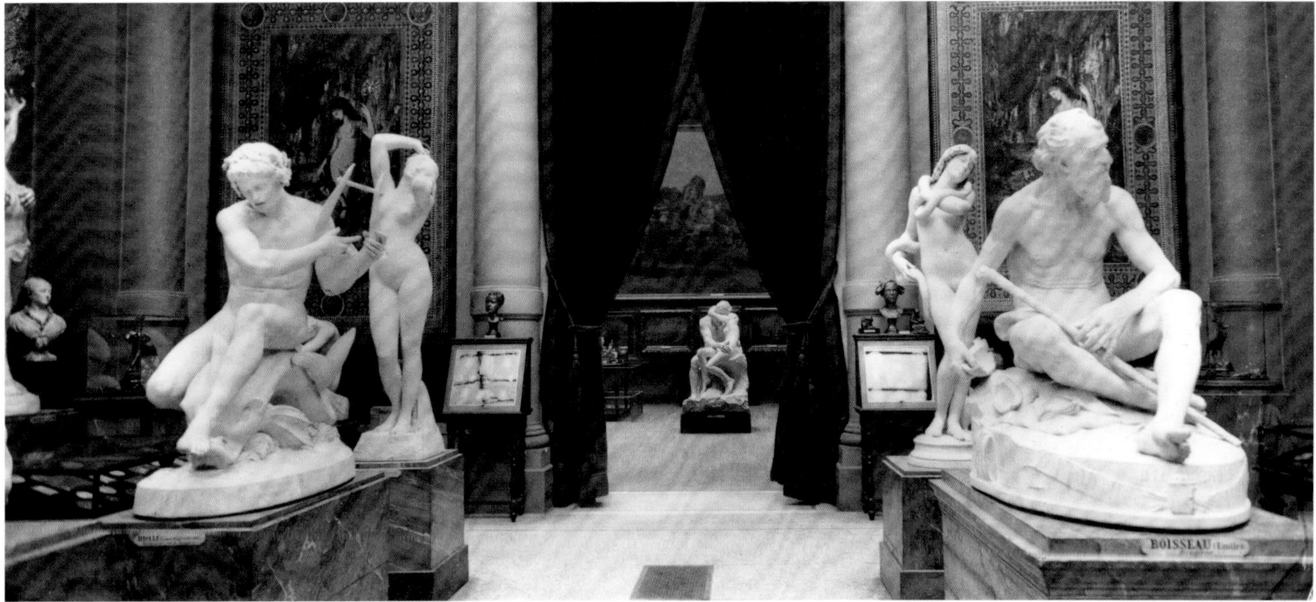

ILL. 4 *Musée du Luxembourg, sculpture hall*, c. 1905. Musée d'Orsay, Paris. DOC-MO-2017-10-63

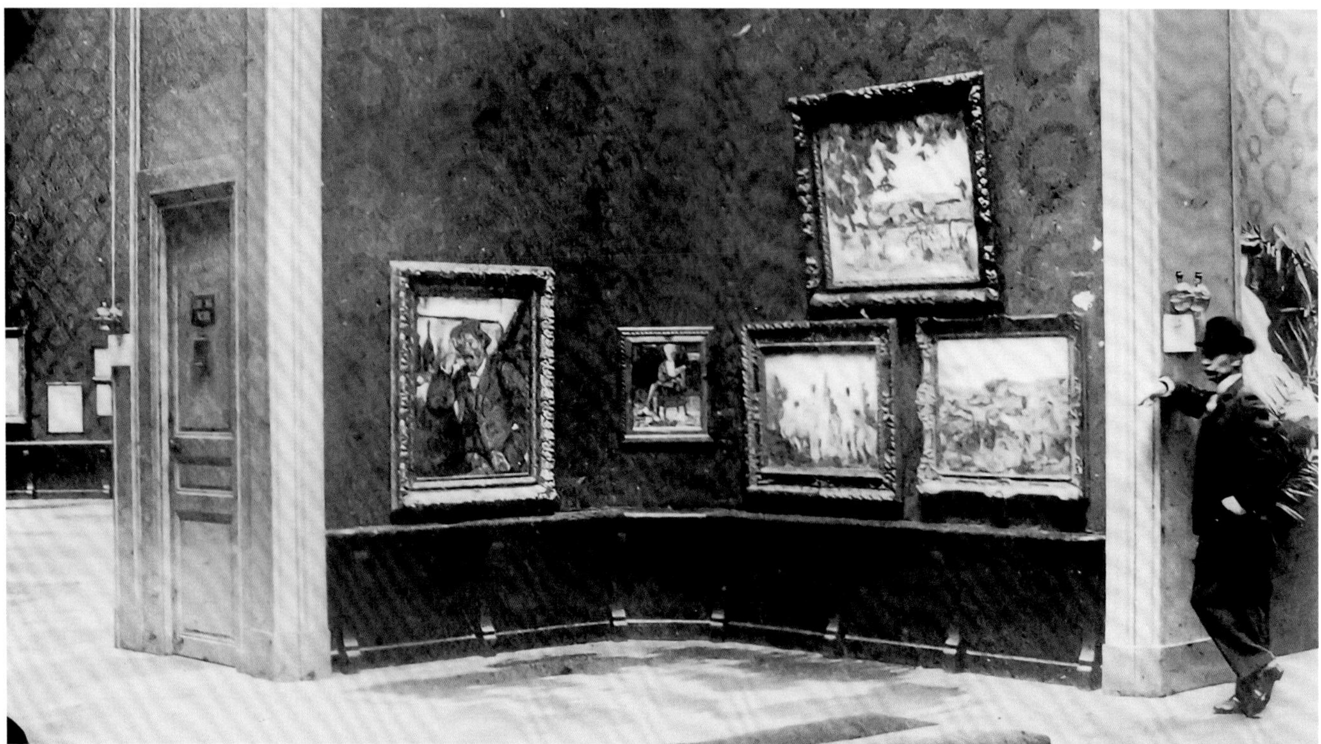

ILL. 5 Ambroise Vollard: *Cézanne exhibition at the 1904 Autumn Salon*, 1904. Musée d'Orsay, Paris.

of revolt was in the air, anticipating the forthcoming Salon, meant that urgent measures were imposed – a simple change in the rules being no longer sufficient – which led to the state withdrawing from the event in 1881. Artists would henceforth be members of a society, the Société des Artistes français, and had to take charge of their own destiny. But this was nothing more than a vain hope, and quarrels and disputes started up again with renewed vigour. Since the state was no longer present to ensure the cohesion of the Salon, the event collapsed shortly after the 1889 Exposition Universelle and a second society was then set up, known as the Société Nationale des Beaux-Arts. But even prior to that, in 1884, a group of artists calling themselves the Groupe des artistes indépendants had organised an event under the auspices of the City of Paris. Its first exhibition ended in uproar – the police had to be called in – but the group was recreated in 1886 under the title of the Société des Artistes indépendants and, depending on the exhibition spaces allotted to it by the Paris city council, it went on to have a peripatetic life. Soon, other events claimed the title of Salon, the last one being of some importance in the period under review: this was the *Salon d'Automne*, which, in 1903, organised its first show in the brand new Petit Palais, built for the 1900 Exposition Universelle, and handed over by the state to the City of Paris in order to create its Musée des Beaux-Arts.

Behind these numerous events with their various titles, which hosted ever greater numbers of artists anxious to be on show in order to launch their careers, different aesthetics were more or less in evidence. The oldest of these was claimed by the Artistes français. As their name might suggest, they were not exactly open to foreign influences: they were strong adherents of the old rules and were very content to accept only those artists who upheld tradition and had gone through the École des Beaux-Arts. The next most sizeable group was that of the Artistes indépendants, in its 1886 form. This group had overturned tradition by stipulating in its rules that exhibitions would in future be held 'without either a jury or an award,' a decision that discarded what had until then been the specific feature of the Salon. However, this freer approach offered to artists did not lead to a huge influx of exhibitors, since many were horrified by the aesthetic principles of the standard bearers, who were defenders of neo-Impressionism. Without being quite so uncompromising, the statutes of the Société Nationale des Beaux-Arts adapted certain articles of the Indépendants, but its organisers, who were from the former Société, ensured that some respect was shown for tradition. This did not, however, prevent them from being more welcoming to foreigners and more open to Naturalism.

Nevertheless, all these upheavals dividing the art world did produce some innovations: the organisation of retrospective exhibitions within different Salons (ILL. 5); recognition of the decorative arts and their exhibition in specially allotted sections; and, finally, the introduction of musical performances at exhibitions, an idea borrowed from the Belgian *Libre Esthétique* exhibitions.

One final feature that should be mentioned in this general review is the fate of the Musée du Luxembourg. From being a simple annexe of the Louvre, it gradually gained independence thanks to the patient work of its curator-director Léonce Bénédite. The museum became a place not only for displaying its permanent collections but also for holding exhibitions. Despite becoming a fully fledged museum, it nevertheless suffered from a lack of funds (for a long time, the expansion of its collections depended on a selection from among the state's often timorous purchases at the Salons), as well as from the power that Academicians continued to exert over its administration. The most striking example of this concerned the difficulties over the French Impressionist painter Gustave Caillebotte's 1894 bequest, which was only presented to the Luxembourg in 1929, and then only in a reserved form.

From 1877 to 1903, Peder Severin Krøyer made numerous visits to Paris, but his almost immediate recognition by the artistic establishment meant that he remained distant from many of these upheavals. His works were officially exhibited from 1878 onwards and from 1884 he held the silver medal, second class, that would allow him to exhibit without appealing to the jury of the Artistes français.[6] Nevertheless, as a foreigner with Naturalist sympathies who was influenced by the zeitgeist, he opted shortly after 1890 for the Secessionist Salon of the Société Nationale des Beaux-Arts, which several of his friends had joined. He also took advantage of the opportunities offered him by galleries, participating on several occasions in the group exhibitions organised by the Galerie Georges Petit, in 1884 under the name *Exposition Internationale de Peinture*, and subsequently the *Exposition Internationale de Peinture et de Sculpture*, at which his friends exhibited and where he met, among others, Auguste Rodin, Claude Monet, and Pierre-Auguste Renoir. Without all these radical changes, his Parisian career would probably not have been the same, and he certainly understood how to use the opportunities created by the changes.

6. See also chapter 2, 28.

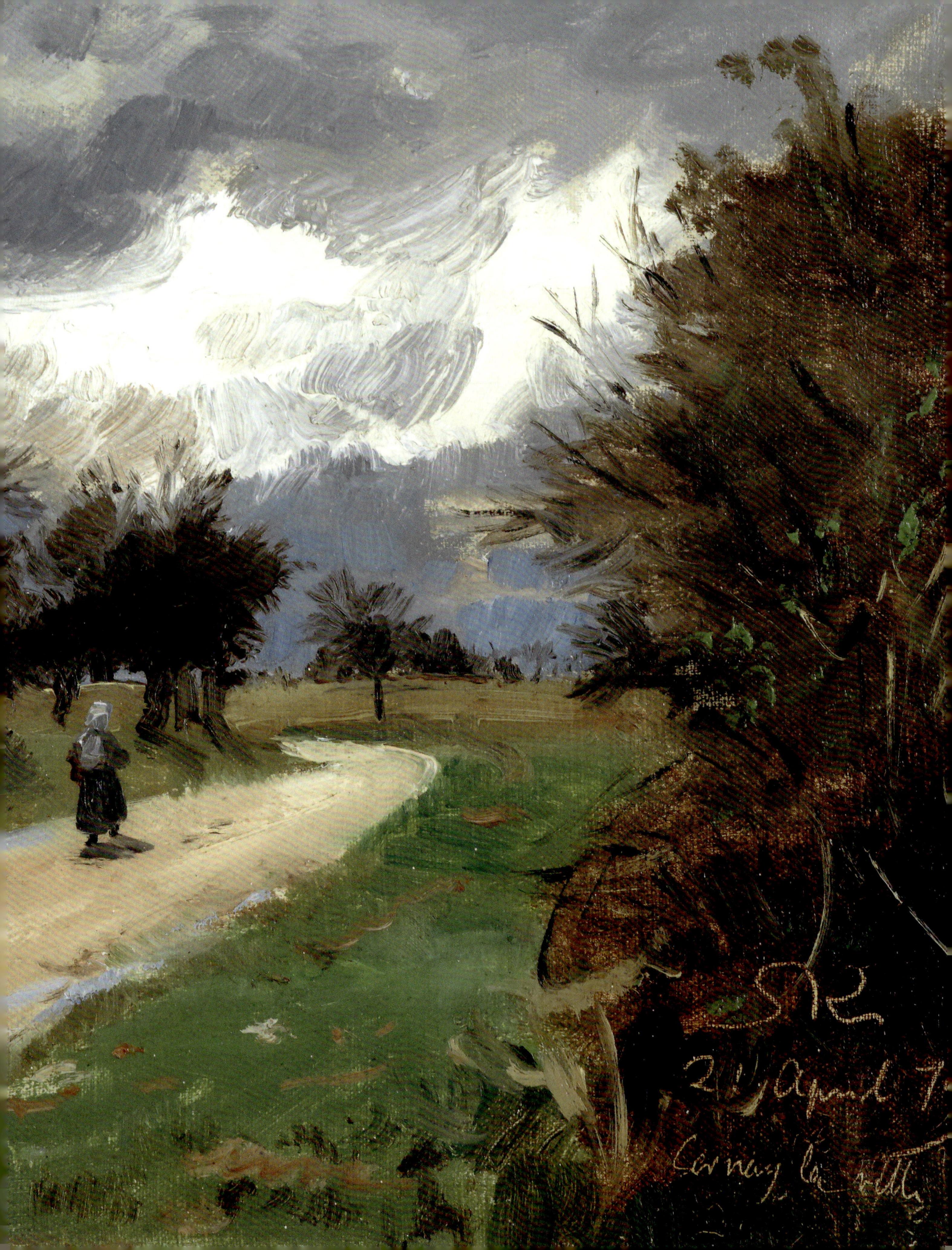
21 April 1
Cernay la ville

Krøyer in France 2

Four years with Paris as his base, 1877–1881

Peder Severin Krøyer's decision to embark on a grand tour of France in 1877 rested on certain elements of an arbitrary nature. This was later described by two of his fellow artists, commenting independently of one another. The Danish painter Laurits Tuxen made the following observation in his autobiography: 'He [Krøyer] felt the urge to go on an extended trip abroad, perhaps for reasons that did not directly concern art, and stated that he would probably do a little work at some artist's studio.'[1] The painter and art historian Karl Madsen went a little further, revealing that 'In 1877, when the gossip in Copenhagen was preoccupied with one of Krøyer's presumed conquests, he decided rather suddenly to make a major trip abroad.'[2]

While both artists can be described as eyewitnesses, their memoirs were written many years later, meaning that hindsight may well have come into play. In any case, Krøyer decided to leave Denmark for a period, and the choice to go to Paris was undoubtedly rooted in professional reasons. Krøyer had also spent the winter before his departure learning French and Italian, suggesting some premeditation.[3] Prior to the trip, the tobacco manufacturer and art collector Heinrich Hirschsprung had also commissioned him to prepare the ground for an exhibition of French art on Danish soil, a plan that never came to fruition.[4]

Among Danish artists, there was growing dissatisfaction with the teaching at the Royal Danish Academy of Fine Art, which they regarded as old-fashioned and obsolete,[5] prompting several of them to look abroad for new inspiration. Some of Krøyer's Danish contemporaries such as Karl Madsen, Laurits Tuxen, and marine painter Carl Locher were already in Paris, as were a wealth of other Scandinavians. The city was the new art capital of choice for young Scandinavian artists.[6] Spending several years abroad was not part of Krøyer's original plan, but as things turned out he did not interrupt his journey until all his money had been spent and financial concerns forced him to do so.[7]

1. Tuxen, *En Malers Arbejde*, 75. He makes another similar statement on p. 190.
2. Madsen, *Skagens Malere og Skagens Museum*, 121.
3. PSK to Viggo Johansen, Copenhagen, 18 December 1876. KB NKS 4192, 4°.
4. See chapter 3.
5. For example, their discontent found expression in missives exchanged via the press between Vilhelm Kyhn, Julius Lange, and Vilhelm Groth. The latter published the leaflet 'Dansk Kunst i Forhold til Udlandets' in 1876.
6. See chapter 1.
7. Hornung, *Peder Severin Krøyer*, 65. His financial troubles can be traced in his correspondence with Heinrich Hirschsprung, culminating in a letter sent by Krøyer from Rome on 3 April 1881: 'I yearn for home. And another thing weighs heavily upon me. My debts are mounting – I need to go back home to save up some money.' Quoted from Mentze, *P.S. Krøyer. Kunstner af stort format*, 95.

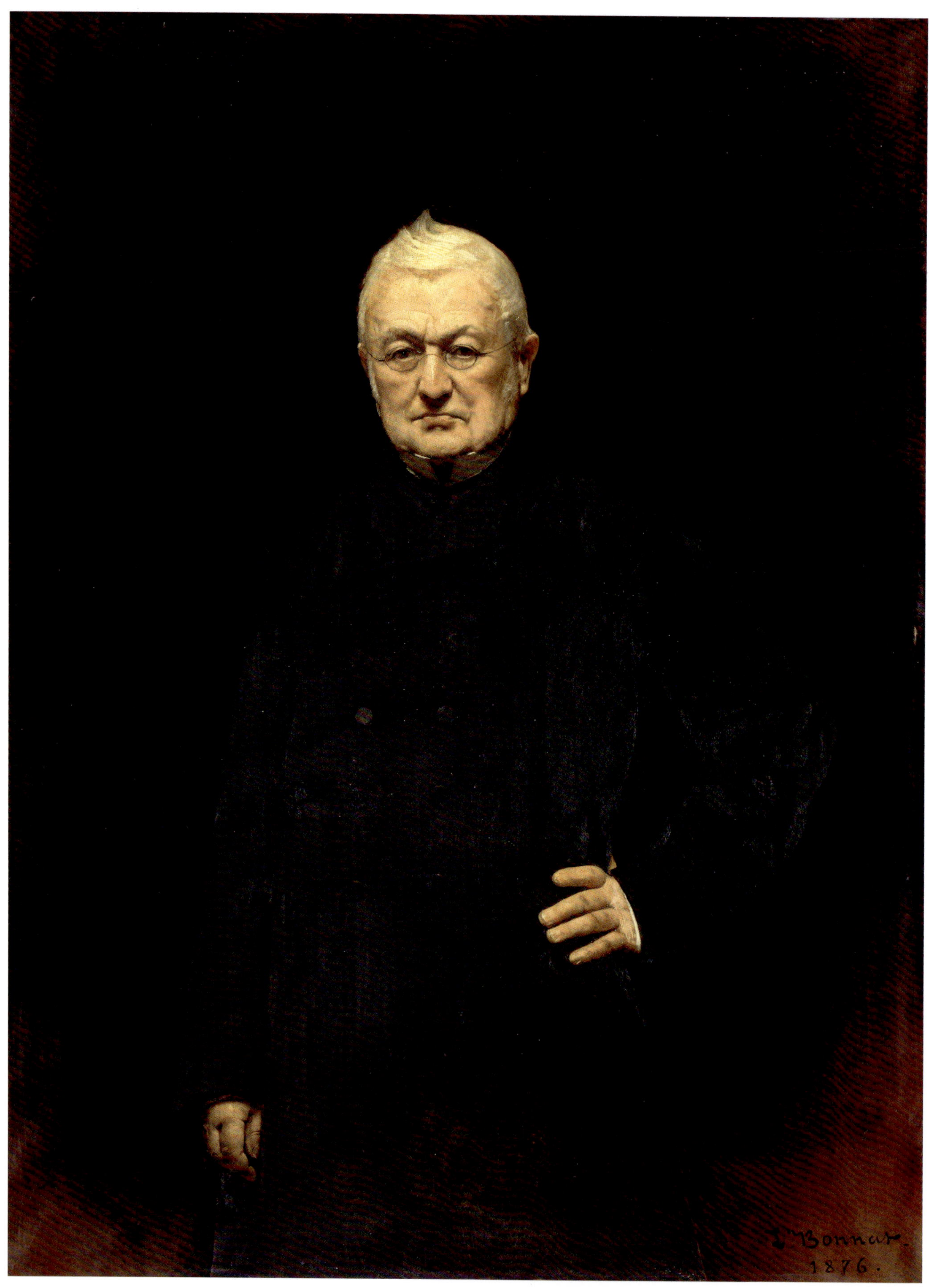

ILL. 6 Léon Bonnat: *Adolphe Thiers*, 1877. Oil on canvas, 126.5×93 cm. Musée du Louvre, Paris. INV 20374

When Krøyer arrived in Paris by train on the morning of Sunday 10 June 1877, he was struck by the vastness of the city, its scope unlike anything he had ever seen before.[8] This in spite of the fact that he had grown up in the Danish capital and had already visited the largest cities in Germany, the Netherlands, and Belgium. In his first letter home he wrote: 'It is a city so colossal that you cannot begin to imagine it. Getting from one end to the other is an entire journey in itself, and there is the most splendid bustling life and traffic.'[9] He rented a small room at 5, Rue de Douai and spent the first fortnight of his stay exploring the city and visiting art exhibitions. He saw the magnificent castles, churches, and public and colossal private buildings, as well as the large department store opposite the Louvre, which fascinated him. He saw the spectacular processions of people going to and from the horse race in the 'Boulogne Forest,' as Krøyer called it – the vast park Bois de Boulogne on the western outskirts of Paris. He saw the lively traffic on the boulevards and the many people sitting outside the cafés drinking coffee, beer, or wine while watching the passers-by, only slightly perturbed that in the City of Light, beer was more expensive than wine.[10] He immediately went to the Salon des Artistes Français to find out more about French art. At first he was overwhelmed, struggling to find meaning in the many impressions. It took him a few days to navigate all these new things and become excited about them.

> One of the things that first struck me when I came to Paris and saw French art was that it was not 'finished'. My attention was drawn to many excellent pictures which seemed to me only sketches; elsewhere I would find a single thing, admittedly the main thing in the picture – very carefully done, with the rest only hinted at – I could not comprehend why the artists would not 'finish it'.[11]

In Denmark at this time, paintings for exhibitions were still expected to be technically fully finished, which in Krøyer's view was not the case in France. In a letter to Hirschsprung back home in Denmark, Krøyer wrote about a couple of the works he liked best at the Salon. These were Léon Bonnat's *Adolphe Thiers* (ILL. 6) and Jules Bastien-Lepage's portraits of the artist's parents (CAT. 13, 14).[12] Among the exhibits at the Musée du Luxembourg – a national museum of contemporary art – he emphasised Henri Regnault's *Juan Prim, 8 October 1868* from 1869 (ILL. 7), Jules Breton, and Jean-François Millet.[13] The Millet in question would have been either *The Church of Gréville* (FIG. 15) or *Two Bathers*, from 1848 (Musée d'Orsay), as these were the only works by this artist at the museum. Even at this early stage, one clearly sees the wide-ranging diversity of Krøyer's sources of inspiration. The works mentioned are very different, but he mostly, though not exclusively, highlights the modern, Realist, and Naturalist painters.

Atelier Bonnat

In the late 1800s, Paris was home to several state-operated and private art schools. Up until now, it has been asserted that in 1876 Karl Madsen had been given a place in Paris at one of the state-run art schools, an École des Beaux-Arts, studying under Jean-Léon Gérôme.[14] In fact, how-

8. PSK in a letter home, Paris, 26 June 1877. PSK Archive 40.
9. PSK in a letter home, Paris, 26 June 1877. PSK Archive 40.
10. PSK in a letter home, Paris, 26 June 1877. PSK Archive 40.
11. Copy of letter: PSK to Frederik Vermehren, Cerney-la-Ville, 20 May 1879. PSK Archive 58.
12. Letter from PSK to Frants Henningsen, Paris, 9 July 1877, reproduced in Mentze, 42–45. The two works are featured in the Salon exhibition catalogue as nos. 243 and 118.
13. PSK to Heinrich Hirschsprung, Paris, 5 November 1877, referenced in Mentze, 51.
14. The Danish encyclopaedia of artists *Weilbachs Kunstnerleksikon*, which is to a great extent based on information provided by the artists themselves, notes this as far back as in its 1896 edition. Karl Madsen did not die until 1935, giving him ample opportunity to change this information.

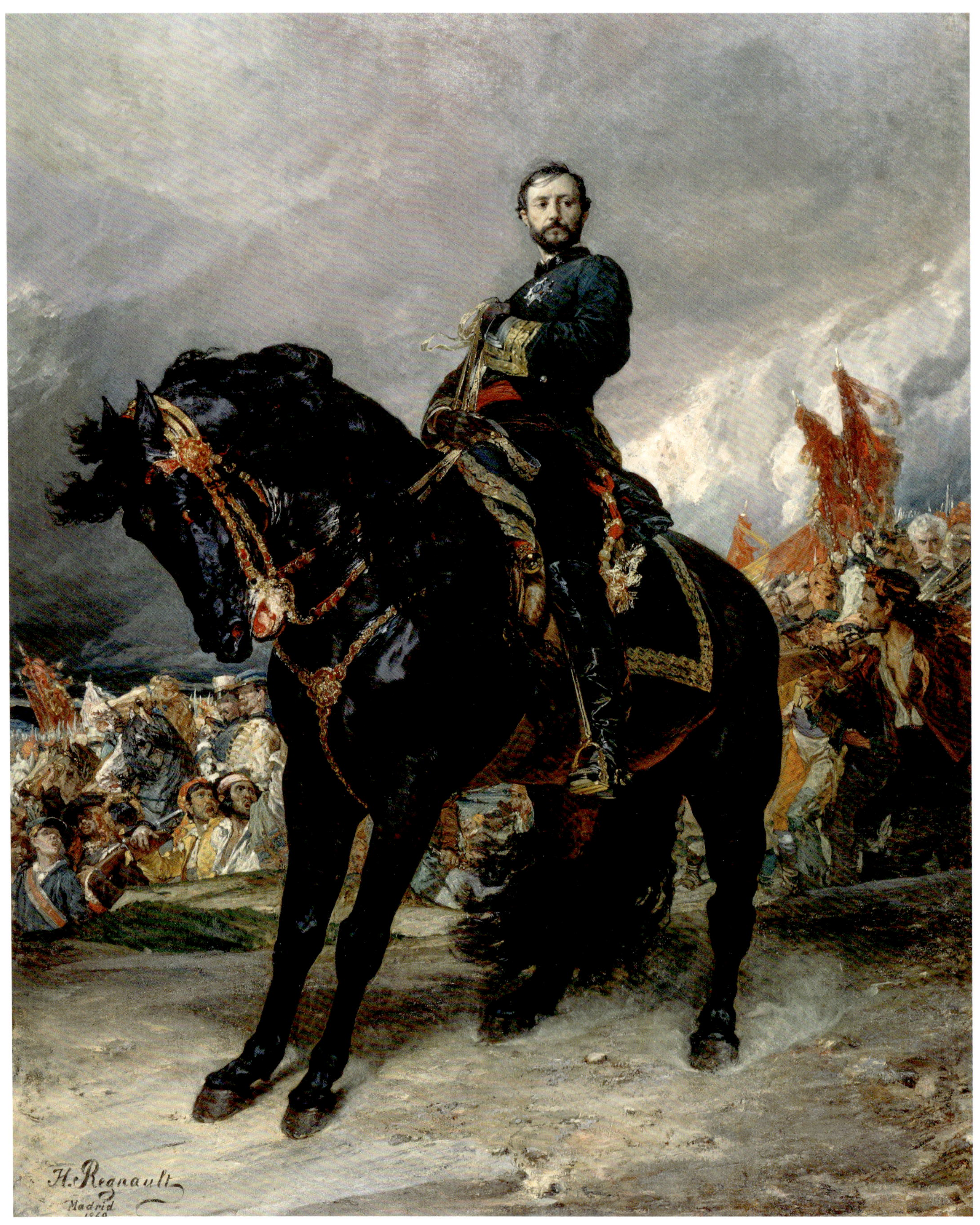

ILL. 7 Henri Regnault: *Juan Prim, October 8, 1868*, 1869. Oil on canvas, 315×258 cm. Musée d'Orsay, Paris. RF 21

ever, the school in question must have been the private Atelier Gérôme, which Gérôme ran as a sideline.[15] In 1875, Laurits Tuxen applied to study under the French painter Alexandre Cabanel at the École, but when no space was available, he chose instead the private school run by the French artist Léon Bonnat.[16] At any rate, it was not necessarily desirable for Scandinavian artists to apply to the state-run schools, as doing so might require a period of waiting when they had little time to spare. At the same time, opting for other solutions meant they could avoid the competitive environment of the crowded studios.[17] Scandinavian students were often dissatisfied with the old-fashioned teaching provided at their native countries' art academies and went in search of training that did not resemble the academic teaching familiar from home. Indeed, the Atelier Bonnat was generally regarded as the best private school among the Scandinavian artists. This information was passed on by word of mouth among the artist community, which is why Bonnat had had 12 Scandinavian students by 1877.[18] According to a letter written in 1867, when he was elected *patron* of the school, Bonnat had planned to poach plenty of students from Gérôme,[19] and the school was to some extent founded with a view to catering to the many foreign painters who visited the city. Bonnat was successful at the Salon, presenting works in a monumental, Naturalist portrait style. Achieving success here was important to the students, even more so than the Prix de Rome, and Bonnat endeavoured to point his pupils in a more commercial direction.[20] This was where Krøyer applied to receive tuition. He knew of the Atelier Bonnat in advance: two of his friends, Carl Locher and Laurits Tuxen, had attended the school in 1875. On 24 June, Krøyer commenced his studies at Atelier Bonnat.

Bonnat was a portrait painter, and his pupils painted after the life in the studio. It follows, then, that this was not where Krøyer learned about French *plein air* and landscape painting. Rather, at Bonnat's he was primarily taught about nude model studies (ILL. 8). As is apparent from Tuxen's painting from the studio in 1877, students sat close to one another, painting after the same model (ILL. 9). Bonnat focused a great deal on the *chiaroscuro* effect, favouring a marked contrast between light and dark, as is also evident in Krøyer's and Tuxen's studies. To promote this effect, the windows in the studio were covered except for a single large window as a source of daylight, and the walls were painted reddish brown so as not to reflect the light back on the model, facilitating a strong effect of light and shadow.[21] The French Naturalism taught here differed from the teaching at the Danish academy by focusing more on the totality than on the details. If you are looking at the model's face, you will quite naturally be unable to maintain the same focus on their foot. In the French style, therefore, the face had to be detailed, while the foot was merely indicated. As regards colours, Bonnat taught *valeur* painting, where each individual colour was modulated by means of black and white rather than by using other colours for areas of light and shadow. Bonnat inspected and corrected his students' work in the morning twice a week and in the evening once a week.[22] Krøyer respected him, and in an 1879 letter to his former teacher at the art academy in Denmark, Frederik Vermehren, he offered the following description of Bonnat: 'he is perhaps the most serious and one of the

15. Gérôme primarily taught French pupils at the École des Beaux-Arts, but one often finds students from abroad stating that they attended that school rather than his private school. On inspection, the records of pupils at the École des Beaux-Arts do not list Karl Madsen. Labat-Poussin and Obert, *Archives de l'Ecole Nationale Supérieure*, 416.

16. Tuxen, 64.

17. Challons-Lipton, *The Scandinavian Pupils*, 39.

18. Challons-Lipton, 67 and Appendix A.

19. Challons-Lipton, 39.

20. Challons-Lipton, 52.

21. Challons-Lipton, 41.

22. Tuxen, 66.

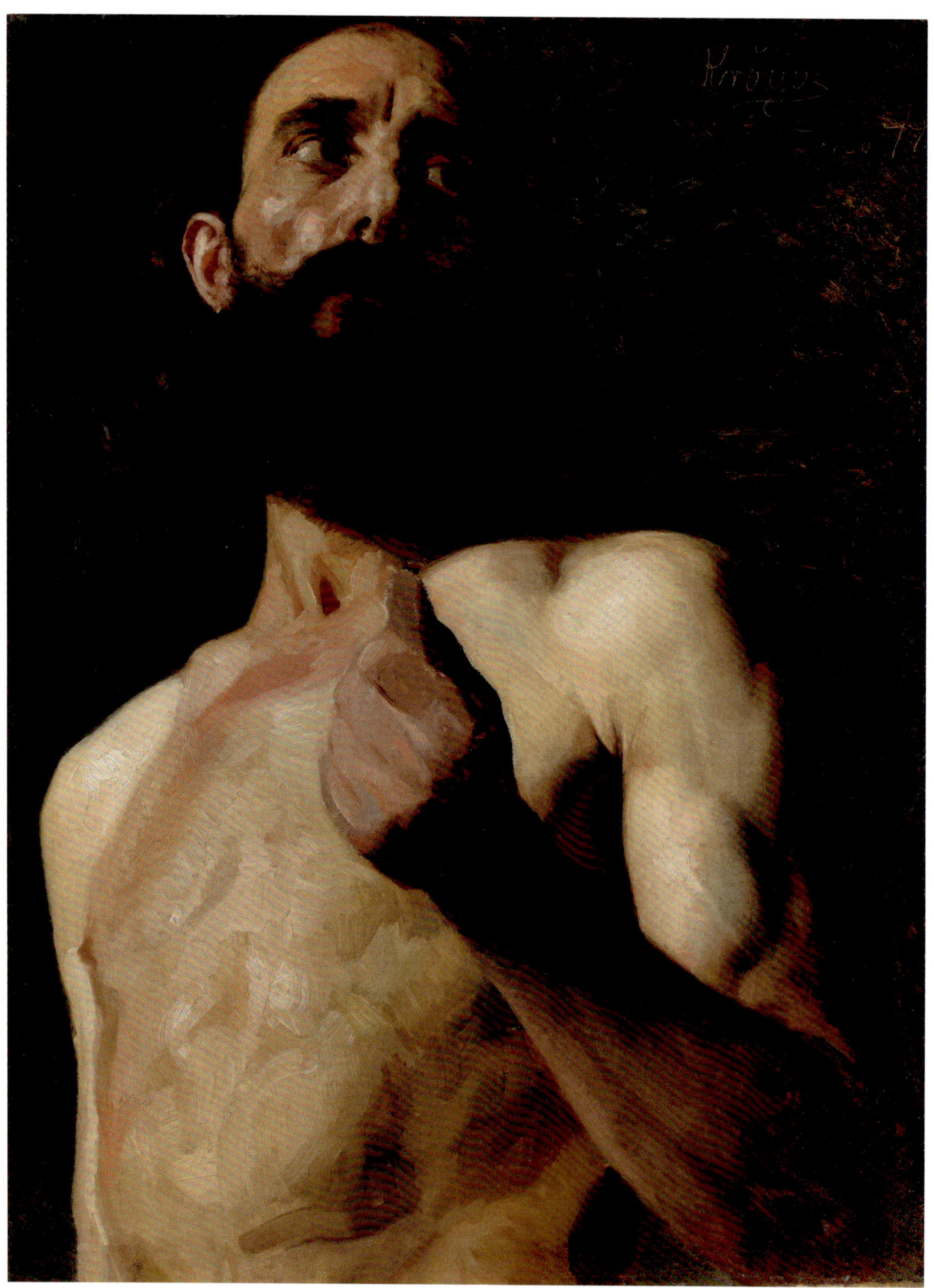

ILL. 8 Peder Severin Krøyer: *Male Model. Half-length*, 1877. Oil on canvas, 59 × 44.6 cm. Skagens Kunstmuseer. SKM12

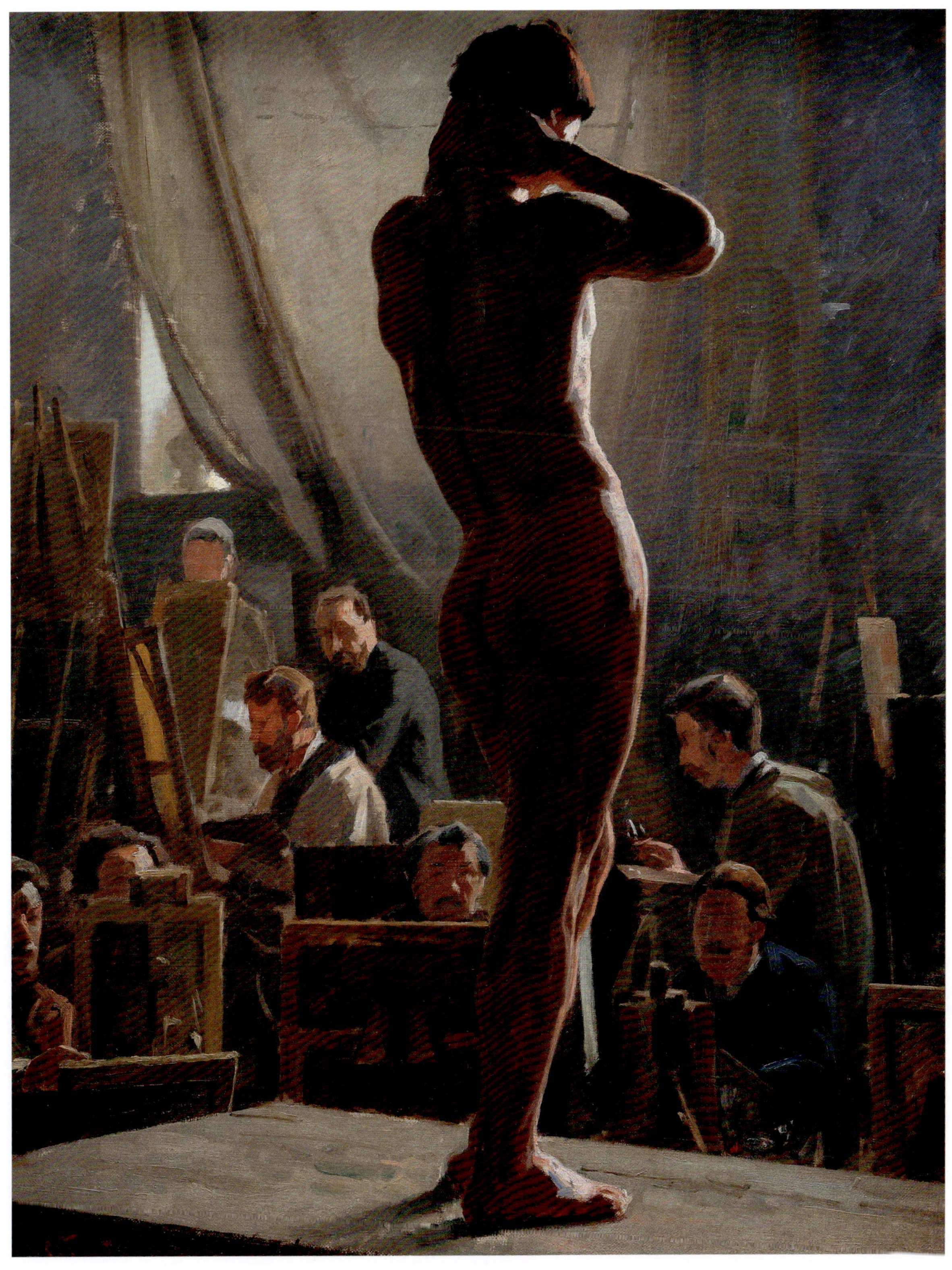

ILL. 9 Laurits Tuxen: *Male Nude in the Studio of Bonnat*, 1877. Oil on canvas, 65.2×50.3 cm. Statens Museum for Kunst, Copenhagen. KMS8266

most talented teachers in France, and he knows how to open his pupils' eyes and to infuse his pupils with energy and a desire to work.'[23] Others shared this opinion, as was made clear when Bonnat was later appointed to teach at the École des Beaux-Arts in 1888 and went on to become its director in 1905. Bonnat also urged his pupils to study old masters such the Dutch painter Rembrandt van Rijn, as well as the Spanish painters Jusepe de Ribera and Diego Velázquez. In his first year in Paris, Krøyer began to copy Rembrandt's *Bathsheba at her Bath* from 1654 at the Louvre.[24] The following year he copied Jean Alaux's *Josias, comte de Rantzau, Maréchal de France*, from 1834 (Versailles), at Versailles outside Paris, having been commissioned to do so by the master brewer Carl Jacobsen of Carlsberg fame. The painting was finished in 1879.[25] Bonnat also recommended going to Spain to copy Velázquez and Ribera, studying their use of light and their naturalism.[26] In that sense, Krøyer's sojourn in Spain in 1878 can be seen as part of Bonnat's teaching. In Spain, Krøyer was particularly interested in Velázquez, whose paintings he studied at the Museo Nacional del Prado in Madrid. Upon his return to Denmark, two of Krøyer's copies after Velázquez adorned the walls of his studio (ILL. 10). Krøyer spent a substantial amount of time in Spain, seven months in all, in the intermittent company of a handful of artist friends. In addition to visiting the Prado, Krøyer went on a journey of discovery into the countryside, subsequently settling in Granada to paint works that could be exhibited and sold. When he returned to Paris in early September 1878, he did so carrying a small fortune in genre paintings that he rolled up and kept under his arm for the entire journey home by train.[27]

The World's Fair in 1878

While Krøyer was travelling through Spain, the Exposition Universelle opened in Paris on 1 May 1878. The exhibition lasted until 10 November, and here Krøyer exhibited his work for the first time ever in Paris, contributing two works to the Danish department in the huge art gallery Palais du Champ-de-Mars. French art took up half of the 219,000 square metres of floor space in the building; the other half was transected by a passage called the Street of Nations on the map of the exhibition, where other countries exhibited their works.

One of Krøyer's two contributions was a commissioned piece, a portrait of the painter Otto Diderich Ottesen from 1873 (Det Nationalhistoriske Museum, Frederiksborg Slot), and the other was *The Smithy at Hornbæk* from 1875 (CAT. 3). Besides Krøyer's paintings and a few other contributions by young artists, the Danish display consisted mostly of works of older date, some even by deceased artists who represented what we now refer to as the Golden Age of Danish painting. For this reason, Denmark's exhibit was not well received by French critics overall, but Krøyer garnered positive responses for his depiction of the smithy, which was skilfully painted.[28]

When Krøyer arrived in Paris in September, he had the opportunity to explore the exhibition complex. He offered an evocative account of his experiences in a letter to his mother:

> This letter to you is long overdue, but you can probably imagine how things are for me here in Paris at this time. In the morning I venture out to the exhibition and spend all day there taking in

23. Copy of letter: PSK to Frederik Vermehren, Cernay-la-Ville, 20 May 1879. PSK Archive 58.

24. Krøyer's copy is reproduced in the Bruun Rasmussen auction catalogue: *Malerier + Antikviteter*, 31–32.

25. PSK in a letter home, Paris, 22 December 1878. PSK Archive 54. PSK in a letter home, Paris, 28 January 1879. PSK Archive 55. PSK to Carl Jacobsen, Paris, 13 January 1879. J.C. Jacobsens Familiearkiv FA 2-008-00021, box F 4.

26. Challons-Lipton, 63.

27. Tuxen, 194.

28. Blanc, *Les Beaux-Arts*, 342.

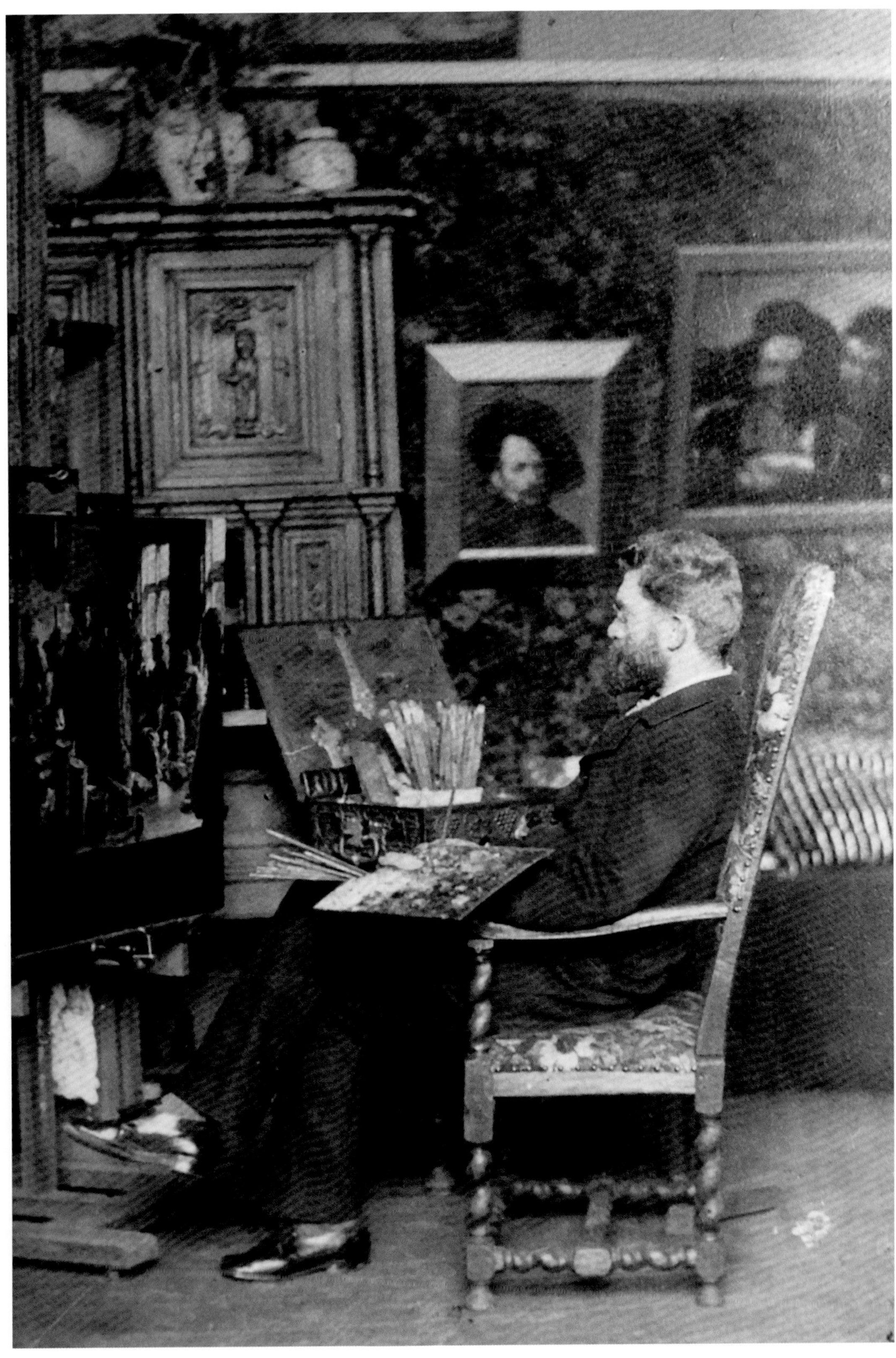

ILL. 10 V. Tillgers atelier, Krøyer in his studio with his copies after Velázquez in the background, c. 1882–1883. Det Kgl. Bibliotek, Copenhagen.

> the sights; it is far away from where I live, so I usually do not eat until seven. After this, those of us comrades still left spend the evening together and discuss all these strange things we have seen. [...]
>
> I have now been here for more than three weeks already, and you may rest assured that I have seen and experienced much. It is, after all, an immensely interesting exhibition and tremendously grand. Simply walking from one end to the other takes almost half an hour. I have mainly viewed the art section, of course, doing more than that would be almost impossible, as it is quite a mouthful in itself. Only now have I truly got to know what French art is and learned to admire it. In the past, it has been more about their principles. There is in particular a portrait by Dubois (pronounced 'Dyboa') depicting his two children, which is undoubtedly the finest that portrait painting has produced in modern times. And a diversity in all directions and a skill on all points, which can certainly flabbergast an ordinary Danish painter like me. And all the training that has preceded my work here in Paris has brought me to a point where I am able to fully understand and enjoy all the good things unclouded by prejudice.[29]

According to this letter, Krøyer was particularly fascinated by Paul Dubois, who was primarily known as a sculptor, and by his painting *My Children* (location unknown). The work depicted a young girl and her older brother as standing, full-length figures, holding hands and looking directly out at the observer. Here was yet another new source of inspiration, this time within the portrait genre, and one which Krøyer describes as modern and praises with enthusiasm. Krøyer later contacted Dubois, and the work was subsequently included in the French exhibition in Copenhagen in 1888, where it is illustrated in the accompanying catalogue.[30]

Daphnis and Chloë

Krøyer returned to Bonnat's school in October 1878, where Bonnat encouraged him to paint a piece that would show what he had learned and which he could exhibit at the Salon. This was to be his first appearance at the Salon since arriving in Paris. The difference between the Salon and the Exposition Universelle was that the jury for the Salon was French, while the exhibition committee for the Danish section at the Exposition Universelle was Danish.

Krøyer rented an apartment at 35, Boulevard Rochechouart together with Carl Locher. They each had a room on the seventh floor and their own studios on the sixth. Krøyer had decided to paint a mythological scene featuring two naked people, a subject he believed might cause offense in Denmark.[31] It is evident from his correspondence with family and friends that he took a long time settling on an exact subject. In a letter to Heinrich Hirschsprung he writes the following about his new surroundings: 'However, I now have a very good and comfortable studio with all the necessary tools in place, with views of the whole of Paris on one side and, on the other, the heights of Montmartre with its picturesque houses and ridges and its light trees reaching up into the air.'[32]

He eventually settled on the ancient Greek pastoral tale of *Daphnis and Chloë* (CAT. 24) as the subject of his Salon picture, and Locher later stated about the further process that Krøyer hired a couple of models, but that the work came into being on the basis of too many undigested theories.[33] When Bonnat saw it in his studio, he was not

29. PSK in a letter to his stepmother, Paris, 4 October 1878. PSK Archive 52.
30. *Illustreret Katalog*, no. 109, 11.
31. PSK to Carl Jacobsen, Paris, 13 January 1879. J.C. Jacobsens Familiearkiv FA 2-008-00021, box F 4.
32. PSK to Heinrich Hirschsprung, Paris, 2 November 1878, reproduced in Mentze, 64.
33. Locher, 'Fra Krøyers Ungdom', 152.

satisfied either. Nevertheless, Krøyer submitted the work at the end of March 1879,[34] and according to Locher, Bonnat used his influence as a member of the jury to make sure it was hung next to the painting *Pastoral Idyll* from 1879 (Musée du Petit Palais, Paris) by the French artist Jean-Jacques Henner, whom Krøyer admired, even though his works were more idyllic and dreamlike than naturalistic.[35] Despite his admiration, Krøyer did not think that the juxtaposition with Henner did his own work any favours. In a letter to Vermehren, he writes:

> I have been so lucky, or unlucky as it happens, to have my painting of Daphnis and Chloé hung next to him. Although my picture is by no means meagre in disposition, in fact it is quite luminously thick and full-bodied, next to him it becomes ever so dry, so hard, so ugly in colour; above all, it lacks simplicity, there are too many small, fussy shapes. But it has been most instructive for me to see my picture thus compared, and that is worth more than if it had hung among poor companions, looking more to its advantage and (perhaps) being sold.[36]

Krøyer's debut at the French Salon was not a great success, and only a single critic noted the work:

> This idyllic image certainly testifies to thorough preparation and a well-thought-out composition, but why has the artist not chosen a more beautiful model than this Daphnis, who is shown seated and playing the pan flute? Chloé, depicted illuminated and in profile, leans against her beloved's shoulder. The two bodies are well drawn and modelled in a thick layer of paint. The picture demonstrates obvious talent and a clear understanding of the subject – a beautiful, powerful, and most strange idyll.[37]

His effort to paint a Naturalist work on a Romantic theme was never fully resolved – he did neither one nor the other with complete precision. At this point, Krøyer almost entirely abandoned 'the great genre' – history painting and mythological scenes – and devoted himself to Naturalism instead.

In connection with the Salon exhibition in 1879, Krøyer's great admiration for one of his near contemporaries, the French artist Jules Bastien-Lepage, flourished. Prior to the exhibition, Krøyer wrote: 'But I was rather discouraged by a picture I saw today by Bastien Lepage. He is ever so good, you know.'[38] Concerning the exhibition, Krøyer wrote, among other things:

> The number one at the salon must unequivocally be Bastien Lepage's potato gatherer [FIG. 39];[39] a picture in a square format, life sized, a girl in a field pouring potatoes into a sack. Her head and hands are admirably done, it is austere and energetic like the old Italians, yet at the same time has all the freshness, power, and realism of modern art. It is a strange picture. The surroundings seem almost sketch-like but are done with great precision and true in colour. There is an immediacy and independent view of nature here which is a veritable joy to see.[40]

It was this Naturalism – the freshness, vitality, and realism of modern art – that Krøyer would pursue that spring.

Travelling around rural France in 1879

By May of 1879, Krøyer had reached greater clarity in his views on the many impressions received from the Parisian art scene during his time in the city. In April he had set out for the French artists' colony in Cernay-la-Ville a little southeast of Paris, from where he wrote a long letter to his

34. Catalogue no. 1704.
35. Catalogue no. 1540. Jean-Jacques Henner: *Eglogue*, c. 1879.
36. Copy of letter: PSK to Frederik Vermehren, Cerney-la-Ville, 20 May 1879. PSK Archive 58.
37. Véron, *Dictionnaire Véron*, 326–327.
38. PSK to Heinrich Hirschsprung, Paris, 12 March 1879. HH Archive 713. Marianne Saabye writes that the passage presumably refers to the work *Hay Making* (Musée d'Orsay), which Krøyer must have seen in the artist's studio; Saabye, 'Krøyer & Bastien-Lepage', 25.
39. *Saison d'octobre*, catalogue no. 164.
40. Copy of letter: PSK to Frederik Vermehren, Cerney-la-Ville, 20 May 1879. PSK Archive 58.

Danish former teacher Frederik Vermehren, demonstrating how he could now put his impressions of the Parisian art scene into perspective.[41] He explained how Bonnat's teaching differed from the teaching provided in Denmark, and how Bonnat emphasised the study of nature – meaning that you painted the model as you saw him, not as you knew he looked.[42] He went on to say:

> [Vilhelm] Kyhn has no cause to mock us because we have chosen Bonnat (whom he, showing such little knowledge of the actual situation, calls a fashion painter) as our tutor, and I hope in time that the results will show that what we have learned are by no means 'tricks' aimed at 'pulling the wool over people's eyes.' I have never received more serious and solid instruction, and Bonnat avoids all mannerisms, tricks, artifice like the plague. It seems quite comical to me when I hear such widespread talk about the technique one is to learn in Paris, 'La Nature Oh je suis esclave de la nature, c'est mon seul maître' [Nature! Oh, I am the slave of nature, it is my only master], Bonnat once said to me.[43]

In the same letter, Krøyer alluded to some of the most important French artists who exhibited at the Salon in 1879. In addition to the aforementioned Bonnat, Henner, and Bastien-Lepage, he brought up precursor of Symbolism Pierre Puvis de Chavannes, landscape painter Charles-François Daubigny, genre painter Gustave Guillaumet, portrait painters Paul Dubois and Carolus-Duran, and the Impressionists. Krøyer simply wrote 'the Impressionists', mentioning no names, but the only one of them to exhibit that year was Pierre-Auguste Renoir, so Krøyer must either have been referring to him or have considered more artists to belong in the category. Alternatively, he may have seen other artists from the group represented elsewhere, perhaps at the fourth Impressionist Exhibition, from 10 April to 11 May 1879. He concluded by stating that there were some lovely landscapes by Benner (Emmanuel or his brother Jean), Antoine Guillemet, Léon Germain Pelouse, Alexandre Defaux, and many others.

The list demonstrates that Krøyer was broadly acquainted with contemporary French art, but Pelouse stands out for the simple reason that Krøyer wrote the letter in Cernay-la-Ville. Pelouse was a self-taught artist who had settled in this town, located in the extensive, wooded area of Vaux-de-Cernay. Despite his lack of formal training, he had achieved success as an artist. He had shown several landscapes at major exhibitions, including the Exposition Universelle in 1878 and the Salon in 1879. In posterity, however, his success has been overshadowed by the Barbizon painters, who had established the first and most famous artists' colony in France in the forest of Fontainebleau a little further south.

In the town of Cernay-la-Ville, Pelouse had gathered a circle of pupils around him. Alongside Danish painter Christian Zacho, Krøyer spent April, May, and June in Cernay with a number of Pelouse's students and other French and American artists, interrupted only by a single, brief trip back to Paris, which was only a few hours away. The French contemporaries with whom Krøyer formed the closest ties included Flavien Peslin, Ernest Baillet, and Léon Joubert. None of them, however, achieved the same position or fame within the contemporary French art world as Pelouse.

One of the first things Krøyer painted in Cernay was *Country Road with Girl Walking. Gathering Storm. Cernay-la-Ville*, dated 21 April 1879 (ILL. 11). All of his newfound Naturalism unfolds in this small *plein air* study. He had done some outdoor painting previously, including in Hornbæk in Denmark and in Granada in Spain, but here another dimension was added in the form of the more fully 'digested' impressions from the art scene in Paris

41. An overview of Krøyer's travels can be obtained through studies of the extensive correspondence that still survives in various archives and publications. Not everything has been preserved, so there are gaps in our knowledge. Jesper Svenningsen provides the best, most comprehensive and elaborate timeline of Krøyer's activities in Svenningsen, 'Chronology – Krøyer's life & movements', 328–333.

42. See also chapter 7.

43. Copy of letter: PSK to Frederik Vermehren, Cerney-la-Ville, 20 May 1879. PSK Archive 58.

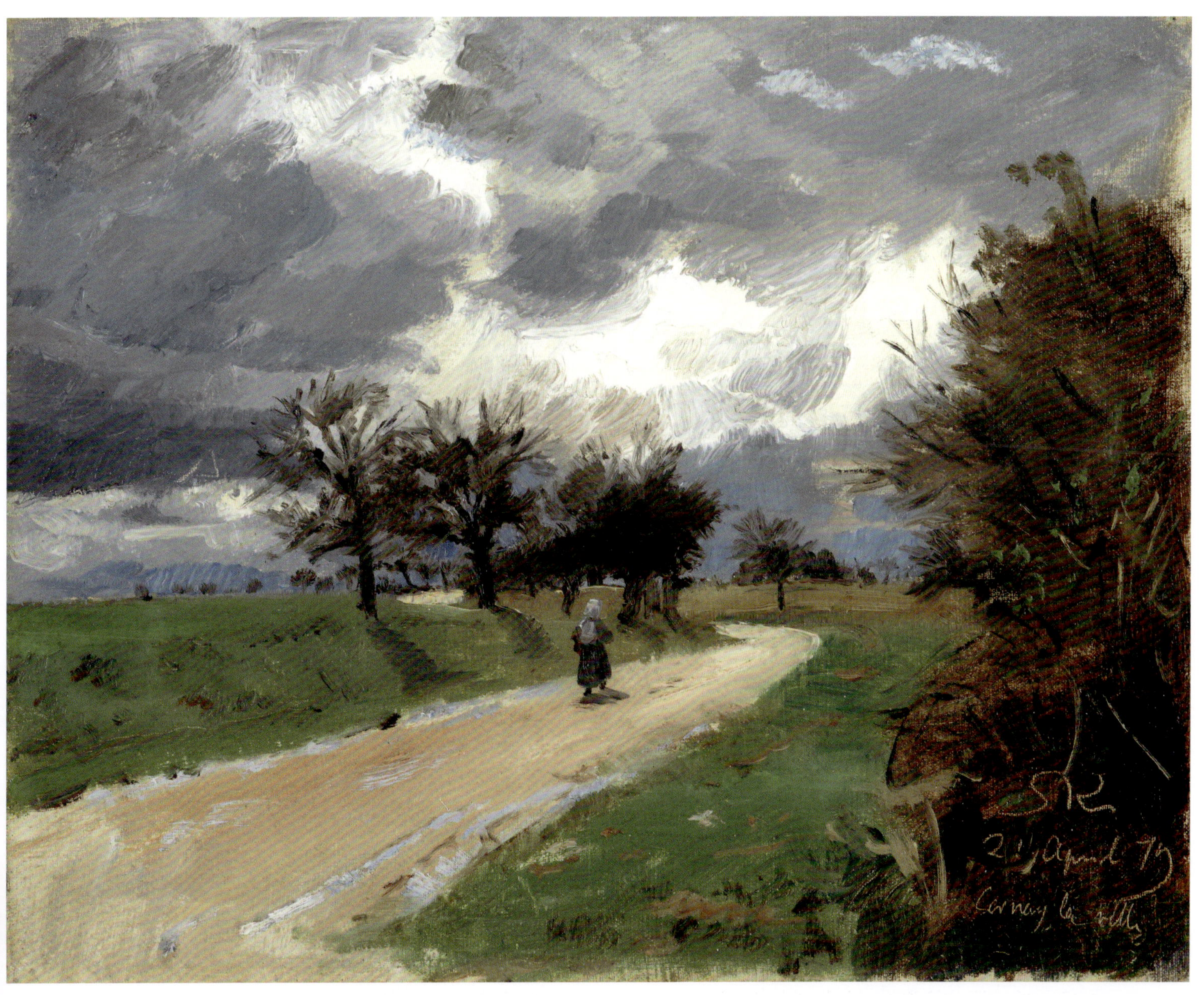

ILL. 11 Peder Severin Krøyer: *Country road with girl walking. Gathering storm. Cernay-la-Ville*, 1879. Oil on canvas, 31.2×39.7 cm. Skagens Kunstmuseer. SKM1178

and his training under Bonnat. This melange was also tinged with the Naturalism of the Scandinavian Modern Breakthrough and with French Naturalism, especially in the form of the influence of Bastien-Lepage and now also Pelouse. The work shows a woman under a stormy sky reflected in the puddles on the gravel road. She has become part of the landscape she inhabits, and her modest size emphasises her interconnectedness with the setting.

Exactly why Krøyer went to Cernay-la-Ville remains unknown, but his decision was presumably prompted by a desire to get out of the city, to find a suitable place for *plein air* painting with lots of company, and to paint a larger work intended for public display, just as he did in Spain the year before. In this case, that larger work was *French Workers on a Sunken Road* (CAT. 25).

Once the large canvas was completed, and after another brief stay in Paris, Krøyer went on to visit Brittany in early July in the company of Zacho and an unidentified French painter of the same age – following in the footsteps of Pelouse, as it were. They travelled by train to Morlaix on the north coast of Brittany, after which they continued on foot for some 90 km south to the artists' colony of Pont-Aven, and then onwards to another artists' colony called Concarneau a short distance away. Pelouse had previously visited and painted scenes from both colonies. The first artists arrived in Pont-Aven in 1866.[44] When Pelouse visited the city in the early 1870s, there were not yet many artists there. When Krøyer arrived, the place had grown somewhat too crowded for Pelouse, but it was not until the 1880s that Paul Gauguin truly put the place on the map. Krøyer stayed in Pont-Aven for a few weeks, making only small studies there.

In Concarneau, Krøyer met up with Tuxen. Wishing to paint a larger *plein air* work, Krøyer settled there for two months until the end of September. The old fishing village had a certain attraction with its authentic fishing environment, and the town was also home to the French artist Alfred Guillou, who laid the foundations of an artists' colony there in the 1870s.[45] Krøyer got to know Guillou during his stay and painted a portrait of him there (Statens Museum for Kunst, Copenhagen). However, several circumstances stood in the way of Krøyer's ambition to engage in *plein air* painting in Concarneau. He wrote the following report to a friend in Denmark, the painter Frants Henningsen:

> So much fuss had been made about the glories of Brittany that I – when, moreover, the season was growing somewhat late – decided to go to Brittany instead of Italy, and I must admit that it is rich and original in terms of landscape as well as figures. However, I would not say that the place I have settled is the most interesting – quite the contrary. Nevertheless, I am by the sea and with my comrades, Zacho among others. First of all, I have had to face the circumstance, less than fortuitous for a figure painter, that it has been almost impossible to get models because it is the great sardine fishing season. And so everyone, men, women, girls, boys are busy for the few months it lasts. I wasted several weeks on vain searches, feeling aggrieved at all existence, until I came upon the idea of trying to paint something in the sardine factories themselves. There I found a very picturesque interior and, using the times of rests and stormy days, I have been able to get the women to model for me. My picture is almost finished and I think it will be much better than the workers [*French Workers on a Sunken Road*]. The colour effect and lighting in particular have proven quite successful.[46]

44. Lübbren, *Rural artists' colonies*, 172.

45. Lübbren, 167.

46. PSK to Frants Henningsen, Concarneau, 2 September 1879. SKMB25.

The interior in question was *A Sardine Curing and Packing Factory in Concarneau* (ILL. 12), and as a substitute for a *plein air* painting it was extremely successful. The composition is well executed with its diagonal view down through the factory hall, the colours of the regional costumes, and the contrast between the dark room and the daylight from the skylights and the door at the end of the hall, reflected in the sardines' shiny scales. The workers are portrayed with great seriousness and respect. As in *French Workers on a Sunken Road*, there is no interaction between the people in the picture; the artist's full attention is focused on the labour, the post-work fatigue, and the setting that surrounds the figures.

By late September 1879, Krøyer was back in Paris. From here he managed to fit in a brief trip to the famous artist colony of Barbizon in the forest of Fontainebleau. Whether he made a day trip or stayed a few days is unknown, but at any rate this meant that he had now visited the most famous French colonies.[47]

In early October 1879, shortly after his trip to Barbizon, Krøyer travelled from Paris to Italy. Once again, he journeyed from the border on the south coast of France to Genoa on foot. These hikes were presumably made due to their inherent opportunities for experiencing nature, enjoying each other's company and making sketches, rather than because of insufficient funds. He spent a month in Florence before travelling to Rome in late November. Here he remained until April, but without painting much. Instead, he enjoyed socialising with several fellow artists from Denmark and other Nordic countries, and engaged in studies of Italian art.[48] He did not paint scenes of urban life in any other cities, whether Copenhagen, Berlin, Paris, or Madrid. He had no interest in the subject, just as he did not paint Parisians of either sex.[49] In that sense he was more like artists such as Millet, Bastien-Lepage, and Pelouse (who took no interest in Paris life either) than Impressionists or certain Naturalists such as Paul-Albert Besnard, Albert Edelfelt, or Anders Zorn, who did.

In early May, Krøyer set out for Sora, southeast of Rome, where there was ample opportunity to paint the magnificent landscape and rural population there. He stayed for a long time, embarking on his largest painting to date, *Italian Field Labourers, Abruzzo* (Kunstmuseum Brandts, Odense), measuring 124.3 x 186 cm. However, his stay was interrupted by a few weeks in Paris in mid-June to see the Salon, to which he had submitted *A Sardine Curing and Packing Factory in Concarneau*. There were various reasons why his stay in Paris did not last longer. In addition to the unfinished picture of the Italian field labourers waiting for him in Sora, there was also a private matter that kept him away from Paris. An acquaintance there, Harald Foss, believed that Krøyer ought to marry a young Scandinavian woman whom Krøyer had met in Rome, but who was now in Paris with her family, the Ditrichsons.[50] By his own admission, Krøyer was fond of the girl, but not in love with her. He therefore asked Tuxen, who was in Paris, to get the lie of the land and find out whether he could even go to Paris that year at all. A lengthy letter to Tuxen on 27 May opens with the following words:

> You lucky thing. Now you can go to the Salon and enjoy Bastien Lepage and Dubois and also dine every day with the sweet, lovable girls, attend the Theatre Francais, etc., etc. And I must remain exiled, imprisoned, for a very dubious crime, forced to give up my long-settled plan to travel to Paris and see my painting at the Salon.[51]

47. The trip to Barbizon is not included on the timeline in Saabye, *Krøyer. An International Perspective*, 328–333. However, the fact that Krøyer did spend time in Barbizon is apparent from two drawings, one depicting the Finnish literary scholar Adolf Fredrik (Fritz) Wetterhoff (The Hirschsprung Collection), the other the Swedish painter Johan Ericson (sold at auction by Bruun Rasmussen on 4 March 2004). The latter is dated 'Barbizon 5 October 1879'.

48. Hornung, 118.

49. PSK to Heinrich Hirschsprung, 35, Boulevard de Rochechouart, Paris, 12 March 1879. HH Archives 713.

50. PSK to Laurits Tuxen, Sora, 21 May 1880. KB NBD 2nd rk.

51. PSK to Laurits Tuxen, Sora, 27 May 1880. KB NKS 2339, 2° 5.

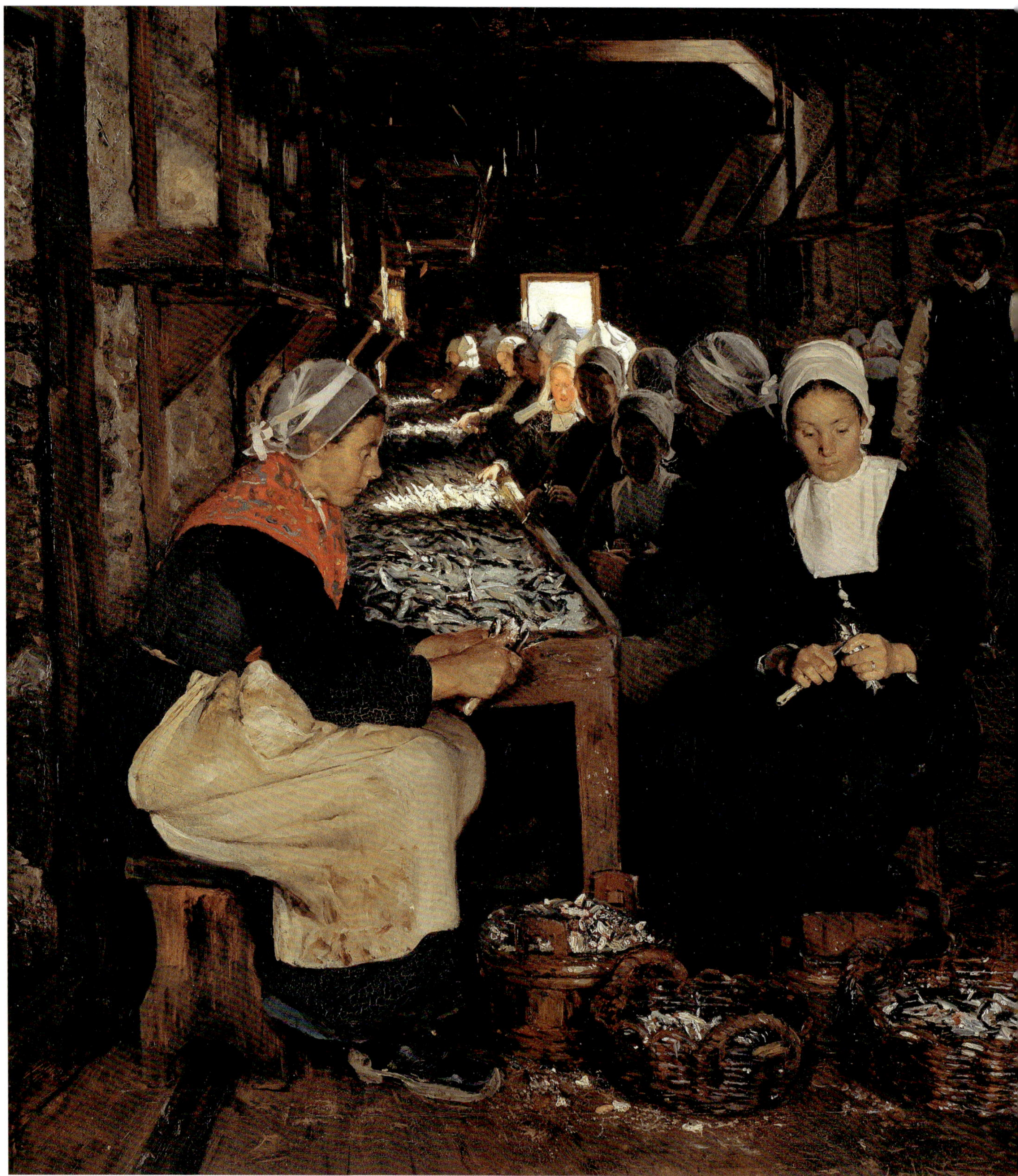

ILL. 12 Peder Severin Krøyer: *A Sardine Curing and Packing Factory in Concarneau*, 1879. Oil on canvas, 101.5×140.5 cm. Statens Museum for Kunst, Copenhagen. KMS3108

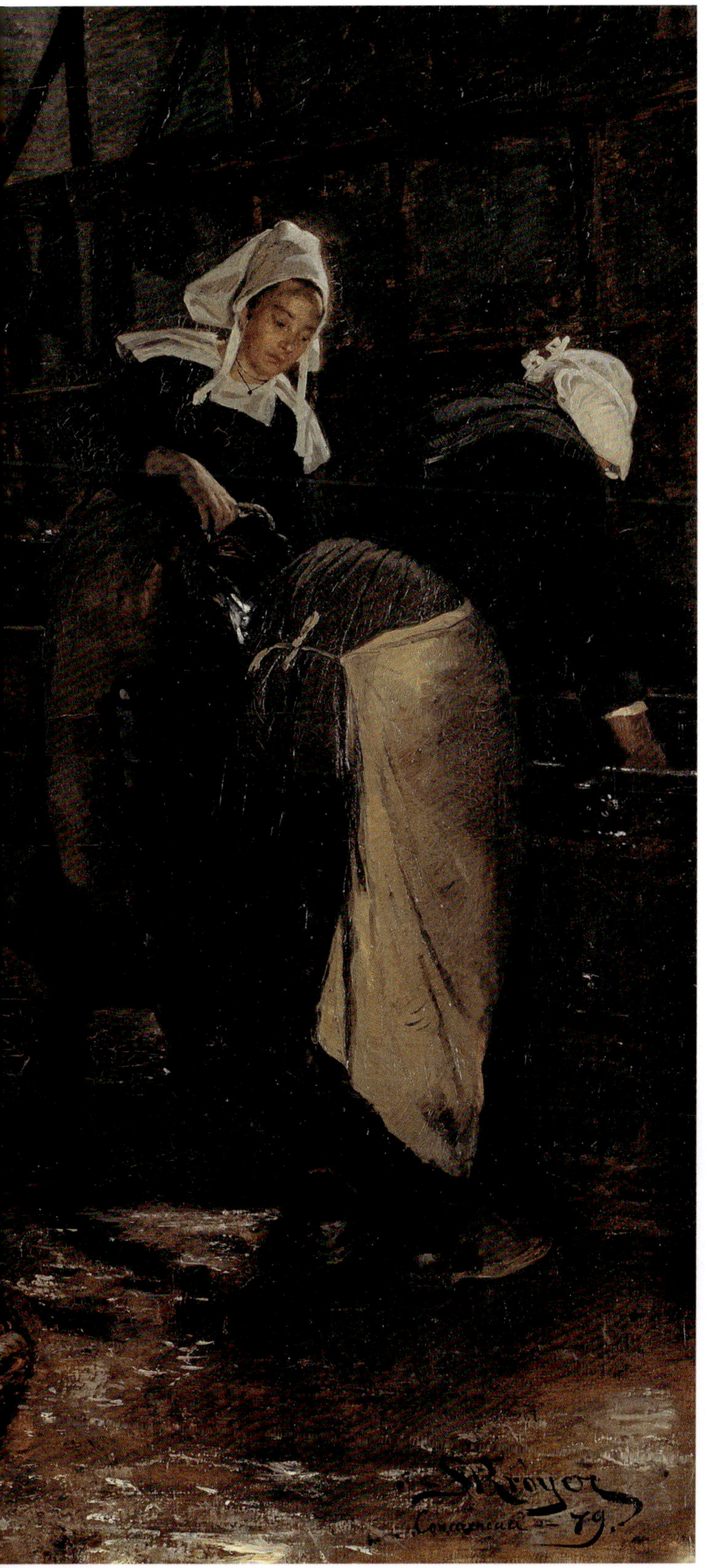

It appears that a brief stay was deemed possible after all. He arrived in Paris around 11 June and stayed until 20 June. One of Krøyer's French friends, the painter Adrien Jourdeuil, had helped him with the practicalities regarding the framing of the work, which had remained in Paris, and Jourdeuil also helped him submit it in time for the exhibition opening so that Krøyer could arrive later. The work received somewhat more attention than *Daphnis and Chloë* did the year before. This time Krøyer received positive mention in several reviews or reports of the exhibition, two of which went so far as to indicate that he should have received a medal.[52]

The French critics did not see Krøyer's work as particularly inspired by French art; on the contrary, they emphasised his unique style and Nordic roots. Several mentioned his treatment of light and the realism in his treatment of working women and men.[53] The French art historian and critic Marius Vachon described the work as follows:

> Although Krøyer spent some time in Bonnat's studio, he retained a distinctively Danish feel and expression in his works. His *A Sardine Curing and Packing Factory in Concarneau* stands out as an example of his exploration of *chiaroscuro* effects, of playing with light falling softly into the space through apertures, and the use of reddish-brown shades, all quite characteristic of the Nordic schools of painting; the artist has intelligently achieved a good result by bringing all these different elements into play.[54]

After almost three and a half months in Sora, interrupted only by his brief trip to Paris in mid-June, Krøyer wrote a letter to his comrade Frants Henningsen, including small drawings of the two paintings he was working on there: *Italian Field Labourers, Abruzzo* and *Italian Village Hatters*

52. The two critics were Olivier Merson, 'Salon de 1880. VI', 9 and Paul Mantz, 'Le Salon. VII', 20 June 1880, [p. 2].

53 Including Havard, 'Le Salon de 1880', 2 and Seigneur, *L'Art et les artistes au Salon de 1880*, 67.

54. Vachon, 'Le Salon de 1880', 3.

(ILL. 13). In the letter, he related that the picture of the field labourers, which was quite large, took longer than expected to paint (CAT. 35), and that he had therefore also begun to paint the hatters, a work which he believed held great promise:

> The lighting and the contrast between the nature of the various naked torsos, the father's lean, characteristic body and the children's, one lean and the other round and plump. It is a pure pleasure to paint.[55]

He also told of his field labourers and hatters in a letter to his patron Heinrich Hirschsprung's wife, Pauline Hirschsprung: 'I am not given to telling stories, except for what might come under the heading of the Zolaesque, for which I make no apologies.'[56] In saying so he meant that he stuck to the kind of naturalistic narratives from real life of which the French author Émile Zola was an exponent, meaning that he eschewed mythological or historical scenes that were far removed from the everyday lives of labourers or fishermen.

After completing the two major works in Sora, Krøyer travelled around Italy. He stayed in Naples for a while, where he shared a studio with the Italian sculptor Pasquale Fosca, whom he had met in Sora.[57] He was back in Rome by December 1880. Here he embarked, perhaps somewhat surprisingly, on a historical scene which he had already considered doing during his first stay. The prompt was that he had been commissioned to do a watercolour of an Italian model.[58] For this task, he had used the model Vittoria. Krøyer knew that she had previously posed for the French painter Aimé Nicolas Morot for his *Medea* (CAT. 7),[59] and for the so-called Gallic amazons in *The Ambrones. Episode of the battle at Eaux-Sextienne* (Musée des Beaux-Arts, Nancy).[60] Krøyer would have had the opportunity to view these at the Paris Salon in 1877 and 1879, respectively.[61] Morot had won the French Prix de Rome in 1873, resulting in a four-year stay at the French Academy's department at Villa Médici in Rome. Krøyer decided to have Vittoria pose for his historic *Messalina* (FIG. 7), which he completed in April 1881. Krøyer described his choices to his colleague, Tuxen:

> I then went on to paint a couple of watercolours and finally my famous *Messalina*. But perhaps you have not heard it mentioned at all? After all, I myself, and most others with me, am so amazed that I, a painter of fishermen and peasants, should be painting a Messalina that I do believe everyone must be astounded by it. Be that as it may, I am painting Messalina, a single figure, in her box at the amphitheatre; she has risen at some exciting moment of the combat below and is animatedly following someone in the arena. In the background is a crowd of people, or next to her background, I should say. She is wearing a light white-blue, pale red robe against a yellow silk drapery with gold fringes, and the side of her in shadow (well, really there is none because it is a flat light) stands out against the golden side of the imperial seat; oriental rugs adorn the edge of the box. The main effect is, then, yellow and gold with a little red. It is a pure portrait of a magnificent, glorious – if a little passée – Roman model, Vittoria. She who posed for Morot's *Medea* and his Gallic amazons.[62]

Messalina was sent to the Nordic Art Exhibition in Gothenburg that same year, whereas *Italian Village Hatters* was sent to the Salon in Paris.

At the end of his four-year stay abroad, Krøyer travelled from Italy to Paris to see the Salon. Here he was awarded the medal that he did not receive the year before. It was

55. PSK to Frants Henningsen, 15 August 1880. SKMB26.
56. PSK to Pauline Hirschsprung, Sora, 8 September 1880. HH Archives 725.
57. Saabye, 'P.S. Krøyer, Pasquale Fosca and the Neapolitan art scene', 143–177.
58. Müller, 'Peter Severin Krøyer', 606.
59. Catalogue no. 1557 at the 1877 Salon.
60. Catalogue no. 2194 at the 1879 Salon 1879.
61. PSK to Laurits Tuxen, Rome, 24 March 1880. KB NKS 2339, 2° 5 and Saabye, '1880–81 Napels, Rome & Paris', 208.
62. PSK to Laurits Tuxen, Rome, 24 March 1880. KB NKS 2339, 2° 5.

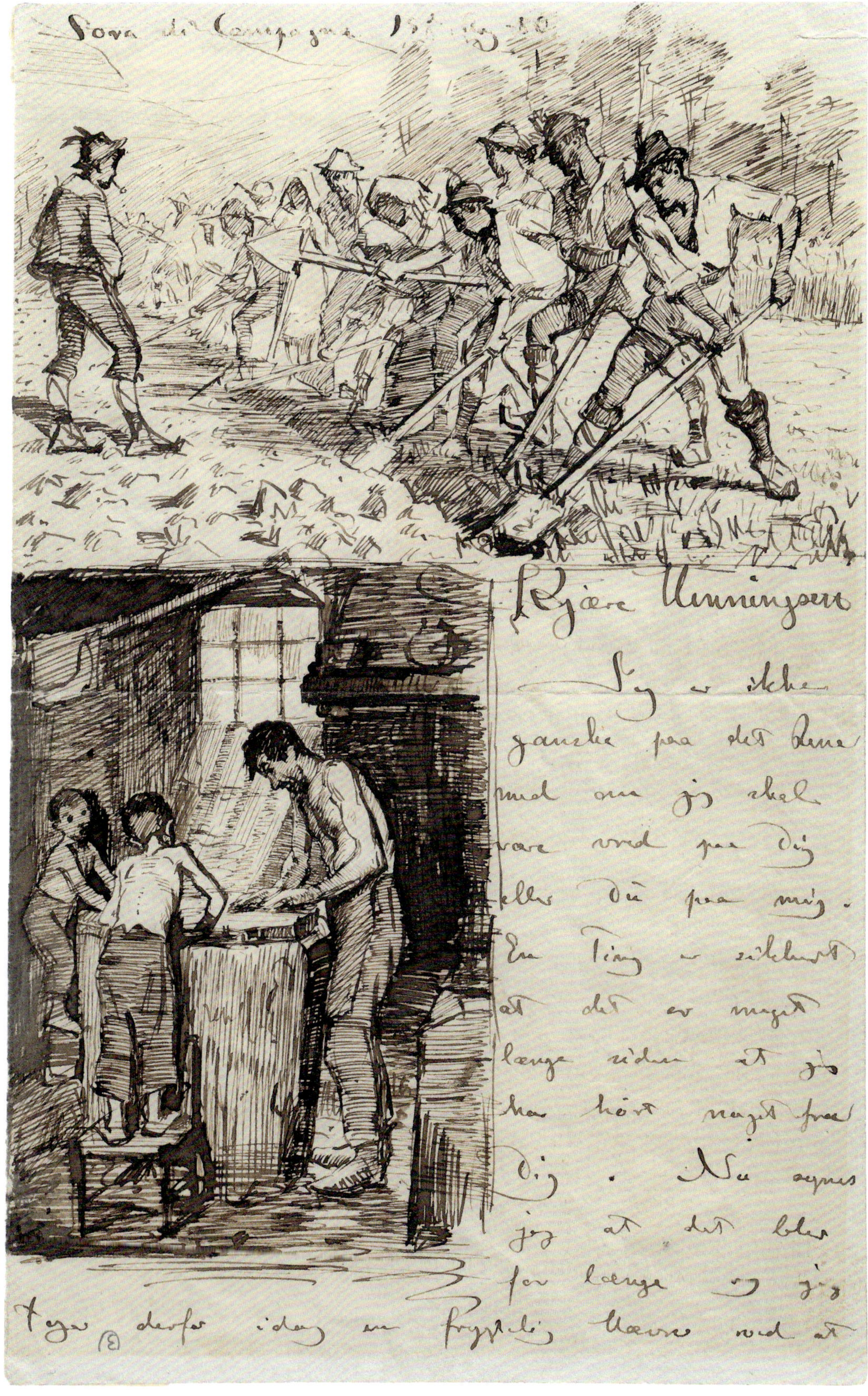

Sora di Campagna

Kjære Henningsen

Jeg er ikke
ganske paa det Rene
med om jeg skal
være vred paa Dig
eller Du paa mig.
En Ting er sikkert
at det er meget
længe siden at jeg
har hört noget fra
Dig. Nu synes
jeg at det bliver
for længe og jeg
tager derfor idag en frygtelig Hævn ved at

ILL. 13 Peder Severin Krøyer, Letter to Frants Henningsen, Sora, 1880. Skagens Kunstmuseer. SKMB26

a third-class medal, quite a feat for a non-French artist, prompting even more numerous reviews and mentions than before. This time Marius Vachon wrote:

> [...] a most original work by Krøyer, the creator of *Sardine Curing and Packing Factory in Concarneau*, which attracted such attention at the Salon last year. It depicts a dark and smoky shop room at the village hatter. We see three workers stripped to the waist, painted in a palette reminiscent of Rembrandt, powerfully executed and with a unique intensity in its portrayal of character.[63]

Krøyer spent three weeks in Paris in May 1881, after which he returned to Copenhagen. Prior to his departure, he painted the small picture *Excursion on the Seine* (ILL. 14). It is a small study that was not intended for exhibition, but more of a note made during his travels. We do not know the identities of the people in the picture, but they are most likely some of Krøyer's acquaintances in Paris, creating a kinship with the Impressionists' range of subject matter and how they often painted scenes of artists socialising in the big city.

Krøyer and France after 1881

Krøyer's hectic travel schedule never stopped. From 1881, he simply divided his year, wintering in Copenhagen and summering in Skagen, where he stayed for the first time in 1882. His connection to the French art scene lasted for many years, but from around 1890 he increasingly visited other European cities. Krøyer now mainly visited Paris for a few weeks in spring to experience the Salon and other exhibitions and museums.

In 1882 he exhibited a full-length portrait of Ferdinand Meldahl (CAT. 41) at the Salon, as well as some drawings in a Scandinavian gallery on Avenue de l'Opera, operated by the Norwegian author H.G. Petersen-Gade, who had settled in Paris.[64] In a departure from his usual habit, Krøyer did not exhibit in Paris in 1883, but nevertheless visited the city. He would faithfully return each year in connection with his exhibition activity until 1889, when he married the painter Marie Triepcke. A small series of four photographs shows a social lunch in Paris in the spring of 1889 in the company of Scandinavian artist friends (ILL. 15).[65] Following this, his visits became more sporadic. He could be found in Paris in the years 1892, 1895, 1898, and 1899, and in 1900 after his mental breakdown. On that occasion he visited the Exposition Universelle, the Danish part of which he had helped to arrange. Afterwards, he visited again in 1902, 1903, and, while passing through, in 1907.

Only a few of his visits during that period were prolonged. One of the more eventful took place in 1884, when he had submitted three works to the Salon: *Fishermen Hauling a Seine Net at Skagen Nordstrand. Late Afternoon* (CAT. 42), *Artists' Luncheon at Brøndum's Hotel* (Skagens Kunstmuseer), and, in the section for works on paper, the pastel *Summer Evening* (Nationalmuseum, Stockholm).[66] The two oils received the most publicity, winning him a second-class medal, of which a total of 12 were awarded. He came close to receiving a first-class medal, of which none were ultimately awarded that year.[67] Still, receiving the silver medal was a considerable achievement, and it came with the huge benefit that from this point on, he could exhibit works of his choice without having to submit them to a jury first. That same spring, he visited the predominantly Swedish artists' colony south of Paris, Grez-sur-Loing, not far from Fontainebleau.[68] Here he immortalised the company in the pastel *Artists' Luncheon in Grez* (Prins Eugens Waldemarsudde, Stockholm).

63. Vachon, 'Le Salon de 1881', 3.
64. Lobstein, '"A Lover of Light"', 53.
65. Left to right: Ursule Tuxen, Ida Schandorph, Michael Ancher, Hanna Rönnberg, Sophus Schandorph, Anna Ancher, Marie Triepcke, and Peder Severin Krøyer.
66. Nos. 1340, 1341, and 2904 at the Salon in 1884.
67. 'Au Salon. Les Deuxième Médailles de la Peinture', 2.
68. Lübbren, 168–169.

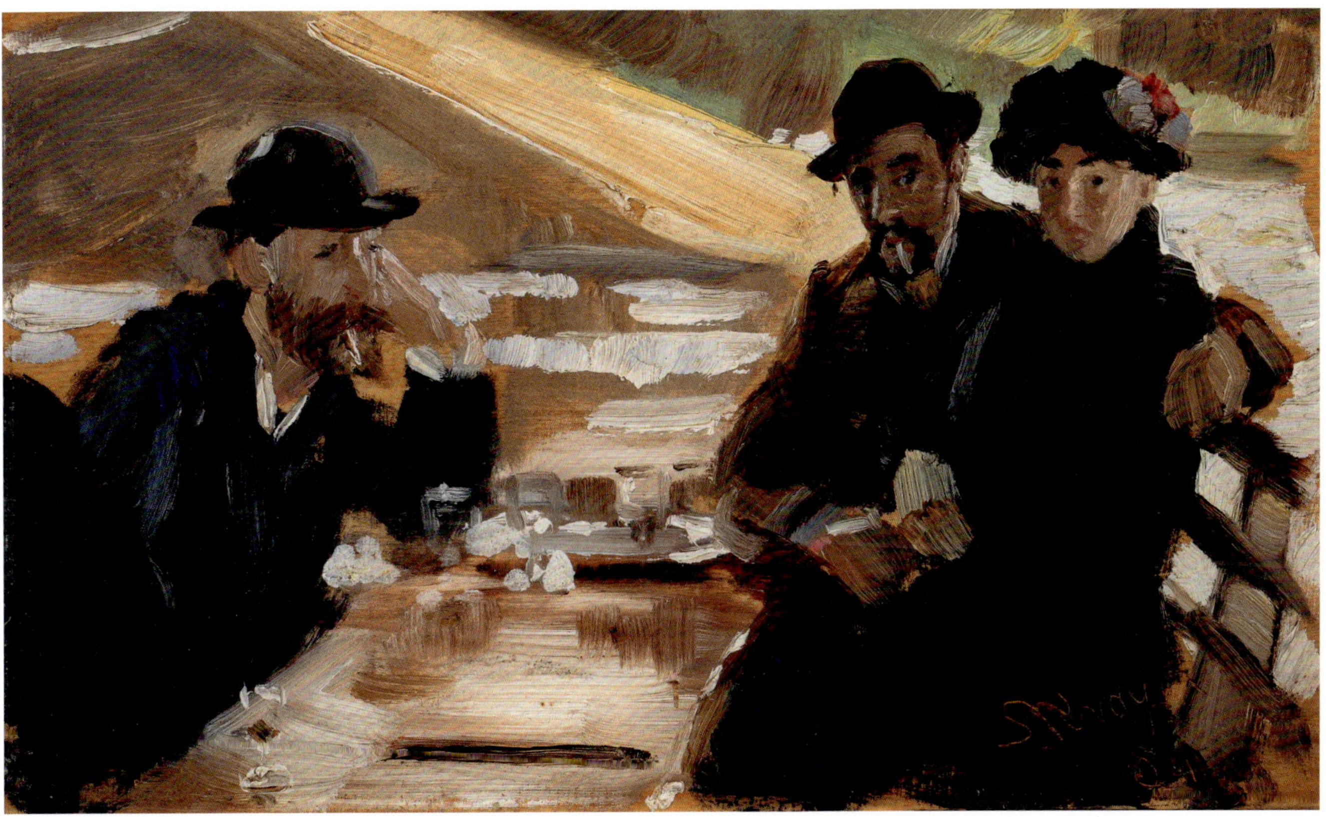

ILL. 14 Peder Severin Krøyer: *Excursion on the Seine*, 1881. Oil on panel, 12.7×21.7 cm. Skagens Kunstmuseer. SKM17

A French contemporary, Paul-Albert Besnard, whom Krøyer had met in Paris, also came to play a major role in Krøyer's career during the 1880s. In 1886, Krøyer exhibited a large painting, *Skagen Men going out Fishing at Night. Late Summer Evening* (CAT. 44), at the Salon in Paris. For practical reasons, he left the large painting with Besnard, and gifted it to him two years later. In 1899, Besnard donated it to the Musée du Luxembourg, which could not afford to buy it. Thus, it was thanks to his good friend Besnard that Krøyer was represented at the museum of contemporary art with such an impressive work. A watercolour depicting his wife, *Marie Krøyer and their daughter Vibeke reading in their home at Skagen* from 1898 (CAT. 55), exhibited at the Exposition Universelle in 1900 in Paris, was subsequently acquired by the Musée du Luxembourg and is now at the Louvre (deposit from Musée d'Orsay).[69]

In 1886 and again in 1889, just before his wedding to Marie Triepcke, Krøyer visited the French city of Luchon in the Pyrenees, close to the Spanish border. This was not the site of an artists' colony but a spa town, which Krøyer visited quite alone. Here he underwent cures with baths and diets to improve his health, and at the same time created small-scale works, including the very atmospheric naturalistic *Labourers at an Inn, Luchon*, created during his first stay (Den Hirschsprungske Samling, Copenhagen).

69. Lobstein, '"A Lover of Light"', 61. The work would have been no. 74 or 75, both of which are listed under the title *Scène d'intérieur – aquarelle* in the exhibition catalogue for the *Exposition Universelle de 1900*.

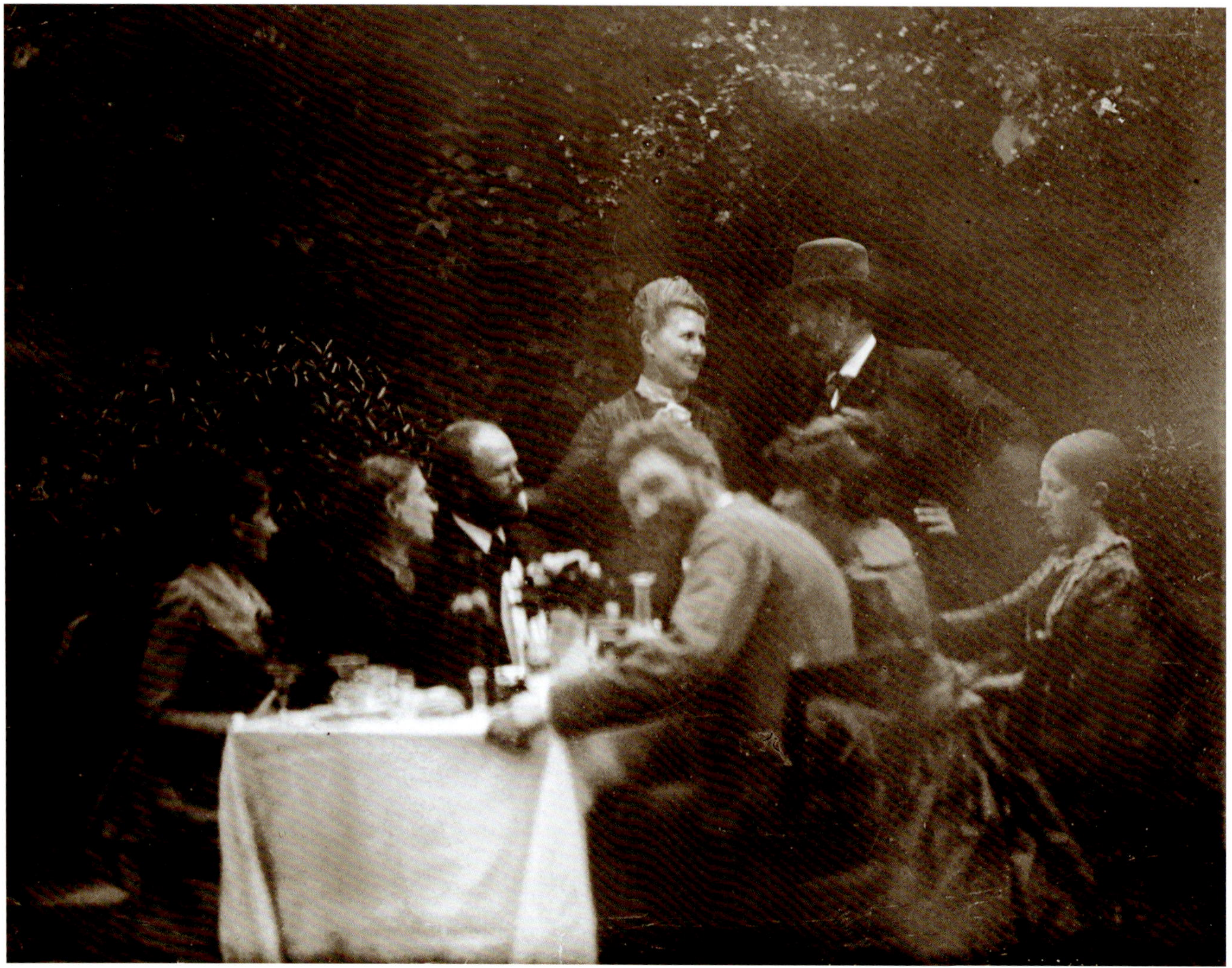

ILL. 15 Peder Severin Krøyer: Luncheon, presumably in Asnières, 1889.

From 1888 to 1889 he made a long stay in Paris, partly in connection with the preparations for the French exhibition in Copenhagen in 1888 and partly to paint and exhibit *Committee for the French Art Exhibition in Copenhagen 1888* (CAT. 47). In 1889 he exhibited at the Salon and at the Exposition Universelle.

As a very special achievement, Krøyer was awarded the French Order the Légion d'honneur twice; first as Chevalier (knight) and then the higher rank as Officier (officer).[70] The Order was awarded twice a year, in January and July, and was not always bestowed in recognition of any particular event. Nor do any documents on the awarding of the Légion d'honneur to foreigners survive in French archives. Krøyer received his first Légion d'honneur on 8 July 1887, and the cover letter states no reason why he was awarded it. Thus, the motivations must

70. The two diplomas pertaining to the Ordre National de la Légion D'Honneur and La Décoration de Chevalier de l'Ordre National de la Légion d'honneur Paris in 1887 and 1901, as well as the covering letters, are in the collection of Skagens Kunstmuseer (Krøyer's insignia and diplomas, nos. 7 and 2).

remain a matter of conjecture, but one possible explanation may be that Krøyer had once again made a name for himself at the Salon in 1887 with the two works *Music in the Studio*, 1886 (Nasjonalmuseet, Oslo), and *Summer Day at Skagen Sønderstrand*, 1884 (Den Hirschsprungske Samling). The second time Krøyer received the Order was 18 January 1901, presumably given due to his involvement in the organisation of the Danish contribution to the 1900 Exposition Universelle. By this time, Krøyer had also (in November 1897) become a Corresponding Academician at the Académie des Beaux-Arts, which was solely an honorary title, and he had won several medals and prizes, the most important being the Grand Prix received for his participation in the Exposition Universelle in Paris in 1889 and 1900.[71]

A career of a thousand connections

In his artistic practice, Krøyer can be described as a nomad navigating through the endless sands of the desert to find ever-shifting oases. Or as a sailor who navigates his way through archipelagos solely by means of his sense of time and place. Krøyer did not live within a closed system, but in an open and changing world, and his art changed along with it. He took something with him from Bonnat's school in terms of his brushwork, *chiaroscuro* effects, and degree of detail, as well as the processing of paint to make it thicker. But he continued to do preliminary studies for his *plein air* paintings in line with the practices he learned at the art academy. He did not relinquish preliminary studies the way the Impressionists did in order to cultivate immediate impressions. In this way, he created a synthesis of what he had learned and absorbed from various sources, adding to this mix his own very special relationship with light, which found expression in interiors, portraits, and landscapes by twilight, in storms, and in bright midday sunshine. He was aware of staying original in his style, ensuring that he did not look like, for example, his French role models. He wrote about this in a letter to his former teacher at the Danish academy of fine arts, Vermehren, in 1879 while describing Bonnat's teaching,[72] and it also found expression in his own teaching of future artists at Kunstnernes Studieskole.

As regards his choice of subject matter, he favoured Naturalist images in the 1870s and 1880s, but also found a distinctly Nordic tone in Skagen during the 1880s and 1890s, seasoning it with dashes of international impulses such as Japonisme, which deeply fascinated Karl Madsen and others;[73] French Symbolism, as in Puvis de Chavannes; and not least the Arts and Crafts movement, inspired by his wife's interest. In 1890, before the couple returned from their combined honeymoon and study trip, Krøyer wrote to the landlord of his studio at 33, Bredgade, Axel Prior, informing him that the studio was now to be painted white in order to accommodate the new works he would paint.[74] After 1900, his *plein air* paintings evolved, using freer, broader brushstrokes, bold colour contrasts, and strong sunlight filtered through the leaves of trees.

71. Appointed Correspondent de l'Institut, Académie des Beaux-Arts, Paris, 20 November 1897; Krøyer's insignia and diplomas, no. 24.

72. Copy of letter: PSK to Frederik Vermehren, Cernay-la-Ville, 20 May 1879. PSK Archive 58.

73. Karl Madsen's first book, *Japansk Malerkunst*, was on Japanese painting.

74. PSK to Axel Prior, Civita d'Antino, 17 June 1890. PSK Archive 125.1. Halkier, 'The studio at Bredgade 33', 68.

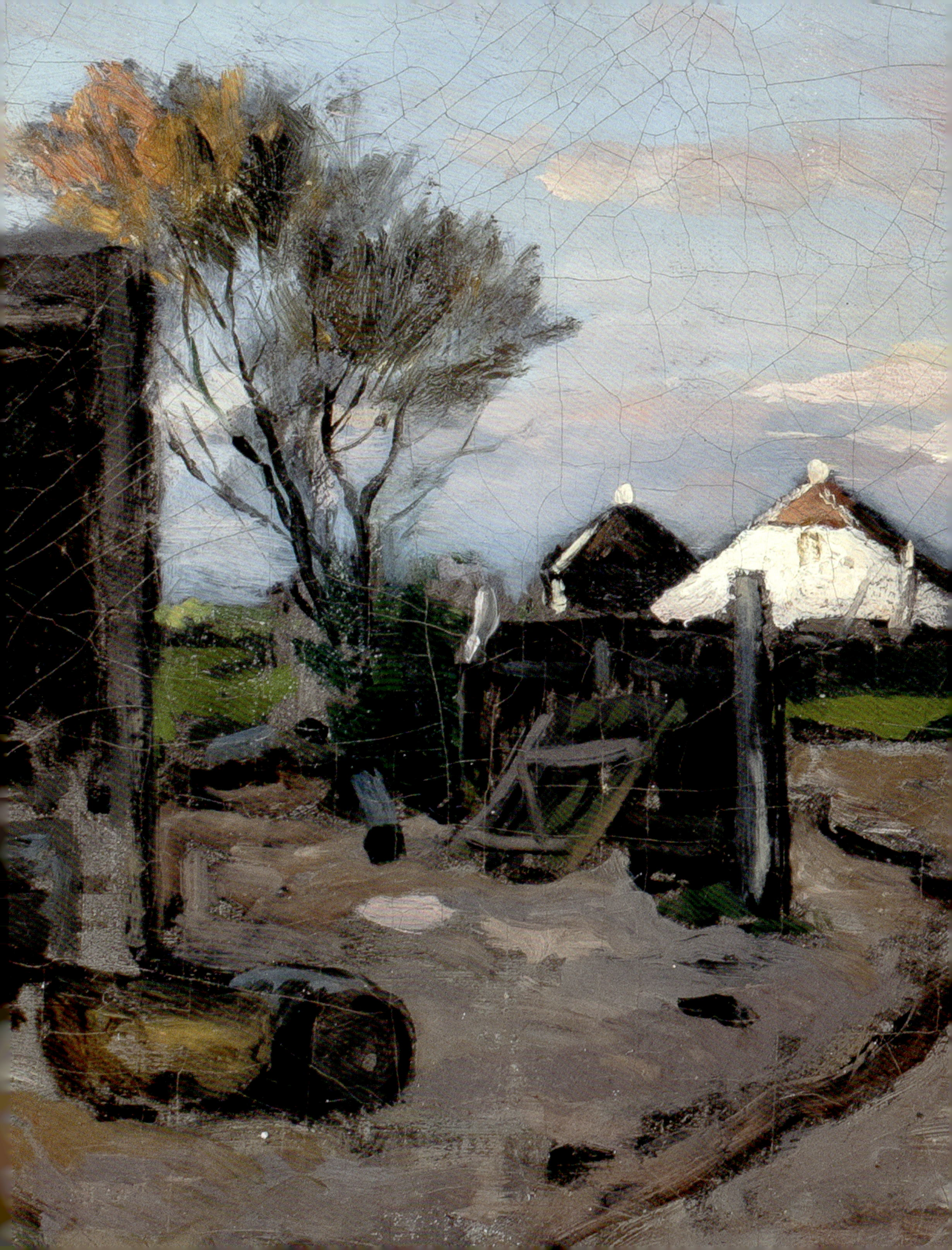

Krøyer and the Scandinavian Artists in Paris

3

The artists' capital

When Peder Severin Krøyer set out for Paris in the spring of 1877, he went against a tradition – one that had been established for decades – of Danish artists going to Rome to study art, grow as artists, and seek out suitable subject matter.[1] The reason Krøyer and several other Danish artists of his generation chose France instead can be found, among other things, in the fact that several Scandinavian artists had already paved the way there. In other words, the French art scene was already open to newly arrived, talented foreign artists. However, the conservative Danish art circles were less receptive to the influence of French art in Denmark. Opinions were divided, to say the least. The number of Scandinavian artists who stayed in Paris, continuing their training or working there, and exhibiting at the Salon around the same time as Krøyer, was quite large; several of them became part of Krøyer's circle of friends for shorter or longer periods of time. Thus, the Scandinavian artists' shared and joint experiences from Paris affected their attitudes towards art. They made informed and decisive choices regarding preferences for a more French or international naturalistic painting style, rather than a distinctively and decidedly national one, and also took a stance regarding their choice of subject matter, which could certainly include scenes from abroad, but even so subjects from the artists' respective home countries were seen to have special advantages.

In the decades before 1873, not many Scandinavian artists had exhibited at the Salon in Paris, which had existed since 1667. The same was true of the international expositions in 1855 or 1867. Only very few names recurred over several years, and the French critics took scarce if any notice of their work. The Danish, Norwegian, and Swedish painters were simply too few in number and exhibited too sporadically for the critics to gain sufficient accumulated knowledge to evaluate their works on a professional basis.[2]

1. Grand, 'Rejsebilleder – Turist i Arkadien?', 202.

2. Lobstein, '"A Lover of Light"', 49.

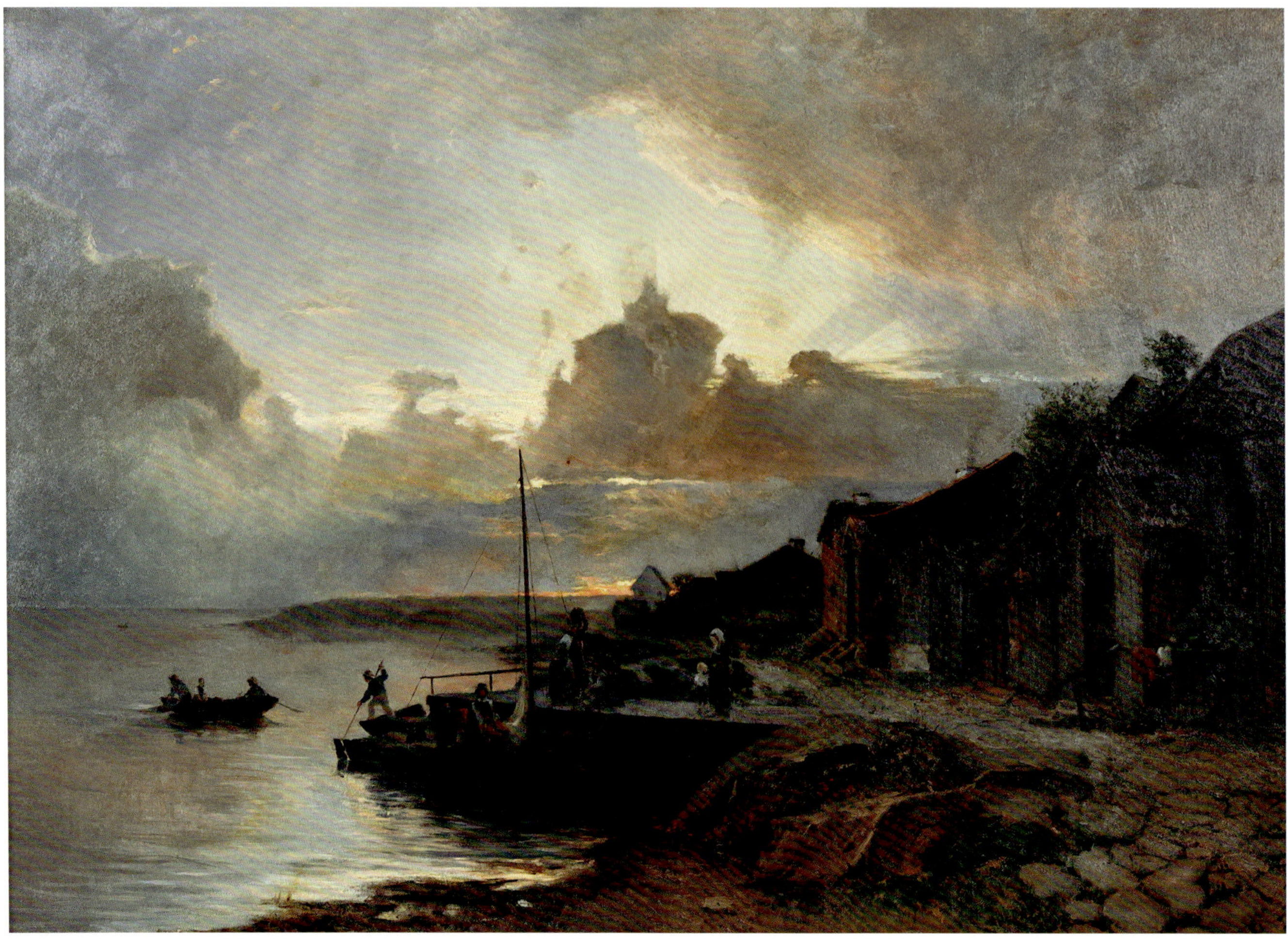

ILL. 16 Alfred Wahlberg (attributed to): *Fishing Village in the Fjällba Region*, 1868. Oil on canvas, 90×130 cm. Location unknown.

During the Second Empire (1852–1870), under the rule of Emperor Napoleon III, French audiences only saw one Scandinavian name regularly at the Salon: the Norwegian painter Jacob Johan Bennetter, who from 1853 faithfully exhibited works there, especially marine paintings stylistically in line with those of his French master, Théodore Gudin, with whom he had trained in Paris. Towards the end of the imperial regime, a few other Scandinavian painters appeared, such as the Norwegian artist Peter Nicolai Arbo in 1864, who introduced France to its very first *Valkyrie* (Nationalmuseum, Stockholm), and Swedish artist Alfred Wahlberg, who exhibited for the first time at the Salon in 1868. Wahlberg exhibited two works, one of which was *Fishing Village in the Fjällba Region* (ILL. 16).[3]

After the Franco-Prussian War of 1870–1871 and the revolutionary rule of the Paris Commune, which prevented the Salon from taking place in 1871, the exhibition was resumed in 1872, by which point Adolphe Thiers had come

3. Catalogue no. 2542. According to Stockholms Auktionsverk, the work cannot definitively be said to be by Wahlberg, as no visible signature is seen on the canvas.

to power as the president of France. In this Third Republic, the Salon aroused growing interest not only among the public but among French and an increasing number of foreign artists, too. This also held true of the Scandinavian artists, with French audiences now having the opportunity to see exhibited works by seven of them in 1873 – one Dane, two Norwegians, and four Swedes – and by no less than 43 in 1880: five Danes, 15 Norwegians, and 23 Swedes.[4]

The reason for the relatively large number of Norwegians and Swedes compared to Danes can be found in the three countries' different traditions in the realms of art and education. The Swedish academy, Kungliga Akademien för de fria konsterna in Stockholm, founded in 1735, was generally more open to French art than its Danish counterpart. When it was founded, the French artist Guillaume Thomas Taraval was chosen as the principal teacher, and so the teaching was arranged according to the French model. From 1856 the Swedish painter Johan Boklund taught at the school, and he was director there from 1867 to 1880. Under his leadership, the teaching was organised according to the schooling he had received in France in the studio of Thomas Couture. During that period, it was not uncommon for pupils to be encouraged to seek out instruction in France, with the Atelier Bonnat as a particular favourite.[5] There were close ties, then, between the Swedish academy's teaching and the French art scene in the years 1850 to 1880, which explains why the Swedish students did not feel quite the same dissatisfaction with their teaching by the end of the period as their Danish counterparts did.

Norway was in a personal union with Sweden under one king from 1814 to 1905; prior to this, it had been in a union with Denmark. Therefore, the country did not have its own art academy until 1909, with Norwegian painter Christian Krohg becoming the nation's first professor of painting. Before this, budding artists could apply to Den kgl. Tegneskole in Oslo – a drawing school founded in 1818 and primarily important in relation to the education of artisans – or they could go abroad to attend the Danish or Swedish art academies.

The Danish academy, Det Kongelige Danske Kunstakademi, was founded in 1754. Denmark, which sided with the French during the Napoleonic Wars, went bankrupt in 1813 due to the wars and had to cede Norway to Sweden at the defeat in 1814. The subsequent Danish crisis led to an inward-looking nationalist focus on Danish history, aiming to build up and reaffirm the Danish self-image. Christoffer Wilhelm Eckersberg became a professor at *modelskolen* (the life class, popularly known as the 'model school') at the Danish academy in 1818, was director in 1827–1829, and made an unmistakable mark on Danish art that would remain in force for many years to come. He himself had received instruction in Paris from the French artist Jacques-Louis David after graduating in Denmark. However, that influence was not enough to permanently push the Danish academy of fine arts in that direction. From around the 1830s, strong political forces held the art academy and the established artists in a firm grip, exercised partly by the art historian Niels Lauritz Høyen, who held a number of key positions in Danish art. As a result, most Danish artists came to support a conservative National Liberal project which insisted that art must do its bit to promote a distinctly Danish identity. After the fall of absolute monarchy in 1848 and the Danish defeat by the Prussians in 1864 – which meant that Denmark once again had to cede a large area of land, this time the duchies of Schleswig, Holstein, and Lauenborg – support for the National Liberal project slowly crumbled, and in the 1870s the younger artists grew increasingly dissatisfied with the older artists' unwavering focus on all things Danish.

4. The figures reflect the nationalities listed in the catalogues, meaning that they are subject to the uncertainties associated with the period's records and registration of the many thousands of artists who took part in the exhibitions.

5. Challons-Lipton, 43.

The first Danish artist to exhibit at the Salon in Paris was Georg Vilhelm Arnold Groth, who found his way there in 1873.[6] It has not proved possible to locate the two works submitted by him, which may be due to the fact that he never achieved any major breakthrough as an artist.[7] The first artist to exhibit a scene from Skagen – two years before Krøyer even visited this northernmost point in Denmark – was the Swedish artist Wilhelm von Gegerfelt, who exhibited *Skagen Beach* (location unknown) in 1880.[8]

Von Gegerfelt had faithfully exhibited at the Salon since 1873, and he visited Skagen in both 1874 and 1879. In connection with his 1879 visit, he brought his French student Émile Barau along to the Danish artists' colony; based on the available knowledge about the artist and close inspection of the subject matter, the museum that currently owns the work Barau exhibited at the Salon in 1880, *Cottages in the Dunes (Denmark)* (CAT. 16), has ascertained that it too was actually painted in Skagen, even though the audiences at the time had no way of knowing this, as the exact location was not identified in the title.[9]

Known to have been created during Gegerfelt's first stay in Skagen, the work *From Skagen Østerby* (ILL. 17) offers an excellent impression of what the small fishing village that would eventually form the setting of Denmark's greatest artists' colony looked like in the early 1870s. Gegerfelt also left his mark on the Danish artists present in Skagen in 1879 by teaching Karl Madsen, Michael Ancher, and Carl Locher how to use asphalt (bitumen) and brown varnish to create intense blacks and a strong effect of depth in dark areas.[10] Krøyer learnt the technique in France that same year from Danish friend and fellow artist Laurits Tuxen, using it in works such as *A Sardine Curing and Packing Factory in Concarneau* from 1879 (CAT. 30).[11]

The connections between the Nordic countries and France thus went two ways. The first Scandinavians paved the way for their successors, preparing the ground and opening the eyes of the French public and the French critics to Nordic artists, and at the same time French impulses were brought back to the Nordic countries and to the artists' colonies, including the colony in Skagen.

From the end of the 18th century and throughout the period known as the Danish Golden Age (approximately 1800–1850), the Danish artists had primarily sought out Rome on their Grand Tours and study trips. These were journeys that were largely dictated – and, through scholarships, often funded – by the Danish art academy. Artists were expected to study the art of classical antiquity and to depict an almost mythological archaic landscape.[12] But after the Franco-Prussian War, France became increasingly popular with young artists, and the 1878 Exposition Universelle in Paris became particularly important for the Danish artists' relationship to French contemporary art.

Warring parties, 1872–1878

In Denmark, the debate about the harmful or beneficial influence of French art on young Danish artists began in the early 1870s as part of a wider discussion concerning the younger artists' dissatisfaction with their established counterparts. In 1872, in connection with *Den nordiske Industri- og Kunstudstilling*, a major Nordic exhibition of industry and art held in Copenhagen, visitors could view works by Swedish artists who had gone to Paris, such as Wahlberg, Boklund, and Hugo Salmson. As has already been mentioned, an early adopter of French impulses among the Danes was William Groth, who went to France

6. He is the first to be registered and therefore known as a Dane, but perusal of the catalogues turns up figures such as the Polish-born Danish artist Elisabeth Jerichau-Baumann, who took part in 1861, and Lorenz Frølich, who lived in Paris for a long time and was best known as an illustrator, in 1868 and 1872. In 1873 another artist is also listed in the catalogue as a Dane, born in Altona, Germany: his name is Ludovic Mendès Monsanto, but whether he was actually Danish cannot be confirmed.

7. Catalogue nos. 684, *View from the Coast of Funen (Denmark)*, and 685, *Misty Morning off the Coast of Zealand (Denmark)*.

8. Catalogue no. 1572.

9. Catalogue no. 155, *Cottages in the Dunes (Denmark)*. At the Musée des Beaux-Arts in Reims the work carries the title *Cottages in the Dunes at Skagen (Denmark)*, inv. no. 907.19.3.

10. Svanholm, *Skagen Leksikon*, 61.

11. PSK to Laurits Tuxen, Sora, 14 May 1880. KB NBD 2. rk.

12. Grand, 'Rejsebilleder – Turist i Arkadien?', 202–212.

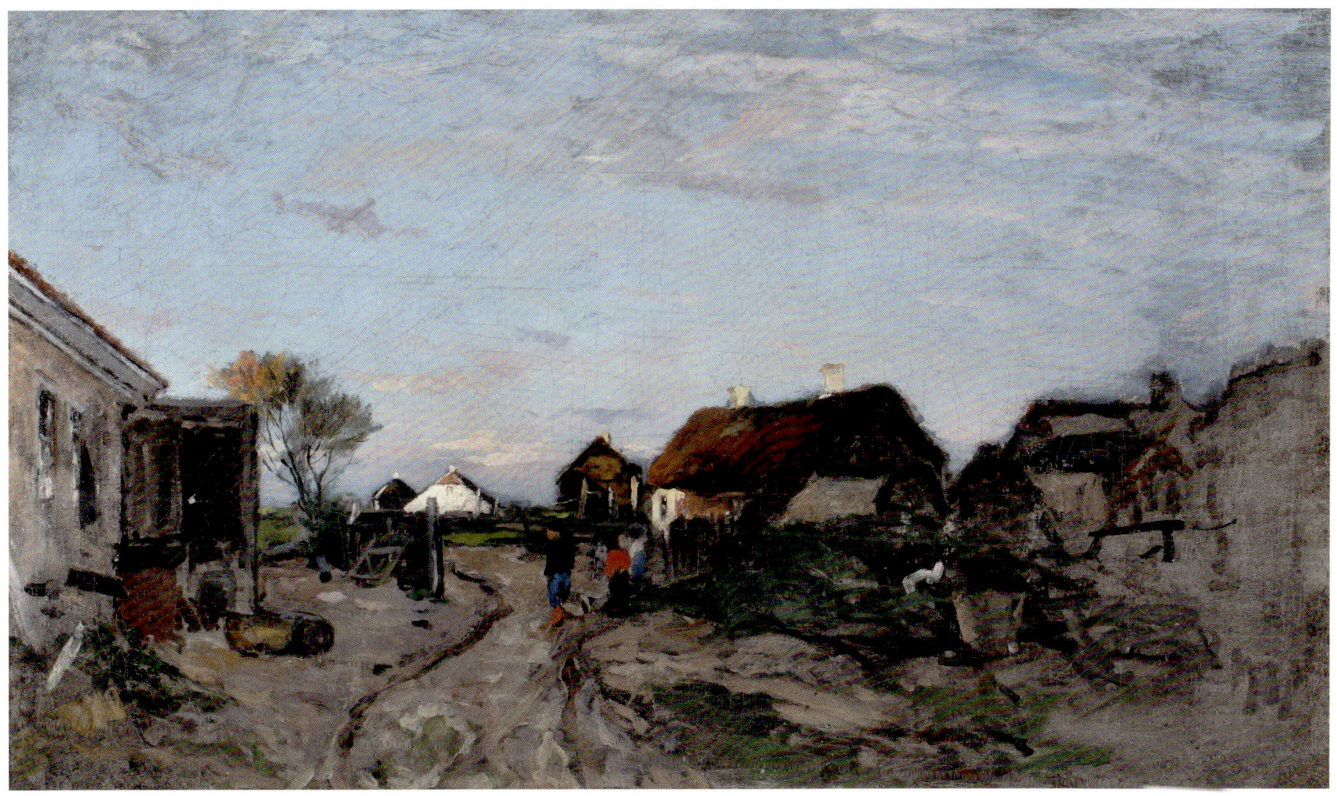

ILL. 17 Wilhelm von Gegerfelt: *From Skagen Østerby*, 1874. Oil on canvas, 41×70 cm. Skagens Kunstmuseer. SKM1649

to learn more. The Danish artist Vilhelm Kyhn was particularly vociferous in defending the distinctive Danish art against what he, in 1874, called 'the French fancies,'[13] and in 1876 and 1877 a fierce debate was enacted in full public view between especially Kyhn and Groth, who wrote small books and pamphlets on the subject. However, the discussion also featured other voices, such as the painter Carl Bloch from the older generation and Holger Drachmann from the younger. Kyhn opened the discussion by writing *Dansk Kunst og Kunstudstillingen på Charlottenborg* (Danish Art and the Exhibition at Charlottenborg), with Groth offering his reply anonymously in *Dansk Kunst i Forhold til Udlandets* (Danish Art Compared to Abroad), but his identity was quickly revealed. Kyhn retaliated with *Dansk Kunst. Svar fra V. Kyhn til den 'danske Kunstner'* (Danish Art. A Reply from V. Kyhn to the 'Danish Artist').[14] Interestingly, both artists took part in the Exposition Universelle in Paris in 1878, where Danish art was expected to triumph, but suffered defeat. Among other things, Kyhn contributed an older work, *A Summer's Day. View from Horneland near Fåborg* from 1869 (ILL. 18), and Groth's submissions

13. Frederiksen, 'Kyhns mareridt', 54.

14. Kyhn, *Dansk Kunst og Kunstudstillingen på Charlottenborg*; En dansk kunstner (A Danish artist (identified as Vilhelm Groth)), *Dansk Kunst i Forhold til Udlandets*; Kyhn, *Dansk Kunst. Svar fra V. Kyhn til den 'danske Kunstner'*.

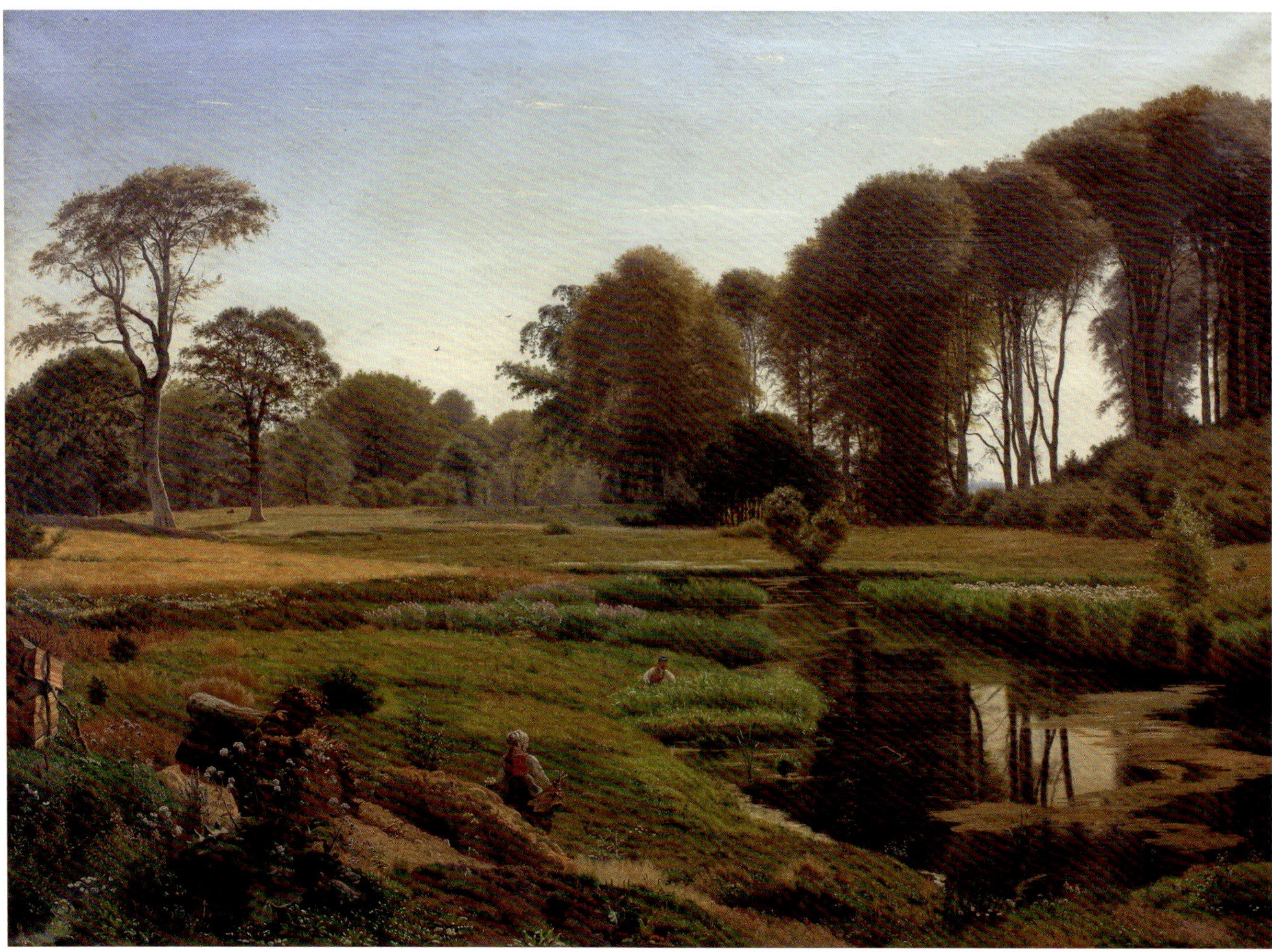

ILL. 18 Vilhelm Kyhn: *A Summer's Day. View from Horneland near Fåborg*, 1869. Oil on canvas, 149.5×200 cm. Statens Museum for Kunst, Copenhagen. KMS866

included the slightly newer work *Heath with a Bog* from 1874 (ILL. 19).[15] Kyhn was a member of the exhibition committee that had put together a selection of works strongly influenced by Danish Golden Age art. Not only were several of the works chosen rather old, but the selection also included numerous artists who were no longer among the living. The Danish contribution fared ill among the critics. In fact, the criticism was so overwhelmingly negative that it prompted thorough subsequent self-examination among the artists in Denmark.

Among the small group of younger painters who exhibited at the Exposition Universelle in 1878, Krøyer received favourable reviews for his *The Smithy in Hornbæk* from 1875 (CAT. 3), as described in chapter 2, but he was not the only one to do so. Kyhn received positive attention too. His *A Summer's Day. View from Horneland near Fåborg*

15. Catalogue nos. 37, *Jour d'été*, and 25, *Paysage des landes*.

attracted the following response from the French reviewer Victor Cherbuliez: 'It has not been raked over; this is not a landscape wearing its Sunday best.'[16]

The defeat at the Exposition Universelle breathed new life into the debate for and against the influence of French art on Danish artists, and a new period of modernity heralded by the Modern Breakthrough in Danish painting had been ushered in, with the writer and literary scholar Georg Brandes as standard bearer. Other voices also entered the discussion, including that of art historian Julius Lange, who in true academic style took up a position somewhere in the middle between the warring parties. In a letter from Copenhagen sent to Krøyer in Paris on 8 May 1879, he wrote:

> But now I notice that I am getting back on one of my hobbyhorses, a theme on which I recently wrote a little book: *Vor Kunst og Udlandets* [Our Art and Foreign Art],[17] which I have long intended to send you without ever picking up the courage to do so, because it has been so strongly gainsaid in all the journals here at home that I fear that it will come across quite wretchedly in Paris. However, I have had the satisfaction of getting approval and support from places where I least expected it, for example from two such avowed Francophiles as Groth and Tuxen.[18]

After 13 years as a member of the Danish art academy, in 1883 Kyhn took his stubborn defence of a distinctly Danish art to its logical conclusion and resigned.[19] By this point he had not attended the meetings of the academy since April 1881, in protest against a proposal to award Krøyer's *Italian Field Labourers. Abruzzo* an exhibition medal at Charlottenborg's juried spring exhibition. According to Kyhn, the painting was too foreign in its manner and its choice of subject matter to merit such an accolade.[20] Back in 1879, Krøyer had shown his resentment of Kyhn's statements in a letter to Vermehren: 'Kyhn has no cause to mock us because we have chosen Bonnat (whom he, showing such little knowledge of facts, calls a fashion painter) as our tutor, and I hope in time that the results will show that what we have learned are by no means "tricks" aimed at "pulling the wool over people's eyes".'[21] But Kyhn remained unconvinced.

Krøyer's Scandinavian circle in Paris

Given the common history of the Scandinavian countries, their various unions through the ages, and their similar languages, it was only natural that Danish, Norwegian, and Swedish artists should seek out each other's company when travelling abroad. They visited each other's apartments in Paris and in the French artists' colonies, they met at cafés that became regular haunts, and they held parties together. In this way, Krøyer gained a large and wide social circle of Scandinavian artists and cultural figures during his times in Paris. It is difficult to form a complete overview of who Krøyer met, when he met them, and exactly how close the various acquaintances became, as the meetings were in several cases only fleeting and not always recorded in written sources. Some of the Finnish, Swedish, and Norwegian artists directly mentioned by Krøyer include Walter Runeberg, Harriet Backer, Alexander Kielland, Bjørnstjerne Bjørnson, and Erik Werenskiold. There were also several Danish artists in Paris, some of whom were close friends, others fleeting acquaintances. Among the Danes with whom he had closer relationships were Christian Zacho, Laurits Tuxen, Holger Drachmann, Carl Locher, Theodor Philipsen, Vilhelm Bissen, and Georg Brandes. Other Scandinavian Naturalist artists and

16. Cherbuliez, 'La peinture à l'Exposition Universelle', 624–626, quoted from Frederiksen, 57.
17. Lange, *Vor Kunst og Udlandets*.
18. Julius Lange to Krøyer, Copenhagen, 8 May 1879, quoted from Købke, 'Breve til Julius Lange', 140–143.
19. Meldahl and Johansen, *Det Kongelige Akademi*, 449–451; Oelsner and Grand, 'Introduktion til Vilhelm Kyhn', 16.
20. Meldahl and Johansen, 449–451.
21. Draft for a letter: PSK to Frederik Vermehren, Cernay-la-Ville, 20 May 1879. PSK Archive 58.

cultural figures associated with the Modern Breakthrough in Norway and Sweden he did not meet in Paris, but elsewhere; they include Carl Larsson, Oscar Björck, Christian Krohg, Kitty Kielland, Henrik Ibsen, Edvard Grieg, Christian Meyer Ross, and Eilif Peterssen, to name just a few.

Some painters should be particularly highlighted for their importance as Scandinavian artists in Paris. They include prominent figures such as the Swedish painter August Hagborg, who distinguished himself at the Paris Salon, exhibiting there regularly from 1876 to 1909. Krøyer may not have met him, but we know that he knew of him. In a letter to Tuxen sent from Sora in May 1880, Krøyer wrote:

> By the way, [Christian] Zacho wrote that Hagborg, Salmson, and Gegerfelt are doing less well this year than last year. The *Figaro*, which was sent to me from Paris, says of Hagborg that 'once you have been successful with a picture, you should not paint the same thing again unless you are able to do it much better'. I should have taken that point more into account when I painted the repetition of my smithy back in the day.[22]

Hagborg was perhaps best known for his Naturalistic scenes from the beaches of Normandy (CAT. 19), but he never stopped painting landscapes from his homeland.[23]

By contrast, Krøyer became personally acquainted with the Norwegian artist Frits Thaulow, who also made his mark in Paris, at an early stage. The two men may have met some time before in Copenhagen in the early 1870s, where they both attended the art academy, albeit at different times.[24] Krøyer graduated in July 1870, and Thaulow began his studies in December 1870, continuing until 1872. Thaulow had wintered in Paris from 1876 to 1879 and later took up more permanent residence there. Accordingly, in 1878 Krøyer was able to write a letter home stating that he would celebrate Christmas in his and Locher's studio in Paris in the company of several other artists and their families, including Thaulow.[25] Similarly, a letter sent during his time in Cernay-la-Ville a little outside Paris in the spring of 1879 states that Thaulow would come to visit with his whole family.[26]

Thaulow also got to know Holger Drachmann during his training in Copenhagen. They visited Skagen together in 1872, making them the very first artists to make this trip among all those who later came to be associated with the upcoming artists' colony there. Thaulow returned to Skagen on several occasions afterwards, including in 1879, at which point Krøyer had left Cernay-la-Ville for Concarneau to spend the summer there. While in Skagen, Thaulow's production included *Fisherman Søren Thy's House, Skagen* (ILL. 20), a work which demonstrates his consistent Naturalism in its depiction of an overturned drying rack for fishing nets in the foreground, the uncultivated nature found in the town, the peeling paint of the house, the bad weather, and the overall sense of poverty.

Krøyer also met the Finnish artist Albert Edelfelt in Paris back in 1877, but their acquaintance did not blossom into a friendship until 1884.[27] They both exhibited in Copenhagen and Paris in the spring of 1884, after which they set out for London together. Before their departure, Edelfeldt wrote the following in a letter from Paris sent to his mother:

22. PSK to Laurits Tuxen, Sora, 14 May 1880. KB NBD 2.rk.

23. Röstorp, 'Third Culture Artist', 178.

24. A portrait of Thaulow drawn by Krøyer in 1872 was up for sale at auction at Blomquist, Oslo, on 12 May 2015.

25. PSK to Vilhelm Krøyer, Paris, 22 December 1878. PSK Archive 48j.

26. PSK to his mother, Cernay-la-Ville, 22 May 1879. PSK Archive 58a.

27. The friendship between Krøyer and Edelfelt is treated in great detail in Saabye, 'Krøyer & Edelfelt', 84–90.

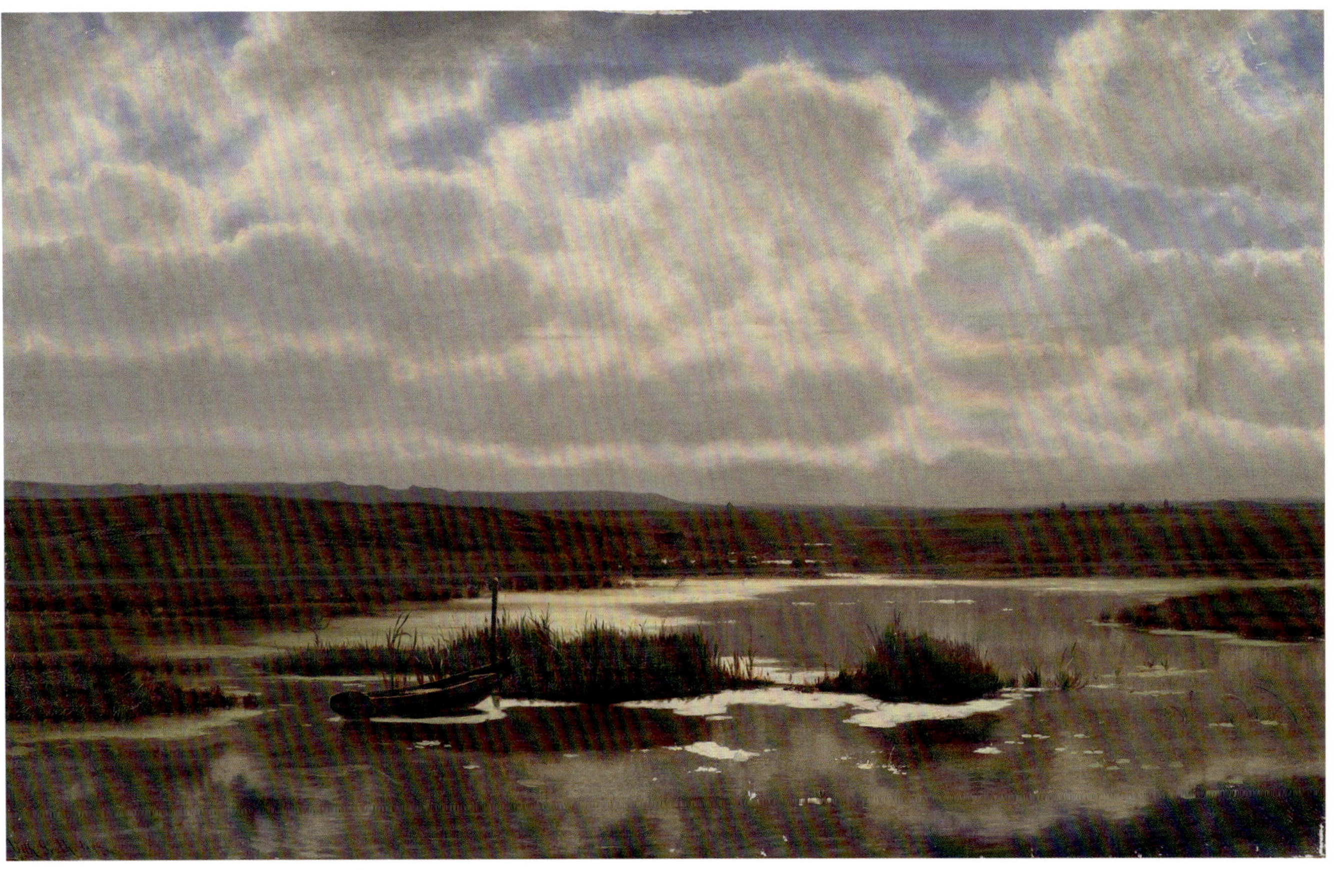

ILL. 19 Vilhelm Groth: *Heath with a Bog*, 1874 (retouched). Oil on canvas, 79.5 × 126.5 cm. Statens Museum for Kunst, Copenhagen. KMS1070

> Krøyer is the most harmonious person I know, enviably harmonious. Happy, fêted, talented, musical; – I cannot conceive of him without Neapolitan songs to guitar accompaniment. He mainly wants to see pictures there, besides roaming the streets, Hyde Park and along the Thames [...].[28]

Edelfelt was fascinated by Krøyer's *plein air* painting, and like Krøyer he was a skilled portrait painter. In his paintings, Edelfelt depicted life in Paris as his fellow Swedish artist Anders Zorn did, but at the same time he, like Hagborg and many other Scandinavian artists, remained anchored in scenes from his homeland, as is reflected in several of his works. Many of the Scandinavian artists who settled in Paris regularly returned to their homeland to paint works that could be exhibited in the French capital. Doing so enabled them stand out from the crowd of Frenchmen by introducing tinges of something exotic.

28. Albert Edelfelt to Alexandra Augusta Edelfelt, Paris, 23 May 1884, Svenska litteratursällskapet i Finland, Axel Berendtson Samling, 364.3, quoted from Saabye, 'Krøyer & Edelfelt', 86.

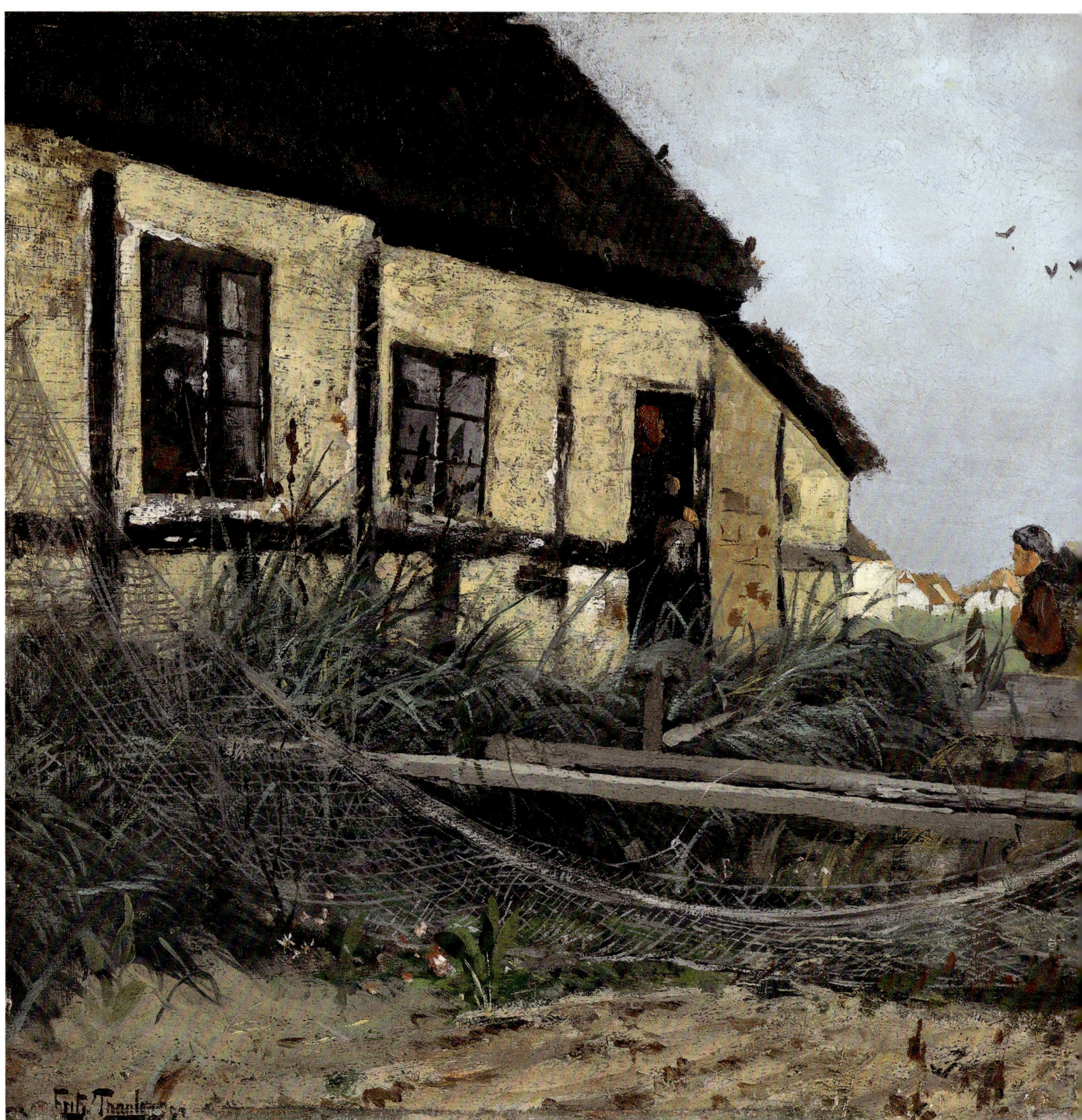

ILL. 20 Frits Thaulow: *Fisherman Søren Thy's house. Skagen*, 1879. Oil on canvas, 34.6×54.2 cm. Skagens Kunstmuseer. SKM409

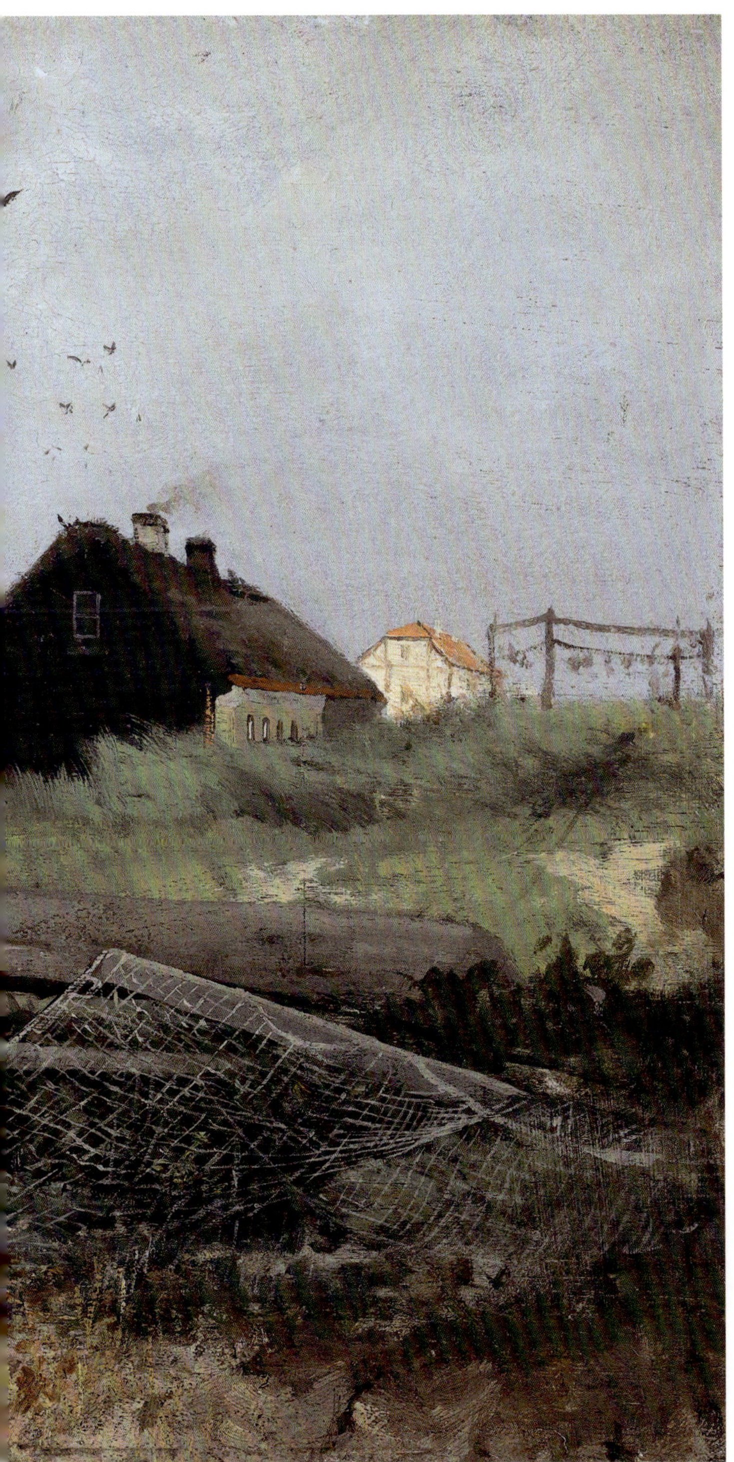

Edelfelt's friendship with Krøyer proved lifelong, and the two artists also exchanged works as gifts: Krøyer dedicated his *Fishermen on Nordstranden a Summer Evening* from 1891 (Skagens Kunstmuseer) to Edelfelt with the words 'To Edelfelt from Krøyer', and Krøyer was given a study of a little girl sitting on a wharf (location unknown), a work done in preparation for *Summer Evening at Hammar's Repair Yard* from 1885 (Statens Museum for Kunst, Copenhagen), where the little girl appears in the middle of the picture.[29]

Zorn made only brief visits to Paris from 1881 until 1888, at which point he took up more permanent residence there and became one of the most prominent Scandinavian artists in France. His first sojourns abroad were to England; he worked extensively in watercolour, and at this time England spearheaded developments in that medium.[30] Krøyer and Zorn could hardly have avoided meeting each other at some point, either in connection with the exhibitions to which they both contributed works, or in the company of mutual friends. However, no correspondence between them has been recorded. Nor does Zorn mention Krøyer in his autobiographical records.[31] Two etchings by Zorn in the Skagens Kunstmuseer collection suggest that a meeting between the two took place in 1889, however, when Krøyer was staying in Paris and borrowed Tuxen's studio. One of the two etchings in question is a self-portrait dated 1889 (FIG. 16), while the other is a *Portrait of the French author Antonin Proust*, also from 1889 (ILL. 21). Both bear the inscription 'To Krøyer / Zorn' done in pencil, and both were bequeathed to the museum from Krøyer's estate in 1918 through Tuxen. Tuxen, who was a

29. *Fishermen on Nordstranden Summer Evening*, inv. no. SKM544. The dedication is on the front in the lower left corner. The little girl on the quay was lot no. 483 at the auction of Krøyer's estate, listed as *Lille pige siddende paa en Brygge* (Little Girl on a Wharf). It had the dedication 'To P. S. Krøyer from A. Edelfeldt'.

30. Regarding the watercolour medium, see: Ohlsen, 'Seks vigtige spørgsmål', 28. Regarding Zorn's movements, see: Röstorp, *Zorn och Frankrike*, 31.

31. Johansen and Jensen, *Zorn besøger Skagen*, 42.

member of the museum's board, wrote the following in a letter to another board member:

> As I recollect, there is an inscription on both of Zorn's etchings 'to Krøyer'. One cannot call them a gift from me. Presumably Krøyer forgot them at my studio in Paris, which he used in the summer of 1889, and they ended up among my papers.[32]

This proves that Krøyer and Zorn met in Paris in 1889, refuting previous assertions that there was no way of documenting that the two artists ever met.

The Nordic contingent in Paris

The Scandinavian artists in Paris incorporated elements of the French manner into the style they had learned beforehand at the art academies in their native countries. French Naturalism was a good fit for the modern Scandinavian art that followed in the wake of the Modern Breakthrough, especially as regards the choice of subject matter and a more socialist worldview. Simplifying matters greatly, artists set out first and foremost to paint what was true rather than what was beautiful. Several artists became integrated into the French art scene, and some settled in France for long periods of time to paint there. Even so, most would continue to depict subjects from their native countries. This trait served to set them apart from the French artists, thereby strengthening their chance of success. Swedish art historian Vibeke Röstorp describes the mode assumed by the Scandinavian artists in Paris as one of 'third culture artists,' borrowing an expression coined by the sociologist Ruth Hill Useem.[33] They represented culture that was not exclusively French nor exclusively national, but precisely a *third* culture – a Nordic community in Paris.

Krøyer held a prominent position among the Scandinavian artists of the 1880s and 1890s. Among his Danish contemporaries, he was one of the most internationally successful. The American associate professor of art history Thor J. Mednick has argued that Krøyer sought to create a visual style that was calibrated to be effective both in Copenhagen and Paris, 'a negotiated modernism that would be at once comfortingly familiar and intriguingly exotic to both audiences.'[34]

For the Exposition Universelle in 1900, three Scandinavian artists were chosen to be honorary members of the art department's jury. The artists selected were Zorn, Thaulow, and Krøyer. This fact is very telling of their status as representatives of the Scandinavian artists in Paris. A Danish journalist wrote:

> As far as Nordic art is concerned, these three names are the most representative on the world market, the most 'European', and in a narrower sense the most French. This is because these artists have most strongly and richly maintained an interaction with the world art that regards Paris as the heart of art, the centre from which the major currents emanate, and to which blood is sucked from all 'cultured countries.'[35]

The Scandinavian artists navigated the French 'world art' and the art of their respective homelands while maintaining their own artistic integrity. In this sense, the third culture (or the Nordic community in Paris) constitutes an enclave of artists who cannot be regarded as a single grouping, yet remain a cluster of individual artists who briefly, in terms of time and place, had certain things in common: a focus on Naturalism and a synthesis of French and Scandinavian painting styles and subject matter.

32. Laurits Tuxen to Victor Klæbel, 30 October 1918. Skagens Kunstmuseer, Hans Klæbel's letter collection, no. 230. The board decided that the work should be credited as follows: 'Gift 1918 from the estate of Krøyer, by Laurits Tuxen'.

33. Röstorp, 'Third Culture Artists', 165–183.

34. Mednick, 87.

35. Soph. M., 'Krøyer og Frits Thaulow'.

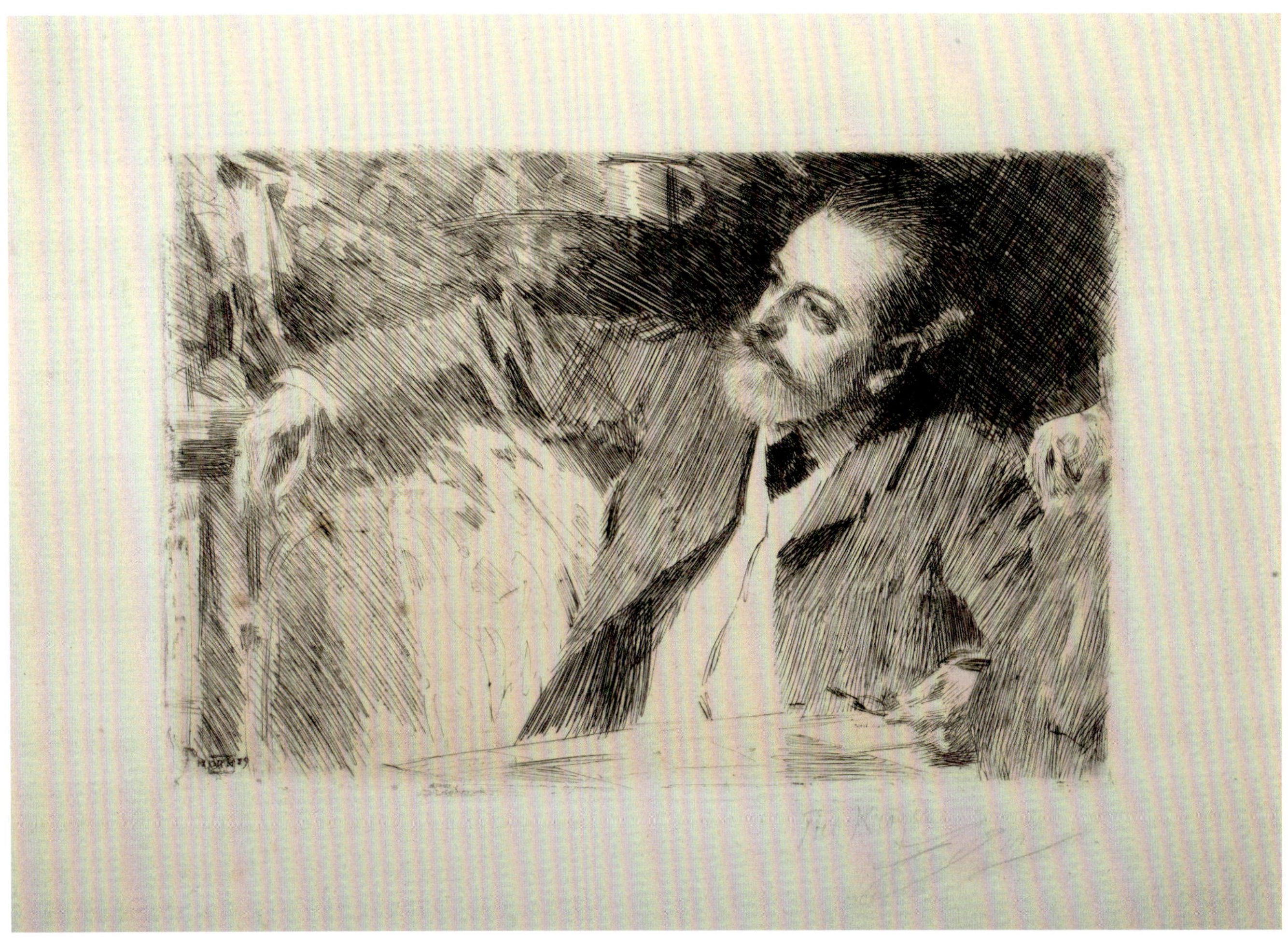

ILL. 21 Anders Zorn: *Portrait of the French author Antonin Proust*, 1889. Etching, 225×313 mm. Skagens Kunstmuseer. SKM185

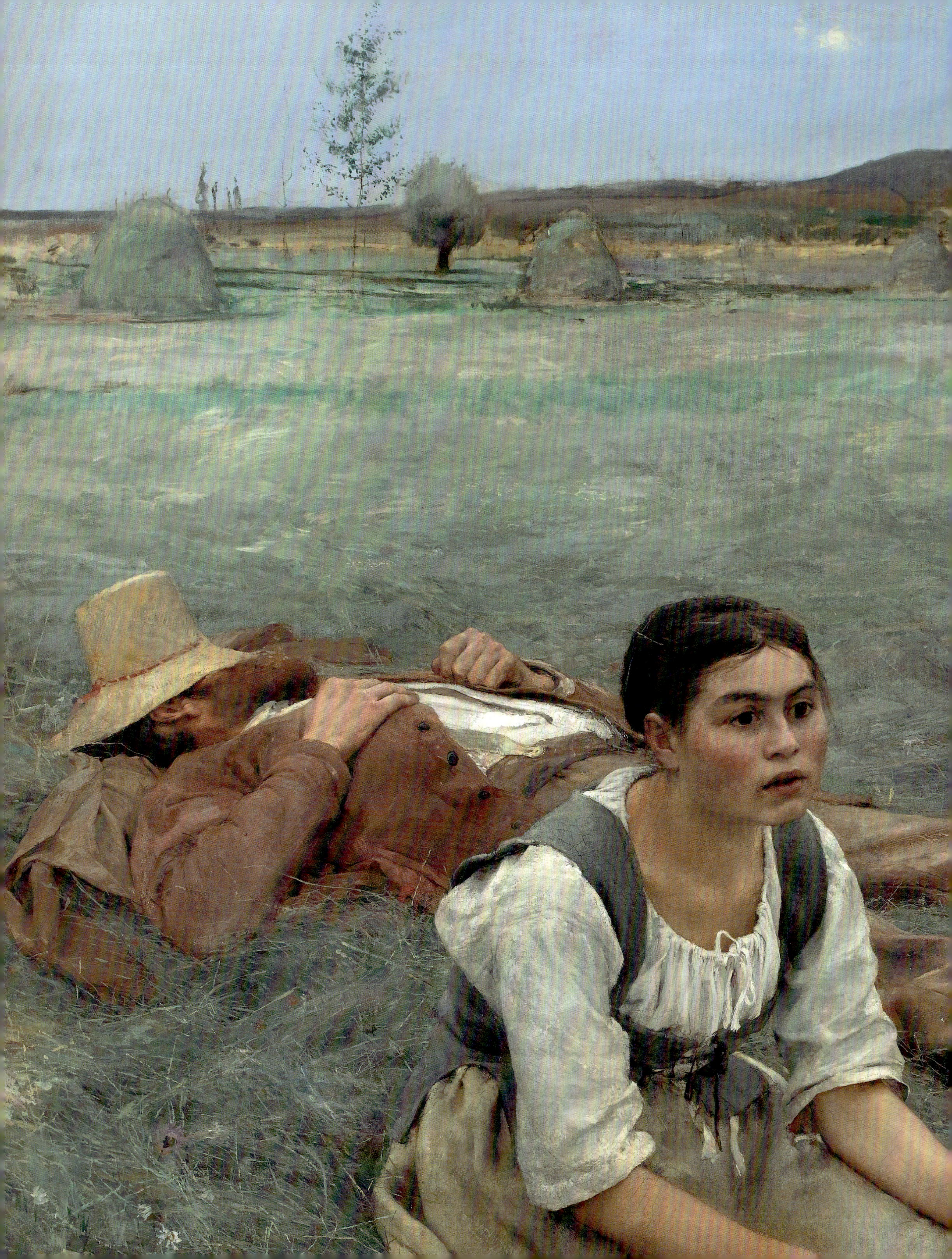

Jules Bastien-Lepage and Naturalism

4

Academic training

Jules Bastien was born on 1 November 1848 at Damvillers in the Meuse, a department in eastern France with part of its border adjoining Germany.[1] He was a studious boy and, from 1859, after attending school in his own village, he continued his secondary education in Verdun, a sub-prefecture of the Meuse and the most densely populated and busiest town of the department. This led him to sit the scientific baccalaureate in 1867. He was briefly tempted by a military career but abandoned this idea and decided to go to Paris and enrol at the École des Beaux-Arts. On 20 June 1870 he passed the competitive examination for places with flying colours, to enter the institution as a star student. He chose to enrol in the studio of Alexandre Cabanel, a painter and teacher who was a defender of the Academic tradition but was admired by his pupils, to whom he allowed great freedom.[2]

Jules Bastien was a regular participant in the École's competitive examinations and was often rewarded with success. This enabled him, in 1870, to attempt the competition for the Prix de Rome, which would allow him to benefit from a four-year scholarship living in the city's Villa Medici. Although he failed the second round, his disappointment must have been tempered by his first acceptance by the Salon, to which he had sent the portrait of one of his architect friends (Musée Bastien-Lepage, Montmédy).[3] But hardly had this official event closed when the Franco-Prussian war broke out, suspending all artistic activity but stirring the patriotic feelings of this son of eastern France.

Classes and competitive examinations resumed in 1872. All his activity was focused on obtaining the Prix de Rome but, once again, he failed at the second hurdle. The following year, he renewed his links with the Salon, to which he remained faithful thereafter, and in 1874 the Fine Arts department purchased one of his works: *Spring*, also called *The Song of Spring* (ILL. 22). It was exhibit number 62, a striking composition in which cherub musicians with butterfly wings – an inheritance from tradition – attempt to distract a young peasant girl with an absent air. The scene takes place against a Meuse landscape, painted in an unexpected way, detailed and yet with a global

1. The compound name Bastien-Lepage only appeared after he started exhibiting at the Salon, when he wished to distinguish himself from other exhibitors named Bastien and so added his mother's maiden name, Lepage, to his father's surname, Bastien.

2. See Lobstein, 'Alexandre Cabanel au Salon', 53–65; Vottero, 'Je leur donne le meilleur', 414–429.

3. Catalogue no. 148. Inv. no. at the museum: CD 95-24-31.

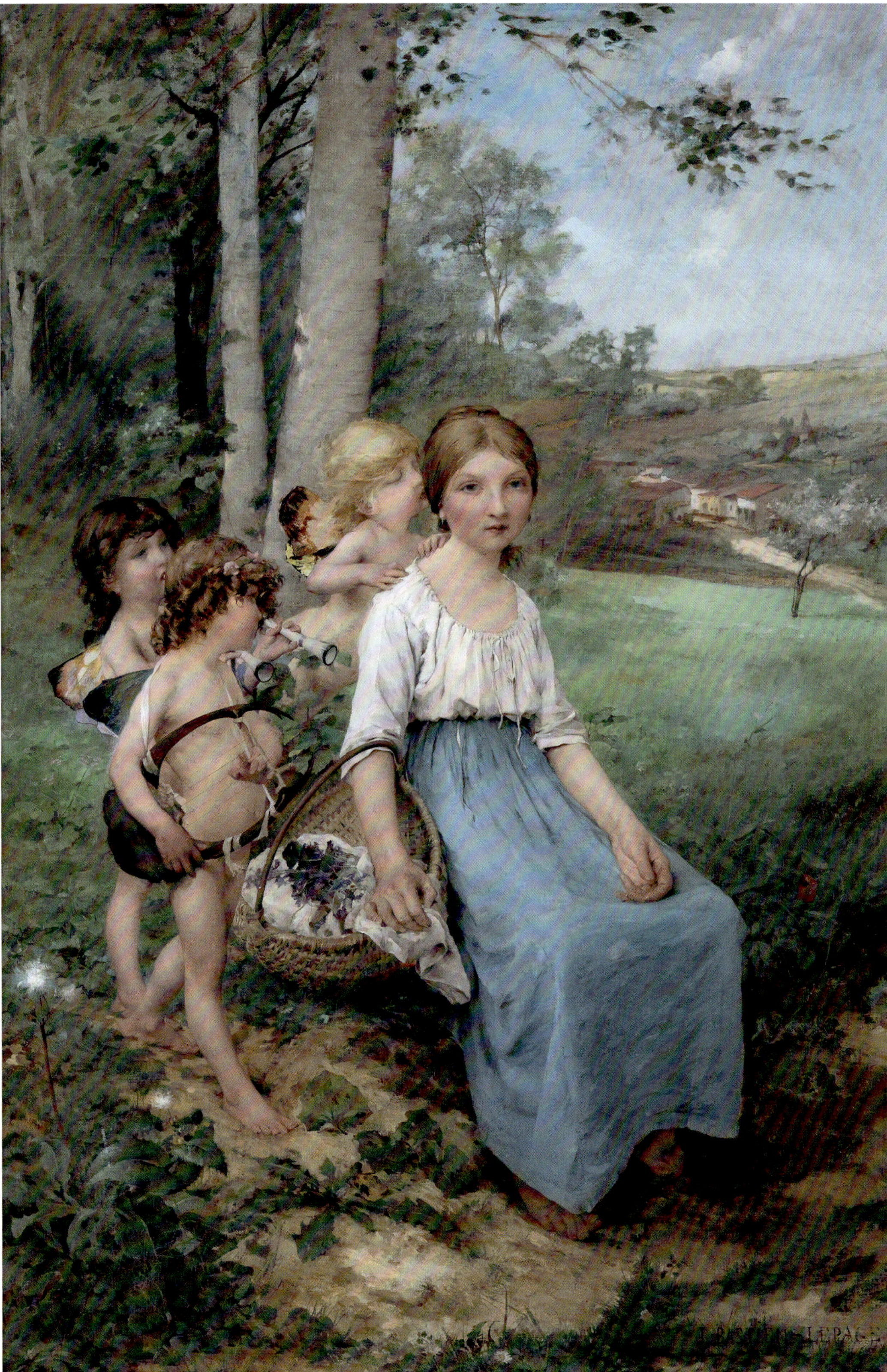

ILL. 22 Jules Bastien-Lepage: *The Song of Spring*, 1874. Oil on canvas, 149×101 cm. Musée de la Princerie, Verdun. 81.1.87

perspective, with rapid brushstrokes throughout, in which the influence of the Barbizon School or the French artist Camille Corot can be discerned. However, this recognition of his work did not extend to his entries for the Prix de Rome, which, each year until 1875, ended in failure.

Towards Naturalism

Alongside Bastien-Lepage's compliance with the tradition imposed by the École, the paintings he sent to the Salon each year revealed an independence that sprang from a variety of sources, in both his portraits and his genre scenes. At the 1875 Salon, for example, he drew attention from both the public and critics with *The Little Communicant* (CAT. 36), which was exhibit no. 96. It was a contemporary portrait of one of his cousins, Lucile Bastien, dressed for her first communion, and referencing artists and well-known paintings from *Anne of Cleves* from 1539 (FIG. 28) by Hans Holbein the Younger to *Mademoiselle Caroline Rivière* (1805, Musée du Louvre, Paris) by Jean-Auguste Dominique Ingres. It is a variation, in white against a blue-grey background, on the model in *The Song of Spring*, with her impassive face, and bears clear marks of the artist's training, whereas her headdress and costume display evidence of a *fa presto* that is new to him (a method that involves working wet-on-wet over toned ground, and some of the ground remains visible in the completed painting).

After his rejection during the second round of the 1875 Prix de Rome, despite critics' expectations that he would carry off the prize, Bastien-Lepage abandoned any aspirations of an Academic art career or of painting in the 'grand manner': rather than mythological, religious, or historical themes, he would henceforth choose to base his work on monumental scenes of daily life.

His first attempt in this style, which brought him to prominence in the contemporary art world, was the painting *The Haymakers* (ILL. 23), exhibited at the 1878 Salon, and its successor, *October*, shown at the 1879 Salon (FIG. 40).[4] Among the numerous comments made about him, the most important came from the future great novelist Émile Zola, and was published in *Le Messager de l'Europe*'s July 1879 edition. In his analysis, Zola refers both to the Salon and to the fourth Impressionist exhibition:

> Here, for example, is Bastien-Lepage, who has quickly achieved great renown by breaking free from the shackles of Academic art and turning to the study of nature. Last year he exhibited *The Haymakers*, a scene of country life, showing a peasant man and woman resting in the mown hay at midday. This year, he has provided a pendant to his picture. A canvas he has named *October* depicts two peasant women gathering potatoes in a landscape formed by the furrows of a ploughed field. Of course, we recognise a grandson of Courbet and Millet. But the influence of the Impressionist painters is also instantly striking.[5]

The intention here was to rank the artist with those independent painters, the Impressionists, but what Zola goes on to say presents a counterbalance to this initial opinion:

> His superiority over the Impressionist painters may be encapsulated thus, that he knows how to produce his impressions. He has very shrewdly understood that a simple question of technique was dividing the public from the innovators. He has therefore retained their originality, while concentrating on the expression and perfection of technique.[6]

4. Catalogue no. 164.

5. Reproduced in: Zola, *Écrits sur l'art*, 401.

6. Zola, *Écrits sur l'art*, 401.

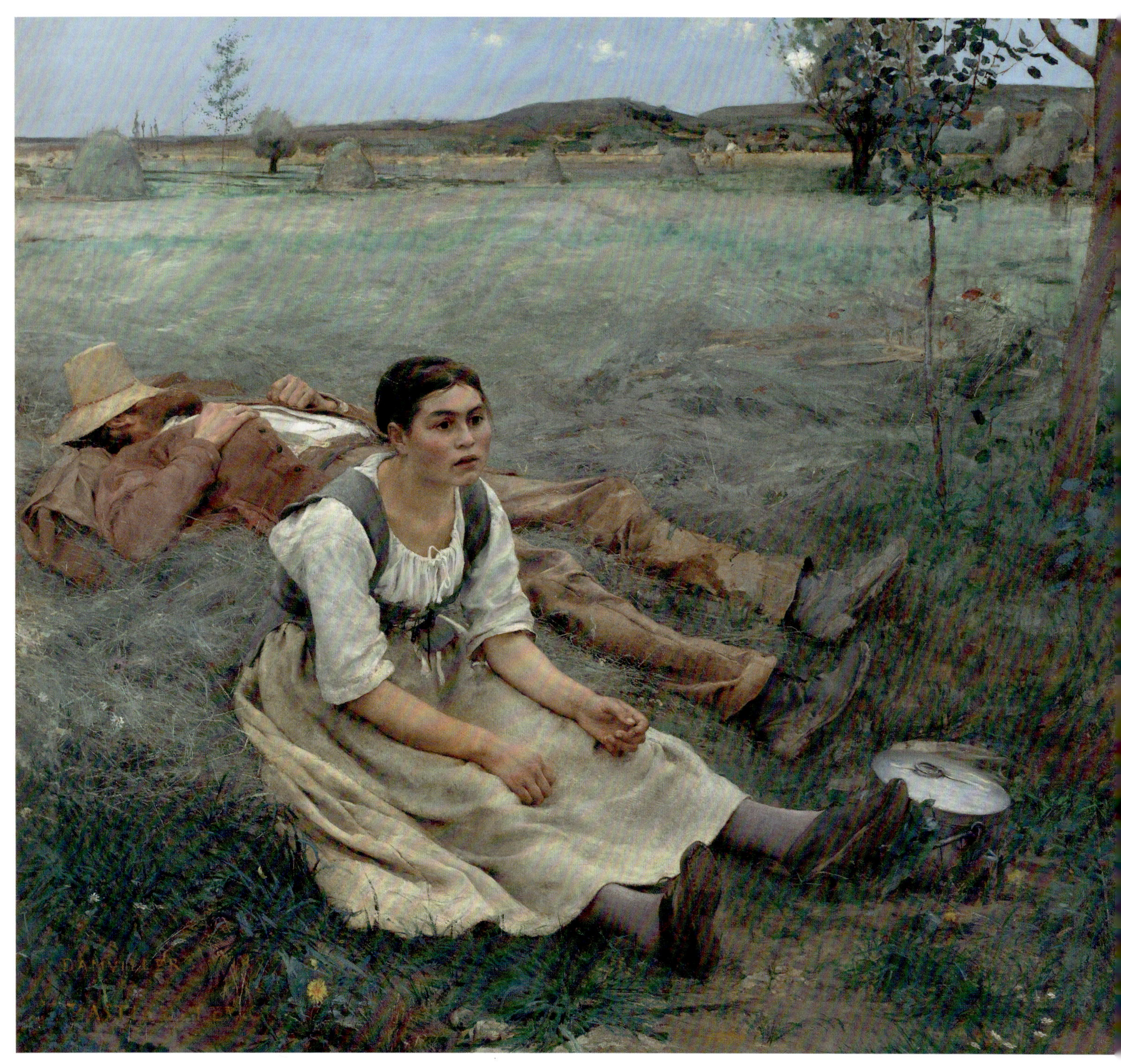

ILL. 23 Jules Bastien-Lepage: *The Haymakers*, 1877. Oil on canvas, 180 × 195 cm. Musée d'Orsay, Paris. RF 2748

The enthusiasm aroused in him by the young artist is moderated in the words that follow, but Zola nevertheless links him to one of his own desires: 'I have said that it was urgent for an artist to appear who is capable of expressing the Naturalist method in such a way that it achieves its full development.'[7] For the critics who came after, Bastien-Lepage would not need to be pigeonholed as an Impressionist in order to see himself defined as a Naturalist artist and the promoter of this movement.

At this stage in Jules Bastien-Lepage's career, it would appear important to define his work and technique in order to clarify what Naturalism represented in the minds of his contemporaries. Apart from his *Joan of Arc* (ILL. 30) in 1880, where his classical training showed through in some of the details, earning him some barbed criticism from Zola,[8] he remained faithful to the spirit of *The Haymakers* in each of the pictures he sent to the Salon. This continued to be the case up until his last great Salon painting of 1883, *Village Love* (Pushkin Museum, Moscow),[9] which preceded his death on 10 December 1884.

Each of his Salon works – apart from portraits, commissioned mainly from the Parisian bourgeoisie, but also his smaller pictures for private clients[10] – focused almost entirely on the landscape and on genre scenes. The context he chose for his evocations was the region where he was born: a great plain dotted with hills and with abundant vegetation and forests, dominated by agriculture that was still largely practised by ordinary, humble people. As a cultured artist who was attentive to anything that might distinguish his work, he abandoned the principles of his masters which had ensured his early success and turned to more contemporary aesthetic ideas, which are visible in *The Haymakers* and subsequent works.

Sources of inspiration

The first innovation of Bastien-Lepage's aesthetic ideas had nothing to do with painting but was related to a practice which, at the time, was struggling to be recognised as an art, namely photography. Framing, to adopt the specific term for this new departure, would give Bastien-Lepage the opportunity to submit some startling compositions, particularly with his increased use of very low viewpoints, or views *di sotto in sù*, from below and upward. This process accentuated the perspective and gave the impression that the landscape was rising towards the canvas to occupy it right up to the skyline, placed very high. And it was as if the characters were stuck on to this background, as in *Poor Fauvette* from 1881 (FIG. 30).

This particular feature, in which the sky occupied the smallest possible space and characters were outlined against a background, should also be considered as a reference to the Japanese prints that were abundant in Paris at the time and collected by many artists. He was to borrow other details from these coloured prints, such as elements cut off by the edge of the canvas and the sensation of an encircling shadow designed to isolate certain components of the composition.

His benchmarks in painting were of two types, depending on whether the models or their surroundings were involved. They are to be found in the works that followed *The Haymakers* in which the faces and hands of the models came from the tradition, whereas the landscapes made reference to Millet and Courbet, as Zola had observed. Given these factors, we need to ask how the term 'Impressionist' came to be used to describe this artist's paintings. If his subjects in all their ordinariness may be

7. Zola, *Écrits sur l'art*, 402.

8. Zola, *Écrits sur l'art*, 427–428.

9. Catalogue no. 131.

10. Aubrun, *Jules Bastien-Lepage, 1848–1884*; Lobstein, 'Jules Bastien-Lepage (Damvillers, 1848–Paris, 1884)', 19–28.

considered as borrowed from daily life, with no references to modern society – there are no crowded cities to be found and no industries with invasive fumes – and he uses the traditional concept of a light source from the north, there is nothing that allows him to be associated with this term in the sense that it was used in the late 1870s and the early 1880s.

Another important difference should also be noted. Impressionist painting at its beginning was apolitical: it is impossible to find in it any reference, or even allusion, to the national and social situation immediately after the 1870 war or to the insurrectional episode of the Paris Commune. Without being militant, the painting of Bastien-Lepage and his followers provides evidence of a greater commitment. By returning to the landscapes of his native soil and depicting its inhabitants and their timeless activities, the painter evokes a golden age prior to industrialisation, an age whose disappearance he deplores. When, next to *The Song of Spring*, he exhibited the portrait of his grandfather (ILL. 24) as number 84 at the 1874 Salon, seated in front of a wood, it was resistance to the invader that he was evoking. In the wake of Bastien-Lepage, these themes of resistance and resilience would provide plentiful subjects for future Naturalists.

We should turn now to the artist's technique. In all probability, it was the foregrounds of his pictures, where nature was treated with rapid and clearly visible brushstrokes, which led to the comparison with the Impressionists. This method of painting could already be seen in the work of Realist painters of the Barbizon School, who applied it to small-format paintings; what was not surprising in Théodore Rousseau or Jean-François Millet – though one should look at the depiction of nature in *Death and the Woodcutter* (1859, Ny Carlsberg Glyptotek, Copenhagen) to see the lineage – becomes more evident in the large-scale paintings of Bastien-Lepage. The method of laying down colour here does not employ the virtuosity aspired to by the Impressionists to achieve a play of light in their works and illuminate their canvases. Given these technical considerations, it has to be recognised that Zola's reservations were well-founded: Bastien-Lepage could have been an Impressionist but he was exclusively and resolutely Naturalist.

Posterity

In 1884, aged 36, Bastien-Lepage died, having trained very few pupils. The exhibition at the École des Beaux-Arts which followed his death,[11] like the studio sale which took place shortly afterwards,[12] met with resounding success. It attracted the curious, but there were also artists of every nationality, among them Peder Severin Krøyer, and each day they crowded into the rooms of the Hôtel de Chimay to admire his paintings and drawings. There were numerous buyers at the Hôtel Drouot, from where his works would be dispersed to all continents,[13] provoking reflection and soon triggering the spread of a movement that would appeal to art lovers the world over.

The artists wishing to follow the principles developed by the recently deceased painter were from diverse backgrounds and had different objectives, and the movement started by Bastien-Lepage would soon have countless offshoots and become widespread. Its ramifications corresponded to the subjects that these new Naturalists would address, extending their repertoire from the countryside to the sea, from the sea to the industrial landscape, and from mines to cities.[14] They would not be satisfied with depicting an Arcadian landscape as their predecessor

11. École des Beaux-Arts, Hôtel de Chimay, Paris, *Exhibition of Works by Jules Bastien-Lepage*, March–April 1885.
12. Galerie Georges Petit, Paris, *Jules Bastien-Lepage Sale*, 11–12 May 1885.
13. The dealer Michael Knoedler, for example, was very active during the sale and sent his purchases to the United States.
14. See, for example: Musée des Beaux-Arts, Dunkirk, *Des plaines à l'usine. Images du travail dans la peinture française de 1870 à 1914* [From the plains to the factory. Images of work in French painting from 1870 to 1914], 20 October 2001–27 January 2002.

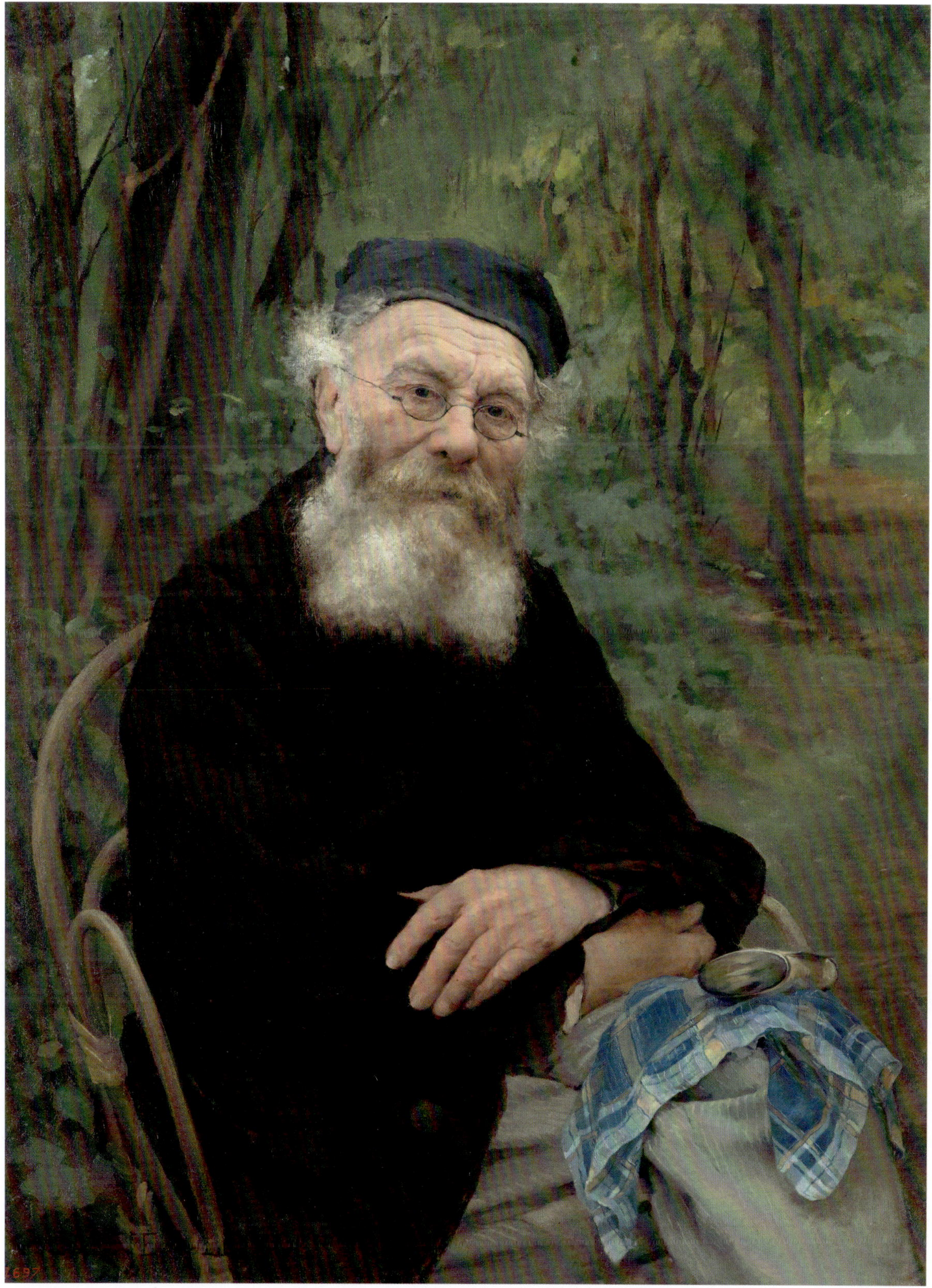

ILL. 24 Jules Bastien-Lepage: *Portrait of the Artist's Grandfather*, 1874. Oil on canvas, 103×77 cm. Musée des Beaux-Arts Jules Chéret, Nice, deposit from Musée d'Orsay, Paris. RF 3984-1

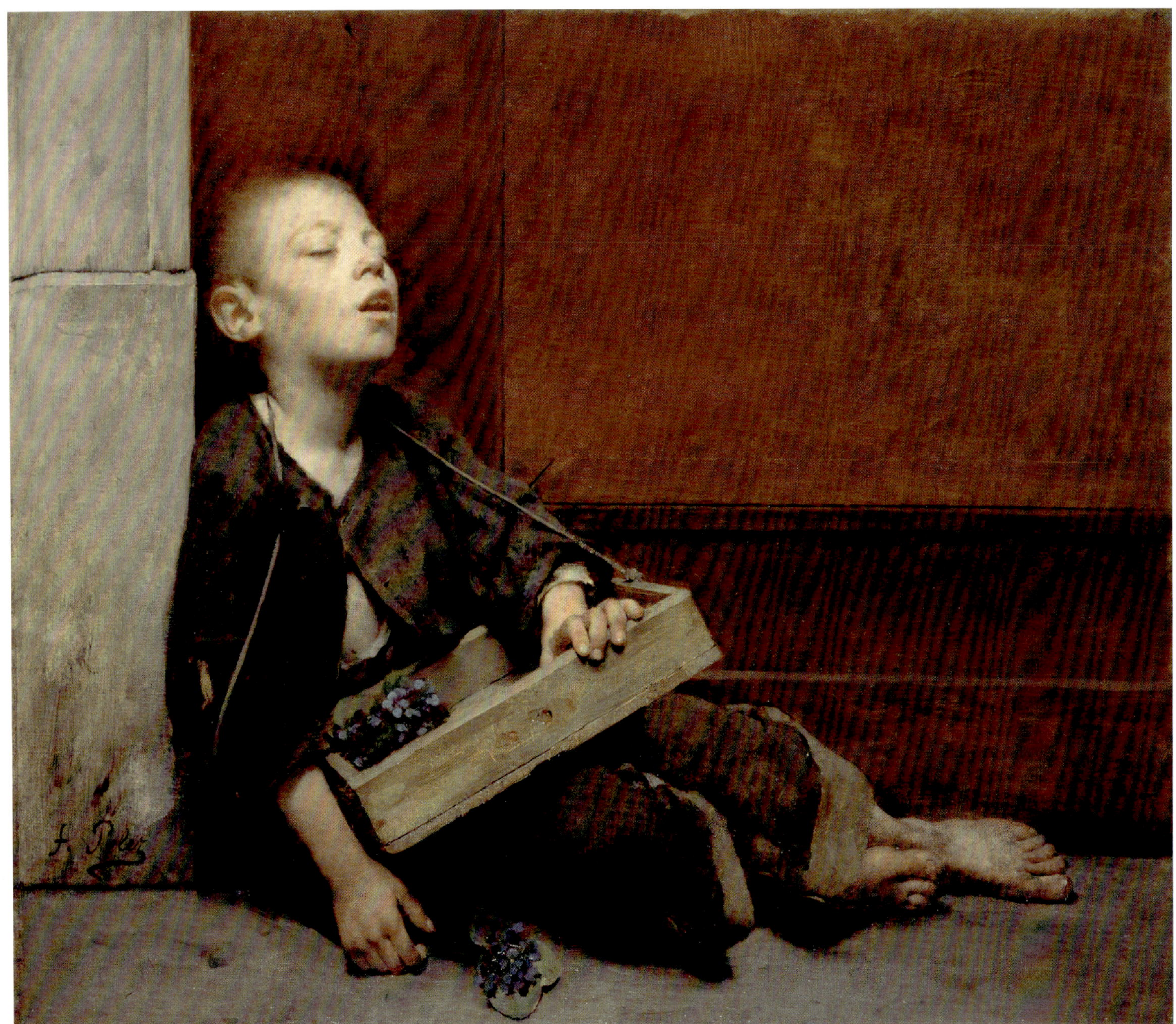

ILL. 25 Fernand Pelez: *A Martyr. The Violet Seller*, c. 1885. Oil on canvas, 87×100 cm. Petit Palais, Musée des Beaux-Arts de la Ville de Paris. PPP592

had done, but would gradually introduce more openly political subjects, together with social resonances (ILL. 25), creating a definitive link with the literary Naturalism created by Zola.

There are few countries that did not experience the effects of Bastien-Lepage's aesthetic innovations;[15] his influence was felt from north to south, throughout Europe and in Russia and the Americas. The varieties of Naturalism that developed in each country from the 1880s onwards can be counted in the hundreds. From 1879, Peder Severin Krøyer was writing to his close contemporaries expressing his admiration for Bastien-Lepage, and long continued to make reference to his work. Beyond his purely artistic interest, he was working to bring together the Scandinavian contributions that were to be involved in the erection of a statue of the deceased artist, created by the sculptor Auguste Rodin, at Damvillers in 1889. For the exhibition he had organised in Copenhagen the previous year, at the request of the brewer Carl Jacobsen, he sent for two large Salon pictures by Bastien-Lepage and negotiated the purchase of *The Beggar* (CAT. 49) from the artist's brother Émile, who was his sole heir.

But the trend developing through a critique of contemporary society could not continue to spread without giving rise to an antidote which would quickly succeed it. A new movement emanating from the literary world, in the form of Symbolism – that depiction of the soul which rejected the materiality of subjects – was about to invade the art galleries, but without forsaking the consensual, eclectic technique instigated by Jules Bastien-Lepage.

15. Weisberg, *Beyond Impressionism*.

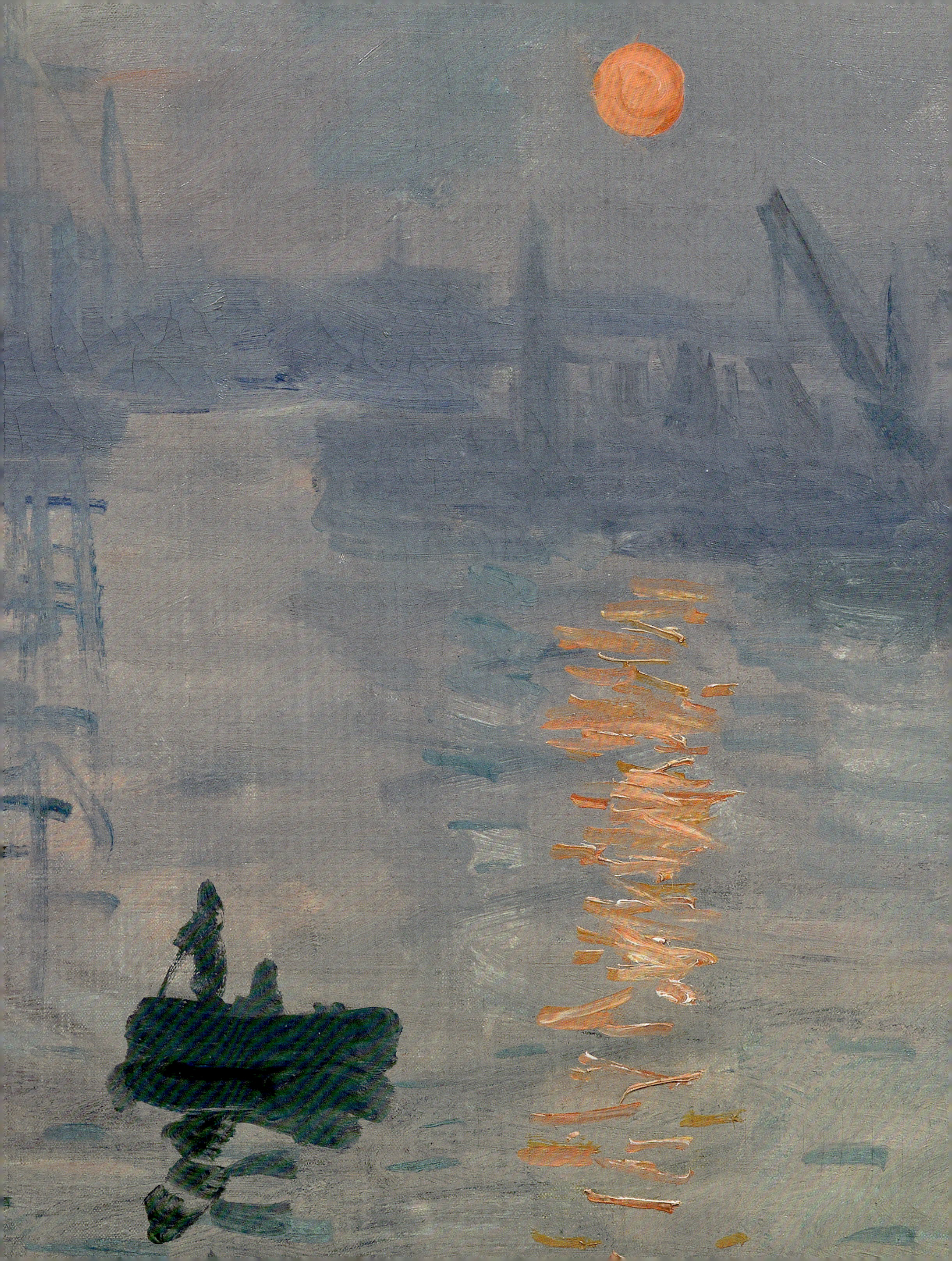

Impressionism and Naturalism

5

The first senses of 'Impression'

The French noun *impression* derives from the Latin *impressio*, while the verb *imprimer* [to (im)print], comes from the Latin *imprimere*: since at least the 14th century, the noun has signified 'the action of pressing on', while the verb, in the modern period, has commonly described the process of book production following the discoveries of Johannes Gutenberg. These words were rarely used initially, and in the century after printing was discovered the French term is used just once, in the celebrated work *The Life of Gargantua* and *of Pantagruel* written in the 16th century by François Rabelais: 'But note that meanwhile he was teaching him to write Gothic style, and he wrote all his books, for the art of printing [*impression*] was not yet in use.'[1]

Gradually, however, the term became more common, and in 1765, in Diderot and d'Alembert's *Encyclopedia*, it became something impalpable, or spiritual. Its definition concluded with this phrase: 'The word impression has a hundred other different meanings, both simple and figurative.' But this was after insisting on its two principal meanings:

> [...] it is generally the mark of an action by one body upon another. Animal feet are printed on the soft earth. A die leaves its impression on a coin. External objects make an impression on our senses. The impressions received in youth resemble the characters carved onto the barks of trees; they grow and become stronger along with the trees.[2]

The 'Impression' conquers art

Much later, in Eugène Delacroix's *Journal*, several quotations, one of them concerning artists, echo the *Encyclopedia*'s definition. On 19 January 1847 the painter wrote: 'I shall often realize the advantage of noting down my impressions in this way; they grow deeper as one recalls them.'[3] With these words, Delacroix was affirming that impressions were merely fleeting and that, for the artist, it was necessary to transpose them into a more material form, nearer to the idea of a sketch, a task that preceded creation, put down as a 'curiosity,'[4] and not, therefore, a completed work. This was to propose the

1. Rabelais, *The Complete Works of François Rabelais*, 38.
2. 'Impression', 205.
3. Wellington, *The Journal of Eugène Delacroix*, 59.
4. For an analysis of the links between 'curiosity' and 'drawing' figures, see, for example: *Dictionnaire encyclopédique*, 392: 'One sometimes draws these lines out of simple curiosity, & in order to have faithful monuments [*evidence*] of beautiful things, that are regarded as studies, & sometimes one makes use of them by copying them.'

notion of grasping something ephemeral. It rejected the supremacy of drawing and composition, conceptions of which had been codified since the Renaissance, and it opposed traditional painting practice and the training of artists, as considered by the Academies. It was no longer Gutenberg's characters that were printed on the paper, but instants stolen from the surrounding world by the artist's eye, without any concern for form, which would then be laid onto paper or canvas and take on their own existence. But to what end?

With the advent of books, thought and knowledge could be preserved on a large scale; for a large number of people they became a personal means of preserving images and, furthermore, the emotions or sentiments spontaneously produced by a motif. The increasing use of the term 'impression' in the language of artists' studios and workshops and in the methods of preparing a work would completely change the way in which subjects were approached and brought to life. Delacroix, for example, who had always considered colour more important than line, had already taken this step in works such as *Sea Viewed from the Heights of Dieppe* (ILL. 26), a painting which the artist must have considered too innovative for his contemporaries: art-lovers and connoisseurs of the time were unable to accept either the sketch or the finished work, so they were never exhibited during his lifetime and

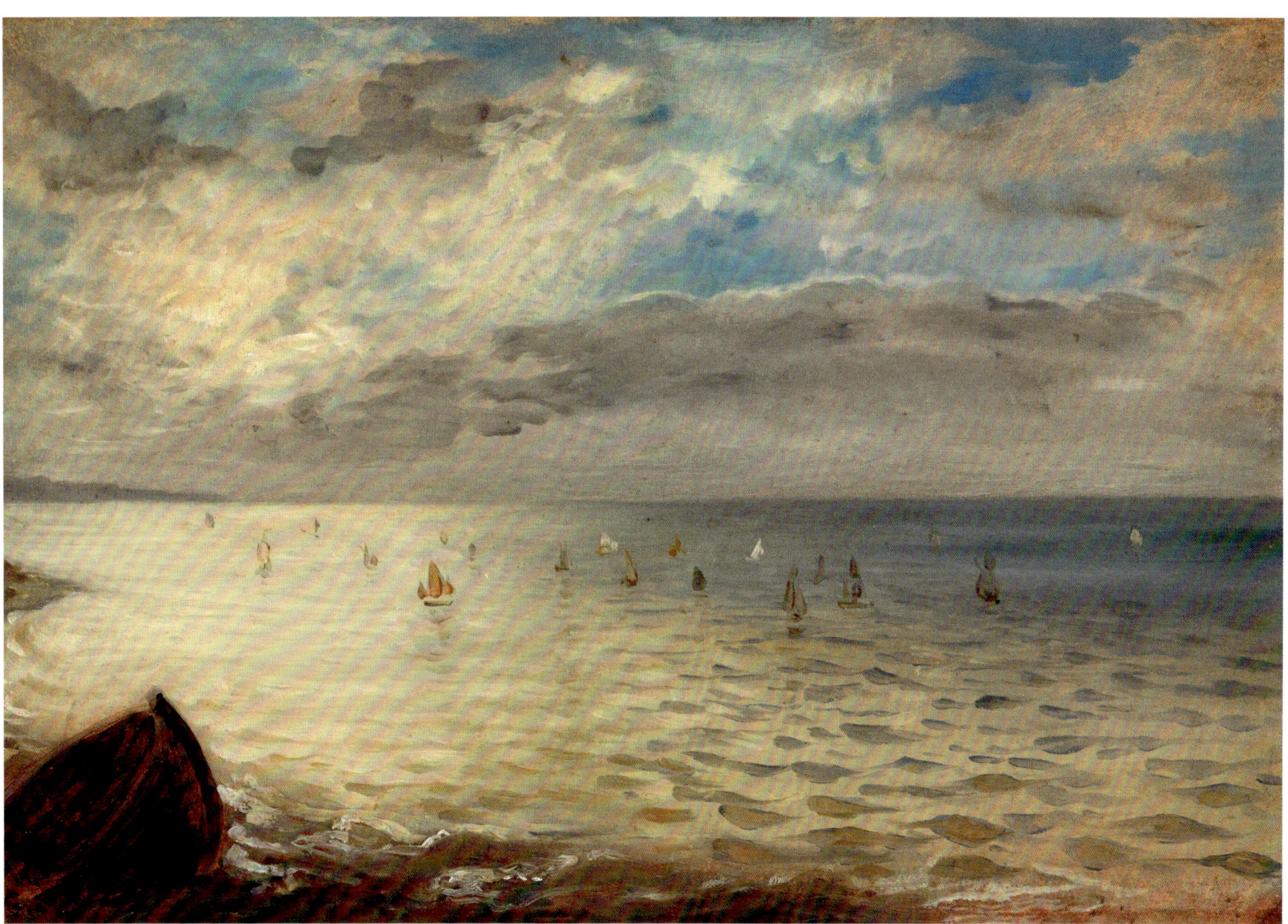

ILL. 26 Eugène Delacroix: *Sea Viewed from the Heights of Dieppe*, c. 1854–1855. Oil on cardboard mounted on wood, 36×52 cm. Musée du Louvre, Paris. RF 1979-46

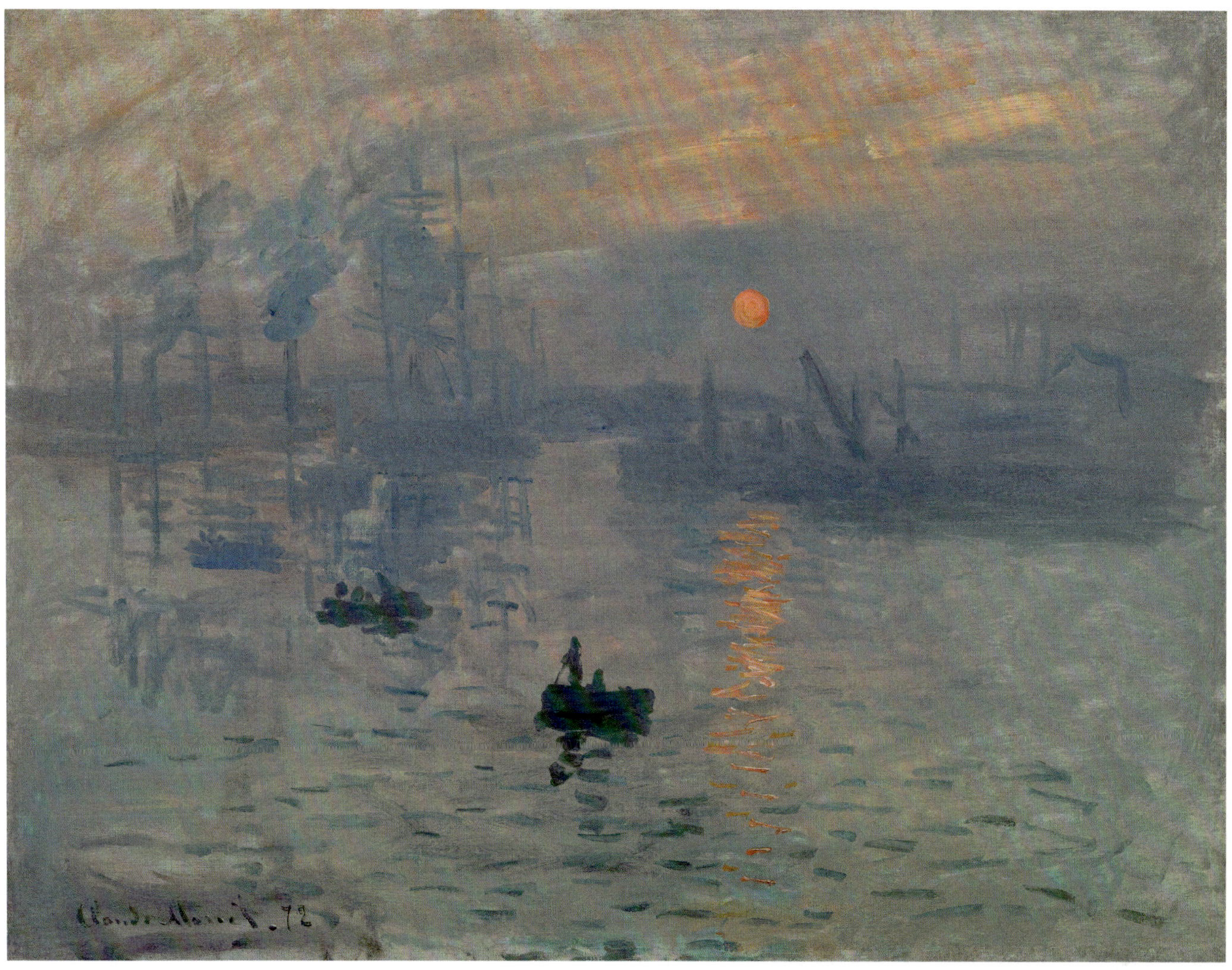

ILL. 27 Claude Monet: *Impression, Sunrise*, 1872. Oil on canvas, 50 × 65 cm. Musée Marmottan Monet, Paris. 4014

only left his studio to appear in the sale following his death, on 17 February 1864.

At a time when the word 'impression' was spreading in fine arts teaching and already giving rise to some new experimentation, we might ask ourselves what Claude Monet was thinking of when he used this term for the exhibition that opened in Paris on 15 April 1874. This event, which would be considered by posterity as the first Impressionist exhibition, took place in the former photographic studios of Nadar, at 35, Boulevard des Capucines. For this event, with its very disparate participants and artworks,[5] Monet presented a picture entitled *Impression, Sunrise* (ILL. 27). He painted this work during a stay in Le Havre, nearly two years earlier,[6] and until that point it

5. Several of the artists present, who are now more or less forgotten – such as Antoine Ferdinand Attendu, Édouard Béliard, Édouard Brandon, and the sculptor Auguste Louis Marie Ottin – belonged to the purest Academic tradition. This disparity was largely due to the manner in which the event functioned, it being the first to take place 'with neither jury nor awards.'

6. For the dating of the work, see: Olson, 'La datation d'*Impression soleil levant*', 80–105.

had probably been referred to by its subject, *View of Le Havre*.[7] The historiography of the work reveals that at the time of the artist's first public exhibition the title changed, and in two stages: at the time of the first change, Monet decided to name his picture *Impression*, as a way of stating that it could be considered an experimental work. This new name disregarded the subject and endowed the work with a new, unusual meaning that called into question the traditional terminology for exhibited works. It was later, at the request of Pierre-Auguste Renoir, who was responsible for displaying the works and editing the catalogue, that Monet added an extension to the title: *Sunrise*, which re-situated the work in a location but nevertheless let an atmospheric phenomenon take precedence over the much more common practice of naming a painting after a place.

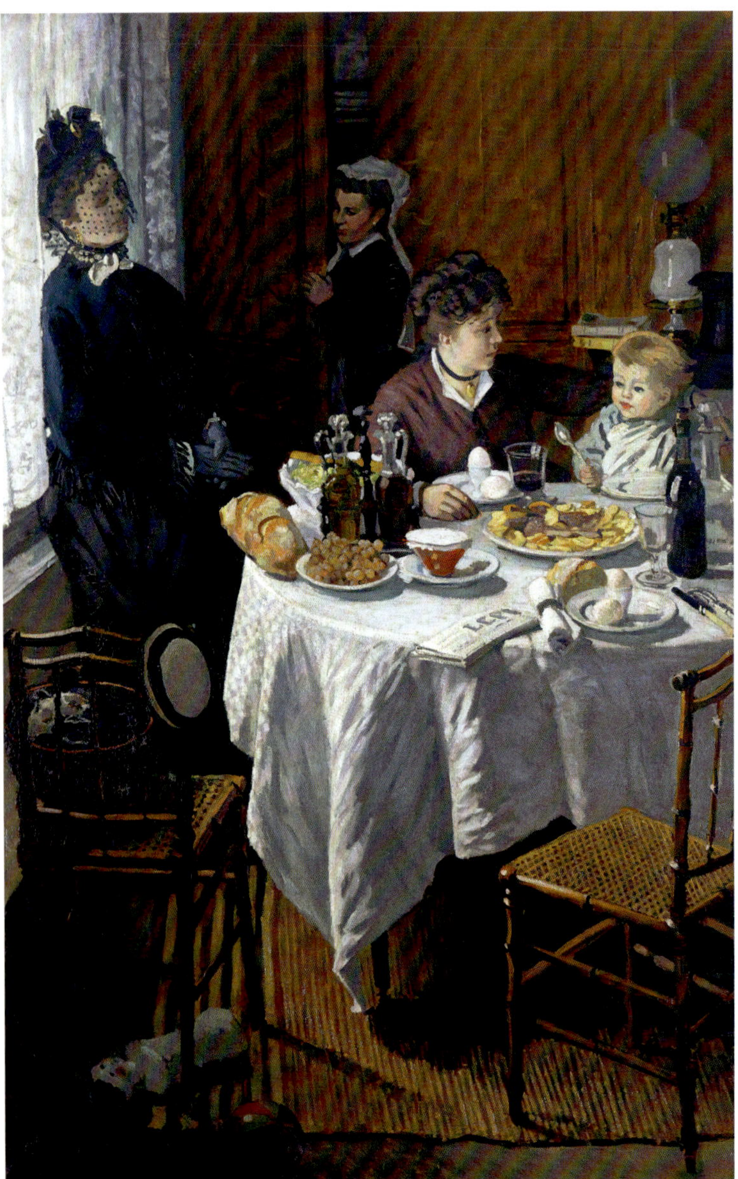

ILL. 28 Claude Monet: *The Lunch*, 1868. Oil on canvas, 231.5×151.5 cm. Städel Museum, Frankfurt am Main. SG 170

In the artist's eyes, the single word 'impression' seems therefore to have been an adequate name for the work, and all the evidence suggests that he borrowed it from the ordinary language of artists' studios. However, it is impossible to say whether or not his action was deliberate. Indeed, why did Monet choose this word for his painting when, at the same time, he was exhibiting five paintings as well as several pastels whose titles all bore the stamp of traditional wording (ILL. 28)? If *Impression, Sunrise* is compared with the other works he sent, a primary difference immediately stands out: the other four pictures are the result of elaborate compositions in which the components are still organised according to traditional principles. The same cannot be said of *Impression*, which depicts a seascape viewed from the front with a precise depiction of a section of the port of Le Havre, even if it is shrouded in mist. Here, Monet's memories of the education he received are reduced to the division between water and land, interrupted by a central canal halfway up the canvas, and to the small boats which create spatial depth on the lower left side. On the other hand, the technique confirms his complete break with tradition, which can be seen in the form of differently sized brushstrokes applied in different directions, with rapid and loose movements. Consequently, we find ourselves looking at a work that

7. Lobstein, 'Ernest Hoschedé et *Impression, soleil levant*', 116–133.

is closer to 'the impression' conceived by Delacroix, quickly painted in order to preserve a memory,[8] and reinforced by the hurried technique and the lack of paint in some areas of the canvas.[9]

Showing that a first 'impression' could become a picture in its own right was groundbreaking, making this work unique among the pictures submitted by the 25 participants in the exhibition. It was also an unusual picture for Monet to send and a departure from the spirit of the other pictures he submitted – whether consciously or not, nobody can say.

Critical reception of *Impression. Sunrise*

Several critics perceived the difference and wrote accounts of this incongruous choice; however, this was not the picture most often mentioned in reviews,[10] nor even the most often cited among the comments devoted to Monet's exhibits.[11]

The historiography of the newly emerging movement gradually materialised, but not without hesitation.[12] Today, it has become only too easy to imitate the approach of the American art historian John Rewald, whose account of Impressionism appeared in 1946,[13] by referring to a single article published while the exhibition was being held. This particular article was written for a humorous and satirical magazine and was supposed to be a record of a conversation between two visitors to the exhibition. The writer was a painter and engraver, as well as a playwright, author, and art critic, named Louis Leroy. He was the oldest of the event's reviewers, being 62 years of age at the time. Among his indulgences was playing on variations of the word 'impression,'[14] of which one – and it must have been a godsend for Rewald's 1946 book – concerned the picture by Monet whose title uses this same noun:

> *Impression*, I was sure of it. I was just saying to myself, if I'm impressed,[15] there must be some impression in there... And what freedom, what fluency in the technique! Wallpaper in its embryonic state is more finished than that seascape![16]

Rewald's reliance on this satirical report, oblivious as it was to the many other sources of information available, thus tended to conceal the multitude of other comments accompanying the event, a multitude in which, it must be stressed, uses of the word 'sketch' abounded.[17] Neither should it be forgotten that contemporary critics of the exhibition were already hesitant about how to define this

8. This idea is repeated several times in the comments on the first Impressionist exhibition of 1874. For example, Émile Cardon speaks in *La Presse* of 28 April 1874 of 'imperfect sketches, hurried impressions' (3). This journalist was also the first, in *La Presse* of the following day, to refer to the state's wish to relinquish its 'management of art exhibitions.' However, this would not become effective until 1881.

9. Chatellier, 'Impression, soleil levant: un autre regard', 194–203.

10. The journalist signing himself E.C. in 'Chronique. Beaux-Arts. Exposition de peintures modernes' lists 12 works that he advises his readers to see in order to understand the groundbreaking nature of the exhibition (254–255). Although two of these paintings were by Monet – *The Poppy Field* and *The Lunch* – no mention was made of *Impression, Sunrise*.

11. Lobstein, 'Claude Monet et l'impressionnisme', 106–115.

12. In order to show how difficult it was to agree on the movement's development, it is pertinent to recall that in 1904 the critic Camille Mauclair wrote: 'But the name [Impressionist] dates from the 1867 Salon, where a setting sun by Monet, under the title *Impressions*, created a scandal' (*L'Impressionnisme. Son histoire. Son Esthétique. Ses maîtres*, 21). He was not the only biographer of the movement to mistake the place, date, and title.

13. Rewald, *The History of Impressionism*.

14. He used the same word to comment on *Study of a landscape with a ploughed field* by Camille Pissarro; *An Orchard* by Alfred Sisley; and Monet's *Boulevard des Capucines*, concluding his text with these words of the visitor-writer whose remarks he is supposedly reproducing: 'I am a walking impression, the vengeful palette knife, Monet's *Boulevard des Capucines*, and *The Hanged Man's House* and *A Modern Olympia* of Mr. Cézanne!'.

15. The original verb derived from the noun 'impression' was 'to [im]print'. The verb 'to impress' (Fr. *impressionner*) only appeared in 1761, meaning 'to affect (someone) with a strong impression' ([Gaudet], *La Bibliothèque des petits maîtres*, 58).

16. Leroy, 'L'Exposition des impressionnistes', 79–80.

17. Étienne Carjat, for example, refers to Berthe Morisot and speaks of a 'sketch to be reviewed when more work has been done,' reserving the term 'Impressionism' for the works of 'Messrs Monet, Pissarro, Cézanne, Sisley, and Guillaumin' ('L'Exposition du boulevard des Capucines', *Le Patriote français*, 27 April 1874, 3). F. de Gantès speaks in his review of 'this innovation, which might also be called an Exhibition of Sketches' ('Courrier artistique: L'Exposition du boulevard' in *La Semaine parisienne*, 23 April 1874, 63–64).

new movement and its representatives. Terms other than 'Impressionism' were used and subsequently abandoned by posterity: 'The New School or the Rebels';[18] 'The Japanese painters';[19] 'The Open Air School';[20] followed by 'The Intransigents';[21] 'The Daredevils';[22] and, finally, 'The Impressionists.'[23]

John Rewald's choice of Louis Leroy's review was therefore one-sided, lending a certain weight to the confusion which, for more than 75 years, has clouded understanding of the multiple stylistic approaches gathered together in the exhibition of April 1874. While the term used to describe the movement should only include works that employed the same technique as Monet's eponymous painting, and perhaps his modern subject matter too, it has continually been extended to aesthetic approaches that more or less bordered on it, provided that they abandoned what had long been considered as the 'grand manner,'[24] were linked to the modern world, and practised a swift execution technique.

Various meanings of 'Impression'

This extended use of the term 'Impressionism' took longer to spread than its appropriation by certain artists who, despite this, never claimed to belong to the Impressionist movement. The use of clearly visible, defined brushstrokes, often well loaded with paint, as seen in the works of Monet, Renoir, Pissarro (ILL. 29), and Sisley at the 1874 exhibition,[25] gave their paintings an extreme mobility when the

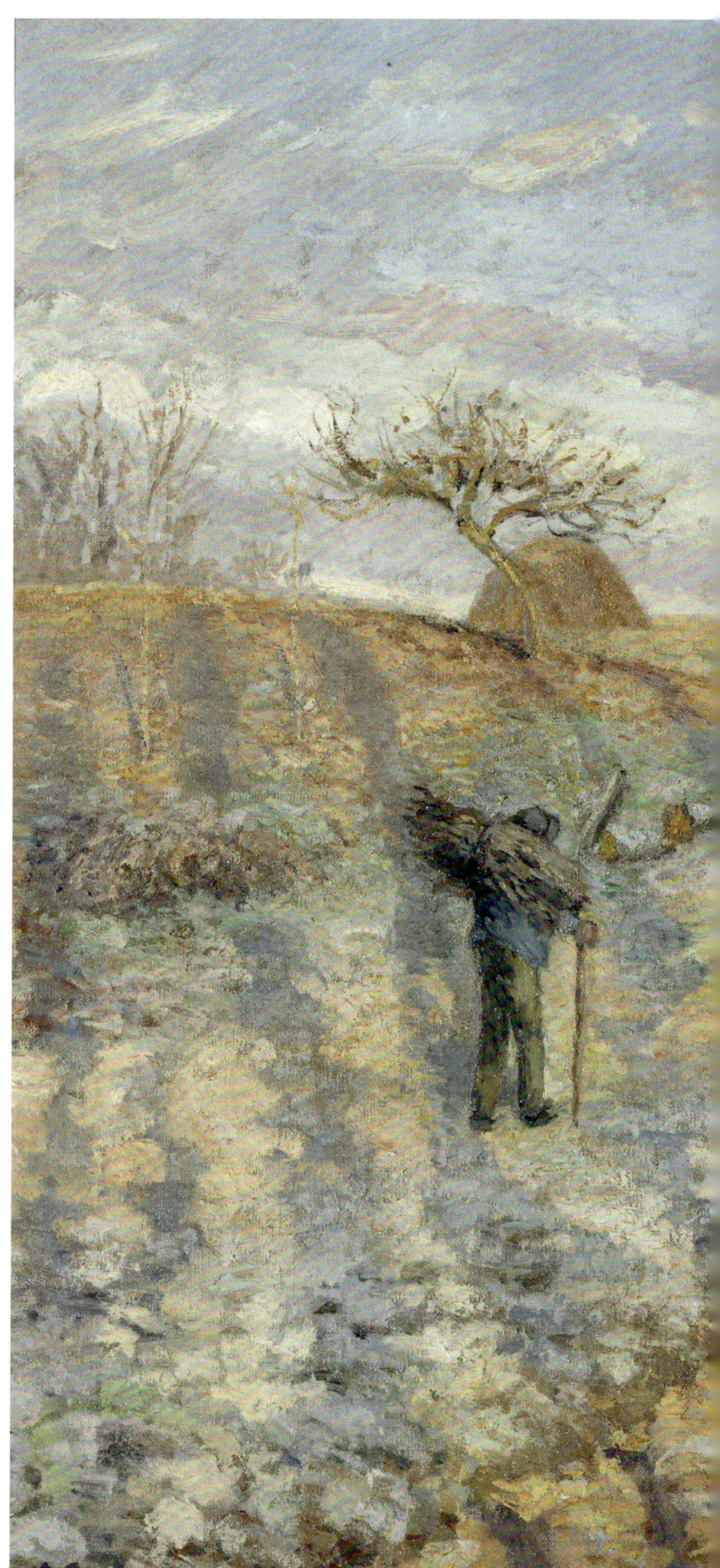

18. Cardon, 'Avant le Salon: l'Exposition des Révoltés', 2–3; Silvestre, 'Chronique des beaux-arts', 2–3.
19. Castagnary, 'Exposition du boulevard des Capucines', 3.
20. Chesneau, 'A côté du Salon: II', 2.
21. Chesneau, 'Au Salon: avertissement préalable', 2; Le Masque de fer [The Iron Mask], 'Echos de Paris', 1; Polday, 'Les Intransigeants', 186–188.
22. Montifaud, 'Exposition du boulevard des Capucines', 307–313.
23. Ariste, 'Salon de 1874 à Paris', 3.
24. In the hierarchy of genres established in 1667 by André Félibien in one of the *Conférences de l'Académie royale de Peinture et de Sculpture*, the supreme purpose of art was mythological, religious, and historical painting – in other words, the 'grand manner.'
25. An important detail because many artists rapidly developed their painting practices in different ways, distancing themselves from 'Impressionism' as it was considered by Rewald.

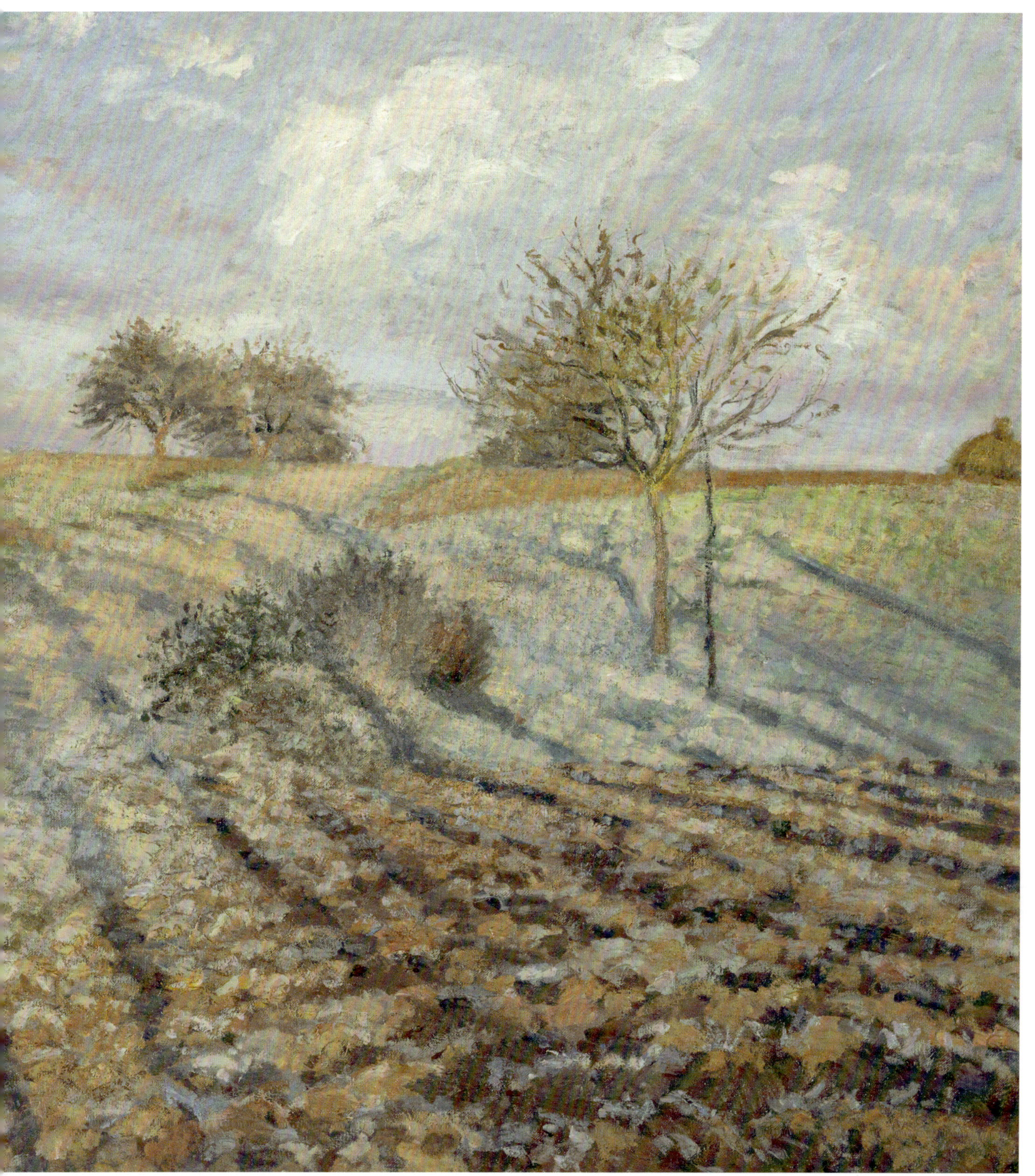

ILL. 29 Camille Pissarro: *Hoarfrost*, 1873. Oil on canvas, 65.5×93.2 cm. Musée d'Orsay, Paris. RF 1972-27

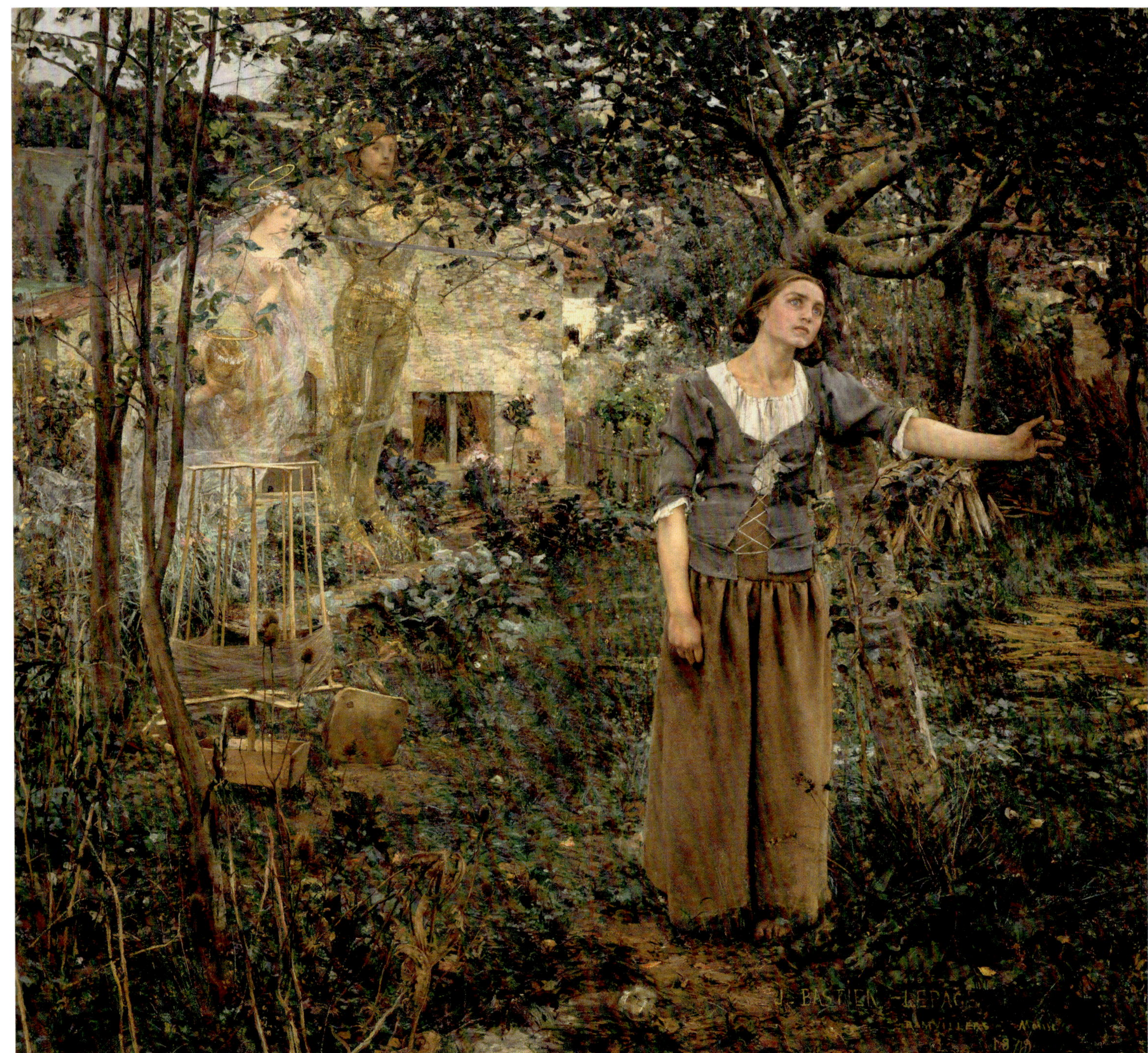

ILL. 30 Jules Bastien-Lepage: *Joan of Arc*, 1879. Oil on canvas, 254×279.4 cm. The Metropolitan Museum of Art, New York. 89.211

light glided over their surface. This method of painting also had the power to vary the way viewers apprehended forms and colours, according to their distance from the painting: it involved an optical phenomenon which had been known since the discoveries of the celebrated chemist Michel Eugène Chevreul and the publication, in 1839, of his comprehensive survey *De la loi du contraste simultané des couleurs et de l'assortiment des objets colorés considéré d'après cette loi dans ses rapports avec la peinture ....* [On the Law of Simultaneous Contrast of Colours].[26] These pictorial practices were picked up and used by artists who had no links with the exhibitors of Boulevard des Capucines. Jules Bastien-Lepage,[27] for example, was very soon inspired by them and, breaking with the Academic training he had received at the École des Beaux-Arts, successfully began uniting all these artistic innovations. In his first Naturalist manifesto picture, *The Haymakers* (ILL. 23), which was presented at the 1878 Salon, it is therefore possible to see a mixed traditional background that bears the marks of Realism and borrowings from photography and Japanese-style painting. The foreground of wild grasses reveals a conspicuously free brushstroke, which is an unmistakable nod towards Impressionism but which does not go as far as the 'broken colour' technique favoured by this movement. Émile Zola, the promoter of literary Naturalism, very clearly articulated Bastien-Lepage's debt towards his young predecessors when, the following year, he wrote: 'Of course, we recognize a grandson of Courbet and Millet. But the influence of the Impressionist painters is also instantly striking.'[28]

The rural scenes depicted by Bastien-Lepage, although they reflected contemporary life in his home region, were already no more than a memory in which time was suspended – almost a historical testimony to a period when the buildings and chimneys of the industrial world were extending their tentacles in and around urban spaces.[29] And when, sometime later, he offered a new vision of the character of *Joan of Arc* (ILL. 30), he resumed painting in the 'grand manner' but without abandoning – quite the contrary – his still more exuberant aesthetic borrowings and vibrant brushwork. Bastien-Lepage died very young, struck down by illness in 1884 at the age of 36, but the path he had chosen was taken up and pursued by many artists who adapted it to a variety of subjects, notably transferring it from the rural to the urban world. This success was not limited to French artists: most of the foreign ones present in Paris during the 1880s who were concerned with establishing a new kind of art – often linked to their search for a national identity – looked towards Naturalism. Many Scandinavian artists paid tribute to Bastien-Lepage; among others, Peder Severin Krøyer was eloquent in his correspondence, expressing admiration for the 'grandson of Courbet and Millet' and the father of pictorial Naturalism, who was godparent to their art.[30]

The only explicit mention among Krøyer's correspondence devoted to Impressionism appears in a letter to Frederik Vermehren of 20 May 1879.[31] It is an ambiguous remark which seeks to vilify the new movement but at the same time considers it destined to be highly influential. Nonetheless, Krøyer's own painting was described as Impressionist on several occasions. Although the parallel appears possible in relation to his subjects and his concern with clear painting, it is impossible to make such a comparison with regard to his technique. Indeed,

26. Chevreul, *De la loi du contraste simultané*.
27. Lobstein, 'Jules Bastien-Lepage (1848–1884)', 15–51.
28. Zola, *Écrits sur l'art*, 401.
29. Bergeron, 'Une France entre deux mondes', 15–25.
30. Preserved at Den Hirschsprungske Samling: PSK to Albert Wolff, Copenhagen, 16 January 1885. PSK Archive 246.
31. Draft for a letter: PSK to Frederik Vermehren, Cernay-la-Ville, 20 May 1879. PSK Archive 58.

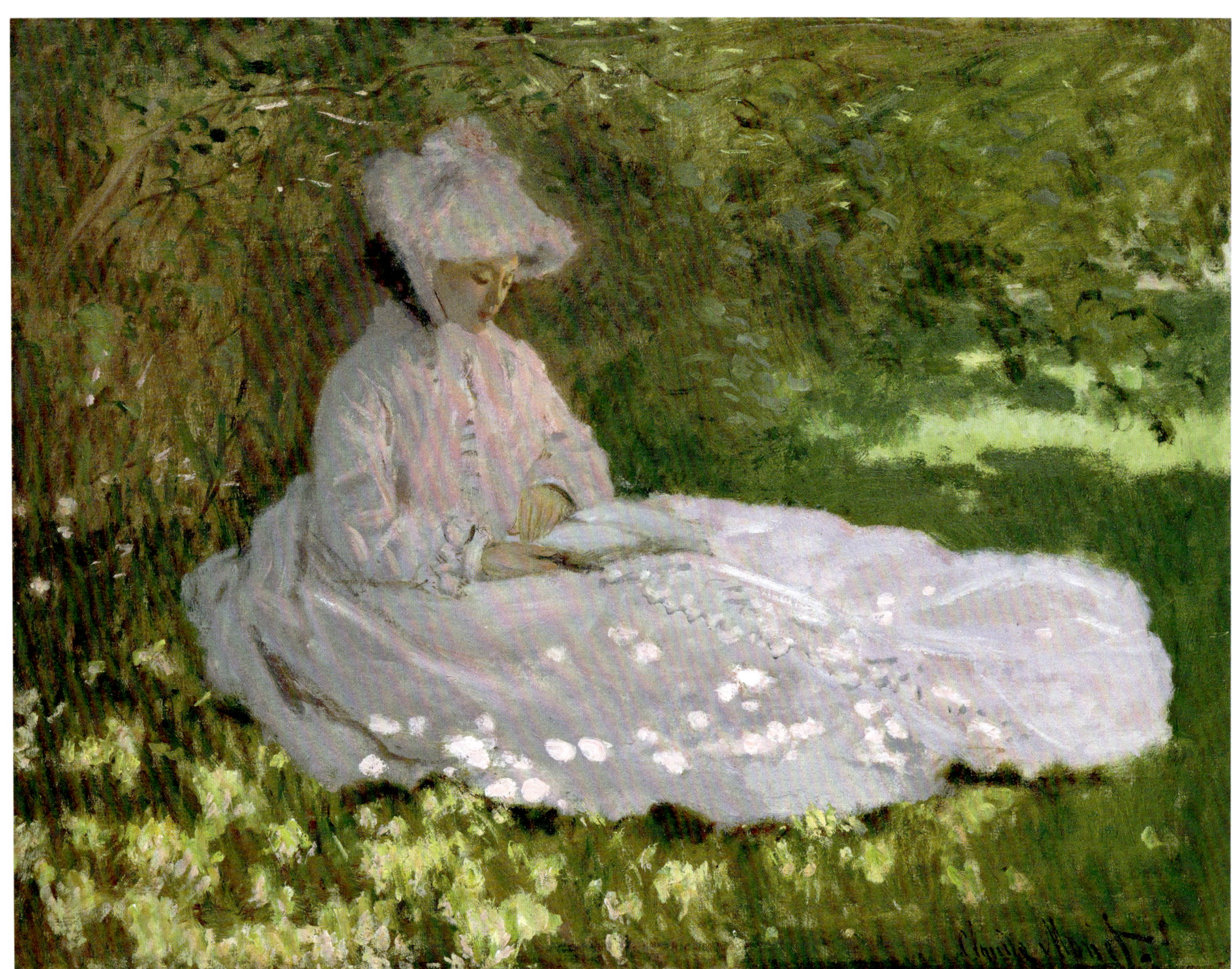

ILL. 31 Claude Monet, *Springtime*, 1872. Oil on canvas, 50 × 65.5 cm. The Walters Art Museum, Baltimore. 37.11

Krøyer never adopted the rapid, close brushstrokes that were characteristic of the paintings submitted by Claude Monet and Pierre-Auguste Renoir to the 1874 exhibition. He remained faithful to the teaching he had received, albeit slightly modified by what Bastien-Lepage had adapted from the Impressionist technique. From this point of view, the comparison between Monet's *Springtime* (ILL. 31) and Krøyer's *Roses* (CAT. 51) is useful: the deft touch of the Danish artist is more delicate, the brush gliding easily over the canvas to create form and movement, without clashes of colour and with great respect for design.

The Naturalist artists were far removed from the objective of Impressionist artists as that was determined by the critic Édouard Drumont: 'To paint what they see, to reproduce nature without interpreting and without organizing it, this seems to be the aim that the artists of the Boulevard des Capucines have set themselves.'[32] However, the two artistic movements continued to be confused with one another, and the picture by Claude Monet which was at the origin of the term 'Impressionism' soon became surrounded by interpretations that were far removed from the criteria defined by Drumont. These now need to be evaluated, while admitting, albeit reluctantly, that Impressionism was no more than a brief spark – but a spark which set art alight, having traversed stylistic periods, led by Naturalism, the movement which, from the outset, succeeded in captivating art lovers.

32. Drumont, 'L'Exposition du boulevard des Capucines', 2.

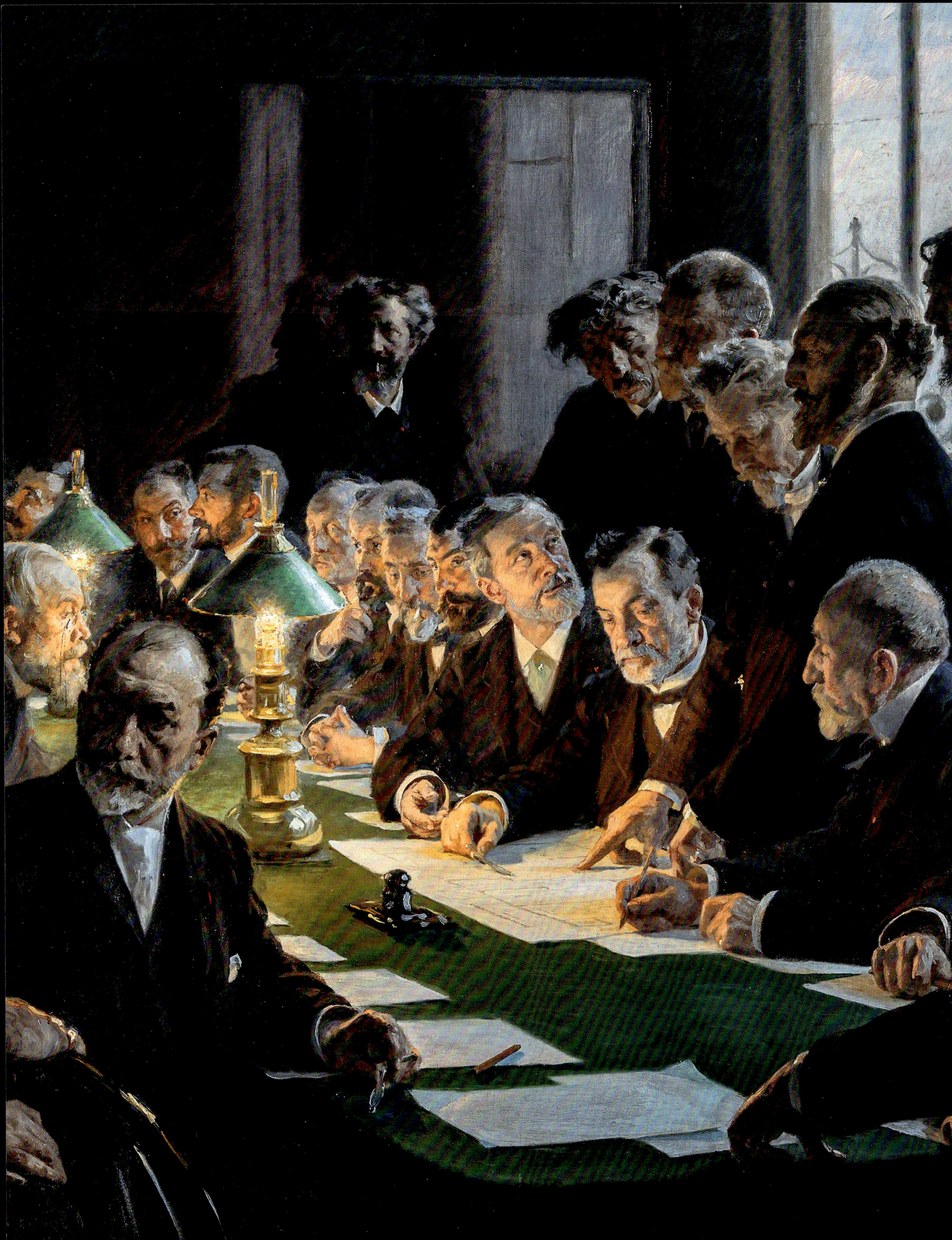

The 1888 French Art Exhibition in Copenhagen

6

At the origins of the exhibition

During the French art exhibition in Copenhagen from 18 May to 16 October 1888, the attendance of Peder Severin Krøyer was not insignificant, as he helped to make the exhibition reality. Thus, it is interesting to look closer at his influences in the choice of works exhibited in relation to the numerous other international art exhibitions organised under the patronage of the French State. Moreover, we will take a look at Krøyer's painting *Committee for the French Art Exhibition in Copenhagen 1888* (ILL. 32) as a symbolic summary of the collaboration.[1]

In 1877, Heinrich Hirschsprung conceived the idea of organising a large exhibition of contemporary French art, to be held in Copenhagen. He gave the painters Peder Severin Krøyer and Laurits Tuxen the task of approaching French painters and sculptors who might be interested in participating, but the matter was not taken any further.[2] However, it was not long before another prominent Danish collector, Carl Jacobsen, took over the initiative and thought of making it more prestigious by twinning it with the Nordic Exhibition of Industry, Agriculture, and Art, due to be held in Copenhagen from 18 May to 4 October 1888. As he was beginning to look for collaborators with an intimate knowledge of French art and Paris art institutions, as well as personal links with artists and government officials, he probably remembered the delegates chosen by Hirschsprung, whom he himself knew. So he invited the painters Peder Severin Krøyer and Laurits Tuxen to fill these roles, along with the architect Vilhelm Klein.

They started to work together in late 1887 and Krøyer was soon sending out the first letters to his contacts, though very few of these communications survive. The first ones were longer and more formal, and on several occasions they were accompanied by New Year greetings, meaning they can be dated around December 1887 and January 1888. Their purpose was to inform the recipients of Jacobsen's decision and to ask for their participation, either as lenders,[3] or as members of the organising com-

1. This essay adopts a French, and, more particularly, a Parisian view of the subject and should be accompanied by the Danish approach which, among others, Nicholas Parkinson treats in the unpublished article "Copenhagen 1888: The First Centennial of French Modern Art".

2. Saabye, *Hirschsprung. Kunstsamler og maecen*, 94–95.

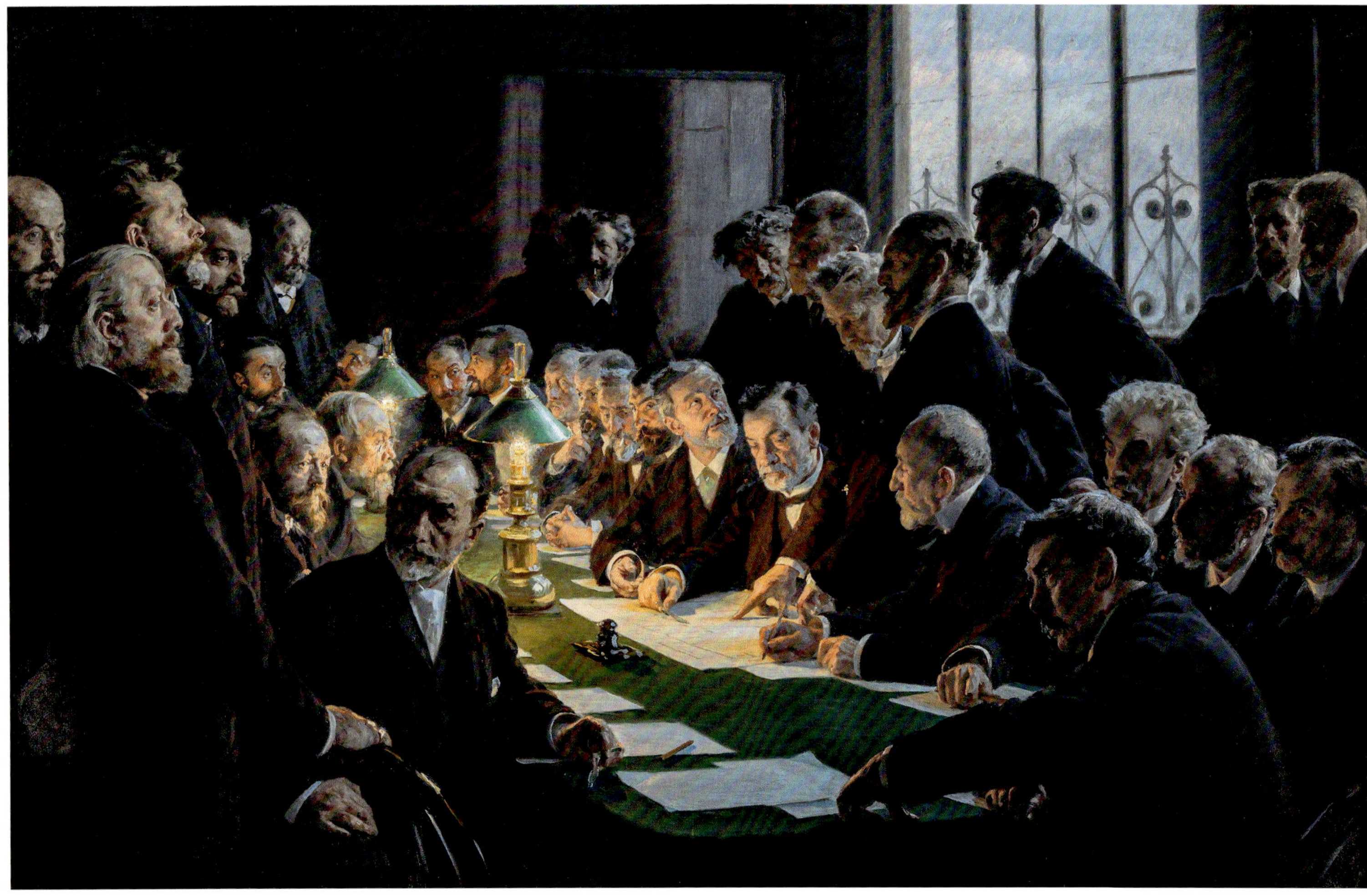

ILL. 32 Peder Severin Krøyer: *Committee of the Copenhagen French Art Exhibition, in 1888*, 1889. Oil on canvas, 144×221 cm. Ny Carlsberg Glyptotek, Copenhagen. MIN 0904

mittee. Some addressees, like Fernand Cormon – with whom Krøyer was on familiar terms, having known him since 1879 – could be asked for their participation in both capacities.[4] In the letter addressed to him, certain details are revealed concerning the construction of a special building for the exhibition and the support given by the Danish government, which had promised to send one of its warships to Le Havre to take delivery of paintings, sculptures, and engravings and bring them back to Copenhagen. The letter also announces that Vilhelm Klein had already left for Paris to make contact with the French government, and to personally meet the members of the future organising committee as Jacobsen had envisioned it. The names found in the letter are those of Count de Moltke, the Danish minister in Paris; Paul Calon, the Danish consul general in Paris; Antonin Proust, a journalist, politician, and future senior official for the Beaux-Arts, who certainly had Scandinavian friends,

3. As in a rough draft of a letter which is undated and carries no indication of the addressee. PSK Archive 240.

4. Undated rough draft of a letter addressed to Fernand Cormon. PSK Archive 242.

since it was precisely that year that he had his portrait painted by the Swede Anders Zorn (ILL. 33); and the scientist Louis Pasteur, whom Jacobsen knew and, in his activity as a brewer, was to benefit from Pasteur's discoveries concerning yeasts. Pasteur was another friend of the Nordic countries, having agreed in 1885 to pose for the Finnish painter Albert Edelfelt (ILL. 34). There was also Louis Eugène Tisserand, listed as a minister but, from 1876 to 1898, simply Director of Agriculture at the ministry; from 1855, he had resided in Denmark, Sweden, and Norway as an agronomist,[5] probably also frequenting Jacobsen. Finally, there was the sculptor Paul Dubois and the painters Léon Bonnat and Fernand Cormon.

Alongside this first task, Krøyer and Tuxen, together with their friends, drew up lists of artists to contact.[6] Clearly determined to assist his friend, Cormon wasted no time in responding:

5. Tisserand, *Études économiques sur le Holstein*.

6. Letter from Cormon to Krøyer. undated, PSK Archive 2852.

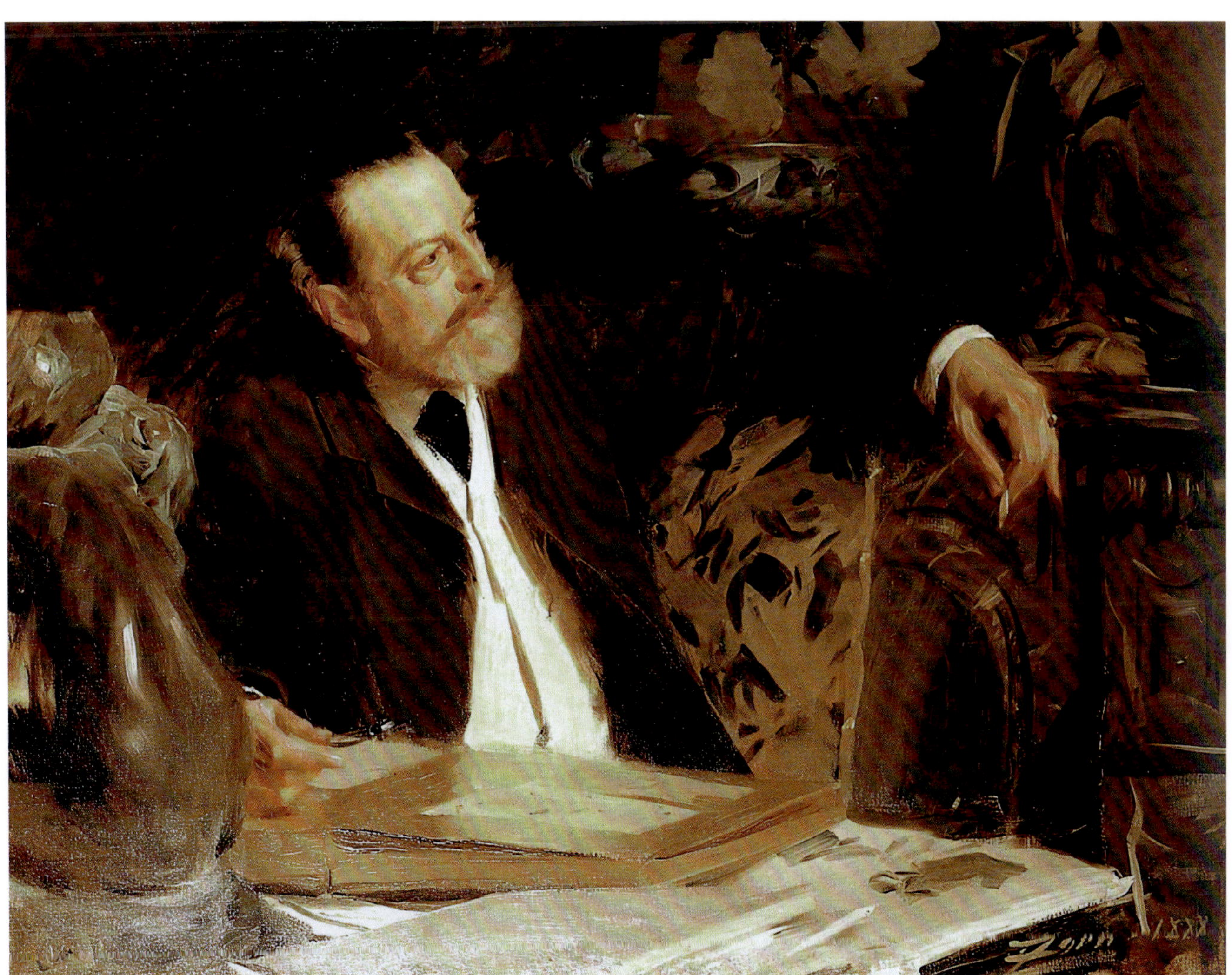

ILL. 33 Anders Zorn: *Antonin Proust*, 1888. Oil on canvas, 106×138 cm. Private collection.

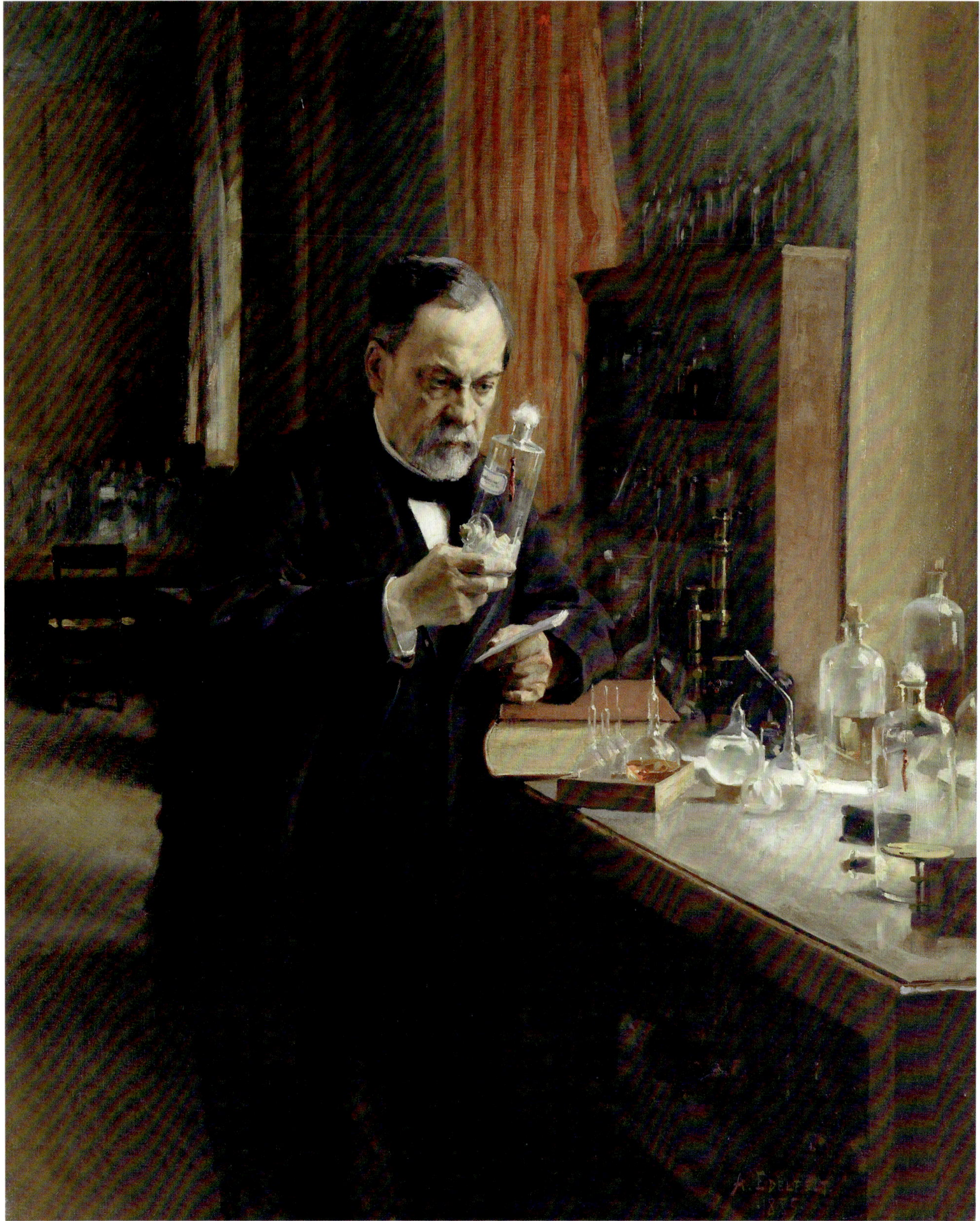

ILL. 34 Albert Edelfelt: *Louis Pasteur*, 1885. Oil on canvas, 155.0 × 127.5 cm. Musée d'Orsay, Paris. DO 1986 16

I have some advice for you. Through our ambassador and Mr Proust, you will certainly have the support of the state. But as for the French artists, you would perhaps be well advised to have the signature of Mr Bailly, President of the Société des Artistes Français, among those of the Committee. He is highly considered, very well liked and, since he is our leader, he is usually the person to whom proposals regarding foreign exhibitions are addressed. As for Harpignies, Busson, and Cazin, do as you think fit. Personally I would prefer Busson,[7] who is my friend and, I think, very superior to the other two, not by virtue of talent but in character. But this is just a personal desire, as I say, and whatever you do will be done well.

A little further on, Cormon completes the list of artists it would be good to invite:

In painting: Carrière, a new [artist], full of talent and originality. And if you put down Jourdeuil, Joubert, and Baillet,[8] don't forget Dameron. Plus Dinet, Marec, and Bordes.[9]

In sculpture: Marqueste, who is enormously talented, and Carriès, who creates striking busts.[10]

This initial advice was followed by a second letter whose contents were more diplomatic, since it mainly listed the top civil servants whose favour it would be useful to win:

1. Leave your card, with your thanks, with our ambassador, Mr Thompson [ambassador to Copenhagen from 1886 to 1891], especially as I spoke about your plans to his brother, the Deputy [Gaston, Deputy for French Algeria from 1877 to 1932], and he, in all probability, has started to attend to the matter. 2. Send your cards to Paris with similar thanks to Mr Spuller, Minister of Fine Arts, to Mr Flourens, Minister of Foreign Affairs, to Mr Mollard [Joseph, or his son Armand, who were 'introducers of ambassadors'] at the Ministry of Foreign Affairs, and to Mr Bonnat, your former patron who has been very kind. Finally, I will ask you to send a special word of thanks to Mr Kaempfen, Director of the Beaux-Arts, 3 rue de Valois, who has dealt with your affair, showing great kindness towards you. I am very keen that you should do this as it may ensure later that one of your canvases is purchased for the Luxembourg.

The letters were sent, either directly or sometimes passed on by mutual friends. The recipients responded and many of them agreed to participate in the project,[11] admitting us, as we read them now, into their lives and revealing their thoughts on Danish art, as Pascal-Adolphe-Jean Dagnan Bouveret later did:

Only today, Sunday 8 April, have I received your letter of 1 March, which Edelfelt has sent to me at Blidah [*sic*]. Why is this? It is because when leaving Blidah [*sic*] on 1 March I forgot to give the hotel my forwarding address, to which they should send any letters that arrived for me. Edelfelt, whom I have seen again recently and who spoke of you and of the strong desire you expressed to have my pictures in Copenhagen, asked me if I had received his letters. I immediately asked in all the post offices of the towns I had passed through in Algeria and today I have received a large number of these letters. Please forgive me, won't you? How I regret, too,

7. Despite this insistence, Busson was not present at the exhibition.
8. With the exception of Jourdeuil, who was present with a *Paysage* (unidentified) priced at 500 francs, these acquaintances from his time in Cernay were absent from the exhibition.
9. None of these three was present at the exhibition.
10. But who was not present at the exhibition.
11. Among artists, it is possible to cite Émile Barau (letter of 19 February 1888, PSK Archive 2803); Alfred Philippe Roll (letter of 20 June 1888, PSK Archive 2933); Léon Germain Pelouse (letter of 20 July 1888, PSK Archive 2923); and, among the committee members, Armand Dayot (letter of 1 March 1888, PSK Archive 2859), author of this important comment: 'The works marked with a cross seem to me to be truly worthy of appearing in your exhibition and I have taken the liberty of drawing M. Proust's particular attention to them.'

> that I have not been able to send you anything other than a study which represents me so badly.
>
> If there were still time, I could send a small-format portrait on a size 6 canvas [41 × 33 cm] which would do me greater honour. Unfortunately, none of my pictures is in Paris. Perhaps you could have been loaned my *Breton Women at a Pardon* from the last Salon, it was Mr Tooth, a picture dealer in London who bought it from me, perhaps he still has it.
>
> I would be very pleased to be well represented in Copenhagen. Perhaps, too, the French Government would lend my pictures from the Luxembourg, *The Consecrated Bread* or *Horses at the Watering Trough*, if the Committee were to submit the request and there was still time.
>
> Nonetheless, please believe me, dear Monsieur Krøyer, when I say that I am very sorry not to be able to take advantage of this opportunity to become known to Danish artists whose artistic research and the feeling they have for Art I greatly admire.[12]

The approaches did not all bear fruit and several artists said they were sorry not to be able to participate in the event.[13] One of these was Jules Breton:

> I am very flattered by your request for the Copenhagen exhibition. I would have been very happy to contribute to it, but unfortunately I have only my canvases for the Paris Salon.
>
> Almost all my pictures are displayed in American collections and it would be pointless to ask for them.
>
> I sincerely regret, therefore, not being able to accommodate a fellow artist whose talent I admire.[14]

All this meant that the first meetings of the Committee of the Copenhagen French Exhibition could now be held. The participants were Antonin Proust, two critics, and the dealer Georges Petit, along with nine painters, seven sculptors, three architects, and one engraver, who were among the most famous of the period.

France and its artistic exhibitions abroad

The Copenhagen French Exhibition was not unique; the files in the French National Archives still preserve records of substantial participation by French artists in foreign exhibitions, under the administrative leadership of the state. This was the case with all the great World's Fairs which took place under the Third Republic, between 1870 and 1940: at the Prater in Vienna, from 1 May to 31 October 1873; at Fairmount Park in Philadelphia from 10 May to 10 November 1876; at Carlton Gardens in Melbourne from 1 October 1880 to 30 April 1881; and then one of exceptional length, from 8 April to 10 December 1888 – the Exposición universal de Barcelona in the Parque. These latter dates speak for themselves, and the Spanish exhibition looked like a formidable competitor to the Danish project. It might be thought that, for many artists, the dilemma of where and what to lend must have been difficult to resolve; as we shall soon see, however, the problem almost never arose.

It is necessary to say a few words about this Spanish exhibition, which appeared in the general catalogue accompanying the event under the title 'Group 23, Fine Arts, Class 178, Drawing, Lithography, Engraving; 179, Painting; 180, Sculpture and Medals.'[15] There were 141 painters who had sent just over 230 works,[16] and only 18 sculptors represented by 26 sculptures in different materials, which appeared to be dominated by statuettes and busts. In contrast to this, at the Danish exhibition there were 133 painters who submitted 301 paintings and watercolours, as well as 63 sculptors with 200 sculptures.

12. Letter from Dagnan-Bouveret to Krøyer, 8 April 1888. PSK Archive 2857.
13. For example, Émile Friant (letter of 2 March 1888, PSK Archive 2878).
14. Letter from Jules Breton to Krøyer, 23 January or February 1888. PSK Archive 2829.
15. République française, 13–36.
16. After a work by Zacharie Zacharian, which is no. 230 in the exhibition, there is a 230a in the name of Carolus-Duran. Some more complete copies of the catalogue have an errata slip, naming five other painters and seven more paintings.

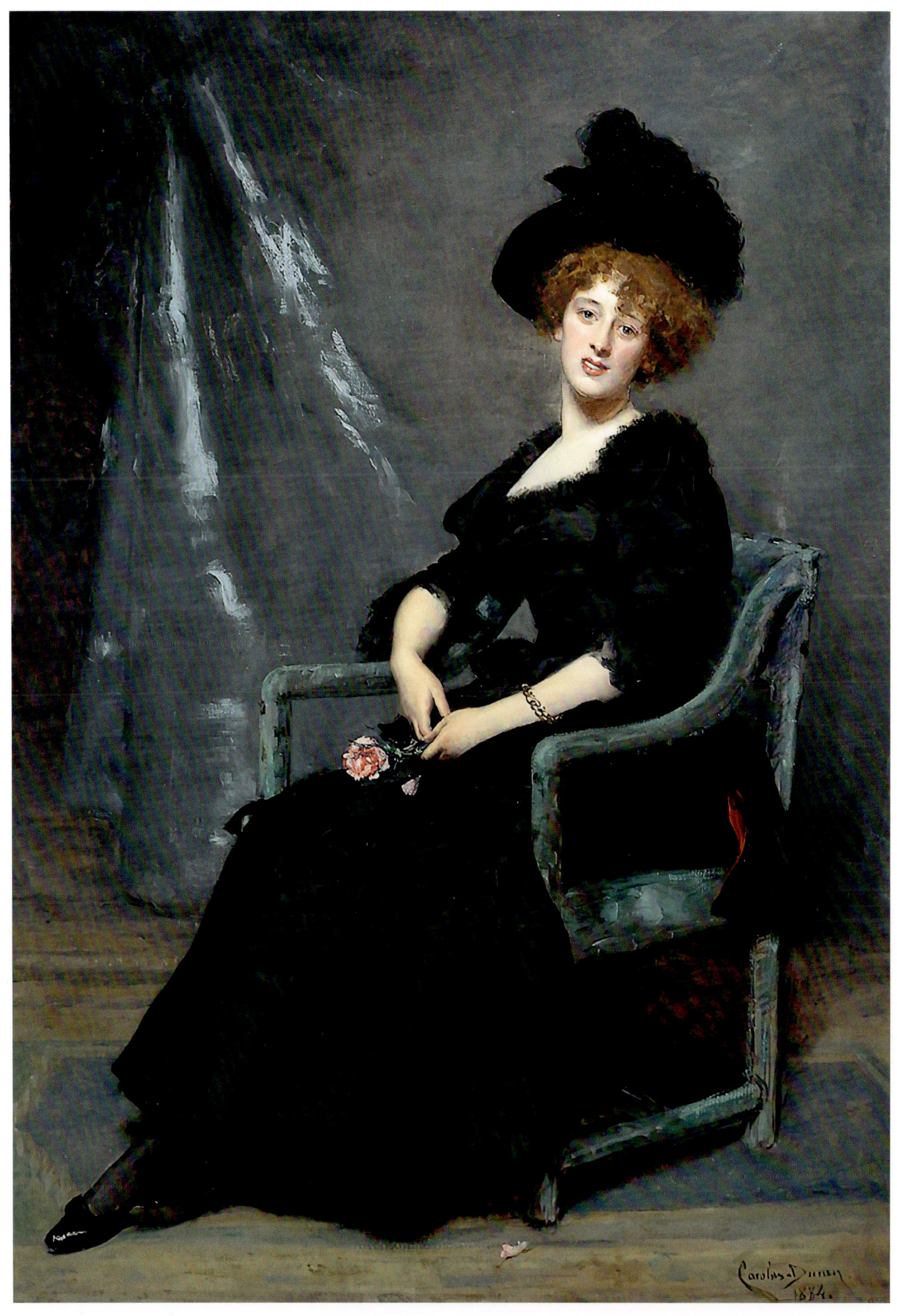

ILL. 35 Carolus-Duran: *Portrait of Lucy Lee-Robbins*, 1884. Oil on canvas, 169.5 × 121.9 cm. Chrysler Museum of Art, Norfolk, Virginia. 71.627

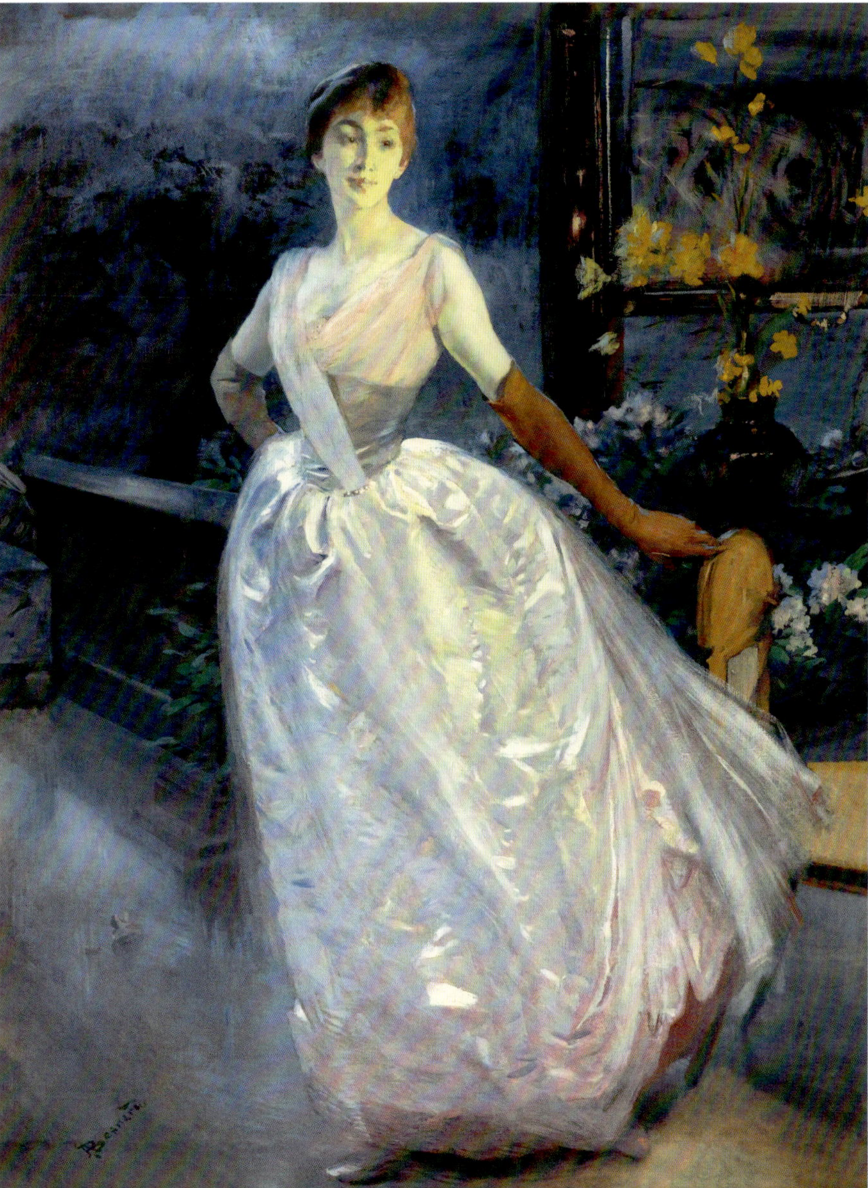

ILL. 36 Albert Besnard: *Mme Roger Jourdain*, 1886. Oil on canvas, 199.0 × 150.5 cm. Musée d'Orsay, Paris. RF 2302

A comparison of the participants in the two events enables us to discern the intentions governing the selection. Only 15 painters and one sculptor were present at both exhibitions, and although they were among the most distinguished of those represented in Barcelona, they were much less so than those who exhibited solely in Copenhagen,[17] among whom were a multitude of recipients of the Légion d'honneur, members of the Institute, and holders of the highest awards of the official Paris Salon (ILL. 35). It often appeared that artworks bought at the Salon were disguised gifts to artists in need and, in view of this fact, it would seem that works sent to foreign

17. *Illustreret katalog*. Krøyer must have helped prepare the catalogue since there are, for example, reproductions of some of his drawings (p. 18); a portrait of Léon Joubert; and a portrait of Léon-Germain Pelouse from 1879, held in Den Hirschsprungske Samling, inv. nos. 840 and 842 (p. 20).

exhibitions organised by the Beaux-Arts served a similar purpose:[18] giving young artists a springboard or enabling older ones who had found it difficult to gain recognition in the official French galleries to exhibit.

In terms of quality, therefore, the French exhibition in Copenhagen far exceeded the Barcelona exhibition, very probably because of the good relations Krøyer maintained with artists like Albert Besnard (ILL. 36)[19] and French gallery owners,[20] but also for other simple, obvious reasons – the first being that the exhibition was not limited to living artists but had the express intention of being retrospective, showing, for example, a version of the *The Death of Sardanapalus* (location unknown) by Eugène Delacroix, *Death and the Woodcutter* by Jean-François Millet (Ny Carlsberg Glyptotek, Copenhagen), and *Spring* by Edouard Manet (ILL. 37). Another advantage of this exhibition was that the number of works per artist does not appear to have been as strictly limited.[21] While no painter sent more than four works, sculptors appear to have had more leeway;[22] Jean Gautherin was a case in point, exhibiting 13 sculptures, some of them in plaster or marble, and on a large scale, like his *Paradise Lost* (1882, Ny Carlsberg Glyptotek, Copenhagen). A third factor likely to attract exhibitors was that, in most cases, the exhibition catalogue indicated the purchase price for each work offered for sale – unless Carl Jacobsen had already bought them, as occurred with Gautherin's aforementioned *Paradise Lost*. A picture by the late Jules Bastien-Lepage (CAT. 49) was on offer for 80,000 francs, one of the highest prices in the exhibition.[23] It had remained in the artist's studio when he died and was lent by his brother, Émile.

Responsibility for the 1888 Danish exhibition was assumed by Carl Jacobsen and his assistants, and everything was financed by him. He took charge of all practical aspects of the event, and although it involved several key figures in the French administration, the exhibition left no trace in the official archives of the French state. For example, in the file preserved in the Pierrefitte National Archives, under the reference F/21/4052, *Commissariat des expositions des Beaux-Arts en France et à l'étranger. 1880–1935*, nowhere is there any reference to this artistic collaboration.

For those on the French side who had been involved in organising the event, several other rewards still awaited them.[24] The first was to be found in the newspapers, which were usually rather circumspect about foreign exhibitions, but in this case some devoted several columns to the event and named the organisers. Charles de Saint-Mesmin wrote about it in *Le Figaro* of 6 June 1888 (p. 4), as did Albert Wolff on the front page of the same newspaper on

18. With the aid of certain artists and collectors. It is surprising to read, on page 10 of the Barcelona catalogue, that Edmond Charles Yon had works exhibited in Copenhagen, though he was not exhibiting in Barcelona.

19. On this special relationship, see: Lobstein and Lehmann, *The Blue Hour*, 104–105.

20. For example, it was through the intermediary of Theo Van Gogh that the pictures of Charles Angrand were lent, as well as those of Manet, Monet, and Alfred Sisley (Vincent Van Gogh, *The Letters*, vols. 4 and 5, Van Gogh Museum et al., 2009). The exhibition did not benefit from the help anticipated to come from Kaempfen and the museums, which was referred to by Cormon. No works from the Musée du Luxembourg appear to have been exhibited. Cormon perhaps forgot to direct Krøyer to Léonce Bénédite, the very powerful curator of this establishment.

21. Whereas in the Barcelona catalogue, apart from a few exceptions in which one or two watercolours were added to one or two oil paintings, it is very clear that Salon principles prevailed, allowing a maximum of two works per artist and per technique.

22. And to have benefited from the exhibition of works of theirs that had been previously bought by Jacobsen.

23. This was indicated at the beginning of the catalogue, after the *Abbréviations*. A letter from Émile Bastien-Lepage of 4 June 1888 reveals that he eventually sold the picture to Jacobsen for 35,000 francs (PSK Archive 2807).

24. Which did not prevent Krøyer receiving some complaints, including one on 11 January 1889 (PSK Archive 1855) from the sculptor Léon Cugnot, whose sculptures *Corybante stifling the cries of Jupiter's Child* (marble, location unknown) and *Young Mercury* (plaster, location unknown) had been damaged. Other artists blamed Krøyer for the fact that no buyers had appeared for their works: 'You told me yourself that there were opportunities, it was partly because of that that I went to great lengths to send you this picture. The exhibition has ended or will end soon. I would be very grateful if you could have it sent back to me as soon as possible and give orders to that effect. On my return to Paris, I am expecting (four illegible words) an art lover who I hope will give a home to it.' (undated letter from Pelouse to Krøyer, PSK Archive 2925).

9 June 1888. This was an opportunity for Wolff to refer to the second benefit of their contribution to the project, in the form of a trip to the very place where the exhibition was being held, which he described as follows:

> Places have been reserved with the Sleeping-Cars Company for Cologne, lunch has been ordered in that city for 11 o'clock tomorrow, two hours before the express for Hamburg departs; the stationmaster at Cologne [...] will reserve a special carriage for our artists; they will arrive in Hamburg at ten in the evening; at midnight they will be in Kiel, where the Danish steamer is being stoked for departure, and on Monday morning, around 10 o'clock, the tourists will enter Copenhagen, where their rooms have been reserved in the best hotels and where the most eminent men of the city will perform the duty of guiding them around.[25]

The journalistic commentary continues in this vein until we arrive at the third and last part of the essay, which concludes thus: 'And in order to preserve a lasting memory of this visit, Mr Jacobsen has commissioned from his compatriot, Mr Krøyer, portraits of all the French guests.'[26]

The aftermath of the exhibition

Before producing the definitive work *Committee for the French Art Exhibition in Copenhagen 1888*, in which not only the committee members would figure but also Louis Pasteur,[27] as well as some of the Danish organisers, Krøyer embarked upon a monumental task which was to occupy him from November 1888 until the summer of 1889, a period in which he visited Paris and travelled in France. He began by dashing off a few sketches for the composition in a sketchbook now preserved in the Hirschsprung Collection.[28] Armed with his initial ideas, he began by gathering together the participants to take a few photos inspired by his early rough sketches (ILL. 38), which would help him settle upon the definitive composition.[29] From that point on, as was his habit where works involving several models were concerned, he started to make individual studies of each face,[30] which would then find their place in several painted sketches (ILL. 39), right up until he was able to paint the final picture in a studio made available to him in the Palais de l'Industrie – where the Salon was usually held. And this was where things became more complicated.

With the exception of a few of the models, such as Puvis de Chavannes ('I am not free before next Thursday; if that day suits you I can offer to meet you at the Palais de l'Industrie for a sitting between 12.30 and 2.30')[31] and Carolus-Duran ('I shall have pleasure in coming to your home next Thursday at 9 o'clock in the morning and staying until 10'),[32] most of his sitters, including Léon Bonnat,[33] for example, were often unavailable for the planned sittings.

With time and patience, Krøyer succeeded in gathering all his subjects together and painting the picture, which he displayed at the eleventh hour, as exhibit number 88, amongst the works in the Danish Fine Arts section of the Exposition Universelle held in Paris in 1889. He did not fail to receive his due share of praise:

25. Many other newspapers published news of this journey: 'The Copenhagen Exhibition', 2; *Gazette du jour*, 3; *Chronique*, [2] (the most important and most detailed on the progress of the visit); 'L'Exposition scandinave', [3].
26. Wolff, 'Courrier de Paris', 1.
27. Michel, 'Le Comité français', 148.
28. PSK sketchbook, inv. no. 7012.
29. There is a scaled-down version of this in the Hirschsprung Collection (inv. no. 212).
30. Since no portrait of the committee members has been recorded in Christensen, *P. S. Krøyer 23. juli 1851–20. november*, we might assume that he proceeded as he did at Cernay, in 1879, and made do with drawings – an assumption which seems justified by the sessions in which each model posed singly. It is nevertheless surprising that none of these drawings is now known.
31. Letter from Puvis de Chavannes to Krøyer, December 1888. PSK Archive 2931.
32. Letter from Carolus-Duran to Krøyer, 15 April 1889. PSK Archive 2870.

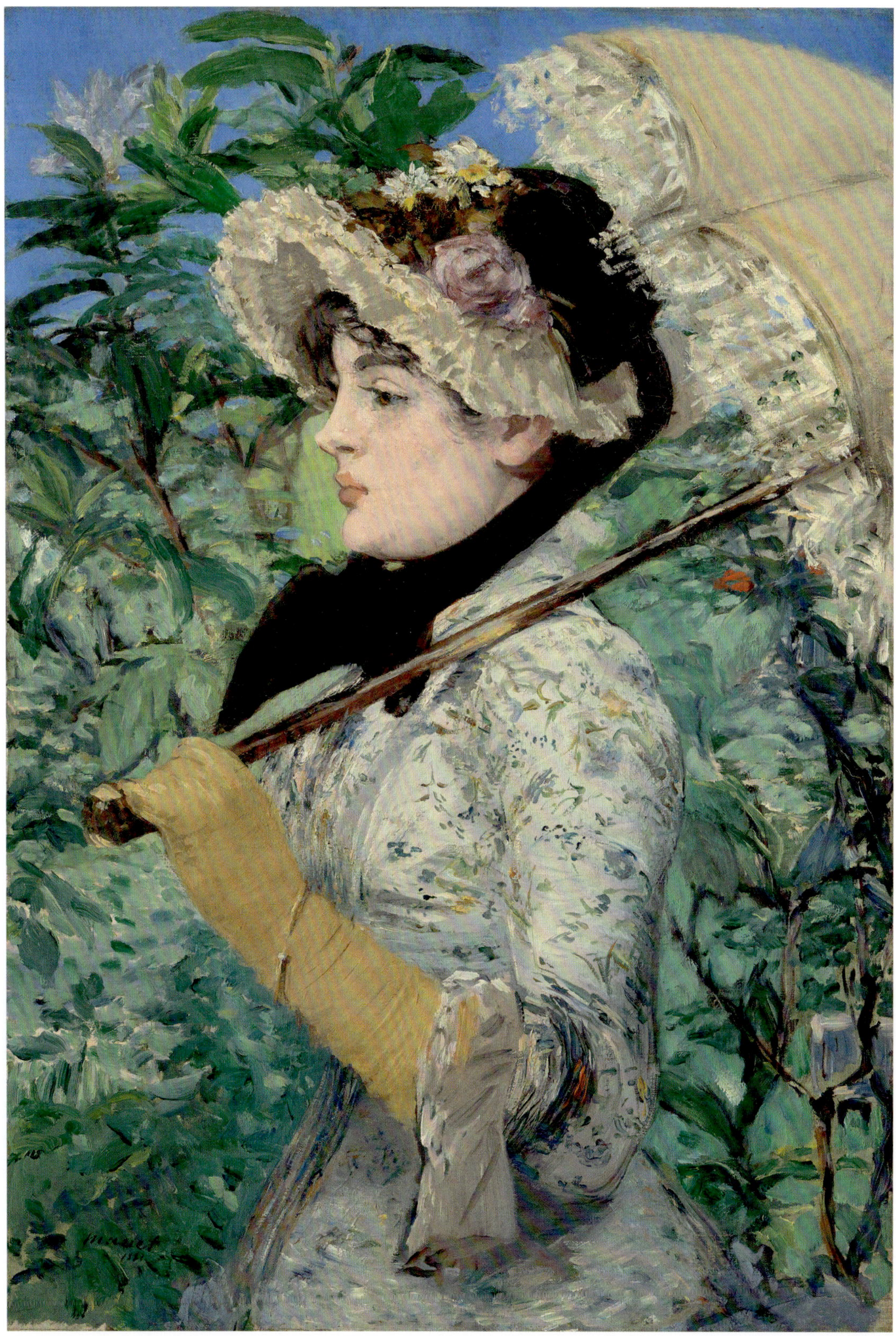

ILL. 37 Edouard Manet: *Spring*, 1881. Oil on canvas, 74 × 51.5 cm. The J. Paul Getty Museum, Los Angeles. 2014.62

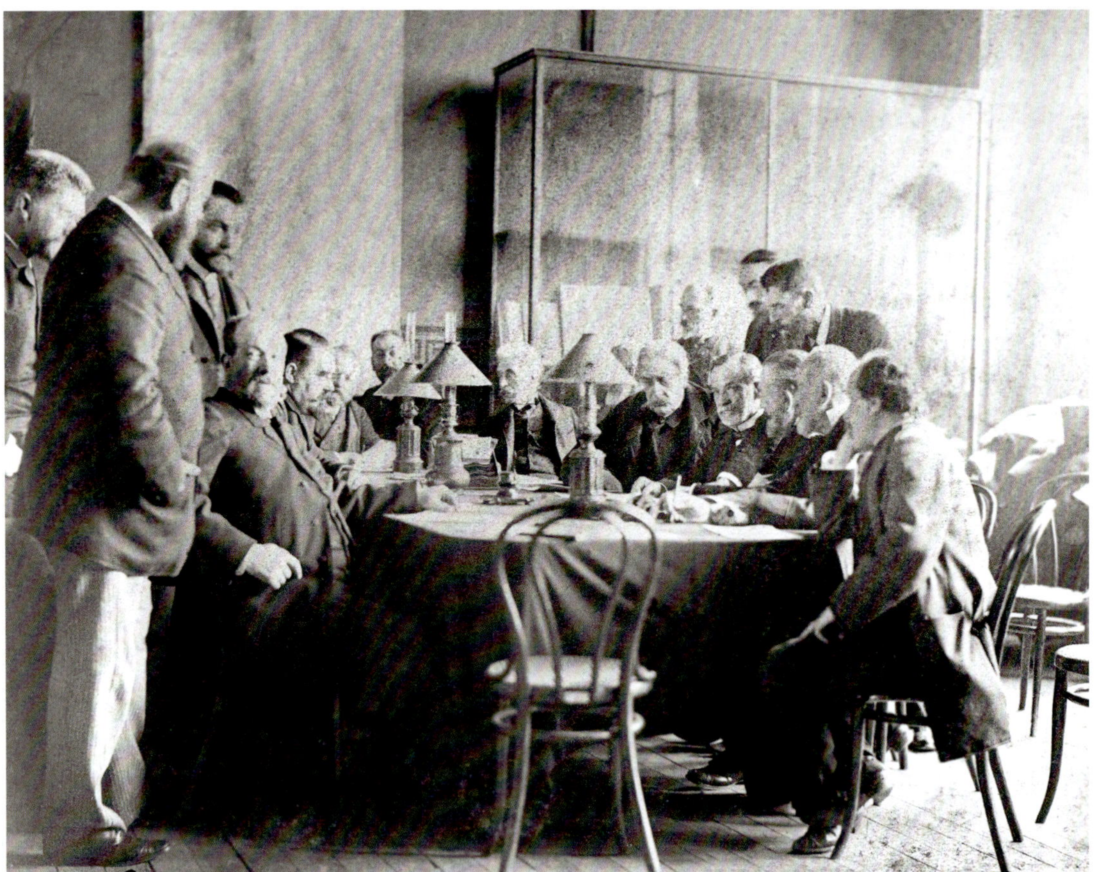

ILL. 38 *Committee of the Copenhagen French Exhibition of 1888*, 1889. Skagens Kunstmuseer.

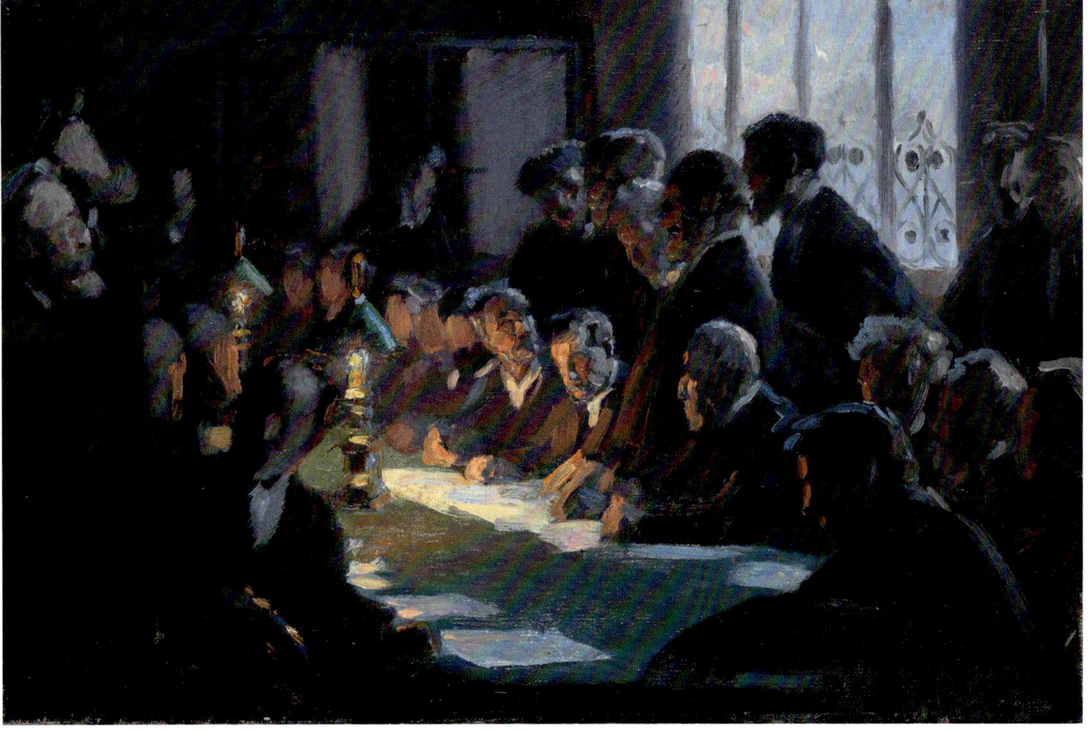

ILL. 39 Peder Severin Krøyer: *The Committee of the Copenhagen French Art Exhibition, in 1888*, 1889. Oil on canvas, 27 × 41 cm. Location unknown.

> One can see all that is both spontaneous and forceful in Krøyer's talent by looking at the portraits he has grouped together in the *Committee for the French Art Exhibition in Copenhagen 1888*. Messrs Pasteur, Jacobsen, Falguière, Dubois, Puvis de Chavannes, Chaplain, Barrias, Bonnat, Gérôme, Roll, etc., are all beautifully drawn.[34]

It was with this deservedly famous painting that the venture ended: a venture to mount one of the most remarkable exhibitions of French art of the 19th century in a foreign country, in which Krøyer played one of the major roles. Denmark could be proud of his qualities as an organiser and coordinator, while France could find in these same attributes a reason to admire him still more. In fact, while enabling the promotion of French artists he had also been an active member of the Danish Fine Arts Committee, which was preparing the Danish entries for the 1889 Exposition Universelle. His qualities appealed both to the public and to critics,[35] and all the way up to the Protocol Department of the Elysée, which invited him, on 20 June 1889, to a dinner with the President of the Republic, Said Carnot, and his wife.[36]

33. Telegram from Bonnat to Krøyer, January 1889. PSK Archive 2824.

34. Michel, 'Feuilleton du *Journal des Débats* du 29 août 1889', [2].

35. 'These magnanimous, simple and open-hearted painters have the secret of making us as keenly interested in the detail of a ray of light or the drama of a shadow as others might do in depicting the rage of Achilles or the pain of Orpheus.' Armand Dayot, 'Exposition Universelle de 1889. XXXIX. L'Exposition décennale étrangère (1878–89)', *Journal official de la République française*, 17 September 1889, 4510.

36. Invitation card sent to Krøyer from the presidential palace, 20 June (1889). PSK Archive 2832.

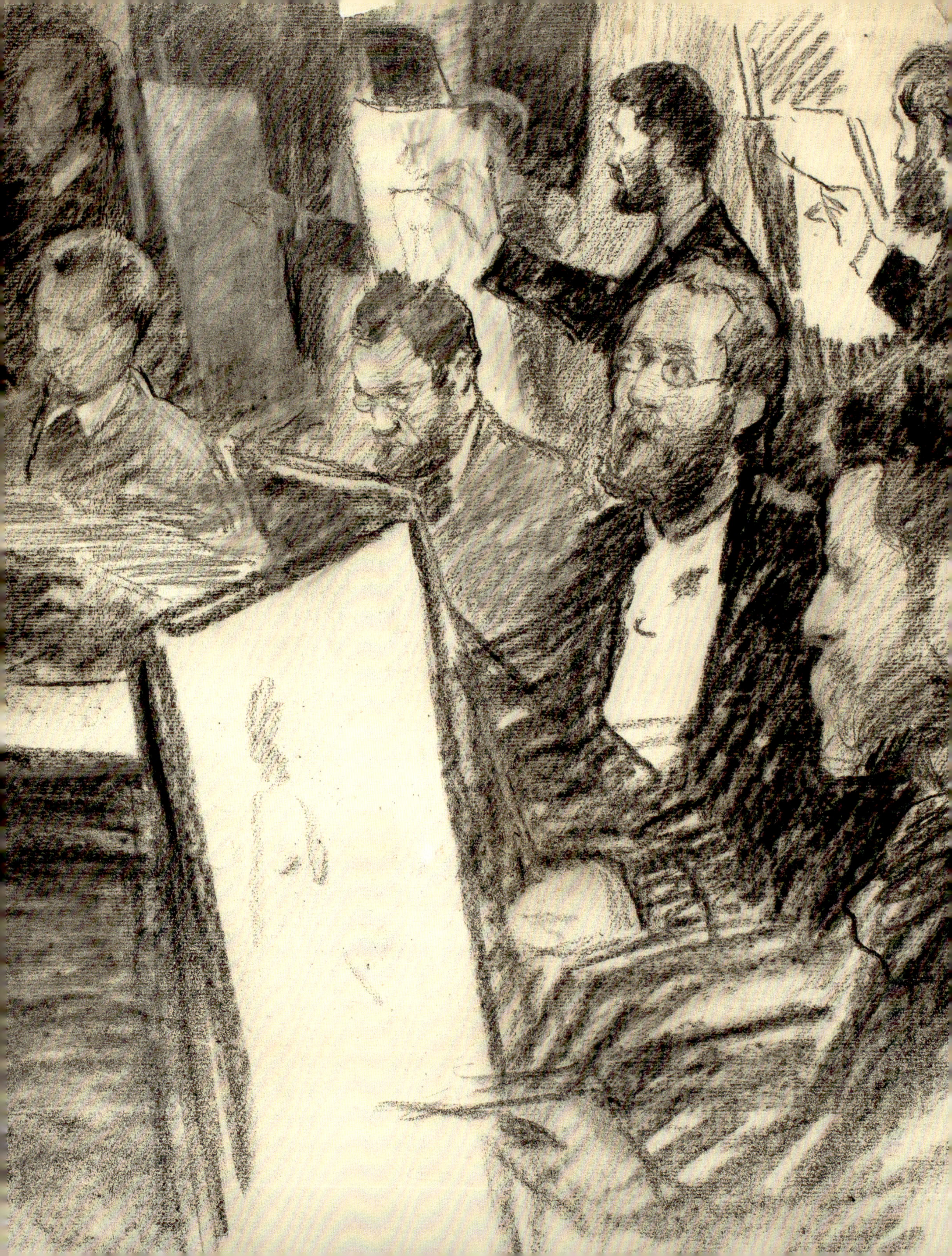

Krøyer's School

7

Krøyer and Kunstnernes Studieskole in Copenhagen

When Peder Severin Krøyer returned to Denmark after his four-year sojourn abroad in 1877–1881, he began teaching at Kunstnernes Studieskole (literally The Artists' Study School); he continued to do so until the turn of the century. His teaching was significantly inspired by what he had learned abroad and by his strong conviction that originality was of vital importance for any artist.[1] His own originality in terms of rendering light would also have set an inspirational example for his pupils. With his involvement in the school, Krøyer contributed to a new departure in the teaching of young artists in Denmark, as the school's presence put Det Kongelige Danske Kunstakademi under pressure to reform its teaching and give younger artists better opportunities for exhibiting their works.

Kunstnernes Studieskole was an educational institution consisting of a number of independent classes and so-called master studios, all located at different addresses but united by a joint board of directors. Master studios were held at a specific place and were always taught by the same artist. There were day classes, evening classes, and classes for advanced students. Some pupils attended only day classes or only evening classes, while others did both; the advanced classes catered to the most talented pupils or previously trained artists, who were taught separately.

The board called the institution Kunstnernes Studieskole in all their internal papers, but posterity has often opted for the more general term Kunstnernes frie Studieskoler (literally The Artists' Independent Study Schools), meaning that the school goes by different names in the literature. The 'independence' concerned the school's autonomy in relation to the art academy, but in fact Kunstnernes Studieskole received state funding from the outset.

The school was established in 1882 in response to a decline in the quality of teaching at the art academy due to a recent academy reform,[2] and reflected the students' wish to have an alternative to the art academy.[3] It was intended for those who already had some practice in the art of painting but lacked proper access to life classes or model studies, and modern teaching methods. The school's first head was Laurits Tuxen, who had already established a life class (known as a 'model school') for graduate artists back in 1879. From the winter of 1880/1881, his school too received a small state subsidy,[4] and the model school subsequently became an integral part of the Studieskole.

1. Krøyer's position on the issue of originality is expressed, for example, in a draft for a letter from PSK to Frederik Vermehren, Cernay-la-Ville, 20 May 1879. PSK Archive 58.

2. Lichtenberg, *Zahrtmanns skole*, 12–13. The reform is also described in Meldahl and Johansen, 455.

3. The history of the school is briefly outlined in the introduction to the exhibition catalogue *Fortegnelse over den af Kunstnernes Studieskole foranstaltede Udstilling*, 3–4.

4. Fabritius, 'Tuxen og de frie studieskoler', 33.

After the summer holidays of 1882, the influx of pupils from the art academy was so great that Krøyer took it upon himself to teach the newcomers.[5] From this point on, the school had two departments offering both day and evening classes: Tuxens Skole, in premises still found at 10, H.C. Andersens Boulevard today, and Krøyer's School, which was first housed in the Industriforeningens Udstillingsbygning near the present-day Rådhuspladsen, the Copenhagen City Hall square. In December 1882, Krøyer made a drawing from Kunstnernes Studieskole showing Tuxen in the foreground (ILL. 40).[6] The scene depicts Tuxen's team of trained painters on 6, Filippavej, and Krøyer arranged his own school in a similar way (ILL. 47).[7] The students sat in a semicircle around the model with large easels at the back and small easels at the front; they were seated alternately on high- and low-legged chairs. In 1880, Tuxen wrote the following to Krøyer about the model school: 'We will draw for three hours every night (5½–8½), and overall we will arrange things in the Parisian manner.'[8] The 'Parisian' arrangements at both schools concerned the teaching methods as well as the practicalities associated with the set-up and facilities. The teaching method involved life classes where students would draw after nude models right from the beginning – unlike at the art academy, where students graduated to the life class last of all. In addition, more frequent changes of model were made, thereby increasing the pace of painting. The practical set-up of Tuxen's classes can be seen in Krøyer's drawing, and one can form a vivid sense of the arrangements at Krøyer's School by reading the inventory list compiled in 1896.[9] On average, the teachers would inspect and correct the pupils' work twice a week, comparing it with the model.[10]

Studieskolen's relationship with Det Kongelige Danske Kunstakademi and the Ministry of Ecclesiastical and Educational Affairs, which was responsible for culture, too, was balanced on a knife edge. In 1882, the school had obtained state support so quickly that the art academy had no time to protest. The fact that the school obtained funding at all may be attributable to A.P. Weis, who was a lawyer and assistant at the ministry and also received tuition in Tuxen's class for advanced learners.[11] The subsidy came with conditions attached: the school must not compete with the art academy in terms of bringing pupils to the point of graduation. Rather, their pupils should be 'advanced', meaning that they should have completed their education, paint only in life classes, and exhibit their works at public exhibitions.[12]

However, the school did not meet these requirements. It took in pupils who were not graduates and who did not quickly proceed to the point where they were ready to exhibit their work. At the same time, the artists were not interested in creating a great rift between the art academy and the Study School; they would rather work to reform the art academy, which did eventually happen. In 1884, however, relations with the academy of fine arts were so strained that, to quote an example, Johannes Larsen, who studied under Frans Schwartz for a few months and then went on to study under Zahrtmann, had to have his parents sign a statement asserting that they would not force him to go to the art academy instead.[13]

Krøyer's teaching

Krøyer's teaching has not previously been described in depth in the literature treating his life, and as other sources

5. Lichtenberg, 16.
6. Front row, left to right: Laurits Tuxen, Tom Petersen, Louis Jensen, Michael Therkildsen, Valdemar Irminger, Edvard Petersen, and Carl Thomsen. Second row, far right: Viggo Pedersen and Niels Skovgaard.
7. Front row, left to right: Johan Rohde, George Seligmann, Gerhard Heilmann, and Wennerberg (Swedish). Second row, left to right: Adolf Heinrich-Hansen, Schellerup (Norwegian), L'Orsa (Norwegian), Otto P. Balle, and J.F. Willumsen.
8. Tuxen to Krøyer, 10 October 1880. PSK Archive 2178.
9. See 'List of inventory, Krøyer's School, 1896', at the end of this chapter.
10. Letter from Kunstnernes Studieskole to the Ministry of Ecclesiastical and Educational Affairs, Copenhagen, August 1885. Archive for Kunstnernes Studieskole 1885–1912, KB NKS 2516, 2°.
11. Fabritius, 'Tuxen og de frie studieskoler', 36.
12. As is apparent from the correspondence between the board of Kunstnernes Studieskole and the Ministry of Culture in the Archive for Kunstnernes Studieskole 1885–1912, KB NKS 2516, 2°. It is also described in Meldahl and Johansen, 456–457.
13. Porsmose, *Johannes Larsen*, 29.

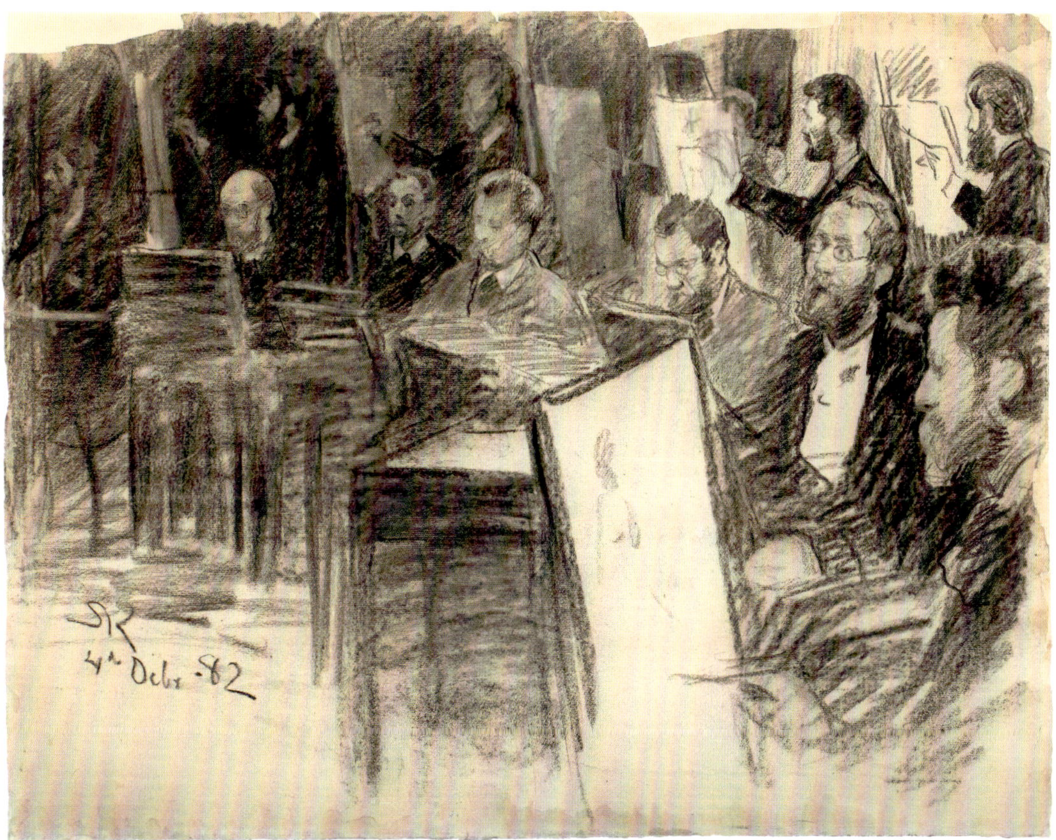

ILL. 40 Peder Severin Krøyer: *Kunstnernes Studieskole*, 1882. Charcoal on paper, 475×620 mm. Skagens Kunstmuseer. SKM200

in the field are sparse, forming a complete overview of his teaching practice is fraught with difficulty. However, if one goes back to the time before he took over as a teacher at Kunstnernes Studieskole, an important source for understanding Krøyer's outlook on studio teaching exists in the form of a detailed letter to his former teacher at the art academy, Frederik Vermehren, from May 1879. By this point, Krøyer had just finished his studies under Léon Bonnat in Paris. He clearly described the differences he saw between the Danish academy teaching and the private studio teaching under Bonnat in France, and how Danish teaching could be improved:

> There can be little doubt that his [Bonnat's] critique of us [his Danish pupils] also, at least to a certain extent, strikes home at our entire Danish school. Back home, many things were never really made clear to me, such as the significance of observing *valeur*, or of overall grand plans, and least of all the term simplicity.
>
> At the [Danish] model school, pupils drew in chalk from head to toe, drawing an infinity of small shapes without sufficient consideration for the whole, setting up reflective papers to be able to draw an equal amount of detail in the shadows, whereby the light turned grey and the shadows restless; indeed the whole figure fell into small pieces. However, I wouldn't call the aid of plaster feet an act of 'beautification' or enhancement of the model. I would, of course, never deny that the strict instruction to overlook nothing can foster great conscientiousness and alertness to nature, but one can so easily lose sight of what is after all the main thing. The point of things. What makes the work of art is much more about the view of the totality rather than minute execution of

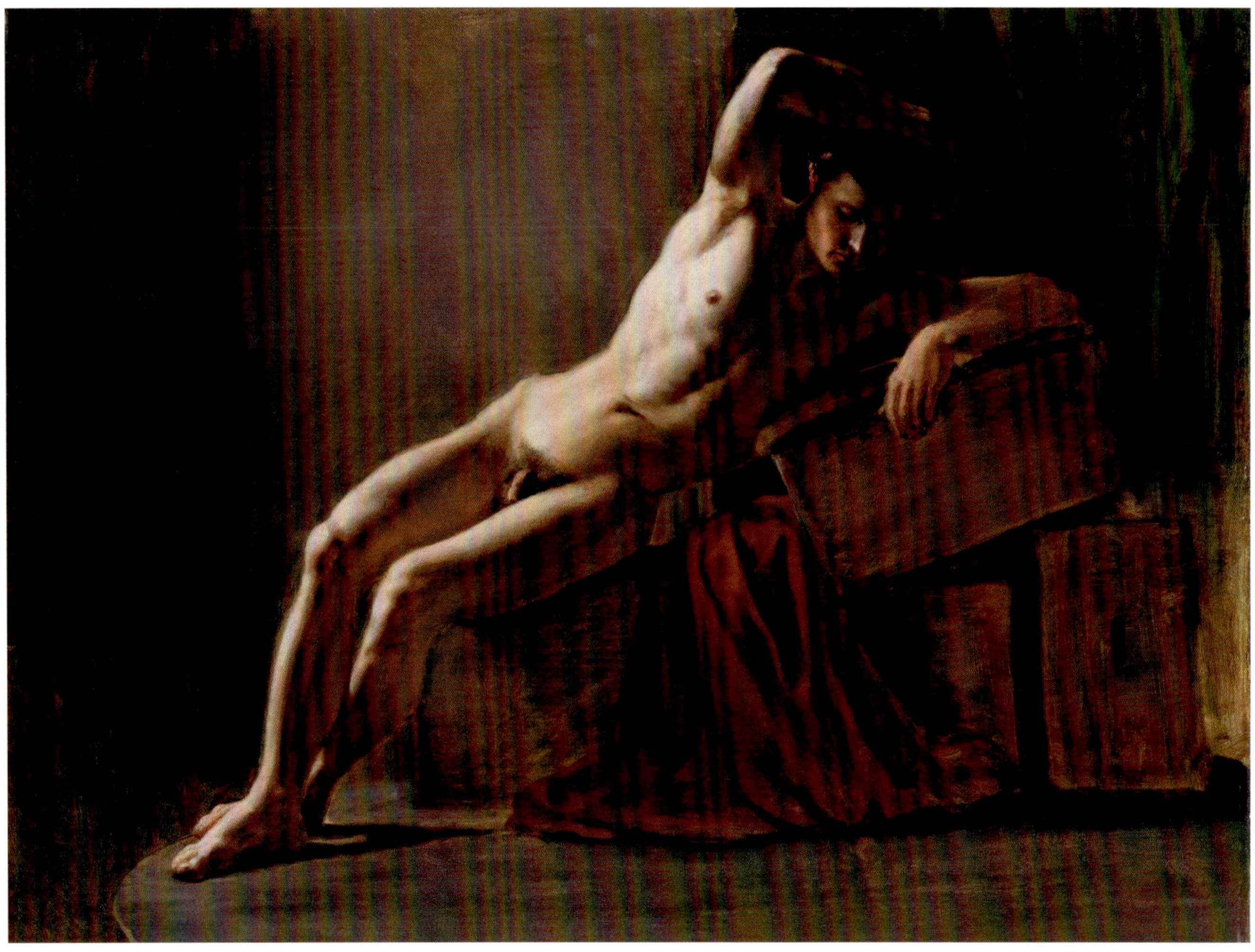

ILL. 41 Peder Severin Krøyer: *Seated Male Model*, 1870. Oil on canvas, 57.7 × 78.5 cm. Skagens Kunstmuseer. SKM4

the finest detail, and there can be as much exquisite finesse in a broadly drawn line as in the one who seeks out all the little forms; indeed, I would say it can have more. [...] Oh, I think it is so much, much more difficult to draw sweeping lines and overall features rather than through detail, and the eye receives so little practice in that back home. That is why I do not quite agree with you when you say that we should not change anything in the direction taken in teaching back home. I believe quite unreservedly that the aspects of the matter of which I have talked here should be made clearer. And what I have written here about the teaching of drawing applies to a much greater degree to our School of Painting at the Academy, especially after Marstrand passed away. One need only refer to the model paintings presented at the school exhibitions in recent years, without light, without colour, without any observation of the great shadows and the wide-ranging scale from white to black, the relationships of light and shade.[14]

14. Draft for a letter: PSK to Frederik Vermehren, Cernay-la-Ville, 20 May 1879. PSK Archive 58.

One of Krøyer's own model studies from his time at the art academy, the 1870 *Seated Male Model* (ILL. 41), exemplifies the very aspects he opposes. Many of the traits he describes are found here: a scrutiny of many details, an illuminated shadow, a contour fully visible all around the body, a certain absence of coherence and consistency in the local colour, and less focus on the whole than on the details. Looking at one of the studies he did at Bonnat, *Male Model. Half-length*, from 1877 (ILL. 8), one sees a much higher degree of coherence in the local colour and '*valeurs*'; the paint is thicker, the contours blurred or absent. Here the focus is on the whole. Krøyer had four such studies hanging in his classroom to serve as role models for his pupils.[15] They were still at the school when it ceased operation, and three of them found their way to Den Hirschsprungske Samling, while one entered the collection at Skagens Museum (CAT. 22).[16]

The pupils at Kunstnernes Studieskole were free to choose which master's studio they wanted to attend, and Krøyer's classes were fully booked right from the outset.[17] He was well liked as a teacher, but of course there were exceptions. In his memoirs, Harald Slott-Møller described how the school's organization, which meant the pupils carried a greater responsibility for the daily running of the school and the teacher was rarely present, could lead to a sense of the pupils being left to their own devices.[18] Rasmus Christiansen, who primarily received instruction from Tuxen but also attended Krøyer's classes, wrote up his memoirs about his time at the school in two articles for *Samleren* in 1928.[19] His first article offers a glimpse of how some pupils might have perceived Krøyer as a teacher:

> Krøyer was harsh and dismissive in his criticism, and he often made his students crestfallen and discouraged. By the time he had finished giving a drawing the once-over, its creator was practically on the brink of suicide, at any rate all desire to continue was gone. It may well be healthy to occasionally be cut down to size that way, but some found it hard. Take, for example, Albert Gottschalk, who became a pupil of Krøyer's; he felt completely terrorised. So anxious was he when Krøyer was expected that he would often hide in the coatroom at the crucial moment.[20]

Albert Gottschalk struggled to settle in, but others greatly benefited from Krøyer's teaching. Krøyer also endeavoured to help his pupils get their work accepted at the Charlottenborg exhibitions and, later, Den frie Udstilling, or to get it sold.

Krøyer's pupils

Providing an accurate overview of Krøyer's pupils year by year is fraught with difficulties. The school's archive, kept in the Manuscript Collection at Det Kgl. Bibliotek in Copenhagen, is not complete and thus lacks many of Krøyer's lists of attendees. From 1885 to 1900, Tuxen and Krøyer merged their departments as far as administrative purposes was concerned. This is to say that Kunstnernes Studieskole had two departments: Krøyer and Tuxen had one, Kristian Zahrtmann the other. Zahrtmann first began teaching at the school in 1885, taking on a preparatory class, but the following year his school became an independent department that took pupils all the way through to the completion of their education. Given that Tuxen's and Krøyer's schools had transitioned to joint administration, even though they each still ran their own school, it is not always possible to clearly distinguish Krøyer's pupils from Tuxen's. In many cases, one must rely on pupils having subsequently stated when they trained there and under whom. Many pupils at the school never achieved any real artistic breakthrough and so have slipped into

15. See 'List of inventory, Krøyer's School, 1896', at the end of this chapter.
16. In 1989, the writer H.P. Rhode gave inv. nos. 3029, 3030, and 3031 to Den Hirschsprungske Samling. In 1920, Skagens Museum received inv. no. SKM199 as a gift from Kunstnernes Studieskole.
17. Meldahl and Johansen, 457. Letter from Kunstnernes Studieskole to the Ministry of Ecclesiastical and Educational Affairs, Copenhagen, August 1885. Archive for Kunstnernes Studieskole 1885–1912, KB NKS 2516, 2°.
18. Harald Slott-Møller's unpublished memoirs. KB NKS 4839, 4°.
19. Christiansen, 'Minder om Samvær og Samarbejde', 5–9, 39–44.
20. Christiansen, 7.

oblivion, their status as students there unconfirmed. No such fate befell one of the early students at Krøyer's School, Vilhelm Hammershøi, who first attended classes there as far back as 1883. Of all the pupils there, he went on to achieve the greatest fame – one that endures to this day, as Hammershøi continues to excite and enthrall audiences. He possessed an originality that must have been unmistakable right from the outset, as can be gathered from various statements made by his contemporaries. At first, Krøyer could not see it. His pupil Albert Repholtz has been quoted as saying:

> Even Krøyer, who as teacher to us young haters of the academy was tasked with correcting Hammerhøj's model drawings, was initially taken aback, even horrified by the idiosyncratic peculiarity of this twenty-year-old youth, admonishingly comparing his blurred figures with 'butter or grease by moonlight' and 'foetuses in spirits'.[21]

In an obituary for Hammershøi in 1916, an anonymous journalist wrote: 'Vilhelm Hammershøi had great respect for Krøyer; and it is said of him and Holsøe that, as a rule, they preferred to disappear on the evenings when Krøyer was to correct their drawings.'[22] Perhaps an understandable reaction, if Krøyer was indeed so harsh in his criticism as reported above. However, Krøyer quickly and markedly changed his mind about Hammershøi. 'I have a pupil who paints quite strangely. I do not understand him, I believe he will become someone of significance, I try not to influence him,' Zahrtmann later recollects Krøyer saying about Hammershøi, when Zahrtmann became a teacher at Kunstnernes Studieskole in 1885.[23]

In 1910, Karl Madsen reported on how Krøyer fought on behalf of the young artists, striving to get them access to the juried exhibitions at Charlottenborg: 'I am sure that mistakes are still made while assessing the submissions; that is quite inevitable. But the malicious intent rife in the old days, with its instinct to crucify anything and anyone that showed a powerful talent, that has been killed off. And Krøyer made a significant contribution toward its demise.'[24]

When Hammershøi was passed over for the prestigious prize Den Neuhausenske Præmie at Charlottenborg's 1885 spring exhibition, where he presented a portrait of his sister, *Portrait of a Young Woman* (ILL. 42), Krøyer wrote a letter full of barely contained outrage to Madsen one Wednesday night:

> Dear Madsen!
> I need to get this off my chest to someone. You are a good fellow and less prudish than most – perhaps not prudish at all. Can we not find some way of blowing up this entire rotten box? Oh, but what happened today was a scandal, – I expect you heard. –
> Are they not idiots, dunderheads, the supreme representatives of prudishness? I urge you, write something against this, full of fire and spirit.
> Spit on them, they deserve it.
> Your P.S. Krøyer[25]

This is to say that Krøyer not only strove to build the technical skills of the young artists, but also to have them preserve their originality whenever doing so led to unique, modern, and beautiful works. And when such originality was not properly understood by the established art scene, he endeavoured to change the art scene rather than the artists.

Valdemar Schønheyder Møller was another pupil who stood out from the crowd. At Krøyer's School, Schønheyder Møller and Hammershøi met and became friends. Schønheyder Møller, who was interested in photography,

21. Quoted from Vad, *Hammershøi*, 23. Sadly, Vad does not state the source of his quote, but it was supposedly said in 1916 on the occasion of Hammershøi's death [according to the reference in Vad's book (certainly in later editions), note 21, the quote was printed in *Ugens Tilskuer*, 25 February 1916].

22. Zahrtmann, 'Om Vilhelm Hammershøi', 5.

23. Zahrtmann, 5.

24. Madsen, 'Krøyer', 209.

25. Quoted from Madsen, 'Krøyer', 209.

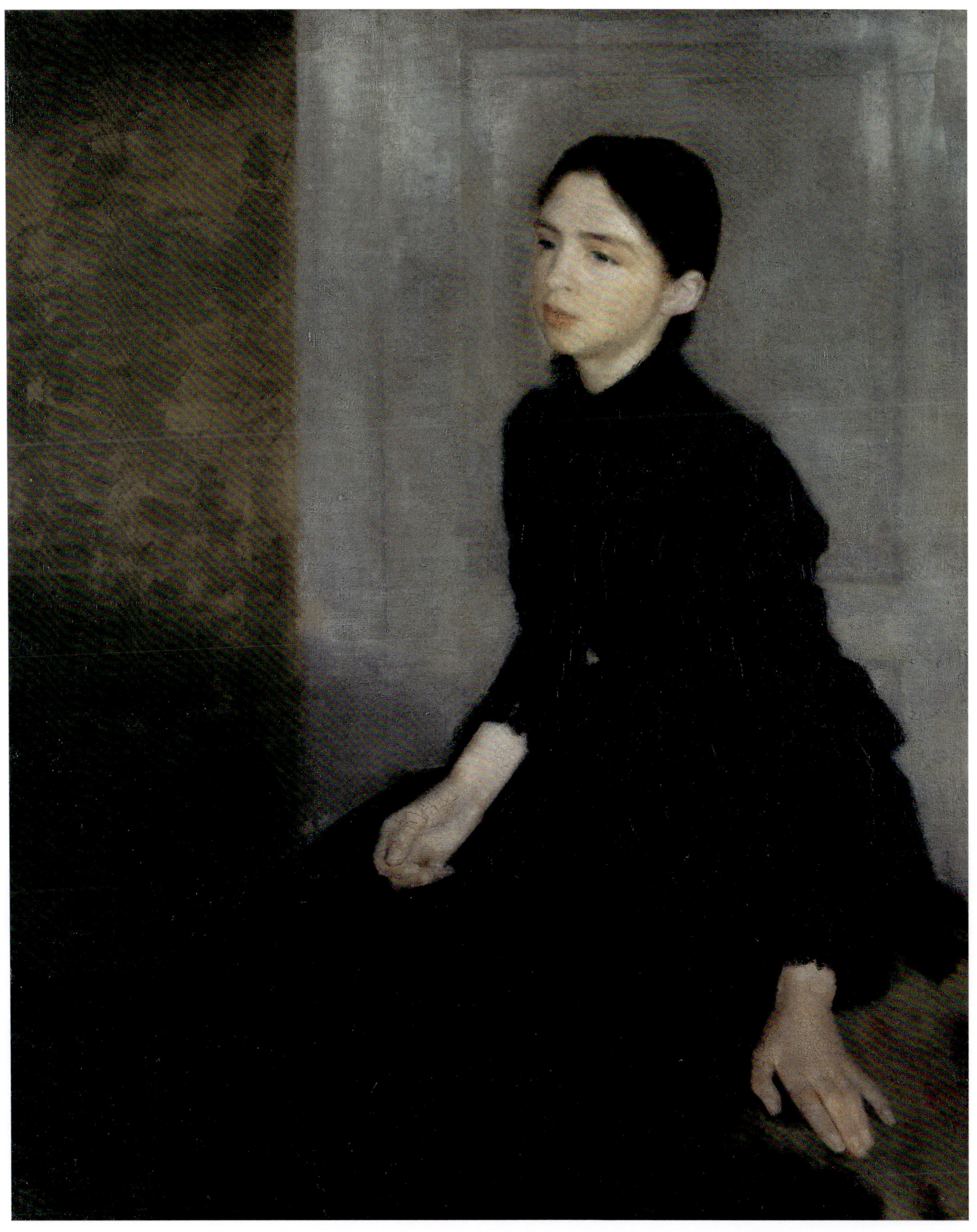

ILL. 42 Vilhelm Hammershøi: *Portrait of a Young Woman. The Artist's Sister, Anna Hammershøi*, 1885. Oil on canvas, 112 × 91.5 cm. Den Hirschsprungske Samling.

took several photographs which Hammershøi used as references for his paintings – including portraits of Hammershøi's sister. In 1891–1893, Schønheyder Møller set out for Skagen each summer to paint, and this was where he became interested in painting the sun (ILL. 46). Michael Ancher later wrote the following about him in his 1893 notebook:

> He walked around quietly, always looking up at the sun, and it became his ceaseless pursuit to paint the sun by day and by evening, bright or behind clouds, playing in the leaves of trees and reflecting in water. He returned on multiple occasions, painted several beautiful things, had a good colour, later went to Paris.[26]

In fact, he did not leave Skagen until January 1894, and he moved to Paris in December of that year. From 1896 he lived in Fontainebleau. Here he painted *Sunset. Fontainebleau* in 1900 (ILL. 43). His works were seen at the Paris Salons from 1895 to 1903, the only exception being 1900.[27] Michael Ancher went on to say: 'His life took a very tragic turn, as he went insane just as one of his pictures caused quite a stir and was sold at the Salon. Having suffered indescribably from poverty, he finally snapped and died in the Aarhus Asylum for the Insane.' According to Ancher, then, Schønheyder Møller also pursued a career in Paris, but did not achieve much success. It is perhaps an understatement to say that he, like Krøyer, was preoccupied with light in his works. In order to paint works like *Sunset. Fontainebleau*, he had to stare directly at the sun to such an extent that by 1901 it had ruined his vision, compelling him to stop painting.[28] He died at the hospital in Aarhus in 1905, only 41 years of age.

In October 1885, the board of Kunstnernes Studieskole received a request from 11 women urging the school to set up a department where they could receive instruction.[29] At this point, it was not yet possible for women to enrol at Det Kongelige Danske Kunstakademi, and the signatories of the letter argued that putting so many obstacles in the way for women wishing to make art their life's work was no longer in keeping with the times. They did not believe that it had ever be proven that women were unable to educate themselves on an equal footing with men. Among the women who later made a name for themselves as artists were Agnes Rambusch (married name Slott-Møller) and Marie Triepcke, who in 1889 married Krøyer. Tuxen wrote to Krøyer, informing him of the petition and stating that for various reasons, he and Zahrtmann did not favour the idea of setting up such a department – partly because 'the reality is that the majority of them end up remaining dilletantes, and there is no reason to support that with public funds.'[30] Nevertheless, the school did indeed set up a department for women. Based on Filippavej and attracting 15 pupils, the classes were taught by Krøyer after some persuasion from Weis.[31] Kunstskolen for Kvinder was part of the Kunstnernes Studieskole organisation for two winters, at which point it was taken over by the art academy.[32] After the first year, Krøyer and Tuxen described the significant progress made by the women in an application for funding for a third year, the winter of 1887–1888, but as things turned out this was not necessary.[33]

26. Michael Ancher, *Notesbog 1893–1894*. KB NKS 1197, 8° - 6. Ancher seems to have begun writing in his notebooks around 1900 and must have concluded them before 1912, and so the note is not a diary entry, as it was written a few years later. See Fabritius, *Michael Anchers ungdom 1865–1880*, 139.
27. He is seen under the names Schönheyder-Möller, Valdemar-Christian, and Waldemar-Christian.
28. Jensen, *Brøndums spisesal*, 160.
29. Margrethe Aagaard, Laura Larsson, Emma Meyer, Minna Meyer, Anne Marie Hansen, Marie Triepcke, Agnes Rambusch, Nathalia Sonneling, Juliane Hammer, Sophie Klofs, and Ida Nielsen to the board of Kunstnernes Studieskole, 10 October 1885. Archive for Kunstnernes Studieskole 1885–1912, KB NKS 2516, 2°.
30. Tuxen to Krøyer, 17 October 1885. PSK Archive 2186.
31. Fabritius, 'Tuxen og de frie studieskoler', 36.
32. The second year of the school is documented in a letter from Nanna Nieger to Frans Schwartz, Copenhagen, 14 October 1886. Archive for Kunstnernes Studieskole 1885–1912, KB NKS 2516, 2°.
33. In July 1886, Krøyer and Tuxen asked the ministry for a subsidy for Kunstskolen for Kvinder for the winter of 1887/1888. PSK Archive 268.

ILL. 43 Valdemar Schønheyder Møller: *Sunset. Fontainebleau*, 1900. Oil on canvas, 116.2 × 88.3 cm. Statens Museum for Kunst, Copenhagen. KMS8079

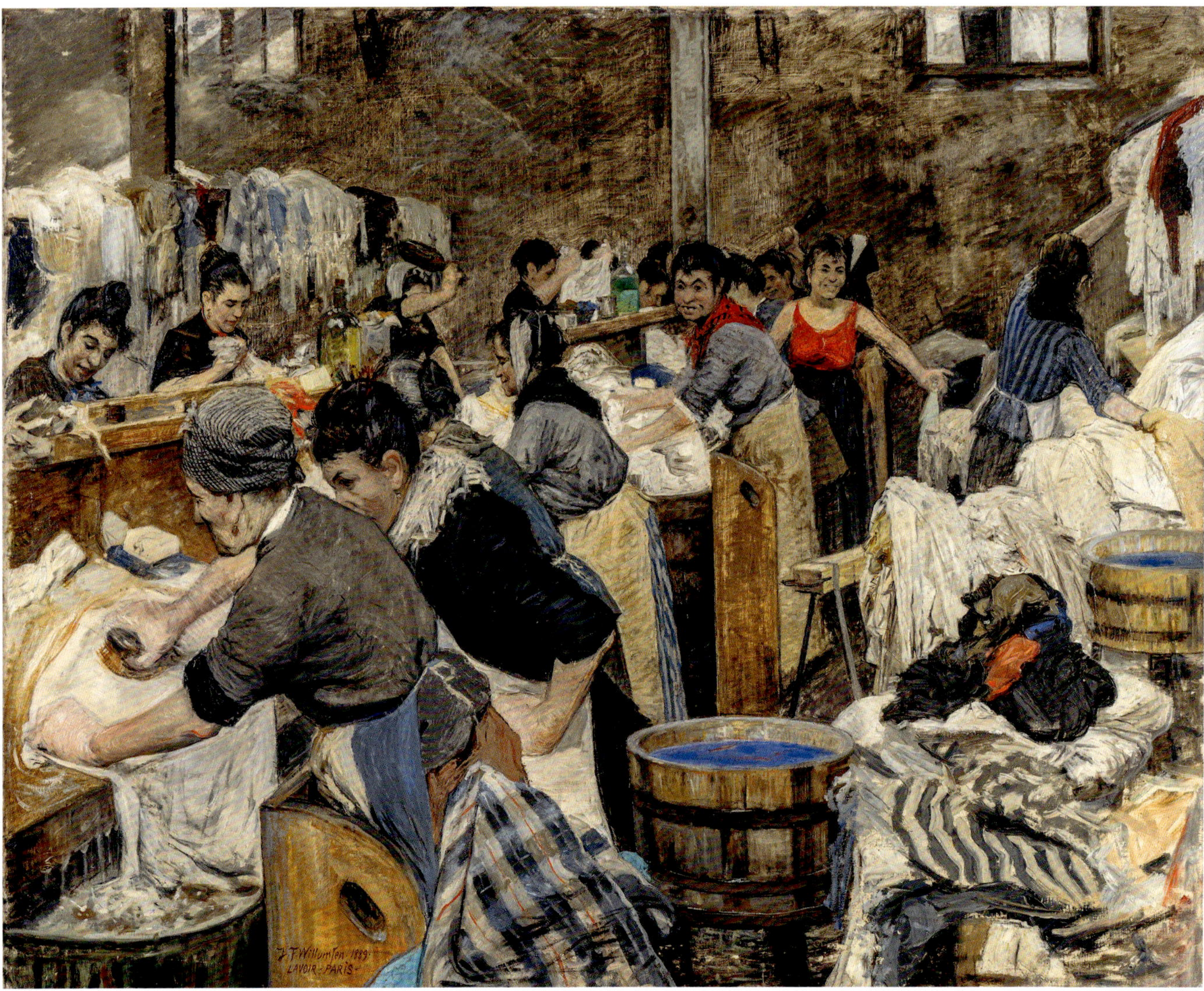

ILL. 44 Jens Ferdinand Willumsen: *In a French Laundry. Paris*, 1989. Oil on canvas, 105 × 133.5 cm. Göteborg Konstmuseum. GKM 0286

In May 1885, J.F. Willumsen left the art academy in favour of Kunstnernes Studieskole. He first attended a few of Tuxen's classes and then switched to Krøyer's School. During his years at the school, Willumsen was still preoccupied with picturesque atmospheres, landscape painting, and the refraction of light in dusty air. As he himself says: 'all those things at which Krøyer excelled, and which he later blamed me for abandoning.'[34]

Having completed his studies at Krøyer's School, Willumsen set out for Paris in 1888, but did not want to attend life classes there, though he was encouraged to do so by several peers. He wished to leave behind the style of

34. Willumsen, *Mine erindringer fortalt til Ernst Mentze*, 24.

painting he had learned and paint directly after reality instead: 'It was the study of life itself that I needed. It was nature and especially people in motion and out in the open air that interested me.'[35] At the same time, he was interested in depicting the difference between the living conditions of the rich and the poor.

Among the cluster of Scandinavian artists in Paris, Willumsen met Marie Triepcke, who had also just arrived in Paris and lived near him. They became friends. He also met Krøyer, who had become engaged to Marie Triepcke in the spring of 1889. At Montmartre, Willumsen painted *In a French Laundry. Paris* in 1889 (ILL. 44). When it was finished, he received an unexpected visit from Krøyer and Michael Ancher. By this time, Willumsen had moved far away from Krøyer's teachings, even though only a year had passed since his Copenhagen school years. Willumsen had followed his own observations and painted the work without visible atmospheric effects, meaning without any visible haze, smoke, or similar. Krøyer immediately saw this and criticised him for it:

> I explained that in the actual laundry there was no steam or mists because the washerwomen used cold water, but Krøyer would not concede that this could be true and was offended by my claim. It should be remembered that Krøyer had just painted the committee scene, a group of gentlemen wreathed in smoke rising from numerous fine cigars. He keenly felt the absence of such tonalities of air and smoke in my laundry, where the air seemed to him far too clean and transparent. But the fashions were thus inclined. Tobacco smoke and heavy air were 'picturesque'. 'You have no joy in painting,' was how Krøyer put it to me, and he would repeat his words many years later at Skagen.
>
> I submitted the laundry, 'Le Lavoir', to the official Paris salon, where it was accepted without any kind of patronage involved, even though this was otherwise always required. Some years later, the picture was exhibited in Gothenburg, where the museum bought it.[36]

The artistic disagreements between Krøyer and Willumsen did not cause a rift between them on a personal level. In Paris, they parted as friends. Several years later, they also met in Skagen, where they both painted, and both appeared in Michael Ancher's *Art Judges* from 1906 (Det Nationalhistoriske Museum, Frederiksborg Slot). Willumsen became a significant, internationally acclaimed artist, and his work very much pointed ahead to a new era and a modernist art.

Several of Krøyer's students not only followed in their master's footsteps in terms of the techniques he taught them, a focus on light, and, in some cases, their choice of subject matter; some also quite literally followed him in geographical terms. Several travelled to Paris for brief or prolonged visits, and some came to Skagen to become more or less permanently associated with the artists' colony there. A group of artists described themselves as 'the circle of younger Skagen painters'. Several of them had trained under either Tuxen or Krøyer, and they rallied around their own exhibition venue called 'Den sorte lade' (The Black Barn), at Krøyers Hus in Skagen Vesterby.[37] Among these artists was Einar Hein, who would become one of Krøyer's last pupils. Hein had visited Skagen back in 1893, but first enrolled at Krøyer's School in 1896; he continued to attend until 1899. He subsequently went to Paris and received instruction from Alfred Philippe Roll, who was one of Krøyer's French acquaintances from the 1890s. Hein must also have gone with Krøyer to Skagen

35. Willumsen, 43.

36. Willumsen, 47. The painting, *La vie du Lavoir*, was exhibited at the Salon des Artistes français 1889 under no. 2732.

37. Lehmann, 'Skagensmaleren Johannes Wilhjelm', 74–76.

on occasion, because he appears in Krøyer's monumental *Skagen Hunters* from 1898 (ARoS Aarhus Kunstmuseum). After Krøyer's death, Hein regularly visited Skagen, and bought a summer cottage there. At Skagen Sønderstrand he painted *Children at the Beach. Skagen* in 1910 (ILL. 45). This work showcases how he simultaneously adheres to both Krøyer's teachings and to his own French schooling. He remains loyal to Krøyer's choice of subject matter and emphasis on light, while at the same time subtly renewing and updating the imagery, following the new idiom of Modernism in a combination of tradition and innovation.

Krøyer's Paris in Denmark

In the winter of 1888/1889, Viggo Johansen substituted for Krøyer while the latter was in Paris, partly in order to work on the Danish contribution to the Exposition Universelle de 1889, which lasted from 6 May to 31 October. A letter from Krøyer to Johansen in January 1889 offers an excellent impression of how passionate Krøyer was about having not only his own pupils, but the entire younger generation of Danish artists be well represented at exhibitions outside Denmark, too.

> I hear from Bache that the number of submissions of pictures for Paris is faring badly. I trust you are being energetic? And working to ensure that at least our younger ones are well represented. You really must work back home. The most important developments in our country have taken place after 1878, when we last exhibited in Paris. On the whole, we have held back from attending the big exhibitions elsewhere, specifically saying no, let us rather wait until there is another World Exposition in Paris and then put our best foot forward. And now it is here. Our art, like our whole country, is beginning to attract some attention in Europe. We are being noticed and things are expected from us. Let us now show that

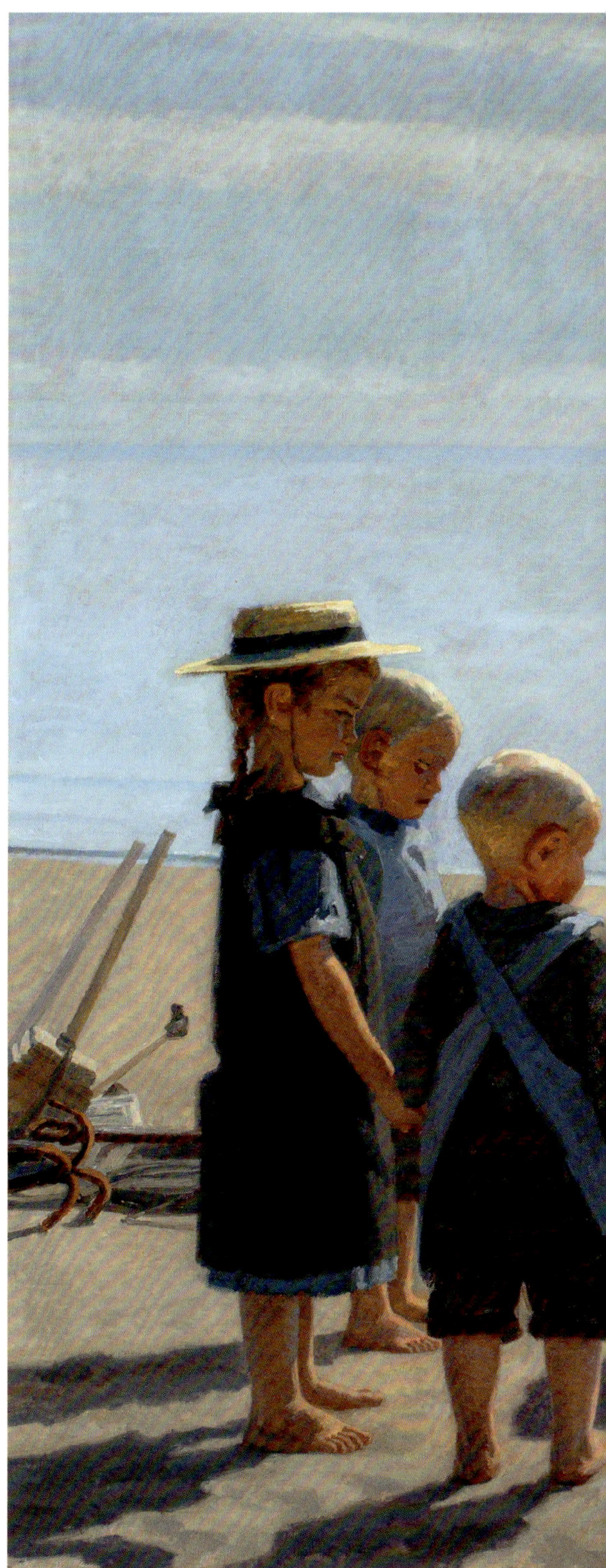

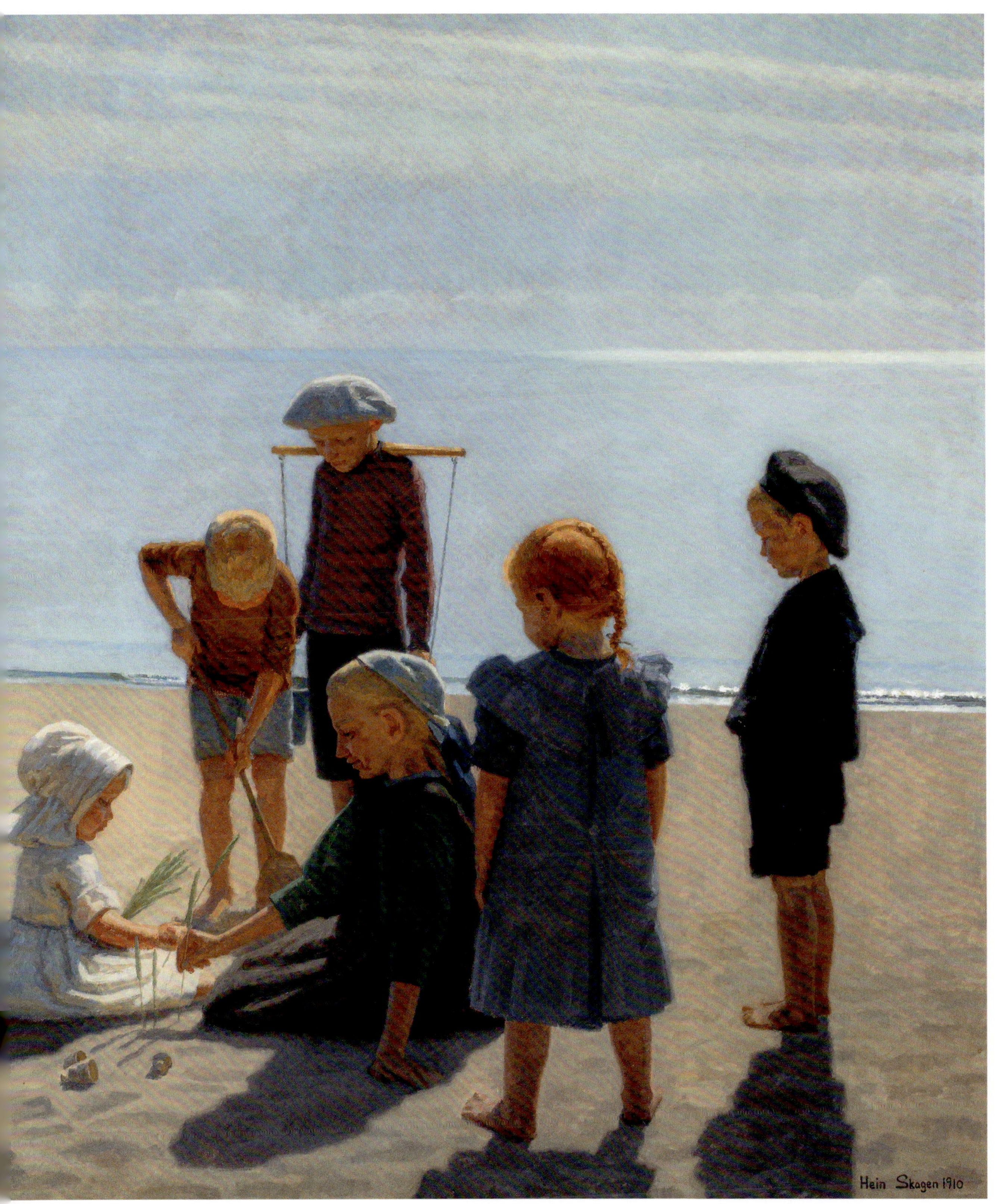

ILL. 45 Einar Hein: *Children at the Beach. Skagen*, 1910. Oil on canvas, 105×136.5 cm. Skagens Kunstmuseer. SKM1212

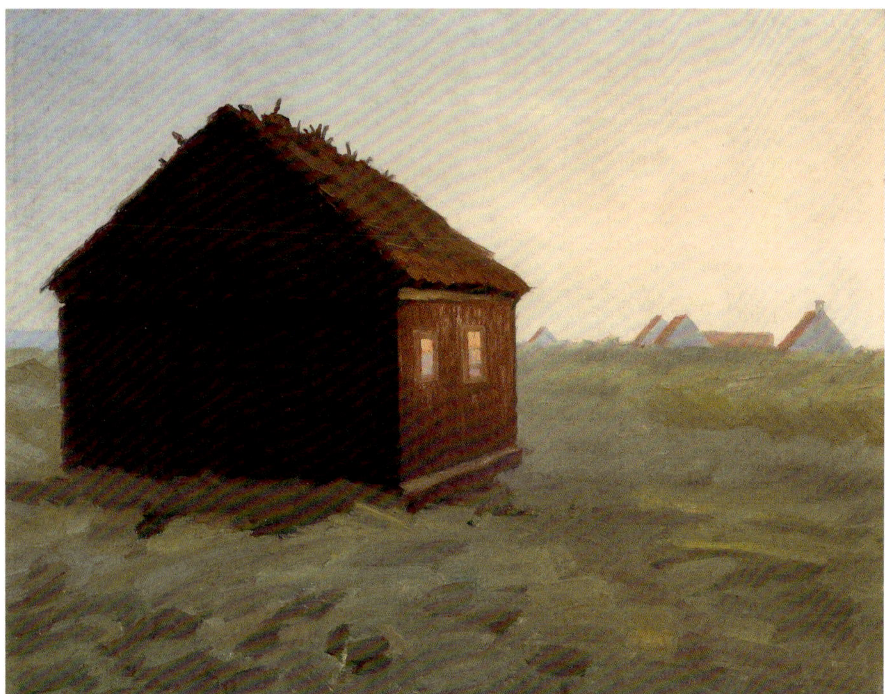

ILL. 46 Valdemar Schønheyder Møller: *Per Bollerhus' Shack*, 1891/93. Oil on canvas, 35.5×45.5 cm. Skagens Kunstmuseer. SKM722

> we deserve this and let us show the best we can. Bache writes that there is a lack of concerted effort and especially petty nonsense. The petty infighting back home in Copenhagen seems even pettier when you are abroad – could you not let go of some of all the quibbling and rally round for this occasion? Even the intransigent Swedes have come together, united by this common matter of showing the nation's art as well and as fully as possible in this 'world centre of art'. Be energetic !!!!! Let me tell you that if all of you do not do everything you can, and right quickly too, I shall consider it a personal insult, having told the French so much about what they are about to see when the Danes arrive.[38]

This passage eloquently reveals how Krøyer's artistic legacy exists on several levels. He left behind many beautiful and much-loved works in museums in his native Denmark and abroad, but he also worked hard to support and develop the entire next generation of Danish artists, helping them evolve their own, unique characteristics that could point into a new artistic era.

The lack of concerted effort among the Danish artists was largely due to the rift that arose between those who exhibited at Charlottenborg and those who, later, showed their works at Den frie Udstilling. The latter venue arose in 1891 in protest against the approach taken by the juried spring exhibitions at Charlottenborg, but the foundations were laid earlier, in 1888, with the first exhibition of pictures rejected by the Charlottenborg jury. The founders of Den frie Udstilling included several of Krøyer's pupils, and Krøyer contributed to their exhibitions to show his support.[39] The new venue would form a framework for the nascent Modernism in Denmark, and seen in that light, it can be said that the Naturalism of which Krøyer was a representative gradually segued into his pupils' Modernist art, a mode of expression which Krøyer saw rising just before his death in 1909. Thus, his legacy is not necessarily visually clear, but it is richly diverse.

38. PSK to Viggo Johansen, 69, Boulevard St. Jacques, 11 January 1889. KB NKS 4192. 4°.

39. Scavenius, *Den frie Udstilling i 100 år*, 7–8.

Timeline for Krøyer's School

1882 Winter: Kunstnernes Studieskole is founded. Frans Schwartz does a little teaching, until Tuxen is home from Paris. Tuxen becomes head of the day classes and continues Kunstnernes Modelskole (life classes, literally 'The Artists' Model School'), which was originally set up 1879 in Søkvæsthuset and received state support from the winter of 1880/1881, having moved to other premises on what was then called Halmtorvet (now 10, H.C. Andersens Boulevard) and become part of Kunstnernes Studieskole.

82/83 Krøyer teaches the new pupils in the exhibition building owned by Industriforeningen, located close to the current Rådhuspladsen (City Hall Square). Krøyer's School is now a reality. Tuxen's School moves to 6, Filippavej at Vodroffsvej.

83/84 Frans Schwartz teaches in a new department, Forberedelsesskolen (The Preparatory School), at 6, Filippavej. Vilhelm Bissen offers instruction for sculptors. The school's board consists of Schwartz, Tuxen, and Bissen.

84/85 Krøyer's School is housed at Atelier-bygningen in 33, Bredgade. Kristian Zahrtmann takes over Forberedelsesskolen as of New Year 1885. He teaches in an attic room at the Hotel Phoenix, 37, Bredgade.

85/86 Tuxen and Krøyer jointly head Krøyer's and Tuxen's School in Bredgade. Tuxen still teaches advanced learners at Filippavej. Forberedelsesskolen becomes Zahrtmanns Skole. A petition from 11 women is received in October – in response, the Kunstskolen for Kvinder (Art School for Women) is set up in November. The new department is active for two winters, housed at Filippavej. Krøyer teaches there during its first year. The school's board comprises Tuxen, Krøyer, and Zahrtmann.

86/87 This is the last year of Kunstskolen for Kvinder. Tuxen gets married and moves to Paris. Krøyer takes over management of Krøyer's and Tuxen's School. The school's board comprises Krøyer, Tuxen, and Carl Thomsen.

87/88 Tuxen's advanced students relocate to 33, Bredgade.

88/89 Krøyer spends the winter in Paris; Viggo Johansen takes over his classes in the meantime. Joakim Skovgaard substitutes for Zahrtmann. The ministry demands that the school present an exhibition of its pupils' work in the spring of 1889, but the school applies for a postponement. The school's board comprises Tuxen, Krøyer, and Zahrtmann, with Frans Schwartz and Johan Rohde as deputies.

89/90 Krøyer is on his honeymoon; Viggo Johansen substitutes for him. Krøyer and Tuxen's School is headed by Tuxen. A public exhibition of the pupil's work is held at Atelierbygningen in 33, Bredgade from Wednesday 28 May to Saturday 31 May 1890. The school's board comprises Tuxen, Krøyer, and Zahrtmann.

1890/91 Krøyer is still on his honeymoon – presumably Viggo Johansen is still substituting. Krøyer and Tuxen's School is headed by Tuxen, but F. Schwartz and Julius Paulsen substitute for him. The school's board comprises Tuxen, Krøyer, and Zahrtmann.

91/92 Krøyer and Tuxen's School is headed by Krøyer until 1900.

92/93

93/94 Krøyer's School relocates to Holckenhus, 86, Vester Voldgade. Zahrtmanns Skole relocates to the Den frie Udstilling building (designed by Bindesbøll and located on what was then called Halmtorvet). A public exhibition of the work of Krøyer and Zahrtmann's pupils is held in the studio of Holckenhus in June of 1894.

94/95

95/96 From 22 December through to January, a major exhibition at Charlottenborg presents works by the school's pupils over the last ten years, to prove the school's worth to the art academy and the ministry.

96/97

97/98 Zahrtmanns Skole moves to Den frie Udstilling's new building, designed by J.F. Willumsen in Aborre-parken (now the railway between the Vesterport and Nørreport stations).

98/99

99/00 This is Krøyer's last year as a teacher at the school. He remains a member of the board until at least 1905.

1900/01 Krøyer travels in Germany, Tyrol, and Italy. Krøyer and Tuxen's School is headed by Tuxen. Zahrtmanns Skole moves to Holckenhus.

01/02 Krøyer travels abroad.

02/03 Krøyer divides his time between Copenhagen and Skagen. Johan Rohde takes over Tuxen's department in the autumn of 1905. Zahrtmann stops in 1908. A croquis drawing school is set up in 1909. Kunstnernes Studieskole closes in 1912.

1903/04

Pupils at Krøyer's School

This list is not exhaustive, as no official list of pupils at the school exists. It is based on information supplied by the individual artists for their entries in the *Weilbachs Kunstnerleksikon*, the catalogue for the Kunstnernes Studieskole exhibition at Charlottenborg in 1886, as well as on sporadic lists in the Kunstnernes Studieskole archive at Det Kgl. Bibliotek. The information has been confirmed and greater detail added where possible.

Achen, Georg Nicolai (1860–1912)	Krøyer's School, winter 1883/1884 and 1884/1885
Agersnap Mortensen, Hans (1857–1925)	Krøyer's School, 1883
Balle, Otto Petersen (1865–1916)	Krøyer's School, at some point between 1885 and 1888
Bentzen-Bilkvist, Fritz Johannes (1865–1934)	Krøyer and Tuxen's School, between 1888 and 1892
Benzon, Bøje Peter Lorentz Alfred (1855–1932)	Krøyer's School of Drawing, evenings 1883–1884
Bonnesen, Niels Christian Julius (1870–1936)	Krøyer and Tuxen's School, after 1892
Christiansen, Rasmus (1863–1940)	Krøyer and Tuxen's School, 1883–1885
Dorph, Niels Vinding (1862–1931)	Krøyer and Tuxen's School, after 1884
Find, Ludvig Frederik (1869–1945)	Krøyer's School (Frans Schwartz), 1888
French, Johan (dates unknown)	Krøyer and Tuxen's School, beginning prior to 1896
Frydensberg, Carl Edvard (1872–1944)	Krøyer's School, 1888–1892
Gottschalk, Albert (1866–1906)	Krøyer's School, 1883–1888
Gretor, Willy (1868–1923)	Krøyer's School, c. 1889
Gudmundsen-Holmgreen, Johan (1858–1912)	Krøyer's School, at some point between 1883 and 1886
Guldbrandsen, Frederik (Frits) Norden (1867–1935)	Krøyer's School, 1888–1889
Hammershøi, Vilhelm (1864–1916)	Krøyer's School, from 1883
Hansen, Ane Marie (1852–1941)	Krøyer's School, winter 1885/1886
Hansen, Peter Marius (1868–1928)	Krøyer and Tuxen's School, 1884
Heilman(n), Gerhard Vilhelm Ernst (1859–1946)	Krøyer and Tuxen's School, after 1883
Hein, Einar (1875–1931)	Krøyer's School, 1896–1899
Heinrich-Hansen, Claus Adolf (1859–1925)	Krøyer's School, c. 1885
Hinrichsen, Lorens (Lorenz) Vilhelm (1865–1929)	Krøyer and Tuxen's School, beginning prior to 1896
Holsøe, Carl Vilhelm (1863–1935)	Krøyer's School, after 1884
Janssen, Luplau (1869–1927)	Krøyer's School, evenings 1887–1891
Jastrau, Viggo (1857–1946)	Krøyer's School, evenings 1886/1887, 1887/1888
Kofoed, Hans Peter (1868–1908)	Krøyer and Tuxen's School, at some point between 1891 and 1896
Kornerup, Valdemar Vincent (1865–1924)	Krøyer's School
Krøyer, Marie Martha Mathilde (born Triepcke, 1867–1940)	Krøyer's School, winter 1885/1886
Lange, Frederik (1870–1941)	Krøyer's School, after 1896
Larsen-Særsløv, Frederik (1870–1942)	Krøyer's School, beginning prior to 1896
L'Orsa (Norway, dates unknown)	Krøyer's School, c. 1885
Meyer, Emma Eleonora (1859–1921)	Krøyer's School, winter 1885/1886
Neandros(s), Sigurd Sørensen (Norway, 1870–1958)	Krøyer's School, beginning prior to 1896
Nørretranders, Johannes Carl Ferdinand (1871–1957)	Krøyer's School, after 1891

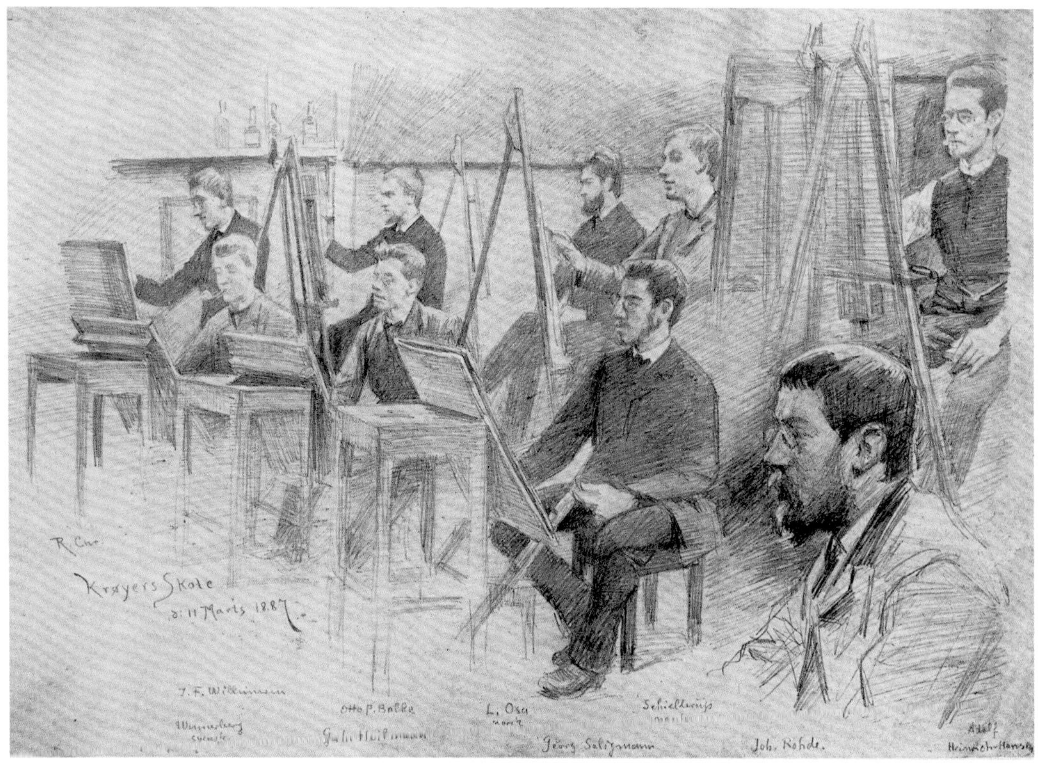

ILL. 47 Rasmus Christiansen: *Krøyer's School in Bredgade*, 1887. From *Samleren*, vol. 5, 1928.

Repholtz, Albert Henrik (1863–1928)	Krøyer and Tuxen's School, before 1896
Resen Steenstrup, Gert Johannes (1868–1921)	Krøyer and Tuxen's School, c. 1894
Ring, Laurits Andersen (1854–1933)	Krøyer's School, 1886
Rohde, Johan Gudmann (1856–1935)	Krøyer and Tuxen's School, 1883/1887
Schellerup (Norway, dates unknown)	Krøyer's School, c. 1885
Schlichtkrull, Johan Christopher (1866–1945)	Krøyer's School, some winters after 1888
Schønheyder-Møller, Valdemar Christian (1864–1905)	Krøyer's School, at some point between 1884 and 1896
Seligmann, Georg Sophus (1866–1924)	Krøyer's School, before 1896
Slott-Møller, Agnes (born Rambusch, 1862–1937)	Krøyer's School, winter 1885/1886
Slott-Møller, Georg Harald, (1864–1937)	Krøyer's School, 1883–1886
Tom-Petersen, Peter (1861–1926)	Krøyer's School, after 1884
Triepcke, Marie (married Krøyer, 1867–1940)	Krøyer's School, winter 1885/1886
Vige, Jens Peder Olsen (1864–1912)	Krøyer's School, winters 1886–1887
Wandahl, William Frederik Vilhelm (1859–1944)	Krøyer and Tuxen's School, before 1896
Wang, Albert Edvard (1864–1930)	Krøyer's School (mainly), 1886–1889
Wennerberg (Sweden, dates unknown)	Krøyer's School, c. 1885
Wilhjelm, Johannes Martin Fasting (1868–1938)	Krøyer's School, 1892–1894
Willumsen, Jens Ferdinand (1863–1958)	Krøyer and Tuxen's School, 1885–1887

List of inventory, Krøyer's School, 1896

The list was made for a contents insurance policy in 1896 when Krøyer's School was located in Holckenhus, an artists' building in Copenhagen. It is archived in the Manuscript Collection at the Royal Danish Library in the archive for Kunstnernes Studieskole.

4 painted model studies by Krøyer
2 painted model studies by Tuxen
8 model drawings by Krøyer
3 model drawings by Tuxen
1 charcoal drawing by Krøyer
10 photographs and reproductions
2 frames with photographs of models
15 three-legged stools
20 tall four-legged chairs
7 low four-legged chairs
9 American chairs
14 large easels
6 small easels
1 washstand
1 washstand chair
1 skeleton
3 curtains
1 curtain for the door
1 curtain for the model's nook
6 draperies
2 coal boxes
2 wooden screens
2 gilt cardboard sheets
1 iron screen
2 daybeds
4 bricks
1 stepladder
1 tin dish
1 tin bucket
1 poker
1 fire tongs
1 coal shovel
1 carafe with one water glass
2 model lamps
11 pendant lamps
10 towels
1 cabinet with shelves
1 large curtain
1 plaster foot
1 manikin
1 mattress
1 leather cushion
1 fabric cushion
2 free-standing drapery holders
2 dumbbells
1 wooden rod
17 drawing folders
1 thermometer
1 basin
1 table
12 drawing boards
1 mirror
2 free-standing clothes racks

And a quantity of knick-knacks and smaller items

ILL. 48 List of inventory, Krøyer's School, 1896. Det Kgl. Bibliotek, Copenhagen.

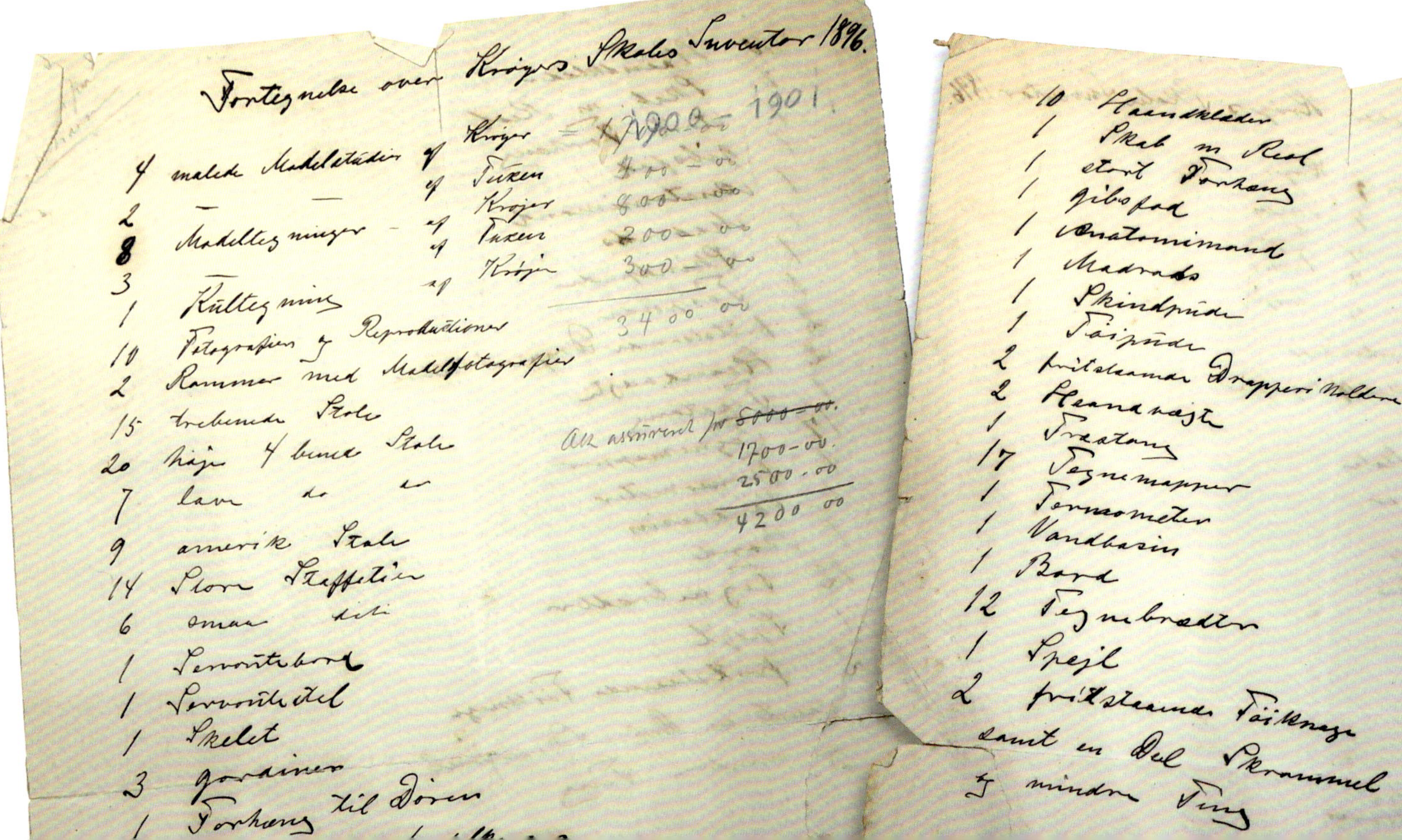

Krøyers Skoles Inventor 1896.

Fortegnelse over

4 malede Modelstudier af Krøyer
2 — — af Tuxen 400-00
8 Modeltegninger af Krøyer 800-00
3 — af Tuxen 200-00
1 Kultegning af Krøyer 300-00
3400 00
10 Fotografier og Reproduktioner
2 Rammer med Modelfotografier
15 trebenede Stole
20 høje 4 benede Stole
7 lave do do
9 amerik. Stole
14 Store Staffelier
6 smaa ditto
1 Servantebord
1 Servantestol
1 Skelet
3 Gardiner
1 Forhang til Døren

Alt assureret for ~~5000-00~~
1700-00
2500-00
4200 00

10 Haandklæder
1 Skab m. Reol
1 stort Forhang
1 Gibsfod
1 Anatomimand
1 Madrads
1 Skindpude
1 Tøjpude
2 fritstaaende Drapperiholdere
2 Haandvægte
1 Træstang
17 Tegnemapper
1 Termometer
1 Vandbasin
1 Bord
12 Tegnebrætter
1 Spejl
2 fritstaaende Tøjknage
samt en Del Skrammel og mindre Ting

Krøyer's Travels in France

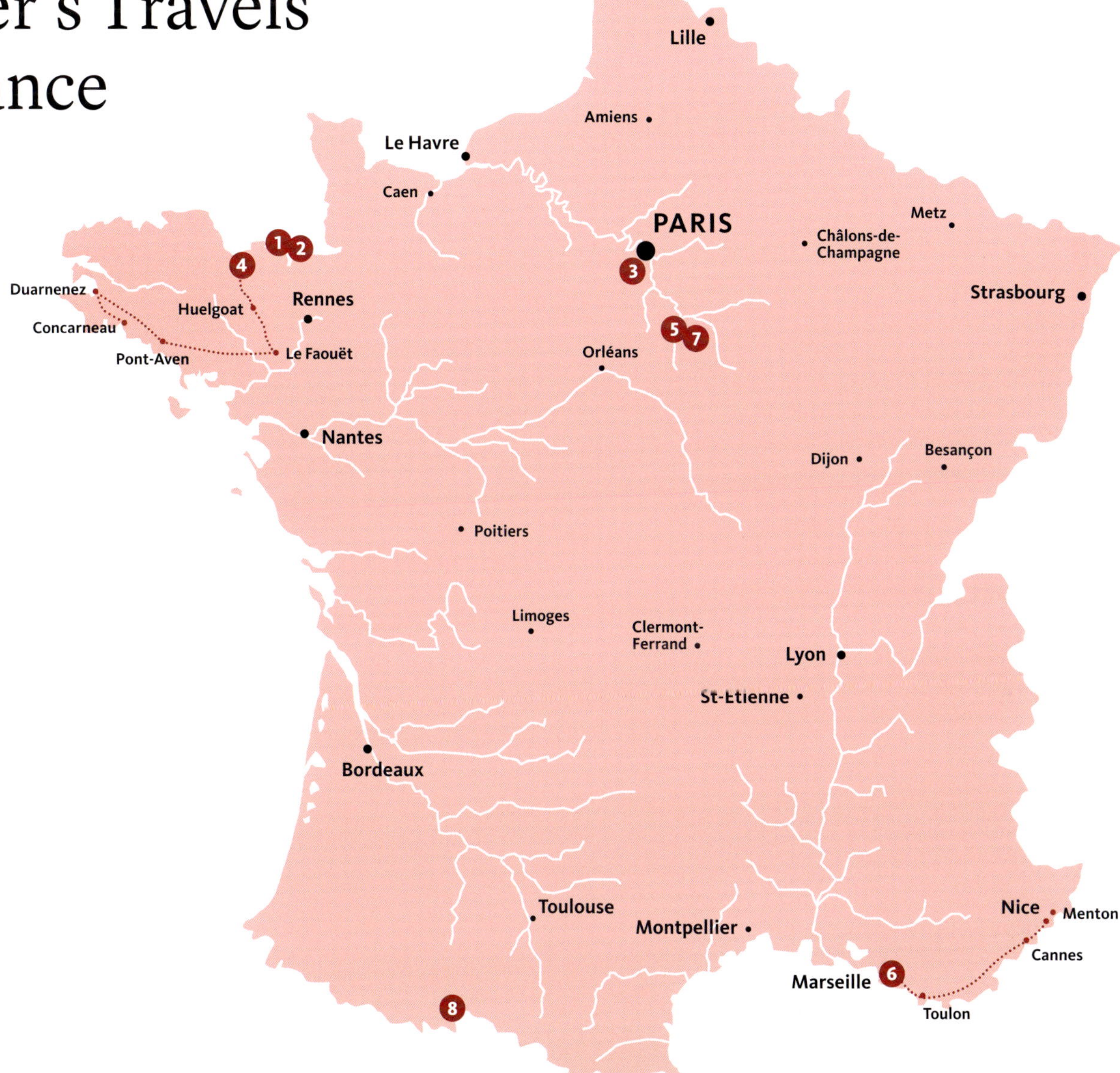

1 **St. Malo** 1877, from 21 or 28 August to 15 or 16 September. Krøyer comes here with Laurits Tuxen for a change of scene from Paris.

2 **Cancale** 1877, 10 September. Krøyer visits for a one-day trip from St. Malo.

3 **Cernay-la-Ville** 1879, before 20 April to c. 24 June. This is the first real artists' colony Krøyer visits in France. His stay is interrupted by a short trip to Paris after 16 May, until no later than 20 May.

4 **Morlaix** 1879, 5 July. Krøyer arrives by train from Paris with Christian Zacho, and continues south by foot:

- 6 July: leaves Morlaix with Zacho and an unidentified French friend.
- Huelgoat, c. 7 July.
- Le Faouët, 9 to 10 July.
- Brief stay at the artists' colony **Pont Aven**, from 11 July to 16 or 17 July.
- Duarnenez, 18 to 19 July
- **Concarneau**, before 22 July to 30 September. The party meets up with Tuxen and stays at the artists' colony for a prolonged visit.

5 **Barbizon** 1879, 5 October or more. Brief stay at the artists' colony in the Fontainebleau Forest.

6 **Marseille**, 1879, 11 October. Travels with Ernst Brandes by train from Paris to Marseilles, bound for Italy.

- Planned trip via Toulon to Nice, 12 October.
- Hike from Menton towards Genoa, mid-October.

7 **Grez-sur-Loing** 1884, c. 16 to 24 May. Visits the artists' colony there, where there are mainly Swedish artists.

8 **Luchon** 1886, from c. 6 June to c. 30 July and again in 1889, 8 June to 2 July. Krøyer visits alone for a recuperative stay in the town, which is picturesquely situated among the mountains of the Pyrenees.

Krøyer in Paris

SOJOURNS AND RESIDENCE

- 1877, 10 June. Krøyer arrives on the sleeper train from Brussels to Paris on Sunday morning at 6 a.m. He remains based in the city until 23 May 1881.
  - Lives in a small room in **5, Rue de Douai** 1 until 15 February 1878, at which point he sets out for Spain.
  - Upon his return from Spain, he stays at **11, Boulevard de Clichy** 2 from 4 to 30 October 1878.
  - Beginning in late October 1878, he and Carl Locher rent premises at **35, Boulevard de Rochechouart** 3. Here they have studios on the sixth floor and separate flats on the seventh floor. Krøyer stays until the spring of 1879, at which point he sets out to travel around France.
  - Krøyer is back in Paris from 30 September to 10 October 1879, once again staying at **5, Rue de Douai** 1, before leaving for Italy.
  - Stays briefly in Paris from c. 11 to 20 June 1880 before returning to Italy.
  - Stays briefly in Paris from c. 1 to 23 May 1881 before returning to Copenhagen.
- 1882, 1 to 17 May.
- 1883, c. 8 to 19 May and c. 23 October to 2 November.
- 1884, 4 to 26 May, interrupted by a trip to Grez-sur-Loing c. 16 to 24 May.
- 1885, 11 to before 25 April. Having visited Copenhagen he is back in Paris on 6 or 13 May to 24 May, alongside Anna and Michael Ancher, as well as Viggo Johansen.
- 1886, 14 May to 4 June alongside Laurits Tuxen. Visits Luchon and is back in Paris 31 July to 1 August.
- 1887, May to 2 June in the company of Martha and Viggo Johansen.
- 1888, 7 to c. 26 February. He is back again on 16 November and stays until 4 July 1889, interrupted by a trip to Luchon from 8 June to 2 July.
  - Krøyer borrows Laurits Tuxen's flat in **69, Boulevard St. Jaques** 4, a small building which is home to only two families. He stays there from November 1888 to May 1889.
  - Has a studio in the **Palais de l'Industrie** 5 in the winter of 1888/1889, painting the many figures featured in *The Committee of the French Exhibition in Copenhagen in 1888*.
  - Moves to **65, Avenue de Wagram** 6 in May 1889.
- 1892, before 23 to c. 31 May.
- 1895, late April.
- 1898, early June.
- 1899, 10 to 18 May, with Laurits Tuxen.
- 1900, 8 to 16 November to see the Exposition Universelle.
- 1902, c. 4 April to 28 May.
- 1903, 14 to 16 or 17 June.
- 1907, 14 to 17 June, with Hans Gyde Petersen.

EXHIBITIONS AND MUSEUMS IN PARIS FROM 1877

- In 1877, Krøyer would have been able to see *Envois de Rome* at the **École nationale et spéciale des Beaux-Arts** 7 at 14, rue Bonaparte. The exhibition featured the winners of the *Prix de Rome*.
- **Exposition Universelle** 8 at Champ-de-Mars in 1878.
- In 1877 and until 1880, the **Salon** at **Palais des Champs-Elysées** 9 was arranged by the Académie des Beaux-Arts. From 1881 it was arranged by the Société des Artistes Français, though it remained at the same venue.
- A new, slightly smaller **Salon** arose in 1890, arranged by the Société Nationale des Beaux-Arts in the **Palais du Champ-de-Mars** 8. The two Salons operated concurrently throughout the rest of Krøyer's lifetime.
- Krøyer first visited the **Musée du Luxembourg** 10, the museum of contemporary art, in 1877. Back then the museum was housed in two wings of the Palais du Luxembourg, where it remained until 1886.
- In 1886 the **Musée du Luxembourg** 11 was moved to the orangery, the present-day Musée du Luxembourg. The museum no longer houses the same collection it did back then; the original collection was distributed among other museums in 1936.
- In 1877 Krøyer visited the **Musée du Louvre** 12, partly in order to study and copy Rembrandt: *Bathsheba at her Bath*, 1654.
- In the winter of 1878/1879, Krøyer worked at the **Château de Versailles**, copying Jean Alaux: *Josias, Count of Rantzau, Marshal of France*, 1834.
- In 1882, Krøyer exhibited a collection of drawings at **H.G. Petersen-Gade, L'Art Scandinave** 13 at a Scandinavian exhibition held at the gallery at 5, Avenue de l'Opera.
- In 1885, 1887, 1890, and 1891, Krøyer exhibited at the **Galerie Georges Petit** 14 in 8, rue de Sèze at the *Exposition Internationale de Peinture*, which also featured artists from the Impressionist group.
- **Exposition Universelle** at Champ-de-Mars 8 in 1889. Construction of the Eiffel Tower.
- **Exposition Universelle** at Champs-Élysées 9 in 1900. Opening of the first metro line; construction of the Petit Palais.
- In 1902, the **Petit Palais** 15 opened as the Musée des Beaux-Arts. It housed the Salon in 1903, to which Krøyer contributed one work.

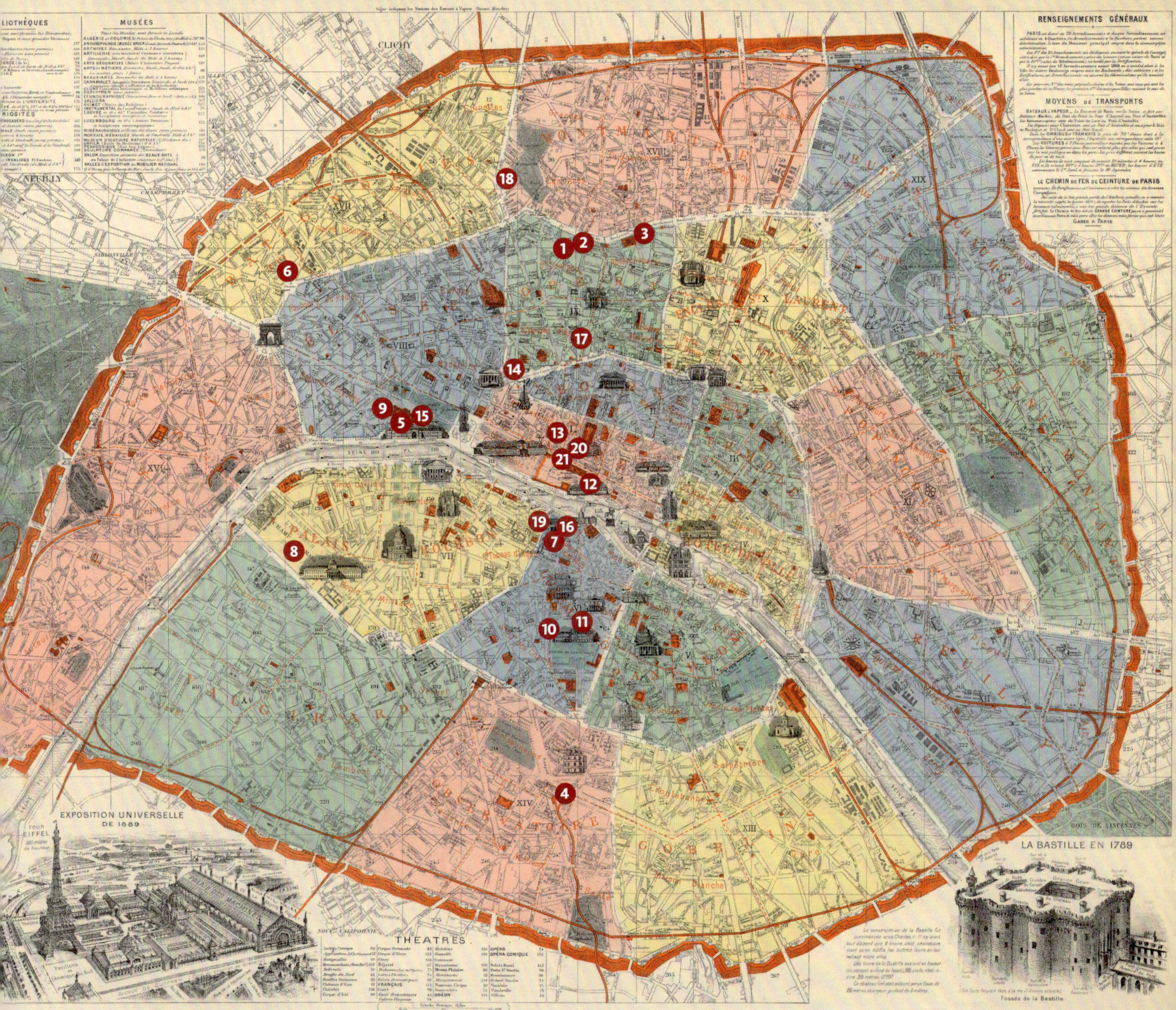

Alexandre Aimé Vuillemin & Charles Dyonnet: Illustrated map of Paris, 1889. Bibliothèque nationale de France.

- Krøyer visited the memorial exhibition ***Exposition des oeuvres de Jules Bastien-Lepage*** in 1885 at the **Hôtel Chimay** on the Quai Malaquais (16). The premises were owned by the École Nationale des Beaux-Arts.
- **The auction of the late Bastien-Lepage's works** was held at the auctioneers Hôtel Drouot, 11–12 May 1885 (17).

PLACES OF NOTE

- **Atelier Bonnat**, the private school run by Léon Bonnat which Krøyer attended in 1877 and in the vinter of 1878/1879. The studio was located in 15, rue Hégésippe Moreau (18).
- Krøyer bought his artist's supplies from shops such as **Sennelier** at 3, Quai Voltaire (19).

- Krøyer was fond of the theatre and attended many performances at the **Théâtre Français** (20).
- **Café de la Régence** (21) – Krøyer was a frequent visitor here.

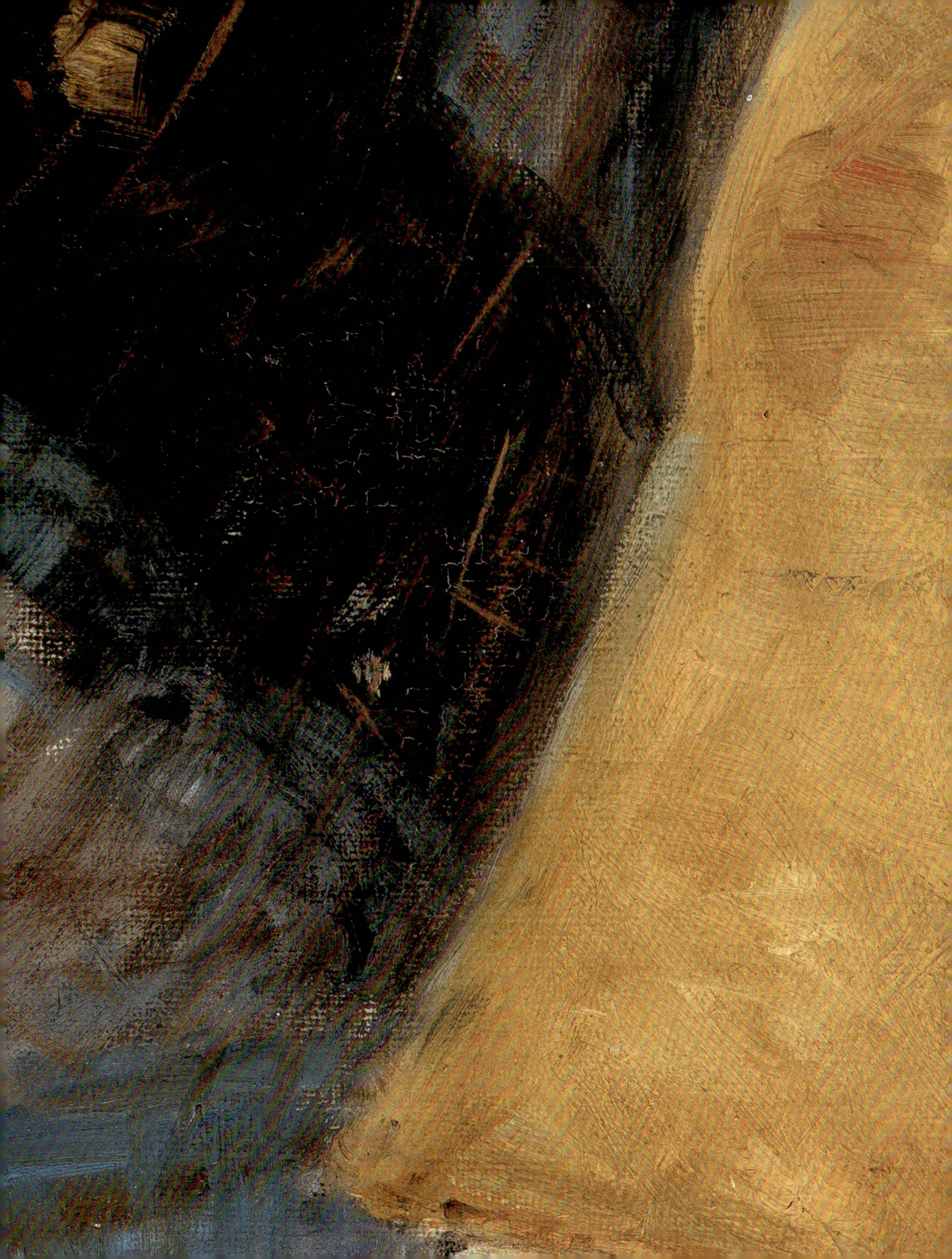

Catalogue

Krøyer Before Paris

CAT. 1 Frederik Vermehren
A Sower, 1859

CAT. 2 Jean-François Millet
Woman Grazing her Cow, 1858

Peder Severin Krøyer attended The Royal Danish Academy of Fine Arts from 1864 to 1870. As was standard for Danish academy students at the time, the last stage of his education was, from 1869, conducted in the life class – known as the model school – where Wilhelm Nicolai Marstrand was professor. The slightly younger painter Johan Frederik Nikolai Vermehren was an assistant teacher at the academy, and of all the teachers there, he was the one with whom Krøyer formed the closest ties. Later correspondence between Krøyer and Vermehren testifies to their respect for each other. In a letter dated 29 June 1879 to Krøyer, who was staying in Cernay-la-Ville in France at the time, Vermehren commented on Krøyer's new teacher, the French painter Léon Joseph Florentin Bonnat:

> I know that I have repeated it a hundred times and a hundred more, so indeed the whole matter is nothing new to me; but it has more bite when a world-famous man [Bonnat] says so than when a mere assistant at our model school [Vermehren] draws attention to it. This is in no way a reproach; for just as you were one of my most able pupils, so too were you one of the most diligent and grateful, one of those for whose sake one can sacrifice time and effort for many of the others for whom teaching is essentially a long, pointless grind. I assure you that you have learned a lot here in Denmark after all, and if you had an instrument with which to measure your skill and distinguish how much of it you owe to Copenhagen, and how much to Paris, I would not fear the outcome as far as we are concerned.[1]

Here, Vermehren argues that Krøyer's Copenhagen training had given him firm foundations prior to his trip to Paris. Vermehren also believes he had said something along the same lines as Bonnat regarding the use of colour and lighting. However, the difference was that Vermehren was a painter of the previous generation, which was very much oriented towards detail and an idealised reproduction of nature. When you depicted a body, you had to know the ideal shape of that body beforehand, and you needed to know and show which shapes were hiding in the shaded areas, regardless of whether you could actually see them or not. Similarly, when one reproduced a landscape, it had to be the God-given landscape.[2] Since an ideal representation was called for, when looking for subjects in the wild, Vermehren would spend a long time finding the perfect

1. Petersen, *Dansk Kunstnerliv i Firserne*, 357–358.

2. Larsen, 'The transcendence of the spirit', 67–87.

landscape. Krøyer and his contemporaries favoured a completely different way of thinking. They wanted to see the world as it was, as perceived by the naked eye, the ugly as well as the beautiful – without always keeping the ideals in mind.

Vermehren's *A Sower* (CAT. 1) from 1855 has a certain degree of naturalism about it, but overall, it is an example of Danish National Romanticism. Delving into the work and its creation, it becomes clear that Vermehren took a somewhat different approach to his chosen subject matter than the one Krøyer was interested in. Vermehren already had an idea of what he wanted to paint before heading out into the countryside to find exactly the landscape he needed for his painting. He studied the movements of the sower, learning them by heart in order to draw them, but found that the farmer himself was not attractive enough. In a letter to his mother-in-law, Vermehren wrote: 'I have looked at many faces but have yet to find a truly handsome man.'[3] He spent quite some time finding a suitable model, ultimately selecting a former soldier.[4] In this sense, the work became an idealised depiction of a sower, despite the studies done in nature beforehand. The painting was bought by Statens Museum for Kunst in 1859 and exhibited at Charlottenborg in 1860. It was also exhibited at the Paris Exposition Universelle in 1878.[5]

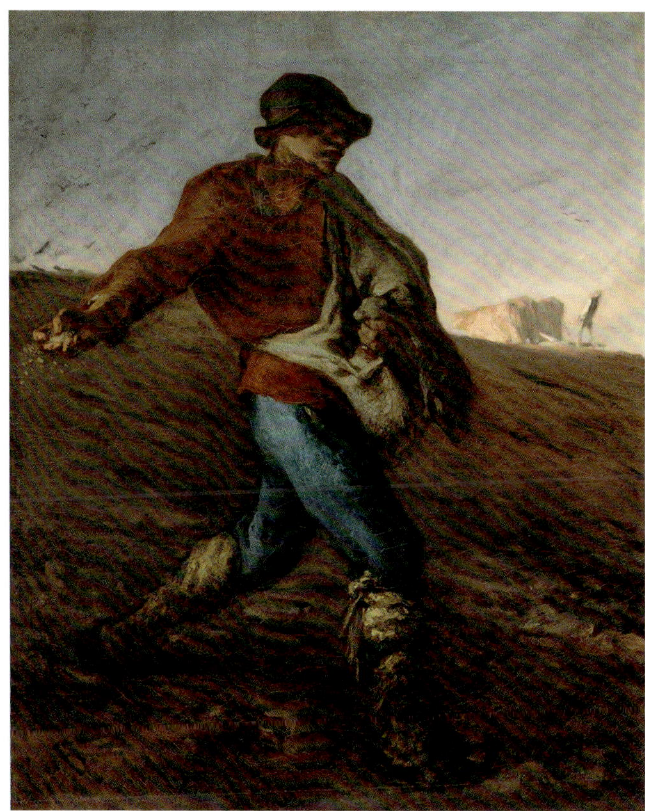

FIG. 1 Jean-François Millet: *The Sower*, 1850. Oil on canvas, 101.6×82.6 cm. Museum of Fine Arts, Boston. 17.1485

At this time, Jean-François Millet was painting works of a comparable nature in France, except with a higher degree of realism – *Woman Grazing her Cow* (CAT. 2) being one example. Whereas Vermehren, who grew up in a bourgeois home, was not interested in the lives and fates of his models, Millet was a farmer's son and could fully empathize with the poverty, hard work, and earthbound existence of rural life. He trained as a farmer and later as an artist in Paris, but then moved to the countryside in Barbizon near the forest of Fontainebleau. His choice of subject matter formed a stark contrast to the romantic and idyllic depictions of country life that prevailed in French art, full of sunshine, smiles, and Sunday celebrations. Millet's social commitment did not make him popular in established art circles in Paris at the time. His *Death and the Woodcutter* from 1858–1859, now owned by the Ny Carlsberg Glyptotek, was rejected at the Paris Salon in 1859, and his final work, *The Church at Gréville* from 1873–1874 (FIG. 15), was the first of his works to be bought by the French nation. Despite this, he would inspire many subsequent artists, including Krøyer's generation, the Skagen Painters, and the artists of the Modern Breakthrough.

3. Quoted from Faaborg, *Johan Frederik Nicolai Vermehren*, 10–11.

4. Larsen, 73.

5. Cat. no. 74.

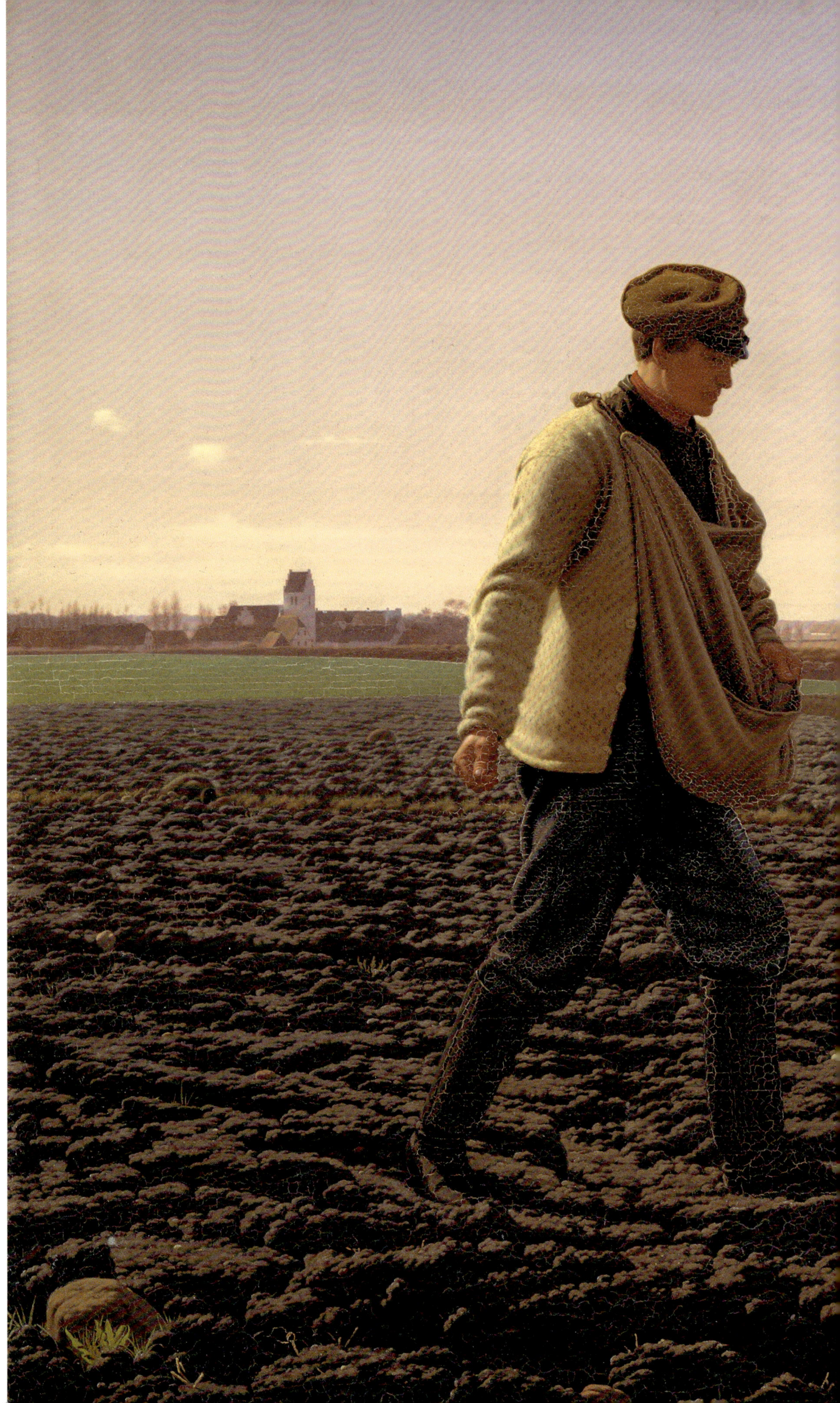

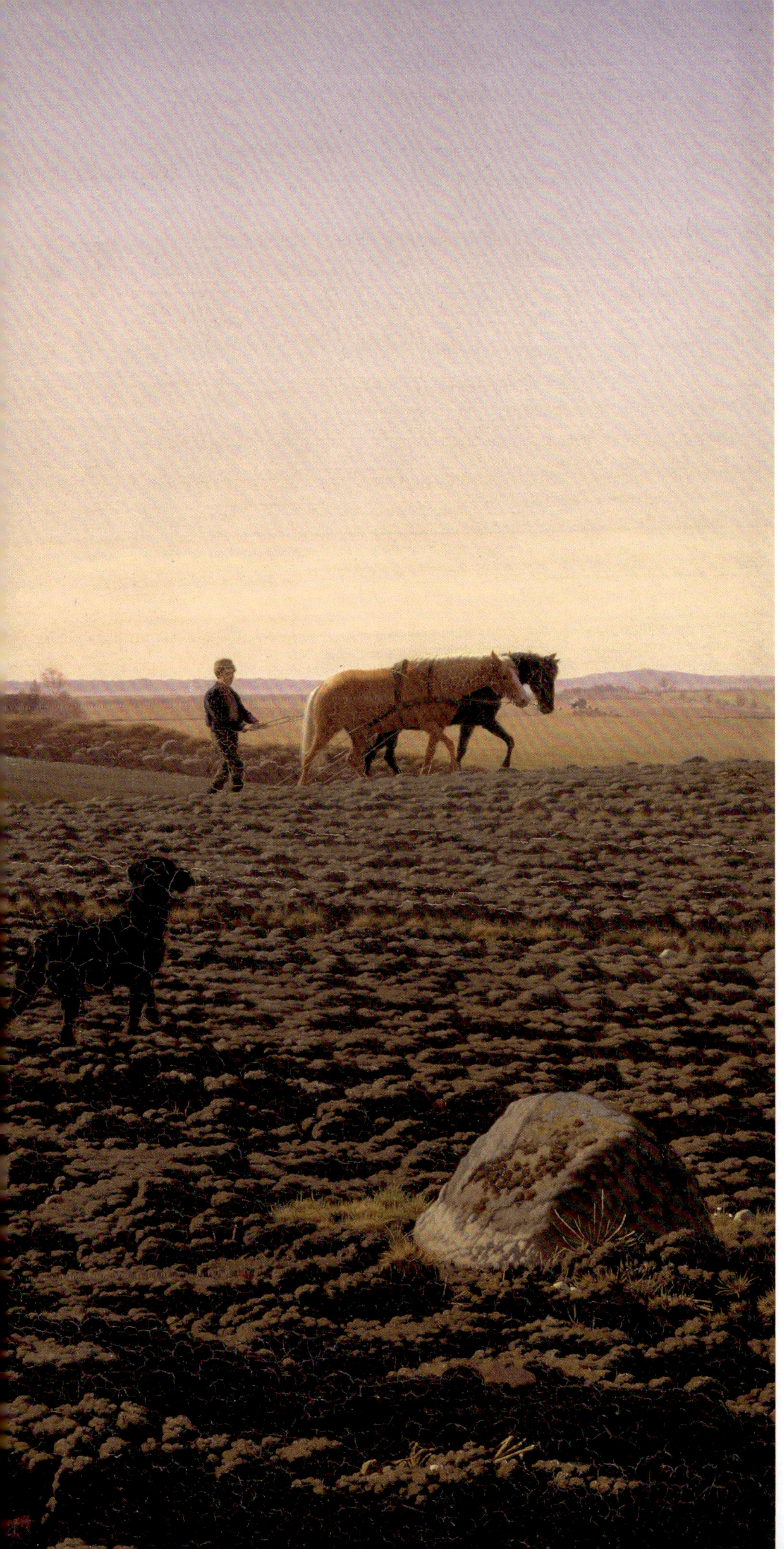

CAT. 1 Frederik Vermehren: *A Sower*, 1859. Oil on canvas, 76 × 89 cm. Statens Museum for Kunst, Copenhagen. KMS753

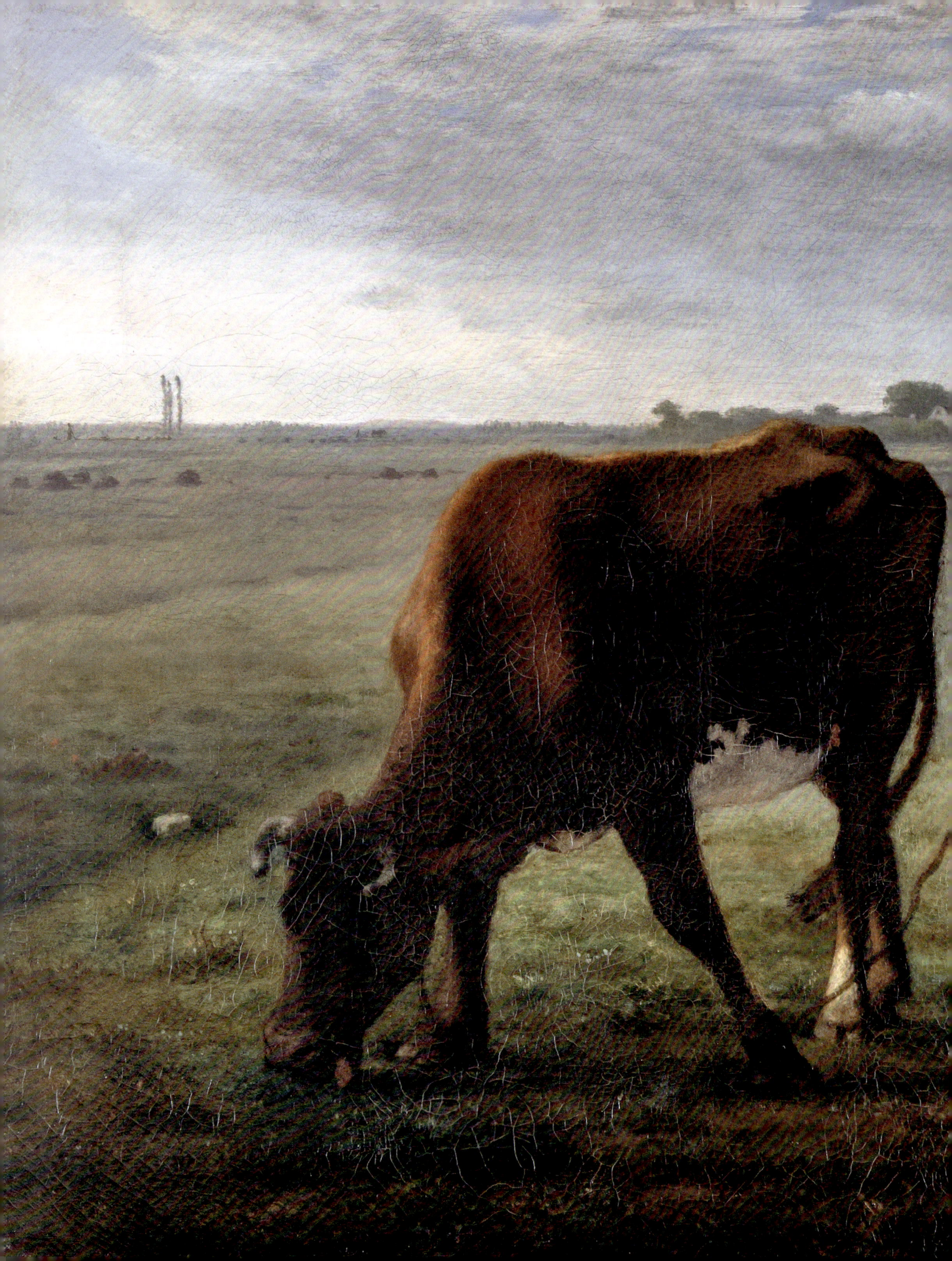

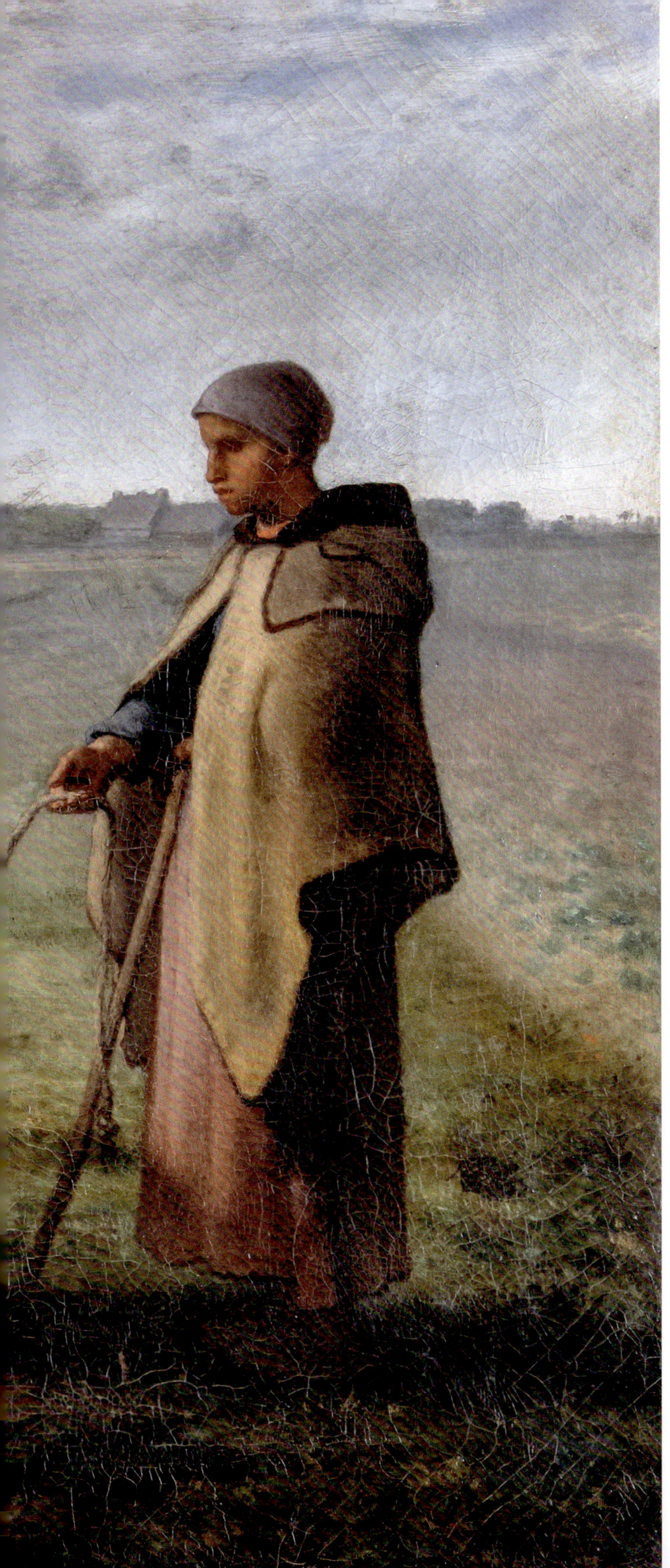

CAT. 2 Jean-François Millet: *Woman Grazing her Cow*, 1858. Oil on canvas, 73 × 93 cm. Musée des Beaux-Arts, Monastère Royal de Brou. 859.1

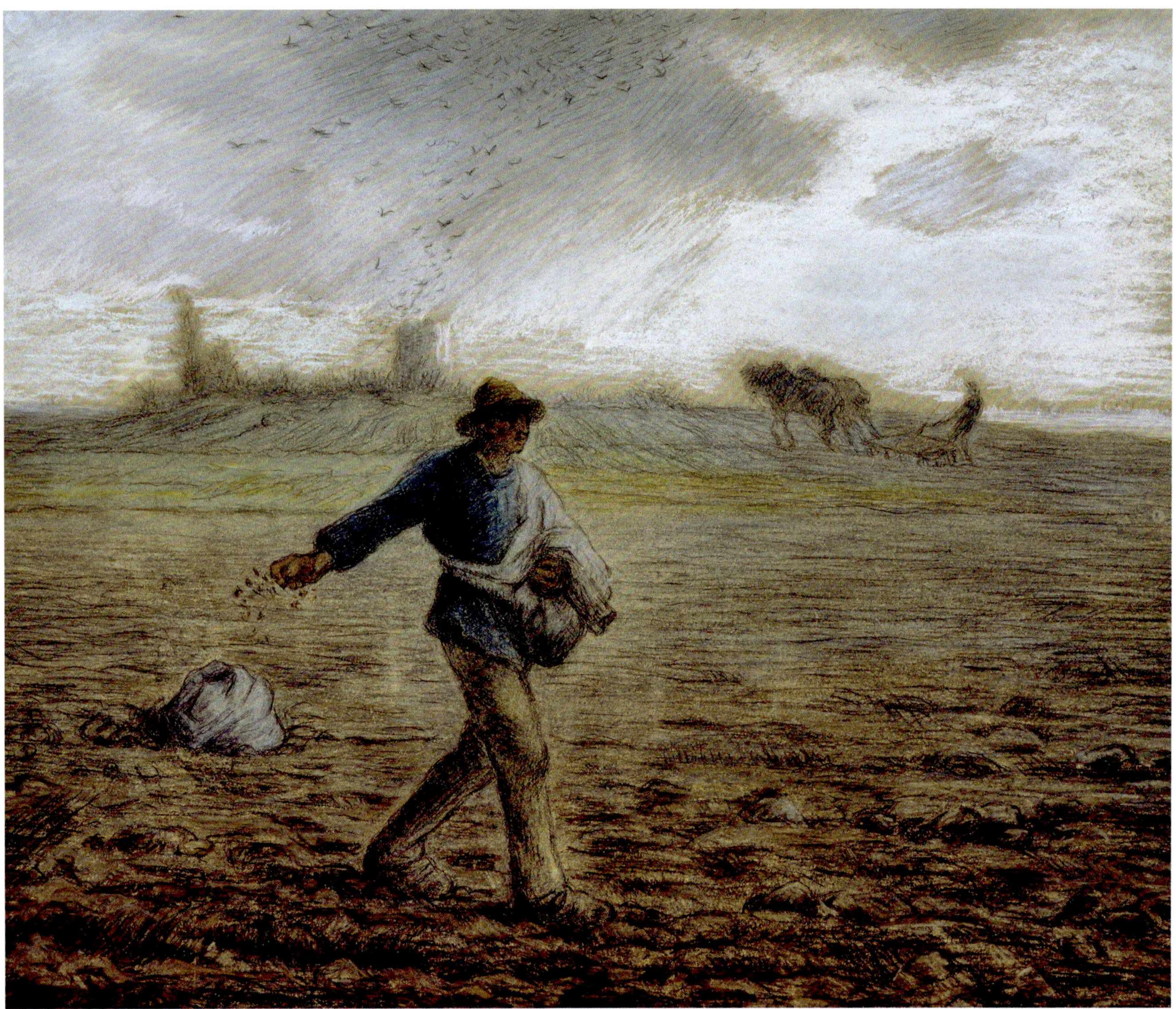

FIG. 2 Jean-François Millet: *The Sower*, c. 1865. Pastel on paper, 43.5×53.5 cm. The Walters Art Museum, Baltimore. 37.905

In 1850, Millet painted *The Sower* (FIG. 1), preceding Vermehren's treatment of the theme by nine years. While Vermehren was in Paris in 1855, he could not have seen the work itself, which had been sold into a private collection. However, he may have seen some of the later printed reproductions.[6] In any case, there is a remarkable similarity between the composition of Vermehren's sower and a drawn version of Millet's sower (FIG. 2). An obvious kinship exists between the two artists in their choice of subject matter and almost religious portrayal of their peasant figures, but the differences were crucial.

Mette Harbo Lehmann

6. Larsen, 77.

CAT. 3 Peder Severin Krøyer: *From the Smithy in Hornbæk*, 1875

From the Smithy in Hornbæk (CAT. 3) was, alongside a portrait (FIG. 3), the first work Krøyer ever exhibited in Paris. He did so at the 1878 Exposition Universelle, and his works were selected by the Danish exhibition committee to be part of the combined Danish contribution, which featured 38 Danish painters. Krøyer's works were painted in 1875 and 1873, respectively, meaning they both dated from the period before he received instruction in France. The smithy was exhibited under the title *La Forge*,[7] stating no specific place, so audiences could only perceive the subject as a generic smithy. The French critics were generally unimpressed with the works shown in the Danish section, and the entire exhibition has since gone down in Danish art history as a defeat that marked a turning point, ushering in a new determination to focus on a more modern art. However, one French critic noted Krøyer and his smithy:

> Today, following the war, when they were abandoned just as we were, the Danes still have artists but they no longer have art. I say artists, and I can name them: [...] M. Krøeyer [*sic*], who has painted an impression of a forge with great *brio* [...] [8]

The critic praised Krøyer for his skilfully executed painting, created before the Danish artist had even had the opportunity to study French art up close and allow it to be reflected in his paintings. There is, of course, no way of telling what Krøyer's career would have looked like if he had not resided in France from 1877 to 1881 and formed lasting ties to the nation, but he would probably have done quite well in any case. The smithy was the first major work purchased by Heinrich Hirschsprung, who would go on to be a key patron of Krøyer. Hirschsprung bought it directly from the artist immediately upon its completion in 1875.[9] That same spring, the work was exhibited at Charlottenborg in Copenhagen, bearing the title *Fra Smedien i Hornbæk* (From the Smithy in Hornbæk).[10] It was shown alongside five other works by Krøyer: two portraits, two figure compositions of fishermen – also from Hornbæk – and a portrait of a fisherman. Danish audiences, unlike the French ones, were informed that the work had been created in Hornbæk. A critic placed the work in that specific context as well:

> This year, for the first time ever, Mr *P.S. Krøyer* has ventured outside the realm of portrait painting; he exhibits a composition rich in figures: *Fishermen at the 'Stokken' Bench in Hornbæk*, and an effective picture focusing on lighting: *From the Smithy in Hornbæk*. As regards the first work, there is perhaps something rather too resigned and meagre in the composition; the many similar heads form an only indifferently agitated line, and the many legs in a row have a somewhat tiring effect. However, such shortcomings are offset by excellent depiction of the figures' character; the artist has penetrated deeply into the peculiarities of these North Zealand fishermen; he understands their physiognomies as well as their modes of movement from the ground up; he knows in the minutest detail how they hold their hands in their pockets, how they lean on a fixed object, how they chat idly with each other. As yet, we have been told nothing about the extent to which the artist is in possession of creative imagination; but the picture of the fisherman and the smithy have both revealed a most unusual keenness of observation; a trait which also gives his portraits their considerable value.[11]

7. Cat. no. 35. The portrait was exhibited under the title *Portrait du peintre O. D. Ottesen*, cat. 36. It was commissioned by the Charlottenborg exhibition committee.
8. Blanc, *Les Beaux-Arts*, 342.
9. Saabye, *Krøyer. An International Perspective*, 155.
10. Cat. no. 385.
11. *Dagbladet*, 28 April 1875, 1–2.

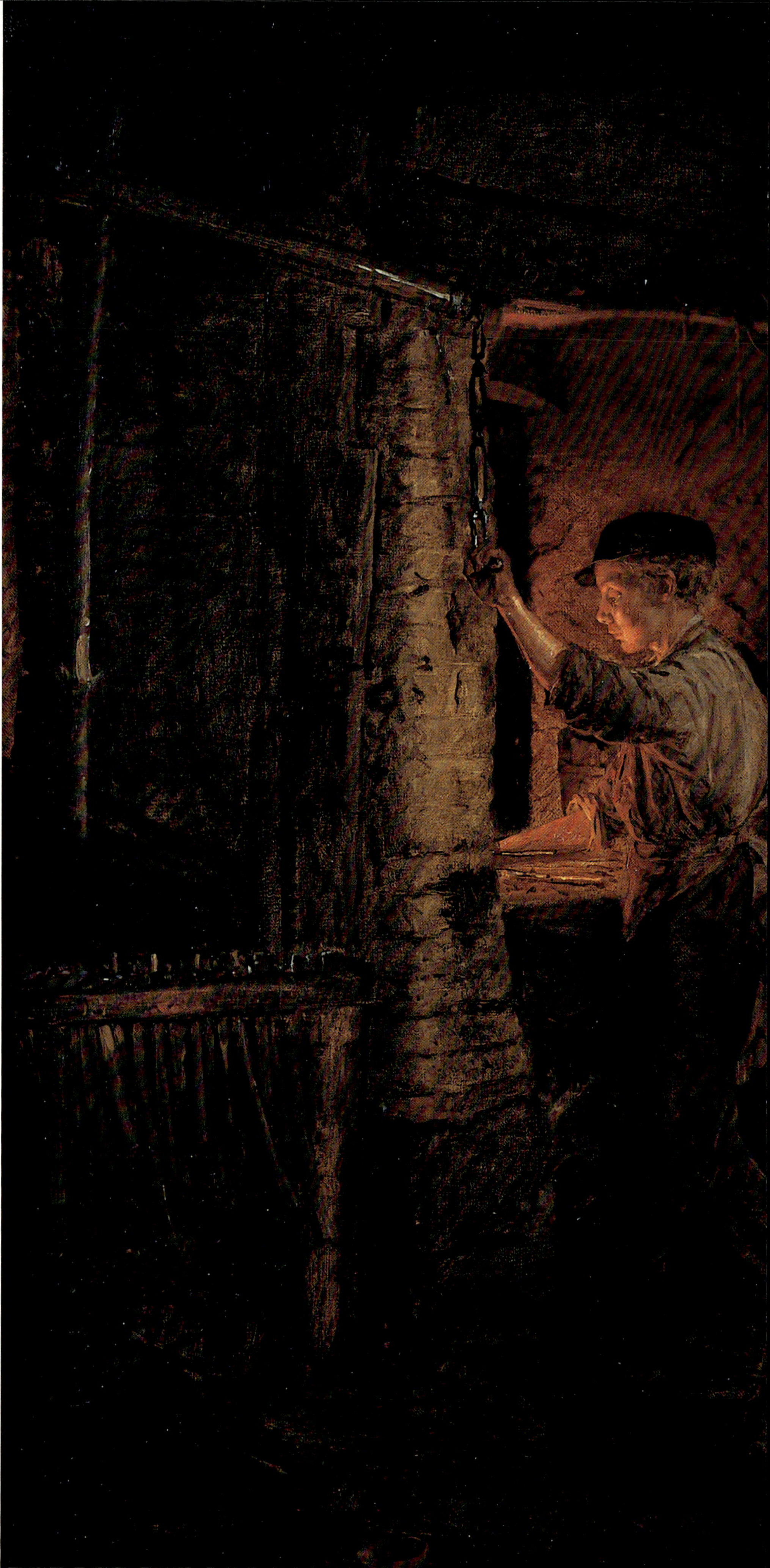

CAT. 3 Peder Severin Krøyer: *From the Smithy in Hornbæk*, 1875. Oil on canvas, 91×118.7 cm. Den Hirschsprungske Samling, Copenhagen. 197

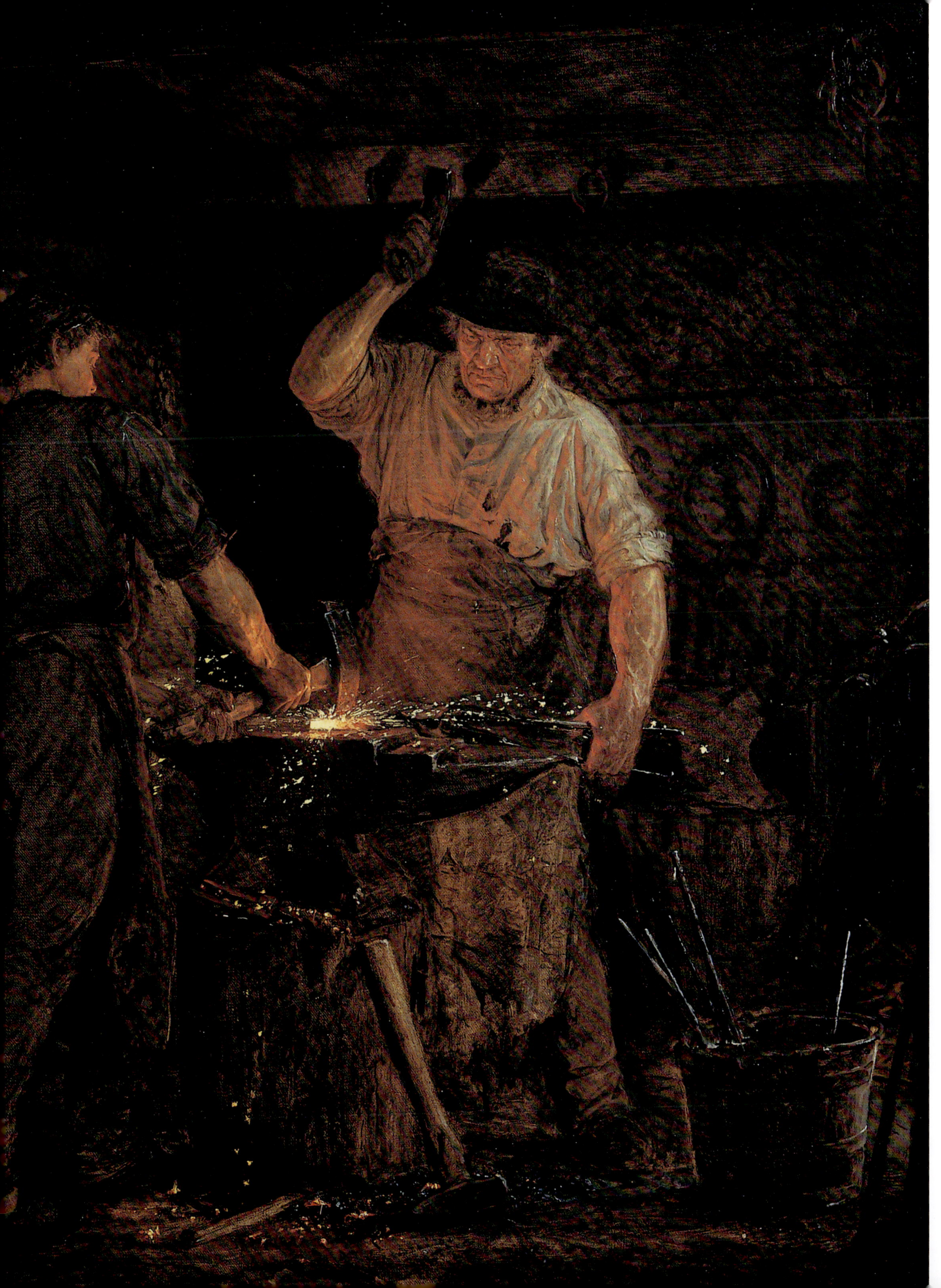

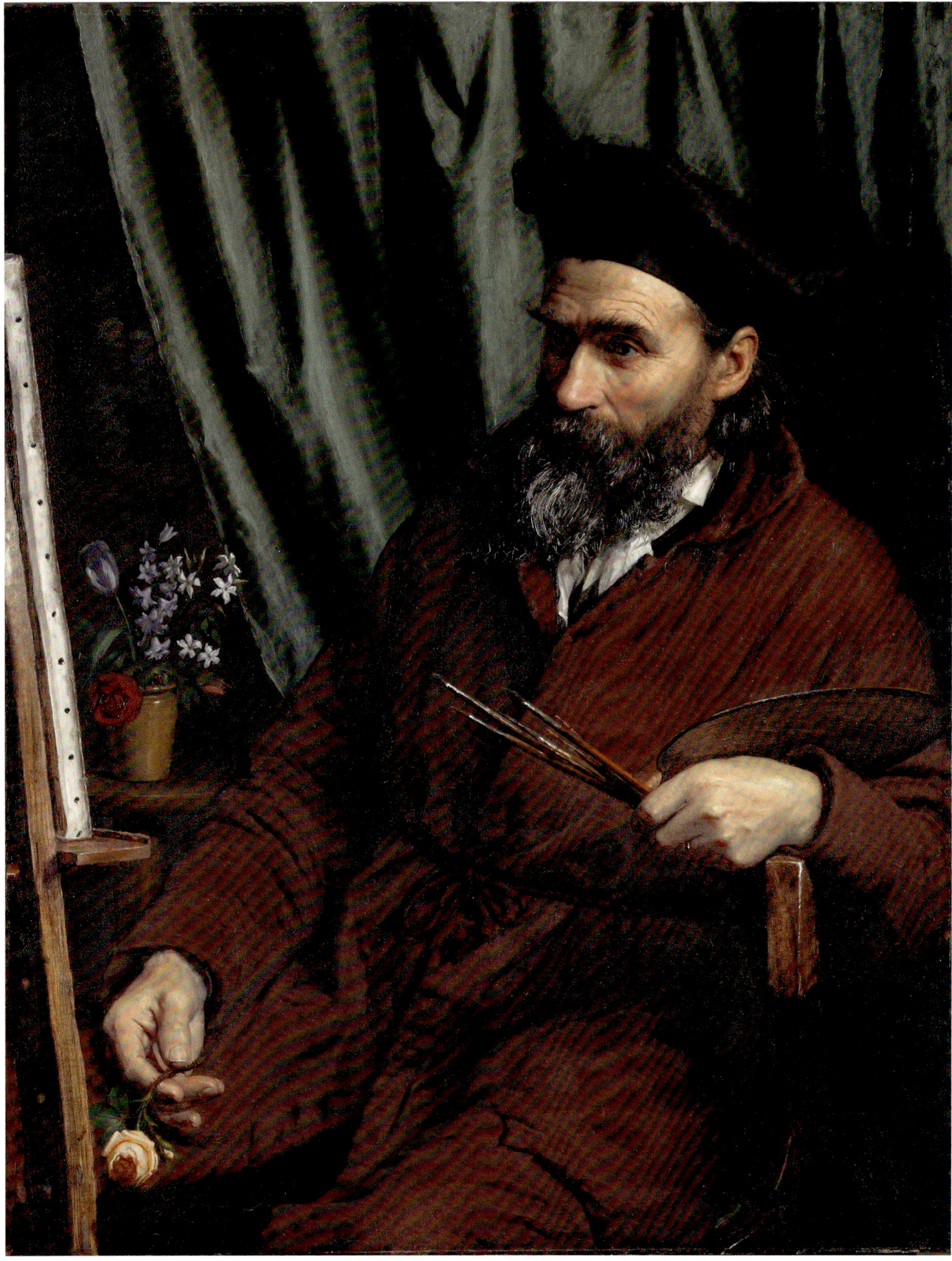

FIG. 3 Peder Severin Krøyer: *Otto Diderich Ottesen*, 1873. Oil on canvas, 86.5 × 70 cm. Det Nationalhistoriske Museum, Frederiksborg Slot. A 9100

The review goes on to appreciatively praise Krøyer's use of colour, as well as his portraits, which are described as vibrant and as excellent likenesses. Overall, the piece is quite a comprehensive review of a young artist's works at a large group exhibition. It is worth noting that the 24-year-old Krøyer is praised for his depiction of light in the smithy and for his ability to accurately and authentically represent the Hornbæk fishermen and their appearance. The question of whether he possesses real imagination may have been raised because he did not exhibit historical or mythological scenes, which would require more imaginary subject matter than the naturalistic depictions of fishermen.

In 1876, Krøyer received a commission from Birmingham for another version of the smithy scene. However, the owner was not happy with the changes Krøyer had made and put it up for auction in London in 1881.[12] This is the situation Krøyer referred to in a letter to Tuxen sent from Sora in Italy on 14 May 1880.

> The *Figaro*, which was sent to me from Paris, says of Hagborg [August] that 'once you have been successful with a picture, you should not paint the same thing again unless you are able to do it <u>much</u> better'. I should have taken that point more into account when I painted the new version of my smithy back in the day.[13]

In 1907, the then owner sold the new version to an American banker. Its current whereabouts are unknown.
Mette Harbo Lehmann

CAT. 4 Peder Severin Krøyer
A Hornbæk Fisherman Sitting on the Gunwale of a Boat, 1876

This Hornbæk fisherman (CAT. 4) is a preliminary study for the painting *Hornbæk Fishermen Catching Herring* from 1877 (private collection). The study is signed 1876 and, despite its later date, this must also have been the year in which most of the work on the main painting was done, because Krøyer was only in Hornbæk in the years 1873 to 1876. Skagens Kunstmuseer also own oil sketches for the fishing boat depicted without any contents or background, for the pile of herring at the bottom, and for the net of herring being pulled in over the railing, as well as two studies of the sky.[14] The museum previously owned a charcoal sketch for the entire composition, sadly lost in the 1954 fire at Brøndums Hotel.[15] Viewed together, all these studies reveal how Krøyer worked on larger canvases immediately after completing his training at the Copenhagen academy and before setting out for France. He would do a sketch of what he wanted the composition to look like in its entirety, and then make separate studies of the individual parts of the work. The charcoal sketch, which was approximately the same size as the finished work, was presumably one of the last things he did before piecing it all together on the final canvas.

The artist is keenly aware of the fisherman's hard toil; it is clear in his work-worn clothes and weathered face. At the same time, the painting is full of fine details such as the light from the sunset reflecting in the wet oilskin trousers speckled with fish scales, the way in which the

12. Saabye, *Krøyer. An International Perspective*, 155.
13. PSK to Laurits Tuxen, Sora, 14 May 1880. KB NBD 2. rk. Also quoted in chapter 3 in the present publication.
14. *The Bow of a Fishing Boat, Study*, SKM9, *Herring in a Fishing Net*, SKM10, *Herring in a Fishing Net*, SKM11, *Evening Sky, Overcast*, SKM7, and *Skyl Study, Evening*, SKM8
15. *Hornbæk Fishermen Catching Herring*, SKM27. From 1934 to 1966, Skagens Museum owned Brøndums Hotel, having received it as a bequest from Anna Ancher's brother, Degn Brøndum. Parts of the hotel were ruined in fires in 1954 and 1959, and on both occasions works of art on display at the hotel were lost.
16. Draft for a letter: PSK to Frederik Vermehren, Cernay-la-Ville, 20 May 1879. PSK Archive 58.

light hits the man's hands, the woollen texture of the sweater, and the hairs of the beard. The face is in shadow yet illuminated by a light which runs slightly contrary to nature.

The study of the Hornbæk fisherman is an example of how Krøyer used relatively thin paint in his works before leaving Denmark for France. His manner of painting is in fact the aspect of his art that changed the most, for his use of naturalism was already present. He began using thicker paints, scaled back the level of detail, and stopped augmenting the light in shaded areas.[16] After studying in France, the shadows in Krøyer's works grew much darker and more intense, and the contrast between areas of light and shadow was more richly contrasted.

The study of the Hornbæk fisherman remained in Krøyer's ownership until his death, upon which Laurits Tuxen bought it. He later sold it to Skagens Museum in 1925. It was exhibited for the first time at Krøyer's solo show at Charlottenborg in 1905 and again at Krøyer's memorial exhibition at Kunstforeningen at Charlottenborg in 1910.

Mette Harbo Lehmann

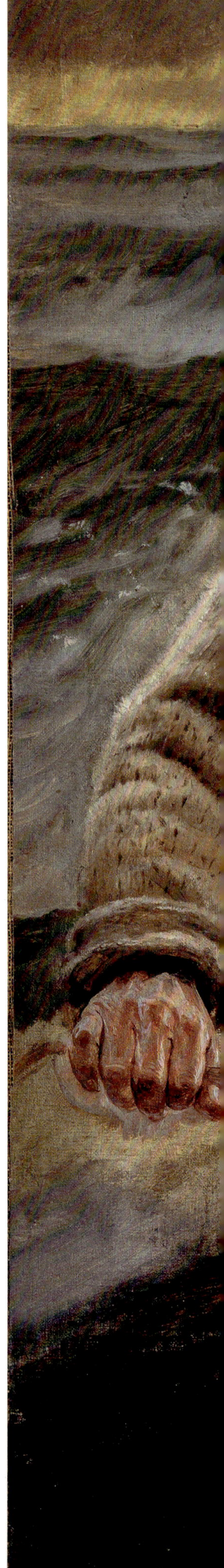

CAT. 4 Peder Severin Krøyer: *A Hornbæk Fisherman Sitting on the Gunwale of a Boat*, 1876. Oil on canvas, 50.2 × 43.6 cm. Skagens Kunstmuseer. SKM221

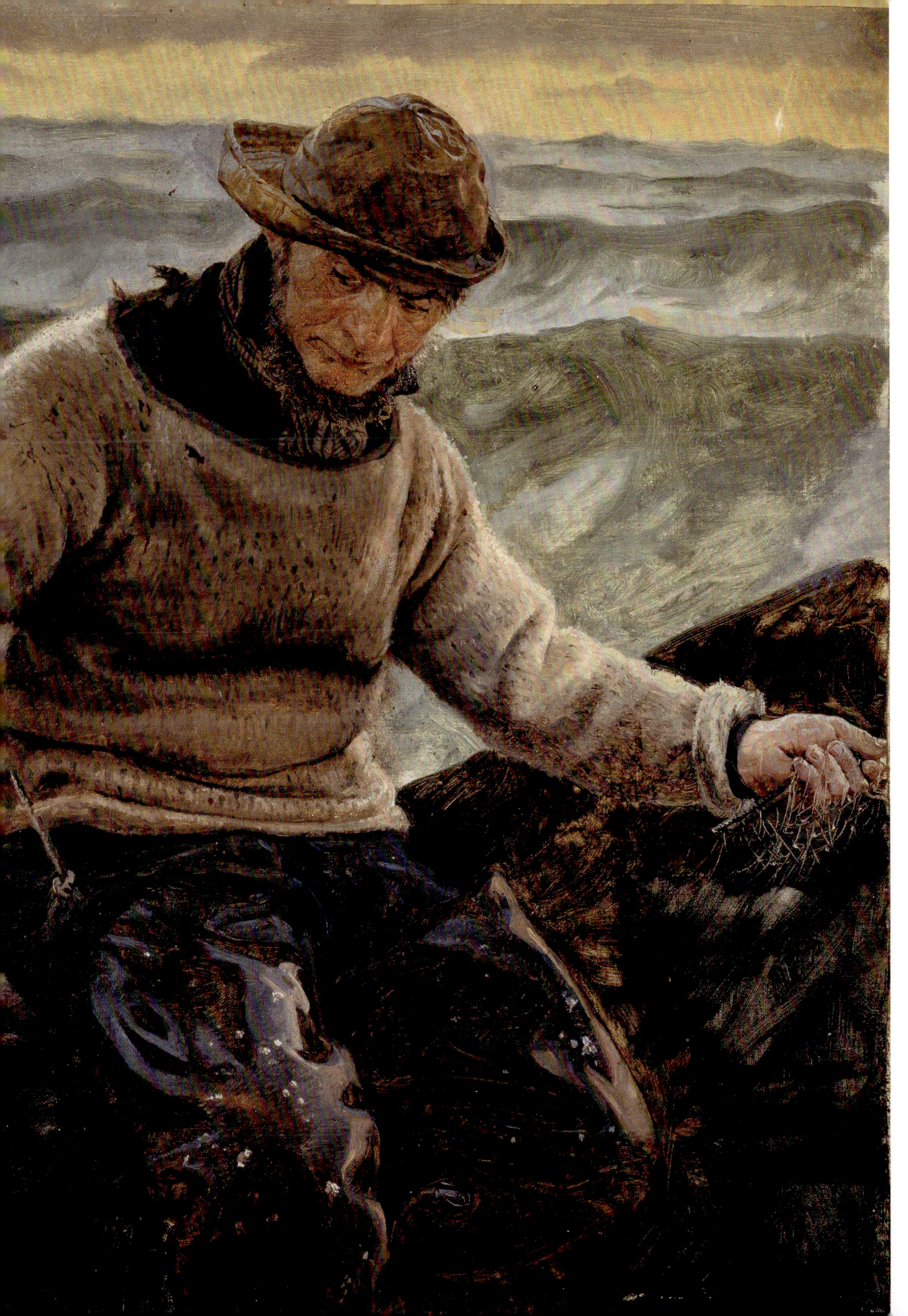

The Salon in Paris

CAT. 5 Théobald Chartran
The Capture of Rome by the Gauls, 1877

In 1663, the Académie Royale de Peinture et de Sculpture organised the first of a series of annual competitions for its pupils. The following year, King Louis XIV undertook to provide the prize-winners with an allowance which would enable them to spend time in Rome and become acquainted with the archetypical models of antiquity and the Renaissance. This period of residence in the Eternal City came into effect in 1666, and from then on, the winners were able to remain there from two to four years. The competition was interrupted by the 1789 Revolution but reorganised by the Institut de France from 1797. It allowed recipients of the prize to stay in the Mancini Palace and subsequently, from 1803, in the Villa Medici, commonly known as the Académie de France à Rome.

The competition began in the spring and was composed of three consecutive tests whose subjects were almost exclusively related to what was then called *grand genre*, the grand manner, which meant painting inspired by mythology, religion, or history. The first stage consisted of producing, within the space of 12 hours, a sketch painted in oils on a biblical or mythological theme. No more than 20 candidates participated in the second stage, for which they had to paint a traditional male nude during four seven-hour sessions. The jury then selected 10 students on the evidence of their sketches and their academic knowledge of the nude. These ten were then permitted to enter *loges*, which were small cubicles where they worked in isolation from the other candidates, giving rise to their name of *logistes*. The final test, which lasted 72 days, was broken down into two sections, once the subject had been announced by the permanent secretary of the Académie. The first consisted of a drawing which established the lines of the final composition; the second involved painting this onto a canvas measuring 113.7 cm by 146.5 cm. Once the paintings were varnished, they were presented, together with the sketches, to a jury composed of academicians who would decide whether or not to deliver various awards, the main one being the Grand Prix, accompanied by the residence in Rome.

Each year, the various stages of this competition were the subject of long commentaries in the press, and the final exhibition of work done by the *logistes* at the *École des Beaux-Arts* was an artistic and fashionable society event widely reported on by columnists. In 1877, the subject of the final test was *The Capture of Rome by the Gauls* and the winner was Théobald Chartran (CAT. 5), who had given proof of a rare determination: he had entered the competition every year from 1870 until 1876. He had thus addressed the themes of *The Death of Messalina* (formerly at the French Embassy in Madrid); *Oedipus Bids Goodbye to the Bodies of his Wife and Son* (Hamilton Art Gallery, Ontario); *A Scene from the Flood* (location unknown); *Captivity of the Jews in Babylon* (location unknown); *The Death of Timophanus, Tyrant of Corinth* (location unknown); *Announcement to the Shepherds* (location

CAT. 5 Théobald Chartran: *The Capture of Rome by the Gauls*, 1877. Oil on canvas, 145 × 113 cm. École Nationale Supérieure des Beaux-Arts, Paris. PRP 128

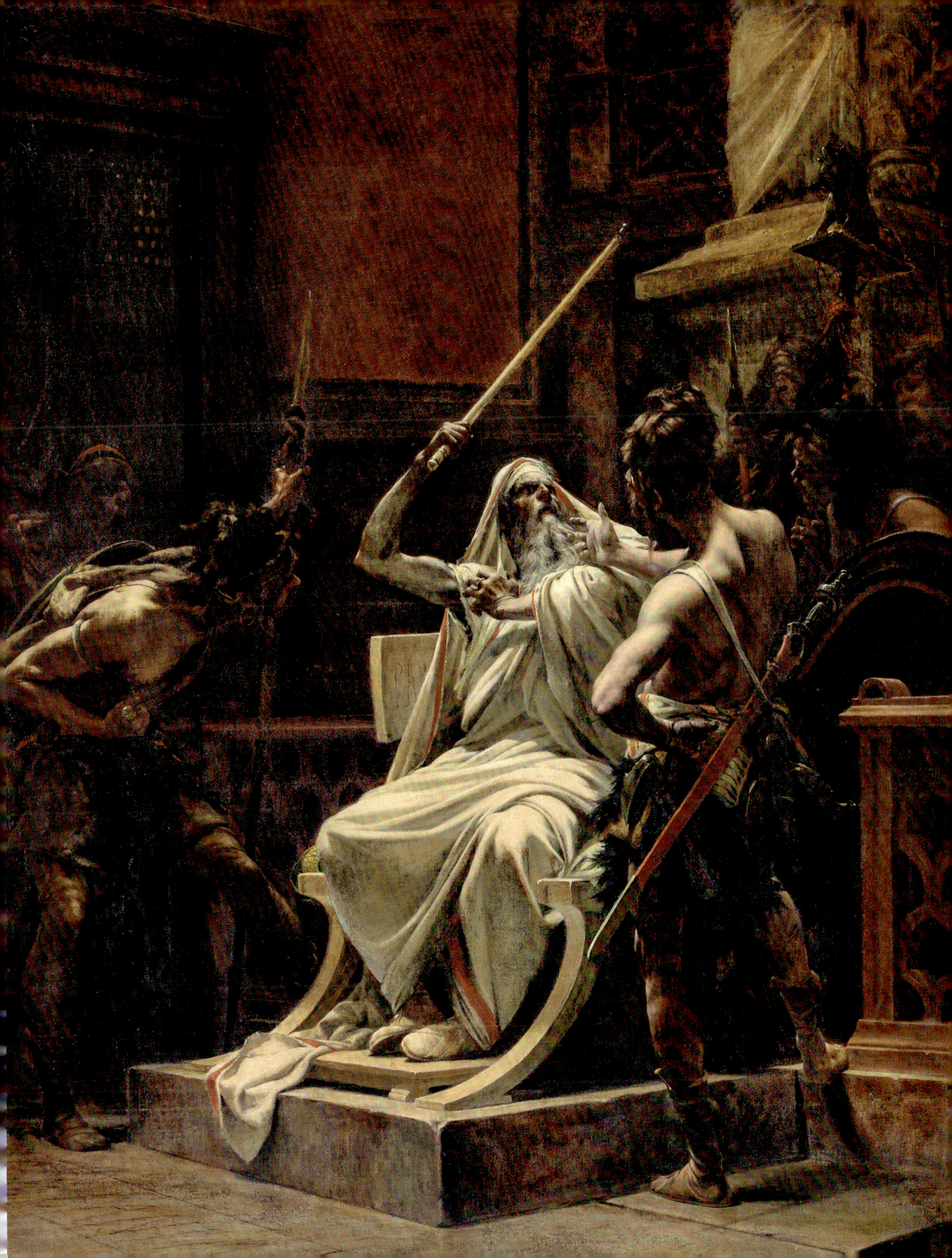

unknown); and *Priam asking Achilles for the Body of Hector* (Petit Palais, Musée des Beaux-Arts de la Ville de Paris). It was also in 1877 that Jules Bastien-Lepage made his last attempt at the prize, after which he abandoned his academic career and the 'grand manner' in order to paint rural life and promote Naturalism.

The works of the 10 candidates selected for the Prix de Rome were shown at the École des Beaux-Arts from late July until early August 1877. Krøyer had arrived for his first stay in Paris on 10 June and would leave the capital on 21 August: he had time, therefore, to see this exhibition, as well as everything else that Paris had to offer in terms of art, including the Salon and the Musée du Luxembourg. Although he appears never to have met Chartran, he did come across several artists in this exhibition who were among the 10 candidates, and whom he would meet again during his subsequent visits to Paris. Worthy of special mention among these are Eugène Carrière and Gustave Courtois, the latter obtaining the second Grand Prix (Hôtel de Ville, Montluçon) in that same year of 1877.
Dominique Lobstein

CAT. 6 William Adolphe Bouguereau
The Day of the Dead, 1859

The Salon had been held every year since 1857 in the former Palais de l'Industrie, built for the 1855 Exposition Universelle, and in its place the Palais des Champs-Elysées was built in 1900. The Salon here brought together the treasures of French art following their acceptance by a jury. Despite frequent reforms of the jury, it still remained much the same, dominated by the defenders of academic principles. It was difficult for artistic innovation to be recognized, given such a jury, and the process still appeared to function according to a 'hierarchy of genres', set by the architect and historiographer André Félibien, who expressed his ideas thus:

> The artist who creates perfect landscapes is superior to another who paints only fruit, flowers, or shells. The artist who paints live animals is more worthy than those who merely depict still life without movement; and as the figure of man is the most perfect work of God on Earth, it is certain that the artist who makes himself the imitator of God by painting human figures is more to be commended than all the others. However, although it is no small thing to make the figure of a man appear alive and to give the appearance of movement where there is none; nevertheless, a painter who paints only portraits has not yet attained this perfect pinnacle of art, and cannot lay claim to the honour which more skilful artists receive. In order to achieve this, it is necessary to move from painting a single figure to depicting a gathering of several figures; it is vital to treat [the subjects of] history and fable; it is essential to represent great actions as historians do, or pleasant subjects in the manner of poets; and rising even higher, through allegorical compositions they should be able to cloak under the veil of fable the virtues of great men and the most lofty mysteries.[17]

This meant, therefore, that the value accorded to artworks varied, ranging from still lifes – the most widely mastered subject – to the 'grand manner', which covered historical, religious, and mythological painting, along with intermediate genres such as landscapes, genre scenes, and portraits, which were becoming increasingly important.

17. *Conférences de l'Académie royal*, 1668.

CAT. 6 William Adolphe Bouguereau: *The Day of the Dead*, 1859. Oil on canvas, 146.5×118.5 cm. Musée des Beaux-Arts, Bordeaux. Bx E 518

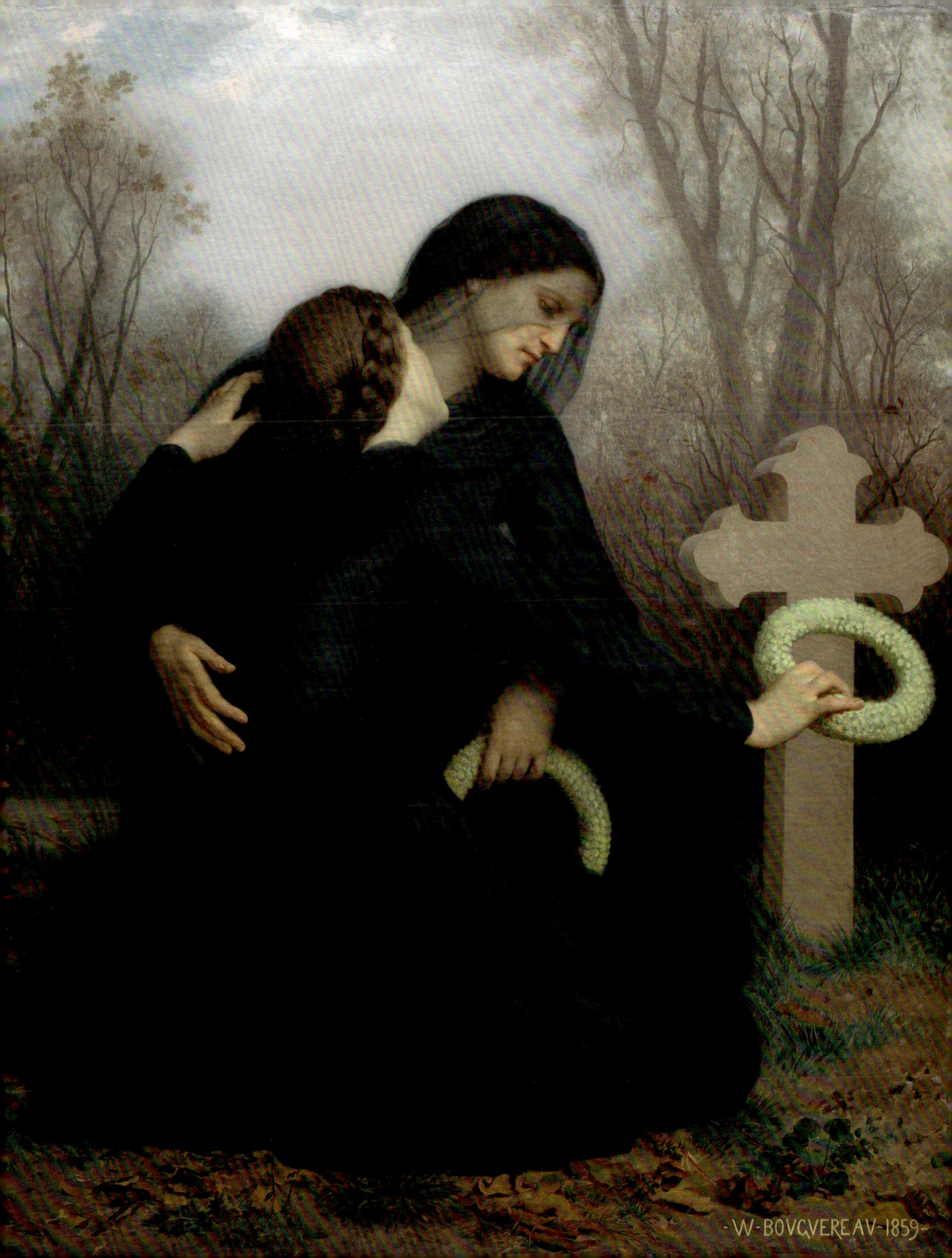
-W-BOVGVEREAV-1859-

Our Lady of Consolation (FIG. 4) by William Adolphe Bouguereau, which Krøyer saw at the 1877 Salon where it was exhibited as number 270, belonged to the most admirable if not the most admired genre. It was impossible to show it because of its monumental size, so it was replaced with an older painting by Bouguereau (CAT. 6), also depicting a religious subject, but with a shift towards the genre scene. This kind of work was not designed for a religious building, but was more like an easel painting with a secular purpose. Indeed, there was no God the Father, no Christ or Virgin, no saints, even, in this 'Commemoration of the faithful departed', which was fixed by the liturgical calendar for All Souls' Day on 2 November but more commonly took place on 1 November, day of the 'Solemnity of All Saints'. The painting of two women in mourning clothes, one of them wearing a black veil, appears to represent a still youthful widow and her daughter at the graveside of a young husband who has died. They are supporting one another as they place wreaths on a newly filled grave, at the head of which has been planted a cross in the shape of a fleur-de-lys.

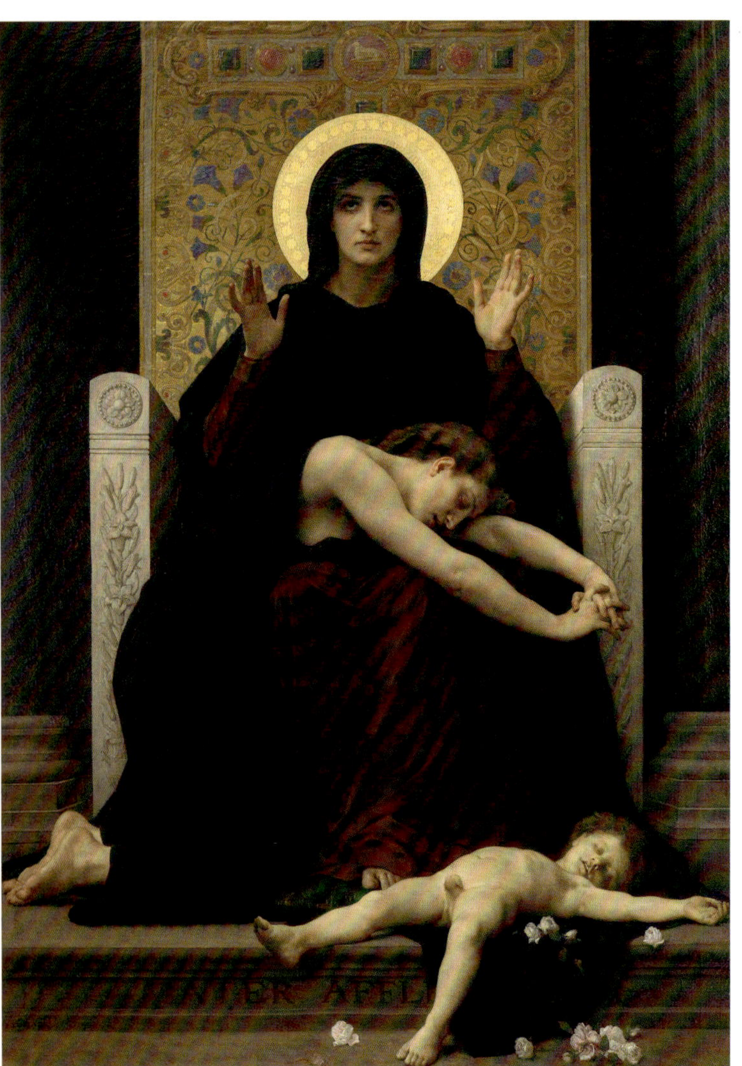

FIG. 4 William Adolphe Bouguereau: *Our Lady of Consolation*, 1877. Oil on canvas, 204×148 cm. Musée des Beaux-Arts, Strasbourg, deposit from Musée d'Orsay. RF 190

Bouguereau had an academic career crowned with honours: having received the Prix de Rome in 1850, he was awarded medals on numerous occasions, elected to the Académie des Beaux-Arts in 1876, and elevated to Grand Officier de la Légion d'honneur in 1903. The pictures he sent to the Salon were increasingly based on religious themes, though these were gradually falling out of favour with critics. Even in 1877, however, certain journalists regarded the maintenance of this tradition as the only possible means by which French art could continue to dominate.

Krøyer was not very susceptible to these arguments; he was much more impressed by the vision put forward by Jules Bastien-Lepage in his *Joan of Arc* (FIG. 5), at the 1880 Salon. For this Danish artist, the era when the 'grand manner' was considered the touchstone was over. Illustration of the contemporary world and his discovery of Skagen, in 1882, were soon sufficient to determine the new direction of his art.

Dominique Lobstein

FIG. 5 Jules Bastien-Lepage: *Joan of Arc*, 1879. Oil on canvas, 254×280 cm. The Metropolitan Museum of Art, New York. 89.21.1

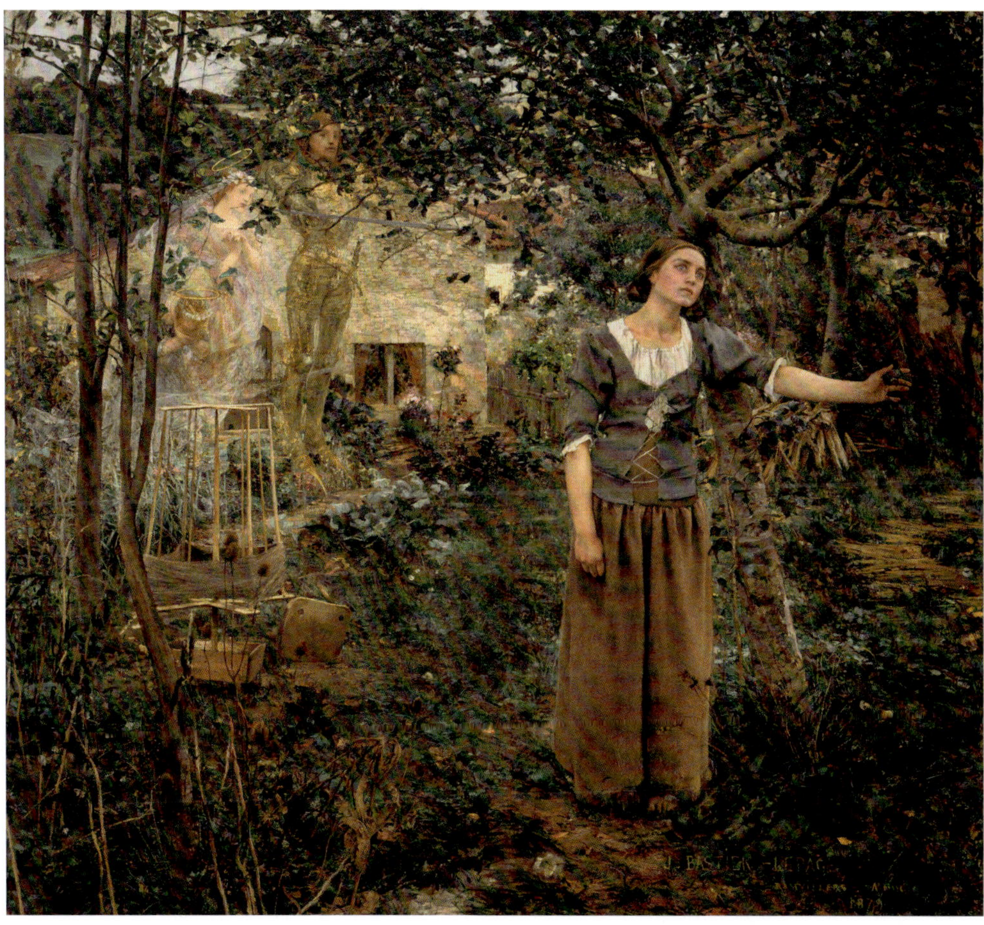

CAT. 7 Aimé Nicolas Morot
Medea, 1876

The painter and sculptor Aimé Morot was born in Nancy on 16 June 1850 and first studied art at the city's school of painting and drawing under the direction of two artists, Émile Thiéry and Charles-Auguste Sellier. The latter, who had studied in Paris and whose name can be found in many Salon catalogues, must have encouraged his pupil to follow his example. In 1869, Morot entered the École des Beaux-Arts, to work in the studio of Alexandre Cabanel. In choosing this teacher he was expressing a wish to follow tradition and to practise in the 'grand manner', implying, therefore, that he would henceforth sit the numerous examinations offered by the school, all leading to the supreme test known as the Grand Prix de Rome. He entered the competition in 1871 and 1872, before emerging as the winner of the three examinations in 1873, with his illustration of *The Captivity of the Jews in Babylon*. In that same year, his work was shown at the Salon for the first time.

As he was busy sending the mandatory artworks to Paris during his residence in Rome, Morot was absent from the 1874 and 1875 Salons, but exhibited there again in 1876, when his painting (*Spring*, unknown location) was awarded a third-class (bronze) medal. The following year, in 1877, he exhibited this *Medea* (CAT. 7), which earned him a second-class (silver) medal, and the Beaux-Arts authorities purchased it for the sum of 3,000 francs. After the impact made by Eugène Delacroix's *Medea* (FIG. 6) at

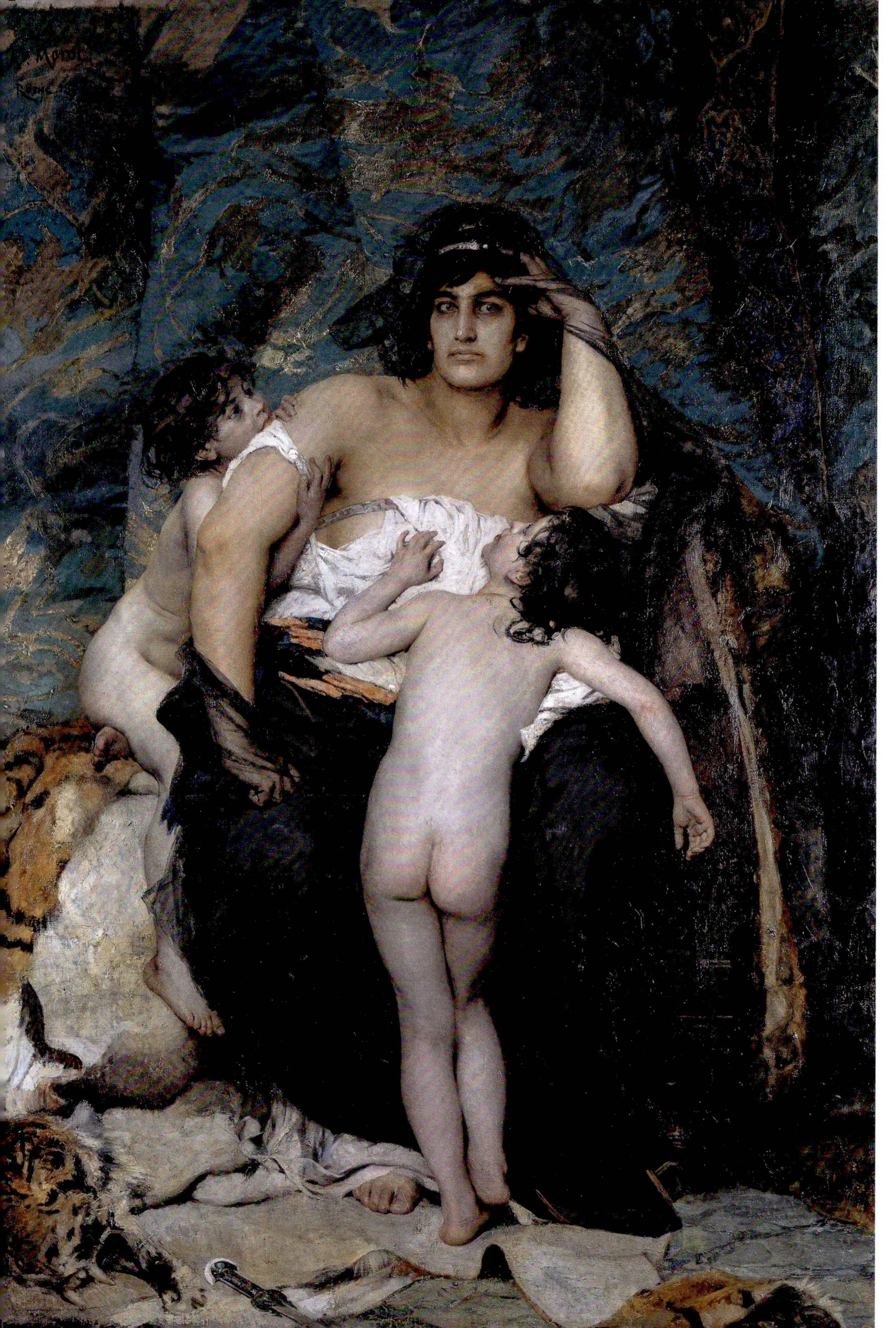

CAT. 7 Aimé Nicolas Morot: *Medea*, 1876. Oil on canvas, 230 × 160 cm. Musée Barrois, Bar-le-Duc. 2007.0.11

FIG. 6 Eugène Delacroix: *Medea*, 1838. Oil on canvas, 260 × 165 cm. Palais des Beaux-Arts, Lille. P. 542

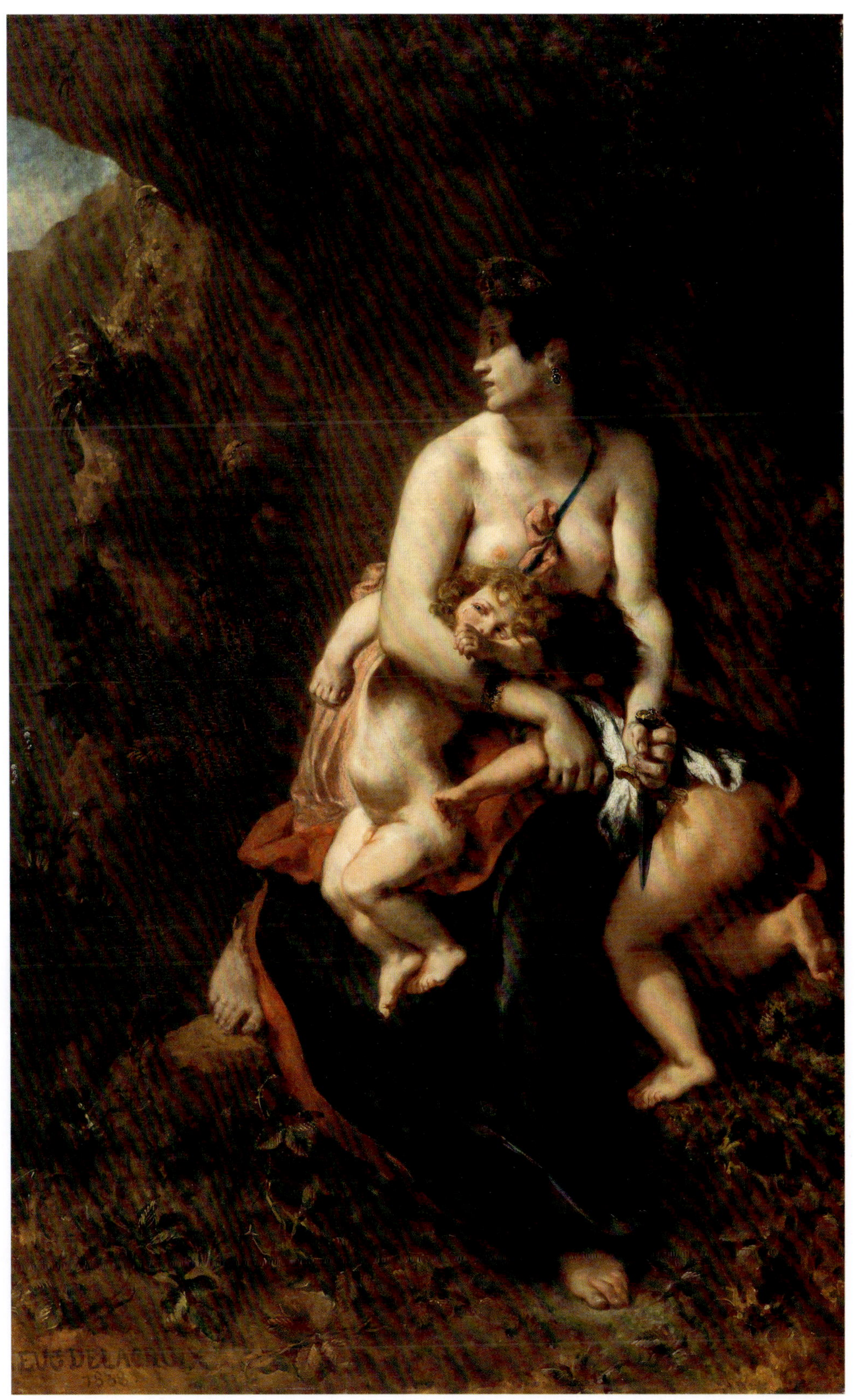

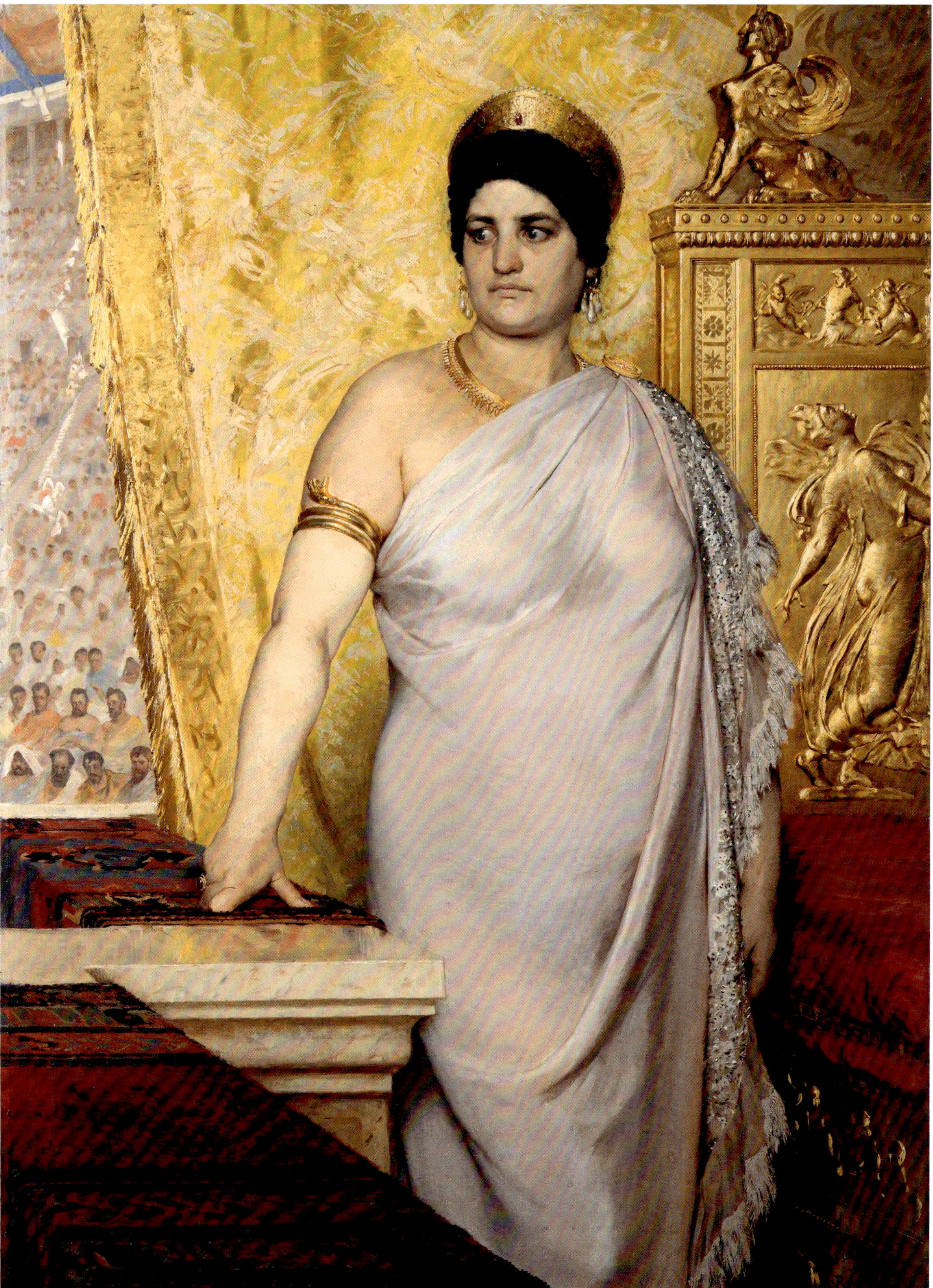

FIG. 7 Peder Severin Krøyer: *Messalina*, 1881. Oil on canvas, 142 × 102 cm. Göteborg konstmuseum. GKM 0173

the 1838 Salon, which was subsequently purchased by the state and deposited in 1839 at the Lille Palais des Beaux-Arts, the response to Morot's cold academicism was very hesitant – even among those who defended academicism, like the critic Olivier Merson:

> In M. Morot's picture, Medea sits in her palace, seething with rage, impervious to her children's caresses and dreaming of the vengeance she will exact on her unfaithful husband. Certainly, the character's attitude and the expression on her mask-like face contain an element of cold ruthlessness which augurs nothing good; one might, however, wonder whether the little children displaying the graceful nudity of their young bodies so naively, the fresh and tender tones contrasting with their mother's pallid flesh, will not emerge safe and sound from the danger that threatens them. The impact of M. Morot's painting is felt more slowly, sensations aroused less immediately than for that of Delacroix.[18]

This painting is one of many works rooted in the French academic tradition that Krøyer was able to examine during his first visit to the Paris Salon. His own training had been similar, which meant he was able to appreciate the picture's subject and the artist's efforts – abortive, if the critics are to be believed – to put his technique at the service of his subject, from the heroine's gaze directed beyond the picture frame, to the omnipresence of cold blues. Nevertheless, Krøyer was certainly disconcerted by this artwork, which was part of a long tradition, and totally remote from contemporary reality. Sensitive as he was to the world of work, as evidenced by his paintings from 1874–1875 depicting the fishermen of Hornbæk and the daily life of the village, he could not but declare his surprise, and even disappointment, in his first letters to his Danish correspondents. Very soon, however, his correspondence revealed the way in which he, having been trained in the 'grand manner', began to analyse these innovations, to understand and appropriate them. Morot's *Medea* perfectly illustrated this process, which Krøyer went on to incorporate into some of his works straight away. Such was the case with his portrayal of *Messalina* (FIG. 7), for which he chose the same model in Rome: Vittoria – 'the woman with the massive neck' was how Merson reproached Morot, in the same 1877 article – whose garments he depicted in cold tones within a setting dominated by yellow and gold.

Dominique Lobstein

CAT. 8 Edmond Lebel
A Trastevere Butcher, Rome, 1874

Although genre scenes – meaning those with an anecdotal or familiar character – were long considered a minor style, they came to occupy an increasingly important place on the walls of official galleries. Before developing into an authentic reflection of contemporary reality in its most intimate aspects, the genre scene endeavoured to continue displaying certain aspects of its creator's academic training. Such was the case with this painting by Edmond Lebel (CAT. 8), which shows a woman in front of a butcher's shop. The painter has transposed his subject to an Italian cityscape and takes characters wearing exotic costumes as his models; this enabled him to touch on the idea of 'fable', so dominant in the text of Félibien, which established the hierarchy of genres. The whole picture is composed, drawn, and painted according to the academic principles taught at the École des Beaux-Arts, making it a kind of intermediate genre: a genre scene that tends towards a history painting.

18. Olivier Merson, 'Salon of 1877. IV', 330.

CAT. 8 Edmond Lebel: *A Trastevere Butcher, Rome*, 1874. Oil on canvas, 98×124 cm. Musée de Picardie, Amiens. M.P.P.222

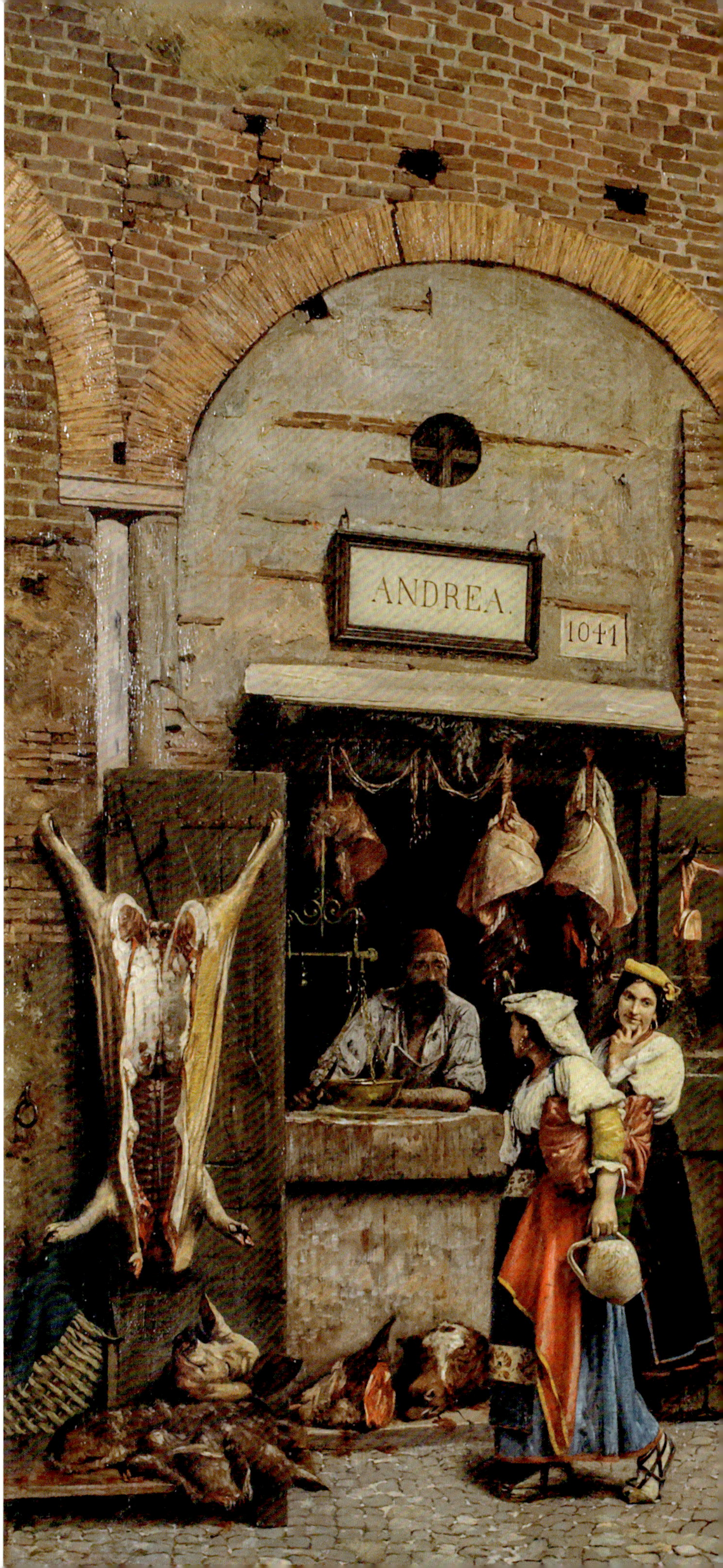

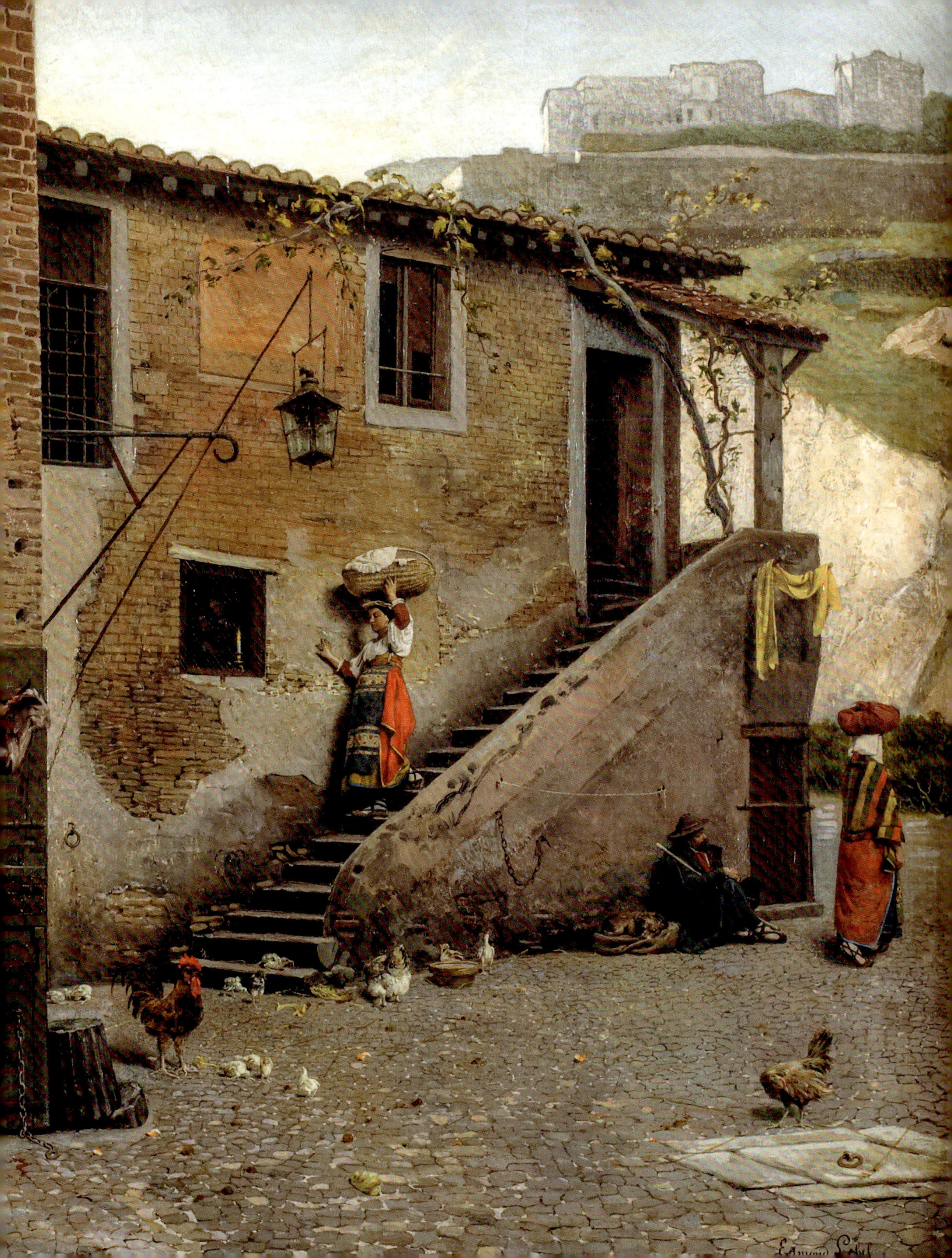

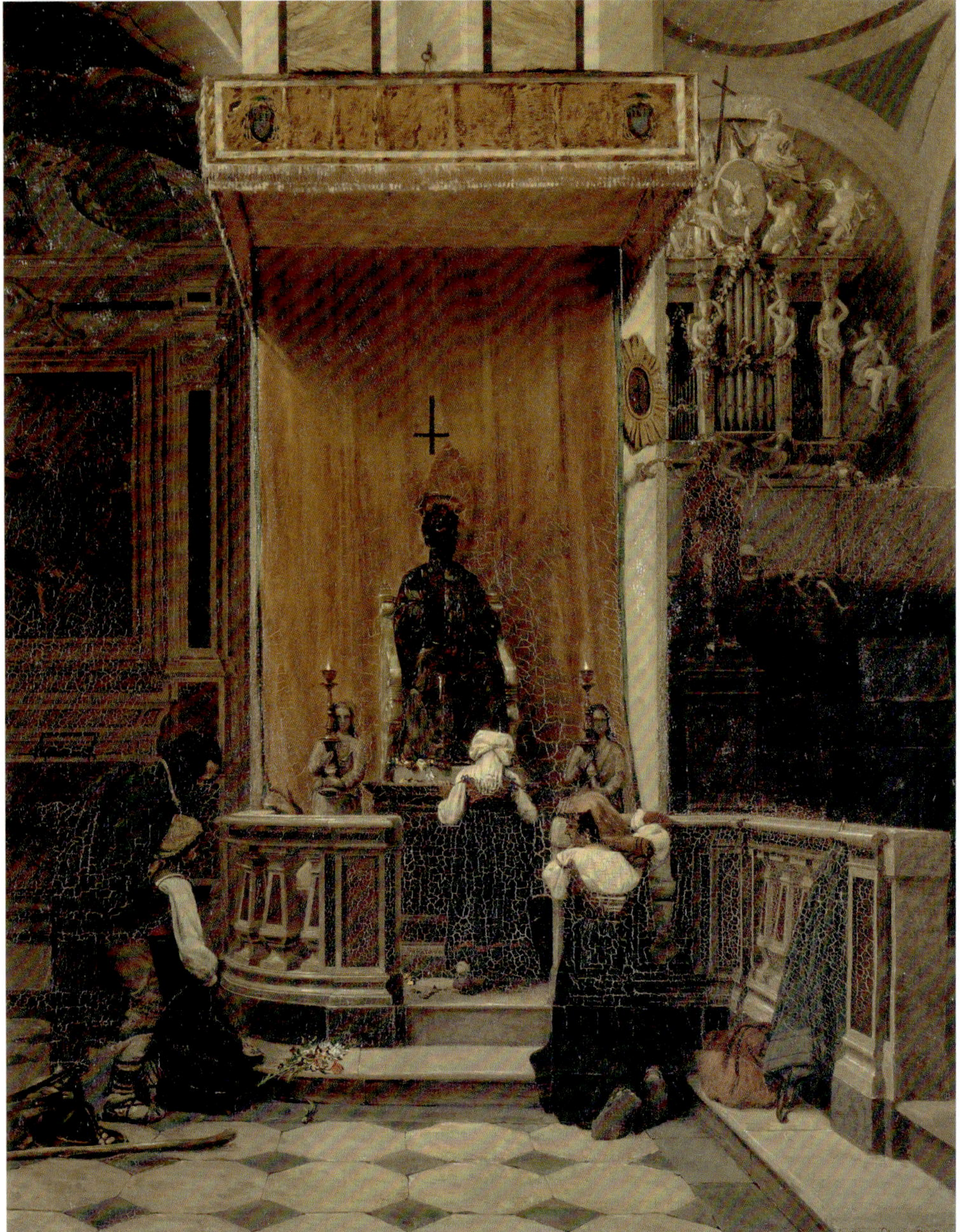

FIG. 8 Edmond Lebel:
A Vow: San Gennaro, Italy, 1872.
Oil on canvas, 94×75 cm.
Musée d'Orsay, Paris. RF 553

Its creator, a pupil of the academic painter Léon Cogniet at the École des Beaux-Arts, made his Salon debut in 1861 with Breton-inspired subjects. In the same year, without even once winning the Prix de Rome, he left for Italy in the company of several fellow students who, while in Rome, became known as the 'Caldarrosti'.[19]

From 1862 onwards, Italian scenes observed in the surroundings of Rome and Naples would dominate the pictures he sent to the Salon. They won him several prizes, such as a silver medal at the 1872 Salon, and a number were purchased by the Beaux-Arts administration. For example, his picture entitled *A Vow: San Gennaro, Italy*,

19. Which may be translated as 'roast chestnuts'.

now in the Musée d'Orsay (FIG. 8), was bought for 3,000 francs from the art dealer Goupil, who had bought it from the painter for 2,000 francs shortly before the exhibition. By adding a religious flavour to a simple genre scene, Lebel was moving a little closer still to the grand manner, a manoeuvre that served him well since his painting was bought and exhibited from 1 January 1874 in the new hanging at the Musée du Luxembourg.

The *Trastevere Butcher* was not so fortunate. Lebel sent a letter to the Beaux-Arts administration asking them to buy his picture, but his request was set aside. The press, horrified by the number of genre scenes in the official galleries, was united in its response to this refusal and so remained very discreet: the longest comment devoted to the work was 'I like Mr Lebel's *Trastevere Butcher*, in which I find the nostalgic charm of personal memories.'[20] The artist had more success in 1877, when he exhibited *A Cardinal, after a Visit to Santa Maria della Pace in Rome, blesses a Family of Pilgrims* (Musée des Beaux Arts, Rouen). Following its showing in Paris, it was exhibited at the 28th exhibition of the Société des Amis des Arts in Rouen, where the museum's curator asked for it to be purchased by the town.

Krøyer saw such works on his regular visits to the Salon but, even during his first stay in Paris, when he would have liked to see greater finish in the works he was viewing (as he told Vermehren), he never made allusion to any of them in his own paintings. He had already decided he would avoid addressing purely invented subjects that were too far removed from those offered by contemporary society; he preferred them to be bound by time-honoured creative principles. An ideal counterpoint to Lebel's conceptions, which revealed the path Krøyer was pursuing, is the small sketch *In a Cellar in Concarneau* (CAT. 31): the figure in the background, wearing contemporary costume, is busy syphoning beer from a barrel, while the upper part of the foreground is full of butchers' carcasses waiting to be cut up – and they are far more impressive than those of Lebel.

Dominique Lobstein

CAT. 9 Jules Breton
The Gleaner, 1877

With the advent of the Realist generation, said to be around 1830, the peasant world found a place in the official galleries, though not without difficulty. Later in the century, such subjects would serve to illustrate what survived of a rural world that was already disappearing in the face of pervasive industrialisation, which was emptying the countryside; at the same time, towns and industrial centres were relentlessly expanding, often to the detriment of those who had newly arrived in them. These depictions of a golden age of the rural world attracted very few admirers as yet. However, after the defeat of France at the hands of Prussia in 1870, and the nation's economic collapse, a new industrial and commercial middle class appeared, which looked to artists who were capable of pursuing Realism but also, henceforth, idealising a rural world that by then had almost disappeared.

Jules Breton, who was from Courrières in the Pas-de-Calais in northern France, spent his childhood in an environment that was still rural but was rapidly being transformed by the mining industry and by metal-working and textile production. He had trained in his native region and in Belgium, and on arriving in Paris became the pupil of Jean-Auguste Dominique Ingres and Horace Vernet. From these supporters of academicism, he would preserve a sense of design and form, but he applied them to quite different subjects from those of his masters. Idealising the peasant world, and protective of moral and fraternal traditions, he very soon made these the exclusive subjects of his pictures. He drew his inspiration from the daily lives

20. Merson, 'Le Salon de 1874. XI', 23.

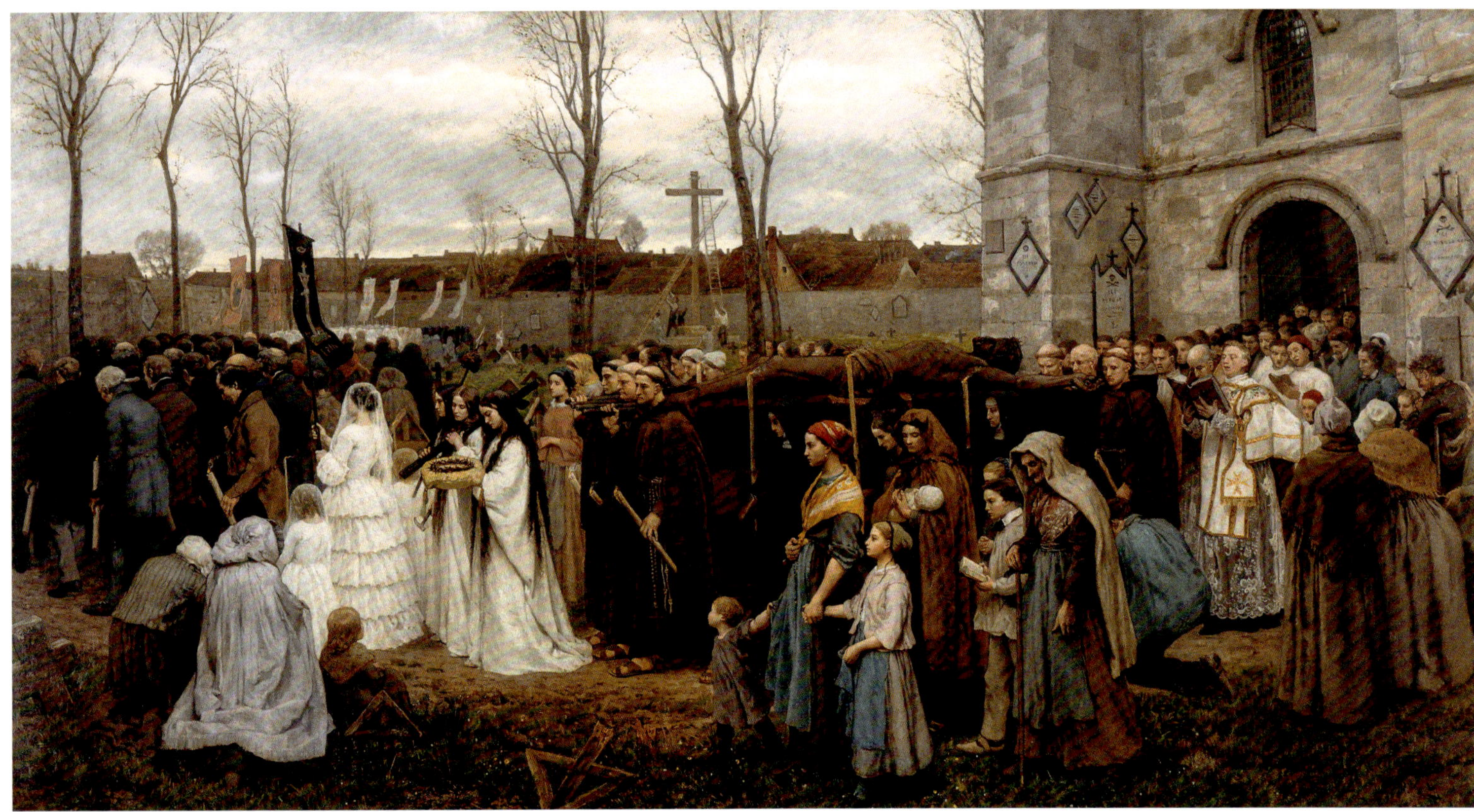

FIG. 9 Jules Breton: *Erecting a Calvary*, 1858. Oil on canvas, 135×250 cm. Palais des Beaux-Arts, Lille. P.1659

of peasants in his native village, not only painting their work in the fields but also revealing their expressions of deep faith (FIG. 9). As a painter of humble people, he often portrayed women burdened by the most thankless work, imbuing them with an unparalleled strength and presence. This was highlighted by critics, who compared some of his female peasants to caryatids, thus bringing together in a single word the sculptures of the Parthenon and the contemporary figures in Breton's paintings.

This *Gleaner* (CAT. 9), the woman who followed behind the reapers at nightfall to gather up stray ears of wheat, is portrayed from the front, in a standing position seen from a low angle, and in a narrow frame. She is an ideal example of Breton's transposition of these semi-divine classical figures. This picture, exhibit no. 302 at the 1877 Salon, attracted many admiring comments and even the satirical magazine the *Journal amusant* showed some respect for it:

> What a masterly figure is this *Gleaner*. An ideal embodied in reality. With her superb silhouette, this beautiful girl, so vividly portrayed, is painted with a sureness of touch that speaks of a master who has arrived at the pinnacle of his art. At the same time, one feels there is a poet in this painter. If the two words did not clash with one another, I would say that Jules Breton's *Gleaner* is a rustic Muse.[21]

This was yet another mark of admiration, linking the painter's work to the finest creations of antiquity.

Another important review points to the kinship between Millet and Breton: 'M. Jules Breton, with Millet,

21. Véron, 'Chronique parisienne. Le Salon de 1877', 2.

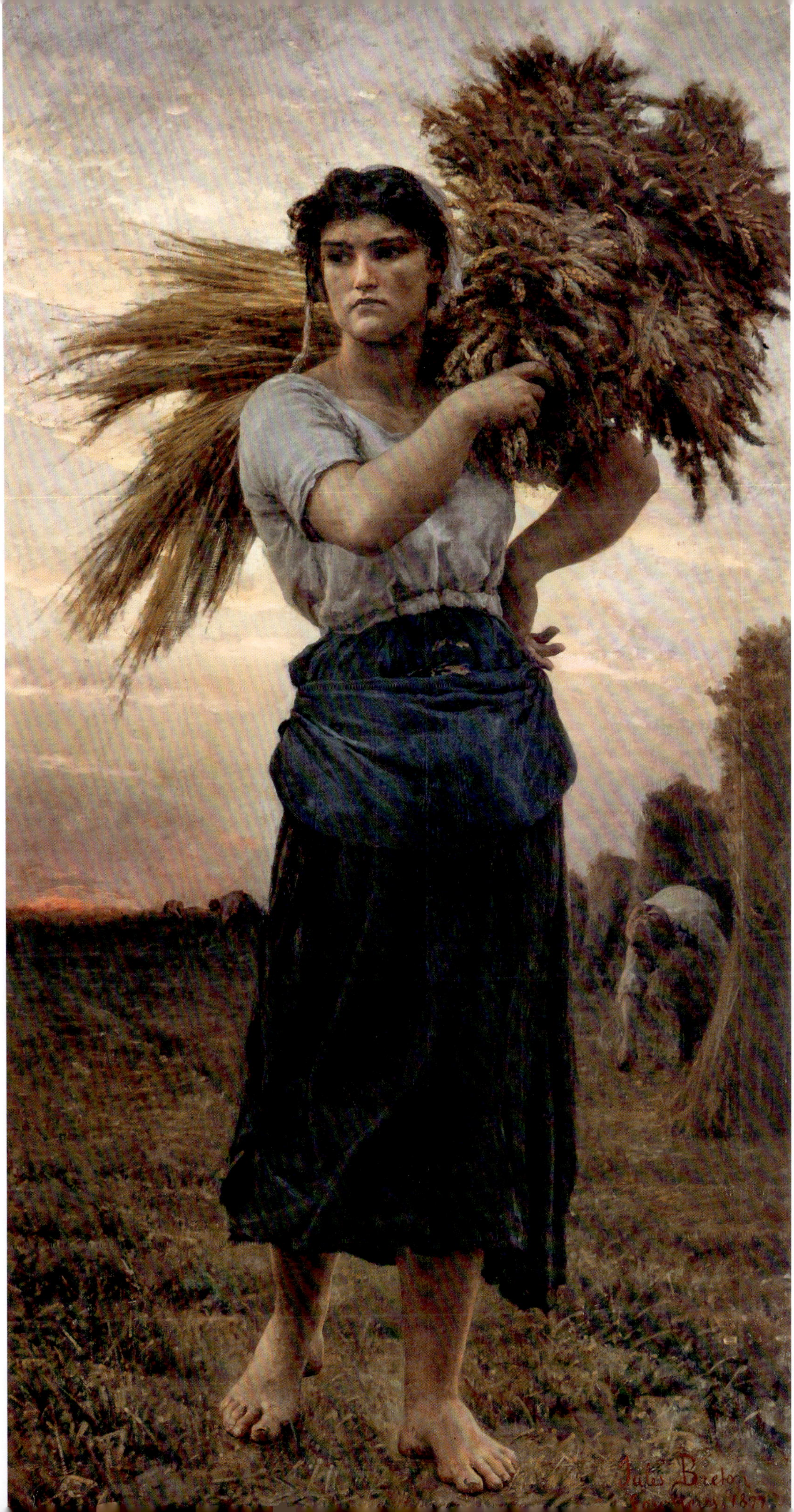

CAT. 9 Jules Breton: *The Gleaner*, 1877. Oil on canvas, 230×124.7 cm. Musée des Beaux-Arts, Arras, deposit from Musée d'Orsay. RF 191

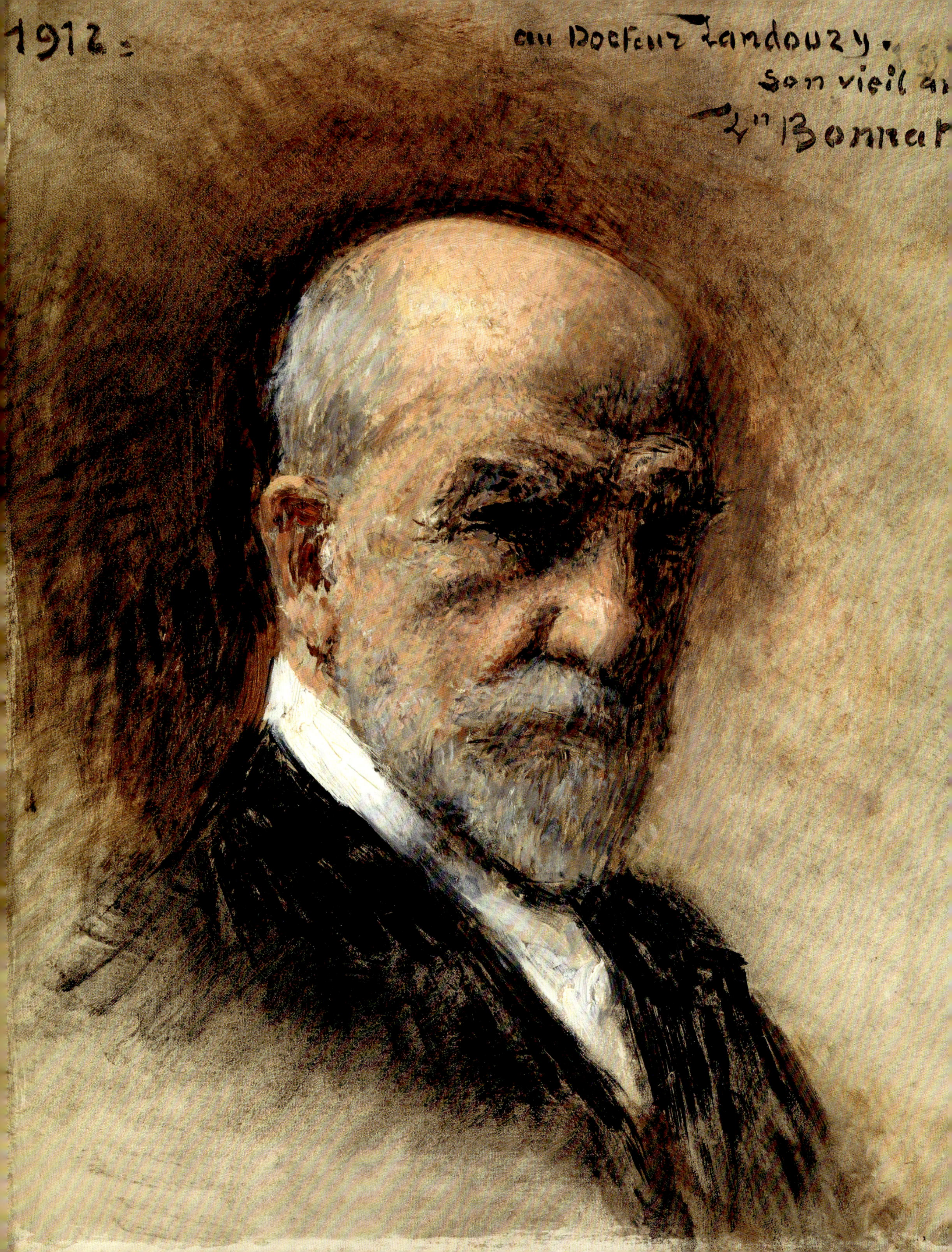
1912
au Docteur Landouzy.
son vieil

is a painter inspired by the life of the fields; but in Millet's work, nature crushes man; in Breton's work, man is of equal stature to nature.'[22]

Following the Danish defeat of 1864, when the country was invaded by Prussia and suffered an economic collapse very similar to the one that France would shortly experience, a comparable new and enriched middle class appeared and set the economy to rights. This new social class also wished to have artists available who were capable of painting the vanishing and apparently happier pre-industrial era. Krøyer was among this elect and, like Jules Breton, offered his patrons the vision they were expecting of a hard, laborious past but one in which the links between people and their connections with the soil – or the sea – seemed to be more harmonious.
Dominique Lobstein

CAT. 10 Léon Bonnat
Self Portrait, 1912

Léon Joseph Florentin Bonnat was born in Bayonne, in southwest France, in 1833. He received his early artistic training from 1846 to 1853, in Madrid, where his father had opened a bookshop. When his father died, he returned to France and moved to Paris where, in 1854, he became a pupil of Léon Cogniet at the École des Beaux-Arts. He entered the competition for the Prix de Rome but was unsuccessful and subsequently turned to the Salon where, from 1857, his knowledge of the Golden Age of Spanish art and his palette of brown tones drew the attention of art lovers. Gradually abandoning the 'grand manner', he increasingly devoted himself to portraits – and to self-portraits, which he continued to paint throughout his life, as illustrated by the 1912 self-portrait exhibited here (CAT. 10) – becoming the official painter of many key figures, including artists and politicians. The trio of his most spectacular successes, which would dictate his future, were portraits of the actress *Madame Pasca*, in 1874 (FIG. 10); of *Adolphe Thiers*, in 1876 (ILL. 6); and of *Victor Hugo*, in 1879 (FIG. 11).

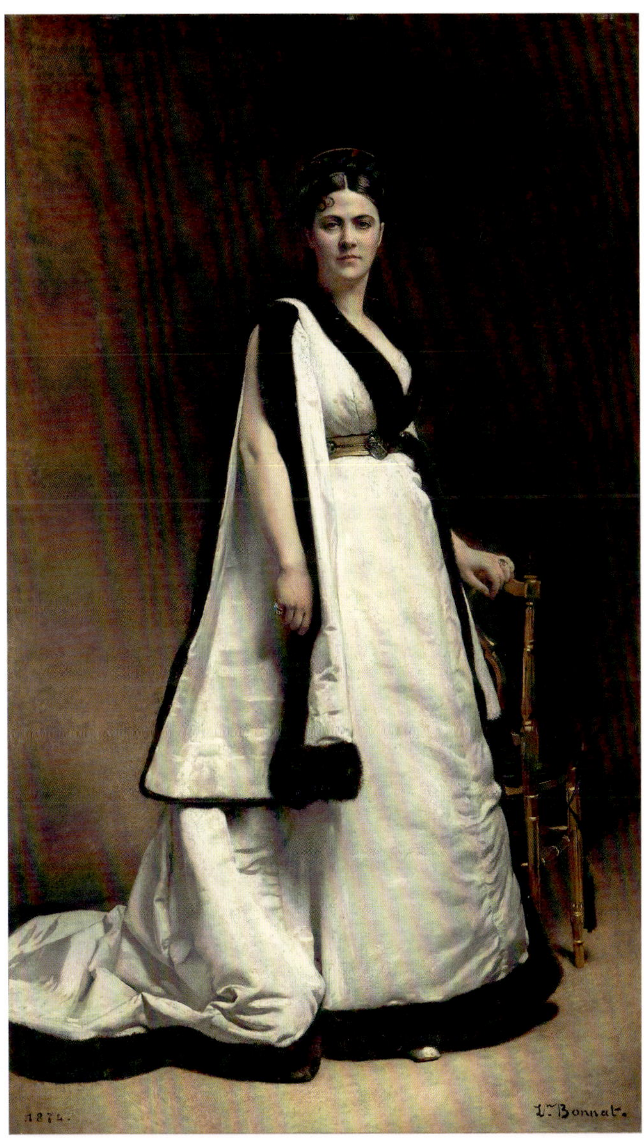

FIG. 10 Léon Bonnat: *Madame Pasca*. 1874. Oil on canvas, 222.5×132 cm. Musée d'Orsay, Paris. 9168

22. Descubes, 'Le Salon de 1877 (suite)', 231.

CAT. 10 Léon Bonnat: *Self Portrait*, 1912. Oil on canvas, 50×41 cm. Bibliothèque de l'Académie nationale de Médecine, Paris. ART 425

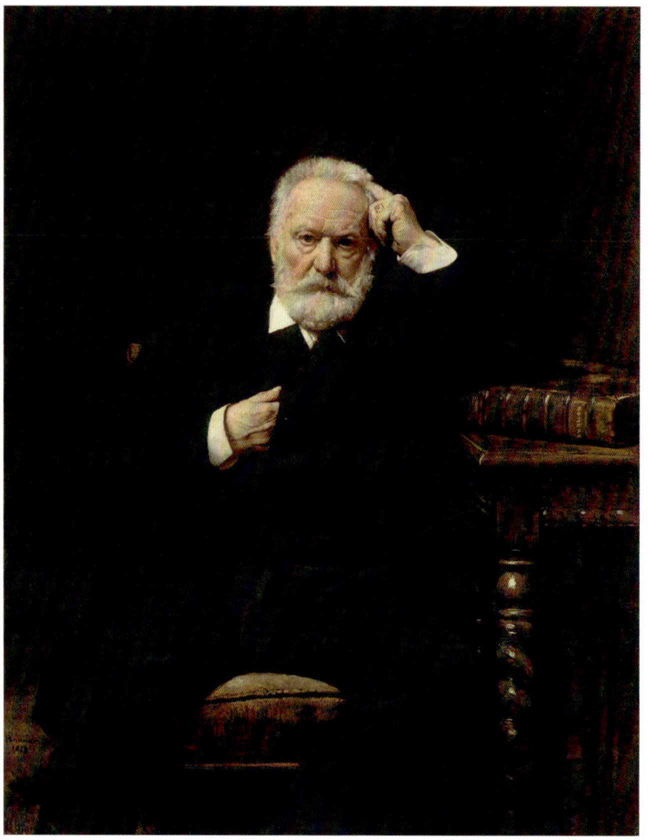

FIG. 11 Léon Bonnat: *Victor Hugo*, 1879. Oil on canvas, 137 × 109 cm. Le château de Versailles. MV 7383

it was due to Bonnat that his *Daphnis and Chloë* (CAT. 24) was exhibited next to Henner's *Eglogue* at the 1879 Salon:

> I was very lucky, or unlucky as one might now say, to have my picture of *Daphnis and Chloë* hung next to it [Henner's picture]. Although my painting is by no means outstanding, it is quite clearly solid and robust, but next [to his] it becomes so dry, so hard, so displeasing in its tones, above all there is a lack of simplicity, too many small shapes. But it is really instructive for me to be able to make this comparison, and that is worth more than if my picture had been hung in impoverished surroundings and appeared good and (perhaps) been sold.[23]

Relations between the French master and his Danish pupil did not stop there, and Krøyer paid many tributes to his skill and to the way in which Bonnat had been able to open his eyes to French art.
Dominique Lobstein

Having achieved success as an official painter, he soon wished to become a teacher. Before obtaining the rewards that would be opened to him by the Académie des Beaux-Arts and the École, where he ran a studio from 1888, he opened up his private studio near the Place Pigalle. It was here that he received several Scandinavian artists, Krøyer among them, from 1877 onwards. Admired by his pupils more for his teaching than for his painting skills, he encouraged them but did not omit to take them to task, sometimes violently. He was, however, supportive, particularly in his role as an established member of the Salon jury, making sure that his pupils were well received and their works well positioned. According to Krøyer himself,

23. Draft for a letter: PSK to Frederik Vermehren, Cernay-la-Ville, 20 May 1879. PSK Archive 58.

CAT. 11 Léon Bonnat
Léon Labbé, 1889

Like all famous portrait painters, Bonnat offered his models a choice between three sizes, which rose in price the larger they were. The resulting picture could be a face, a head and shoulders, or a full-length portrait. The next choice involved the surroundings and the position to be adopted, and once agreement was reached, the sittings could begin.

Léon Labbé (CAT. 11) obtained his medical doctorate in 1861, then became a professor of medicine (*agrégé*) in 1863 and a hospital surgeon in 1864. His brilliant career in various Paris hospitals was crowned with successes, and he published many scientific works. He continued his ceaseless activity until 1914, when at the age of 82

CAT. 11 Léon Bonnat: *Léon Labbé*, 1889. Oil on canvas, 70 × 58 cm. Bibliothèque de l'Académie nationale de Médecine, Paris. ART 305

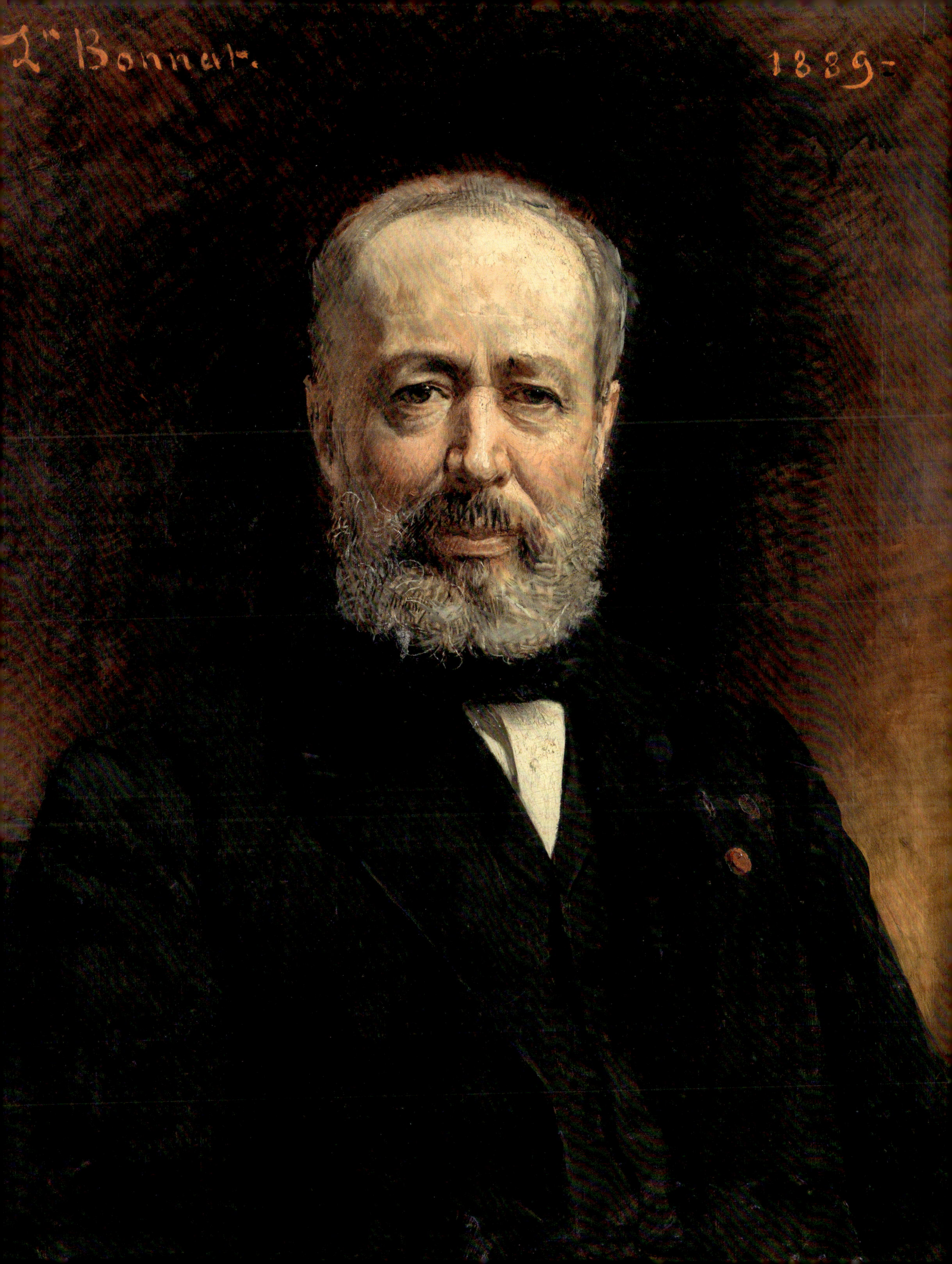

Ln Bonnat. 1889.

he asked to be appointed inspector of hospitals and ambulances, and was rewarded with various honours, as is clearly shown in Bonnat's portrait by the red rosette of the Légion d'honneur on his jacket. The honours continued to pour in with elections to important posts, such as president of the Académie de Médecine for 1909.

In addition to his commitment to medicine, he entered politics around 1890, becoming a member of the Groupe Républicain and a constant participant in all sections dealing with social matters, as well as introducing bills designed to protect public health.

This portrait was exhibited at the 1895 Cercle artistique et littéraire, held at Rue Volney, in Paris, prior to the opening of the Salon. It was heralded as a remarkable work, despite the fact that art lovers considered there to be too much use of impasto. This criticism was particularly aimed at the model's face and might equally be applied to the work in some of Krøyer's portraits, such as *Alfred Benzon's Two Daughters* (1897, Faenoe Estate, Denmark).
Dominique Lobstein

CAT. 12 Jules Bastien-Lepage
The Song of Spring, 1874

CAT. 13 Jules Bastien-Lepage
Portrait of the Artist's Mother, 1877

CAT. 14 Jules Bastien-Lepage
Portrait of the Artist's Father, 1877

Jules Bastien-Lepage was born in 1848 at Damvillers, a village of the Meuse department in eastern France, into a family of smallholders and farmers. After attending school in his village, he continued his studies in Verdun, before going to Paris in 1867. His ambition was to become a painter, but he had a difficult start – until he passed the competitive examination of the École des Beaux-Arts with flying colours in October 1868 and entered the studio of Alexandre Cabanel. A studious pupil, he was rewarded with success on several occasions and decided to enter his work for the official art event, the Salon, to which he was admitted in 1870 with his portrait of a fellow Beaux-Arts student. This was the future architect Joseph Gustave Lemarchand (Musée Bastien-Lepage, Montmédy), who was unknown to critics. There was no Salon in 1871 and Bastien-Lepage did not exhibit in 1872, but his name reappeared in 1873, linked to a picture entitled *Spring* (location unknown), of which nothing is known. The following year, in 1874, he exhibited the *Portrait of the Artist's grandfather* (FIG. 12), appraised as 'of extraordinary accomplishment and startling in its truthfulness.'[24] In the same year, he presented *The Song of Spring* (CAT. 12), which was judged 'very inferior to his portrait.'[25] The two works nevertheless caught the attention of both the critics and the Beaux-Arts administration; the artist was awarded a third-class medal and his picture was purchased by the state.

From that moment on, Bastien-Lepage's success was assured with, for example, in 1875, his painting *The Little Communicant* (CAT. 36) and his portrait of Mr Simon Hayem (FIG. 27), which earned him a second-class medal. The rules stipulated that the winners of an award which was at least equivalent to a second-class medal were exempted from presenting their works to a jury, since they were automatically accepted. As a result of this prerogative, but oblivious of another paragraph in these same regulations which limited the number of works that could be sent to just two, Bastien-Lepage dispatched three portraits to the 1877 Salon: that of *Lady L...* (location unknown) and those of his parents (CAT. 13 and 14). The jury asked him to withdraw one of his pictures but he refused to comply. Instead, he sewed together the paintings depicting his father and mother and did a little touch-

24. Élie de Mont [Élizé Louis de Montagnac], *Les Beaux-Arts au palais de l'Industrie. Exposition 1874*, 8.

25. Élie de Mont, 8.

CAT. 12 Jules Bastien-Lepage: *The Song of Spring*, 1874. Oil on canvas, 149 × 101 cm. Musée de la Princerie, Verdun. 81.1.87

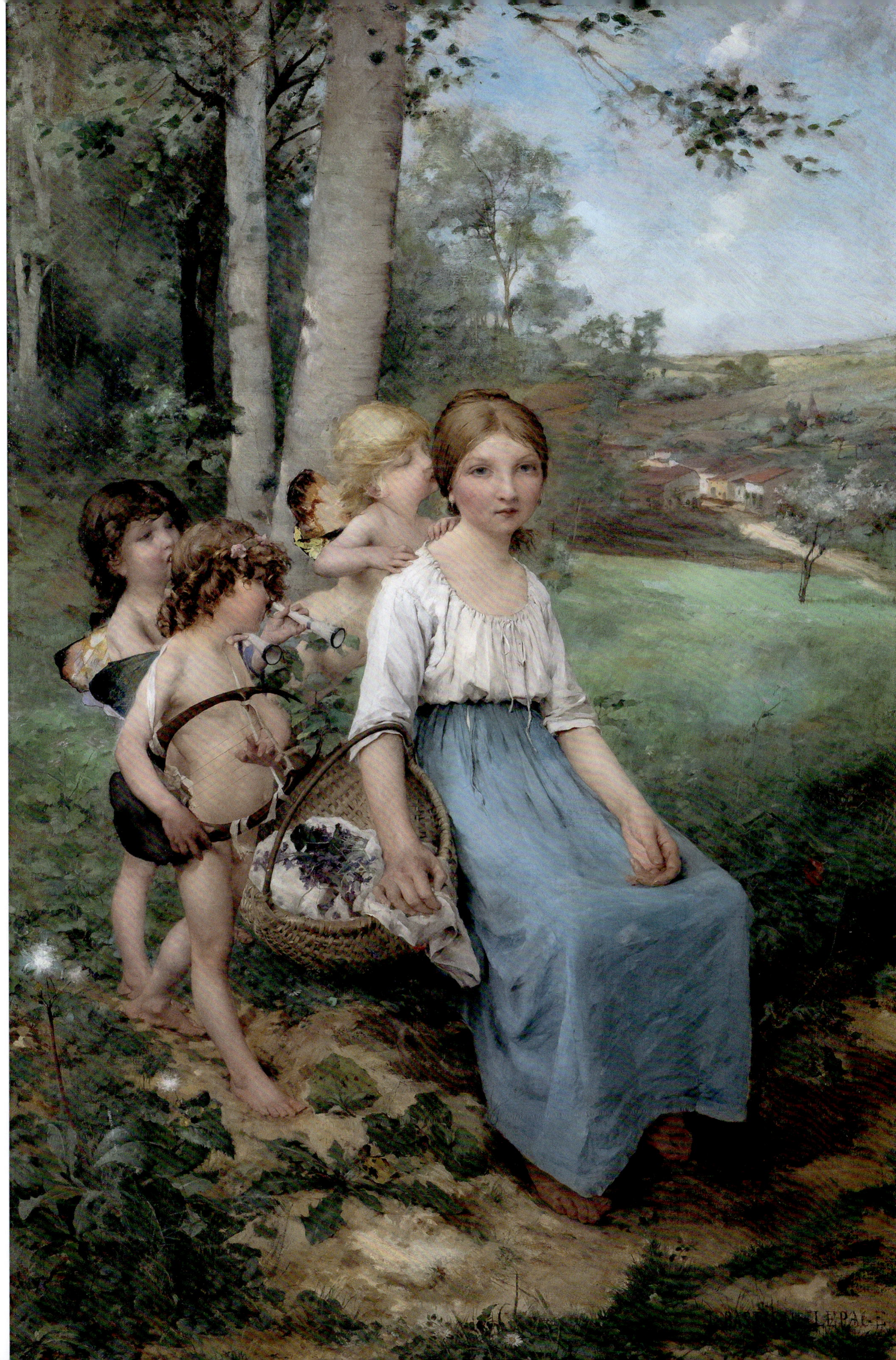

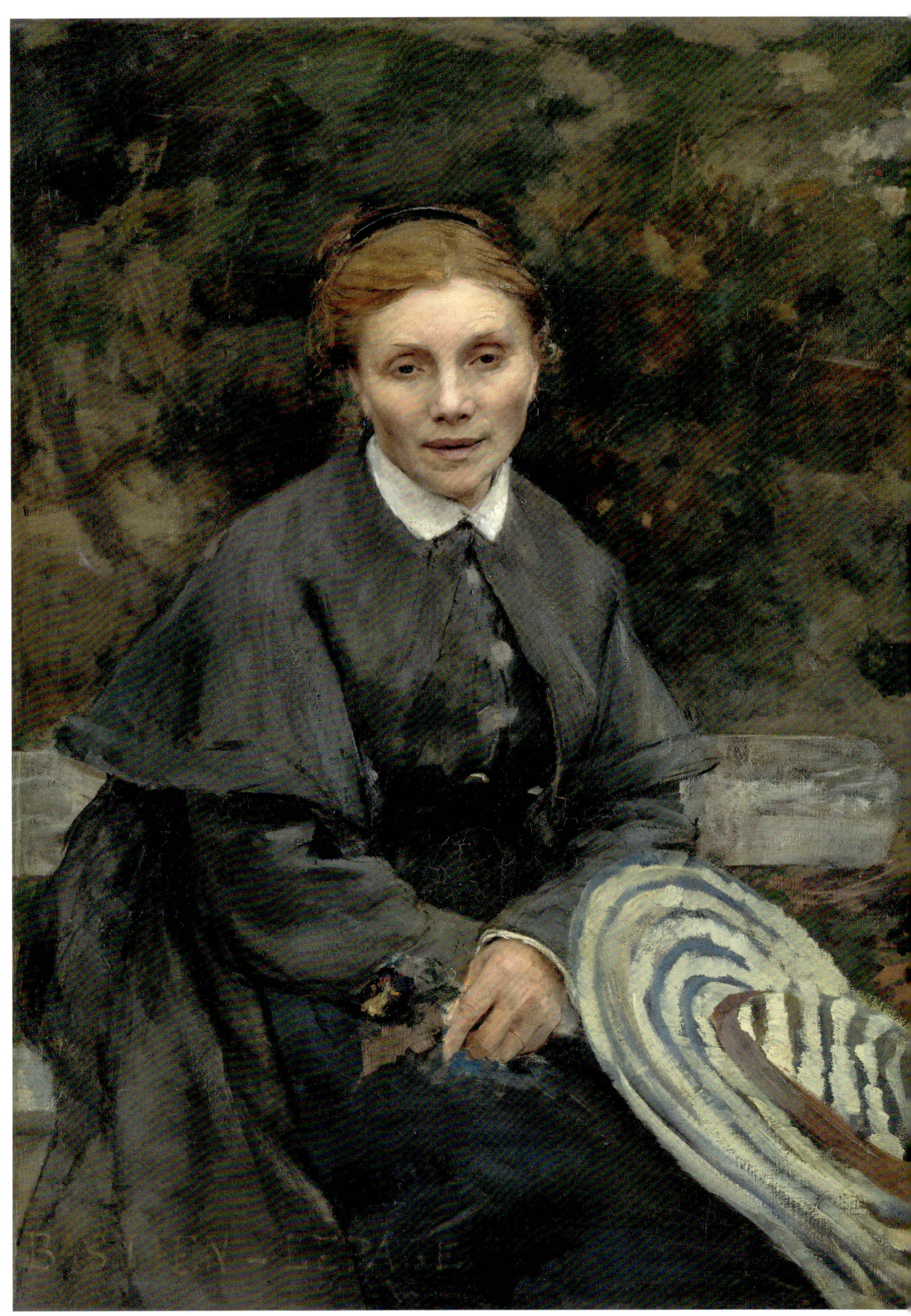

CAT. 13 Jules Bastien-Lepage: *Portrait of the Artist's Mother*, 1877. Oil on canvas, 103×77 cm. Musée des Beaux-Arts, Nice, deposit from Musée d'Orsay. RF 3985

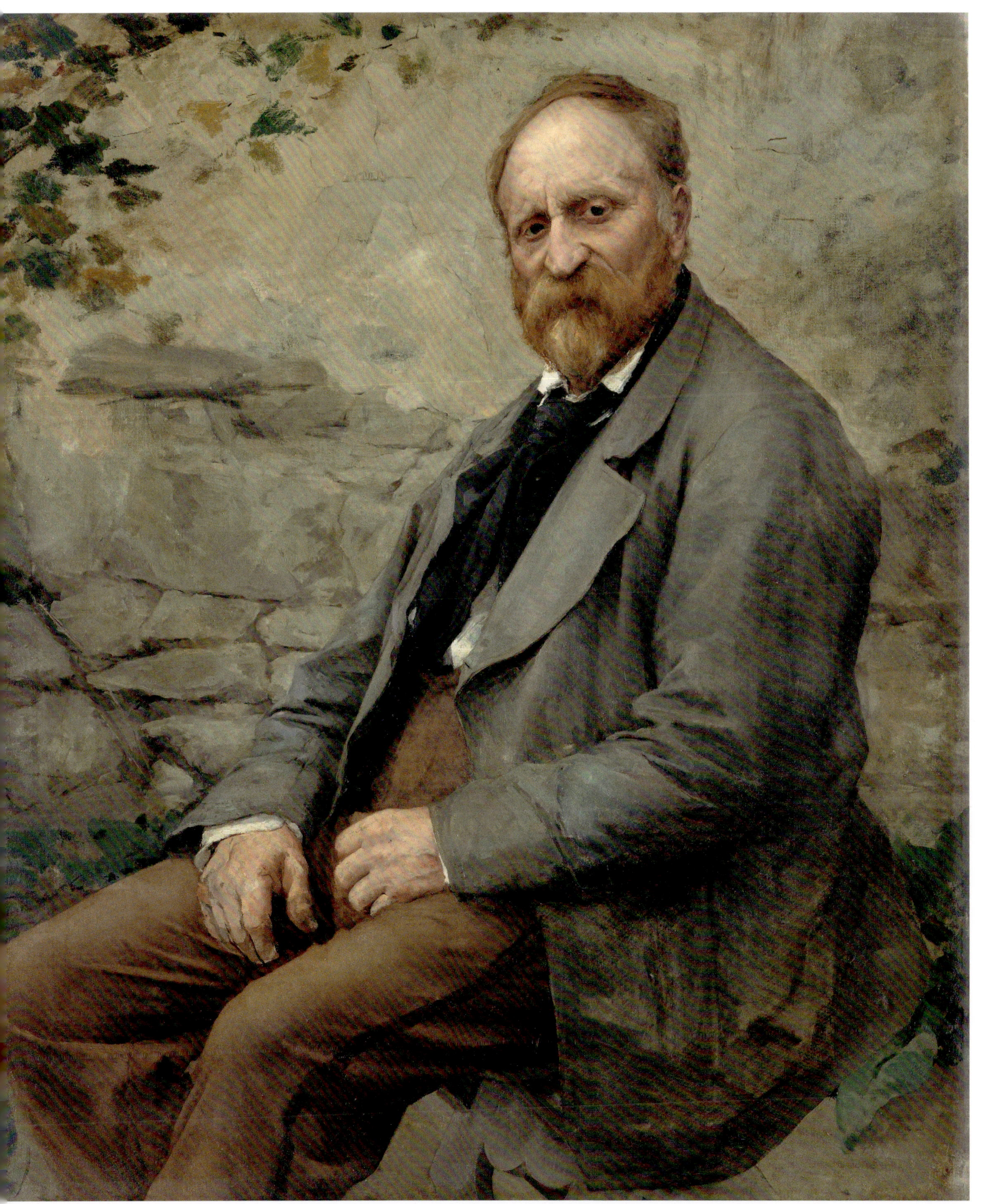

CAT. 14 Jules Bastien-Lepage: *Portrait of the Artist's Father*, 1877. Oil on canvas, 106×90 cm. Musée des Beaux-Arts, Nice, deposit from Musée d'Orsay. RF 3986

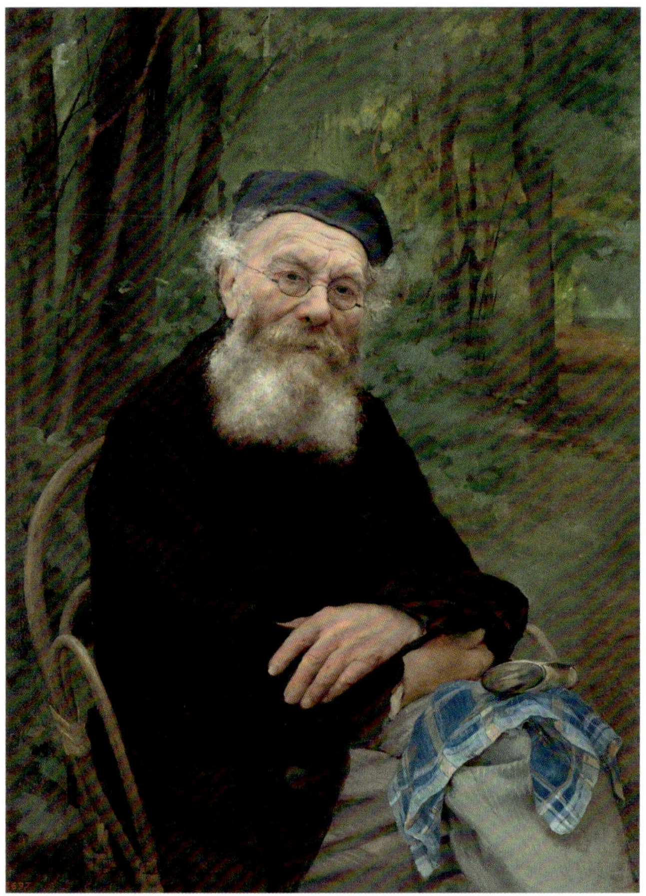

FIG. 12 Jules Bastien-Lepage: *Portrait of the Artist's Grandfather*, 1874. Oil on canvas, 103×77 cm. Musée des Beaux-Arts Jules Chéret, Nice, deposit from Musée d'Orsay. RF 3984 A

ing up to blend the surroundings of the two figures, which enabled him to present just two works. The format of the second was rather unusual and it gained approval from all the critics. Paul Mantz, for example, wrote:

> We know neither the father nor mother of M. Bastien-Lepage; but we declare them to be good likenesses because the painter has portrayed them in such a lifelike way, in their humble everyday attire and under the authentic rays of a provincial sun. Nothing is hidden; nothing is embellished, so the lips and the eyes are full of life. It is when he paints with such utter candour that M. Bastien-Lepage acquires the naïve tone of the masters he loves.[26]

Krøyer saw these pictures on the walls of the Palais des Champs-Elysées and was immediately attracted by the offerings of his young fellow artist, as he was to state on several occasions. During his second stay in Paris, for example, he mentioned Bastien-Lepage three times in a letter he addressed to Vermehren on 20 May, which he began by writing 'Number one in the Salon is the Potato Gatherers [*October*, FIG. 40] by Bastien-Lepage,' a phrase he repeated in an almost identical manner a little further on in his letter. Summarising his comments at the end of the letter, he once again cites Bastien-Lepage among his favourite artists, together with Léon Bonnat, who that year painted the portraits of *Adolphe Thiers* (ILL. 6), Élie Delaunay, and Albert Besnard.
Dominique Lobstein

CAT. 15 Ludovic Napoléon Lepic
Berck Beach (Pas-de-Calais), around 1877

The town of Berck is situated in the Pas-de-Calais department of the Hauts-de-France region. It was initially a fishing port, before becoming a seaside resort famous for its exceptionally long beach. Its reputation grew under the Second Empire, when the therapeutic benefits of sea-bathing for the treatment of tuberculosis were discovered; its first hospital was opened by Empress Eugénie and her son, the Prince Imperial, in 1869. Shortly afterwards, artists began to arrive to paint the first marine views – like Édouard Manet, in 1873 (Wallraf-Richartz Museum, Cologne). He set a precedent, and his fellow artists joined him in making these views a subject for Salon pictures from 1874 onwards. By this date, the

26. Mantz, 'Le Salon. IV', 27 May 1877, [2].

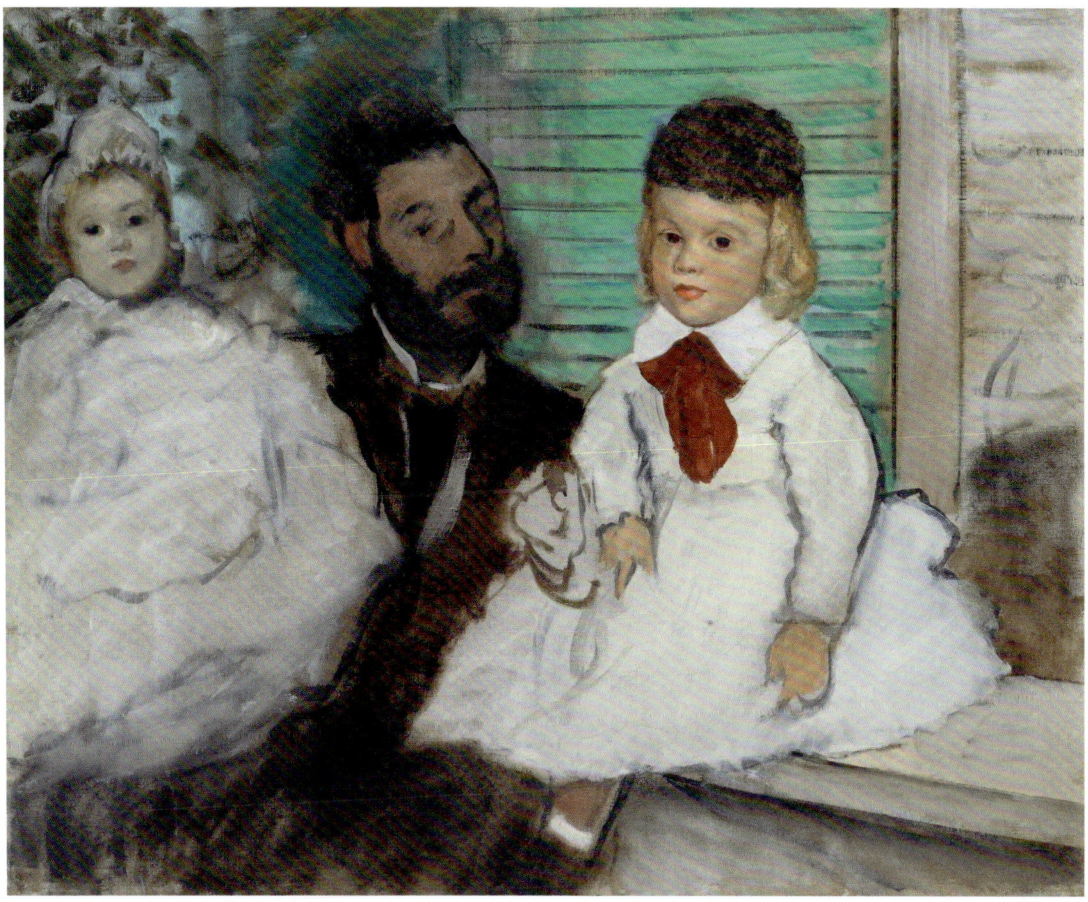

FIG. 13 Edgar Degas: *Ludovic Lepic and his Daughters*, 1870. Oil on canvas, 65×81 cm. Kunsthaus Zürich, deposit from Sammlung Emil Bührle, Zürich. 36

name of Berck had become linked to painters like Louis Latouche and Louis Lemaire, while the architect Émile Lavezzari was presenting plans for a new hospital. At the same time, Louis Latouche took part in the first Impressionist event, for which he painted a *Church Tower at Berck (Pas-de-Calais)* (location unknown) and a *Beach, Low Tide at Berck (Pas-de-Calais)* (location unknown), which the critic Etienne Carjat considered to be 'of excellent colour and striking realism.'[27]

Virtually every year, the name of this location was to be found in the official art galleries, and it also found its way onto the walls of the second Impressionist exhibition, where Ludovic Napoléon Lepic had several pictures on display: *Boats on Berck Beach* (location unknown), *Berck Beach (Pas-de-Calais)* (location unknown), and *The Christ of Berck Beach* (location unknown). These were mentioned by the journalist Alexandre Pothey in an article where he revealed the painter's method of working: 'Each year, M. Ludovic Lepic spends five or six months on the deck of a boat, where he learns about the lives of seafarers. The *plein air* studies he brings back from these excursions are highly distinctive.'[28] Although he was a close friend of Edgar Degas (FIG. 13), who was to paint him on several occasions, his relationship with Impressionist circles ceased at this date. From then on, he broke free of Impressionist events and turned to the official Salon, while at the same time hosting an artists' colony which he attracted to Berck. The titles of the pictures he sent to the

27. Carjat, 'L'Exposition du boulevard des Capucines', 3.

28. Pothey, 'Chronique', 3.

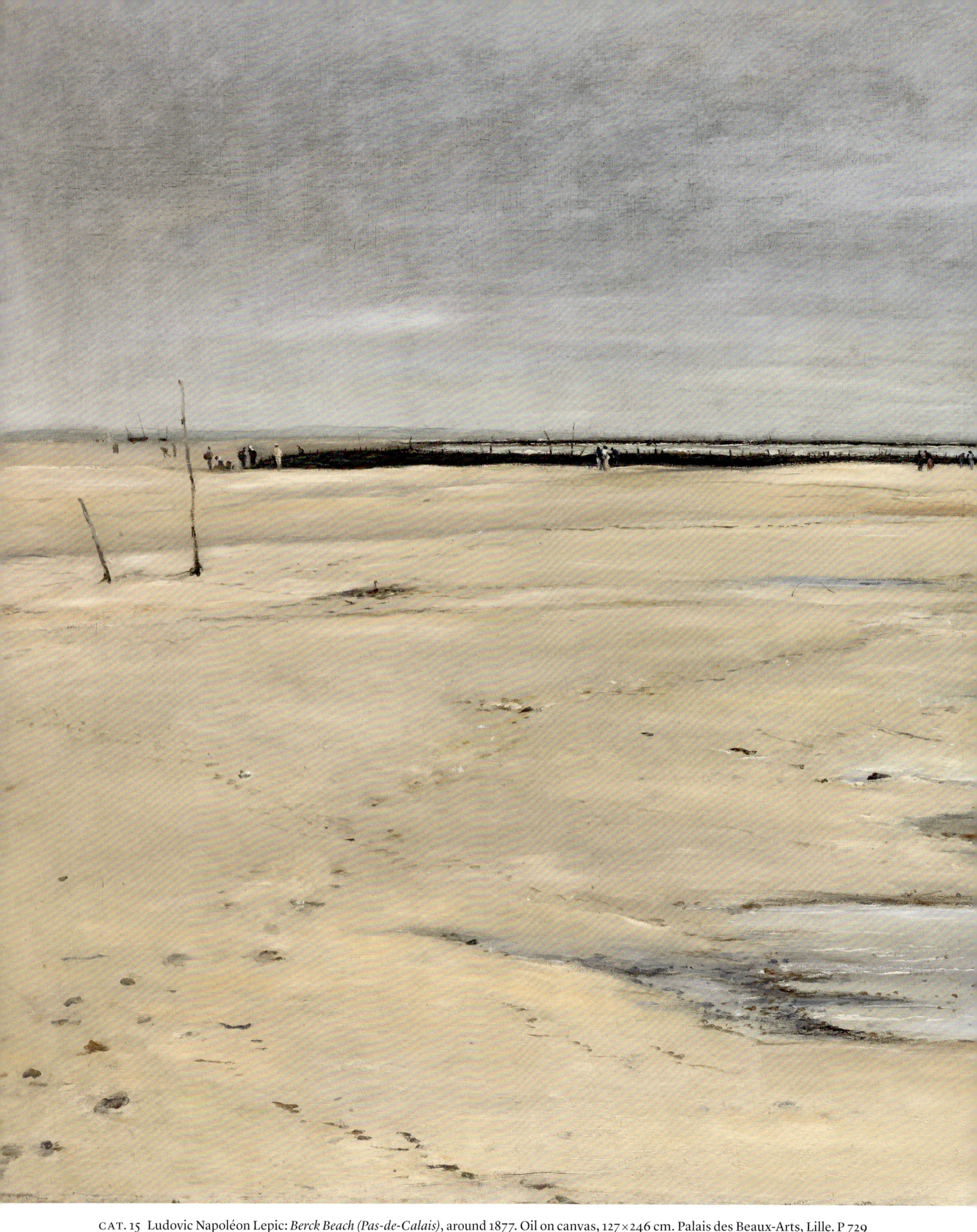

CAT. 15 Ludovic Napoléon Lepic: *Berck Beach (Pas-de-Calais)*, around 1877. Oil on canvas, 127×246 cm. Palais des Beaux-Arts, Lille. P 729

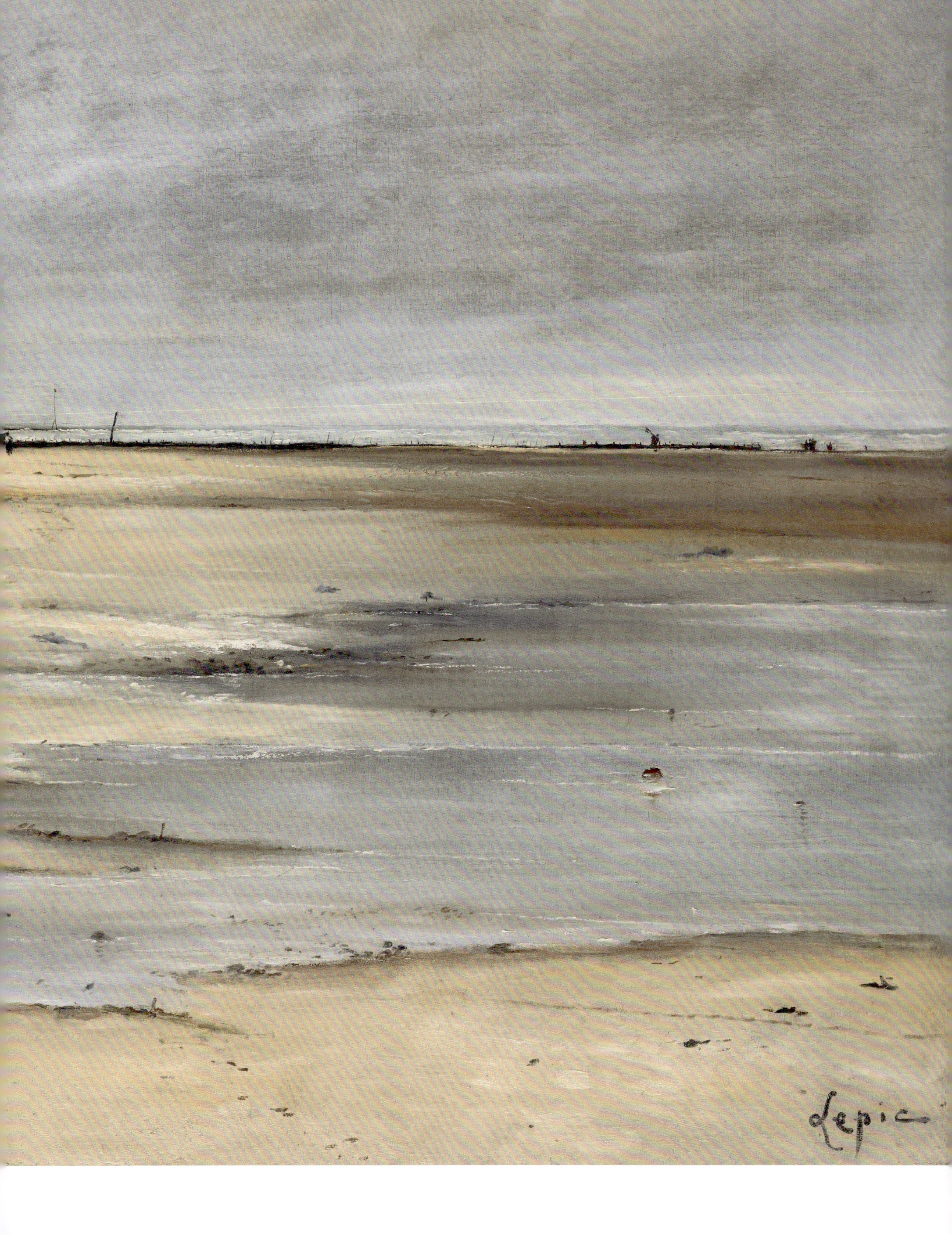
Lepic

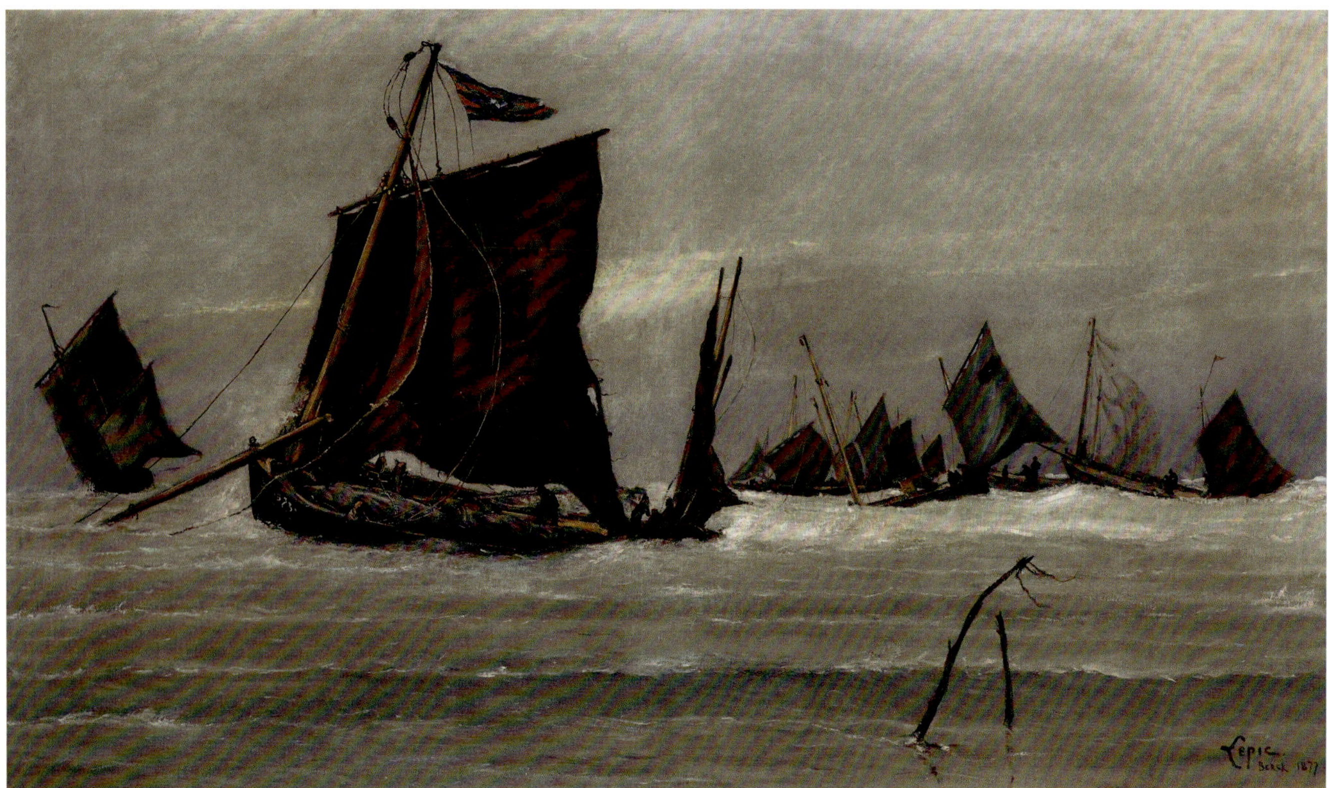

FIG. 14 Ludovic Napoléon Lepic: *Fishing Boats Returning to Berck (Pas-de-Calais)*, around 1877. Oil on canvas, 127×246 cm. Palais des Beaux-Arts, Lille. P 730

Palais des Champs-Elysées were often vague and insufficiently described by critics, who showed precious little interest in the artist, making it impossible to attribute the picture exhibited (CAT. 15) to one of the annual events that took place in the resort. It would also have been difficult to date if it had not been discreetly offered by the artist to the Lille Museum where it was deposited, together with a *Fishing Boats Returning to Berck (Pas-de-Calais)* (FIG. 14), under the pseudonym of Van der Hoost.

Ludovic Napoléon Lepic's name does not appear in Krøyer's correspondence, although the Dane had ample opportunity to view his works at the Salon. Neither was Lepic among the artists whom Krøyer recruited for his 1888 exhibition. Lepic's death, in 1889, meant that the two men were never able to meet – though any meeting would probably have been facilitated by the warm relations they both had with Albert Besnard. Nevertheless, it is highly likely that Krøyer knew Berck in the years between 1895 and 1901, a period during which Besnard often stayed in the resort with his family, initially to obtain treatment for his youngest son and, subsequently, to carry out the decoration (preserved *in situ*) of the Saint Elizabeth of Hungary chapel in the Cazin-Perrochaud hospital. It is even possible that Krøyer may have visited this place which, out of everywhere he visited in France, was most likely to remind him of Skagen with its vast beach and the changing light of its skies.

Dominique Lobstein

CAT. 16 Émile Barau
Cottages in the Dunes at Skagen (Denmark), 1880

The French painter Émile Barau was among the first artists to exhibit a scene from Skagen at the Salon des Artistes français in Paris, presenting *Cottages in the Dunes at Skagen (Denmark)* (CAT. 16). When it was exhibited in 1880, it was simply called *Cottages in the Dunes*, meaning that the audience had no way of knowing that the subject was Skagen.[29] At the same Salon, the Swedish artist Wilhelm von Gegerfelt exhibited the work *Skagen Beach* (unknown location), making him the first to explicitly mention Skagen to a French audience.[30]

Krøyer visited Skagen for the first time in 1882, so he would have been able to see Barau's painting at the Salon in Paris two years before seeing the real thing himself. Krøyer always spent several days viewing the Salon's many works with great thoroughness, so he would certainly have seen the work, even though he makes no mention of it in his letters home.

Barau was born in Reims as the son of a wealthy cork manufacturer, and his family supported his choice to become a painter. He worked in the family business until his father's death in 1872 and then studied under the Austrian painter Eugen Jettel and then Jean-Léon Gérôme at the École nationale des Beaux-Arts in Paris.[31] He painted landscapes, including from his home region of Reims, several examples of which can now be found in the collection of the Musée des Beaux-Arts in Reims. In his own day, he was represented at a few French museums, including the Musée du Luxembourg in Paris and the Musée des Beaux-Arts de Tours, and he exhibited at Galerie Georges Petit in 1889 (*Exposition des 33*) and 1890 (*Exposition internationale de Peinture*), on the latter occasion together with Krøyer, among others. In 1888, Barau also exhibited three works at the French art exhibition in Copenhagen.

Upon completing his studies, Barau set out for the Netherlands and Denmark to paint. In Skagen, he signed the guest book at Brøndums Hotel on 28 July 1879.[32] Michael Ancher noted about Barau's visit that he came there as a pupil of Gegerfelt's, and that he had a 'fine sensibility and colour'.[33] A passionate hunter, Michael Ancher also noted that 'we went hunting, mostly Barau and I.' Barau was, then, part of the artists' colony in Skagen in 1879 and presumably also painted his picture that same year; however, it was not dated until 1880, when it was due to be exhibited. The picture does not show the fishing town of Skagen as an idyllic setting, but rather as a harsh environment. The sky is overcast, and the painting focuses on the sandy soil, the dilapidated buildings, and a small stream that would also have acted as a gutter for the settlement. The picture presents it as a dirty, ramshackle place with sparse, scattered buildings, clearly observing one of the less flattering sides of the community. Barau was not alone in opting for this aesthetic. The approach was widespread in the artist's colony during its first years, especially in 1879, where one sees the back of the settlement in the works of Wilhelm von Gegerfelt and several other artists there. The theme 'Skagen Østerby after Rain' is a recurring feature of several works, with another popular motif being fishermen labouring in harsh weather on windswept beaches.

Mette Harbo Lehmann

29. *Chaumières dans les dunes (Danemark)*, cat. no. 155 at the 1880 Salon. At the Musée des Beaux-Arts in Reims, the work is called *Chaumières dans les dunes à Skagen (Danemark)*, inv. no. 907.19.3.

30. The work was cat. no. 1572: *La Plage de Skagen (Danemark)*.

31. Sureau, *Les rues de Reims*.

32. Jensen, *Brøndums spisesal*, 292.

33. Michael Ancher, *Notesbog 1879, 1880 og 1881*. KB NKS 1197,8° - 6.

CAT. 16 OVER LEAF: Émile Barau: *Cottages in the Dunes at Skagen (Denmark)*, 1880. Oil on canvas, 70 × 111 cm. Musée des Beaux-Arts, Reims. 907.19.3

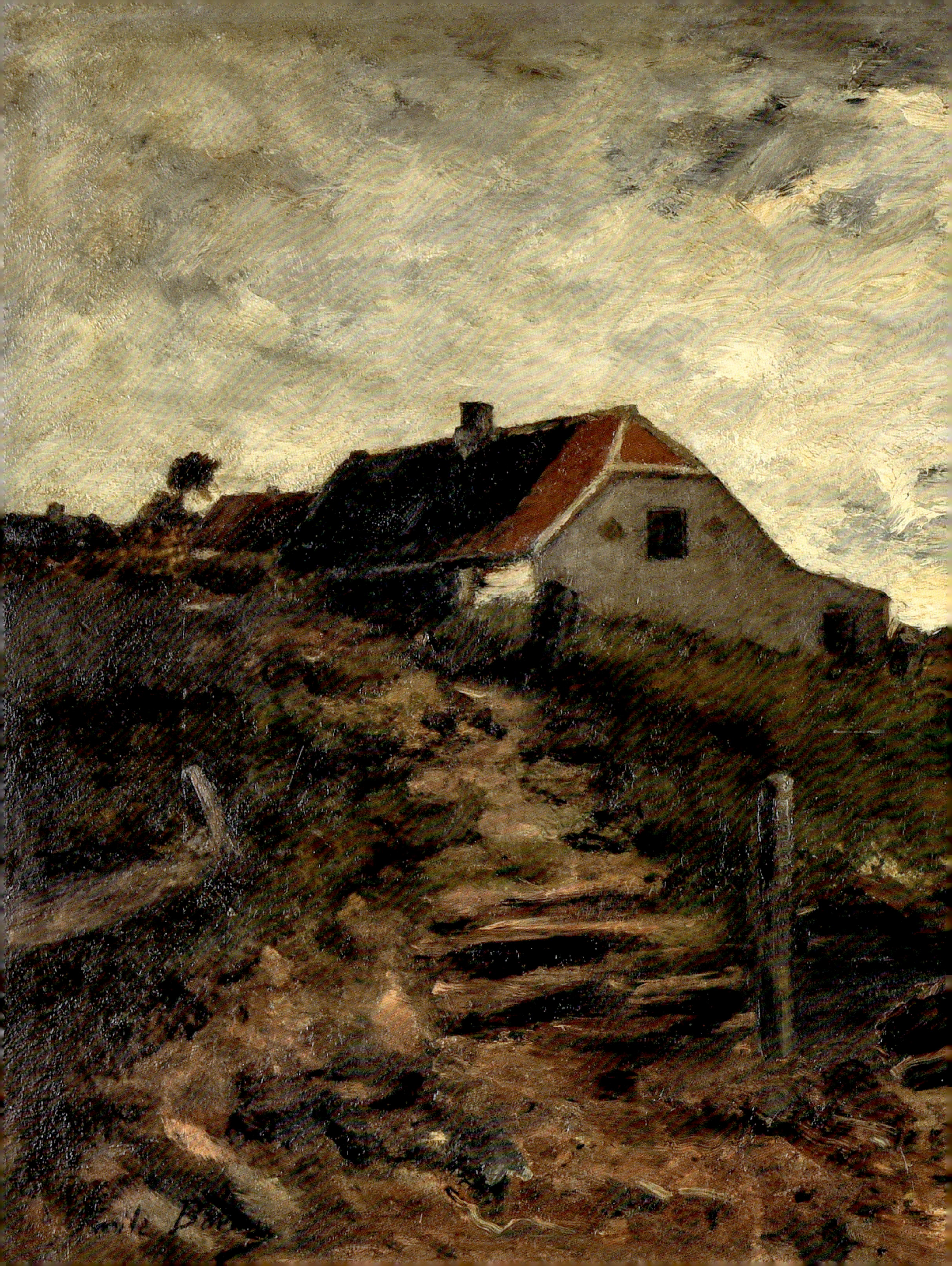

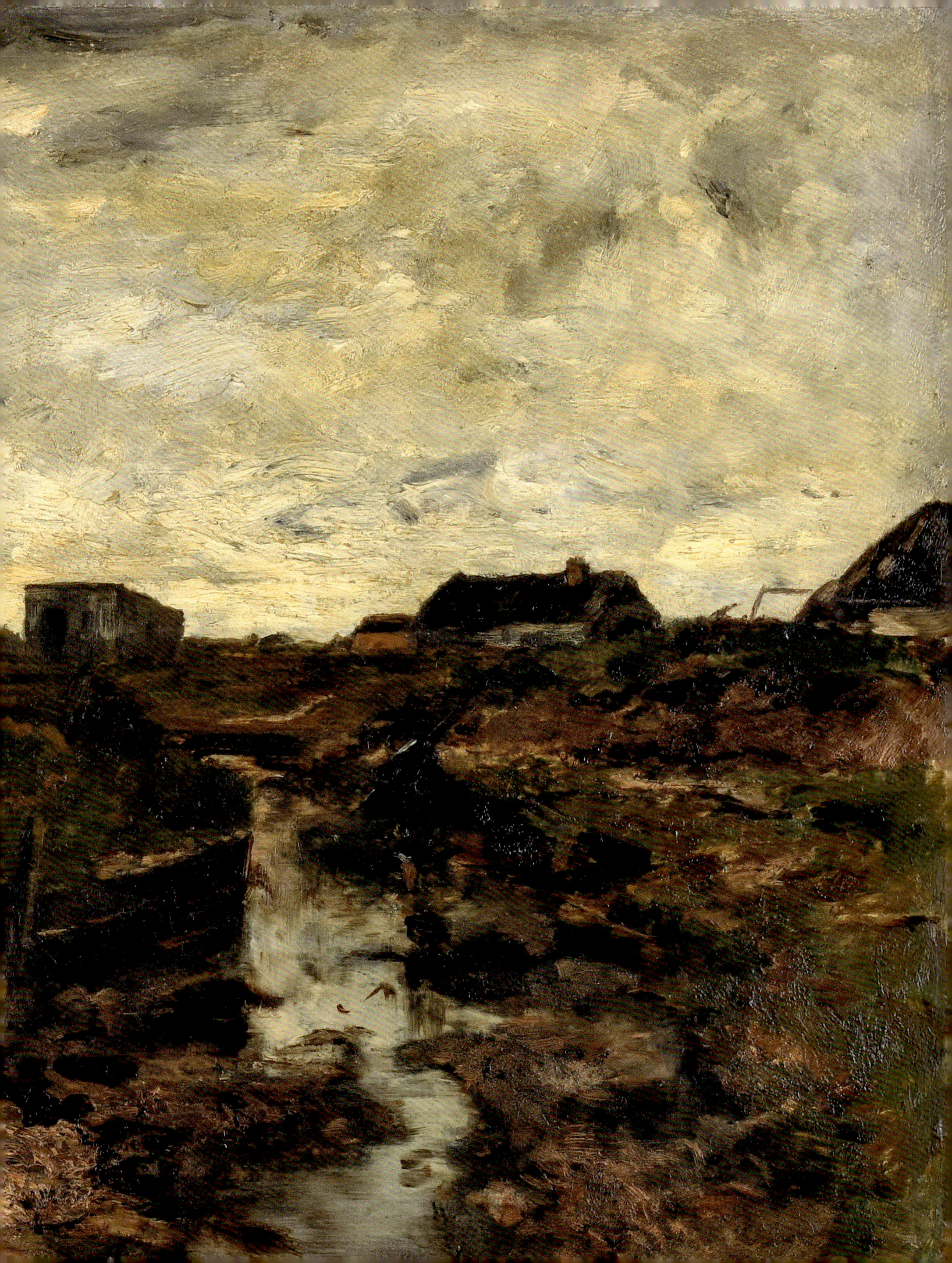

Musée du Luxembourg

CAT. 17 Jean-Jacques Henner
Idyll, around 1872

When it first opened, the Musée du Luxembourg was located in the very same palace that Marie de Médicis had commissioned to be built in 1615, and it remained there until 1886, when it moved to the adjoining orangery, built in 1839. Its role, as the *Moniteur universel* defined it at its opening, was to 'form a link between the Salon, where pupils were placed next to masters, and the Musée Royal [the Louvre], where France received the *chefs d'oeuvre* of great masters worldwide, once universal opinion had confirmed their reputation after their death.'[34] In administrative terms, it meant that this museum was merely a short-term location and that, five or ten years after the artists had died, their work would be sent either to the Louvre, implying that their reputation was established, or to a provincial museum or administration, a less enviable fate.

Despite its ambiguous status – the Musée du Luxembourg was merely a department of the Louvre[35] and did not have its own collection – it rapidly built up its acquisitions to the point where, as early as the Second Empire, its administrators were bemoaning the lack of space and the overflowing exhibition rooms. New works, which were added to the collection each year, were mainly acquired during the Salon by the Beaux-Arts administrators and belonged to the academic tradition. When he first visited, Krøyer would therefore have encountered a selection of artists and artworks of which France was particularly proud. Several years later, when Léonce Bénédite was appointed head of the Luxembourg, its status would change, but its director still had to face the same logistical problems.

Under the Second Empire the Salon had been reorganised and, among the various changes made, it had been decided that this event, normally lasting around two months, would terminate after a month. During the few days when the public was not admitted, the big institutional buyers would come and make their purchases; the works acquired were exhibited separately, and the hanging of the others was changed. On 20 June 1872, the painter Jean-Jacques Henner was told that the Beaux-Arts administrators wished to purchase the picture entitled *Idyll* (CAT. 17) which had been registered as number 789 in the exhibition catalogue. They were offering the substantial sum of 4,000 francs to this celebrated artist who, at 43 years of age, had already won many awards – a sum which he accepted, and the picture thus made its official entry into the museum's inventories on 10 June 1874. It would remain there until it was transferred to the Louvre on 17 December 1885, not because the artist had died but to be replaced by another painting acquired from him. Fifteen years later, judging it to be of greater interest, Bénédite arranged for *Idyll* to be returned to the

34. 'Musée de la Chambre des Pairs', 696.

35. Which Krøyer also visited and commented upon, specifically in a letter to Vermehren of 20 May 1879. PSK Archive 58.

CAT. 17 Jean-Jacques Henner: *Idyll*, around 1872. Oil on canvas, 74 × 61.5 cm. Musée Jean-Jacques Henner, Paris, deposit from Musée d'Orsay. RF 95

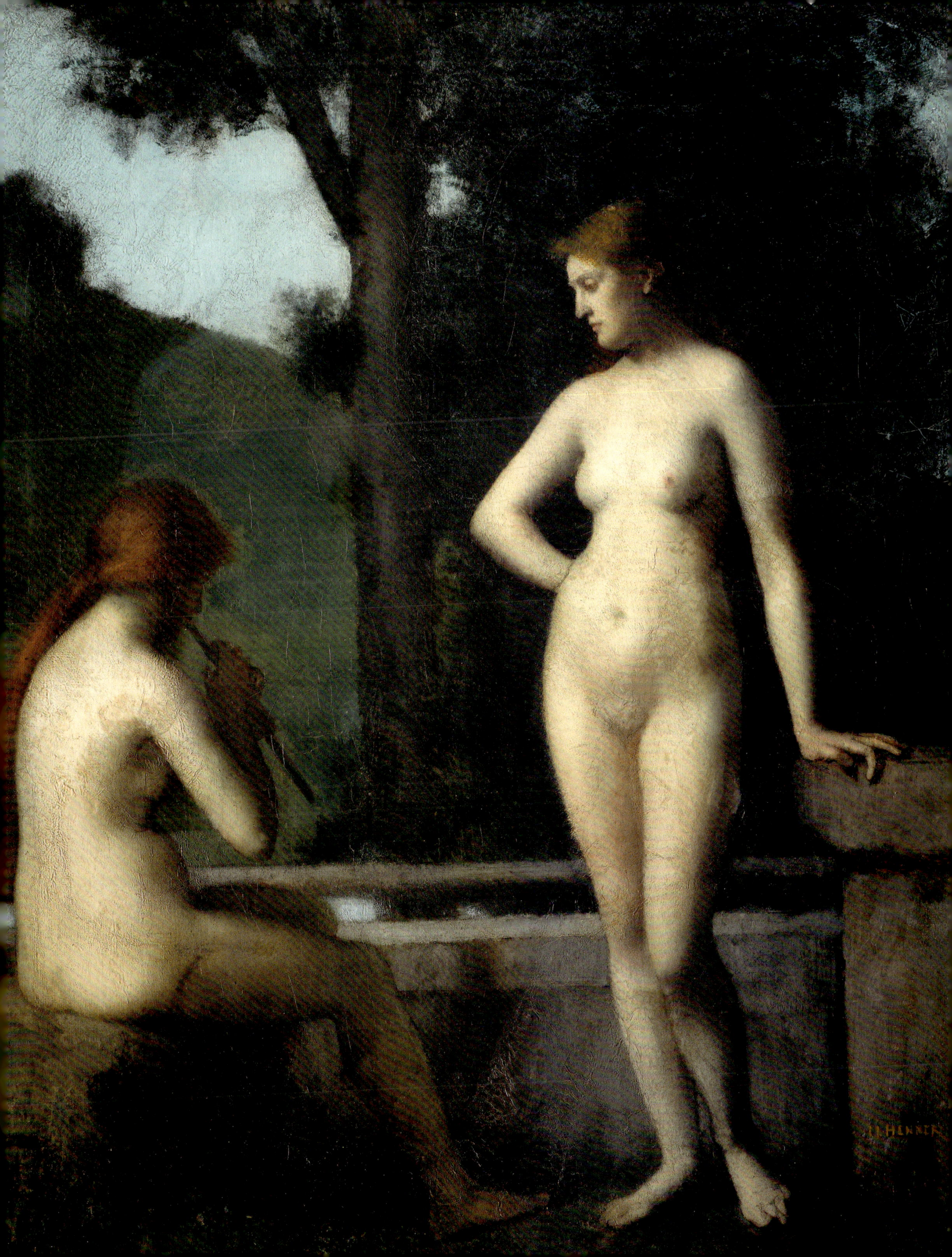

Luxembourg, where he remained as director until 1923.

The critics' reactions varied: despite the *Journal amusant* changing its title to 'Idyll at the edge of a bathtub, or cleanliness and clarinet',[36] the more general tendency was to praise the work:

> The impression given by Henner's idyll is mystical as well as sensual, very profound. At the edge of a marble pool stand two naked women. One of them is standing, listening to the other who, seated at the edge of the pool, is gently blowing into a flute; her averted profile can hardly be distinguished. Seeing this, one thinks of Giorgione; indeed, the shadows are warm, blond under their brown tones. [...] Great charm emanates from this picture; nature is there to be loved in these cool waters and in the song of this flute which the ears cannot perceive.[37]

The charm of this picture also affected Krøyer, who particularly referred to its creator, mentioning him three times in the letter he sent to Vermehren on 20 May 1879. Alluding to the *Eglogue*, from 1879 (Petit Palais, Musée des Beaux-Arts de la Ville de Paris), another encounter between two naked women in a landscape which was presented at the Salon, he wrote:

> What fascinated me most was Henner's two *Nymphs* (you probably remember his burial and his pictures of nymphs at the Exposition Universelle), with its luminous colour, its incredible plenitude and simplicity of form, reminiscent of Correggio, and especially his strange woodland poetry, although it is not at all naturalistic – but that's Henner.[38]

Dominique Lobstein

CAT. 18 Jean-François Mille
Cousin's Hamlet in Gréville, 1854–1873

Given a rough ride by the critics and ignored by the Beaux-Arts administrators, Millet's original work was set in the peasant world that was then disappearing, but gradually attracted interest from various art lovers. His death, on 23 January 1875, was very soon followed by a sale of the works that had remained in his studio. His demise overcame the former hesitance of the administrators who, that very day, purchased two paintings and several drawings for the Musée du Luxembourg. This meant that on Krøyer's first visit to this museum devoted to the most contemporary art, he was able to meet *The Church at Gréville* (FIG. 15), a picture that had occupied the final years of the artist's life and would be admired by generations to come, including Paul Cézanne for example, who owned a photograph of it.

During his subsequent trips, Krøyer, who insisted on going to Barbizon in 1879, discovered other works by the artist. In 1885, for example, when he arrived in Paris to see the exhibitions of Delacroix and Bastien-Lepage, he was also able to admire 30 works by Millet at the Galerie Georges Petit, in the first exhibition of the Société des Pastellistes. These had been lent by private collectors, some of whom were in the city of Reims. Two years later, the large retrospective of Jean-François Millet held from 10 May until 20 June 1887 at the École des Beaux-Arts gave him access to more than 260 pictures, pastels, watercolours, drawings, and etchings. It is certain that, accompanied by Viggo Johansen and his wife, Krøyer arrived in Paris during the early days of May and stayed until 2 June, when he left for London. Everything points to the fact that

36. Stop, 'Le Salon de 1872', 4.

37. Aicard, 'Salon de 1872', 83.

38. Draft for a letter: PSK to Frederik Vermehren, Cernay-la-Ville, 20 May 1879. PSK Archive 58.

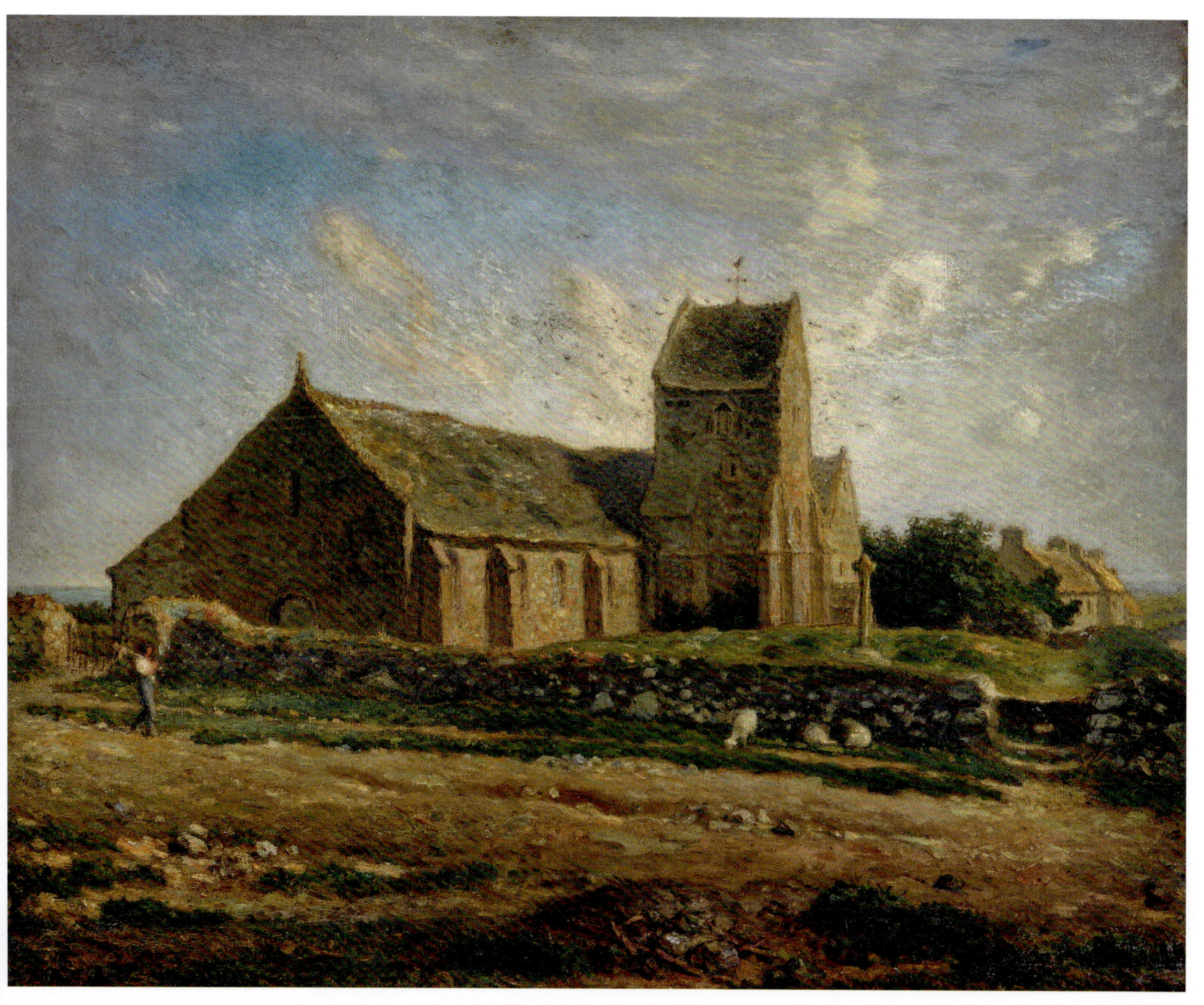

FIG. 15 Jean-François Millet: *The Church at Gréville*, 1871–1874. Oil on canvas, 60×73.4 cm. Musée d'Orsay, Paris. RF 140

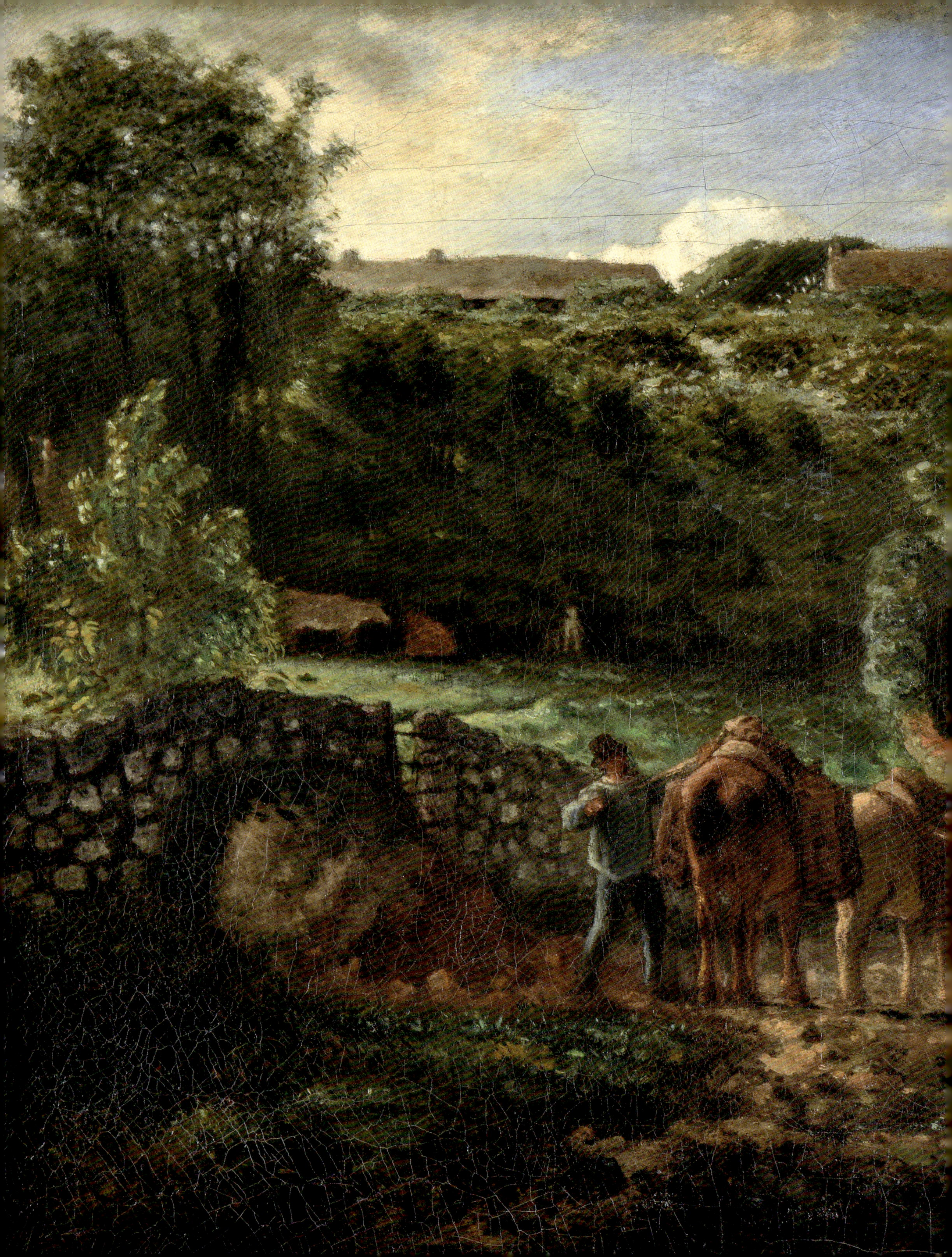

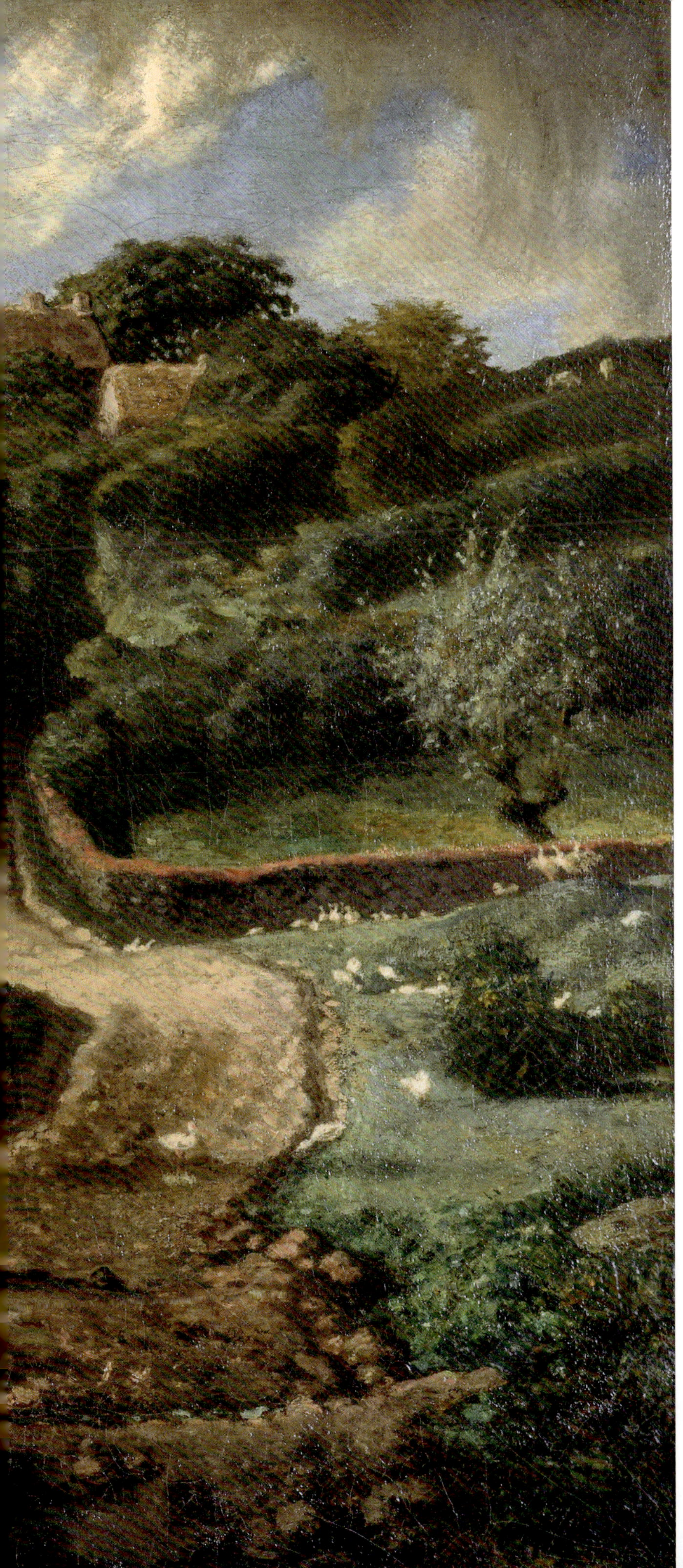

CAT. 18 Jean-François Millet: *Cousin's Hamlet in Gréville,* 1854–1873. Oil on canvas, 74.1×92.3 cm. Musée des Beaux-Arts, Reims. 907.19.190

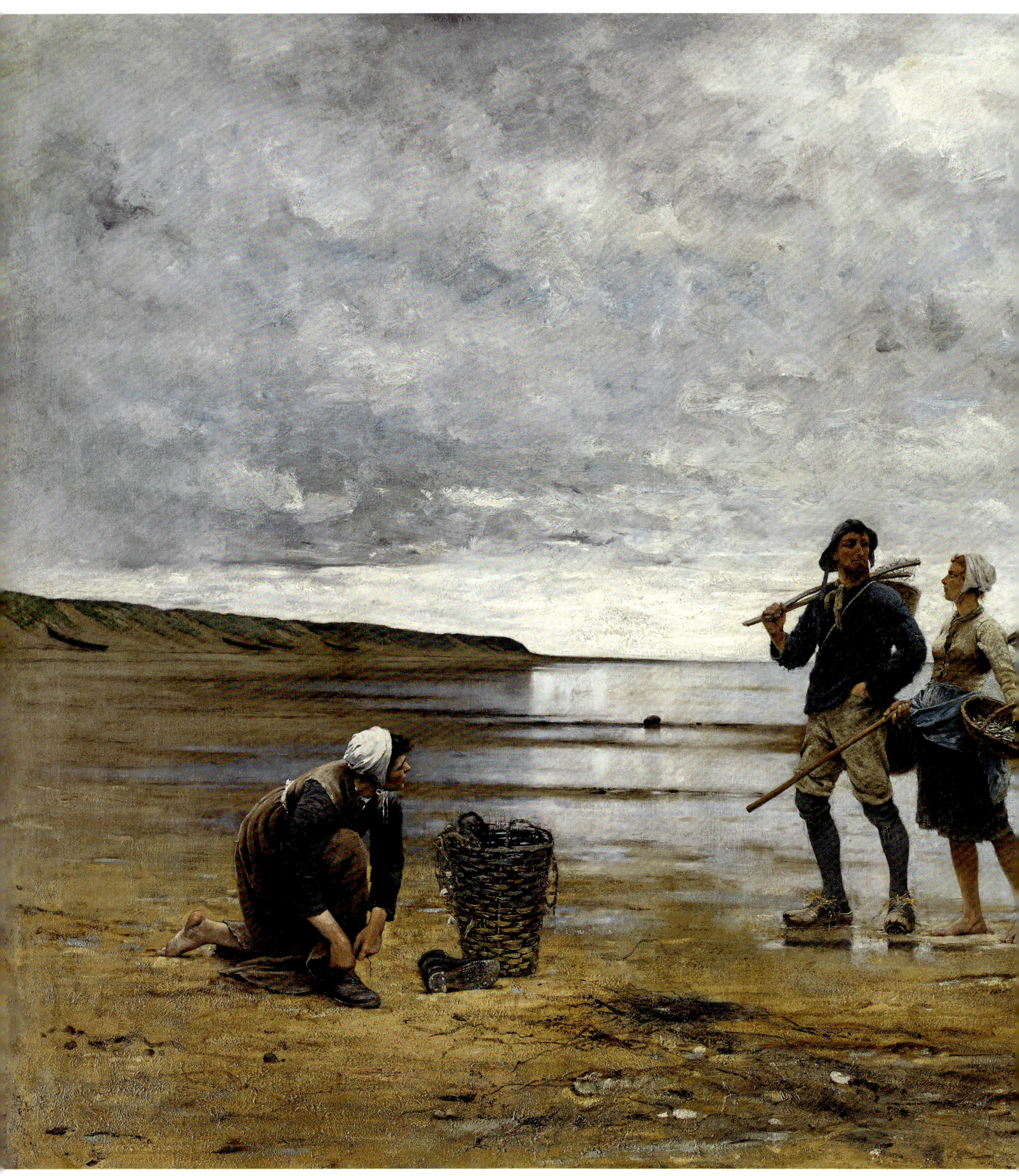

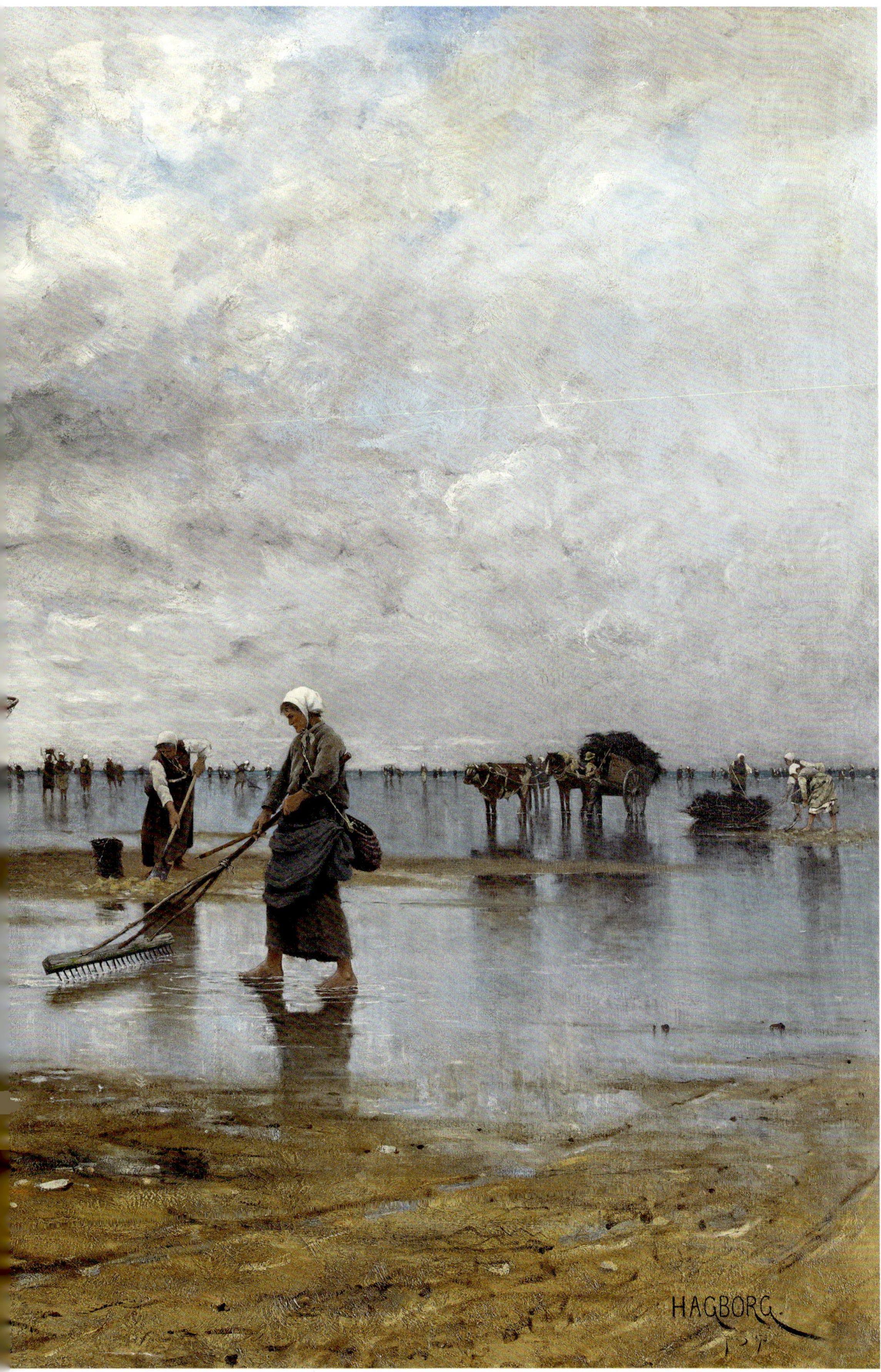

CAT. 19 August Hagborg: *Low Tide in the Channel*, 1879. Oil on canvas, 166 × 267 cm. Musée de Saint-Maur, Villa Médicis, deposit from Musée d'Orsay. RF 248

he visited the Quai Malaquais, the headquarters of the École des Beaux-Arts, so that he could admire the work exhibited there, which was still owned by Adolphe Tavernier, a fencer, writer, journalist, and art critic, who was renowned for his collection of Impressionist painting. After the exhibition, Tavernier sold the painting *Cousin's Hamlet in Gréville* (CAT. 18) for 40,000 francs to an intermediary, Louis Guyotin (dates unknown), a member of the Société des Amis des Arts in Reims and a middleman between the Paris art market and the upper bourgeoisie of Reims, which had grown rich on the back of the champagne trade. Guyotin immediately resold it for 50,000 francs. Two collectors clubbed together to pay this sum: Mme Pommery, owner of the Pommery champagne house – which would donate Millet's *Gleaners* to the Musée du Luxembourg – and Henry Vasnier, a partner in this same firm. Upon Mme Pommery's death, the work passed to Vasnier, who left it to the Musée de Reims together with five pastels and several drawings.

Thanks to Millet's paintings, Krøyer had access to what is sometimes called the '1830 School', also known as the 'Barbizon School' after the name of a hamlet at the edge of the forest of Fontainebleau; it was here that a colony of artists gathered who wished to depict the landscape in a more realistic manner, if necessary setting up their easels facing their subject, which led to their being dubbed Realist. But the Realism of Millet's early years was not quite what it was in his later years, when it seemed to augur fresh changes and point to the revolution being brought about by Impressionism. This style of painting recurred several times in his oeuvre over almost 30 years, revealing a method that espoused both a traditional and an innovative approach. Typical of Millet's early years of training was the deep-toned preparation onto which the paint was laid, which became lighter as time went on. His later experiments led to his method of laying on the paint in thinner brushstrokes, in a range of colours where he unhesitatingly placed brilliant reds side by side with saturated greens in graduated shades from yellow-green to blue-green.

Although Krøyer admired the artist – as evidenced by the fact that he mentioned Millet several times in letters to his Danish correspondents – he never adopted or adapted this technique or colour palette, working in a light that was very different from that of Normandy.
Dominique Lobstein

CAT. 19 August Hagborg
Low Tide in the Channel, 1879

CAT. 20 Anders Zorn
A Fisherman at Saint-Yves, 1888

Vilhelm Nikolaus August Hagborg was born in Gothenburg. He attended the Swedish academy of fine arts from 1871 to 1874, studying under Professor Johan Christoffer Boklund. As a Naturalistic artist, he preferred to paint subjects from everyday life. In the autumn of 1875, he set out for Paris, and the following year he exhibited for the first time at the Salon in Paris, presenting *Le Gavroshe* (location unknown): a life-sized depiction of a street urchin sitting out of doors, reading the newspaper *Le Figaro*. The painting was later bought by King Oscar II of Sweden. In 1877, Hagborg exhibited the first of what would be many scenes portraying the lives of fishermen, *Waiting* (location unknown). Presented at the Salon in Paris, the painting shows a young Swedish fisherwoman on a quay with a child on her arm, looking out at the sea.[39] These first works attracted some attention, but his real

39. Cat. no. 1026: *L'attente; souvenir de Suède*. The work is reproduced in *Illustreret Tidende*, 8 July 1882, no. 1241.

CAT. 20 Anders Zorn: *A Fisherman at Saint-Yves*, 1888. Oil on canvas, 128 × 86 cm. Musée des Braux-Arts, Pau, deposit from Musée d'Orsay. RF564

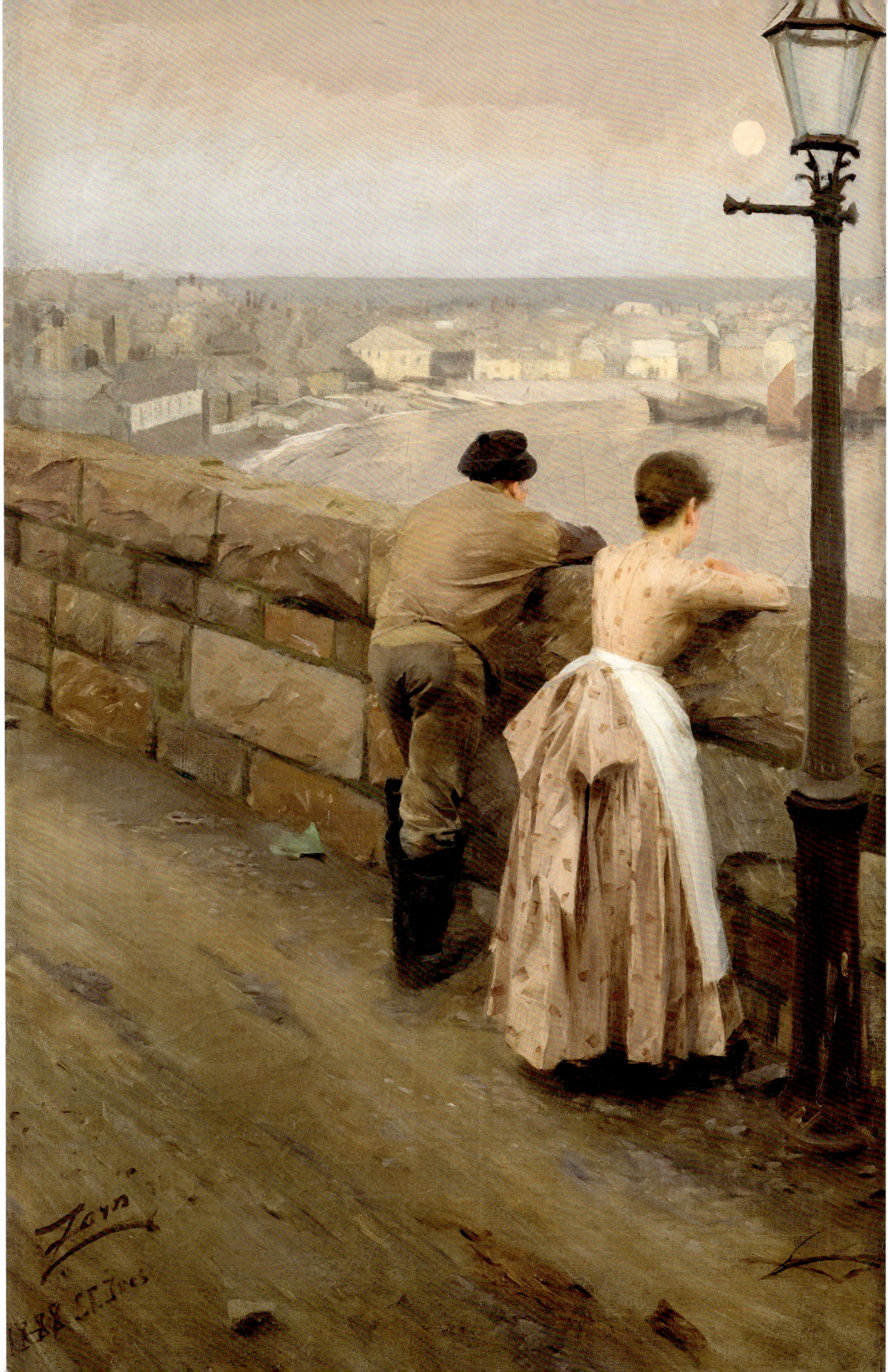
Zorn

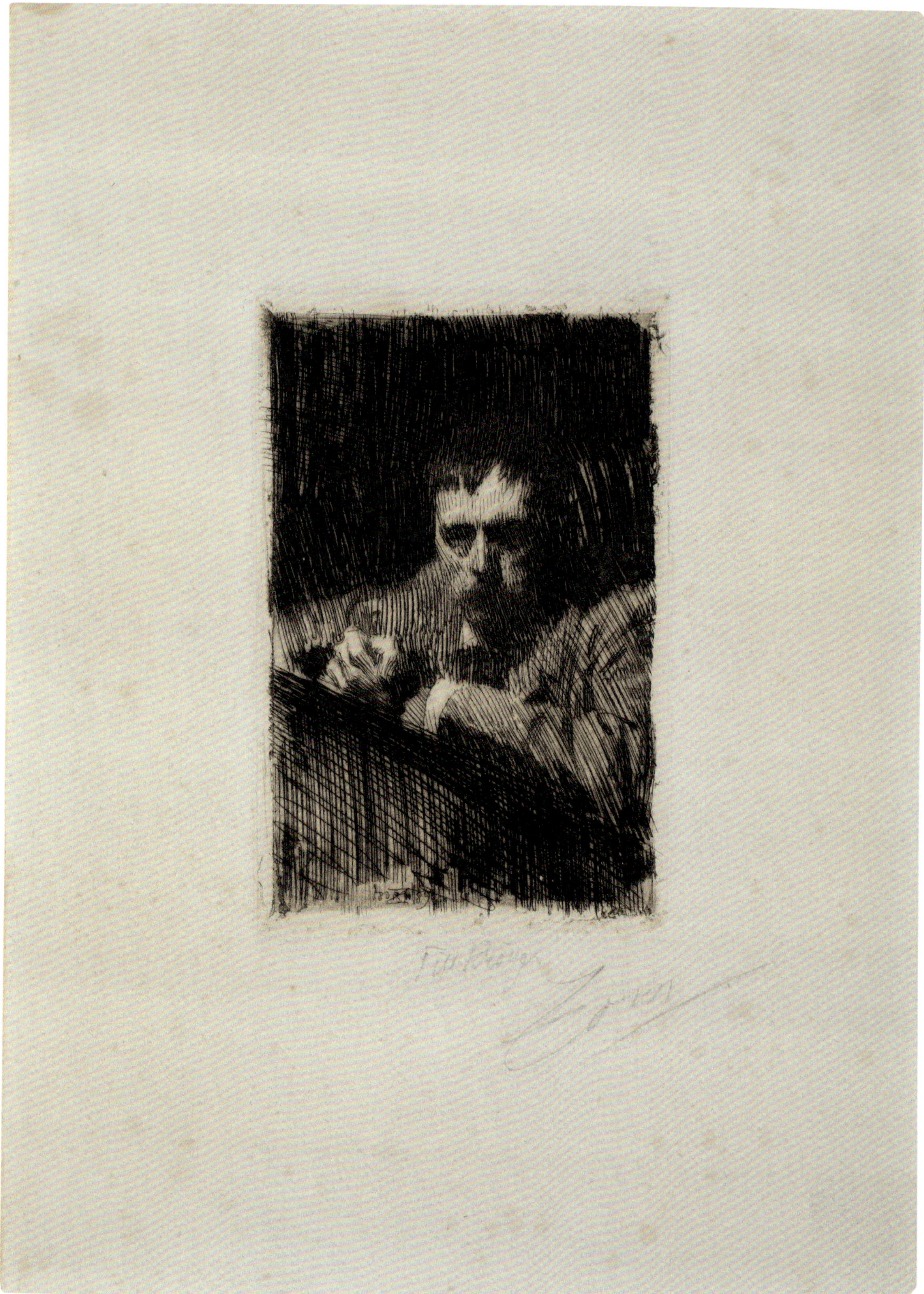

FIG. 16 Anders Zorn: *Self-portrait*, undated. Etching, 240×175 mm. Skagens Kunstmuseer. SKM184

breakthrough came with the picture he exhibited in 1879, *Low Tide in the Channel* (CAT. 19), a scene from the French north coast of Normandy. The painting not only won a third-class medal, but also enjoyed the good fortune of being bought by the Musée du Luxembourg, the French nation's museum of contemporary art. The work depicts oyster-gatherers on the wide beach at low tide. Its popularity meant that it was reproduced many times as an etching and on postcards, thereby reaching larger audiences. At the 1879 Salon, another Swedish artist, Hugo Salmson, exhibited *The Arrest in Picardie* (Musée de Picardie, Amiens, deposit from Musée d'Orsay), which depicts a woman being arrested for infanticide.[40] It, too, was awarded a prize and purchased by the Musée du Luxembourg. Seeing these two extraordinary events at one and the same Salon may have been particularly instrumental in attracting the French public's attention to Scandinavian artists. In 1880, Hagborg exhibited *On the Beach at Agon in Manche* at the Salon in Paris, which, as noted by Krøyer, received bad reviews.[41] However, the artist's success was reinstated the following year.

At the art academy, Hagborg had been friends with several fellow pupils who went on to become famous painters, such as Carl Larsson, Georg Pauli, Ernst Josephson, and Anders Zorn, all of whom would be his lifelong friends. Hagborg became part of Opponenterna, a group of Swedish artists in Paris who stood in opposition to the Stockholm academy in the mid-1880s, forming the Konstnärsförbundet in Sweden. By the early 1880s Hagborg had won international acclaim, and he received lavish praise for his exhibits at the 1878, 1889, and 1900 Expositions Universelles in Paris. He became best known for his paintings from Normandy and Brittany, but also created many paintings during his frequent visits to his homeland, often in connection with exhibitions. He is represented at several museums, including Nationalmuseum in Stockholm, Göteborgs konstmuseum, Bergen Museum, and several museums in France, the UK, Germany, and the United States.

Anders Zorn attended the art academy in Stockholm from 1875 to 1881. Although he was younger than Krøyer, many parallels can be drawn between the two artists. They were both among the most successful artists in their home countries in their own lifetimes; they were both devoted to Naturalistic painting; and they both won international acclaim. In addition to this, they both forged close ties to Paris.

Zorn painted the work *A Fisherman at Saint-Yves* (CAT. 20) in 1888 in Cornwall and exhibited it at the Salon in Paris the same year. It was his Parisian breakthrough, and the work was purchased by the French nation for the Musée du Luxembourg.[42] A few critics, however, poked fun at the fact that the French title was 'A Fisherman', as there were clearly two people in the picture. The following year he won a third-class medal at the Salon, and at the world exhibition – where he also exhibited *A Fisherman at Saint-Yves* among other works – he received a gold medal and was awarded the Legion of Honour, just as Krøyer had been two years before.[43] He settled in Paris from the autumn of 1888 to 1896 (summering in Sweden), which made him one of the prominent Scandinavians in Paris in the 1880s and 1890s. The years 1888 and 1889, so crucially important for Zorn, were also years in which Krøyer lived in Paris. They must have met each other at this time, as evidenced by two etchings signed 'To Krøyer / Zorn' in the Skagens Kunstmuseer collection (FIG. 16).[44]

Mette Harbo Lehmann

40. *Une arrestation dans un village de Picardie*, cat. no. 2687.

41. *Sur la plage d'Agon (Manche)*, cat. no. 1770, 190 × 300 cm. See chapter 3.

42. *Un pêcheur*, cat. no. 2580.

43. Röstorp, *Zorn och Frankrike*, 134–135.

44. See chapter 3, 'Krøyer and the Scandinavian Artists in Paris'.

A Matter of Technique

CAT. 21 Peder Severin Krøyer
A Young Italian Woman, 1877

CAT. 22 Peder Severin Krøyer
Female Model. Half-length, 1878

Krøyer's small picture *A Young Italian Woman* (CAT. 21) was painted during his time studying at Atelier Bonnat in Paris. In 2020, Skagens Kunstmuseer had the opportunity to acquire the work, which contributes some new knowledge about what Krøyer learned from Léon Bonnat and about Krøyer's movements in the summer of 1877. Krøyer painted the work in Paris on 17 September, likely the day of his return to Paris after having spent a few weeks in St. Malo. The timeline of Krøyer's life provided in the book *Krøyer: An International Perspective* states that he arrived in St. Malo between 21 and 28 August and returned around 22 September. But another of Krøyer's paintings of an Italian model, *A Young Italian Girl* (location unknown), suggests that Krøyer was still in Paris on 20 August, and according to the inscription on the museum's new work, *A Young Italian Woman*, he was back on 17 September.[45] This is to say that the trip to St. Malo was shorter in duration than previously assumed. Given that Krøyer only had a small room in Rue de Douai, the model was presumably hired for Atelier Bonnat. The theory is supported by the fact that Bonnat also painted Italian models, and further corroborated by Laurits Tuxen's *Italian Girl* from 1878 (location unknown), painted while he was still in Paris and receiving instruction from Bonnat.[46] The many artists arriving in Paris and the many public and private art schools in the city created a thriving market for models, who let themselves be hired by the artists. They included a large group of Italians who, clad in traditional Italian costumes, would wait in the street to be hired.[47]

Models dressing in regional costumes and waiting to be hired by visiting artists who wanted to depict the typical population of a given place was not a new phenomenon; they could be found in many European cities and artists' colonies, but the fact that there were Italian models in France, with no real connection to the place, has not yet been thoroughly treated in the literature. The French artist Félix-Hilaire Buhot depicted a couple of such models sitting on a staircase in his etching *Place Pigalle in 1878* (FIG. 17). The square is located right on the edge of Montmartre, not far from Krøyer's apartment, or from Atelier Bonnat on the Boulevard de Clichy. Some of the models also achieved a certain level of celebrity, such as Agostina Segatori, who posed for artists such as Édouard Manet, Vincent Van Gogh, and Pierre-Auguste Renoir, as well as many other prominent figures. A memorial plaque

45. Saabye, *Krøyer: An International Perspective*. Peder Severin Krøyer: *Young Italian Girl*, current owner unknown, is reproduced in the photo collection at Danmarks Kunstbibliotek (Christensen, *P.S. Krøyer. 23. juli 1851-20*, HCC165).

46. The work is reproduced in the photo collection at Danmarks Kunstbibliotek.

47. 'Les Modèles, la petite histoire', 25 November 2017.

CAT. 21 Peder Severin Krøyer: *A Young Italian Woman*, 1877. Oil on canvas, 27 × 20.7 cm. Skagens Kunstmuseer. SKM2090

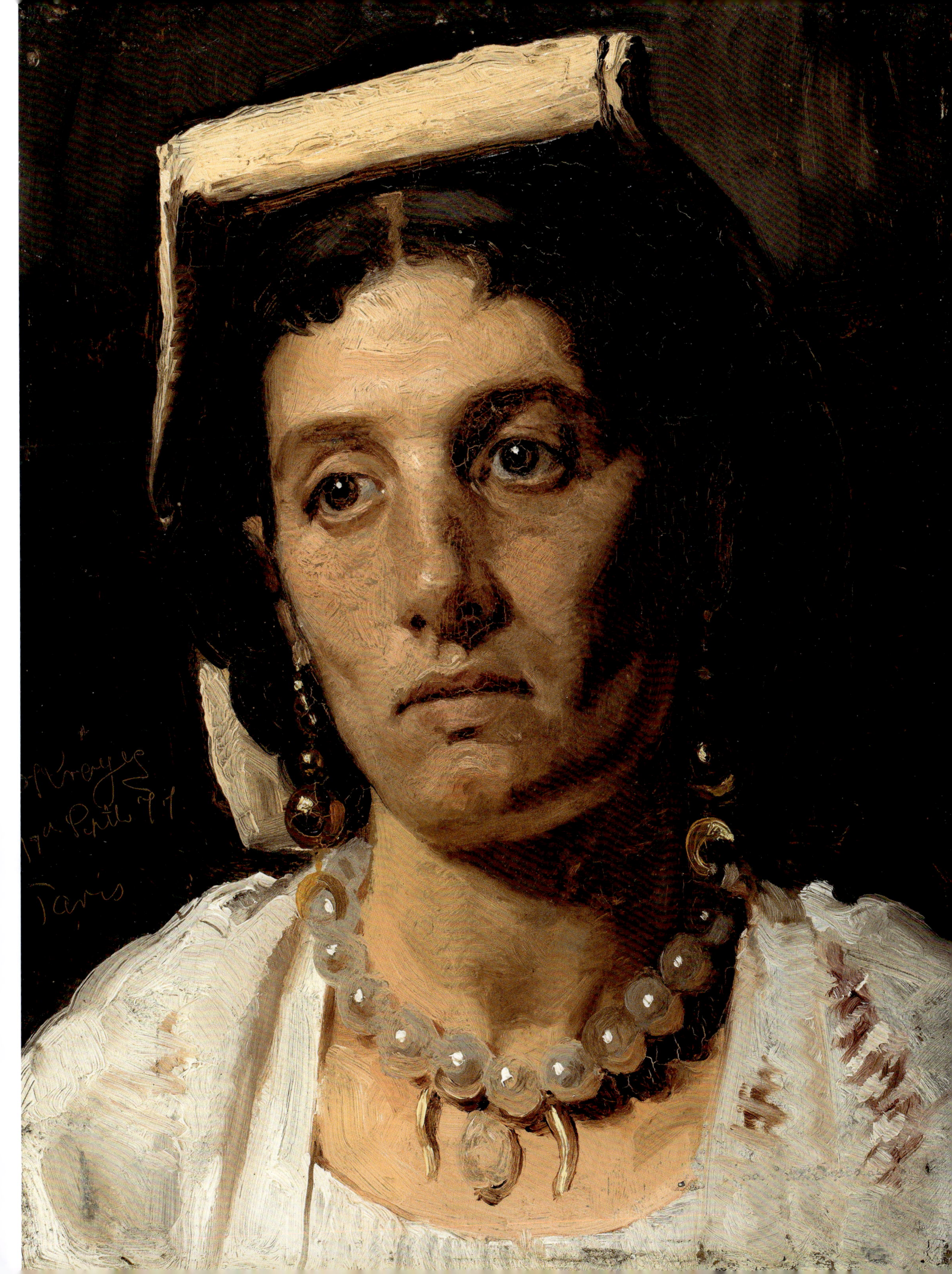

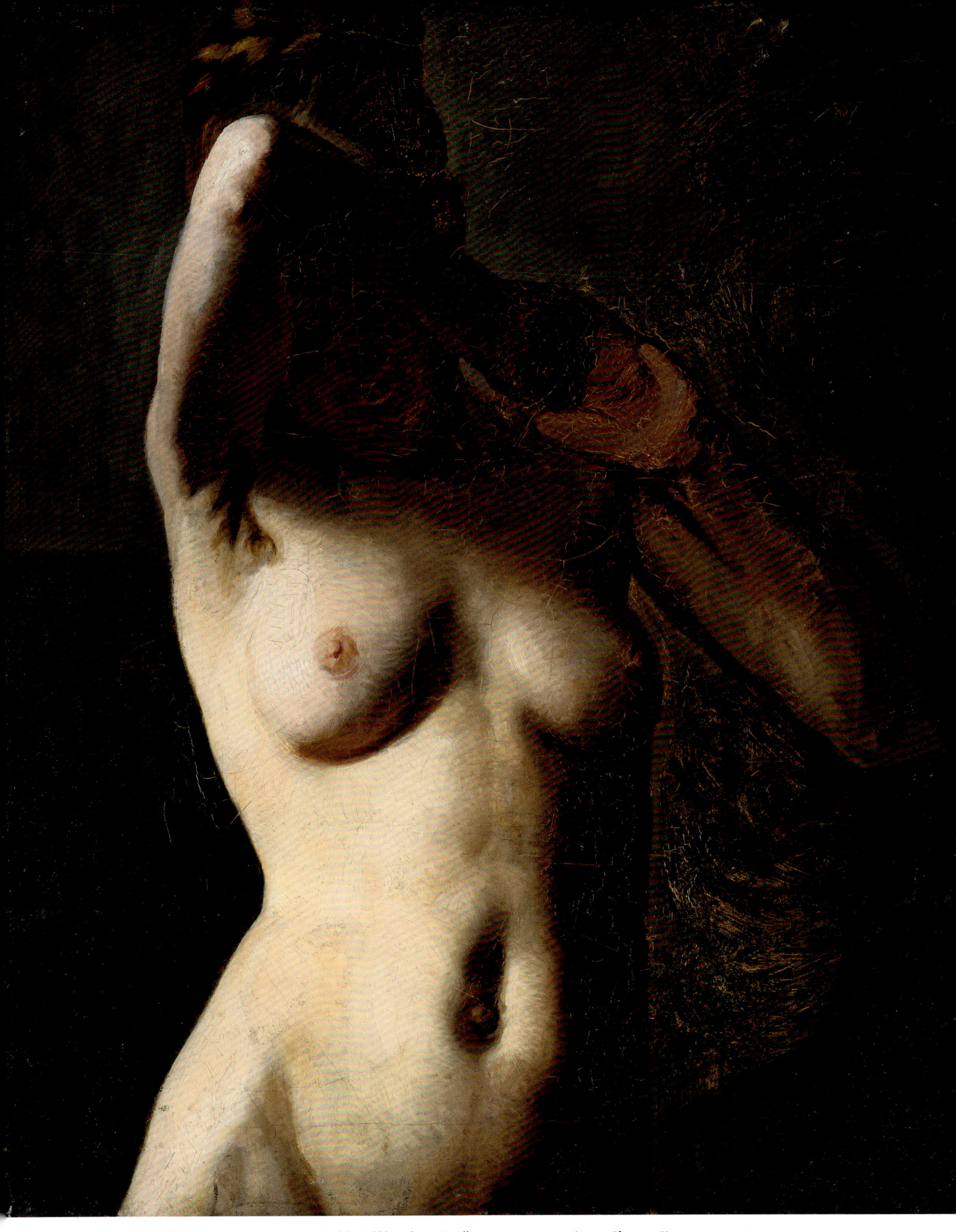

CAT. 22 Peder Severin Krøyer: *Female Model. Half-length*, 1878. Oil on canvas, 54.5 × 46.1 cm. Skagens Kunstmuseer. SKM199

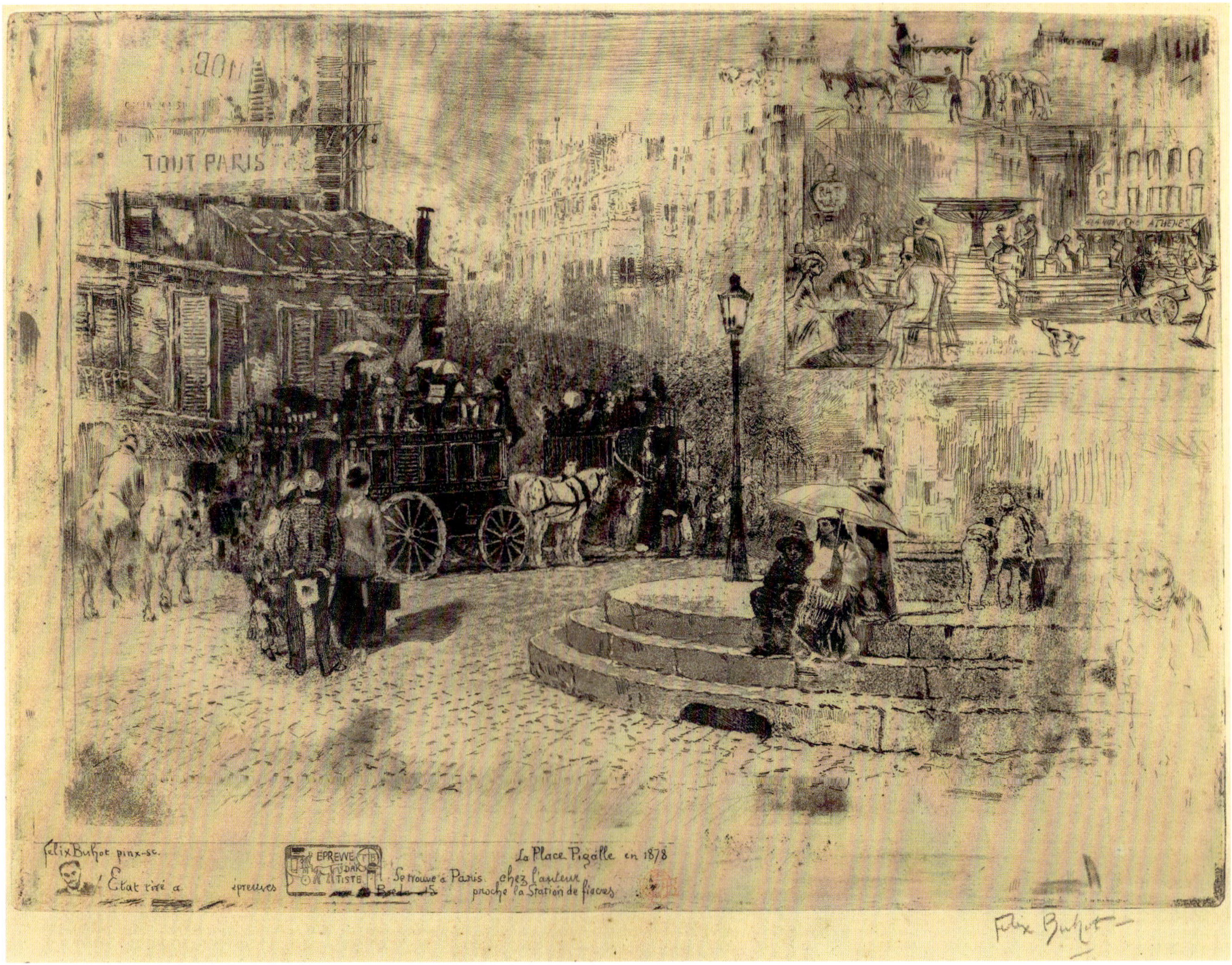

FIG. 17 Félix-Hilaire Buhot: *Place Pigalle in 1878*, 1878. Etching, aquatint, drypoint, and roulette in black on toned paper. National Gallery of Art, Washington. 1943.3.1238

at 62, Boulevard de Clichy, where she opened the Café du Tambourin, describes her as a Parisian model.

Behind Krøyer's Italian model we see the studio's dark brown background and the light illuminating her left side, simultaneously casting dark shadows on her right side to create a *chiaroscuro* effect. In line with the teaching received at Bonnat's studio, the artist has maintained a focus on her face and the pearl necklace, leaving the rest blurry, and the colour is modulated according to the principles of *valeur* painting. The painting is a portrait, but at the same time it prepared the artist for painting larger figure compositions, such as interiors or *plein air* paintings in the countryside or at artists' colonies, depicting many different types of people. While the work has focused on technique, one also sees definite signs of the artist empathising with the model, giving her sad eyes but the hint of a smile darting around her lips.

The study *Female model. Half-length* (CAT. 22) also shows a Parisian model and was made during classes at Atelier Bonnat, presumably the year after *A Young Italian*

Woman.[48] Here we see the same dark background and a spotlight falling onto the left side of the model, accentuating the contrast between light and shadow. Krøyer subsequently used the work as a reference when teaching at his own school in Copenhagen, where it hung until the school closed in 1912. Eight years later, it was donated to Skagens Museum by Kunstnernes Studieskoler.[49]
Mette Harbo Lehmann

CAT. 23 Raphaël Collin
Daphnis and Chloe, 1877

CAT. 24 Peder Severin Krøyer
Daphnis and Chloë, 187

> There is talent, and a great deal of it, in M. Raphaël Collin's picture *Daphnis and Chloe*. The general aspect is pleasing and the composition naïve. The two figures are elegant, and the flesh tints of the virgin and ephebe are agreeably varied. I would have wished Chloe's face to be less soft, and Daphnis's torso, bulging under his arm, forms a kind of bagpipes of human skin. The ground and especially the rocks are too soft, the landscape is vaguely rumpled, the blue drapery is stiff, like plaster; but the two heads form a well-chosen silhouette of rare distinction.[50]

With a few reservations, the critic Edmond About was here expressing as much, if not more, a criticism of Collin's work (CAT. 23) as a denunciation of what the demands of the 'grand manner' had become. There was an obligation for the work to be treated according to the principles taught by the École des Beaux-Arts. The bodies, for example, had to be based on the most beautiful models bequeathed by classical sculpture, which the students at this school studied from plaster copies. Journalists were therefore on the alert for any limb that was poorly attached to the body or any badly placed muscle, in order to denounce it, even if it meant quickly revising their judgment and admiring the overall result, as About did here.

This picture was presented at the 1877 Salon and Krøyer probably saw it, even if it was not among the works and painters that he mentioned in his letters that summer. After the 1888 Copenhagen exhibition, at which Collin exhibited four pictures, the artist would become well known to Krøyer and appear many times in his correspondence. They would not have any formal relationship, but maintained a frank cordiality which, for example, brought them together on 5 January 1889 for a dinner with Émile, the brother of Jules Bastien-Lepage, and the American painter Thomas Alexander Harrison.[51] That same year, at the end of the Exposition Universelle, this familiarity was again expressed in an undated letter from Collin:

> My dear Krøyer, forgive me for not replying to you: I had lost your address but as I am now in Paris, I am taking the opportunity to congratulate you, both on your forthcoming marriage and your *Médaille d'honneur*. I understand only too well the happy situation you are now in for me to want to trouble your happiness in any way. But if you can find a moment, we would all be very glad, both myself and my entire family, to see you and your fiancée either for dinner or for luncheon at Fontenay-aux-Roses. If you have a moment it would be very kind of you to let us know. I still have your study in my studio and will find one or two days when I can come and pose for you in the afternoon.[52]

Two years after Raphaël Collin had exhibited his *Daphnis and Chloe* (CAT. 23), Krøyer presented his version of the

48. The date is not stated on the work, but it is listed under the year 1878 in Christensen, *P.S. Krøyer. 23. juli 1851–20*, HCC179.

49. We do not know for certain where the work was during the eight years between when the school closed and when it ended up in the museum's ownership, but the donor wanted it to be credited as 'Gift 1920 from Kunstnernes Studieskoler'.

50. About, 'Salon de 1877', [3].

51. Émile Bastien-Lepage to PSK, Paris, 5 January 1889. PSK Archive 2808.

52. Raphaël Collin to PSK, [probably Fontenay-aux-Roses], no date. PSK Archive 2847.

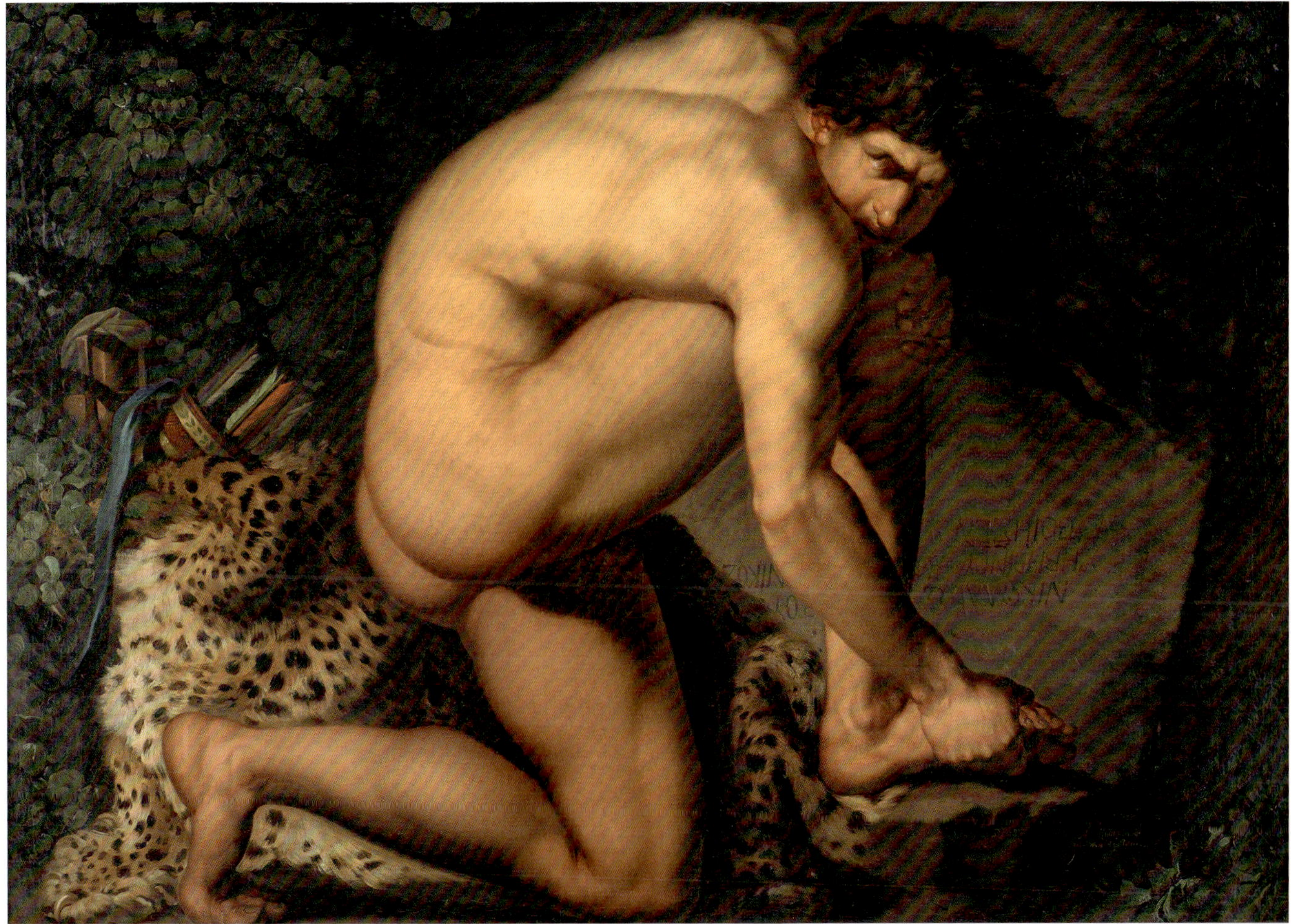

FIG. 18 Nicolai Abraham Abildgaard: *The Wounded Philoctetes*, 1775. Oil on canvas, 123×175.5 cm. Statens Museum for Kunst, Copenhagen. KMS586

same scene, on the advice of Léon Bonnat. The subject appears to have been suggested to him by Karl Madsen, who had just read the Greek pastoral prose romance by Longus, but perhaps we can see a trace of Collin in the way the characters are presented, in profile and from the front, close together. However, the resemblance stops there, and Krøyer's technique proves to be more spontaneous, his colours stronger and more varied. Above all, his models' anatomies are more realistic – closer to the Scandinavian tradition and the bodies fashioned by Nicolai Abraham Abildgaard (FIG. 18), for example. When it was shown at the 1879 Salon, under number 1704, the work disconcerted the critics who had heaped praise on *From the Smithy in Hornbæk* (CAT. 3), presented the previous year at the Exposition Universelle, one of them declaring: 'This *Smithy* by M. Krøyer, to which we have returned many times without ever being able to find fault with it; a master work.'[53] The die was cast, and Krøyer would no longer try to acknowledge the 'grand manner' on the walls of the Paris art galleries.

Dominique Lobstein

53. Proth, *Voyage au pays des peintres*, 225.

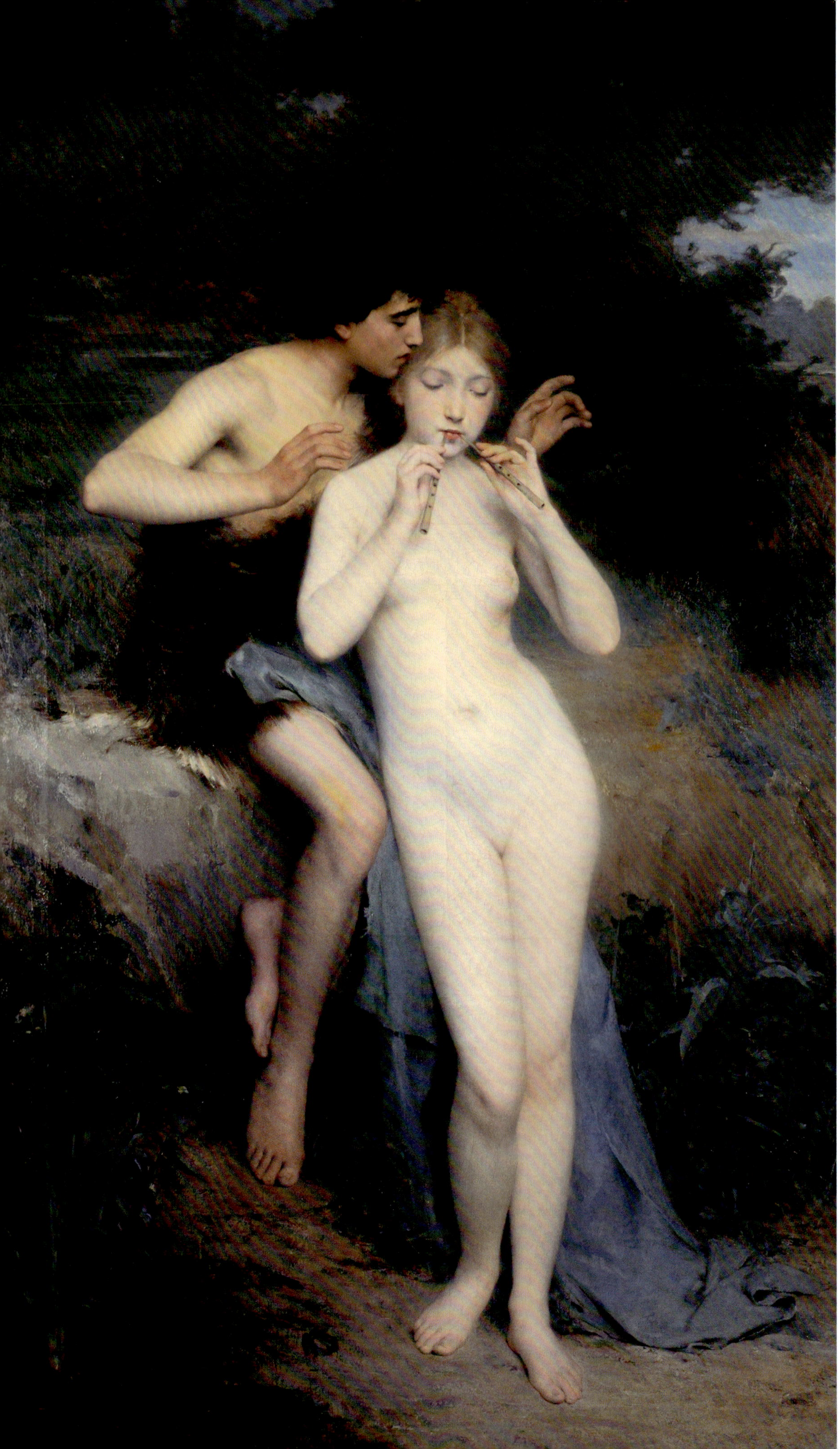

CAT. 23 Raphaël Collin: *Daphnis and Chloe*, 1877. Oil on canvas, 205 × 128.5 cm. Musée des Beaux-Arts et de la Dentelle, Alençon. 2013.1.18

CAT. 24 Peder Severin Krøyer: *Daphnis and Chloë*, 1879. Oil on canvas, 164 × 123 cm. Ulrik Bach and Berit Rosenvinge.

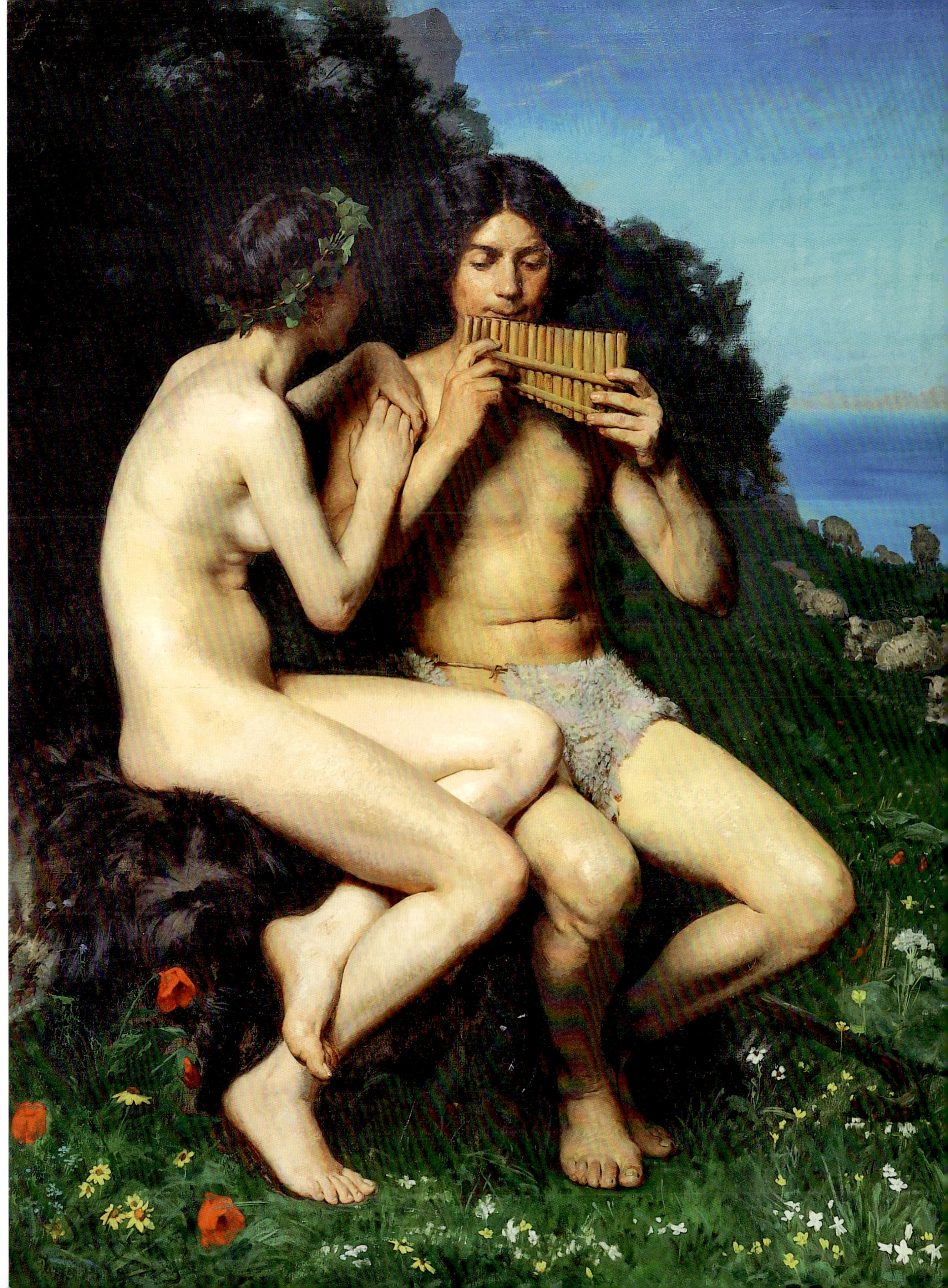

Artists' Colonies and Landscape Painting

CAT. 25 Peder Severin Krøyer
French Workers on a Sunken Road, 1879

Peder Severin Krøyer's first visit to a French artists' colony took place in the spring of 1879, when he set out for the small village of Cernay-la-Ville, located in a scenic area complete with forests, fields, streams, and a rural population, all of it just 40 km southeast of Paris. Two years previously, he had made a brief visit to the small town of St. Malo, a picturesque, fortified island on the north coast of France, but not an artists' colony. Indeed, not all *plein air* painters gathered in actual artists' colonies. Several painted on their own by the coast or in the countryside, and in 1877 Krøyer was only accompanied by Laurits Tuxen. By that point, Krøyer had been in France no more than a few months and had painted only small-scale studies. The second time Krøyer set out for the French countryside was, then, in April 1879, when he visited what had become an actual, if small, artists' colony in Cernay-la-Ville, home to many French painters and a few other nationalities besides. Here he was determined to paint an intensively studied outdoor painting. The result was *French Workers on a Sunken Road* (CAT. 25). The work is interesting because it is Krøyer's first *plein air* painting from France that was to become an exhibition work. In a letter to his teacher from the art academy in Copenhagen, Krøyer wrote:

> I am currently painting a small figure scene (figures one foot tall) of workers returning home at sunset from labouring in the forest. In this picture I seek to showcase all my talent, to pour all my energy into it and especially to complete my figures to the utmost reaches of my ability.[54]

Krøyer's statement supports the view that this was the first time his newfound Naturalism came to the fore. Here we see, for the first time ever in a work intended for exhibition, the painting technique he learned from Bonnat in Paris combined with both French and Danish Naturalism expressed in a *plein air* study.

He began work on the painting in the early spring when there were no leaves on the trees yet, and he maintained this look even though the trees had come into leaf before the work was finished. The men in the picture are road workers from a quarry some distance away, returning home from a hard day's work making cobblestones. They carry picks and shovels over their shoulders, their tired eyes glancing in several directions without seeking out each other's faces. They appear too fatigued for small talk. When the work was exhibited in Denmark, it was given the title *Forest Workers*, for reasons that remain unknown. Perhaps Krøyer found the sound of forest workers more appealing than road workers. However, contemporary

54. Draft for a letter: PSK to Frederik Vermehren, Cernay-la-Ville, 20 May 1879. PSK Archive 58.

sources also refer to them as 'workers' or 'road workers'.[55] In a letter to a friend and fellow artist back home in Denmark, Krøyer wrote: 'Speaking of which: I am puzzled that you found the landscape the best aspect of the picture of the workers; I thought that was the least successful – to me, it seems that the best thing was the heads.'[56]

The landscape was carefully chosen and important, but to Krøyer the people in the picture were the most important aspect. These are real workers. There is nothing romantic or idyllic about the way they are portrayed. They are worn out, dirty, and tired. The bare branches and earthy colours of the landscape do not invite a romantic view of them; rather, they are placed deep inside the landscape, down in the hollow road, firmly connected to the earth. The workers are positioned rhythmically, alternately in front and behind each other, with different shades in the colours of their clothes helping to differentiate them from each other, and yet their blue work clothes convey an impression of a uniform army of workers. Krøyer deliberately works with and accentuates the light in all his canvases, and this is no exception. Here, the sunset serves a dual purpose: it casts a soft, mitigating light that gives the entire scene a gentler air, and at the same time it highlights the workers' long working day and meagre free time – their toil takes up all the daylight hours.

Mette Harbo Lehmann

CAT. 26 François Louis Français
The Painters on the Banks of the Ru des Vaux-de-Cernay, 1870

The place name Cernay appeared for the first time in a charter of 768 and, from then on, there are documents enabling us to follow the development of this village, which had the benefit of water supplies, forests well stocked with game, and farmland. In the early 12th century, its fame increased when a Cistercian abbey made its home there and proceeded to drain a swamp, and the place soon appeared in documents under the name of Vaux-de-Cernay, after that of the Vaux stream, which had been canalised. The ecclesiastical buildings expanded over time and the abbey became an intellectual centre with close links to the French court. With the Hundred Years War (1337–1453) the site was abandoned and the buildings deteriorated. But monastic life resumed in the 16th century, and both the abbey and the village regained a certain importance, despite the vagaries of time – until, in 1791, the Revolution led to the dispersal of the monastic community and seizure of the ecclesiastical property. It was not until 1873 that the place recovered from this desertion, when Baroness Nathaniel de Rothschild purchased the site of Vaux-de-Cernay and had it restored, constructing various buildings which are still standing today.

Artists had already arrived in the region prior to this; they stayed in the inns of Cernay and set up their easels to draw and paint in the picturesque forest of Vaux-de-Cernay, which was still crossed by a stream that ran between the rocks (FIG. 19). The first depictions of the place began to figure in the official galleries from the early 1820s: Théodore Caruelle d'Aligny, for example, sent an early view of the site to the 1822 Salon, portraying it again in 1827, then in 1831, and, finally, almost every year for the following 30 years. This artist was a pioneer, arousing the interest of others, and his successors arrived in large numbers about 20 years later, before the great wave of invasion of the village and forests under the Second Empire. There they found a site that was a little like Fontainebleau, but closer to Paris. Somewhat earlier,

55. Saabye, '1879 Cernay-la-Ville', 182.

56. PSK to Frants Henningsen, Concarneau, 2 September 1879. SKMB25.

CAT. 25 Peder Severin Krøyer: *French Workers on a Sunken Road*, 1879. Oil on canvas, 80×100 cm. Ribe Kunstmuseum. RKM0492

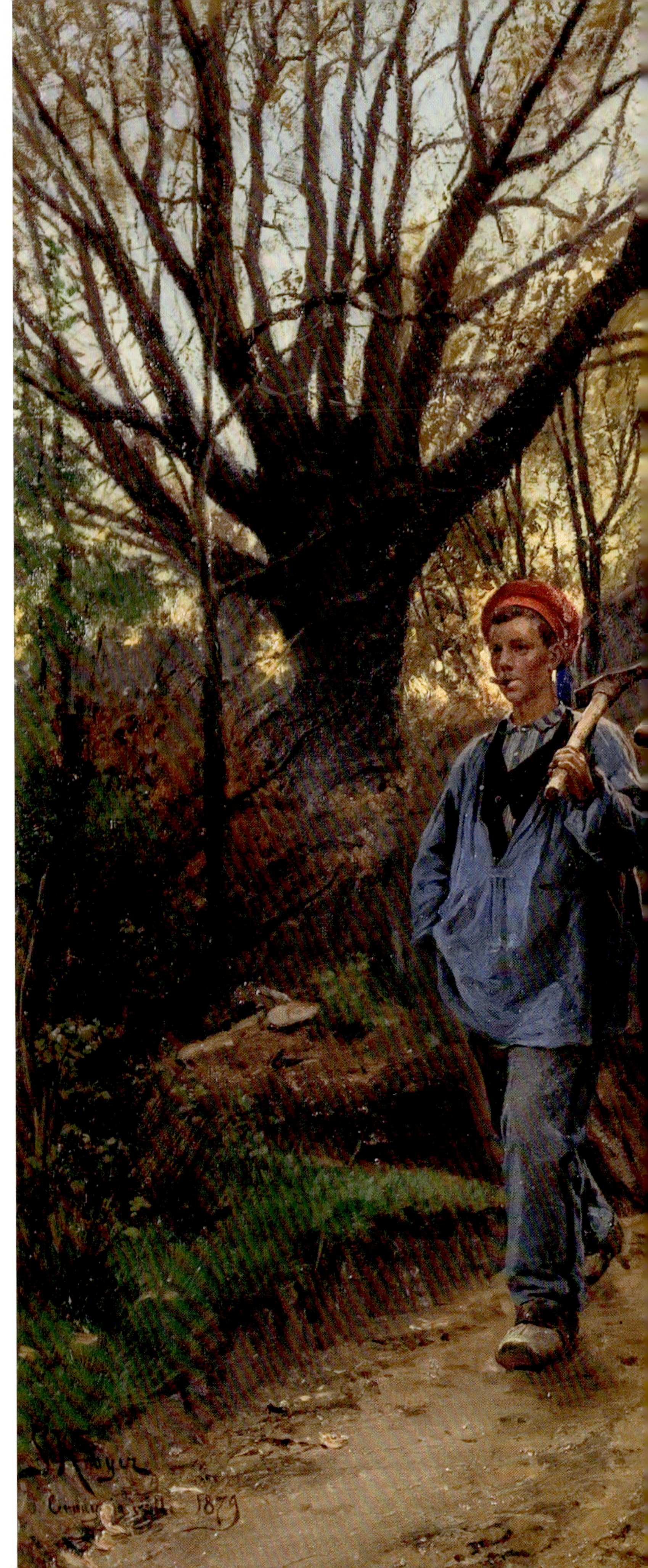

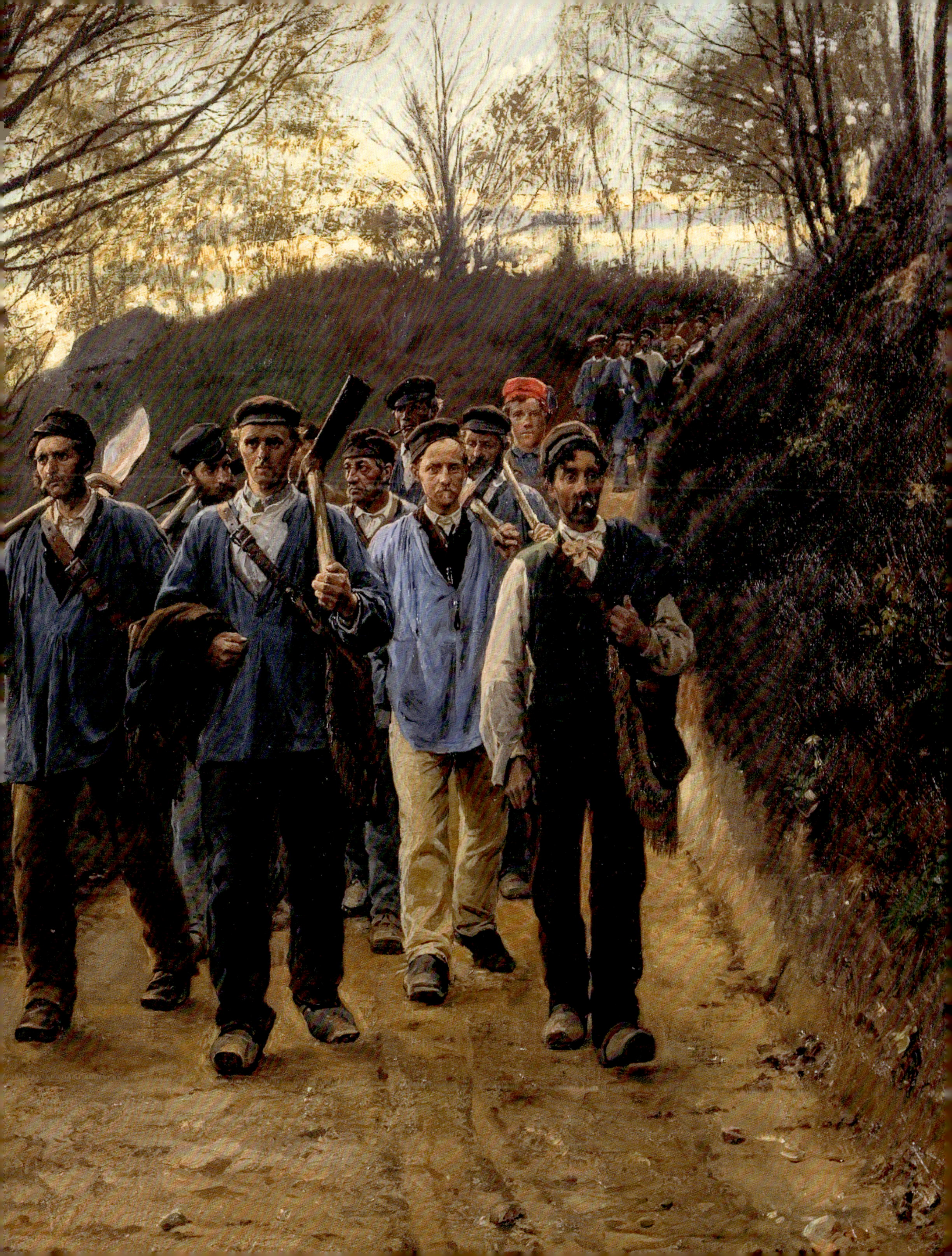

CAT. 26 François Louis Français: *The Painters on the Banks of the Ru des Vaux-de-Cernay*, 1870. Oil on canvas, 45×56 cm. Musée Charles de Bruyères, Remiremont. 92.1.5

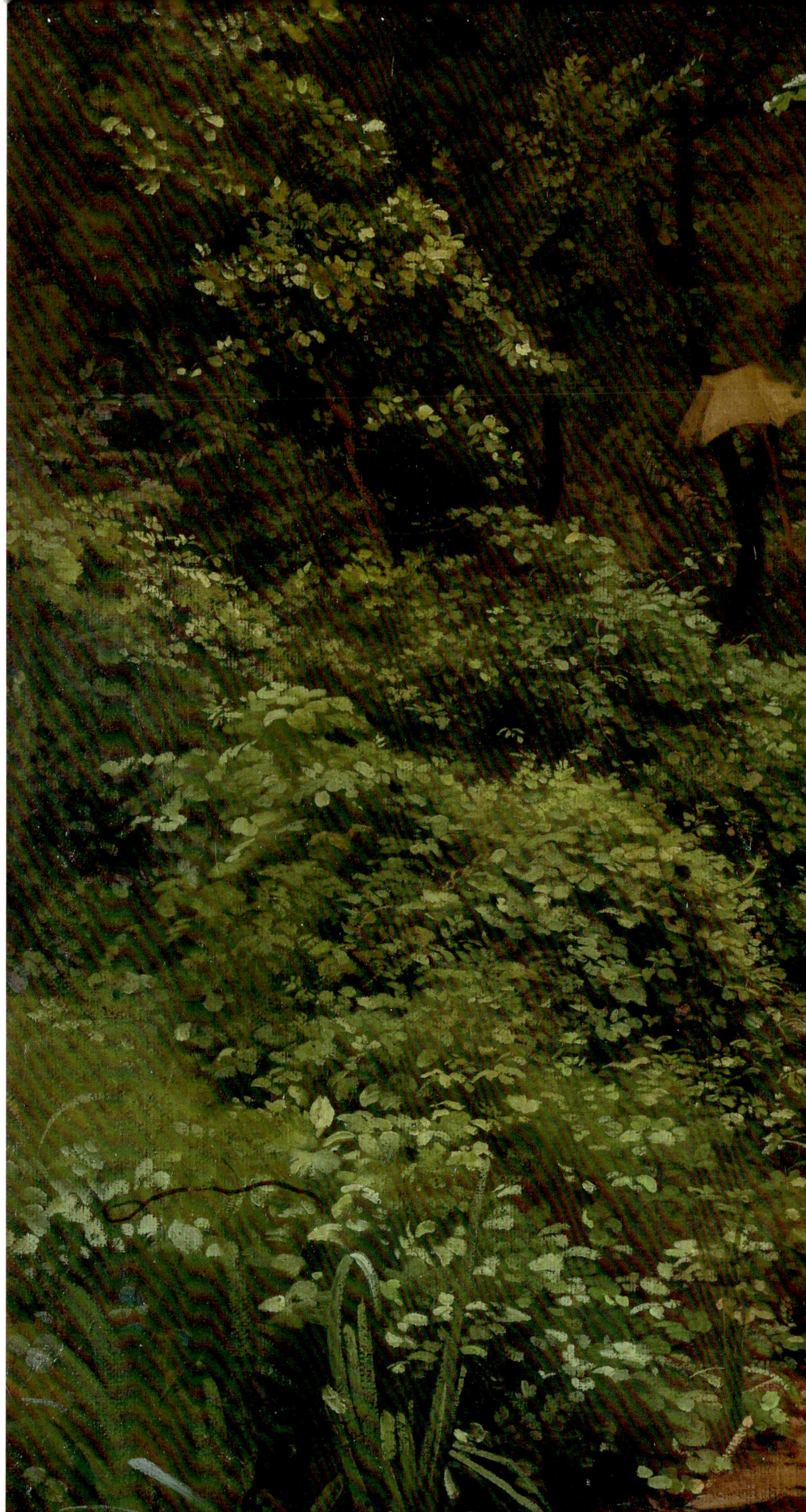

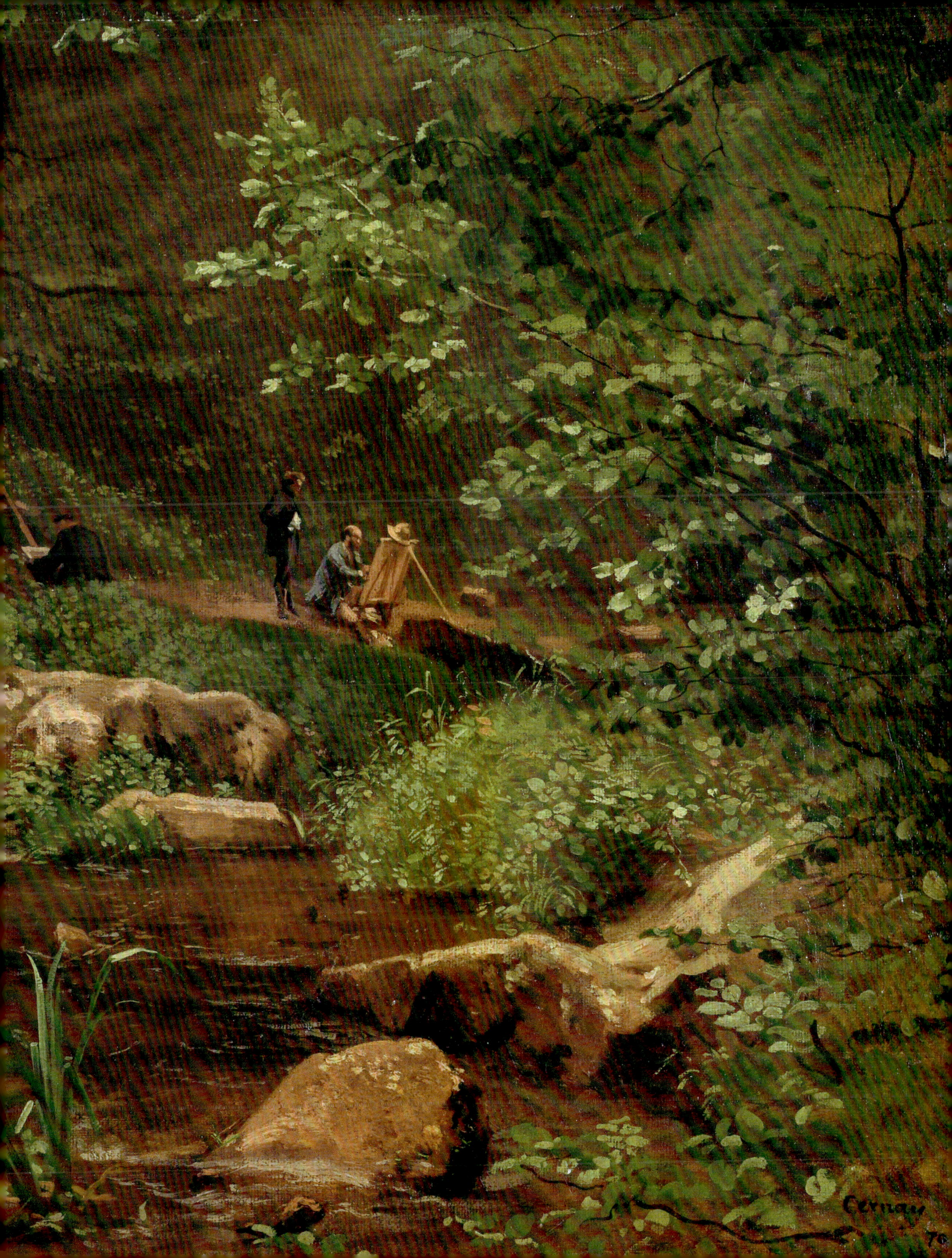

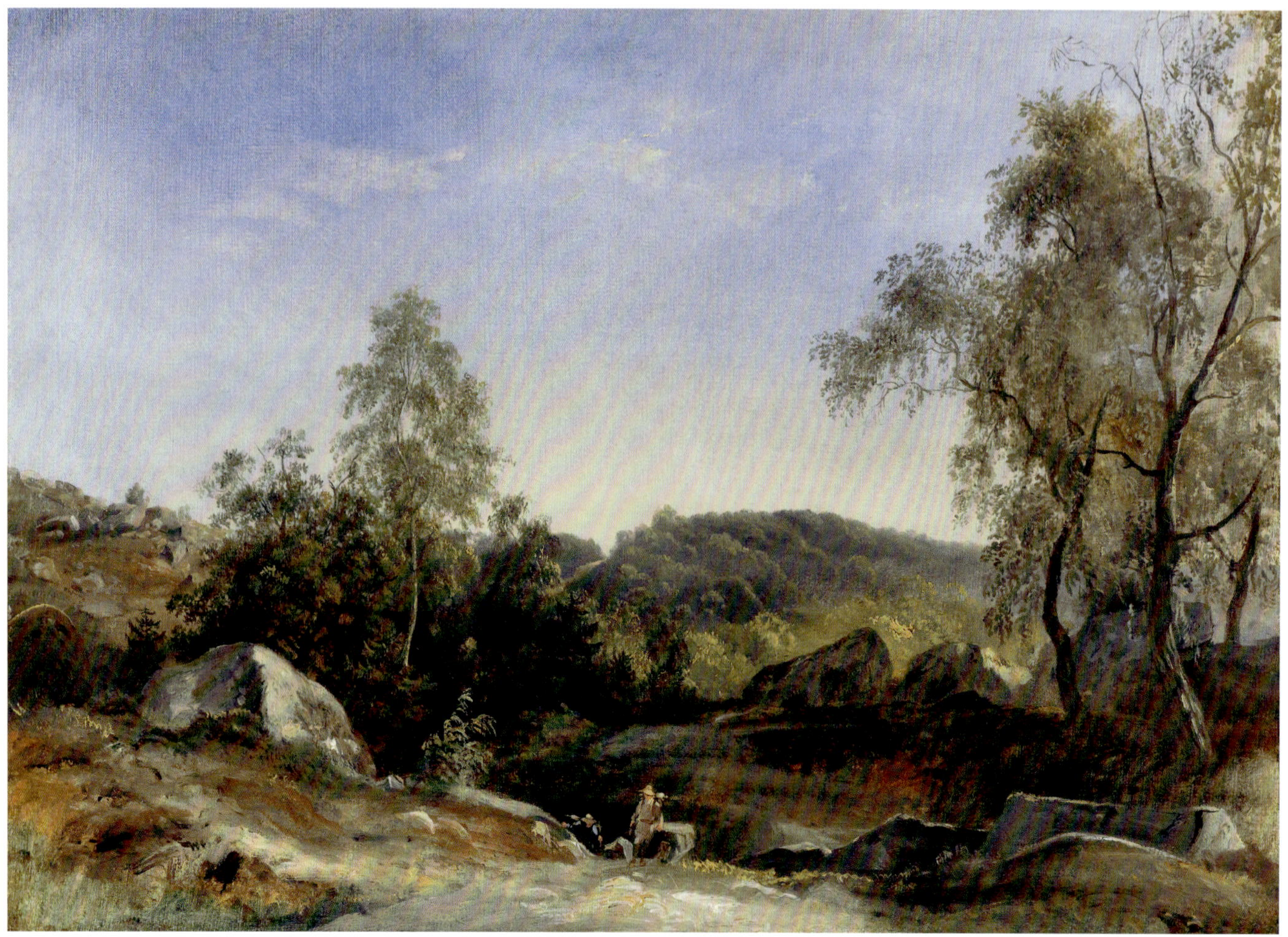

FIG. 19 Auguste Xavier Leprince: *Painters Resting, Fontainebleau*, c. 1824. Oil on paper mounted on canvas, 35.7×50.5 cm. Musée départemental de l'Oise, Beauvais. 998.10.38

in 1791, Fontainebleau had attracted painters such as Lazare Bruandet, who sent a *Landscape. In the Forest of Fontainebleau* (location unknown) to the Salon de la Jeunesse.

François Louis Français, who received an academic training but was also a pupil of Camille Corot, among others, was an inveterate traveller whose landscapes, inspired by a variety of French regions, were successfully exhibited at the Salon between 1838 and 1897. From 1870, he numbered among the Vaux's wave of admirers, although he did not send many works relating to Cernay to the Salon. The work exhibited here, for example, although it is probably his greatest success in this genre, never attained the honour of inclusion in a prestigious exhibition.

His early landscapes, in accordance with academic principles, were composed from diverse elements; mediated through Corot, he was also influenced by Lazard Bruandet, Théodore Rousseau, and the Realist painters, devoting himself to painting subjects as they appeared. Remembering also his master's paintings and those of his friends, he liked to bring his compositions to life by portraying his fellow artists at work (CAT. 26). Thus, in the picture exhibited, beyond the pool and rocks in the foreground, it is possible to glimpse two artists fully engaged in their task; they have arrived at their place of work bearing all the modern equipment of a painter, in the form of paint boxes, stools, and folding easels.

Krøyer and Zacho probably carried the same equipment as they followed in the footsteps of their young fellow artists, whom they met on arrival at Cernay-la-Ville, on 20 April 1879. Having settled in with them at one of the village inns, run by Léopold Lequesne – hence its nickname of Auberge Léopold – they would work in collaboration with young French artists whom they very quickly came to consider as friends.
Dominique Lobstein

CAT. 27 Léon Joubert
The Rustéphan Road under the Snow, Finistère, 1880

Thanks to the preparatory drawings on wood panel for the *Artists' Luncheon in Cernay-la-Ville* (FIG. 26), which Krøyer offered to Léopold Lequesne to decorate the dining room of his inn, we know the names of the other artists – around a dozen of them – who were more or less his age and were staying at Cernay at the same time as him, between April and June 1879. For Krøyer, this stay was interrupted in May, when he went to Paris to visit the Salon. Some of these artists accompanied him or would soon meet him at Concarneau, where they were to form the 'Brittany Group'. Among them was Léon Joubert (FIG. 21), whom Krøyer had perhaps known earlier because both they and the painter Ernest Baillet lived a stone's throw from one another between the Rue d'Orsel and the Boulevard Rochechouart at the foot of the hill of the Sacré-Coeur, not far from the Place Pigalle or Léon Bonnat's studio.

Joubert's presence in Brittany was easier to understand because he was originally from Quimper. Having trained in his hometown, he was exhibiting at the Salon from 1876 onwards and already presenting himself as a pupil of

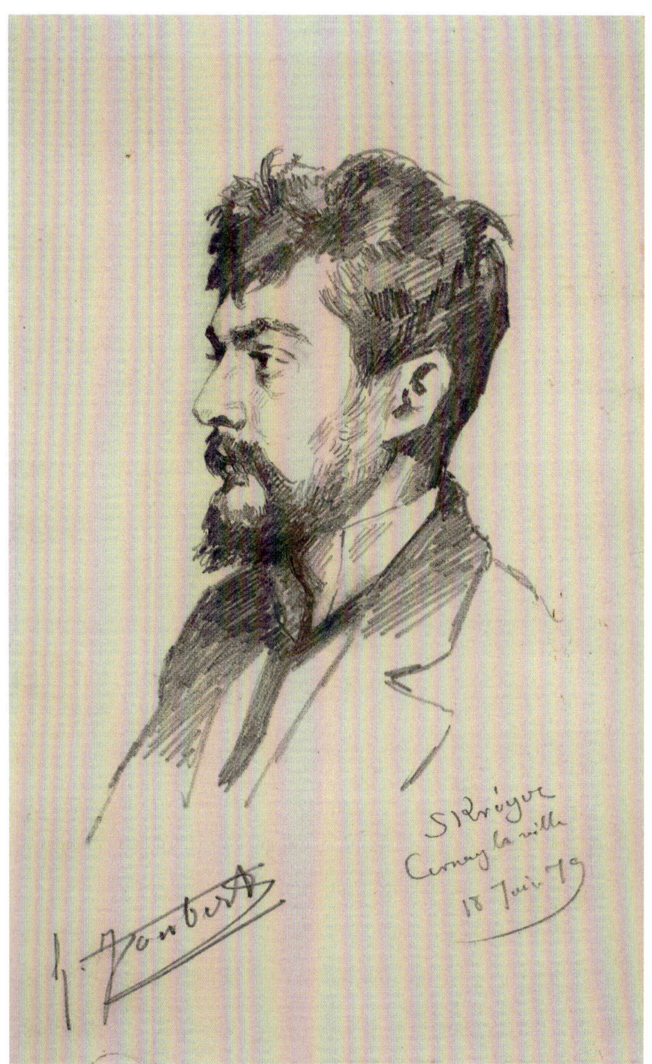

FIG. 21 Peder Severin Krøyer: *Portrait of Léon Joubert*, 18 June 1879. Pencil on paper, 190 × 119 mm. Den Hirschsprungske Samling, Copenhagen. 840

Pelouse, as well as of Alfred Guillou, his elder by seven years. Guillou was also a Breton, from Concarneau, and he was a regular visitor to Cernay, where Krøyer painted his portrait (Statens Museum for Kunst, Copenhagen) in 1879. In the first picture he sent to the Salon (location unknown), Joubert paid homage to the Chevreuse valley in which Cernay lay – and whose name he gave as his place of residence – by having it registered in the catalogue as *The Cottun Mill, in the Valley of the Chevreuse (Seine-*

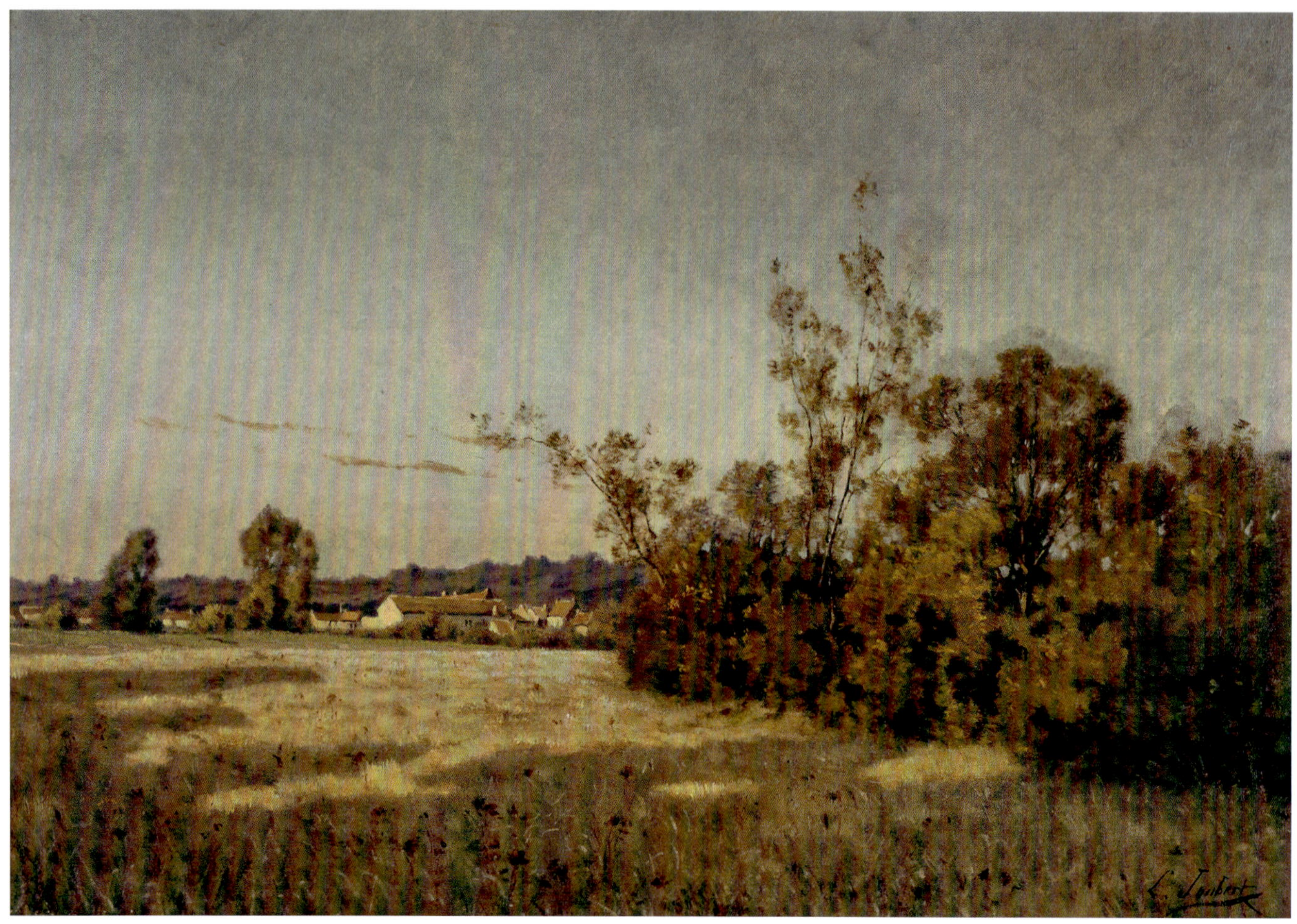

FIG. 20 Léon Joubert: *Autumn at Clairefontaine*, 1891. Oil on canvas, 259×204 cm. Musée d'art et d'histoire des Côtes-d'Amor, Saint-Brieuc. 80

et-Oise). Joubert returned to this place many times to paint pictures for exhibitions; he also painted in smaller formats for clients who were art lovers, his *Autumn at Clairefontaine* (FIG. 20) of 1892, depicting a site in the nearby forest of Rambouillet, being one such example. The artist's style remained the same and each of his pictures seems to have been painted in homage to the master whose teaching he followed.

Returning to his origins, in 1877, while still claiming Cernay as his place of residence, Joubert referenced the region of his birth by exhibiting *Kerensgosquer Heath, near Pont-Aven (Finistère)* (location unknown) under the number 1127.

Some years later he painted a place nearby, *The Rustéphan Road under the Snow, Finistère* (CAT. 27), which he sent to the 1880 Salon.[57] This picture must have reminded more than one person of the same subject painted by Pelouse several years earlier. It surprised Salon visitors with its vertical format and the dramatic aspect of its winter scene, infused with warm tones in its upper part by the red foliage of the trees and a distant sunset, towards which leads a sinuous, snowy road, with blue shadows.

57. Cat. no. 1977.

CAT. 27 Léon Joubert: *The Rustéphan Road under the Snow, Finistère*, 1880. Oil on canvas, 259×204 cm. Musée des Beaux-Arts, Quimper. 55-114

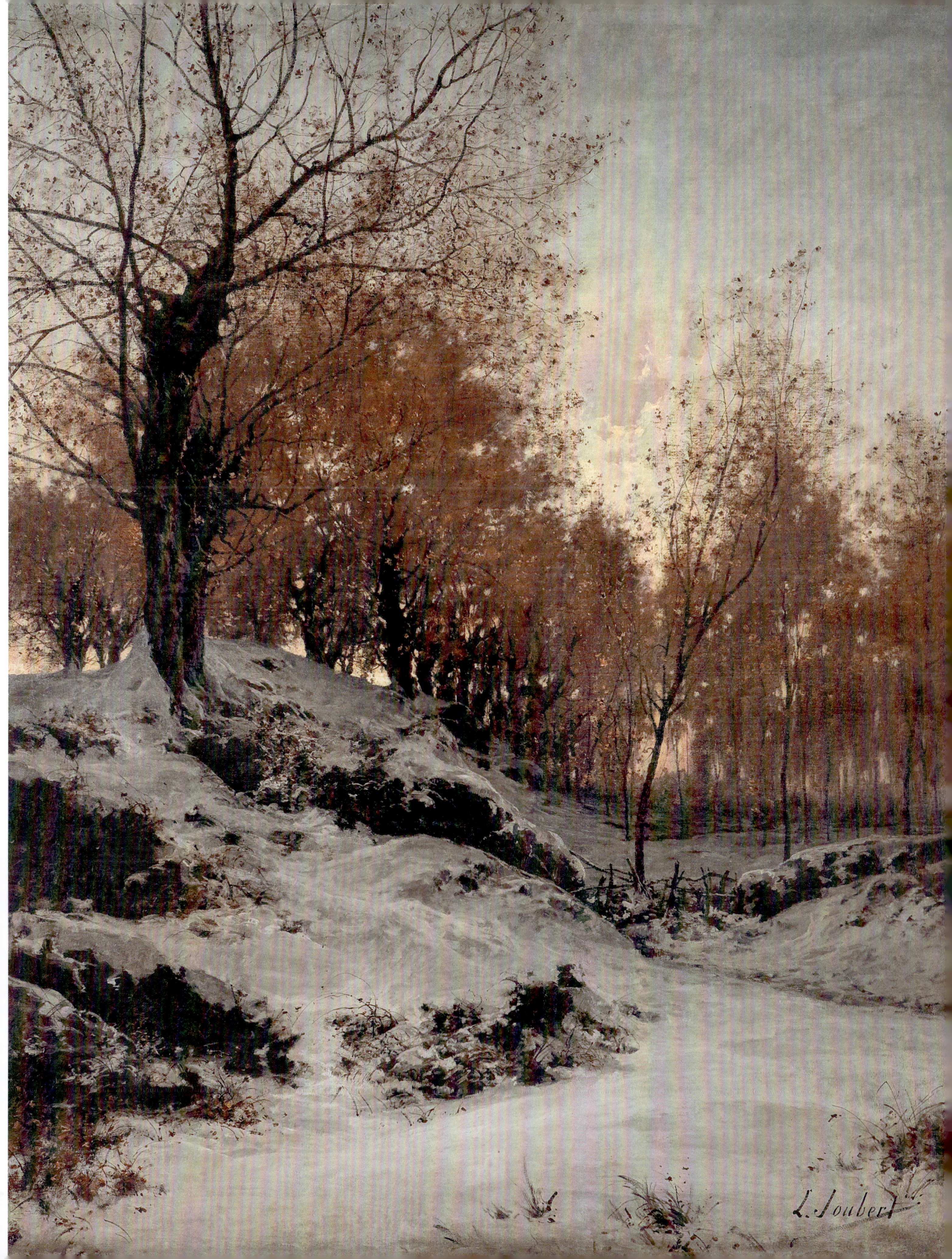
L. Joubert

Krøyer's relationships with these first French friends would continue throughout his life. Many letters preserve the memory of these relationships: naturally, they mention painting, but also the ordering of art materials, for which his Parisian friends took responsibility. When he was organising the French art exhibition in Copenhagen, in 1888, Krøyer would not forget these friends of his youth: Joubert was present with a landscape, as was Guillou with his *The Arrival of the Pardon of Sainte-Anne-de-Fouesnant at Concarneau* (1887, Musée des Beaux-Arts, Quimper); nor was Pelouse forgotten – the master of them all – with his exhibit of *Charcoal Burners by the Banks of the River Doubs* (location unknown).
Dominique Lobstein

CAT. 28 Léon Germain Pelouse
The Path from Lanriec to Concarneau, by Moonlight, 1878

CAT. 29 Léon Germain Pelouse
Veaux de Cernay, undated

Somewhat older than the other painters staying at Cernay, Léon Germaine Pelouse had adopted the role of leader of the little artists' colony which gathered in the village before scattering into the surrounding forests to set up their easels.

Pelouse was born in 1838 in a village named Pierrelaye, in the Paris region, where his father was a carpenter. He was still living there when he embarked on his professional career, becoming a commercial traveller for businesses in northern France. Later, having travelled to every corner of France, he taught himself to paint, before going to Paris and trying his luck at the Salon. Since records of the event from the early 1850s are no longer extant, it is impossible to know the date from which he tried to gain access to it. However, given that he exhibited his first picture there in 1865 – aged 27, therefore – it is possible that he may have been rejected prior to that date. This first attempt was not a resounding success. According to the information in the catalogue, he exhibited just one work, entitled *Near Précy (Oise): Autumn Evening* (location unknown). It met with such a cool reception that Pelouse's name disappeared from the 1866 and 1867 Salons – whether through his own doing or that of the jury is unclear. But he reappeared in 1868 and figured regularly in the catalogue thereafter. That year he exhibited *A Foreshore at Low Tide: Brittany Coast* (location unknown). According to the information in the catalogue, the work was owned by a collector named Puissant, which proves that while awaiting a favourable reception by the critics, his work was already of interest to some art lovers. It was not until 1872, when one of his works was first purchased by the Beaux-Arts administration (FIG. 22), that his situation changed. In 1873, and again thanks to a work from Cernay, an article in the newspaper *Le Figaro* finally paid homage to him:

> The painters who have arrived should not monopolise our attention. Besides the names that are listed, new talents are springing forth and I know of nothing more interesting than to take an artist who is just setting out and to follow him.
>
> Among the latecomers, a special place should be reserved for M. Pelouse, who is exhibiting a landscape of great interest. Everything is in its place in this very fine picture of the *Valley of Cernay*, the prettiest landscape of the young school. An excellent understanding of nature, a sobriety of method, and a perfect harmony are the dominant qualities of this young landscape artist who has a promising future.[58]

This first recognition by a critic brought institutional rewards: a second-class medal – exempting him henceforth from appearing in front of the jury in order to exhibit – and, the following year, the purchase of his picture *Through the Woods, an October Morning*, sent to the Musée de Rennes in 1875.

58. Wolff, 'Le Salon de 1873', 2.

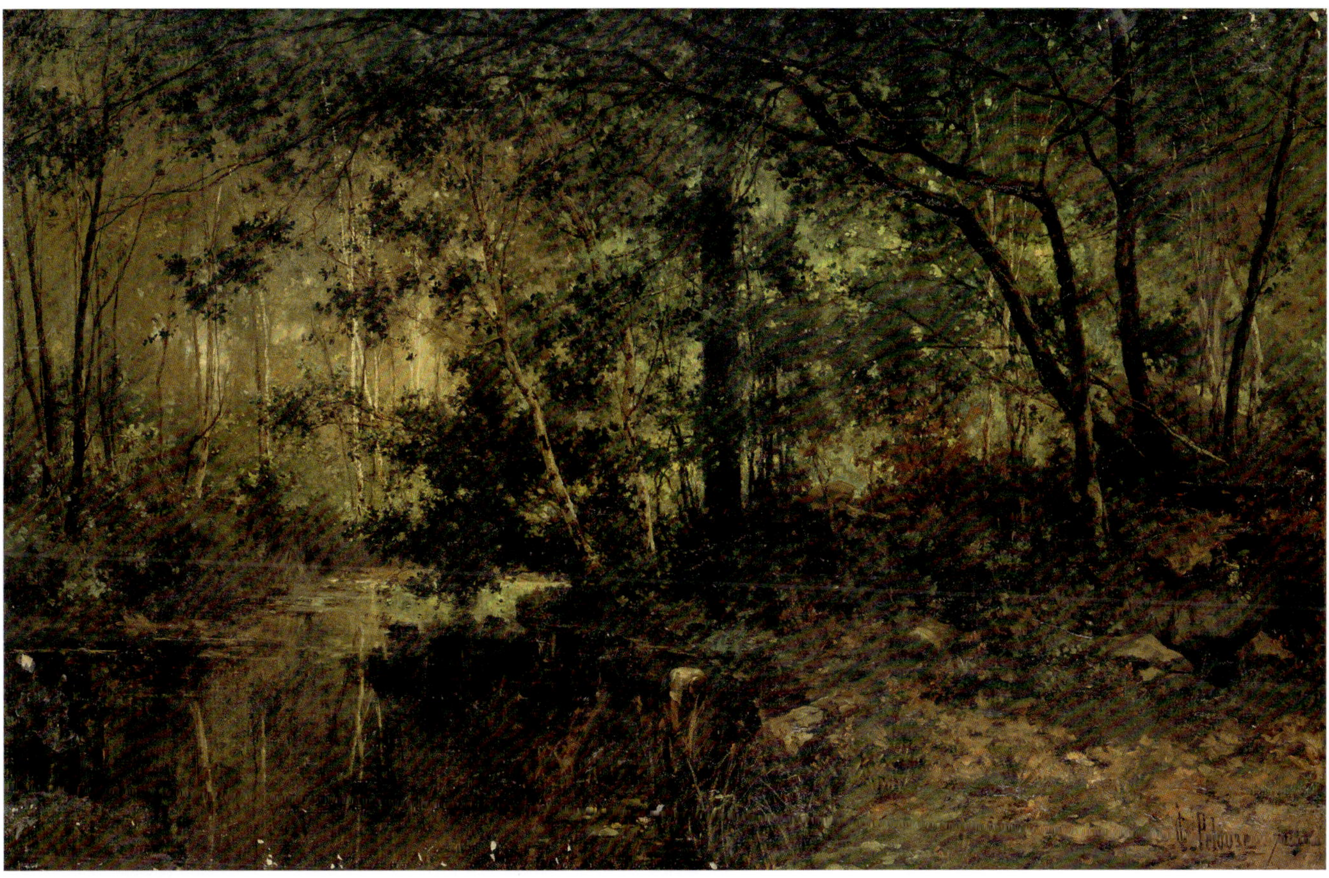

FIG. 22 Léon Germain Pelouse: *Souvenir of Cernay*, 1872. Oil on canvas, 81×128 cm. Musée d'Orsay, Paris. INV 20112

By 1872, Pelouse had already been living in Cernay for some time. He arrived there in 1870 but was quickly driven out by the Prussian invasion, before returning once more. The place became the most common subject of his paintings, and he varied the views of Vaux-de-Cernay – like the example in the Musée des Beaux-Arts in Bordeaux – throughout the seasons, intent on rendering the vegetation under skies that were worked on with close attention (CAT. 29). The valley of the Chevreuse was not his only subject; he occasionally followed his young fellow artists to Brittany, bringing back mementos such as *The Path from Lanriec to Concarneau, by Moonlight* (CAT. 28), which he exhibited at the 1878 Salon and subsequently at the Société des Amis des Arts in Rouen, where it was acquired for the city museum.

With his reputation growing, he very soon began to attract young artists who wished to become landscape painters but were not much tempted by the training offered them by the École des Beaux-Arts. Thus it was that what we now know as the 'Cernay colony' began. Having more of a classical bent than his associates at Fontainebleau and Barbizon, Pelouse was only a moderate supporter of Realism and, both in his paintings and in the advice he gave, stood in a tradition in which Krøyer – who had seen the pictures he sent to the 1877 Salon – seems little interested, in view of his French creations of the period (such as CAT. 25). However, this did not prevent him from making frequent references to Pelouse in his correspondence,[59] and inviting him to exhibit in Copenhagen in 1888.
Dominique Lobstein

59. For example in a letter: PSK to Frederik Vermehren, Cernay-la-Ville, 20 May 1879. PSK Archive 58.

CAT. 28 Léon Germain Pelouse: *The Path from Lanriec to Concarneau, by Moonlight*, 1878. Oil on canvas, 131×163 cm. Musée des Beaux-Arts, Rouen. 1880.8

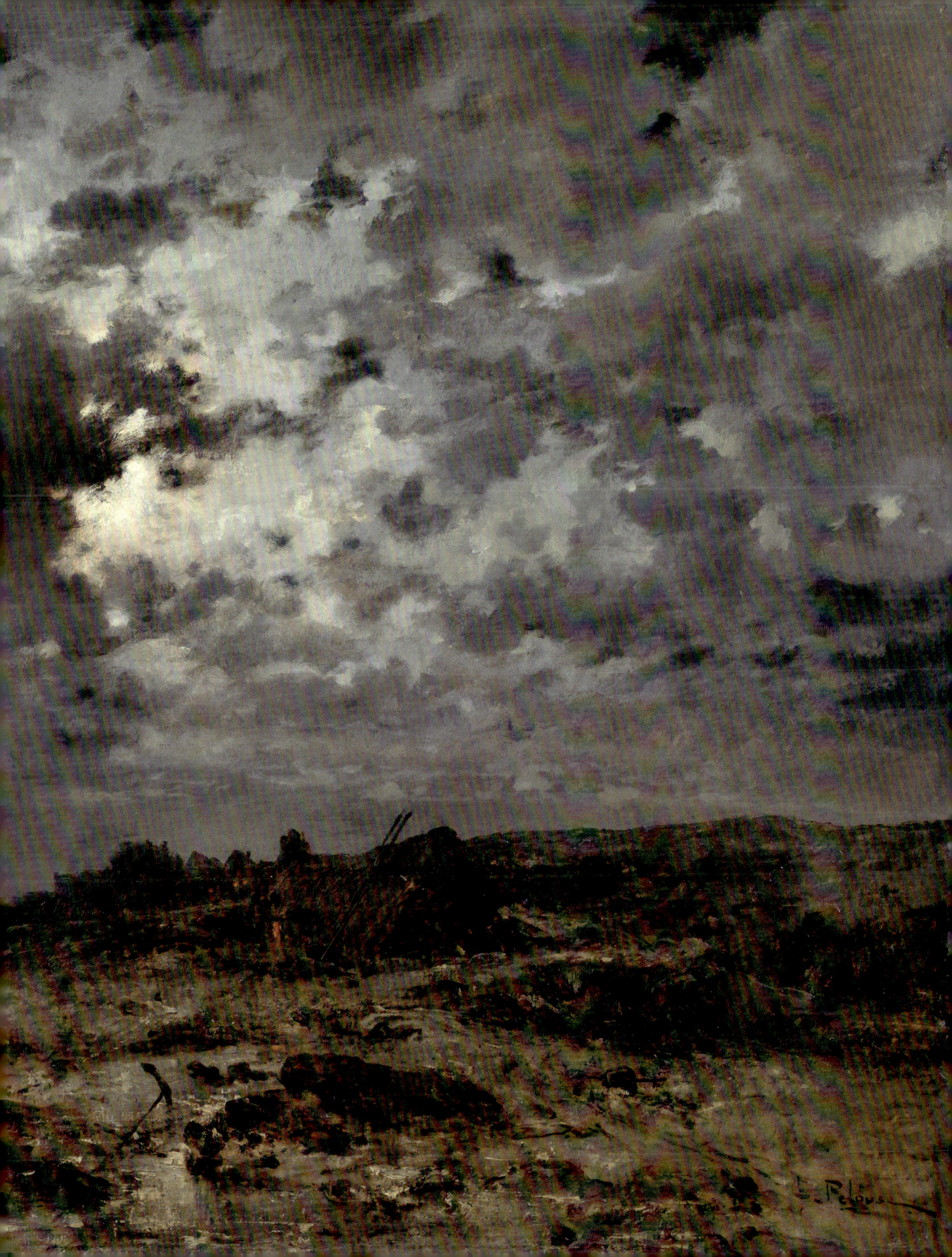

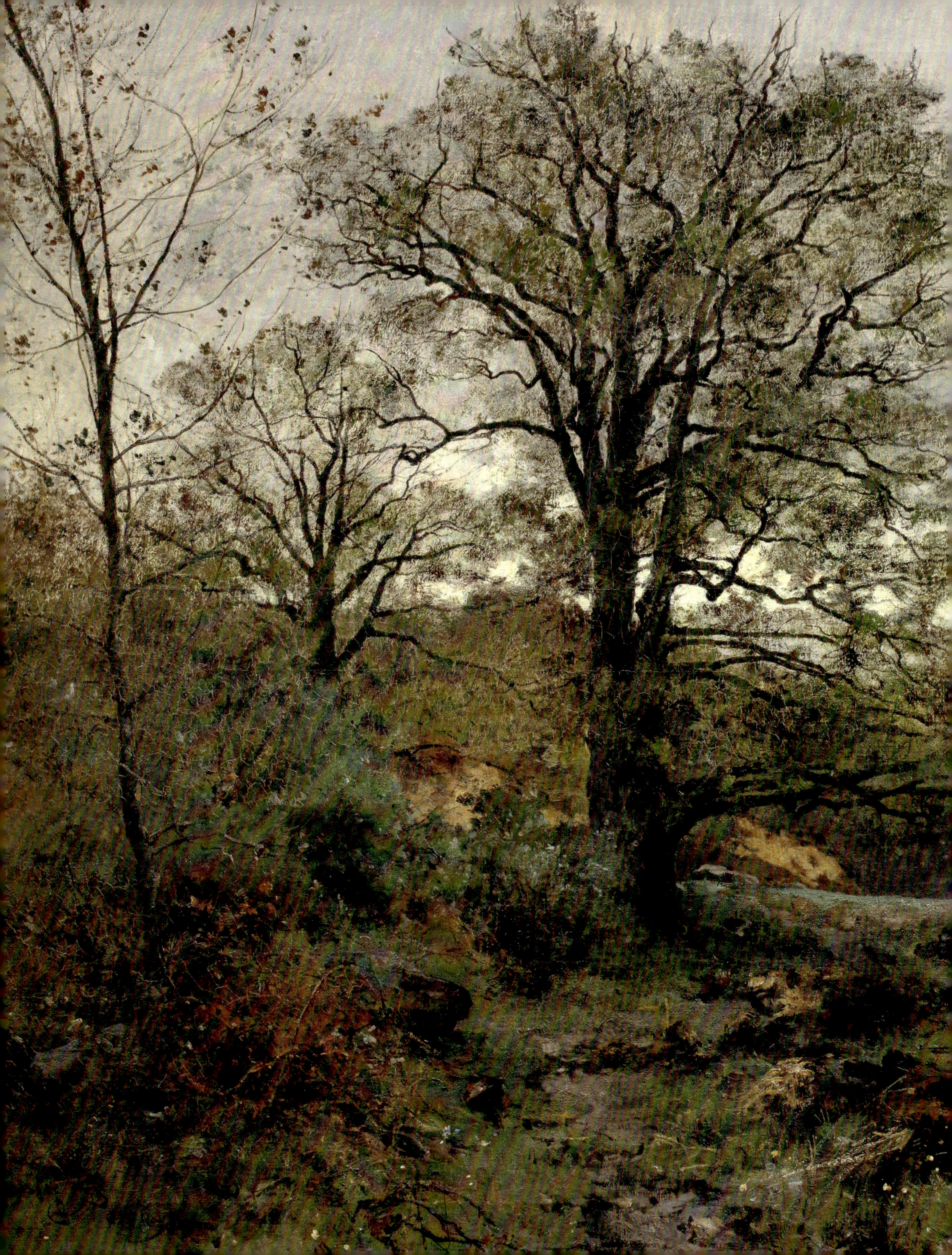

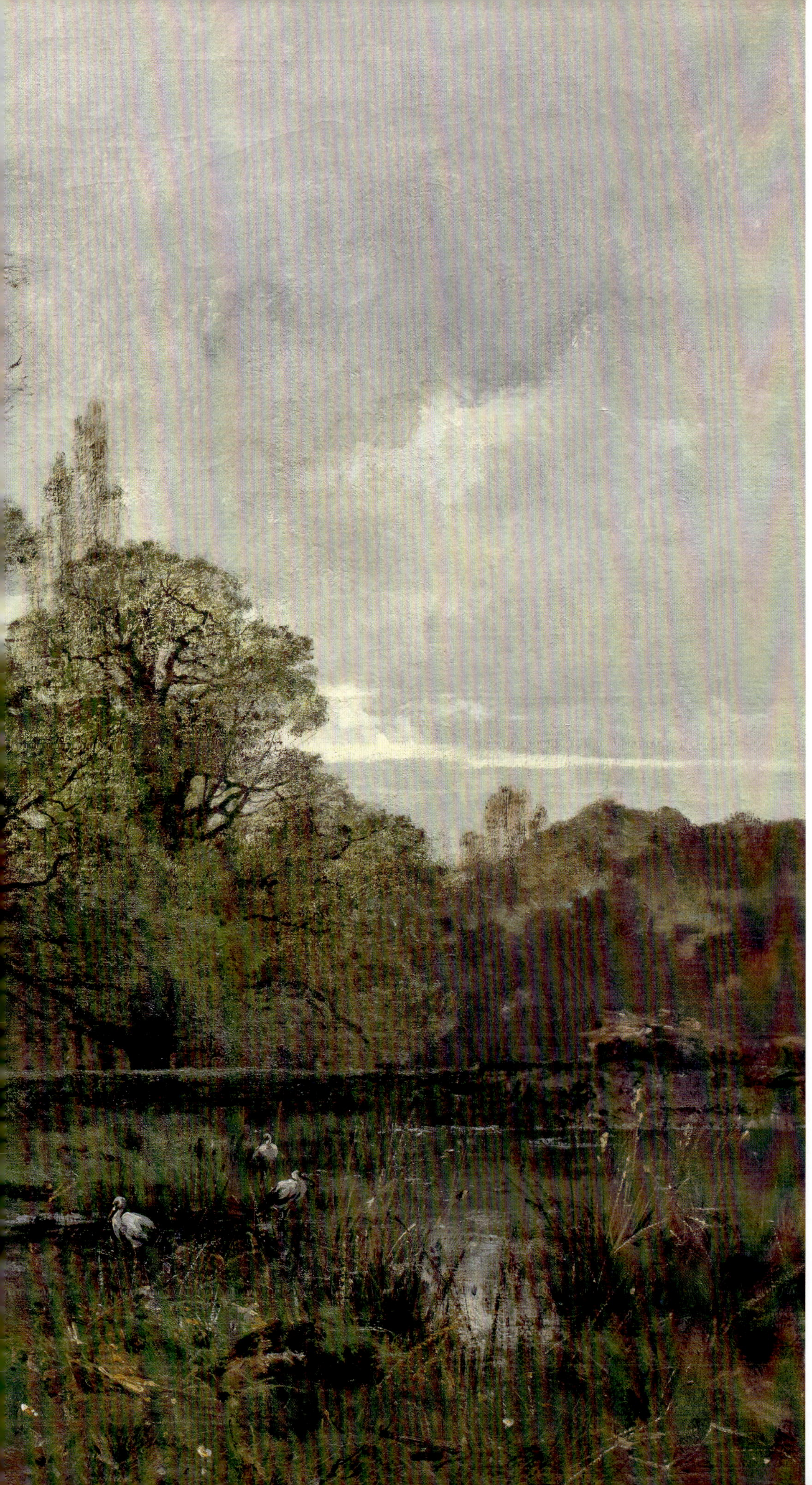

CAT. 29 Léon Germain Pelouse: *Veaux de Cernay*, undated. Oil on canvas, 100.5×135.5 cm. Musée des Beaux-Arts, Bordeaux. Bx E 1091

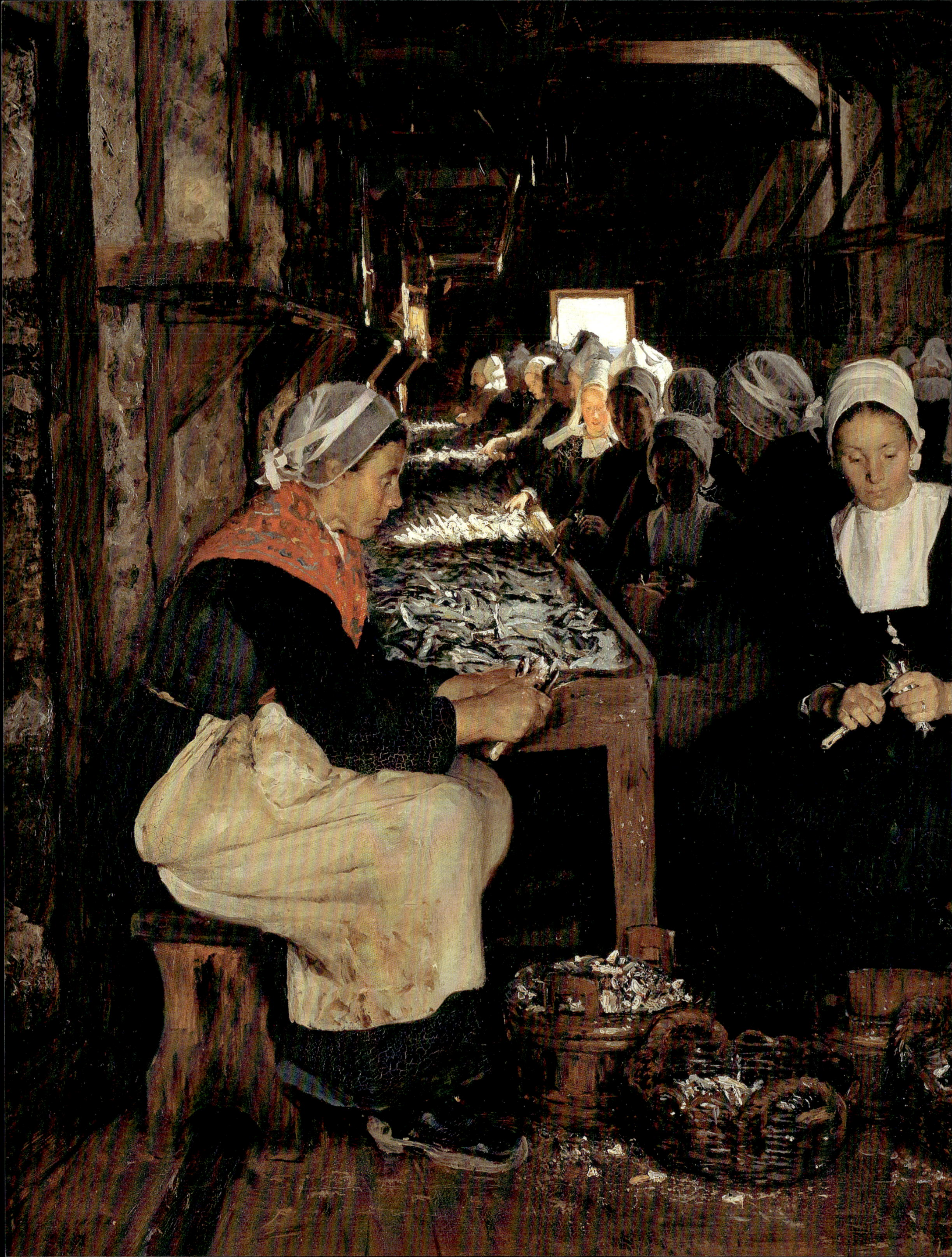

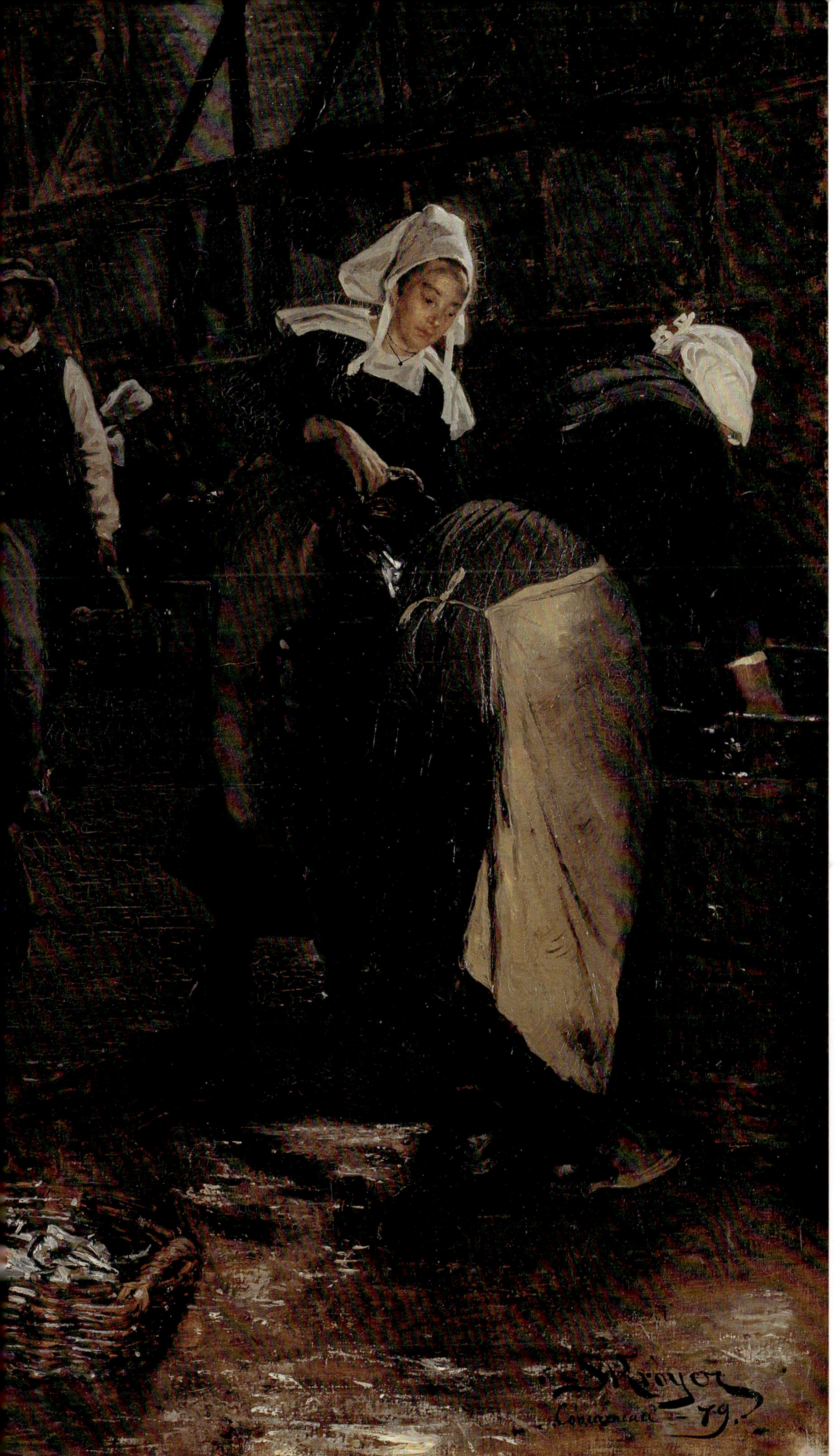

CAT. 30 Peder Severin Krøyer: *A Sardine Curing and Packing Factory in Concarneau*, 1879. Oil on canvas, 101.5×140.5 cm. Statens Museum for Kunst, Copenhagen. KMS3108

CAT. 30 Peder Severin Krøyer
A Sardine Curing and Packing Factory in Concarneau, 1879

CAT. 31 Peder Severin Krøyer
In a Cellar in Concarneau, 1879

The second time Krøyer exhibited at the Salon in Paris, he presented *A Sardine Curing and Packing Factory in Concarneau* (CAT. 30). This was a so-called genre painting, an everyday scene from contemporary ordinary life. The work was created during Krøyer's sojourn in Brittany in the summer of 1879, after his stay in Cernay-la-Ville. Like St. Malo, Concarneau began as a medieval fortification around an island, gradually developing into a fishing village. However, Concarneau is located on the south coast of Brittany rather than the north. It was home to a small colony of artists and to the French painter Alfred Marie Guillou, who had grown up there but trained in Paris. Krøyer met Guillou and a few other artists during his time there, as evidenced by several drawn and painted portraits. Similarly, the small, atmospheric study *In a Cellar in Concarneau* (CAT. 31) testifies to the artist's pursuit of good subjects – and shows what the innkeeper could serve up in terms of food and drink. Krøyer had arrived at Concarneau with the intention of painting a *plein air* scene with figures but was forced by circumstances to paint inside a large hall where the fish were processed. Krøyer himself described the place as follows:

> Concarneau, where I am now staying, is a larger fishing village which is currently very busy as this is the high season of sardine fishing. There are about 1,000 boats in operation, and it is a magnificent spectacle to see them all head out at once or return with the catch. There are large factories here where the sardines are prepared in different ways, and I am currently painting a picture of that, rather large. Incidentally, the weather has been very bad until recently, with almost constant rain and very cool. Now we have had warm and beautiful weather for the last week. Just like in Cernay, there are quite a few of us painters together here, and we have a very nice time. I thoroughly enjoy being back at the sea and swimming in salt water again; almost two years have passed since I last saw the sea up close.[60]

Krøyer submitted the work for the Salon in Paris, where it was exhibited in the spring of 1880, while Krøyer himself had gone on to Italy. However, he did take a trip back to Paris to see the Salon. Here, several reviews from the exhibition had been published in newspapers and magazines, praising Krøyer's work. In this example, the French critic Paul Mantz made the following comment in one of the most important newspapers of the time in Paris, *Le Temps*:

> It will perhaps be recalled that at the Champ-de-Mars Exhibition [The World's Fair in 1878], the Danes appeared very weak. Some of them were even producing paintings after the fashion of 1820, which is perhaps not a crime, but certainly a mistake. It will be a pleasure to learn that not all Danish artists are quite so backward-looking. Here is a painter who is new to us, M. Krøyer. A pupil of the Copenhagen Academy, M. Krøyer has conducted himself like an American: he went to Concarneau, for it is undoubtedly there that the ideal resides. The picture he brought back is full of exceptional promise. It shows the interior of a *Sardine Factory* [*sic*]. In the half-light of a workshop whose particular aroma can be sensed from far off, women are busily preparing silver-bellied sardines. M. Krøyer is a realist; he has an energetic hand, which insists on registering character with boldness. The jury members do not seem to have looked closely enough at this dynamic painting.[61]

60. PSK in a letter home: Concarneau, 14 August 1879. PSK Archive 60.

61. Mantz, 'Le Salon. VII', 20 June 1880, [2].

CAT. 31 Peder Severin Krøyer: *In a Cellar in Concarneau*, 1879.
Oil on canvas on cardboard, 28 × 22 cm. Skagens Kunstmuseer. SKM2091

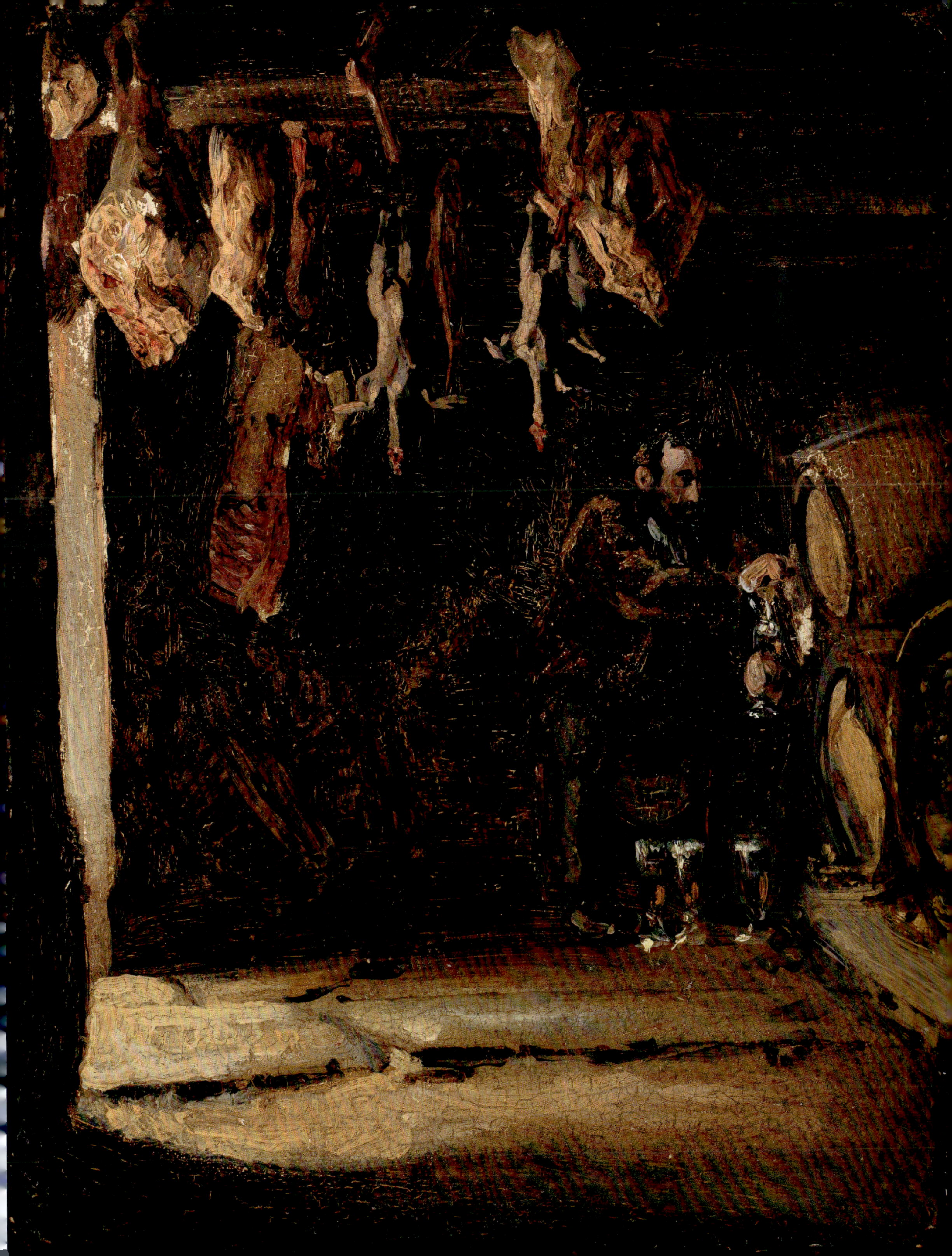

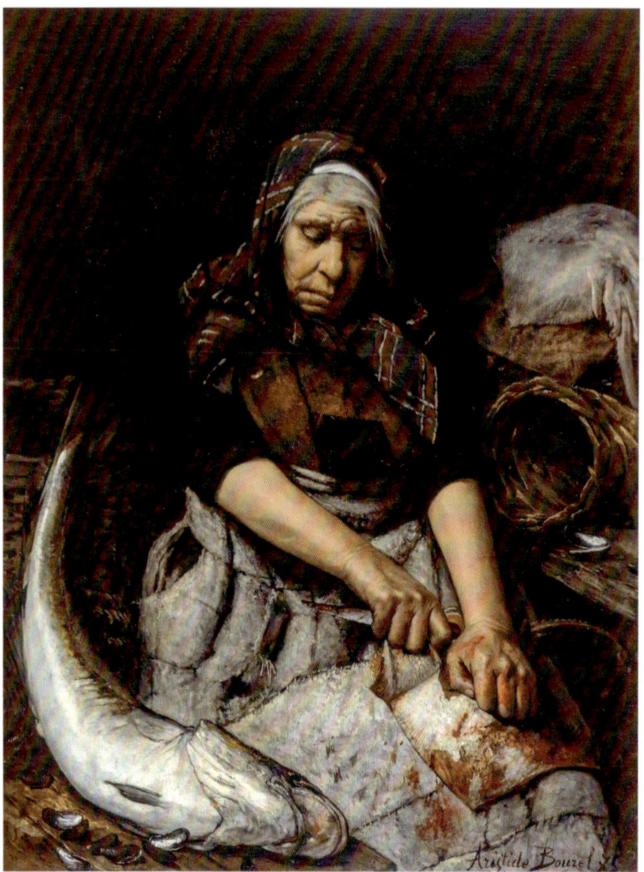

FIG. 23 Aristide Bourel: *Woman Skinning a Skate*, 1875. Oil on canvas. 137×107 cm. Musée des Beaux-Arts, Dunkerque. BA.P 364

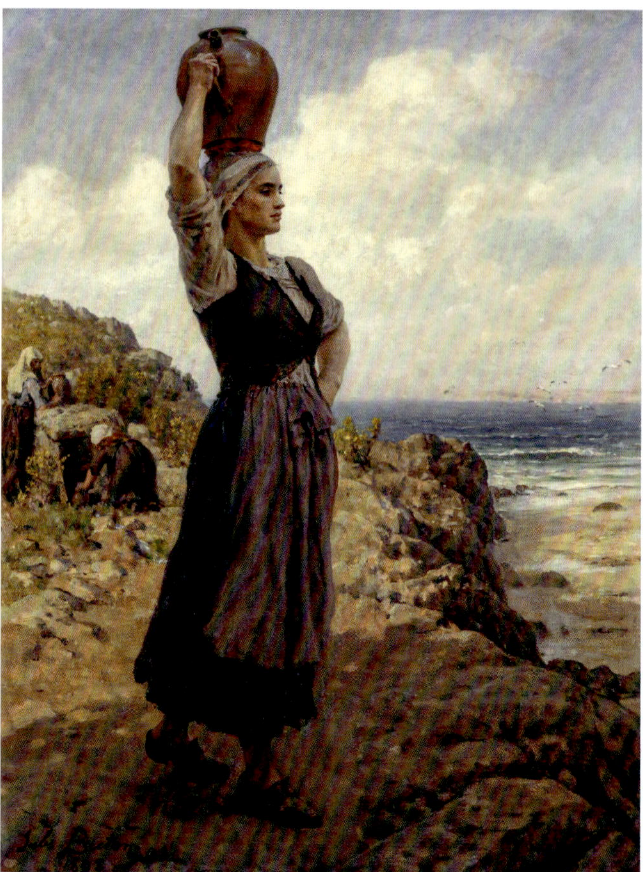

FIG. 24 Jules Breton: *At the Fountain*, 1892. Oil on canvas. 90.5×68.5 cm. Musée des Beaux-Arts, Quimper. 55-78

Here we see Krøyer as a modern artist who does not look back in time for inspiration, thereby countering the general impression conveyed to the French public when they saw the Danish contribution to the Exposition Universelle in 1878 in Paris. Krøyer is highlighted as a Realist who paints his models with honesty. The mention of members of the jury having failed to look closely enough at the painting is an allusion to the fact that several French critics had predicted that Krøyer would receive a medal, which he did not. Many of the other reviews highlighted Krøyer's ability to capture the daylight falling in through the factory windows.[62]

Mette Harbo Lehmann

62. For example, Vachon, 'Le Salon de 1880', 3.

CAT. 32 Gaston Édouard Le Senechal de Kerdreoret
Oyster Gatherer in Cancale, 1890

There were many references to maritime occupations to be found on the walls of the Salon, and women often figured strongly in these. They were present when their sailor husbands departed and when they returned, present too on the quaysides awaiting unlikely returns; their silhouettes were visible in many works. Jules Breton, along with a very few other painters, still made his subjects stand in for classical figures: his picture *At the Fountain* (FIG. 24), for example, portrayed a caryatid facing the ocean. Most, however, did not attempt to idealise them, depicting them worn out by the painful conditions of their lives (FIG. 25), ageless, and dressed in rags, enslaved by their hard work. This was also the case in the two works which were exhibited at the Salon. The painting by Aristide Bourel (FIG. 23) concentrates on a single figure, close-framed and engrossed in her task; it is as much a portrait as a genre scene. Viewed from below, the woman skinning the skate appears monumental while the still life presented by the sea fish attains prominence in the foreground – another speciality of this artist; in the midst of this, the woman's hands are busily moving and, holding the knife that has enabled her to make an incision in the skin, she carefully separates it from the flesh. This special care and precise cutting operation are designed to retrieve the flesh for consumption and the skin for manufacturing shagreen, a precious material used for covering certain luxury objects.

Le Sénéchal de Kerdréoret, on the other hand, adopts a panoramic view (CAT. 32) and places his subjects on a beach at low tide, transforming them into sea harvesters, gathering oysters that the storm has torn from their breeding beds and abandoned on the beach. These then become the property of whoever finds them. The painter depicts this uncomfortable work, with its uncertain outcome, at nightfall under a seemingly menacing sky.

These are examples of the kind of pictures Krøyer saw during his visits to the Paris Salon, enabling him to compare his own creations in this vein with those of certain French artists and to consider what united and separated them. Generally, the subjects tackled by Krøyer, compared with those of artists such as Bourel and Le Sénéchal de Kerdréoret, seem more measured, whether they were portraits or genre scenes. Without representing an ideal of happiness, the lives of his subjects seem easier, and time does not appear to weigh as heavily on their bodies and faces. His fishermen drawing their nets or hoisting their sails do not betray the difficult nature of their work in their gestures or attitudes. Krøyer's working women – of whom there were far fewer in Denmark than in France – seem not to suffer from their condition: *A Sardine Curing and Packing Factory in Concarneau* (CAT. 30), for example, must have surprised the Parisian public, since the harshness of their working conditions seems effaced by the youthfulness of these young women preparing the sardines, with their light, clean clothes and the reserve in the evocation of their work.

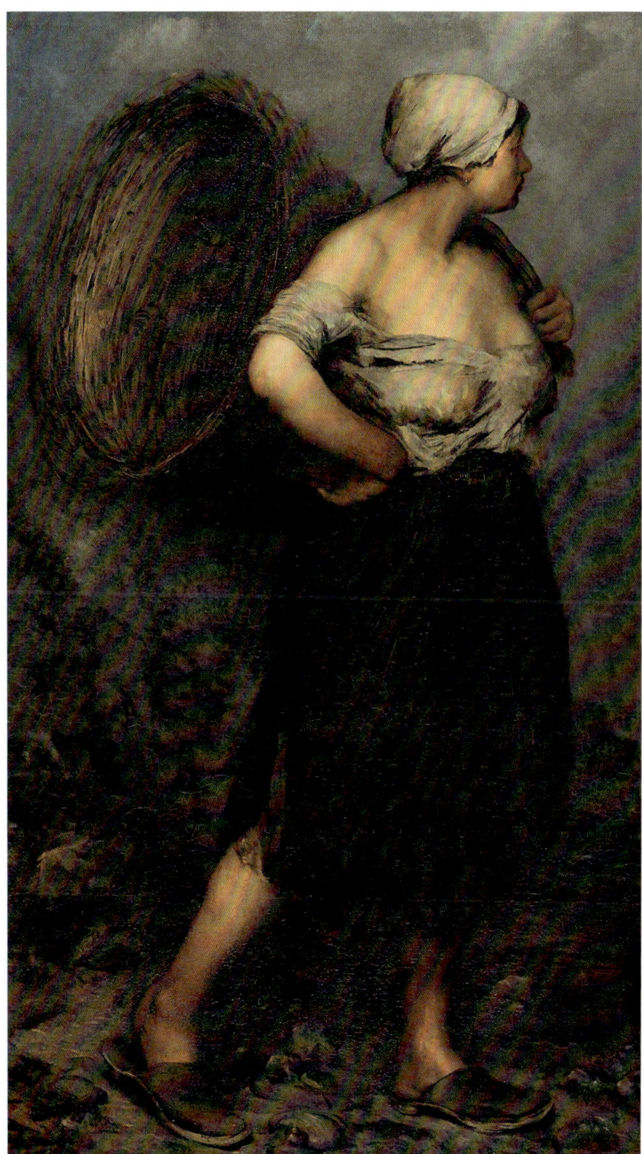

FIG. 25 Antoine Vollon: *Woman of Le Pollet, in Dieppe*, 1876. Oil on canvas, 183 × 105 cm. Kunstmuseum Den Haag. 0333805

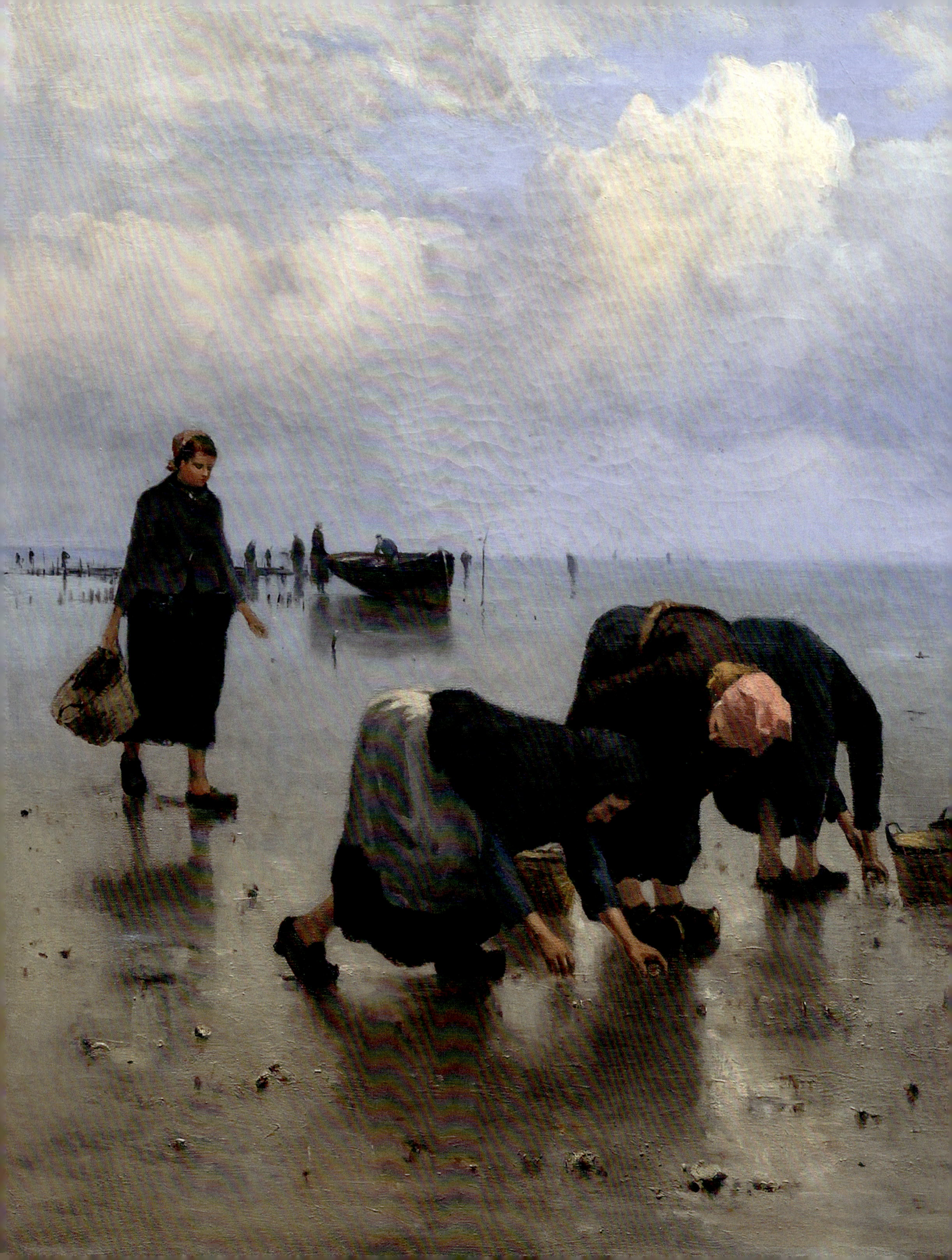

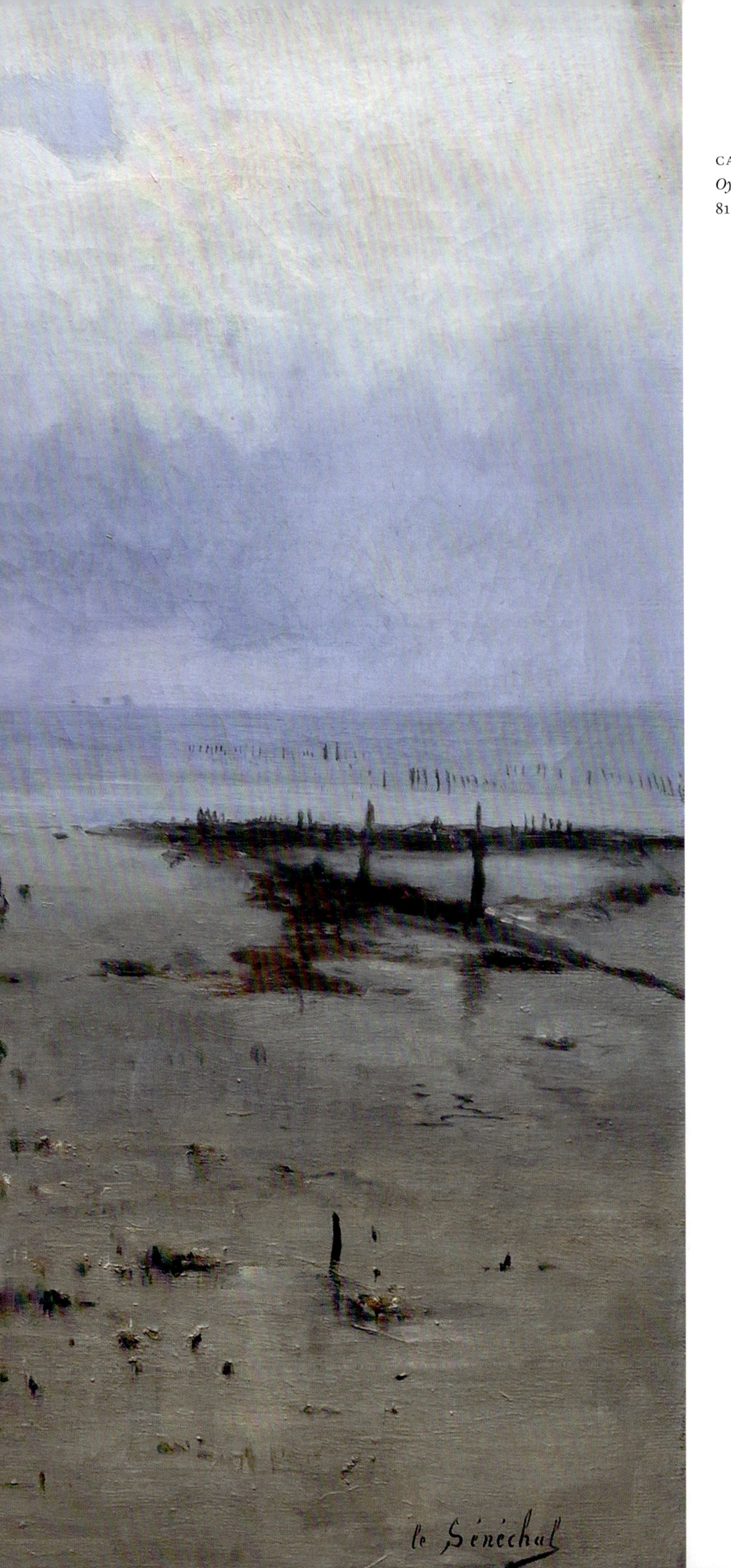

CAT. 32 Gaston Édouard Le Senechal de Kerdréoret: *Oyster Gatherer in Cancale*, 1890. Oil on canvas, 81×100 cm. Musée d'Art et d'Histoire, Évreux. 8070

The differences are also due to Krøyer's method of painting: his brush is much more pliant, his colours more varied and often animated by warm notes and bright touches of white; and the clear light with which he surrounds portraits and genre scenes seeks not so much to dramatise his subjects as to immerse them in an almost ideal environment. There may be several explanations for these differences: the first is the artist's academic training, which was constantly in his mind – as indeed it was for Bastien-Lepage – while another is his interest in Italian art, which he would encounter in October 1879, following his stay in France. But perhaps more important than either of these factors, we should note the links uniting Krøyer with some of his earlier painter friends – those he had met in Cernay-la-Ville and with whom he then went to Concarneau.

Dominique Lobstein

CAT. 33 Flavien Louis Peslin
The Spinner, 1881

CAT. 34 Alfred Marie Guillou
Landing of Tuna at Concarneau, 1879

As in the previous account, two different pictures have been brought together here. The first depicts a single figure at work indoors, while the second shows a number of people at work by the sea.

The first, *The Spinner* (CAT. 33), was painted by Flavien Louis Peslin – of whom there is a portrait, drawn by Krøyer, in the Hirschsprung Collection, and who figures among the artists gathered together in the picture *Artists' Luncheon in Cernay-la-Ville* (FIG. 26). Peslin was also, and notably, the painter of the portrait that shows Krøyer sketching the faces of his companions in the lower left corner of this painting. The granting of this privilege reveals an early friendship which was to last several years, as testified by certain elements of their correspondence that have been preserved. Having left for Concarneau with his compatriot Christian Zacho and another Cernay painter, probably Ernest Baillet, Krøyer was joined by some of his other role models such as Peslin who, for the following Salon in 1880, would send a scene of Breton life and, in 1881, the picture shown here.

Against the décor of what might have been the principal room of a Breton dwelling, depicted in great detail, a young woman in regional costume is spinning on a traditional spinning wheel; she has been placed slightly to the left of the composition so that the whole right-hand side of the canvas is devoted to portraying an immense hearth. There is abundant light coming from the left of the picture, so that each meticulous and subtly painted element is precisely highlighted. Unlike the atmosphere that Aristide Bourel (FIG. 23) wished to create, Peslin idealises his scene, and the woman he depicts is sitting in clean and colourful surroundings; she is young, and her work appears effortless.

The second picture (CAT. 34) is a work by Alfred Marie Guillou, another Cernay habitué depicted by Krøyer, who had joined him in July at the Hôtel de la Marine in Concarneau where the 'Brittany Group', mentioned in the correspondence of Zacho and Krøyer, was formed.[63] The picture captures the arrival of tuna boats in the port of Concarneau; it is skilfully composed around a diagonal that gives greater depth to the painting, with its unusual vertical format. There is a large crowd which has been carefully arranged to highlight the main lines of the composition: sailors and young women, tastefully dressed, appear to take pleasure in their work and devote themselves to it without effort, unlike the subjects of Le Sénéchal de Kerdréoret (CAT. 32). Here too, the colours are varied, contrasting but predominantly warm, and the paint is

63. For example, in a letter: PSK to Heinrich Hirschsprung, [Concarneau], 6 October 1879. PSK Archive 715.

CAT. 33 Flavien Louis Peslin: *The Spinner*, 1881. Oil on canvas, 138.5 × 104 cm. Musée de Pont-Aven. 2016.2.1

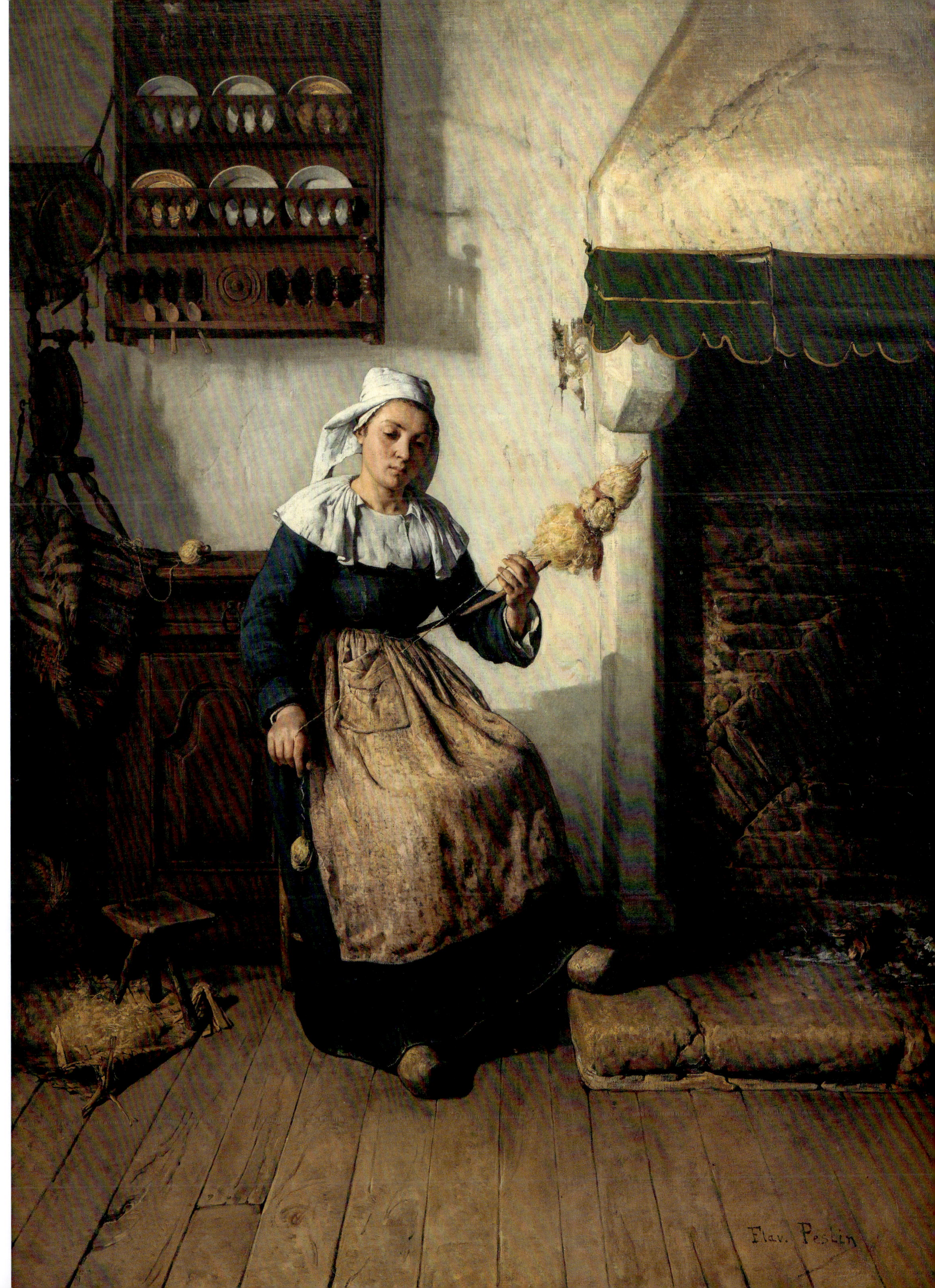
Flav. Peslin

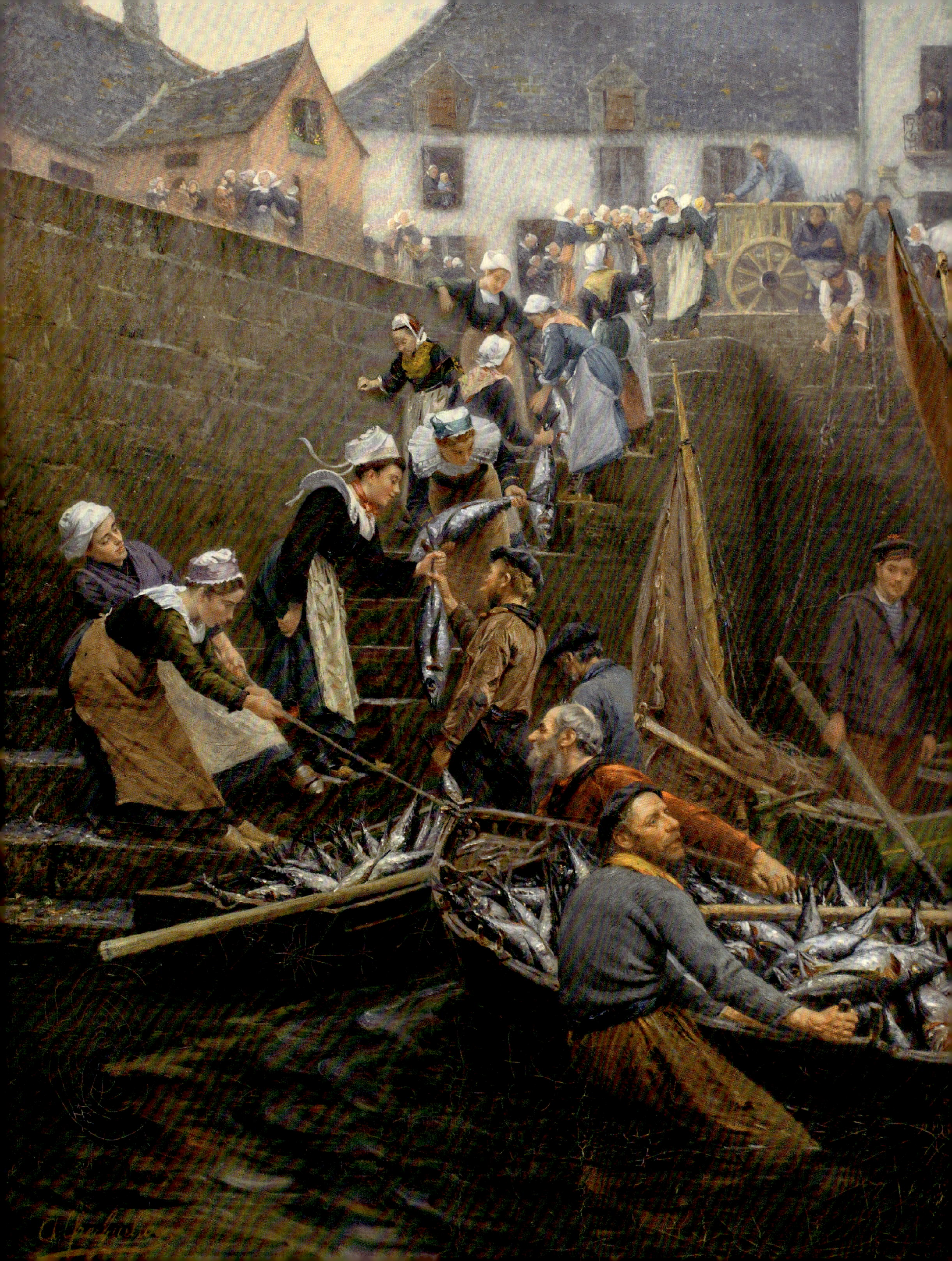

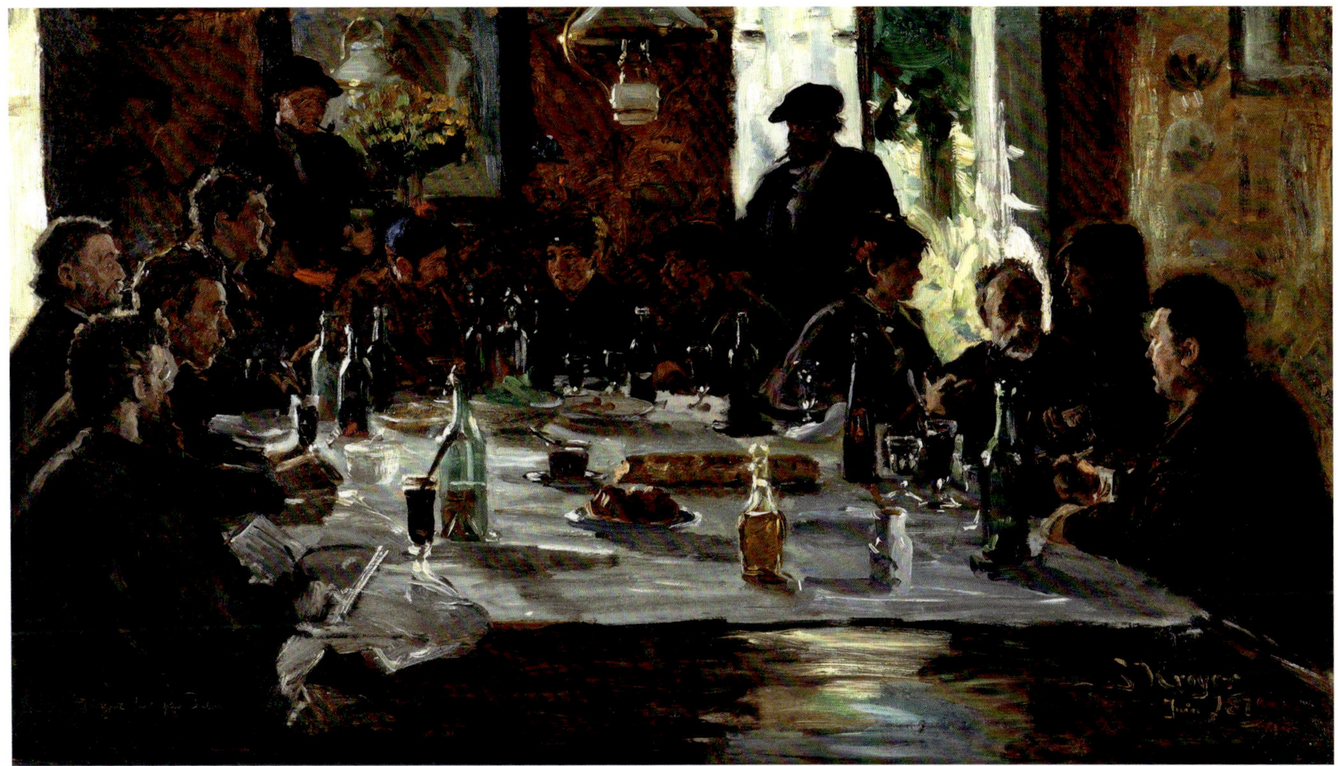

FIG. 26 Peder Severin Krøyer: *Artists' Luncheon in Cernay-la-Ville*, 1879. Oil on wood, 53×95 cm. Skagens Kunstmuseer. SKM1096

applied gently, allowing the light to glide over the surface of the canvas without being inhibited by patches of impasto.

These artists were closer to the tradition of academic training than to the example set by the Realist school, and both they and their works appear to have become benchmarks for Krøyer immediately after his arrival in France. This was the case right up until the following year, when his landscapes and Italian scenes demonstrate an identical way of working. However, his discovery of Skagen, in 1882, and his association with the artists who resided there, would very quickly encourage Krøyer to develop his palette and technique. In the gatherings of unoccupied fishermen (CAT. 43) his colours would become more dramatic, with graduated browns and skilful backlighting being applied to evoke the difficulties resulting from the impossibility of putting out to sea. Fishing scenes would be marked in a similar way, in the positions, gestures, and features of the sailors, and by a greater tension in the menacing sky as the day declines. At the same time, he made increasing use of white impasto to mark the foam at the edge of the waves, changing the way in which the light glides over the canvas, as, for example, in *Fishermen Hauling a Seine Net at Skagen Nordstrand. Late afternoon*, 1882 (CAT. 42).

Dominique Lobstein

CAT. 35 Peder Severin Krøyer
Italian Village Hatters, 1880

Italian Village Hatters (CAT. 35) is an iconic work that greatly contributed to Krøyer's breakthrough as a Naturalist painter. It was the only work he showed at the

CAT. 34 Alfred Marie Guillou: *Landing of Tuna at Concarneau*, 1879.
Oil on canvas, 136 cm×106 cm. Musée d'art et d'histoire des Côtes d'Armor, Saint-Brieuc. 137

Salon in 1881, where it was very well received.[64] The painting was created in Italy, and while working on it Krøyer sent a letter to Pauline Hirschsprung, wife of his patron Heinrich Hirschsprung, describing his current project:

> You have expressed a desire to know what I am painting. I have tried to convey some idea with these vignettes, but with little success. Also, these subjects are in a genre reminiscent of older art – and the painting I sent home represents my true circle of activity. I feel that more and more. I am not given to telling stories, except for what might come under the heading of the Zolaesque, for which I make no apologies.[65]

The two paintings Krøyer was working on were *Italian Field Labourers. Abruzzo* (Kunstmuseum Brandts, Odense) and *Italian Village Hatters* (CAT. 35). The painting that Krøyer mentions having sent home must be *French Workers on a Sunken Road* (CAT. 25), from the year before.[66] 'The Zolaesque' is a homespun term used here to refer to the author Émile Zola, who was the standard-bearer of Naturalism in France, portraying people from the top to the very bottom rungs of society in his art. As regards the works mentioned by Krøyer, their titles alone highlight his focus on the working and rural population. At the Salon in Paris, Krøyer received a third-class medal for *Italian Village Hatters*. A total of 20 third-class medals were awarded that year, along with 12 second-class medals, but no first-class medals at all.[67] But it should be noted that the medal was a great achievement for Krøyer: there were 3,614 exhibitors that year, showing a total of 4,982 works. Two of the reviews of Krøyer's work at the exhibition read as follows:

> A highly original picture by M. Krøyer, the painter of *A Sardine Factory*, which attracted so much attention at last year's Salon; it depicts the dark, smoky interior of a country hatter's shop; in it are three figures of workers who are stripped to the waist, painted in tones reminiscent of Rembrandt with a singular intensity of character and very robust modelling.[68]

> M. Krøyer is a highly talented painter of interiors. His *Village Hatter's Workshop* is a marvel of concise, close drawing and, at the same time, precise colouring. The scene is rendered with an astonishing intensity of expression. It is reality itself, conveyed by the brush of a true artist.[69]

The reviews focused on the people depicted in the painting, acknowledging their toil and poverty. They also accentuated the artist's talent and not least the rendition of light in the picture, which is markedly rich in contrast between the scorching sun outside the window and the dark workshop. Having been shown at yet another exhibition in Paris, *Exposition internationale d'Électricité*,[70] the work was exhibited in Denmark the following year to a rather different response: here, the painting sparked heated discussion. Audiences and critics were divided. Many were outraged by the painting's Realism, and it also attracted criticism for not being Danish enough. The older cultural elite leaned towards the views of the National Liberal political movement and still wished to see art celebrating all things Danish, whereas the younger cultural radicals (a later term used to describe what were then considered 'modern' views) wanted to see new art gain ground, regardless of whether it had been painted in Denmark or abroad.[71] These first French and Italian works by Krøyer were also among the first to truly give visual form to the Modern Breakthrough in Danish art.

Mette Harbo Lehmann

64. Cat. no. 1266.
65. PSK to Pauline Hirschsprung, Sora, 8 September 1880. HH Archive 725.
66. Saabye, *Krøyer: An International Perspective*, 181–182.
67. 'Nouvelles diverses', 3; 'Nouvelles du jour. Les récompenses du Salon', 2.
68. Vachon, 'Le Salon de 1881', 3.
69. A.E., 'Au Salon. Les tableaux de genre', 2.
70. Krøyer refers to the work being at 'the electric exhibition' in Paris in the autumn of 1881. It is not listed in the exhibition catalogue nor mentioned in reviews, but the artist can only have been referring to the *Exposition internationale d'Électricité*, on from 15 August to 15 November at the Palais de l'Industrie. PSK to Laurits Tuxen, Copenhagen, 11 November 1881. KB NKS 2339, 2° 5.
71. Hornung, *Peder Severin Krøyer*, 151–154.

CAT. 35 Peder Severin Krøyer: *Italian Village Hatters*, 1880. Oil on canvas, 135.3 × 107 cm. Den Hirschsprungske Samling, Copenhagen. 206

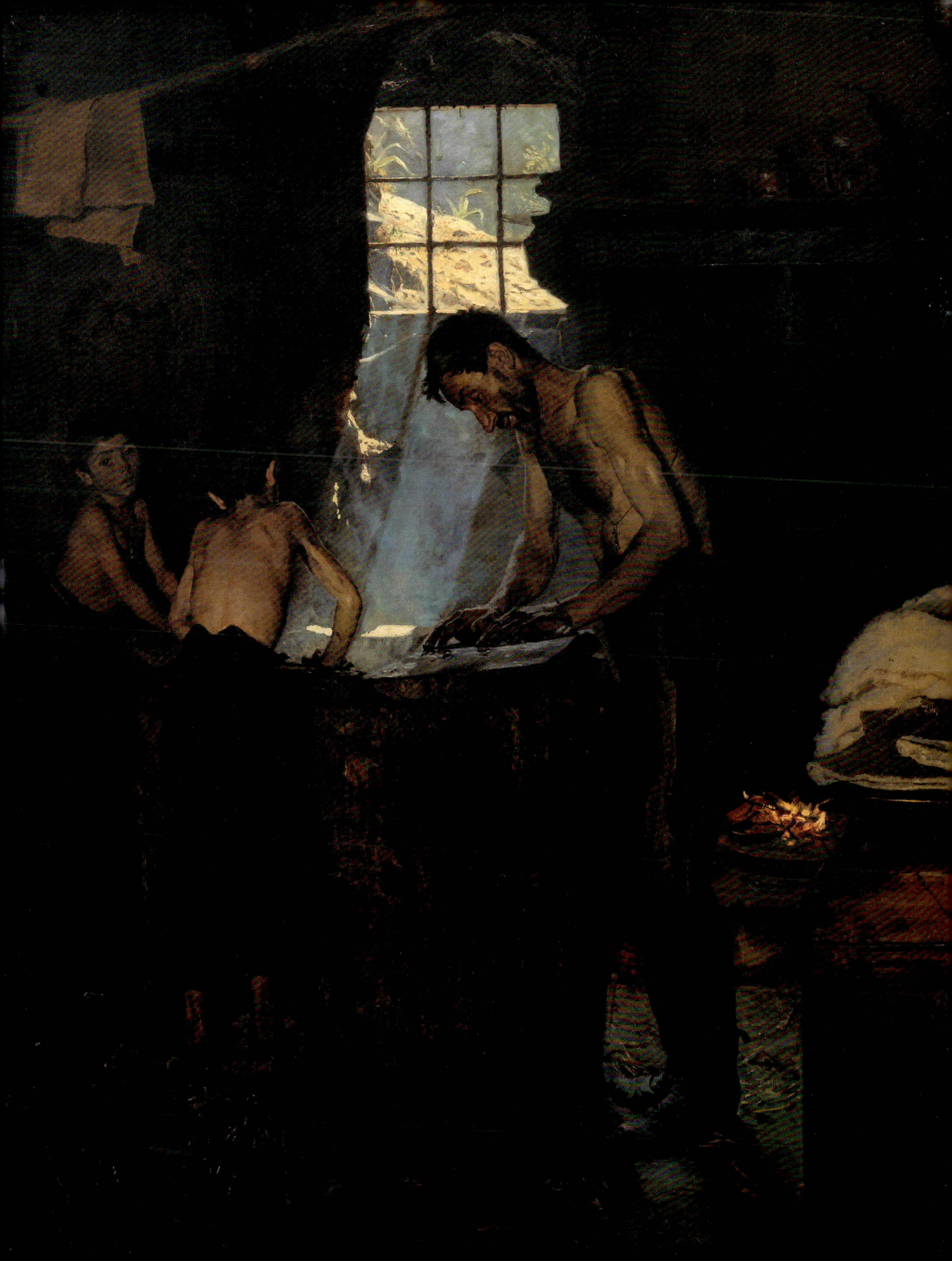

Krøyer's Idol

CAT. 36 Jules Bastien-Lepage
The Little Communicant, 1875

While working hard to prepare for the Prix de Rome examinations, Bastien-Lepage was still able to present two pictures at the 1875 Salon, exhibiting *The Little Communicant* (CAT. 36) and the *Portrait of M.H. ...*, also called *Portrait of Simon Hayem* (FIG. 27).[72] Rarely had an artist united two works in this way, illustrating moments so distant from everyday life in such contrasting tonalities and with such distinct references.

The older of the models was widely known, although the painter gave only his initials: he was Simon Hayem, who had made a fortune by inventing the celluloid collar-tie. His shirt emporium in the Sentier district, with its sign *Maison du Phénix*, was a supplier to the aristocracy and bourgeoisie, not only in Paris but from the provinces and abroad. Hayem, aged 64, is closely framed and appears to emerge from the shadows. He is comfortably seated in an armchair, his head slightly tilted and his gaze fixed upon the artist. The air of presence given to the model, which must have reminded visitors to the Salon of that accorded to *M. Bertin* (1832, Musée du Louvre, Paris) by Ingres, held people's attention, and the picture was highly praised:

> This portrait of M. Hayem seated is perhaps the best male portrait in the Salon from the point of view of its life; the model has been captured true to life, in that familiar and brusque yet easeful pose of people who handle big business and are always rushed.[73]

The second work, a portrait of a cousin of the artist, was smaller: the model is Lucie Bastien, aged between 12 and 14 years, in her first communion dress. Because of her severe, full-frontal depiction at the centre of the canvas, the tension that was visible in Hayem's portrait is here replaced by an almost expressionless immobility; nevertheless, this is overlaid with a palette of whites whose bluish reflections accentuate the cold tones of the background. The models that Bastien-Lepage appears to have consulted were more varied than those he used for the portrait of M. Hayem. The hieratical pose and inexpressive face, for example, seem borrowed from Hans Holbein the Younger's *Anne of Cleves* in the Musée du Louvre (FIG. 28). Ingres is not far distant either, and Bastien-Lepage was in all likelihood inspired by him: this symphony in white is probably a reference to the portrait of *Mademoiselle Rivière* from 1806 (Musée du Louvre, Paris). The critic Castagnary did not hesitate to state his preference for Bastien-Lepage over the older master: '*The Little Communicant* by the same painter astonishes by the delicacy of its drawing, and the naivety of the expression. M. Ingres has some-

72. Cat. nos. 96 and 97 at the Salon.

73. Montaiglon, 'Le Salon de 1875', 498.

CAT. 36 Jules Bastien-Lepage: *The Little Communicant*, 1875.
Oil on canvas, 50 × 33 cm. Musée des Beaux-Arts, Tournai.

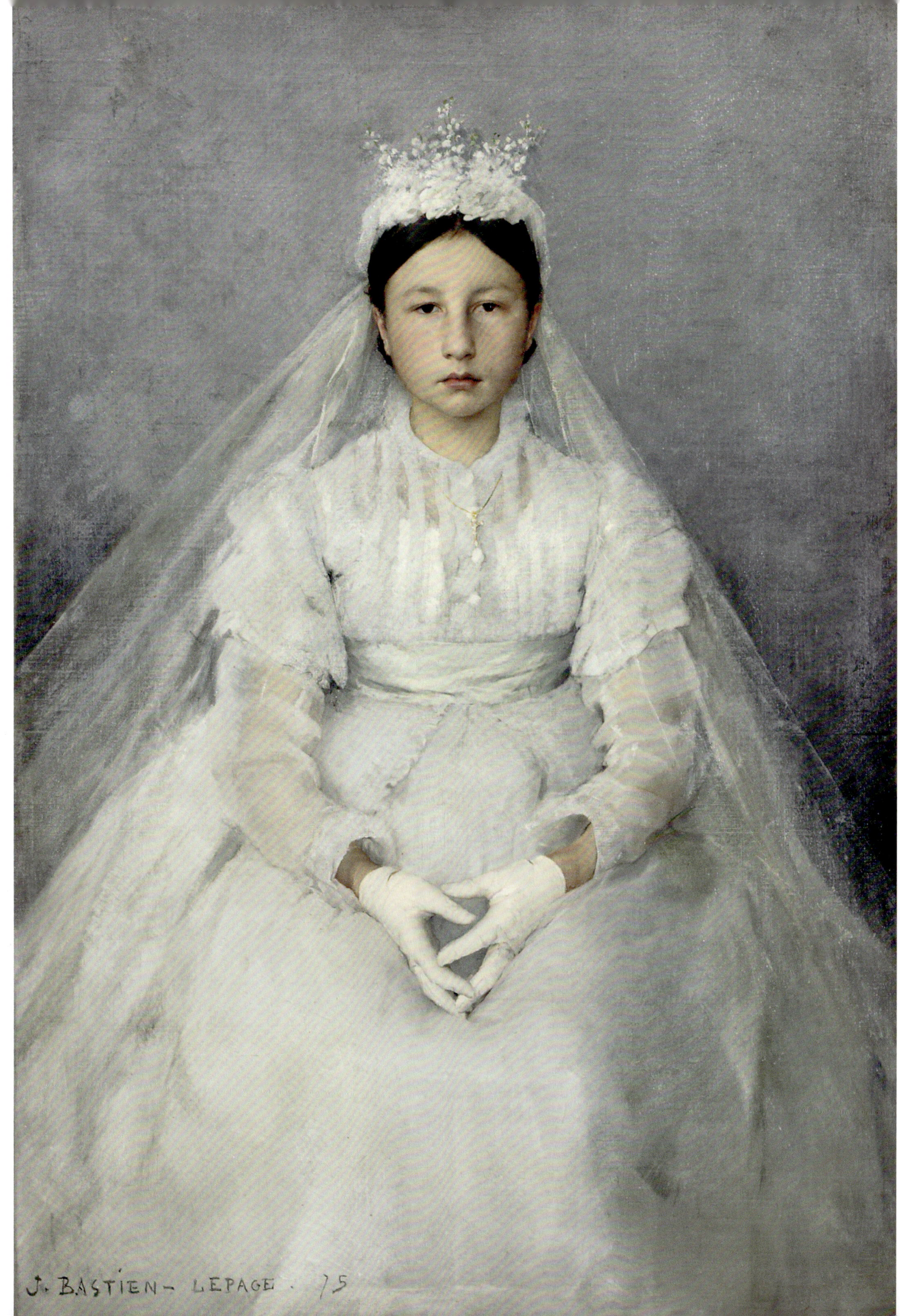
J. BASTIEN- LEPAGE . 75

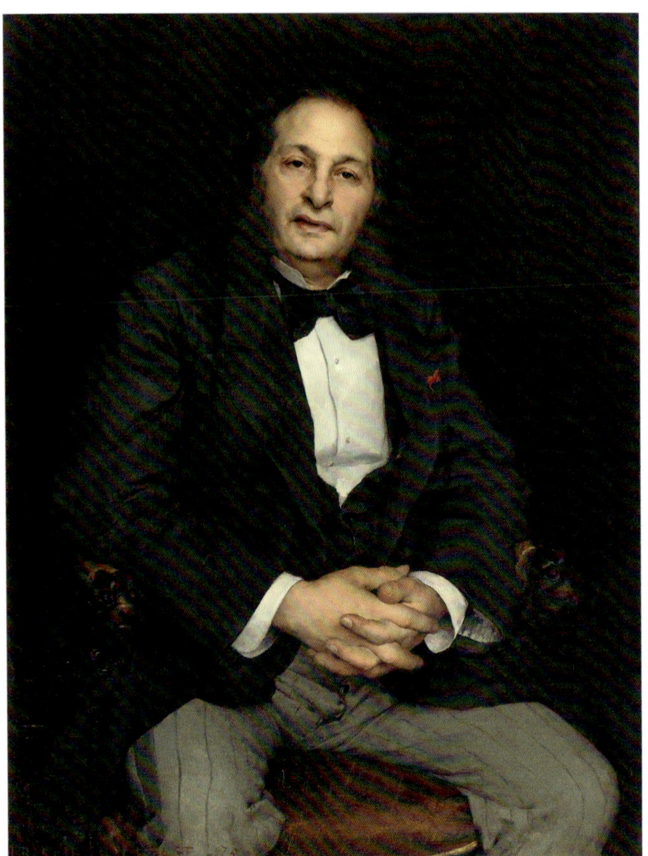

FIG. 27 Jules Bastien-Lepage: *Portrait of Simon Hayem*, 1875. Oil on canvas, 105×80 cm. Musée Municipal, Hazebrouck, deposit from Musée d'Orsay. RF 2747

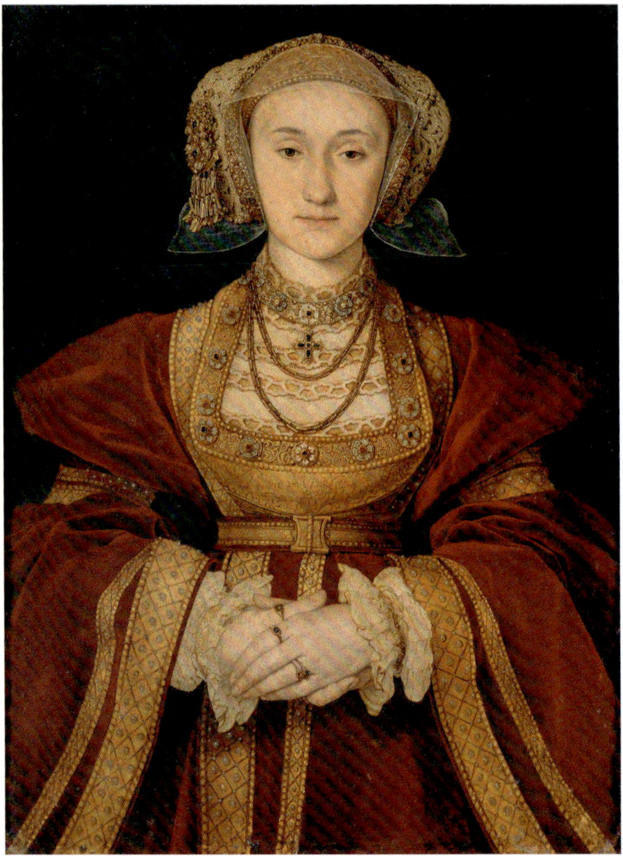

FIG. 28 Hans Holbein the Younger: *Portrait of Anne of Cleves (1515–1557) Queen of England, fourth wife of Henry VIII*, 1539. Vellum glued on canvas, 65×48 cm. Musée du Louvre, Paris. INV 1348

times sketched as delicately, [but] never with as much charm.'[74]

In 1885, at the retrospective exhibition following Bastien-Lepage's death, Krøyer had the opportunity to see these two pictures,[75] and *Portrait of Simon Hayem* in particular appears to have had the most fruitful and rapid influence on Krøyer's work, especially after 1890 when he adopted a sitting position for his models, portraying them to below the knees and particularly emphasising the head and hands, as in the *Portrait of Baron Otto Ditlev Rosenorn-Lehn* from 1891 (Statens Museum for Kunst, Copenhagen). However, unlike Bastien-Lepage, he always set his portraits against a panelled background which, with its pattern and colours, served as a showcase for the work. The lesson learned from *The Little Communicant* appears to have been abandoned in the portrait of Marie Krøyer in *Two Women in the Garden. Marie Krøyer and her Mother. Skagen* from 1891 (Museum Behnhaus Drägerhaus, Lübeck), in which the model's long white dress, as she sits under the foliage but facing the sun, reflects all the ambient shadows.

Krøyer got to see many of Bastien-Lepage's paintings, but his encounters with the artist himself were somewhat more sporadic. Upon Bastien-Lepage's death on 12 December 1884, Martinus Galschiøt wrote a substantial obituary in *Illustreret Tidende*.[76] Prior to this, he contacted

74. Castagnary, *Salons (1872–1879)*, 167.

75. *The Little Communicant*, cat. no. 32; *Portrait of M.H. ...*, cat. no. 34.

Krøyer to ask whether he would contribute a text about the artist.[77] In response, Krøyer penned some loosely written notes that never saw print.[78]

> In 1881 at the Salon, Le jour de vernissage, I was standing in front of my 'Hatters' with a couple of French friends. Then someone tapped me on the shoulder and I saw a young man – small, blond, pale (beard and hair and face all approximately the same shade), yet sturdy, energetically built, who introduced himself to me as Bastien Lepage. He paid me some of the usual 'compliments' at which [I] was however highly delighted precisely because they came from Bastian Lepage, whom I already considered part of the front rank among the French artists. He was most winsome and amiable, a straightforward man, and [I] decided not to let this acquaintance lie idle. As I recollect, this was the same year he had exhibited his *Joan of Arc*, one of the most beautiful and strange modern pictures I know.
>
> However, due to the brevity of the visits I made to Paris in those years, I only managed a few visits to his studio, and since was he most certainly not among the most talkative of fellows and also did not let himself be interrupted in his work by visitors ... the acquaintance remained cursory.
>
> I remember the last time I was there, in his *Ateliers* ... It was in the spring of '83. The situation when I entered was as follows: Bastien was seated, painting a portrait. The model was posing as directed, and next to Bastien sat a famous soubrette from the Th.[eatre] Franc.[ais] (do not be alarmed: ... 'anciens amis d'enfance'), perusing the Munich exhibition catalogue. The situation did not change much upon my arrival. After exchanging the usual greetings: comment allez vous – et vous – je vous r'mecie, all three of them carried on as before, and I ambled around the room and looked at his pictures. They were still there, most of them: The Annunciation to the Shepherds, which was hung in the third Row at the Salon (1877), Awakening in the Field from the Salon 78 (again exhibited in Vienna), les ramasseuse des pommes de terres, de moissonneurs and so on, all his unsold pictures which, back then, found very little understanding among the 'old' and the general public.[79]

Krøyer was not the only Dane to have taken note of Bastien-Lepage. The French artist had attracted widespread fame and admiration among young Danish artists and critics. In his obituary, Galshiøt opened by stating that: 'In recent years, whenever one asked younger French painters or foreigners who had studied in Paris to name those they considered most prominent among them, Bastien-Lepage was almost always mentioned without hesitation.' Five years after Bastien-Lepage's death, the critic Karl Madsen, who had himself stayed in Paris as a young painter in 1879, wrote a mixed review of his works in connection with the Exposition Universelle in Paris in 1889, where Bastien-Lepage was richly represented. Madsen was partly critical of Bastien-Lepage, stating that as a personality he could not aspire to the high rank of Millet. Conversely, he did acknowledge the artist's importance to Danish peers during his own lifetime.

> When Bastien-Lepage died – which he did, as the reader is no doubt aware, at a very young age – Danish artists sent a wreath. Perhaps he enjoyed even greater acclaim in Denmark than in France while alive. For the small audience here in Denmark

76. Galschiøt, 'Bastien-Lepage', 187–189.
77. Galschiøt to PSK, Elsinore, 25 December 1884. PSK Archive 1132.
78. The circumstances are comprehensively described in Saabye, 'Krøyer & Bastien-Lepage', 29.
79. Sketchbook of Peder Severin Krøyer, no. 42, Den Hirschsprungske Samling, inv. no. 7042. Saabye, 'Krøyer & Bastien-Lepage', 29–30 has identified the referenced works as follows: the picture of Joan of Arc was not exhibited in 1881, but at the Salon the preceding year; *The Annunciation to the Shepherds* (1875, National Gallery of Victoria, Melbourne); Awakening in the Field (*Hay Making*, 1877, Musée d'Orsay, Paris); *Les ramasseuse des pommes de terres* (*October*, 1879, National Gallery of Victoria, Melbourne); *Peasants Sharpening their Scythes* (1881, current owner unknown).

> who had some knowledge of the art produced abroad, whether through first-hand knowledge or by way of reproductions, his name was among those mentioned with the greatest reverence. He stood before us as the supreme representative of Youth in French art, indeed, of Youth in the art of all countries.[80]

Soon afterwards, the Danish art historian Julius Lange wrote what amounted to a short dissertation on Bastien-Lepage. Here the artist was thoroughly treated in analyses of his portraits and descriptions of his colour schemes, which in the case of landscapes were governed by his outdoor painting. Lange began his description of Bastien-Lepage as follows: 'His art is in fact every bit as "modern" as that of our own painters, Michael Ancher, Krøyer, Viggo Johansen – to name just a few artists who are close to him in age and, partly, in terms of their artistic direction too.'[81] He presumably did so in order to make it easier for Danish readers to place Bastien-Lepage. Still, Lange could not resist commenting on Madsen's article:

> In an article in *Tilskueren* about the centennial Exhibition of French Art, Karl Madsen was not, in my opinion, quite fair in his comments about Bastien-Lepage. Madsen states that he was by no means a personality of Millet's rank, more of a talent than a genius, and so on. Certainly, much can be said both for and against Bastien-Lepage; but in the end he will, in my opinion, stand as a first-rate artist as fully as Millet or any other of the French artists of our century.[82]

There can be no mistaking his recognition that Bastien-Lepage was an important artist during the period and a key source of inspiration for the Danish artists of the day, especially Krøyer.

Dominique Lobstein and Mette Harbo Lehmann

CAT. 37 Jules Bastien-Lepage
The Small Peddler Asleep, 1882

CAT. 38 Jules Bastien-Lepage
London Shoeshine Boy, 1882

CAT. 39 Auguste Rodin
Maquette for the statue of Jules Bastien-Lepage, 1885

Having been praised by the critics for his pictures inspired by the countryside, Bastien-Lepage attempted to adapt the Naturalist vision to the 'grand manner'. He embarked upon the creation of a painting that was both historical and religious, featuring the character of Joan of Arc (FIG. 29). Originally from Lorraine, her memory had been revived after the battle of Sedan in 1870, when France was defeated by Prussia during the Franco-Prussian war. She is shown in the garden of the artist's parents – none other than a garden in Damvillers, his native village – where, during the Hundred Years War, she hears the voices of Archangel Michael and Saints Margaret and Catherine, commanding her to free France from English oppression and lead the *dauphin* Charles to the throne. Bastien-Lepage depicts his heroine in extremely modest attire, at the moment when she has just abandoned her spinning wheel and is standing, eyes wide and fixed on a point in front of her, listening to her voices. However, this is not the direction from which the voices come: their source can just be distinguished against the light-coloured gable of the house in the background. The very erect archangel, dressed in gold armour, appears to be levitating beside the two female saints, who seem to be flying alongside him, wearing gauze with circlets of flowers on their heads. Such a combination of Realism and invention did not please the critics. Émile Zola, for example, who had written the first article praising Bastien-Lepage – while at the same time expressing some concern over how a pupil of Alexandre Cabanel might develop – gave vent to his feelings:

80. Madsen, 'Indtryk fra Verdensudstillingen', 785.

81. Lange, *Bastien Lepage*, 2.

82. Lange, *Bastien Lepage*, 30.

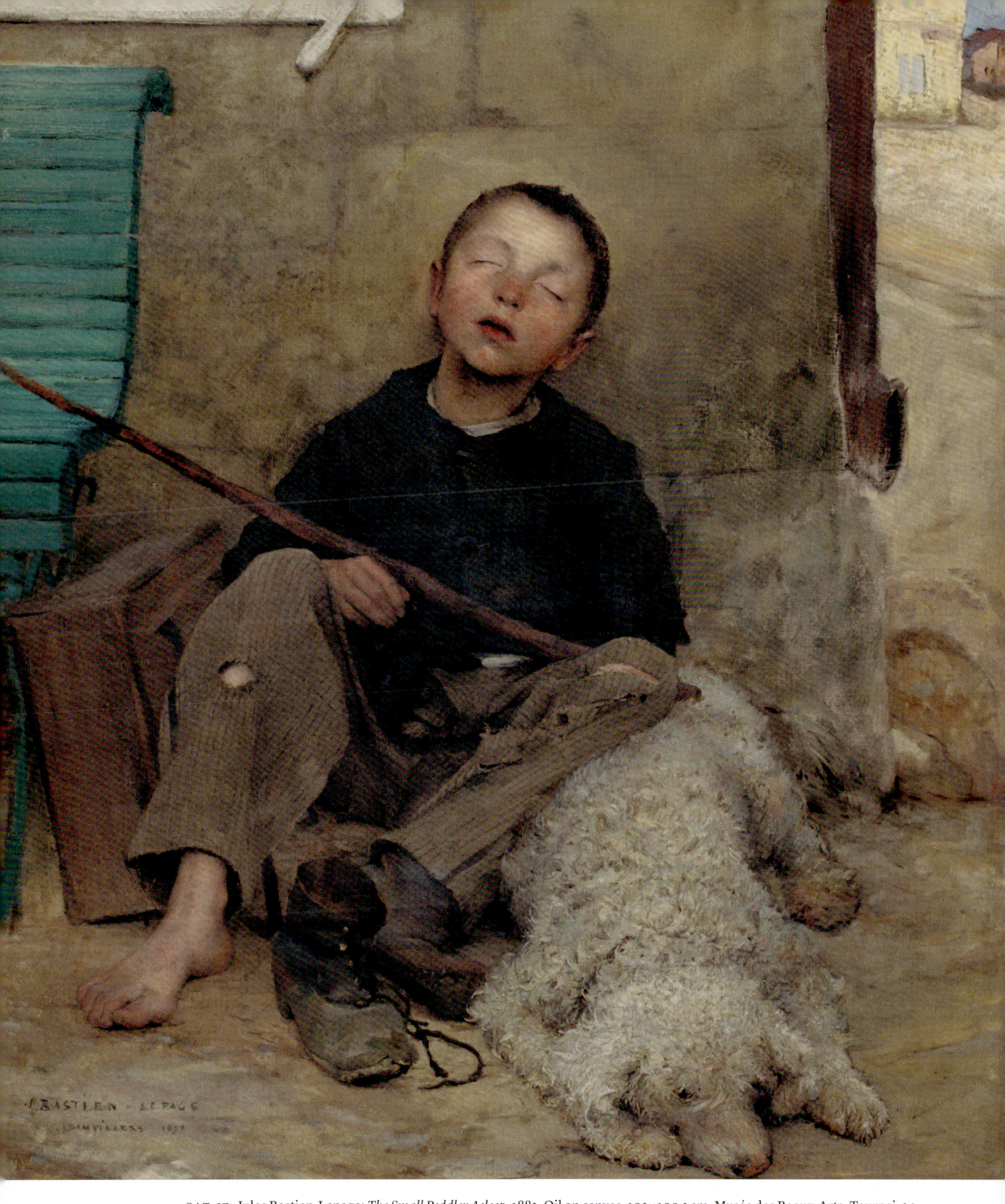

CAT. 37 Jules Bastien-Lepage: *The Small Peddler Asleep*, 1882. Oil on canvas, 103×109.3 cm. Musée des Beaux-Arts, Tournai. 34

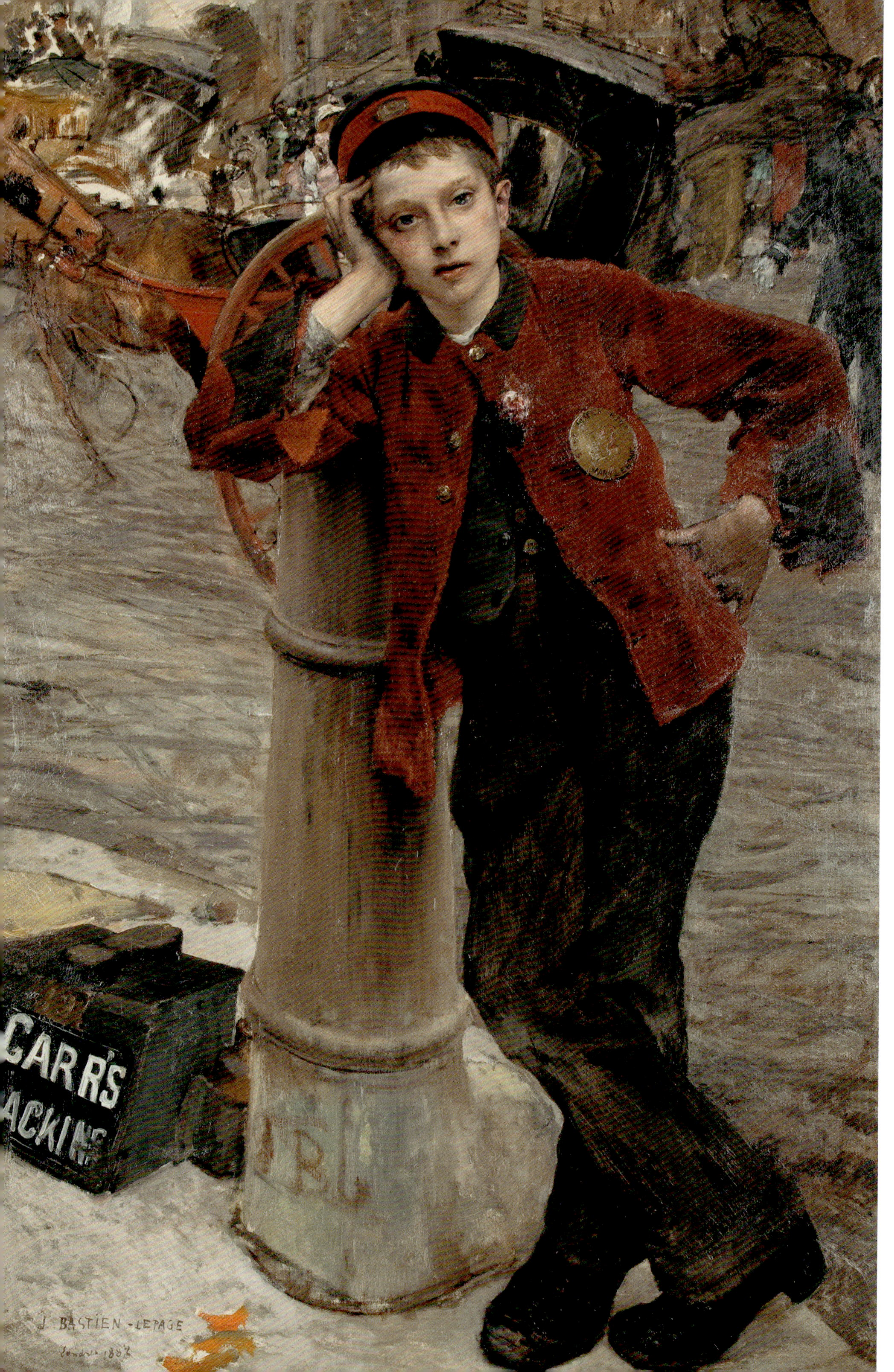
CARR'S
ACKIN
J. BASTIEN-LEPAGE

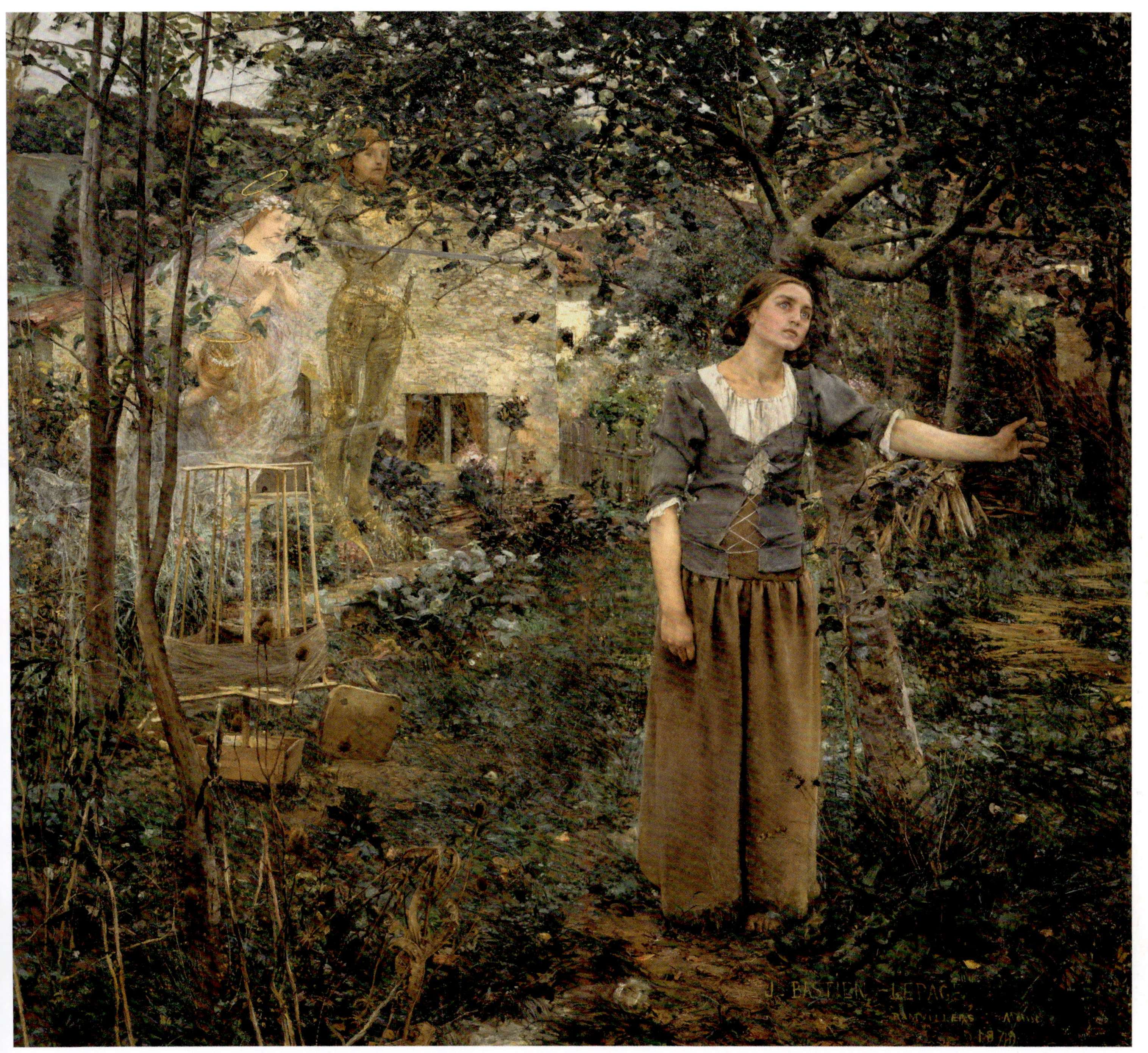

FIG. 29 Jules Bastien-Lepage: *Joan of Arc*, 1879. Oil on canvas, 254×279.4 cm. The Metropolitan Museum of Art, New York. 89.2.11

CAT. 38 Jules Bastien-Lepage: *London Shoeshine Boy*, 1882.
Oil on canvas, 132×89 cm. Musée des Arts décoratifs, Paris. 34363

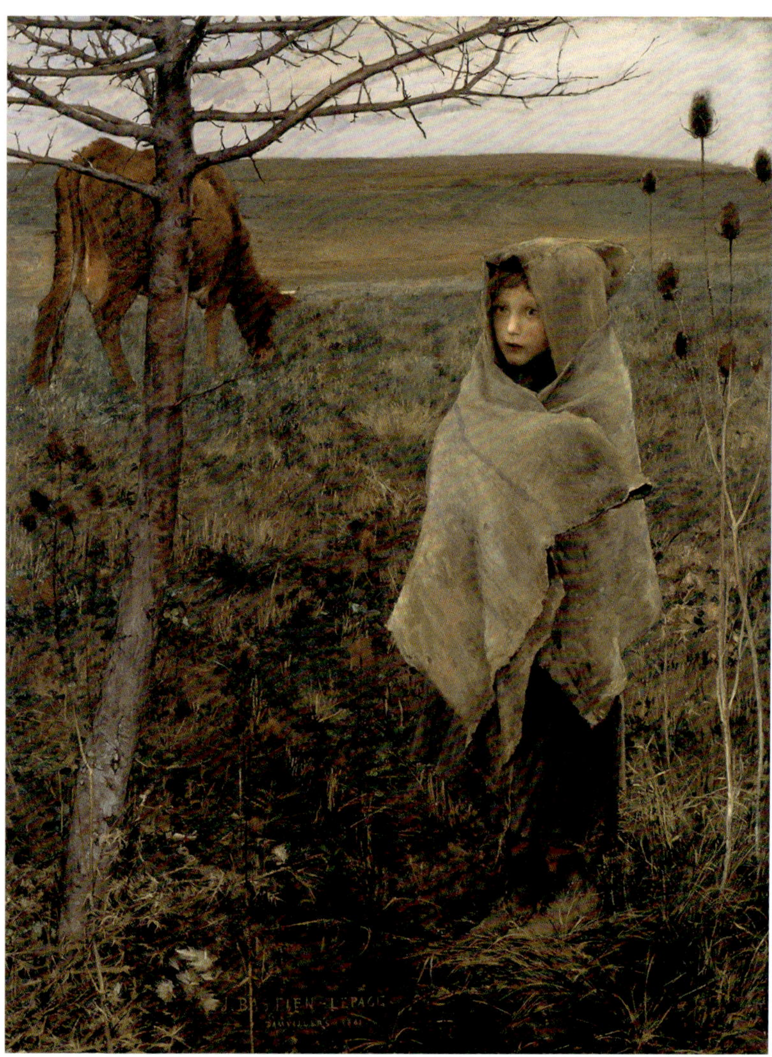

FIG. 30 Jules Bastien-Lepage: *Poor Fauvette*, 1881. Kelvingrove Art Gallery and Museum, Glasgow. 1323

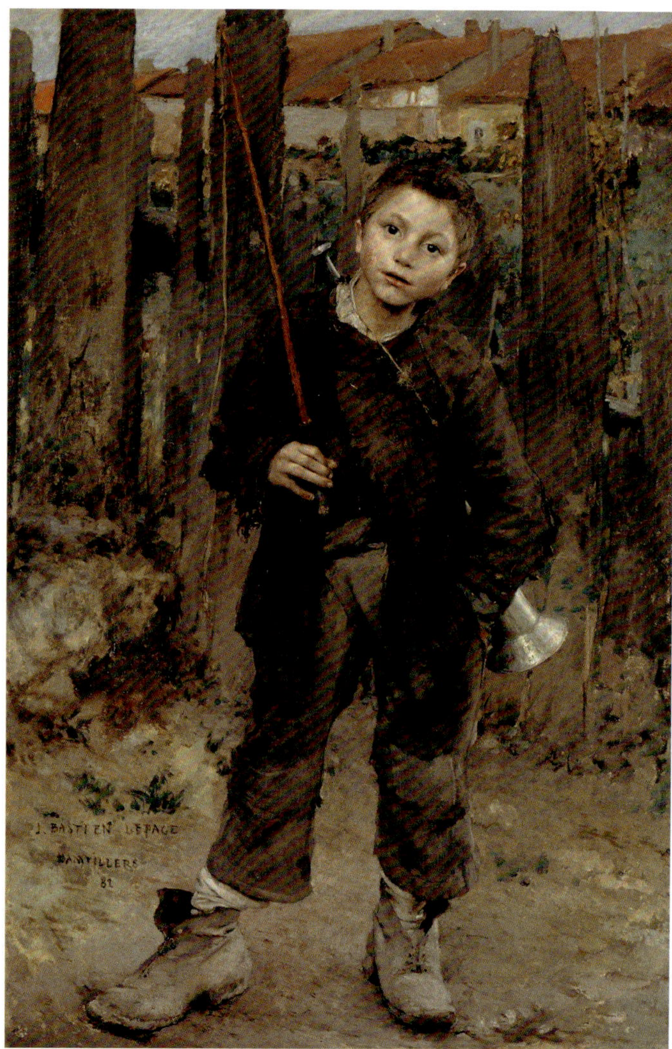

FIG. 31 Jules Bastien-Lepage: *Nothing doing*, 1882. National Galleries of Scotland, Edinburgh. NG 1133

CAT. 39 Auguste Rodin: *Model for the statue of Jules Bastien-Lepage*, 1885. Bronze, 35×26×21 cm. Musée Marmottan Monet, Paris. 3046

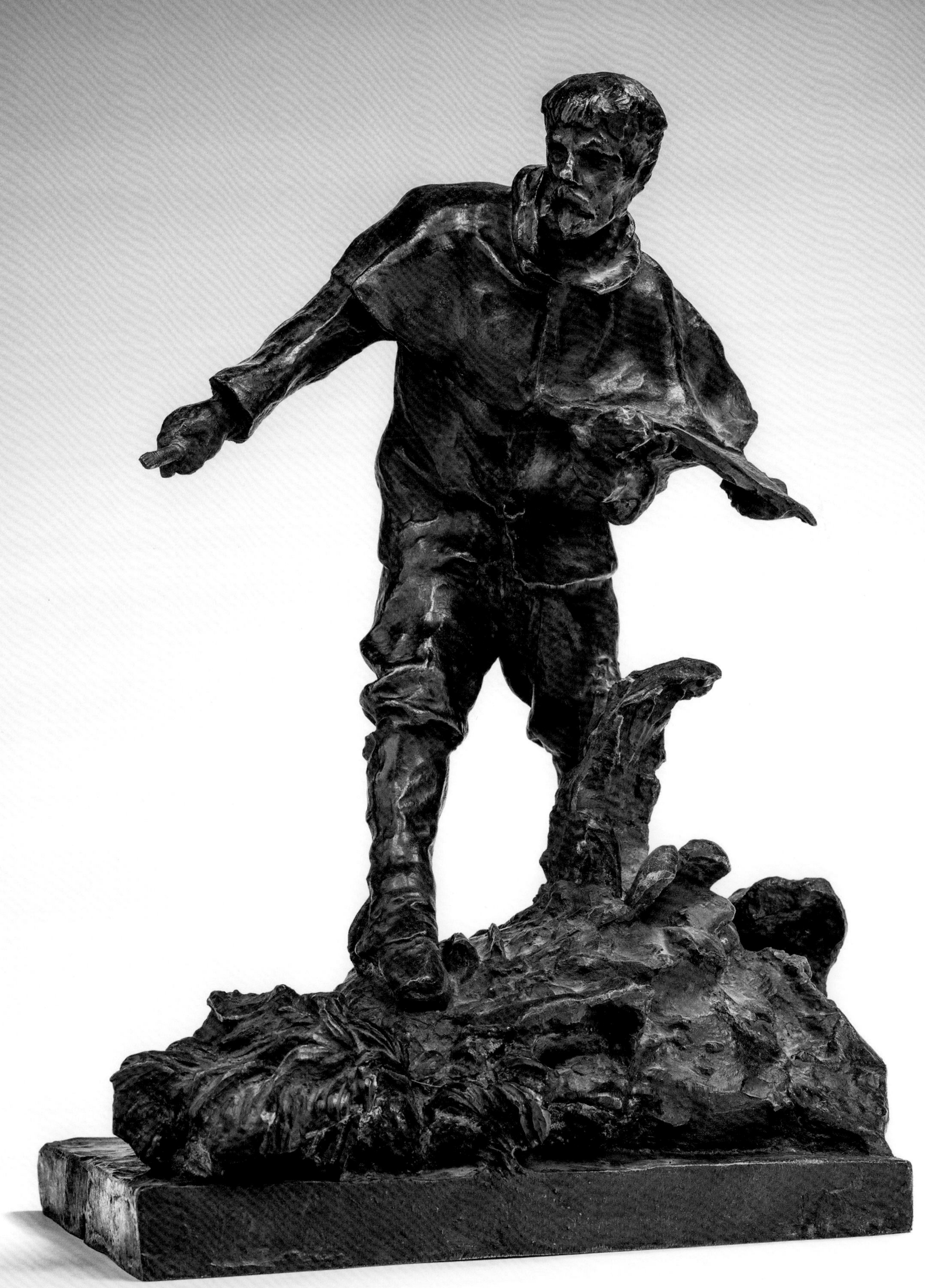

> This year, the painter has been overtaken by a higher ambition. Reflecting on the historic figure of our Joan of Arc, he thought that no painter had yet had the idea of giving us a real Joan of Arc, a simple peasant girl in the setting of her little garden in Lorraine. [...] M. Bastien-Lepage, doubtless to make his subject more intelligible, took it into his head to paint the young girl's vision of two saints and a knight in gold armour in the branches of an apple tree. In my view, this concern is regrettable; Joan's bearing, her gestures, her hallucinated eyes were sufficient to tell us the story; and this childish floating apparition is nothing but a pleonasm, a useless and cumbersome device. It displeases me, especially as it ruins all the fine naturalist unity of the subject.[83]

Bastien-Lepage was deeply affected by these comments, and that summer left France for London where he took up residence at 104, Regent Street and rediscovered such British acquaintances as Alma-Tadema, Burne-Jones, and Dorothy Tennant, but also some French ones like Sarah Bernhardt. He participated in artistic life by exhibiting at the Royal Academy, and established ties with the London galleries, which commissioned pictures from him for art lovers. This gave rise to some rare genre scenes inspired by London life (*London Shoeshine Boy*, CAT. 38), as well as many more tender evocations of his native Lorraine countryside (CAT. 37), some of which remained in the United Kingdom (*Poor Fauvette*, FIG. 30, and the enigmatic *Nothing doing*, FIG. 31). Krøyer would see all these works at the 1885 exhibition, and they would reinforce his idea that the Scandinavian painters who admired this French artist who had died prematurely should honour him with some kind of gesture. Krøyer gave concrete expression to this gesture by starting a fund which would enable them to offer a memento to be added to the monument planned for the artist at Damvillers. However, there was limited participation and, finally, rather than offering an overly modest gift, the Scandinavian donors transferred their contribution so that it could be added to the money collected in France under the aegis of the critic Albert Wolff, as revealed in a letter from Krøyer to Wolff dated 16 January 1885.[84] In this way they were able to participate in the commissioning of the monument which Rodin dedicated to his young fellow artist, and of which several sketches were produced in different sizes. An example of these is the one in the Musée Marmottan Monet donated by the artist's brother, Émile Bastien-Lepage (CAT. 39).
Dominique Lobstein

CAT. 40 Philippe Alfred Roll
Louise Cattel, Wet Nurse, 1892

In a brief letter of 21 February 1889 addressed to his friend the Danish architect Thorvald Bindesbøll, Krøyer added a short sentence at the end, which assures us of the amicable relationship he then had with Paul Albert Besnard – something that was also evident from other letters well before this – and with Alfred Philippe Roll: 'I get on very well with Besnard and Roll.'[85] This was not the first mention of a relationship between the two artists; there were countless opportunities to meet in the building where Roll lived and where Krøyer attended Bonnat's classes, in 1877, or behind the scenes at the Salon, where Roll was elected to the jury in 1881. A reliable document has been preserved in the archives, providing evidence of a meeting between these two artists, among others: it is a telegram sent to Krøyer by Roll and three of his *confrères* – Ernest-Ange Duez, Henri Gervex, and Jean-Charles Cazin – congratulating him on the painting he had sent to the 1884 Salon.[86]

Between these two sets of correspondence, the year 1888 would probably have provided opportunity for

83. Zola, 'Le Naturalisme au Salon', [3].
84. PSK to Albert Wolff, Copenhagen, 16 January 1885. PSK Archive 246.
85. 'Besnard og Roll omgaaes jeg meget'. PSK to Thorvald Bindesbøll, Paris, 21 February 1889. KB NKS 4192,4° 7.
86. Telegram from Alfred Roll, Ernest-Ange Duez, Henri Gervex, and Jean-Charles Cazin to PSK, Paris, [probably May or June 1884]. PSK Archive 2638.

CAT. 40 Philippe Alfred Roll: *Louise Cattel, Wet Nurse*, 1892. Oil on canvas, 157×74 cm. Palais des Beaux-Arts, Lille. P 550

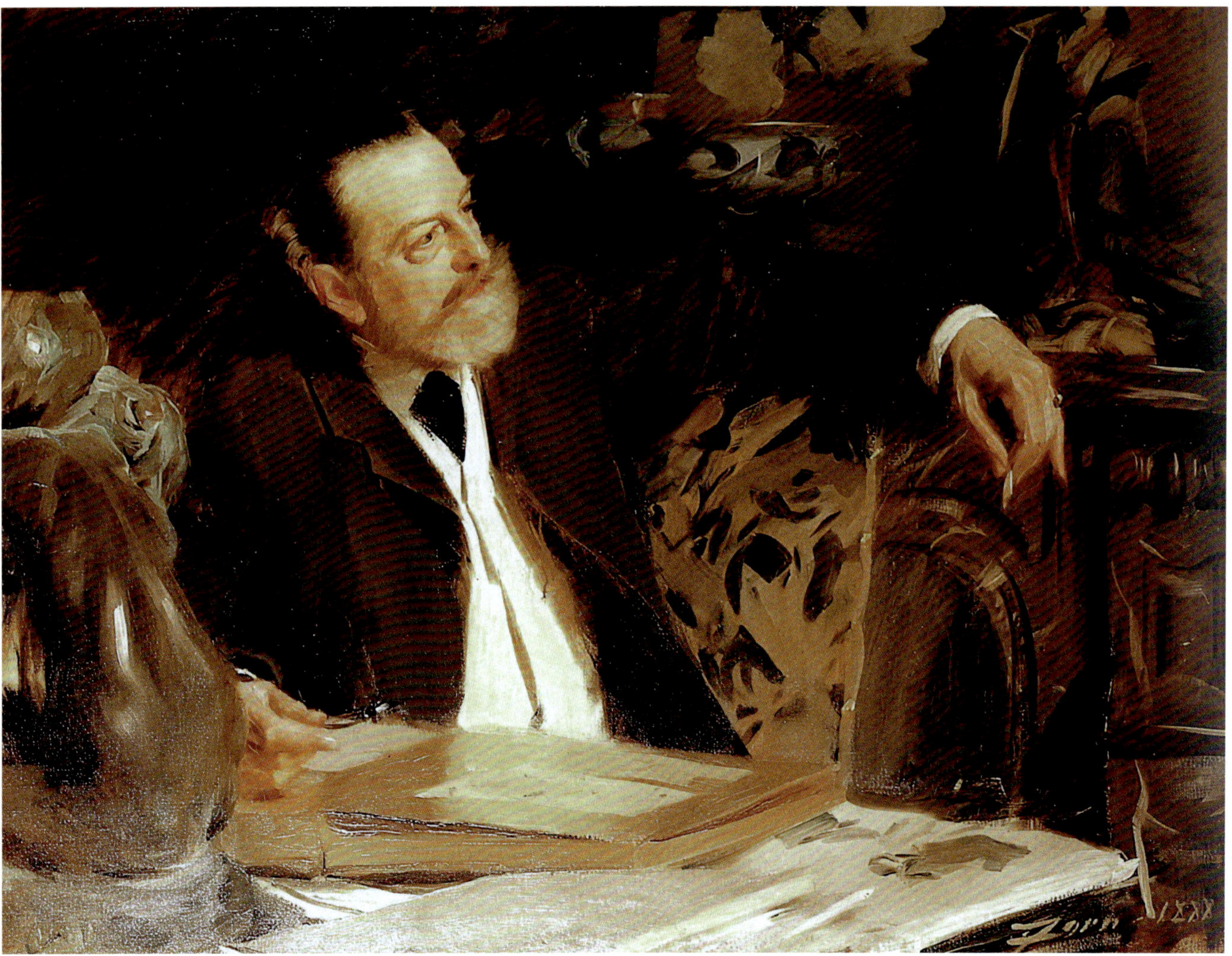

FIG. 32 Anders Zorn: *Portrait of Antonin Proust*, 1888. Oil on canvas, 106 × 138 cm. Private collection.

more frequent contacts – namely those leading up to the Copenhagen exhibition – but on these the archives are silent. Krøyer's first approaches were made with the intention of gathering together a committee, which he was able to do thanks to the support of Antonin Proust, the former minister for the Beaux-Arts in 1881–1882. Although called to other duties, he had never abandoned the art world. An additional asset was that he maintained excellent relations with Scandinavian artists: with Krøyer, from whom he had bought a pastel at the close of the 1886 Salon, or else with Anders Zorn, for whom he had agreed to pose in 1888 (FIG. 32). On Proust's advice, Krøyer began to approach a number of French artists, among them Roll. The collaboration paid off and Roll indeed became part of the organising committee, as well as exhibiting four of his recent works at the exhibition itself: among these were *Man at Work* (1885, Musée d'art et d'histoire, Cognac) and *Portrait of Pierre-Emmanuel Damoye* (FIG. 33). The latter was also a painter, present both on the committee and in the exhibition, as well as having a hand in the painting commemorating the event (CAT. 47).

Born in 1848, Roll trained at the École des Beaux-Arts and exhibited at the Salon from 1869 onwards. He was initially a landscape painter, but it was not until 1875 that he achieved success with his scene of *The Flood at Toulouse*, in 1875 (1877, Musée d'art moderne André Malraux, Le Havre). This painting bears the marks of Romanticism in its composition, but of Courbet and the Realists in its brushwork. Success and its rewards followed, opening the doors to public commissions and the decoration of several monuments. He turned to figure painting in order to bring life to his décors and then soon moved to painting portraits, thereafter influenced more by Bastien-Lepage than by Courbet, which served only to increase his success.

Like many of those who emulated Bastien-Lepage, Roll left the Salon des Artistes français in 1890 to help create the Salon de la Société Nationale des Beaux-Arts, which, from the following year, would receive works by Krøyer. This new society placed no limit on the number of works and even accepted older ones: in 1890, for example, *High Tide* (location unknown) could be seen there, even though it had been exhibited in Copenhagen in 1888, together with a portrait of the actress Jane Hading from 1890 (Petit Palais, Musée des Beaux-Arts de la Ville de Paris), and a few, more laboured, anonymous pictures. From then on, there would be a succession of narrow pictures of vertical format in which unknown people would be given an identity, such as *Louise Cattel, Wet Nurse* (CAT. 40), which appeared at the exhibition of the Société Nationale des Beaux-Arts in 1894, under number 989. These likenesses of anonymous models painted in the format of historical portraits, using light tones and bold brushstrokes, would have many descendants in the work of painters who were followers of Naturalism. Krøyer does not appear to have yielded to this type of painting; he was probably too busy with the many commissions for portraits that occupied his visits to Copenhagen, where his brushwork nevertheless became gradually freer, enabling him to try more daring colour combinations.

Dominique Lobstein

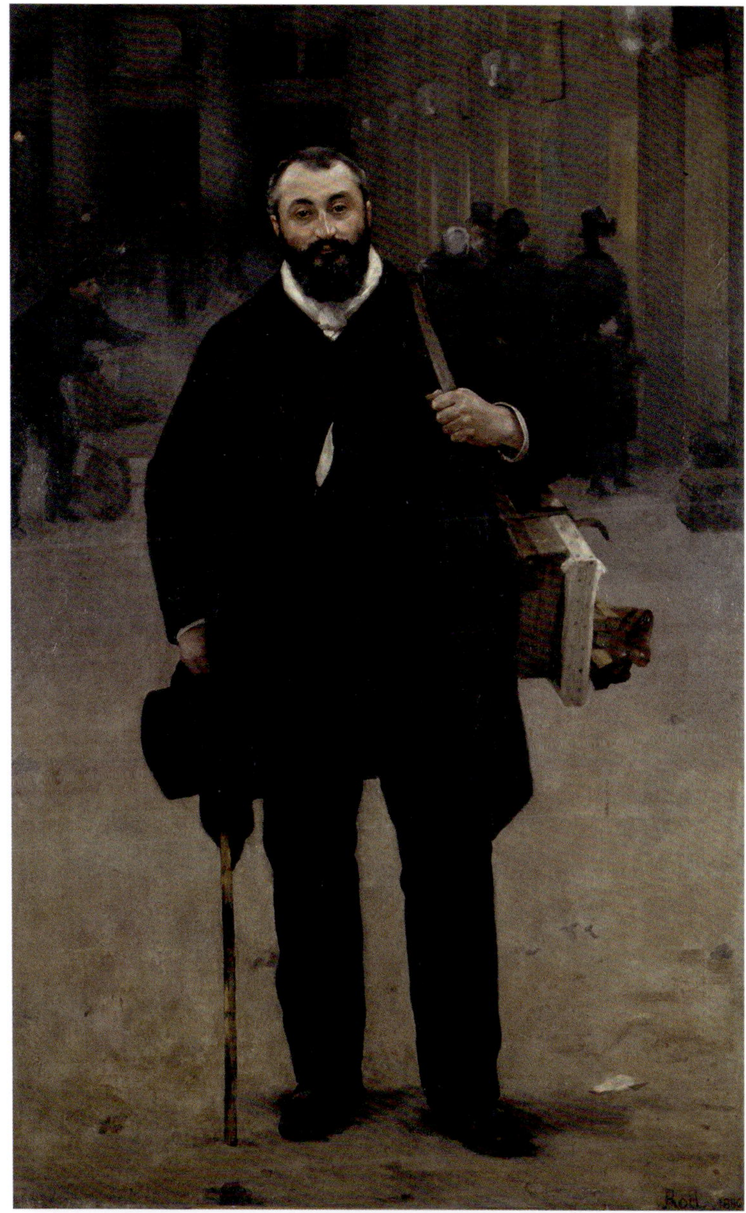

FIG. 33 Alfred Philippe Roll: *Portrait of the painter Pierre-Emmanuel Damoye*, 1886. Oil on canvas, 217 × 138.5 cm. Musée de Picardie, Amiens, deposit from Musée d'Orsay. LUX 995

A Name in Paris

CAT. 41 Peder Severin Krøyer
Ferdinand Meldahl (1827–1908), 1882

It was not long before Krøyer saw Paris again, after his long sojourn abroad: the year after his return to Denmark, he set out to see the Salon in May 1882, to which he contributed a single work: *Ferdinand Meldahl (1827–1908)* (CAT. 41). Once again, the French audiences were thrilled. However, its reception in Denmark would be rather different.

When Krøyer returned to Denmark in the summer of 1881 after his long stay abroad, he once again began accepting commissions for portraits. The practice brought in a stable income, and so it was a major aspect of his artistic work. At the same time, he challenged the genre by experimenting with light, composition, background, and expression. He marked the fact that he had further honed and developed the genre during his time abroad by raising his fees upon his return: 'I am raising my prices at home. I take 3000 kroner for a whole-length portrait, 2000 for a half-length and 1400 for a bust-length.'[87] To offer some perspective on this, a labourer in Copenhagen made no more than approximately 700 kroner a year in 1881.[88] Krøyer's target audience was obviously somewhat higher up the social ladder.

Krøyer immediately sought out his friends in Copenhagen. It was a happy reunion, one which very quickly led to him being admitted to an association of radical literati and painters known as 'Bogstaveligheden'. Writing to his friend Laurits Tuxen, who was still in Paris, Krøyer said:

> Well – now I'm home and I enjoy it tremendously – of course – I have arrived here at the loveliest time of year, everyone welcomes me with open arms, my friends are doubly amiable. I have already been admitted into 'Bogstaveligheden' at a dinner at the Hermitage – the reddest radicalism you could imagine.[89]

Krøyer's sympathy for 'the reddest radicalism', in spite of the salaries he claimed for himself, may have been the thorny issue that caused such differences of opinion in the reception of the portrait of Meldahl. Ferdinand Meldahl was the most prominent architect in Denmark at the time. He held a number of important positions due to his political commitment and his professional standing as an architect, and had been director of the Royal Danish Academy of Fine Arts since 1873. Normally, a portrait of such a prominent architect would showcase his position by incorporating attributes indicative of his profession or status. Examples of such symbols might be compasses and rulers, architectural drawings, models of ongoing projects, or perhaps a uniform, a dignified pose, and the wearing of various insignia. No such accoutrements can be

87. PSK to Laurits Tuxen, Copenhagen, 11 November 1881. KB NKS 2339, 2° 5.

88. Dalgaard, 'Arbejderklassens Økonomiske Kaar', 112.

89. PSK to Laurits Tuxen, Copenhagen, 4 June 1881. KB NKS 2339, 2° 5.

CAT. 41 Peder Severin Krøyer: *Ferdinand Meldahl (1827–1908)*, 1882. Oil on canvas, 195 × 113.5 cm. Den Hirschsprungske Samling, Copenhagen, deposit from Statens Museum for Kunst. KMS1475

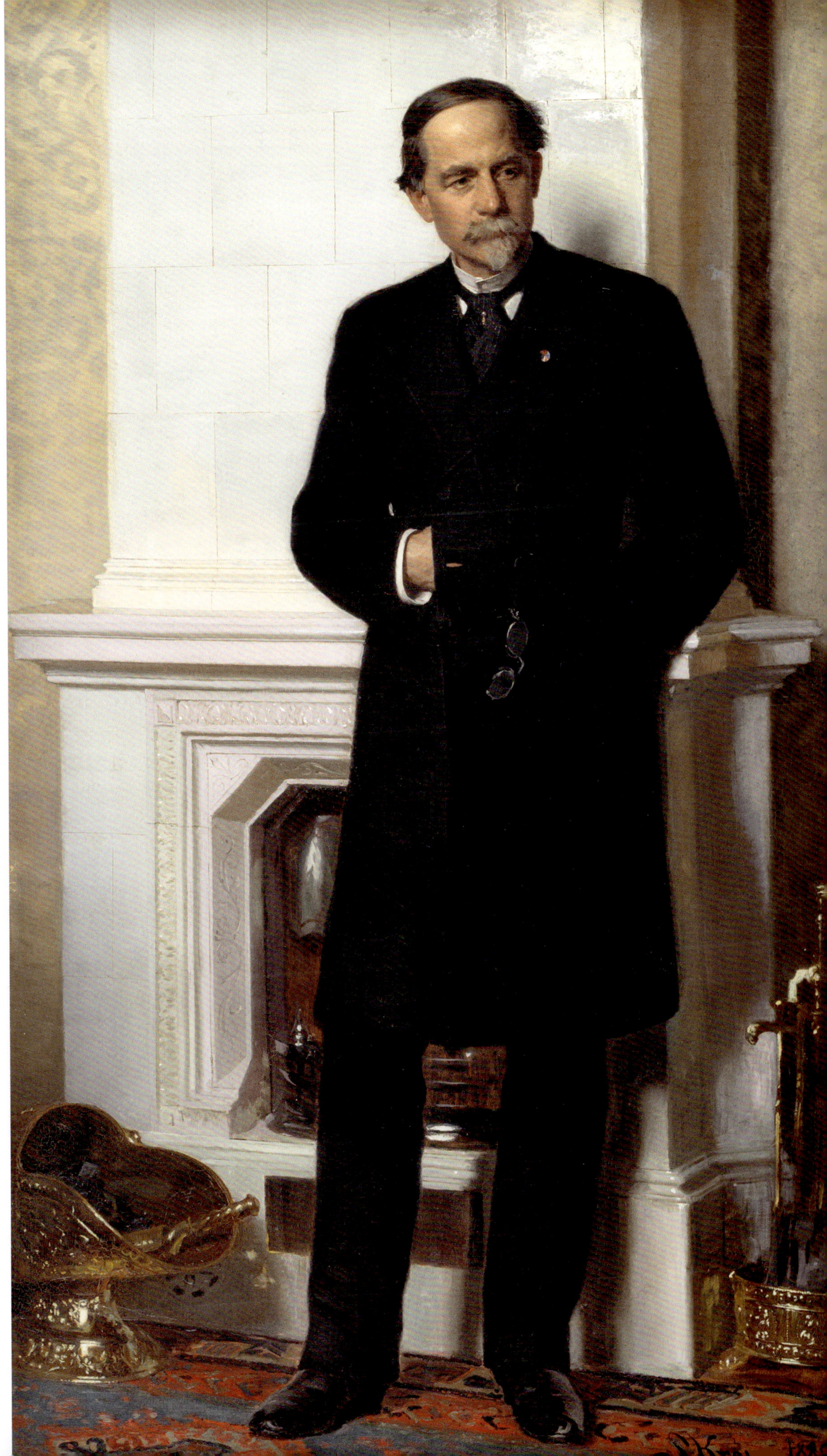

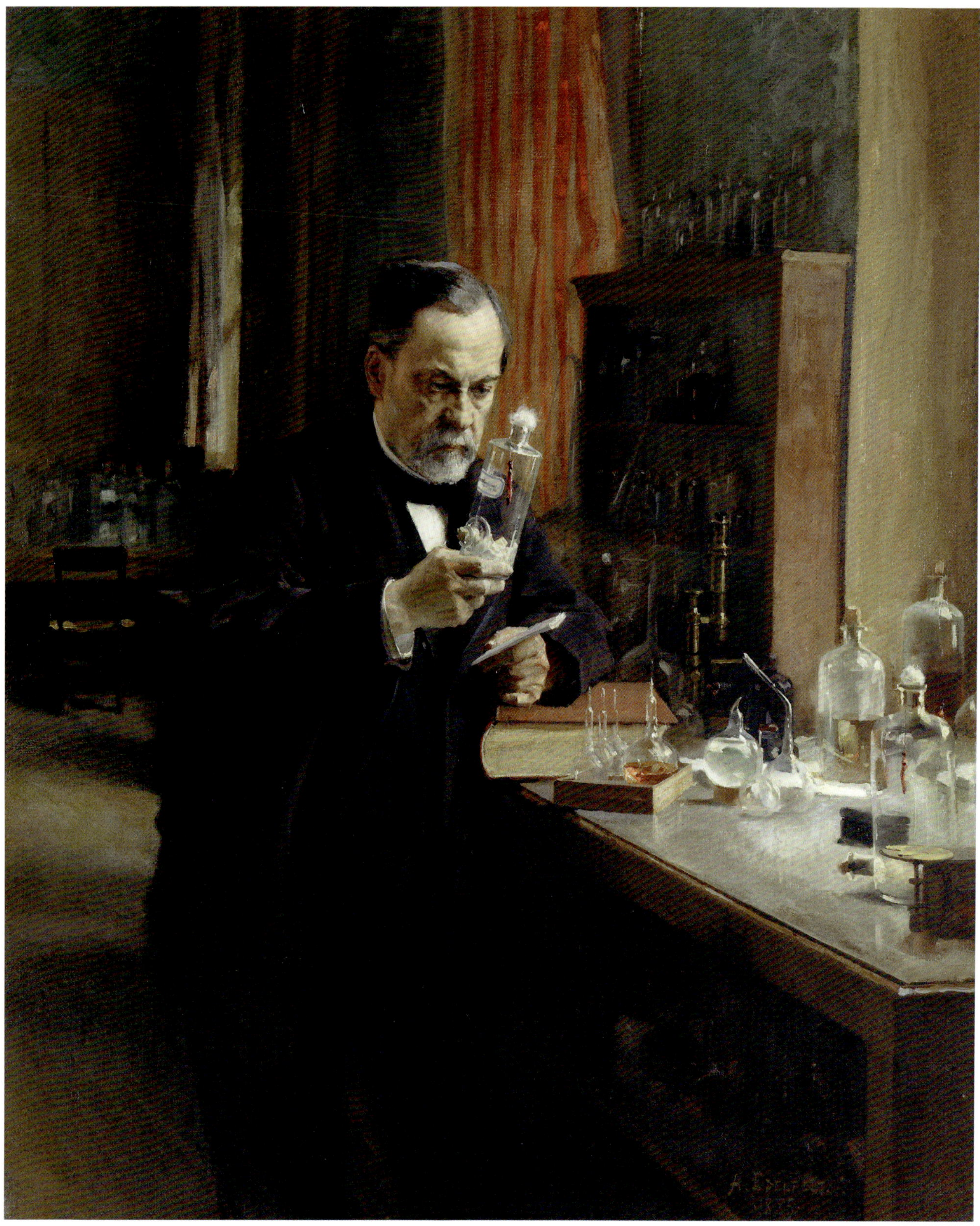

FIG. 34 Albert Edelfelt: *Louis Pasteur*, 1885. Oil on canvas, 155 × 127.5 cm. Musée d'Orsay, Paris. DO 1986 16

found in this portrait, leaving only a man dressed in fine, but not extraordinary clothes.

The work was commissioned by Meldahl's wife, which is to say that it was intended for a private home, but when she saw the result, she did not want it on her walls.[90] Meldahl himself was not keen on it either, and after a few years it was acquired by Den Kongelige Malerisamling (the present-day Statens Museum for Kunst) in 1893. Krøyer himself was very pleased with the painting, as were the French.[91] Having no idea who Meldahl was, they simply saw a portrait characterised by an innovative composition, impressive renditions of light, and a distinctive Nordic stove covered in porcelain tiles.[92]

In 1885, the Finnish painter Albert Edelfelt, one of the more established Nordic artists in Paris, painted a portrait of the scientist Louis Pasteur, who was quite the national treasure in France (FIG. 34). Edelfelt and Krøyer first met in 1877, and their acquaintance grew into a friendship in 1884 when they went on a trip to England together.[93] Unlike Krøyer, Edelfelt included a range of attributes in his portrait of Pasteur, enabling us to recognise him as an important chemist and microbiologist. Here is a large laboratory, bottles, flasks, and preparations, and a thick book and notepad, hinting at important scientific achievements. By this point in time, Pasteur had invented the process of pasteurisation, which makes milk and other foods keep longer; he had cultivated pure yeast cells that made it far easier to control the brewing of beer; and he had developed a vaccine against anthrax and one against rabies, which was previously a deadly disease. The cultivation of pure yeast cells made him a figure of particular importance to Krøyer's patron, the brewer Carl Jacobsen. That is why Pasteur also appears in Krøyer's *The Committee of the French Art Exhibition in Copenhagen in 1888* (CAT. 47), a painting commissioned by Jacobsen. Still Edelfelt's portrait of Pasteur differed from typical French portraits by focusing more on composition than on symbols of the sitter's status, a trait he shared with the other Nordic artists. The work was exhibited at the Salon de la Société des Artistes Français in 1886, where he was awarded a prize and received the Légion d'honneur. The French state subsequently bought the work in 1887 for the Sorbonne, the University of Paris, and today it is owned by the Musée d'Orsay. Edelfelt was thus among the Nordic artists who achieved great success in Paris, just like Hagborg, Zorn, Thaulow, and Krøyer, thereby making it easier for other Scandinavian artists to break through on the French art scene. On a par with his fellow artists, Edelfelt contributed to the Scandinavian artists forging ties and establishing their own community in Paris.
Mette Harbo Lehmann

CAT. 42 Peder Severin Krøyer
Fishermen Hauling a Seine Net at Skagen Nordstrand. Late Afternoon, 1883

Krøyer's large painting of Skagen fishermen hauling a net (CAT. 42) was exhibited at the Salon de la Société des Artistes Français in Paris in 1884. Presented alongside two other works depicting scenes from Skagen – the painting *Artists' Luncheon at Brøndum's Hotel* from 1883 (Skagens Kunstmuseer) and, in the section for works on paper, the pastel *Summer Evening* from 1884 (Nationalmuseum, Stockholm) – this became a turning point in Krøyer's career in France.[94] The reviews were extremely favourable, and Krøyer received a second-class medal, which meant that in future he could submit works to the Salon without bringing them before the jury first.[95] This is to say that he was free to decide what he wanted to exhibit with no danger of having his works rejected.

90. Mentze, 120–121; Hornung, 145–148.
91. PSK to Laurits Tuxen, Copenhagen, 11 November 1881. KB NKS 2339, 2° 5.
92. Saabye, *Krøyer. An International Perspective*, 240.
93. Saabye, 'Krøyer & Edelfelt', 84–90.
94. Cat. no. 1340: *Pêcheurs de Skagen (Danemark); coucher de soleil*, cat. no. 1341: *Le déjeuner des artistes, à Skagen*, and cat. no. 2904: *Sur la plage de Skagen (Danemark), crépuscule* (pastel).
95. Lobstein, '"A Lover of Light"', 55.

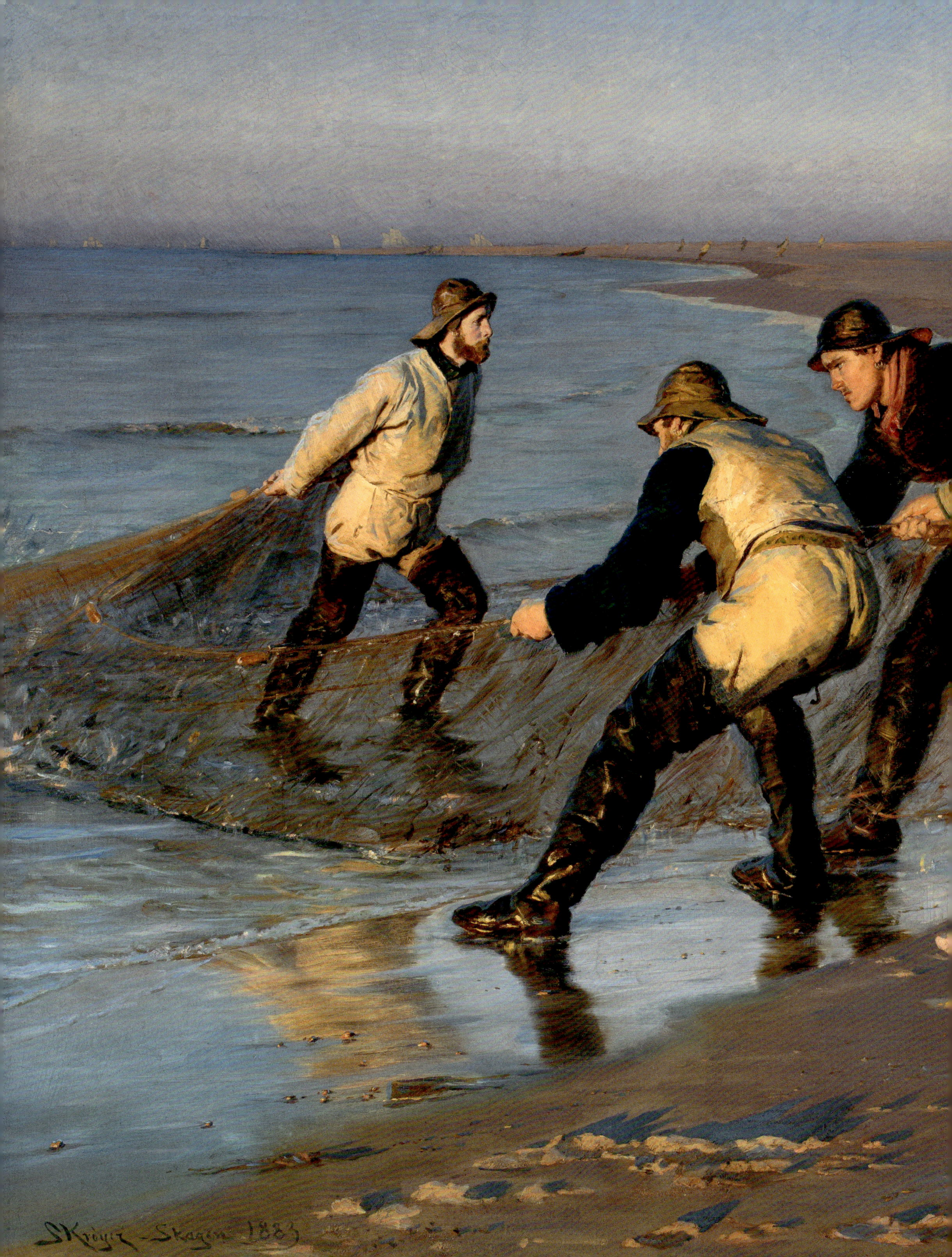
SKrøyer - Skagen 1883

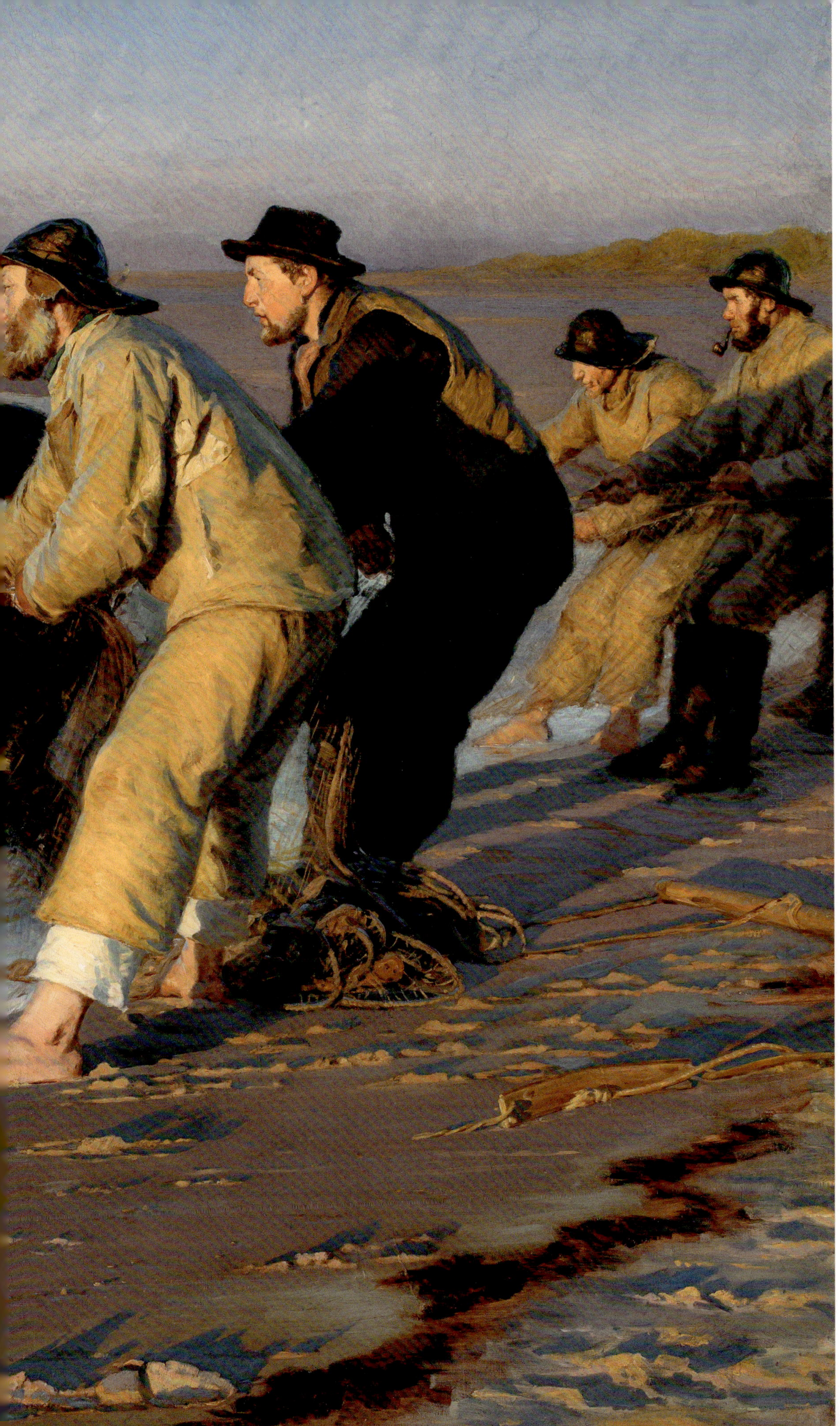

CAT. 42 Peder Severin Krøyer: *Fishermen Hauling a Seine Net at Skagen Nordstrand. Late Afternoon*, 1883. Oil on canvas, 135×190.5 cm. Skagens Kunstmuseer. SKM1486

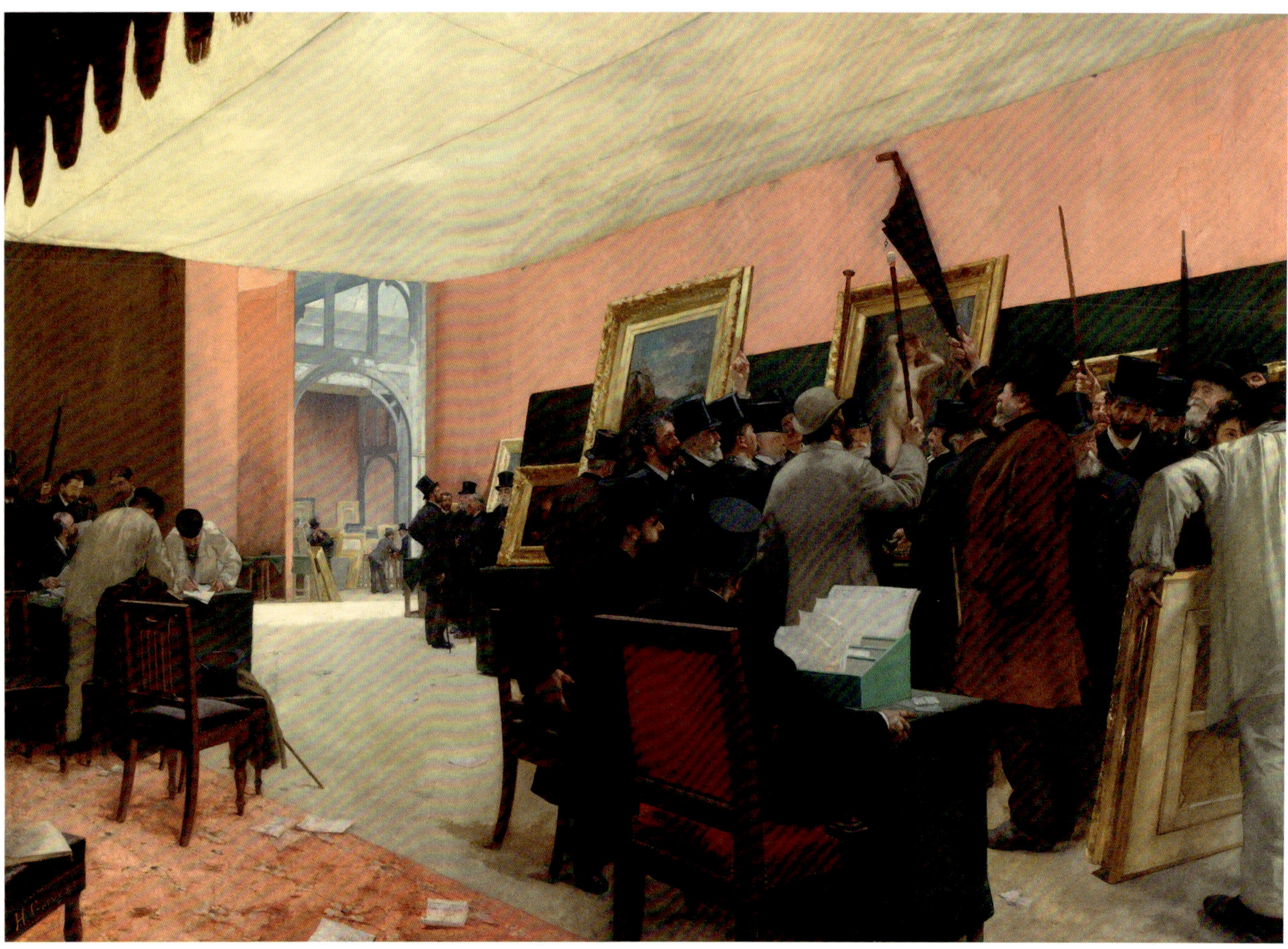

FIG. 35 Henri Gervex: *A Session of the Painting Jury*, before 1885. Oil on canvas, 300 cm × 419 cm. Musée d'Orsay, Paris. RF 726

That year, the jury, comprising 40 artists, had a very hard time agreeing on their assessments:

> Voting for awards in the painting section was laborious. The members of the jury met at nine o'clock in the morning, under the chairmanship of Mr. Bouguereau, and did not complete their operations until five o'clock. Yet the jurors only awarded second-class medals, having decided not to award first-class medals this year. Voters numbered 40.
>
> The first 12 medals were awarded to MM. de Lalaing, by 30 votes; Schommer, 29; Auguin, 28; de Thoren, 28; Kreyder, 28; Bonnefoy, 27; Delahaye, 26; Damoye, 24; Krøyer, 23; Barillot, 22; Escalier, 22; and Durst, 20.[96]

This is to say that among the several thousand artists who exhibited at the Salon, Krøyer was ranked the ninth best of all. The following year, the French artist Henri Gervex

96. Dangeau, 'Nouvelles du jour. La ville', [1].

exhibited a huge painting at the Salon, showing the jury in the process of judging work in 1883 (FIG. 35). It offers an impression of the chaotic nature of the sessions with the many assembled jurors, all of them acclaimed painters, holding up their canes and umbrellas to cast their votes, all while someone intrudes on the proceedings to proffer a work he would like to have judged; scraps of notes are strewn haphazardly across the floor.

Fishermen Hauling a Seine Net at Skagen Nordstrand. Late Afternoon is one of Krøyer's first large-scale figure paintings from the beaches at Skagen. He began working on the subject during his first summer in Skagen in 1882. As large as the canvas was, the painting was mostly painted out in the open air. In a letter sent to his patron Heinrich Hirschsprung in August, he wrote:

> This afternoon I went out to the North Beach for the first time with my big picture, driving there with all my odds and ends. It was such a pleasure. The sea was entirely calm and the skies clear, which is really important to me. Otherwise, I have only done minor studies on the spot itself – which does, by the way, go somewhat against the grain of my principles, but then what are principles for? – other than that, I paint in the field behind my house.[97]

The house was a two-storey building at 5, Oddevej. By the end of the summer, the weather was too bad to allow him to finish painting the picture, and the fishermen were too busy fishing to model for him. The picture had to be put aside for the winter while Krøyer fulfilled his obligations in Copenhagen, where he taught for the first time at Kunstnernes Studieskole. He then took a trip to Paris in early May 1883. On 25 May, Krøyer picked up work on his Skagen scene again, finishing it soon after. On 15 June 1883, he was able to write the following message to his mother:

> I am coming home again, probably on Tuesday morning. At any rate, my intention is to leave here Monday morning. I have had such incredibly clement weather it's downright amazing. So I finished the big picture in good time. I have been able to work outside on the beach every day since I came here, it's been calm and clear every afternoon, very rare here in Skagen.[98]

He thus felt compelled to go to Skagen in order to complete the picture on site before it was to be presented at the Nordic Art Exhibition in Copenhagen, which opened at the beginning of July. When he submitted the painting to the Salon in Paris the following year, it was still unsold, but Krøyer's account book reveals that it was sold through a French art dealer, Adolphe Goupil, to a private owner in England.[99] It was acquired by Skagens Museum in 1991.

Mette Harbo Lehmann

CAT. 43 Peder Severin Krøyer
At the Victualler's when there is no fishing, 1882

At the Victualler's when there is no fishing (CAT. 43) was one of the four works Krøyer presented at his first exhibition at the Galerie Georges Petit in Paris, the fourth *Exposition Internationale de Peinture*, which opened on 15 May 1885. The other three works were entitled *Marine*, *On the Beach*, and *Marine (Sunset over the Sea)*, and given that the catalogue stated no dimensions or dates for works and contained no reproductions, identifying them is virtually impossible.[100] Krøyer exhibited here along with a small selection of other artists: Jean Béraud, Albert Besnard, Léon Bonnat, Boutet de Monvel, J.C. Cazin, J. Chelmonski, Domingo, Albert Edelfelt, R. de Egusquiza, Henri Gervex, M. Libermann, Claude Monet, J.F. Raffaëlli,

97. Krøyer to Heinrich Hirschsprung, 9 August 1882, Skagen. HH Archive 746.

98. Krøyer to his adoptive mother, 15 June 1883, Skagen. PSK Archive 90.

99. Saabye, *Krøyer. An international perspective*, 215.

100. Cat. no. 59: *Dans le Cabaret de pêcheheurs*. Cat. no. 60: *Marine*. Cat. no. 61: *Marine (Coup de Soleil sur la mer)*. Cat. no. 62: *Sur la Plage*.

CAT. 43 Peder Severin Krøyer: *At the Victualler's when there is no fishing*, 1882. Oil on canvas, 79.5 × 109.8 cm. Den Hirschsprungske Samling, Copenhagen. 3083

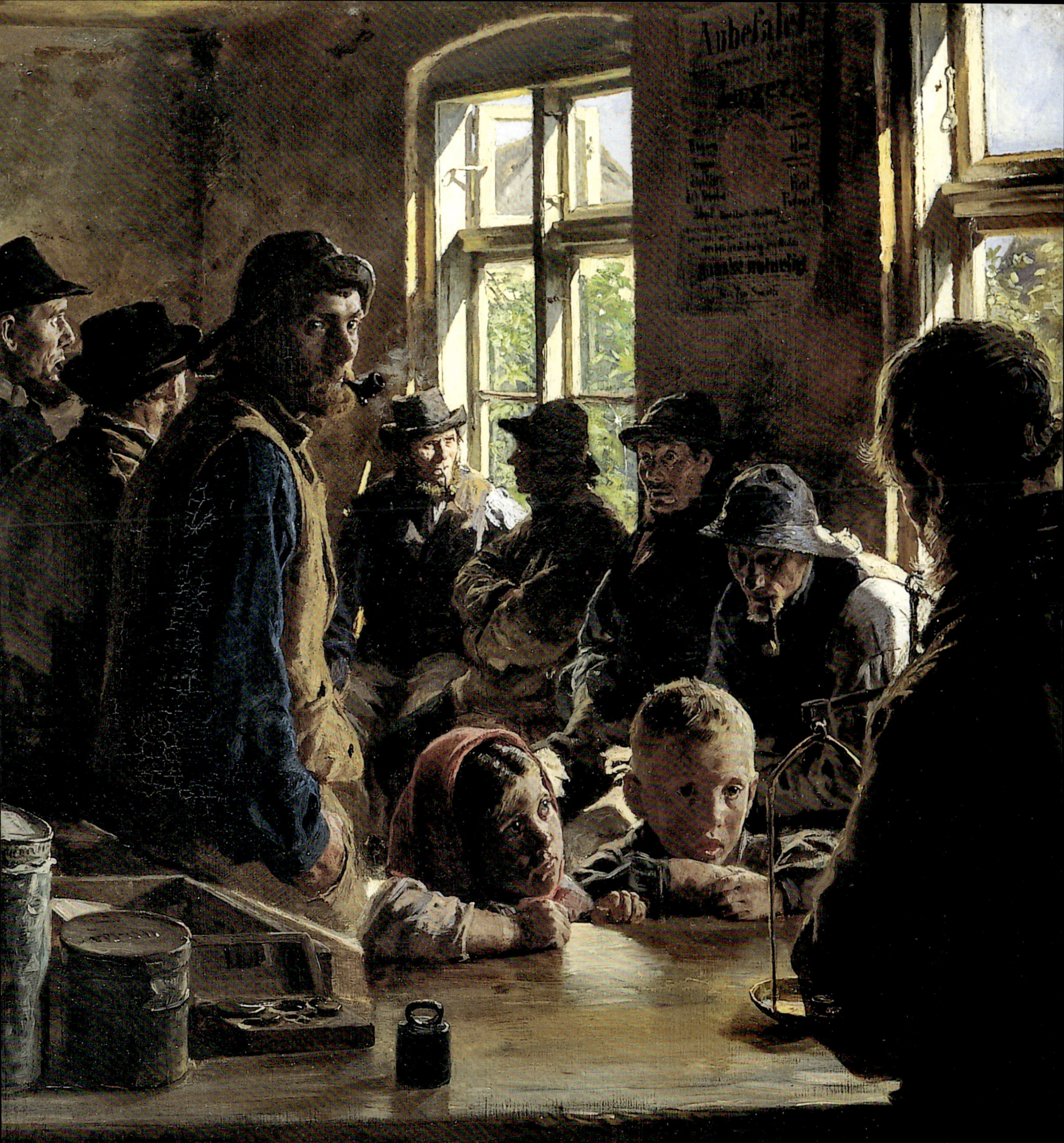

John S. Sargent, Alfred Stevens, Jan van Beers, W. Wyllie, and Mrs Berthe Cazin.[101] Several of these artists were or would soon become part of Krøyer's circle of acquaintances in France. Bonnat was his teacher in France; Besnard and Edelfelt were among those who eventually became his friends. But whether he ever met Claude Monet in connection with the exhibition (or since then) has never been proven. No correspondence mentioning Monet has been found from Krøyer's hand, even though Monet took part in the French exhibition in Copenhagen in 1888, where Krøyer played a major role in the exhibition jury. In any case, Krøyer was a Naturalist painter who may well have noted the paintings created by the French Impressionists, but paid greater attention to artists such as Edelfelt and Besnard. That spring, Krøyer was joined in Paris by fellow Danish artists Viggo Johansen and Anna and Michael Ancher. He presumably viewed the exhibition with them, and they would all undoubtedly have discussed the paintings there.

The exhibition at Georges Petit was significantly less important than the Expositions Universelles in which Krøyer participated in Paris in 1878, 1889, and 1900, or the Salon in Paris, where he exhibited almost every year. The gallery exhibition featured just 19 artists, while thousands of artists were represented at the two major exhibitions. There was also a difference between exhibiting in private, commercial settings like galleries and on the established art scene, which enjoyed far greater attention among audiences and critics alike. Accordingly, the Krøyer exhibition at the gallery consisted of smaller-scale paintings, pastels, and drawings.

At the Victualler's when there is no fishing dates from Krøyer's first visit to the artists' colony in Skagen in 1882. Michael Ancher, who had lived in Skagen for a long time, was not happy about Krøyer's sudden presence there, fearing that the other artists would impinge on his specialised subject matter. Ancher was the first to paint the fishermen from Skagen, and he wanted to keep his subjects all to himself. His ties to the place were further reaffirmed by the fact that he had married into a Skagen family. For example, the shop shown in the painting actually belonged to Michael Ancher's in-laws, and Ancher had been planning to paint his own picture of the place. Michael Ancher waited to vent his frustrations until he sent a letter to Krøyer in September 1882, after the latter had departed from Skagen.[102] Yet despite recurring frictions between the two, they remained friends. Krøyer reacted mostly with kindness and understanding whenever the 'Skagen Jealousy' flared up and Michael Ancher felt that his territory was being encroached upon.[103]

The work had been sold to a private collection back in 1882, meaning that it was presented for display only at the 1885 exhibition in Paris. Krøyer received several inquiries from interested buyers at the exhibition but, as he wrote in a letter home, the pictures were not for sale.[104]

Mette Harbo Lehmann

CAT. 44 Peder Severin Krøyer

Skagen Men going out Fishing at Night. Late Summer Evening, 1884

The history of how Krøyer's picture *Skagen Men going out Fishing at Night. Late Summer Evening* (CAT. 44) entered the collections of the Musée du Luxembourg, and its links with *Return from Fishing, Towing of the Boat* (FIG. 36) by the Spanish painter Joaquín Sorolla y Bastida, covers a period of around 15 years and a series of events with unexpected outcomes which are only partially revealed by the archives.

101. Sanchez, *Les expositions de la Galerie Georges Petit*, 9.
102. Michael Ancher to Krøyer, 5 September 1882, Skagen. PSK Archive 573.
103. Krøyer uses the term 'Skagen Jealousy' to describe Ancher's recurring frustrations in 1901, when Tuxen bought a house in Skagen. PSK to Michael Ancher, Schloss St. Valentin, Eppan, South Tirol, 25 November 1901. HAF dep. KB NKS 4572,4°.
104. PSK in a letter home, Paris, 23 May 1885. PSK Archive 107.

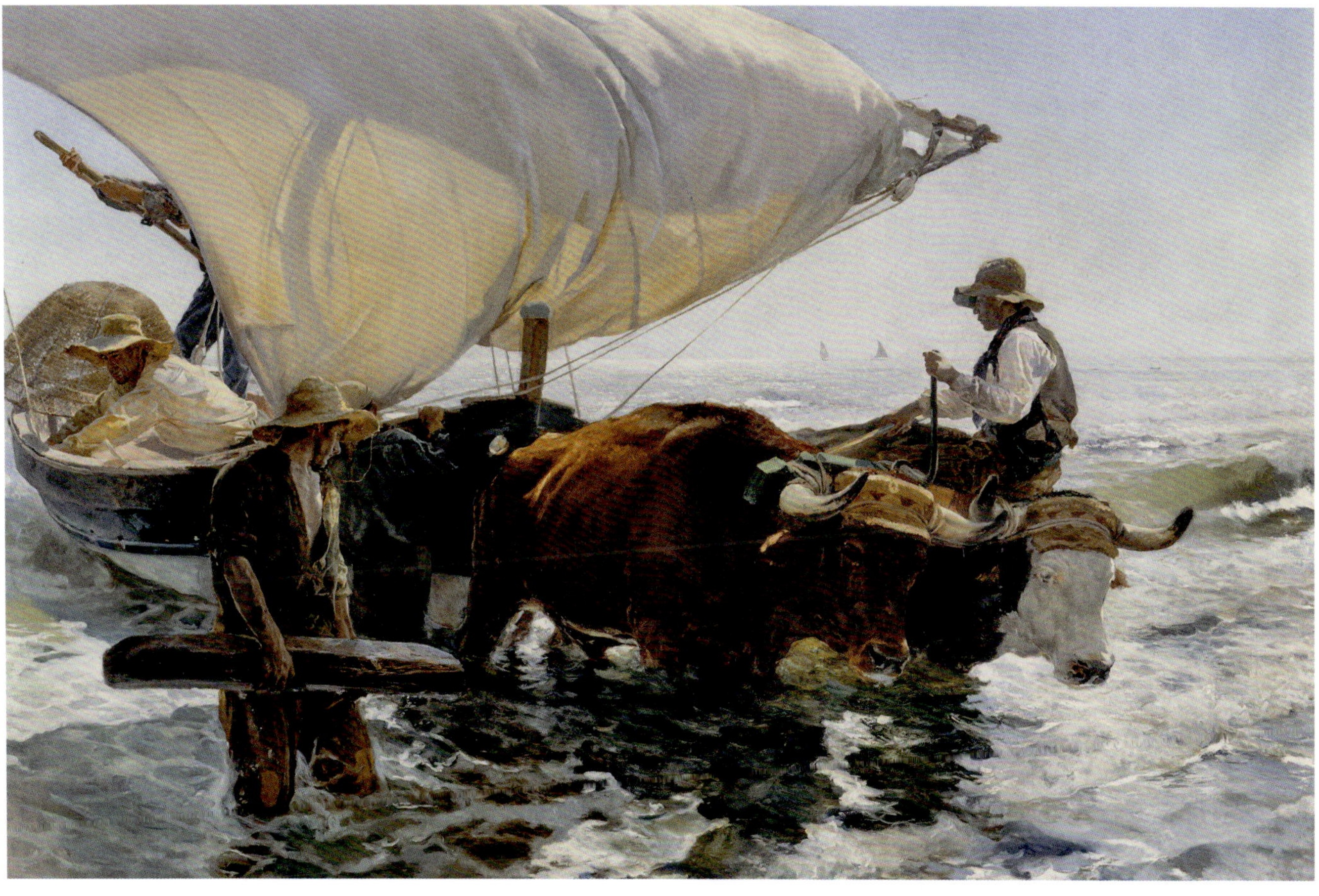

FIG. 36 Joaquín Sorolla y Batisda: *Return from Fishing, Towing of the Boat*, 1895. Oil on canvas, 265×403.5 cm. Musée d'Orsay, Paris. RF 948, LUX 736

It all began with the presentation of the Danish picture at the 1886 Paris Salon,[105] at the same time as *The Iron Foundry, Burmeister and Wain*, also by Krøyer (1885, Statens Museum for Kunst, Copenhagen).[106] Although this evocation of an industrial world did not arouse enthusiasm, the fishing scene was admired by critics, such as Alfred de Lostalot,[107] for example, in the most prestigious French art magazine. After an abortive attempt by the state to purchase the picture, which at that time was called *The Departure of the Fishing Fleet*, it continued its travels and, in all probability, was shown at the Continental Gallery in London in December 1886; at the Nordic Exhibition in Copenhagen, from May to October 1888; and perhaps, again, at the Fritz Gurlitt Gallery in Berlin.

A letter in the archives of Den Hirschsprungske Samling enables us to see the date when the French painter Albert Besnard made his appearance in this series of events. On 7 July 1888 he wrote to Krøyer and added, as a postscript, a rather enigmatic phrase: 'I am thinking of your picture, you will find it on your journey this autumn.'[108] This laconic remark becomes clearer in the light of a subsequent letter, dated December 1889, which says:

105. Cat. no. 1300: *Bateaux de pêche.*

106. Cat. no. 1299.

107. Lostalot, 'Le Salon de 1886', 472, 474.

108. Paul Albert Besnard to PSK, Paris, 7 July 1888. PSK Archive 2817.

CAT. 44 OVER LEAF: Peder Severin Krøyer: *Skagen Men going out Fishing at Night. Late Summer Evening*, 1888. Oil on canvas, 160×245 cm. Musée d'Orsay, Paris. RF 1977 204

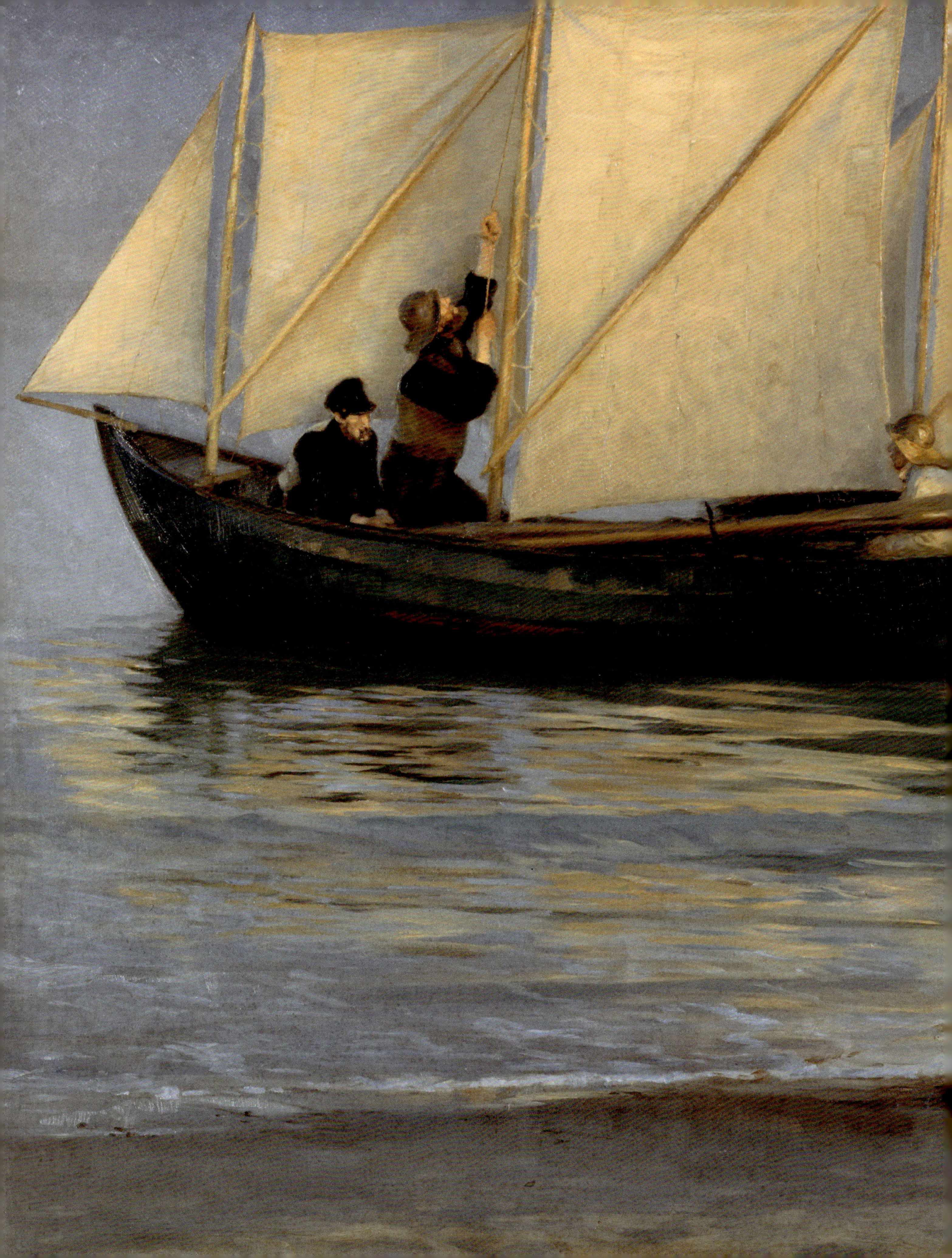

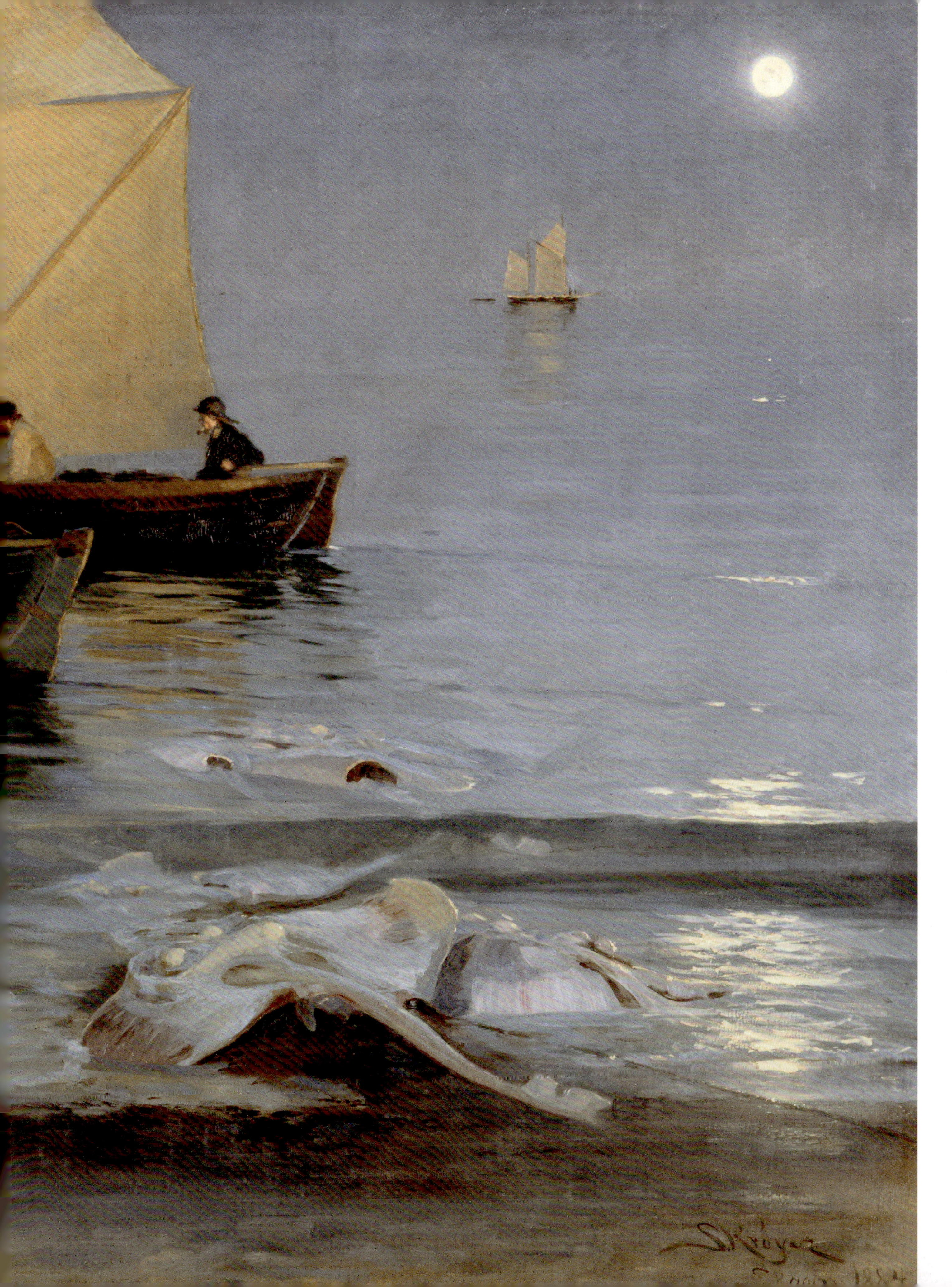

> Your delightful masterpiece has been at my house since the exhibition closed, and my daughter Rose will arrive with the same post that returns your picture. Your representative has proved to be most amiable.
>
> You have given me here a work of great value and inspired elegance.
>
> I thank you again my dear Krøyer, both on my own behalf and that of my wife, to whom you have given great happiness by leaving with us this memory of yourself and this proof of your very great talent.[109]

This text might be understood in the following way: when the World Fair ended, Krøyer's picture – shown in the catalogue as already belonging to Besnard – was sent to his town house; Besnard would shortly send Krøyer one of his own pictures, known today as *The Siren* (CAT. 45), which would leave for Copenhagen together with the work to be returned to him, which was probably the portrait of Ferdinand Meldahl, who was director of the Kongelige Danske Kunstakademi in Copenhagen (CAT. 41).[110] Sincere and profound thanks from the French painter and his wife, a sculptor, born Charlotte Dubray, were to follow.

For several years, nothing happened. The most that can be said is that in 1895, the Musée du Luxembourg bought Sorolla's picture after it had been shown in the official galleries. As the next Exposition Universelle approached, due to be held in 1900, Besnard decided to offer *Skagen Men going out Fishing at Night. Late Summer Evening* to the Musée du Luxembourg. There may have been several reasons for this gesture. The first certainly lay in the fact that Besnard wished the work to be exhibited at the Exposition Universelle, which was contrary to the decision that foreign artists could only appear at the Decennial Exhibition – the picture, dated 1884, was therefore too old. The second, more personal reason, stemmed from Besnard's attachment to the European idea: through this gesture, he would be reuniting Krøyer and Sorolla or, in other words, the north and south of Europe. But his approach came to nothing since the two paintings remained in the Musée du Luxembourg, while the exhibition commemorating the century just past was held on the other bank of the Seine.
Dominique Lobstein

CAT. 45 Albert Besnard
The Siren, 1889

Paul Albert Besnard was born in Paris on 2 June 1849; his father was a painter of historical subjects and his mother a miniaturist. So his path was already mapped out: in 1866, he was enrolled at the École des Beaux-Arts, from which he emerged brilliantly, having won the Prix de Rome with his illustration of the *Death of Timophanes, Tyrant of Corinth*. This initial award would be followed by many others which would lead him first to the Académie des Beaux-Arts, of which he became a member in 1912, then to the Académie française, which he joined in 1924, followed by the directorship of the Villa Medici in Rome, in 1913; finally he became director of the École des Beaux-Arts in Paris, in 1922. The distinctions would culminate with his nomination to the rank of Grand-Croix de la Légion d'honneur, in 1926.

As a painter, but also a pastellist and engraver, his works were many and varied, with portraits of women and well-known or exemplary figures occupying a prime place. *The Siren* (CAT. 45) exhibited here was created for Peder Severin Krøyer in 1889, in thanks for the gift of his picture *Skagen Men going out Fishing at Night. Late Summer Evening*

109. Paul Albert Besnard to PSK, Paris, December 1889. PSK Archive 2818.

110. Cat. no. 83 in the Danish section of the Decennial Exhibition of the 1889 Exposition Universelle.

CAT. 45 Albert Besnard: *The Siren*, 1889. Oil on canvas, 163.5 × 121 cm. Ny Carlsberg Glyptotek, Copenhagen. MIN1591

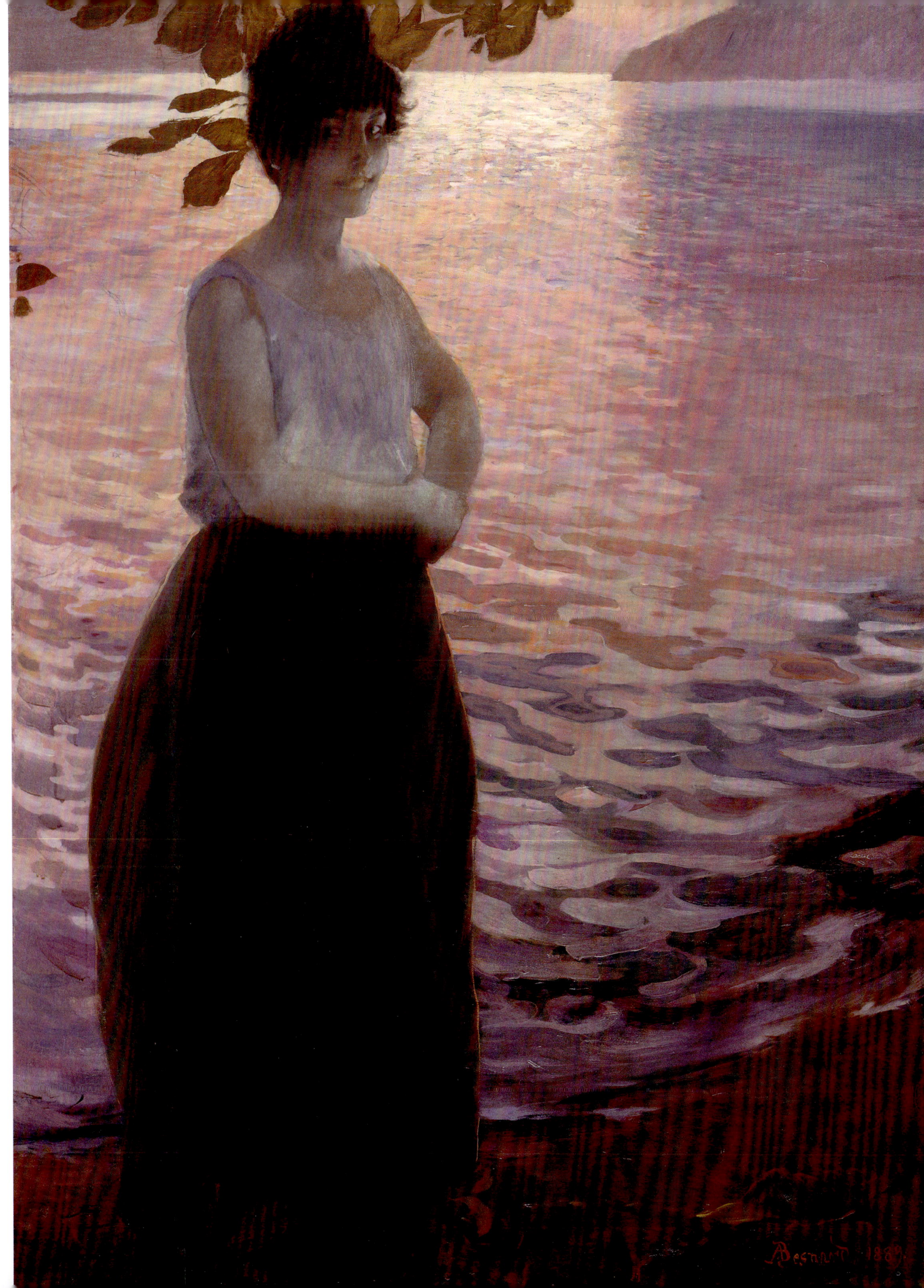

(CAT. 44), but it is one of Besnard's least known pictures. The painter sent it directly to Krøyer in Copenhagen, where it remained in his collection. In 1910, it was among the works that were broken up in a public sale by the firm Winkel and Magnussen, acting on behalf of Krøyer's daughter. The work was bought by the collector Carl Jacobsen for the museum which owed him so much, but it seems never to have been exhibited since that time.

The 'daughter Rose' mentioned by Besnard in a letter of 1888 refers to one of his paintings inspired by the setting of Lake Annecy in the Haute-Savoie region of France, which he had discovered in 1889. Having fallen in love with the place, he bought a piece of land in the commune of Talloires, where he had a villa built between November 1887 and June 1888, although it was not finally completed until 1889. From that moment on, the house also served as a studio and certain pictures would then travel between the Haute-Savoie and Paris before being completed. This was probably the case with *The Siren*, which, at the time Besnard was writing about it, appeared to be in his Paris studio.

Besnard placed his model on the shore of the lake, below his house. The picture appears to be more of an allegory than a portrait, a feeling that is reinforced by the title of the work. The woman's silhouette is outlined against the shifting reflections of the water, which extends to cover almost the whole height of the canvas. While the sun seems to be setting on the horizon, the monumental woman in the foreground is illuminated from behind, her features partly hidden in shadow. However, her mouth seems to be smiling and her eyes sparkle, giving her face an enticing look which is also a little strange. A wide, dark-coloured skirt hides the lower part of her body, making her look like the mythological sea monster after which the picture is named; the upper half of her body is scantily covered by a chemise with shoulder straps, leaving her arms bare, and looking more like an undergarment than an item for wearing in public. The colours Besnard has used reinforce the figure's allegorical aspect, her white top with its bluish reflections standing out against the background colours, which vary from red to yellow. By naming his picture *The Siren*, in homage to Krøyer, Besnard was probably making reference to the half-woman, half-fish siren of Nordic mythology rather than to the half-woman, half-bird chimera of Greek imagination. Over and above this, the artist was perhaps highlighting the danger that this woman represented – probably fatal, as she rises suddenly from the water, at dusk, in the fading daylight. This cannot fail to surprise when we know that the work was intended as a gift for a young husband, Peder Severin Krøyer having married Marie Triepcke on 23 July 1889.

Dominique Lobstein

CAT. 46 Peder Severin Krøyer
Osteria in Ravello, 1890

Osteria in Ravello (CAT. 46) was among the works presented by Krøyer at his penultimate exhibition at the Galerie Georges Petit in 1890.[111] He had already exhibited at Petit's *Exposition Internationale de Peinture* in 1885, 1887, and 1890, and would take part for the last time in 1891. The 1890 exhibition opened on 20 December and closed on 28 January, enabling him to exhibit a work created during his and Marie's honeymoon in Italy the same year. It is one of the few works exhibited there that can be conclusively identified. Less than half of the works Krøyer showed at Georges Petit can be identified today. The rest are hidden under less-than-specific titles such as *Danish*

111. Sanchez, 1071. Cat. no. 74.

Fisherman, *Group of Fishermen*, *Interior*, and *Marine*, all of which are subjects to which Krøyer returned repeatedly. Once again, the group of exhibiting artists was an exclusive circle comprising 19 people, including Albert Edelfeldt, Anders Zorn, and Alfred Sisley.

This scene from an Italian inn in Ravello is an interesting counterpart to *At the Victualler's when there is no fishing* from 1882, a scene from Skagen which Krøyer exhibited at Petit's 1885 exhibition (CAT. 43). They both represent watering holes where local residents come to spend time, conversation is brisk, and time passes slowly. But this is where the similarities end. One depicts a scene from northern climes and the other is from the south; also, the décor, the people's attire, and especially the light are all different. In addition to this, Krøyer's style of painting had changed since he first exhibited at the Galerie Georges Petit. By this point, he often presented sketches for larger paintings, works on paper, and other works done more quickly and with a freer hand than before. These pieces were generally a little smaller than those he exhibited at the Salon in Paris, at Charlottenborg in Copenhagen, and at other major exhibition venues. In 1887, Krøyer had exhibited alongside fellow artists such as the Impressionists Berthe Morisot, Camille Pissarro, Pierre-Auguste Renoir, Claude Monet, and Alfred Sisley, as well as sculptor Auguste Rodin, English artist James-Abbott McNeill Whistler, and Nordic artists Albert Edelfeldt and Carl Larsson. The encounter with the many French Impressionists at Georges Petit's exhibitions may explain the slightly altered style seen in 1890. He may have selected precisely those works from his Naturalist production that best suited the company.

Since 1878, Galerie Georges Petit had sold and promoted the Impressionists alongside other contemporary artists of the time. In the years that followed, the Impressionists had gone from being outsiders with low earnings to becoming increasingly popular. In 1886 the group held their last exhibition together, and their individual careers took over. From that point on, they exhibited their works separately in solo shows, and around the same time several other artists began to incorporate elements of their style into their own Naturalist paintings. However, Krøyer's *Osteria in Ravello* is still far removed from the Impressionist painting style.

In 1890, Krøyer did not exhibit at the Salon in Paris, perhaps because he was in Italy with Marie Krøyer, but critics still wrote about his participation at the Salon and the Exposition Universelle the year before. The timing of Georges Petit's exhibition opening in December was better, and Krøyer's new works were probably a better fit for it, but even so his three works at the exhibition failed to attract a single review.[112] Krøyer had previously tried his luck at other private galleries in Paris, and in 1888 he was able to write to his mother: 'Yesterday, I quite unexpectedly sold a small charcoal drawing from Skagen, which has sat undisturbed at an art dealer here in Paris for years, for 300 Francs. A most pleasing and amusing event, as it was so unexpected.'[113]

Mette Harbo Lehmann

112. The three works were cat. no. 73: *Le Comité de l'Exposition Française à Copenhague. Etude*; cat. no. 74: *Dans un cabaret italien*, owned by Heinrich Hirschsprung; and cat. no. 75: *Marie, esquisse*.

113. PSK in a letter home, Paris, [date unknown] 1888. PSK Archive 141.

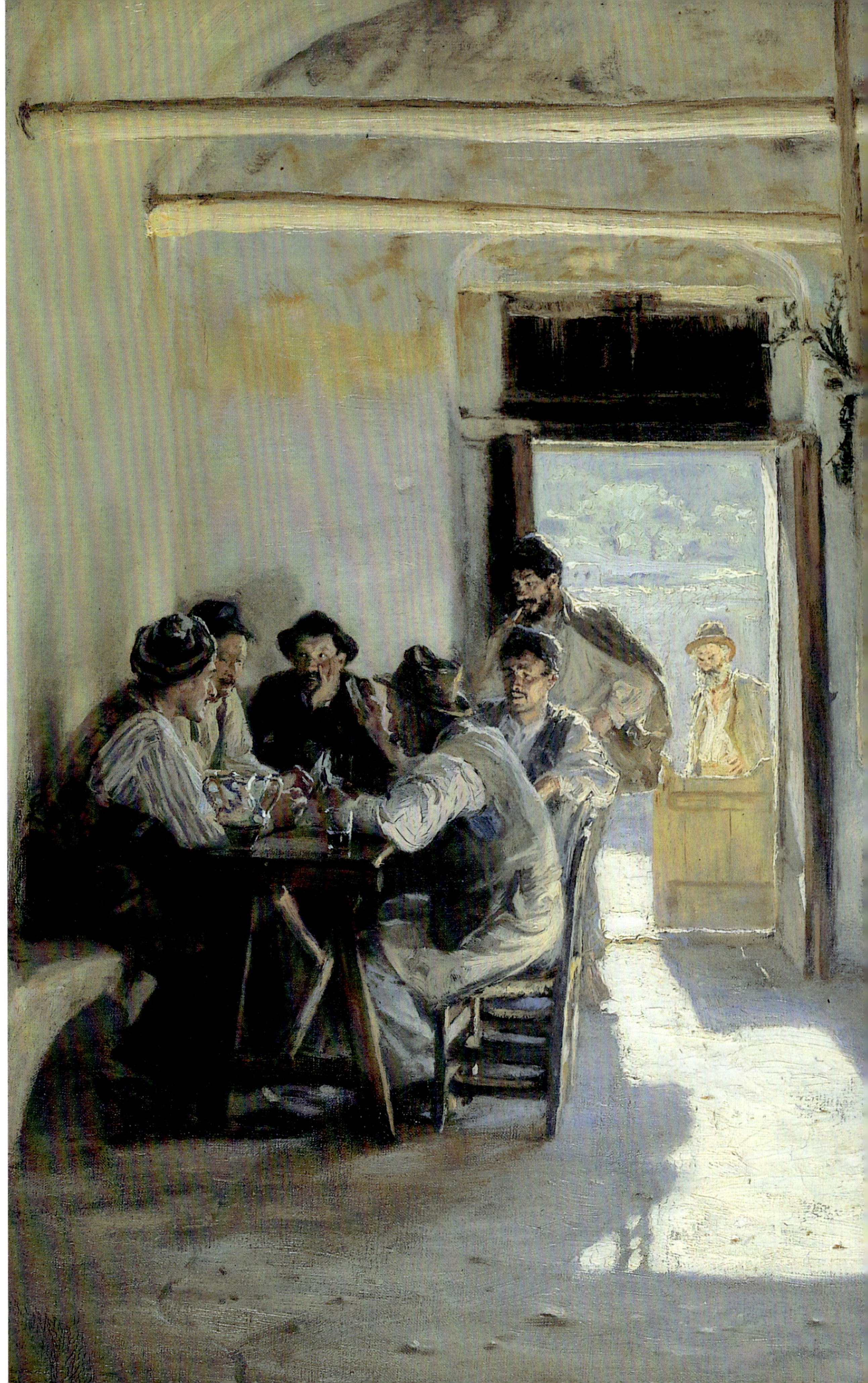

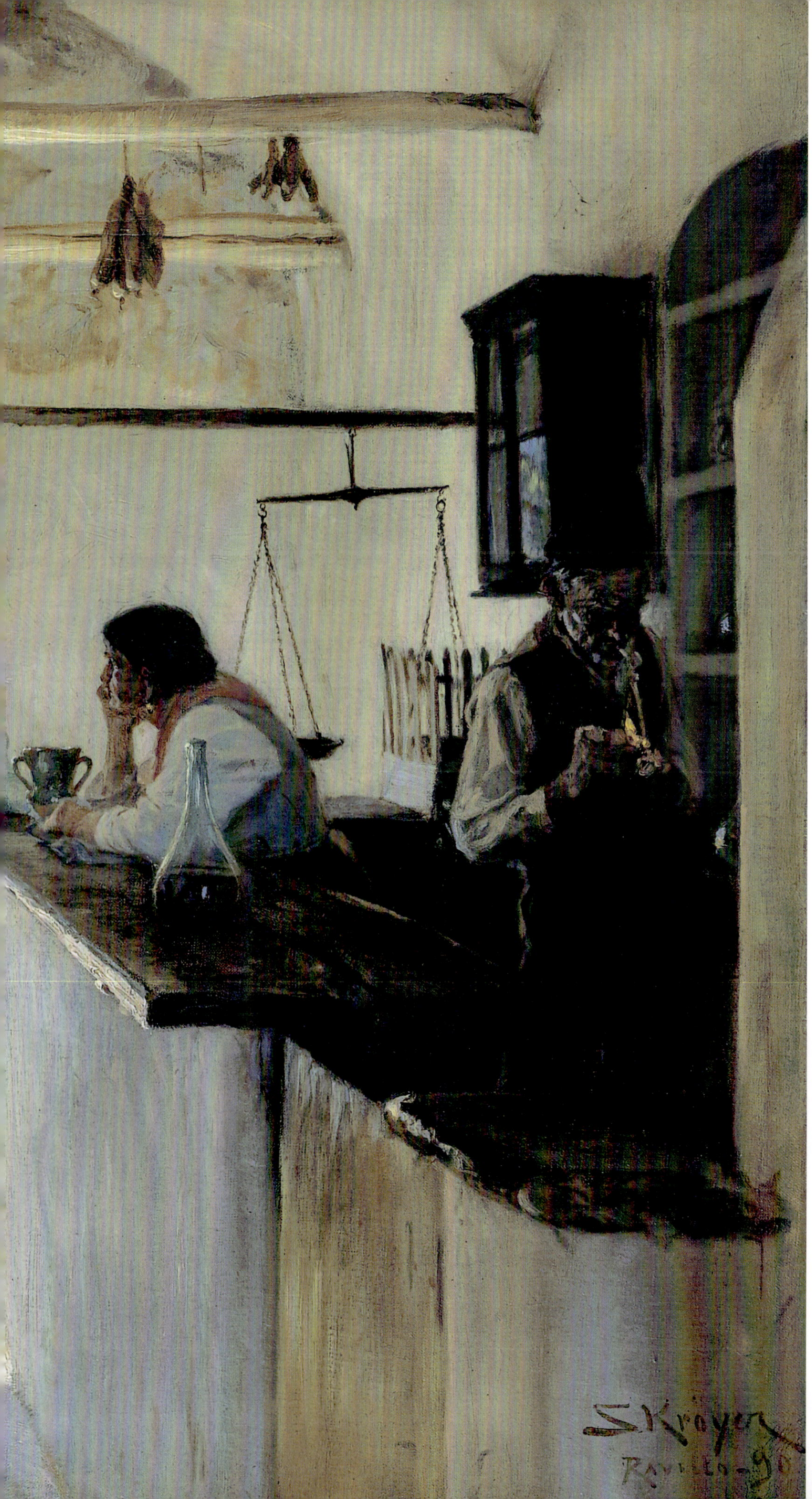

CAT. 46 Peder Severin Krøyer: *Osteria in Ravello*, 1890. Oil on canvas, 48 × 60.3 cm. Den Hirschsprungske Samling, Copenhagen. 214

French Masterpieces to Denmark

CAT. 47 Peder Severin Krøyer
Committee for the French Art Exhibition in Copenhagen 1888, 1889

This picture (CAT. 47) has been mentioned several times already and is the subject of an essay in this catalogue. It is the final outcome of an exceptional event which Krøyer was charged with organising and which, at the request of Carl Jacobsen, brought numerous French artists to the Danish capital in 1888. The work was exhibited in Paris at the 1889 Exposition Universelle under number 88, and led to many enthusiastic reviews in the most important journals. The critic André Michel wrote not only a chronicle of the exhibition but a panegyric on Franco-Danish relations, extracts from which provide a useful substitute for explanations that might entail needless repetition:

> The presence of M. Pasteur amid this group of artists should not trouble the amiable reader ... There is no allusion here to the stormy incidents of the last general assembly of French artists; this is not a vaccination session, but the most fraternal debate *within the compass* of the most peaceable commission. – M. Pasteur was here as president of honour ... And it is hardly necessary to say why. Indeed, everyone knows how the great Danish brewer, M. Carl Jacobsen, has the deepest admiration for our illustrious compatriot, and through what delicate tributes he has wished to prove this to him. His portrait and that of his granddaughter, commissioned from Léon Bonnat [Musée Pasteur, Paris], have been presented to Mme Pasteur; his bust, set in a place of honour at the Ny-Carlsberg factories, recalls the debt and endorses the homage of all brewers to the man who instigated research into fermentation; and finally, the list of founders of the Institut Pasteur, if it were consulted, would complete the account of the extent to which this gratitude and admiration of a foreign friend have borne fruit.
>
> But M. Jacobsen does not refrain from going further still; this brewer is also a passionate art lover. The Ny-Carlsberg Glyptotek is no less famous than his brewery, and the works of our sculptors are gloriously represented there. When the Danish government decreed that an international exhibition of industrial art should take place, to celebrate King Christian IX's Silver Jubilee and the centenary of the 1788 edicts – which, by abolishing forced residence and extending property rights, established the emancipation of the peasantry – M. Jacobsen wished for French art to be part of it. He therefore sent out a joint invitation to French artists and,

at the same time, had an elegant pavilion built and fitted out in order to exhibit their works.

A committee set up in Paris was tasked with receiving applications and gathering together pictures, statues, engravings, medals, and drawings; the presidency of honour was awarded to Pasteur, the actual presidency to M. Antonin Proust, and, to perpetuate the memory of the committee's transient meetings, M. Jacobsen asked a Danish artist, M. P.-S. Krøyer – who needs no introduction to readers of the *Gazette des Beaux-Arts* – to paint a picture of its members from life, as a kind of corporate body, in the Dutch style. The result is this picture – which has already been seen and admired at the Exposition Universelle – where Krøyer, with his wonderful gift of capturing close likenesses of people and things in a few distinctive strokes, has ingeniously grouped together so many portraits, revealing the way they appear in the light and the ambient atmosphere [...]

So here we are introduced into one of the committee's sessions. Judging from the gravity and concentration of those present, the proceedings must have been very important and have lasted late into the afternoon. Lamps have just been brought in and the faces are lit by the contrasting rays of artificial light and the fading daylight in the still luminous sky, seen through the glass of the large bay-windows. We know how delicately and with what bold frankness Krøyer approached these subtle problems and how his brush and eye gave free play to them. M. Pasteur is seated at the centre, following, on a plan, the explanations being given by Professor Klein, an architect and member of Det Kongelige Danske Kunstakademi, whose good grace and unfailing kindness were experienced on countless occasions by all those who had travelled to Copenhagen. M. Jacobsen stands behind him, near to Charles Garnier; Paul Dubois is seated to his right with his head turned towards M. Jacobsen. M. Antonin Proust is standing, presiding over the session, and our friend Lucien Magne, who was the amiable companion and faithful recorder of our journey, has briefly interrupted his à parte with Krøyer (who has remained discreetly in a corner with his friend Tuxen) to glance at the plans laid out on the table.

Certainly, these deliberations were thorough, and this committee must have been a microcosm of all the parliamentary virtues, just as it brought together all the finest talents. Puvis de Chavannes was taking notes; Falguière, impressed by these administrative proceedings, looks like a minister, his head bowed in deep thought; Chaplain, Barrias, and Gérôme assist him; on the opposite side, Bonnat appears to want to restrain an excitable group, while Cazin and Roll, pensive, stand next to Besnard and Gervex ... Antonin Mercié, Chapu, Carolus-Duran, Delplanche, Gautherin, and others are following the proceedings attentively, but without participating.

Krøyer has recounted all this with his elegant brush in a way that is spontaneous and skilful, full of life and vigour, all at the same time; he is able to reconcile ancient Dutch bonhomie with modern anxiety, in a rare but delightful union [...].[114]

Everything has been said; there is nothing to add.
Dominique Lobstein

114. Michel, 'Le Comité français à l'Exposition de Copenhague', 148–151.

CAT. 47 OVER LEAF: Peder Severin Krøyer: *Committee for the French Art Exhibition in Copenhagen 1888*, 1889. Oil on canvas, 144×221 cm. Ny Carlsberg Glyptotek, Copenhagen. MIN 0904

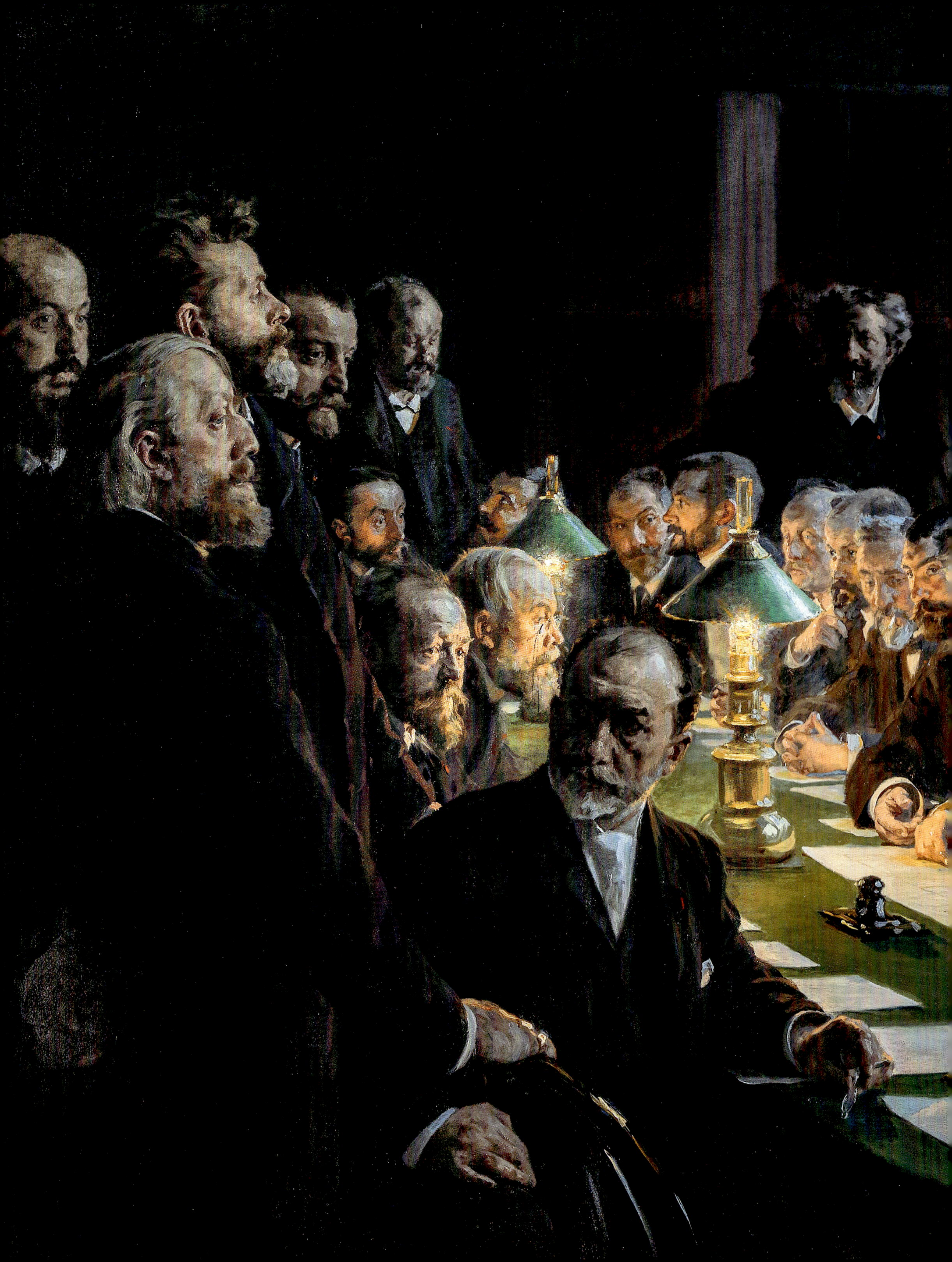

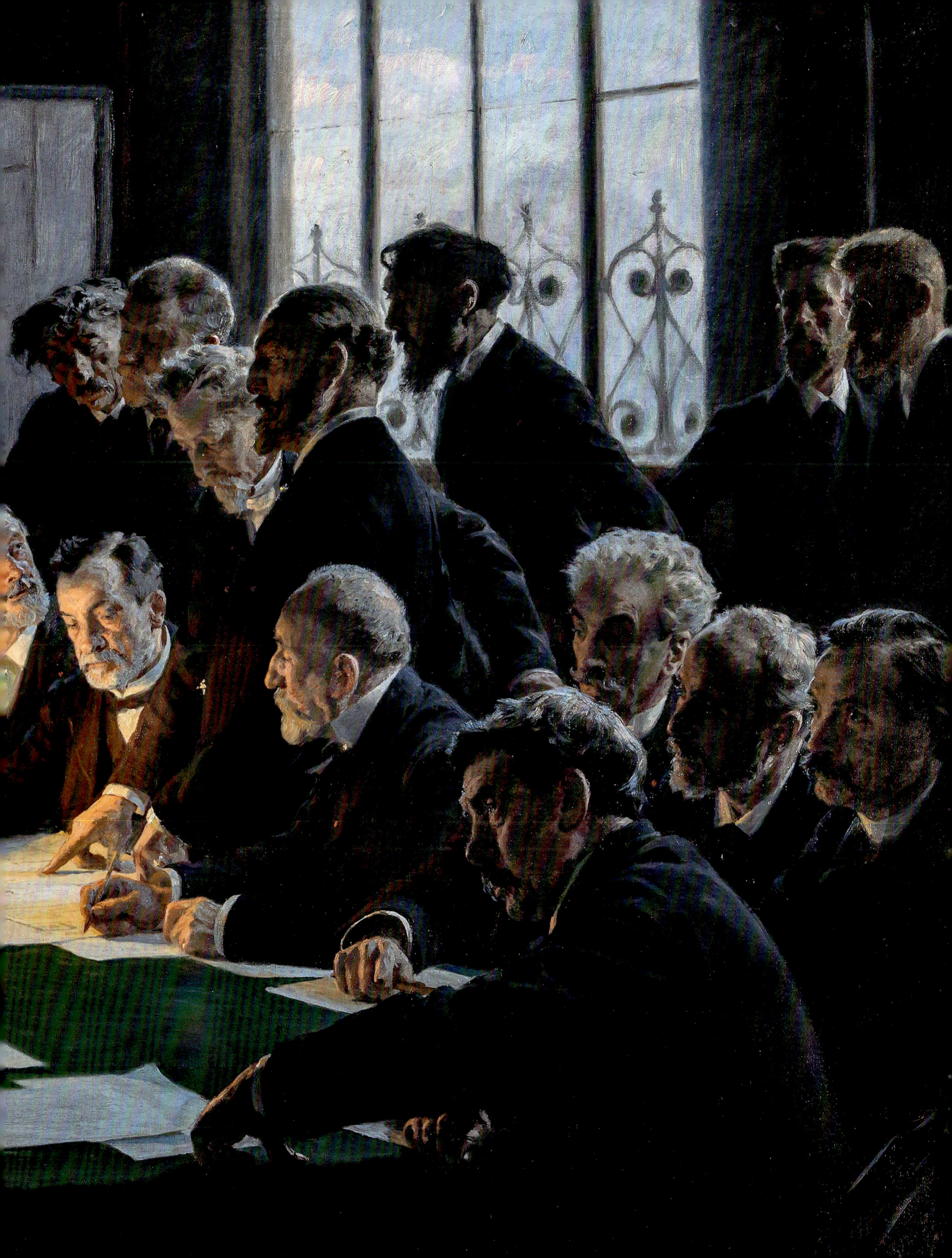

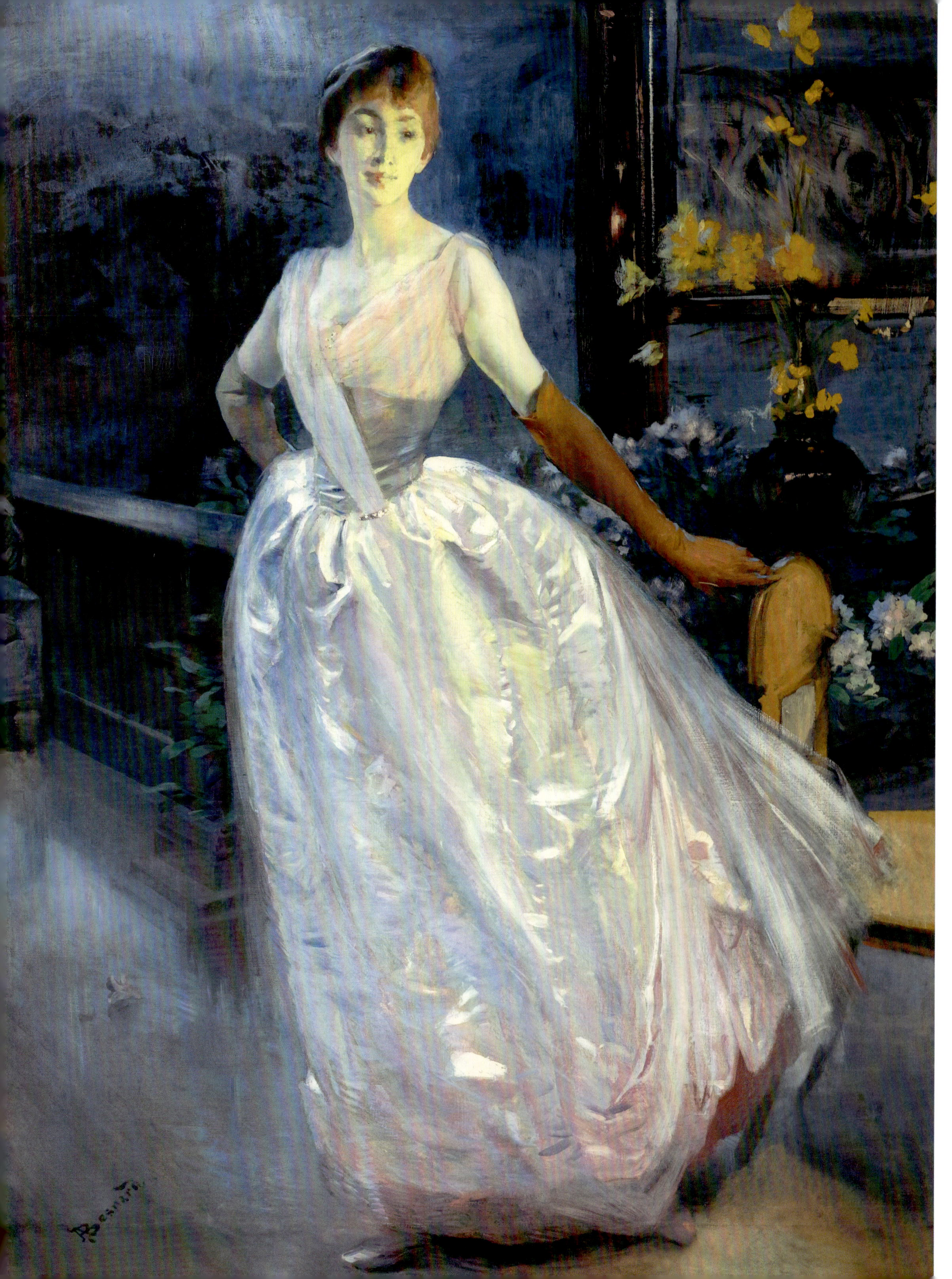

CAT. 48 Albert Besnard
Madame Roger Jourdain, 1886

While Bastien-Lepage was the deceased artist to whom Krøyer was most attached, Besnard, of a similar age to him, was probably the living artist with whom he had the friendliest relationship. The affability of this French painter, his open-mindedness, and his deep belief in a united Europe which led him to travel beyond French borders far more than was common, meeting other artists of all nationalities, must certainly have counted for much. Their letters that have been preserved (many more than were exchanged with other French artists) testify to this unfailing friendship, which also united the wives of these artists – Charlotte in Paris and Marie in Copenhagen – although direct evidence arising from the works exhibited is rare.

The existence of an engraving (FIG. 37), signed by Krøyer and reproducing Besnard's portrait of *Madame Roger Jourdain* (CAT. 48), published on page 91 of the 1888 exhibition catalogue, was a mark of his admiration, sufficient to indicate that he himself would have liked to include the painting in this exhibition, and for us to try and understand why this portrait interested the Danish artist.

The work was exhibited at the 1886 Salon, and depicted Henriette Marie Dubois de Moulignon, wife of the painter Roger Jourdain, when she was aged 24, that is to say a few years after her marriage, which had been celebrated on 31 December 1881. As a well-known figure in Parisian high society, the model for this picture, presented as number 208 and bearing the mysterious title *Portrait of Mme R.J.*, very soon lost her anonymity. The fact that such a person could lend herself to the artistic experiment that this work represented drew additional attention from the critics and, in the case of many, their animosity; the violent contrast between the cold natural light and the brightness of a lamp emanating from outside the picture frame – directed towards the model more than towards the flow-

CAT. 48 Albert Besnard: *Madame Roger Jourdain*, 1886.
Oil on canvas, 199 × 150.5 cm. Musée d'Orsay, Paris. LUX 1352, RF 2302

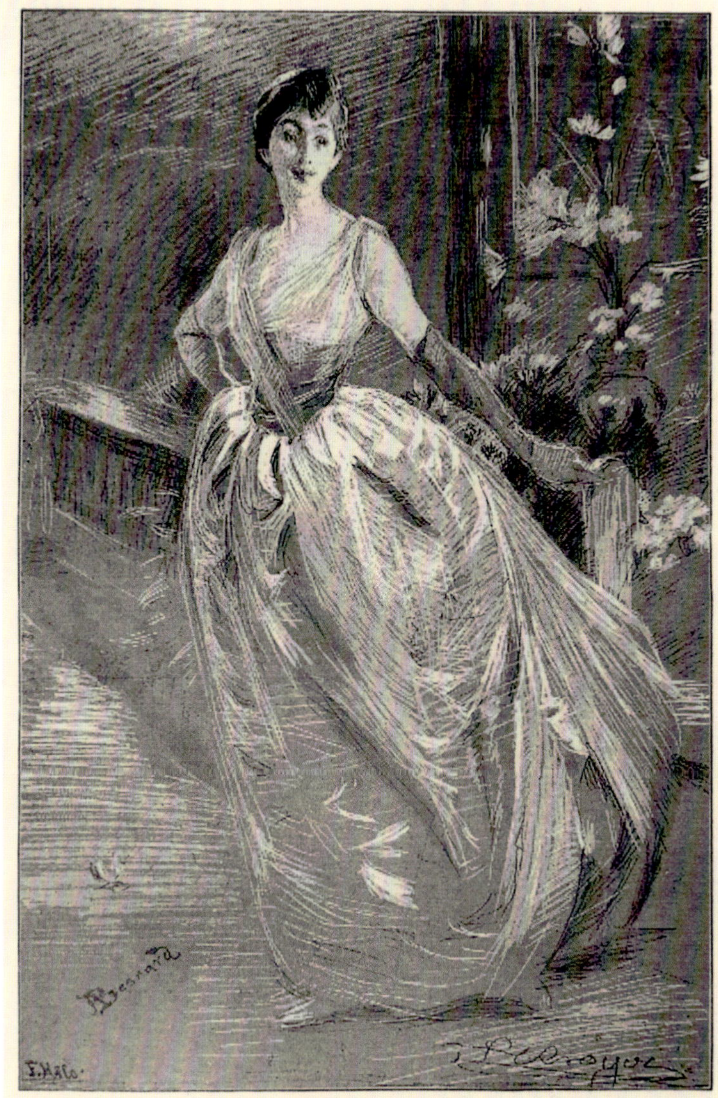
A. BESNARD. Portrait de Mme R. J.
Tegnet af P. S. Krøyer.

FIG. 37 Peder Severin Krøyer: *Drawing after Besnard's painting 'Portrait of Madame Jourdain'*, reproduced in the catalogue for the 1888 French Art Exhibition in Copenhagen. Det Kgl. Bibliotek, Copenhagen.

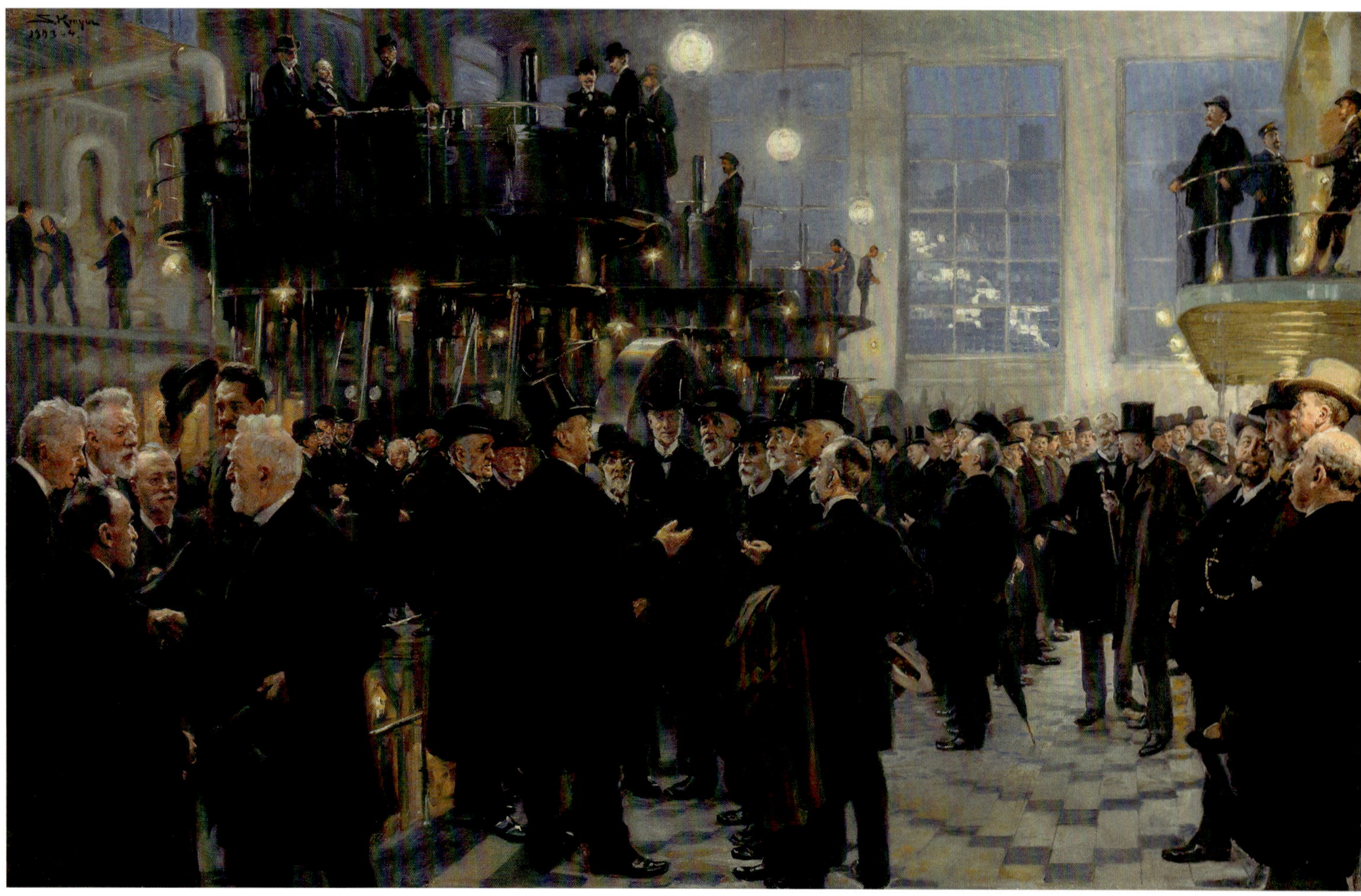

FIG. 38 Peder Severin Krøyer: *The Men of Industry*, 1903–1904. Oil on canvas, 116×185 cm. Frederiksborg Nationalhistoriske Museum, Hillerød. A 7348

ers and yellow banquette, whose tones it might have enlivened – meant that the model's name was quickly forgotten and the picture was simply named *The woman in blue and yellow*.

Among the manifold comments that accompanied this stormy reception, it is possible to cite a few extracts:

> As for M. Besnard, 1874 Prix de Rome, and showered with medals, he is now thumbing his nose at the École in such a way that it makes one double up with laughter; he has lapsed into a pictorial Wagnerism which must mightily grieve his teachers and I have positively heard people ask for his head, one Sunday, in front of his portrait of Mme Roger Jourdain.[115]

Or this:

> M. Albert Besnard, who is not renowned for his timidity, and whose audacity long ago stunned Rome, has imagined for Mme R.J. ... lighting effects that are both scientific and exceptional. The young woman is standing, on the terrace of a house where Yablochkov and Ruggieri [inventor of the arc lamp and famous pyrotechnician] have united in order to conduct their experiments.[116]

115. Christophe, 'Le Salon intime', 206.

116. Mantz, 'Le Salon. IV', 30 May 1886, [2].

Or again:

> At each exhibition, M. Besnard delights in displaying a new side or unexpected aspect of his multiple and proven talent.
>
> At present he is showing us a yellow portrait. It is not the background that is yellow, nor the dress: it is the face, it is the carnations.
>
> Why? – For nothing. Because M. Besnard doubtless finds it very amusing to play difficult tunes: so are they not then impossible?[117]

Even if everything suggests that he admired this work, Krøyer never attempted to rival an experiment of this type, probably because those who commissioned his portraits would never have given him leave to do so. Nevertheless, with the passing of time, he did, albeit timidly, adopt this almost unreal contrast between cold and warm colours as, for example, in his picture *The Men of Industry* (FIG. 38).
Dominique Lobstein

CAT. 49 Jules Bastien-Lepage
The Beggar, 1880

While busy raising funds to honour the memory of Jules Bastien-Lepage, Krøyer had the opportunity to make the acquaintance of Émile Bastien-Lepage (FIG. 39), his younger brother and heir. Following in his brother's footsteps, Émile was a painter, and exhibited at the Salon de la Société des Artistes Français from 1883 and then, from 1890, at the Salon de la Société Nationale des Beaux-Arts. He presented himself to these societies as a pupil of his older brother and mainly sent in landscapes of their native region, but without ever arousing the admiration that his brother had known. He had also studied architecture, from which he made his living.

When Jules Bastien-Lepage died, in 1884, his studio was still full of sketches, easel paintings, and large paintings of the countryside which had been shown at the Salon from 1878 to 1883. Very soon after his death, the Beaux-Arts administration expressed the wish to acquire one of his pictures for the Musée du Luxembourg, as it did each time an important artist had died. According to certain press articles, the choice was uncertain: the administrators wavered between the oldest picture, *The Haymakers* (ILL. 23), and *October*, the picture exhibited in 1879, more commonly known as *The Potato Harvest* (FIG. 40). Finally, and under pressure from several other suggestions for acquisition, *The Haymakers* was purchased for 25,000 francs. This meant that Émile Bastien-Lepage remained in possession of *October*, from the 1879 Salon; *Joan of Arc* (FIG. 29), from the 1880 Salon; *The Beggar* (CAT. 49); *The Wood Gatherer* (1882, Milwaukee Art Museum), exhibited in 1882; and *Village Love* (1882, Pushkin Museum, Moscow), presented in 1883. These were major pieces and their owner attempted to sell them quickly by offering them to the *Vente après décès* held at the Hôtel Drouot on 11 and 12 May 1885. The results did not match his hopes, if we are to believe these extracts from the report of the sale:

> *Potato Gatherers*, from the 1879 Salon, one of the finest works by the young master, was sold for 29,100 francs; the valuer had specified 30,000 francs [...]. *The Beggar*, from the 1881 Salon, remained 4,000 francs below the reserve price of 25,000 francs.[118]

Émile Bastien-Lepage had wanted to sell his pictures at a premium and continued to ask high prices, which had the effect of slowing down sales considerably. In order to show to best advantage the works that still belonged to him, he had no hesitation in allowing them to travel elsewhere. He was therefore very interested when Krøyer's request arrived and had no hesitation in accepting it,

117. Hervet, 'Le Salon. XI', [2].

118. 'Mouvement des arts. Oeuvres de Bastien-Lepage', 154.

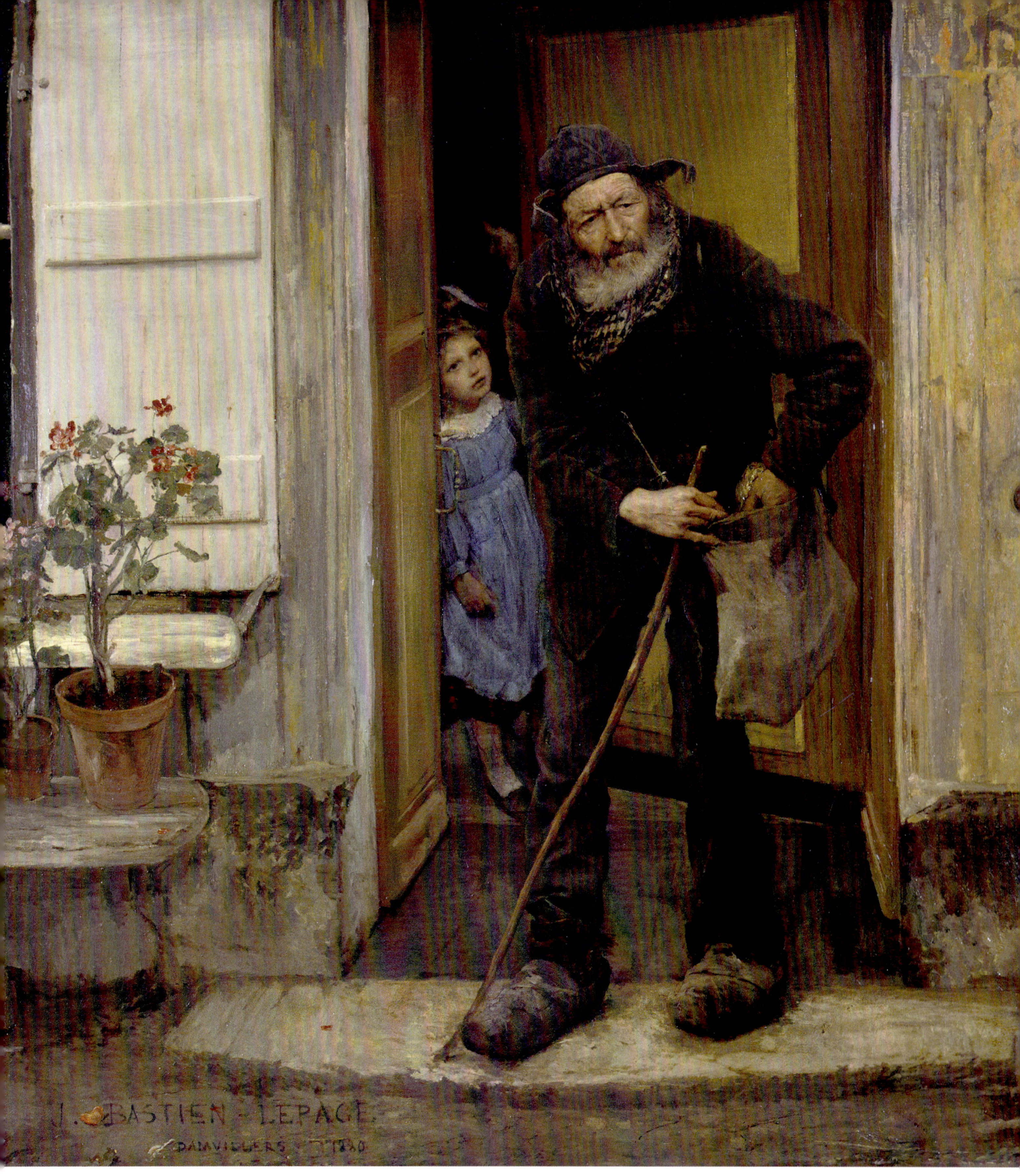

CAT. 49 Jules Bastien-Lepage: *The Beggar*, 1880. Oil on canvas, 199 × 181 cm. Ny Carlsberg Glyptotek, Copenhagen. MIN 0956

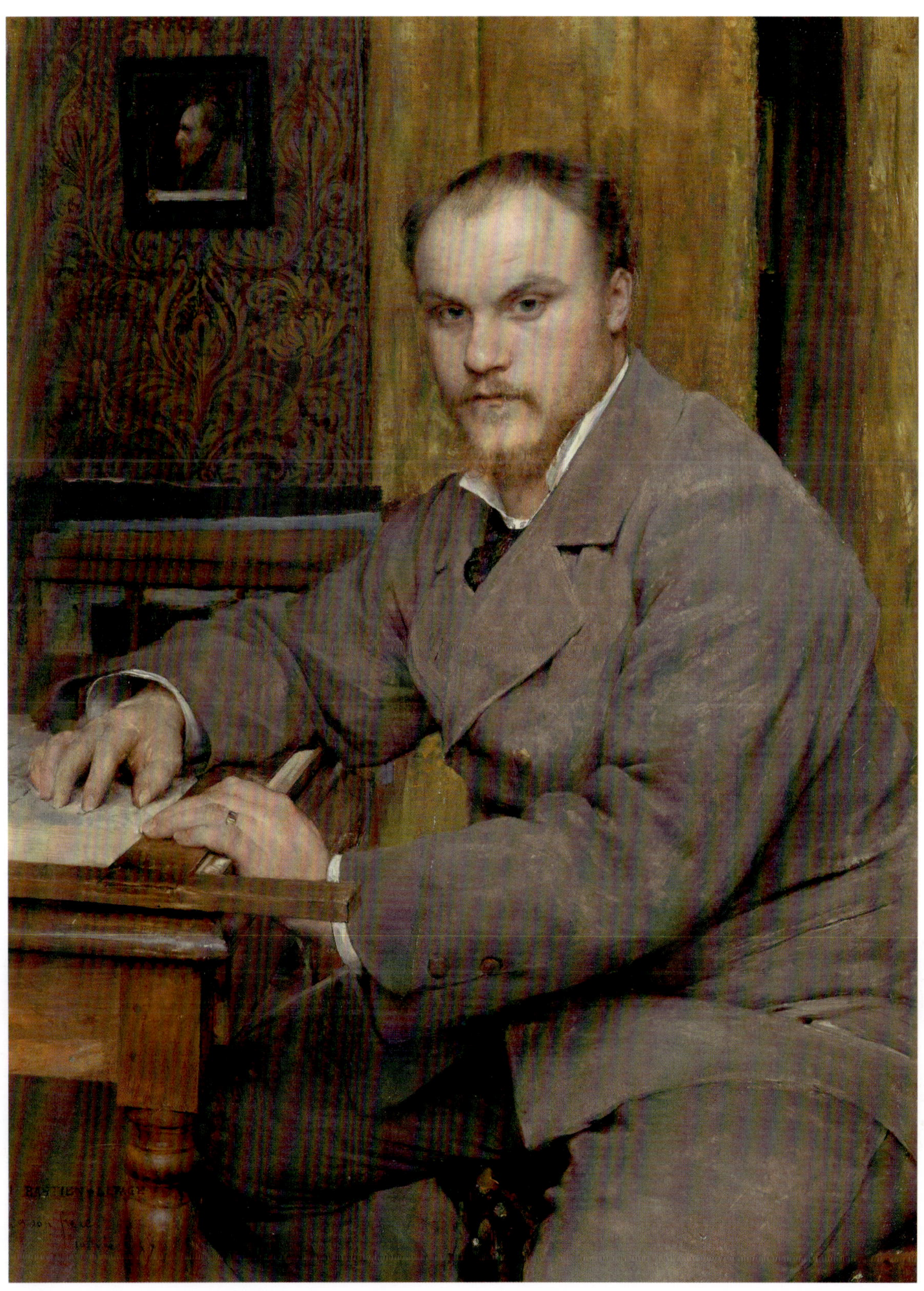

FIG. 39 Jules Bastien-Lepage: *Émile Bastien-Lepage*, 1879.
Musée des Beaux-Arts, Nancy, deposit from Musée d'Orsay. RF 3986

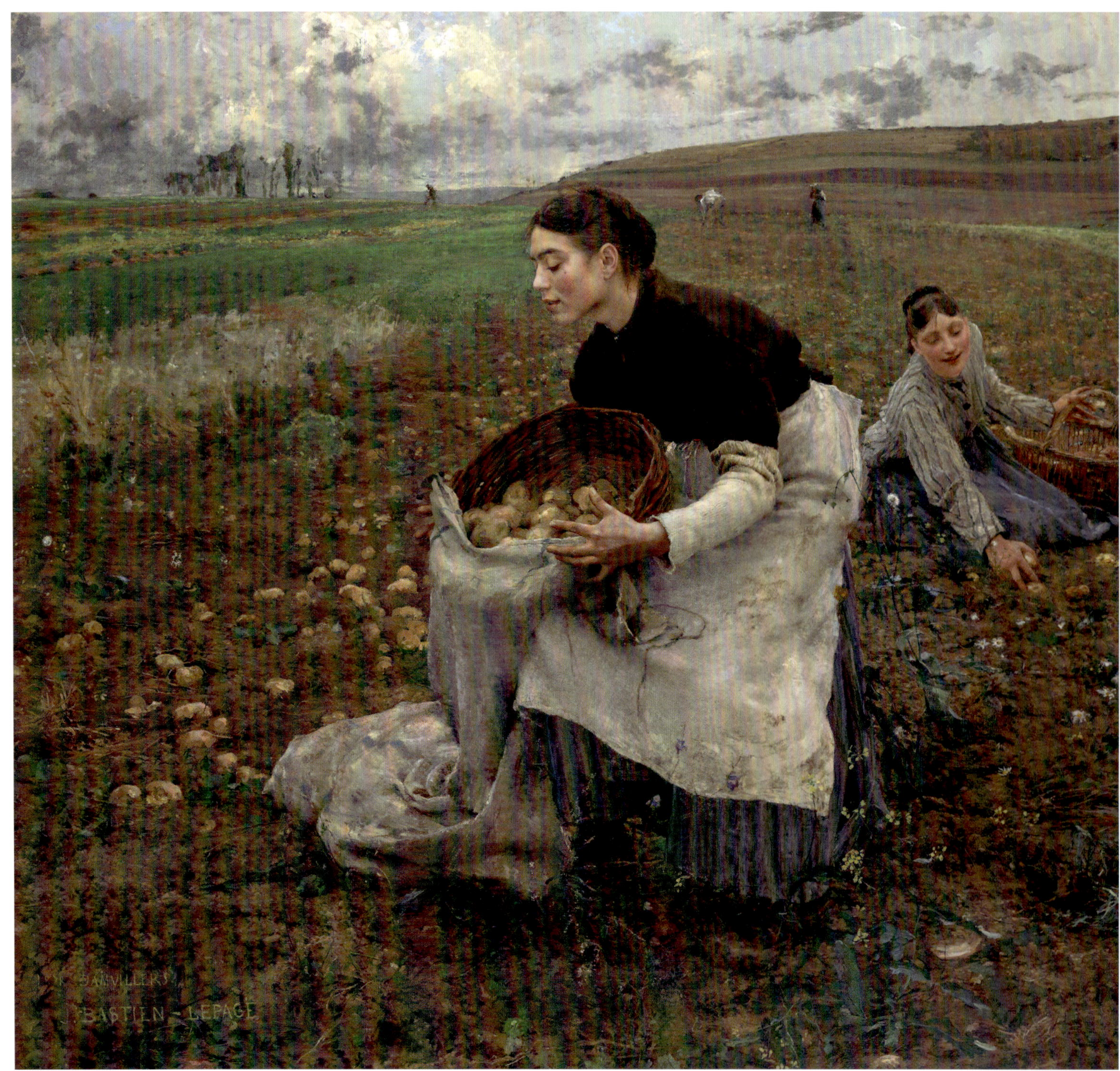

FIG. 40 Jules Bastien-Lepage: *October*, 1878–1879. Oil on canvas, 180.7 × 196 cm. National Gallery of Victoria, Melbourne. 3678-3

agreeing to part with the pictures from the 1878 and 1880 Salons, which he was offering for 80,000 and 40,000 francs respectively. At Krøyer's prompting, Carl Jacobsen became interested in *The Beggar* but it was Krøyer who approached Émile Bastien-Lepage and negotiated the purchase. The latter's final answer arrived on 4 June 1888, accepting the reduced price of 35,000 francs 'in memory of the marks of sympathy shown by Danish artists to the genius of Jules Bastien-Lepage and with the assurance of seeing this picture offered to the Copenhagen museum.'[119] It was not until 25 July 1889 that Émile Bastien-Lepage acknowledged receipt of the balance for the sale of this painting.[120]

Relations between Krøyer and Émile Bastien-Lepage did not cease with the closure of the Danish exhibition. There are some later letters preserved in the archives of the Hirschsprung Collection which reveal that the Danish painter was still received courteously at the Paris apartment in Rue de Phalsbourg and in the town house in Rue de Chézy, at Neuilly,[121] but also at Damvillers for the unveiling of the statue by Rodin depicting Jules Bastien-Lepage at work painting in the countryside (CAT. 39). A letter of 24 September 1889, for example, states:

> My dear friend,
> The unveiling of my brother's statue will take place at Damvillers on 29 September.
> In memory of what you have done to commemorate this dear artist, I hope you will do us the pleasure of accepting our invitation to this ceremony.
> In the hope of a positive reply, I send you my kindest regards.[122]

However, Krøyer did not go to the unveiling; he was on his honeymoon with his young wife, the painter Marie Krøyer, in the remote village of Stenbjerg on the west coast of Jutland in Denmark at the time.

Dominique Lobstein

119. Émile Bastien-Lepage to PSK, Paris, 4 June 1888. PSK Archive 2807.

120. Lobstein, 'Jules Bastien-Lepage (1848–1884)', 132–134.

121. Émile Bastien-Lepage to PSK, Paris, 5 January 1889. PSK Archive 2808.

122. Émile Bastien-Lepage to PSK, Paris, 11 September [1889]. PSK Archive 2810.

The Greatest Succes

CAT. 50 Peder Severin Krøyer
Summer Evening at Skagen, 1892

S*ummer Evening at Skagen* (CAT. 50) cemented Krøyer's fame in Paris. He contributed this painting – and only this one – to the *Exposition de la Société nationale des Beaux-Arts* at Champ-de-Mars in 1894. Since 1891 he had exhibited scenes from the serene, blue-tinted summer evenings in North Jutland and Skagen depicted on large canvases at the exhibitions in Paris. The first was *August Evening in Thy* (1889, private collection) in 1891, followed by *A Group of Fishermen on Skagen Beach* (1891, private collection) in 1892. One of the reviews described the shift evident in Krøyer's production between 1891 and 1894, when *Summer Evening at Skagen* was exhibited:

> A portrait by M. Krøyer, of a young woman by the shore, will, with its elegance and lightness, surprise all those who, until now, had been accustomed to a harsher style from the hand of the Danish master: it is one of the finest portraits of the Salon.[123]

The French critics were not informed of the identity of the woman in the picture, as the title of the work was simply given as *Portrait de Mme K ...* .[124] Accordingly, the reviews focused on the beautiful woman, the composition, the light, and the colours. Enraptured, one of the reviewers wrote:

> For charm that is both skillful and naïve, grace that is youthful and profound, M. Krøyer's portrait of a young woman seems to me to be among the finest. She stands by the shoreline, wearing an ecru gown. The sea is that North Sea which, in the enchantment of long summer sunsets, has such caressing silences, such harmonious drowsiness. From the distant horizon, where the sea almost merges with the luminous nocturnal sky, its bluish satiny expanse unfolds, its surface barely ruffled by the few undulations fringed with orange beneath the moonlight. She has paused to enjoy the ineffable charm of this hour; and, from head to foot, the mellow light envelops her in its soft caress: her charming profile; her light gown gathered in at the waist by a yellow ribbon, retains an impalpable bluish tint in its dark folds; the straw hat she holds in her hand; all are gently transfigured against this infinite backdrop of calm blue sea. She appears as if in a radiance of tenderness and harmony. It is a charming fullness, in which the whole of nature, the softness of the damp air, the peaceful splendour of the sky, the deep and veiled conjunction of blue waves conspire in an amorous and pure apotheosis, in I know not what sweet spell ... One feels that the painter's art has an abundance of resources, armed with all the subtleties of modern impressionism, and yet is simplified, becalmed, unfettered, and tender; and the portrait, in this natural setting of sky and ocean, remains intimate as a secret, discreet as an avowal.[125]

123. Wyzewa, 'Le Salon de 1894 (premier article)', 464.

124. Cat. no. 666.

125. Michel, 'Feuilleton du *Journal des Débats*', 8 June 1894, 1.

CAT. 50 Peder Severin Krøyer: *Summer Evening at Skagen*, 1892. Oil on canvas, 206×123 cm. Skagens Kunstmuseer, deposit from Ny Carlsberg Glyptotek. MIN 905

With this work, Krøyer also focused less on a strict Naturalist approach in favour of greater emphasis on decorative lines and atmosphere. The perspective has been manipulated so that the figure's legs are longer than expected and the horizon line unnaturally high, giving the long-limbed woman a flat blue background. With this painting, it becomes clear that Krøyer is taking his work in a new direction where there is less focus on an exact reproduction of the chosen subject matter and more on pensive and emotional aspects.

During the exhibition period, the members of the Société nationale des Beaux-Arts, the association behind the exhibition of French art, convened under the leadership of chairman Puvis de Chavannes to elect new members to the society. Krøyer, who was a close acquaintance of Puvis de Chavannes, was admitted as a member on this occasion.[126] In this way, Krøyer was once again tangibly and more closely linked to French artists and French art.

Summer Evening at Skagen achieved a distinguished exhibition history in very little time. It was exhibited in Denmark for the first time in 1893 – not at Charlottenborg's juried spring exhibition, as one might have imagined, but at Den frie Udstilling, which several of Krøyer's pupils at Kunstnernes Studieskole had contributed to founding in 1891.[127] Here, Krøyer exhibited alongside a younger generation of Danish painters as well as a richly represented Paul Gauguin, who briefly lived in Denmark in 1885 with his Danish wife Mette Gad, and an equally lavishly featured Vincent van Gogh, who had died in 1890. Later that year, *Summer Evening at Skagen* was exhibited at the Secession in Munich, where it was sold to a private collector in Germany. After the exhibition in Paris, the work was exhibited at *P.S. Krøyers Portræt-Udstilling* at Kunstforeningen in Copenhagen 1894, in Berlin in 1895, and at the exhibition of Scandinavian art in St Petersburg in 1897. In 1902 the owner of the painting sold it to the Ny Carlsberg Glyptotek, and it has been on a permanent loan to Skagens Museum since 1937.

Mette Harbo Lehmann

CAT. 51 Peder Severin Krøyer
Roses, 1893

CAT. 52 Gaston La Touche
Phlox, 1889

Roses (CAT. 51) ranks among Krøyer's masterpieces. It was painted during one of his summer sojourns in Skagen with his wife, where they took lodgings in a house on the western outskirts of the town, the sandy heathland spreading out right on the other side of the hedge. Given this location, the garden is unusually lush with its sheltered, windless, enclosed greenery. In terms of subject matter, the work has a close kinship with the flourishing gardens favoured by the French Impressionists, especially Claude Monet's famous works, but Krøyer's manner of painting remains rooted in Naturalism.[128] The level of detail and the colour scheme employed are significantly different from those of the French Impressionists, a fact of which Krøyer may himself have been aware. In any case, he did not exhibit the work in Paris, where it could have been shown side by side with Impressionist works, offering a point of comparison for audiences well acquainted with the group. Instead, he chose to send the painting to the World's Columbian Exposition in Chicago in 1893, and then to Charlottenborg in Copenhagen in 1895, Chicago again in 1895, Cincinnati in 1896, and Venice at the Biennale in 1909.[129]

A more Impressionist feel can be found in *Phlox* by French painter Gaston La Touche (CAT. 52), a painting comparable in composition to *Roses*. Here, too, the large cluster of white flowers in the foreground gives the work

126. 'Informations', 18 June 1894, 3.

127. See chapter 8.

128. Lobstein and Lehmann, *The Blue Hour of Peder Severin Krøyer*, 168–169.

129. Saabye, *Krøyer. An International Perspective*, 296.

its title. Like Krøyer's flowering rose bush, the beautiful white phlox are more prominently featured than the figures in the background of the picture. Viewing the works next to each other offers excellent opportunities for spotting differences and similarities in their style and execution.

Even though Krøyer and La Touche were about the same age and contributed art to some of the same exhibitions, there is no indication that they ever met each other. La Touche, who had received only drawing instruction in his youth, meaning that he was not a fully trained painter, started his career as a Naturalist artist, showing dark and somewhat sombre scenes in the Salon's section for paintings from 1880 onwards.[130] He later became acquainted with Édouard Manet and other artists who were part of the Impressionist group. As a result, La Touche gradually made his images brighter, employed a freer hand, and chose more cheerful subject matter. He exhibited *Phlox* at the Salon de Société Nationale des Beaux-Arts in 1890, which was one of the few salon exhibitions Krøyer neither saw nor participated in, as he was on a combined honeymoon and study trip in Italy with his wife.

While we know that the figure reading the newspaper in a deck chair under the large, flowering rose Alba Maxima is Krøyer's wife Marie, depicted in the garden of what would later become known as Tuxen's villa Dagminne in Skagen, La Touche's garden and people are more anonymous. Given that we know La Touche's own appearance from portraits, we can ascertain that he did not include himself in the picture, and in 1889, when the picture was created, he had not yet had children. Therefore, it cannot be La Touche's own family sitting around the table in the garden, but perhaps some other family in a garden from the Saint-Cloud area just west of Paris, where La Touche and other members of his family lived.

Mette Harbo Lehmann

CAT. 53 Peder Severin Krøyer
The Author Sophus Schandorph, 1895

CAT. 54 Albert Besnard
Francis Magnard, 1884

Eleven years separate the creation of Albert Besnard's portrait of French writer and journalist Francis Magnard from 1884 (CAT. 54) and Krøyer's portrait of Danish author Sophus Schandorph from 1895 (CAT. 53). Nevertheless, seeing the paintings next to each other is interesting as they show the two artist friends' similar approaches to the subject.

> When Besnard painted his portrait, Magnard was editor-in-chief of one of France's most popular newspapers, *Le Figaro*. Magnard is shown sitting at his desk in his place of work, and in the background the open door offers a glimpse of the printing press with a worker carrying paper for that day's newspaper. In the foreground is a prominently featured part of the furniture Magnard is seated at, creating a sense of depth and a diagonal perspective reaching back into the pictorial space. Magnard was someone whom the critics could recognize, and as the portrait was skilfully executed, it prompted favourable reviews:
>
> M. Besnard has left M. Francis Magnard in the setting that was appropriate to him; *Le Figaro*'s Editor-in-Chief is writing, and behind him are the corridors and staircases of the printing house; a worker is passing, carrying a pile of paper; in addition to this, the physiognomy is very true to life and the picture is of a pleasing grey harmony.[131]

Magnard was depicted going about his daily work, facilitating easier recognition, and perhaps that is why critics praised this picture for being an honest and personal portrait:

130. The following information on Gaston La Touche appears in Lobstein, 'xxxx', 62.

131. Geffroy, 'Salon de 1884. Portraits. II', 1.

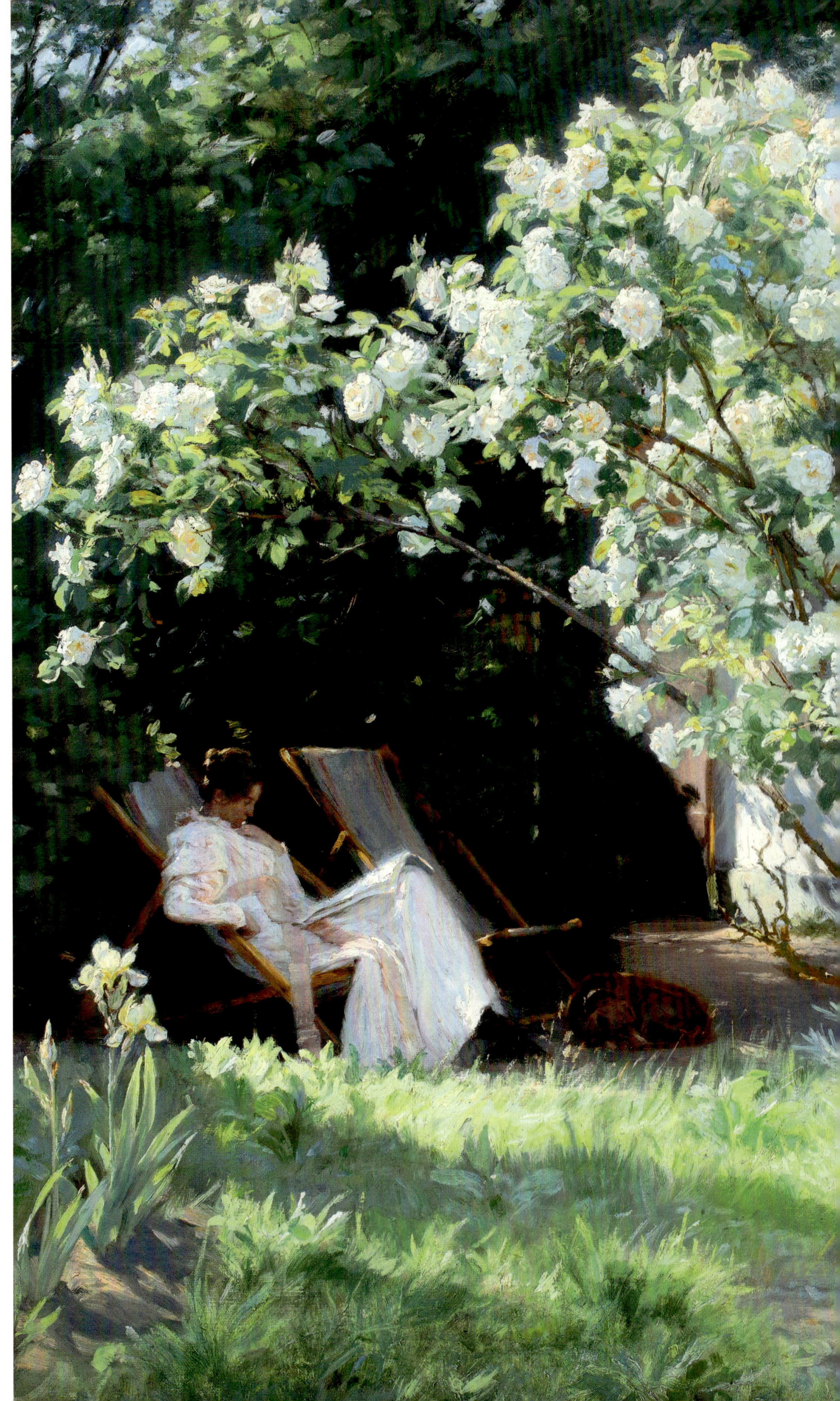

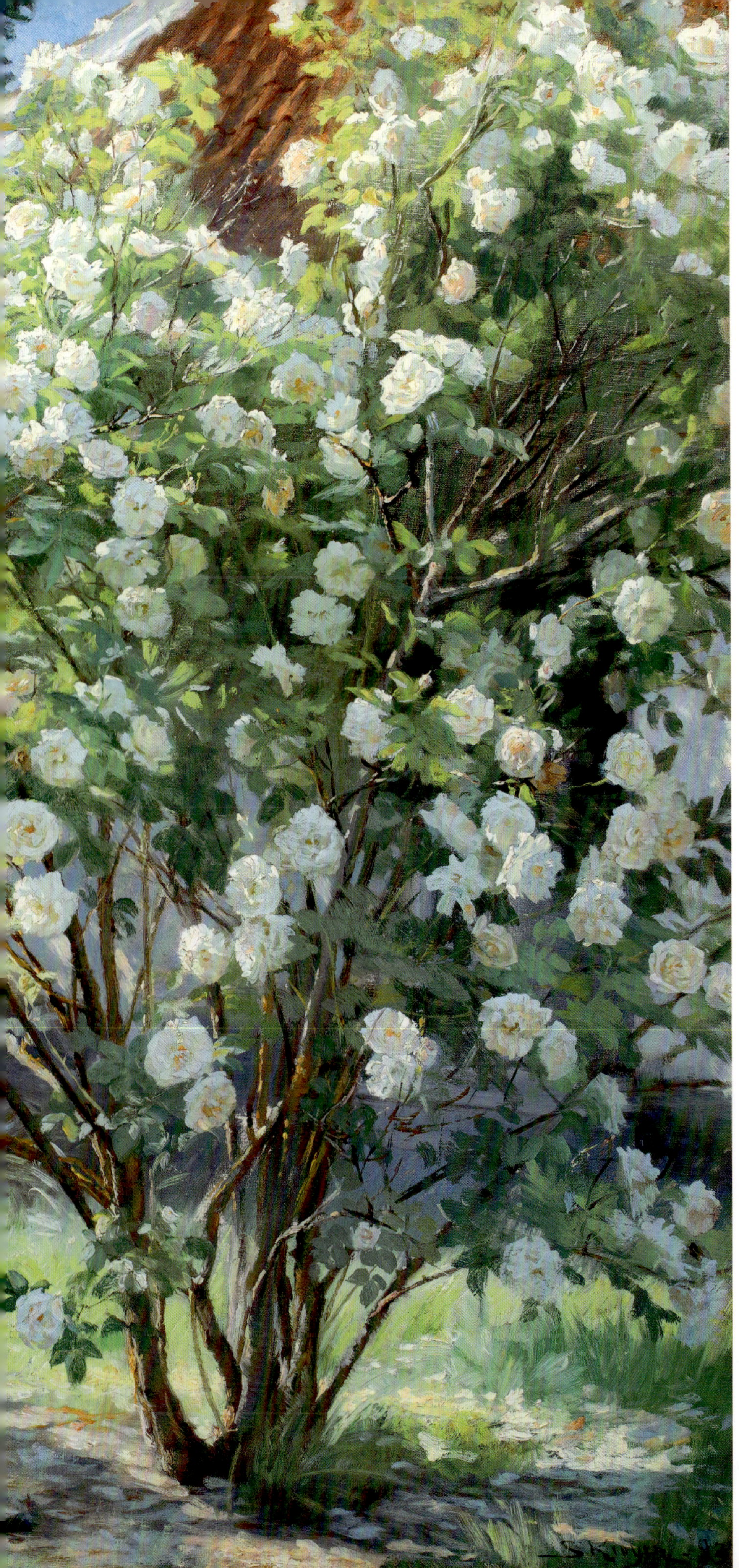

CAT. 51 Peder Severin Krøyer:
Roses, 1893. Oil on canvas, 67.5×76.5 cm.
Skagens Kunstmuseer. SKM1851

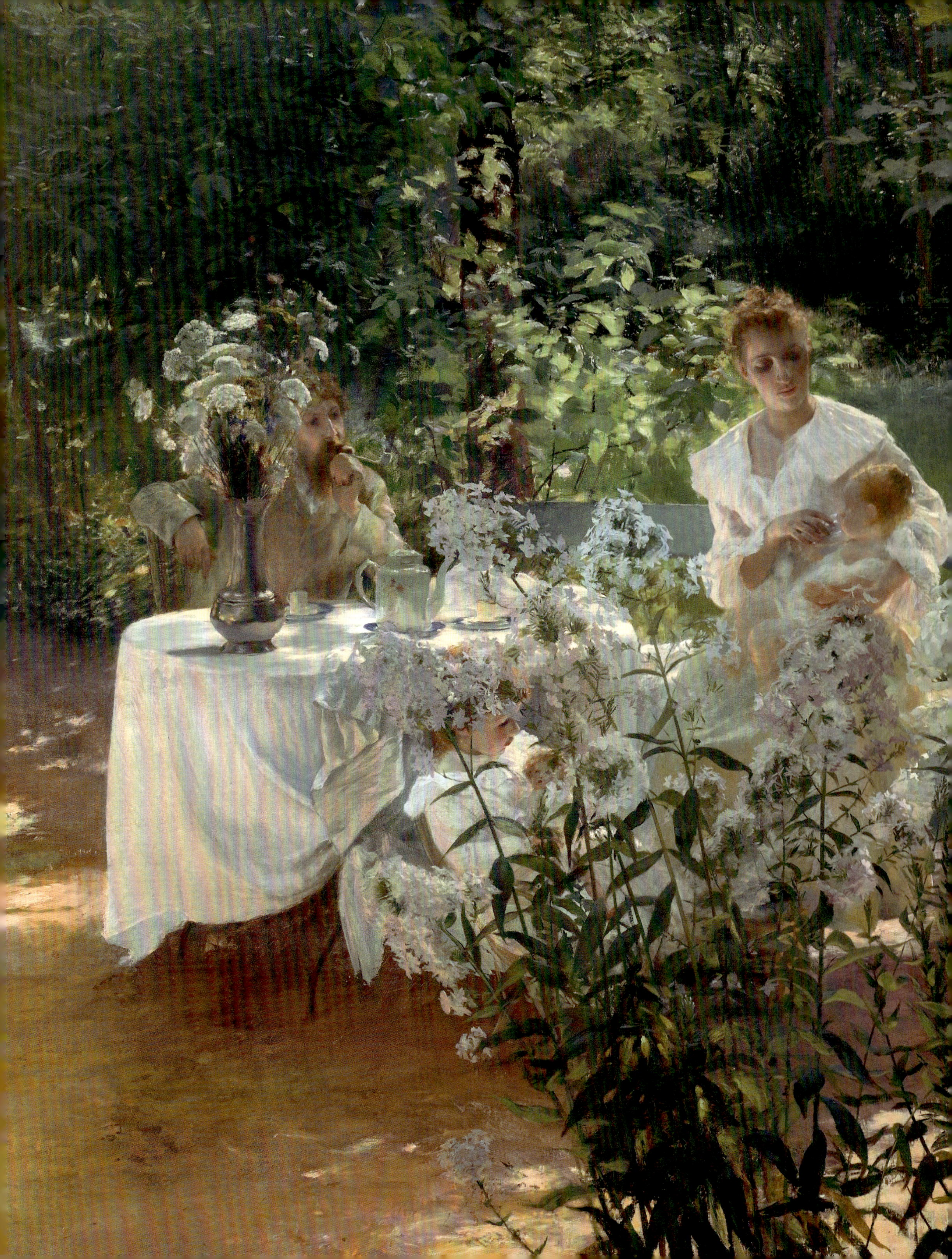

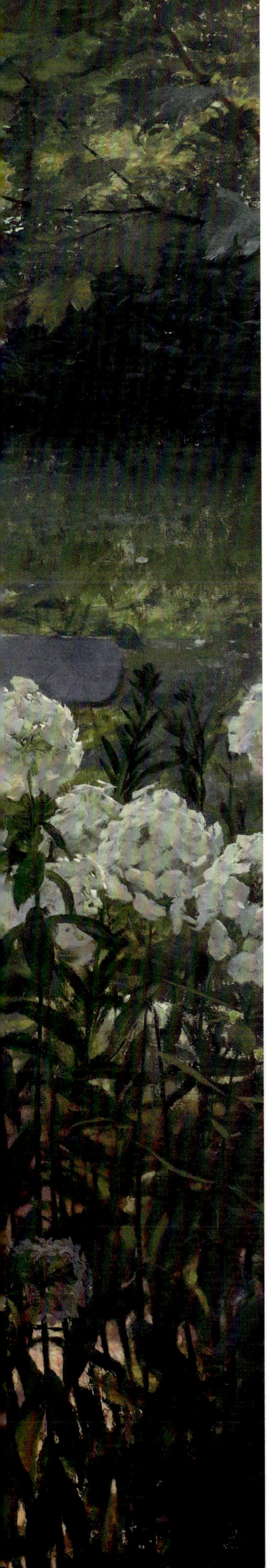

CAT. 52 Gaston La Touche: *Phlox*, 1889. Oil on canvas, 160×160 cm. Musée Lodève, deposit from Musée municipal La Roche-sur-Yon. 2012.6.10

> The portrait of M. Francis Magnard, by M. BESNARD, is very candidly and freely executed, in a palette of grey tones that makes an agreeable change from the usual blacks. It is one of the good portraits at the Salon.[132]

Krøyer exhibited his portrait of Schandorph at the *Exposition de la Société nationale des Beaux-Arts* in 1898 alongside a portrait of Holger Drachmann (FIG. 41). Krøyer's two portraits were the first in a series of five author portraits commissioned by Jacob Hegel, publisher and director of the publishing house Gyldendal in Denmark and Norway. Hegel wanted portraits of some of the most prominent writers associated with the publishing house; the range of such depictions would later include Georg Brandes in 1900, Bjørnstjerne Bjørnson in 1901, and Jonas Lie in 1902.[133] Krøyer himself was pleased with the portraits and would repeatedly borrow them from Hegel – especially the first two – to be presented at many different exhibitions at home and abroad. Portraits were an important part of Krøyer's production and business, and these works were valuable as showcases of his most successful portrait painting.

When considering the range of works that Krøyer sent to the salons in Paris throughout his career, one sees that he took great pains to show different aspects of his production. If he sent a landscape painting, he also sent an interior scene; in this case, where he sent two author portraits, he made sure that one was done in the pale Nordic light on Skagen beach with wind ruffling the sitter's hair, while the other was done in a dark living room with heavy furniture and with a lamp as the only light source. One critic had this response:

> These two portraits might be called *The Lamp* and *The Sun*. The two figures are lit from the same side – that is to say their right side – but one of them only by the glow of the lamp, while the other is also illuminated by the diffuse daylight; one by the artificial

132. Paul Mantz, 'Le Salon. I', 11 May 1884, [2].

133. Saabye, *Krøyer. An International Perspective*, 254–263.

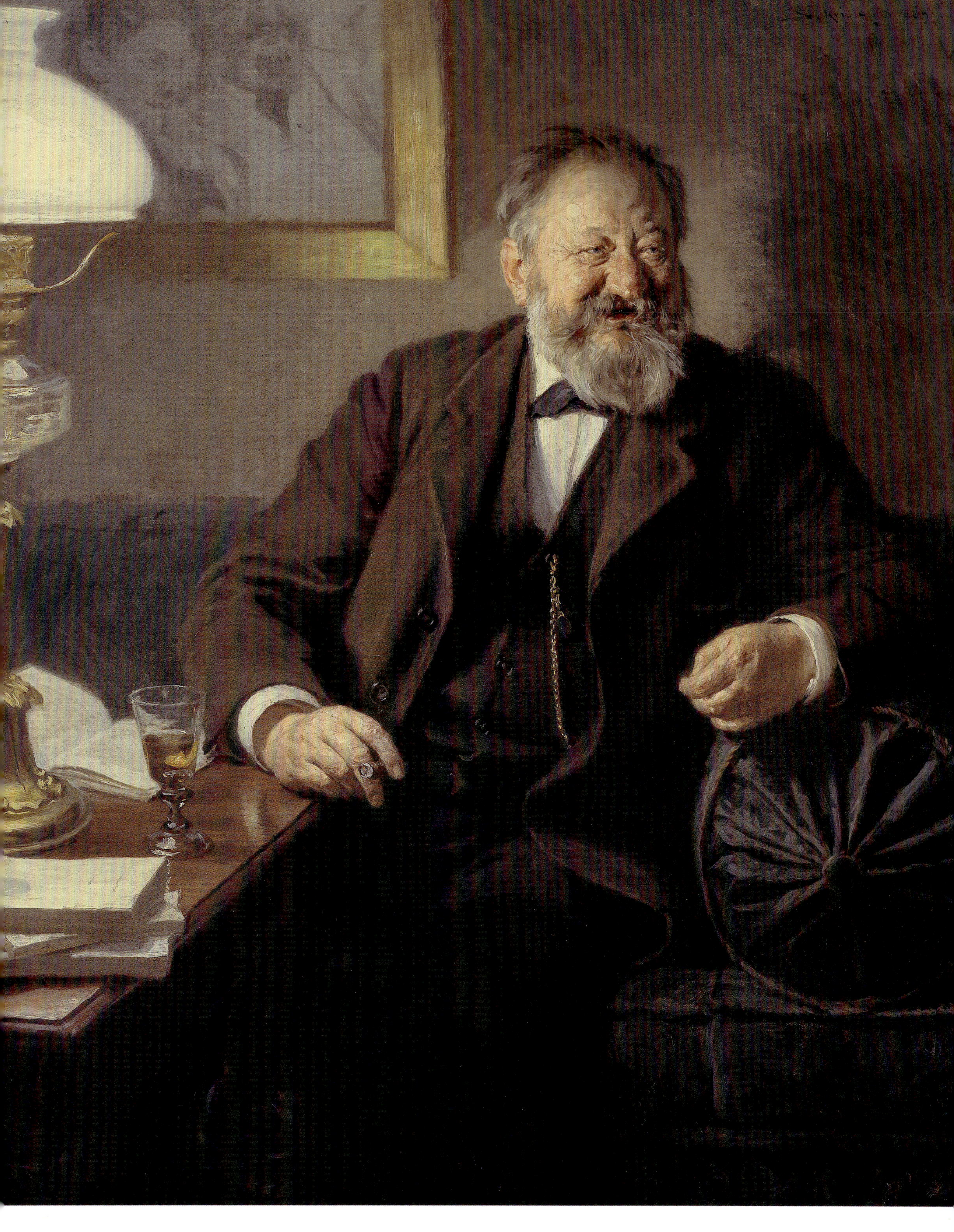

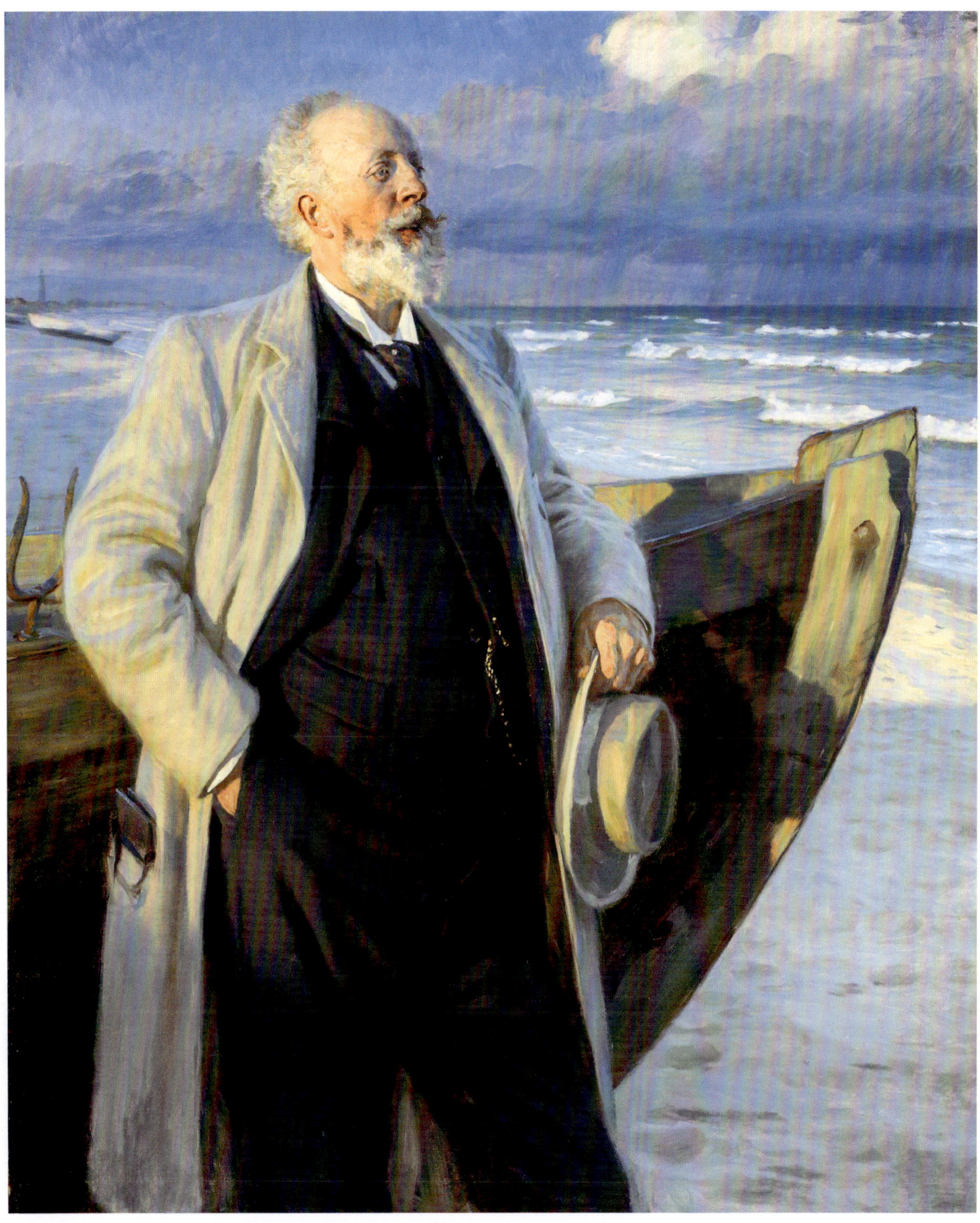

FIG. 41 Peder Severin Krøyer: *Holger Drachmann*, 1895. Oil on canvas, 167×140 cm. Skagens Kunstmuseer. SKM444

CAT. 53 Peder Severin Krøyer: *The Author Sophus Schandorph*, 1895.
Oil on canvas, 130.5×110 cm. Statens Museum for Kunst, Copenhagen. KMS6858

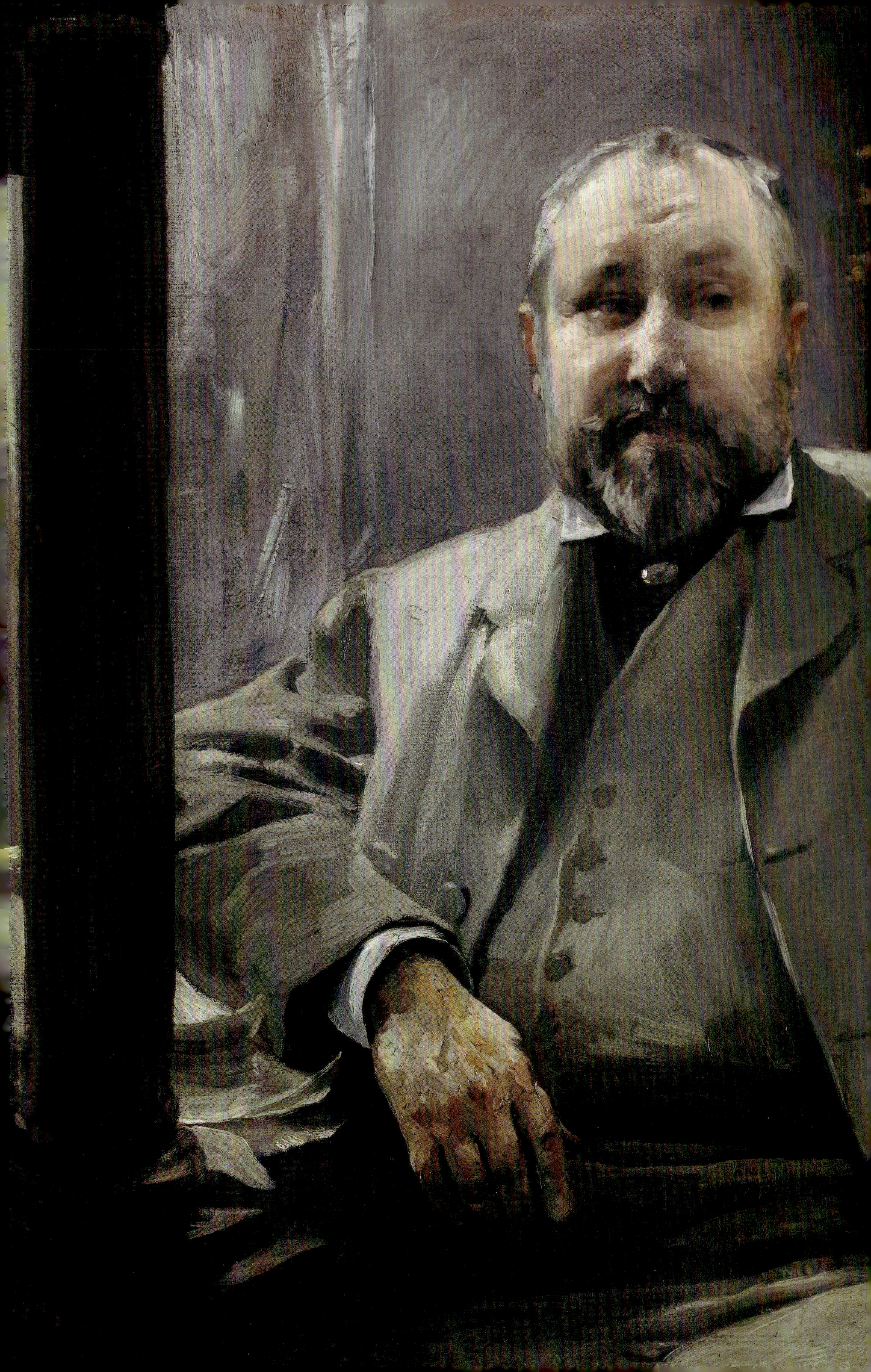

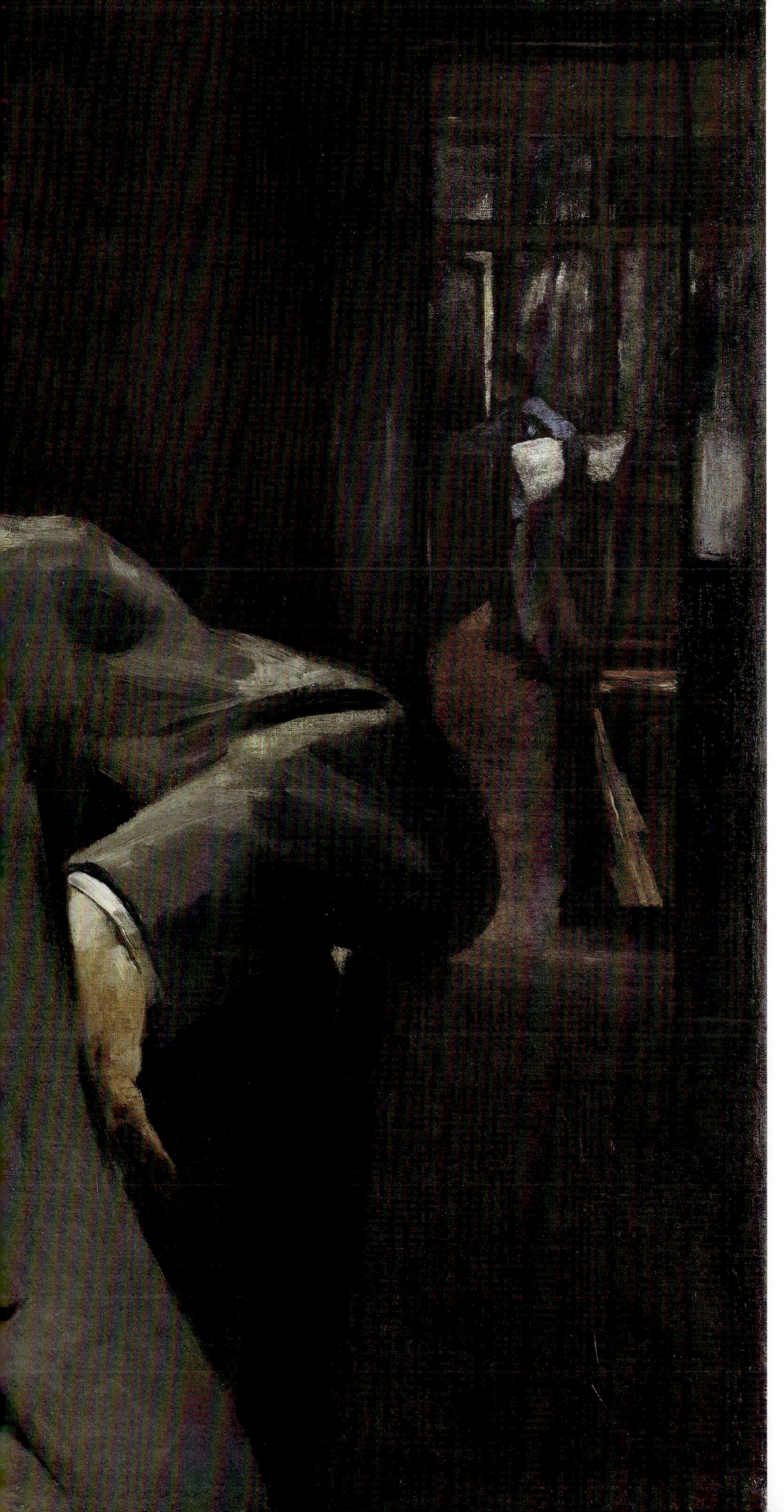

CAT. 54 Albert Besnard: *Francis Magnard*, 1884. Oil on canvas, 82.5×109.5 cm. Petit Palais, Musée des Beaux-Arts de la Ville de Paris. PPP514

> glow which enlightens only in the sense that knowledge does, the other by that natural light which not only enlightens, but warms in the manner of love.[134]

Even though the French knew neither Drachmann nor Schandorph, the Drachmann portrait in particular received rave reviews. The stately, white-bearded person and the unusual background of Skagen on a windy day prompted great enthusiasm, with critics especially noting the cold blue light offset by the warm shades of the author's clothes.
Mette Harbo Lehmann

CAT. 55 Peder Severin Krøyer
Marie and Vibeke reading at the home in Skagen, 1898

The last great Parisian success of Krøyer's career was the Exposition Universelle in 1900. Here he exhibited five paintings, six watercolours and drawings, three etchings, and a plaster bust. In recognition of his overall efforts, Krøyer was awarded the highest prize, the Grand Prix, which also resulted in him receiving a higher rank of the Legion d'honneur the following year. Having been Chevalier, he now became Officier de Legion d'honneur. Importantly, one of his watercolours – *Marie and Vibeke reading at the home in Skagen*, which depicts Marie Krøyer lying on a sofa in the living room in Krøyers Hus in Skagen with the couple's daughter Vibeke next to her – was bought by the Musée du Luxembourg. It was one of a series of four watercolours of which Skagens Kunstmuseer owns the last three. Thus Krøyer achieved the distinction of being represented at the prestigious French museum with two works: *Marie and Vibeke reading at the home in Skagen* and *Skagen Men going out Fishing at Night. Late Summer Evening*, the latter from 1884.
Mette Harbo Lehmann

CAT. 56 Peder Severin Krøyer
Summer Evening on Skagen Sønderstrand, 1893

The depiction of two white-clad women ambling along the beach in Skagen in the bluish light of dusk is widely regarded as Krøyer's most iconic work today. It was created in 1893, the same year as *Roses* and a year after the large full-length portrait of Marie Krøyer with her husband's dog by her side, *Summer Evening at Skagen* (CAT. 50) This was a period in Krøyer's life that saw several of his most famous works leaving his studio.

Summer Evening on Skagen Sønderstrand (CAT. 56), with the two walking women, was exhibited for the first time at the *Exposition de la Société nationale des Beaux-Arts* in Paris in 1895, alongside three studies for the monumental group portrait *From the Copenhagen Stock Exchange* (Dansk Erhverv, Copenhagen), presumably in the form of individual, full-length portraits. Considering that this was the fourth time in a row that Krøyer had exhibited a large, blue-tinted painting from the beaches in Skagen, the work received good reviews. The more critical voices noted that there was nothing new to see here, and as far as the portraits went, some reviewers had difficulty disregarding the fact that the men portrayed were of Jewish origin.[135] However, most critics were positive:

> Krøyer, a charming, restful, and captivating twilight, *Summer Evening on Skagen Sønderstrand*; [...][136]

> Denmark has M. Krøyer as its representative, a painter who is skilled in luminism. His portraits of people and his *Summer Evening on Skagen Sønderstrand* show what he has always been, namely a steadily sympathetic, delicately fine observer of nature. Like the Swedish group, he tends towards the French in art.[137]

134. Sizeranne, 'Les Portraits d'homme aux Salons de 1898', 624.

135. Fouquier, 'Le Salon du Champ de Mars', [1]; Méry, 'Le Salon du Champs-de-Mars', 2.

136. A.M. [André Michel], 'Le Tour du Salon (Champ-de-Mars)', 2.

137. Thiébault-Sisson, 'Le Salon du Champ de Mars', [1].

> Look closely at a picture by M. Krøyer: on a quiet beach, in a pure, calm light, a little mist in the air, two women, seen from behind, are slowly walking. It is a time for whispered secrets, and the picture is exquisite.[138]

The most elaborate and enthusiastic review of the work came from André Michel:

> and M. Krøyer's *Summer Evening on Skagen Sønderstrand*; oh yes! A calm and delightful evening; the satiny-blue sea, painted with long, softly waving, horizontal brushstrokes, sleeps beneath a sky which seems to merge with it at the horizon; the blond sand close to the blue sea catches the reflections of the inexpressible light of northern nights; a line of flat dunes disappears in the distance in an imperceptible gradation of subdued tones, while on the shore are two late walkers, ladies in mauve and white gowns with orangey-yellow sashes, gently transfigured against this background of blue sea. Without troubling it by their presence or the bright note they provide, they animate this supremely harmonious and meditative seascape.[139]

In this painting, Krøyer has reduced the contrasts compared to what one would see in a strictly Naturalist work. Unimportant elements like rocks, seaweed, or fishing gear on the beach have been removed, and the tone of the work is extremely harmonious and blue. The sensibility thus arising in the picture takes on a universal feel for almost any viewer, as most viewers, regardless of time period, will be able to put themselves in the place of these women on a beach on a calm summer evening.

One might well imagine the work instantly gaining star status, travelling from one exhibition to the next on the international art scene, but this was in no way the case. In fact, the painting was only exhibited twice during Krøyer's lifetime. The second time was later that year at the Secession in Munich, in 1895. Here the work was sold to Lilli Lehmann-Kalisch in Berlin, a German opera singer who was famous at the time, thus disappearing from the public eye and memory.

Summer Evening on Skagen Sønderstrand first appeared in public again more than 80 years later, when it was put up for sale at Bruun Rasmussen's Auctions in 1978 and sold for a staggering DKK 520,000, the highest bid for a work by Krøyer ever. At the time, Skagens Museum bid on the work, but had to let it go to the German businessman and publisher Axel Springer, who was able to bid significantly more than the museum. The event attracted considerable media attention, and in Denmark there was palpable disappointment that the work would once again disappear out of the country. When Springer realised that Skagens Museum had wanted to acquire the painting, he chose to donate it to the museum on the proviso that he could keep it in his home for 20 years. However, Springer died before then, in 1985, and the following year his widow chose to donate it to the museum. It arrived in Skagen in 1986, once again attracting great media attention. The story of the return of this unknown and forgotten, but extremely valuable masterpiece was very popular.

In the early 1980s, the work began to reappear in the literature about Krøyer, and with this sudden success a wide range of reproductions appeared, on all sorts of merchandise from posters to cookie jars, umbrellas and pens to book covers. It even appeared in the perennially popular Danish 'Donald Duck' comic book. The most reproduced work by Krøyer to date, it continues to enthrall audiences today.

Mette Harbo Lehmann

138. Mitchi, 'Notes sur les Salons. Champ-de-Mars', 236.

139. Michel, 'Feuilleton du Journal des Débats', 24 May 1895, 2.

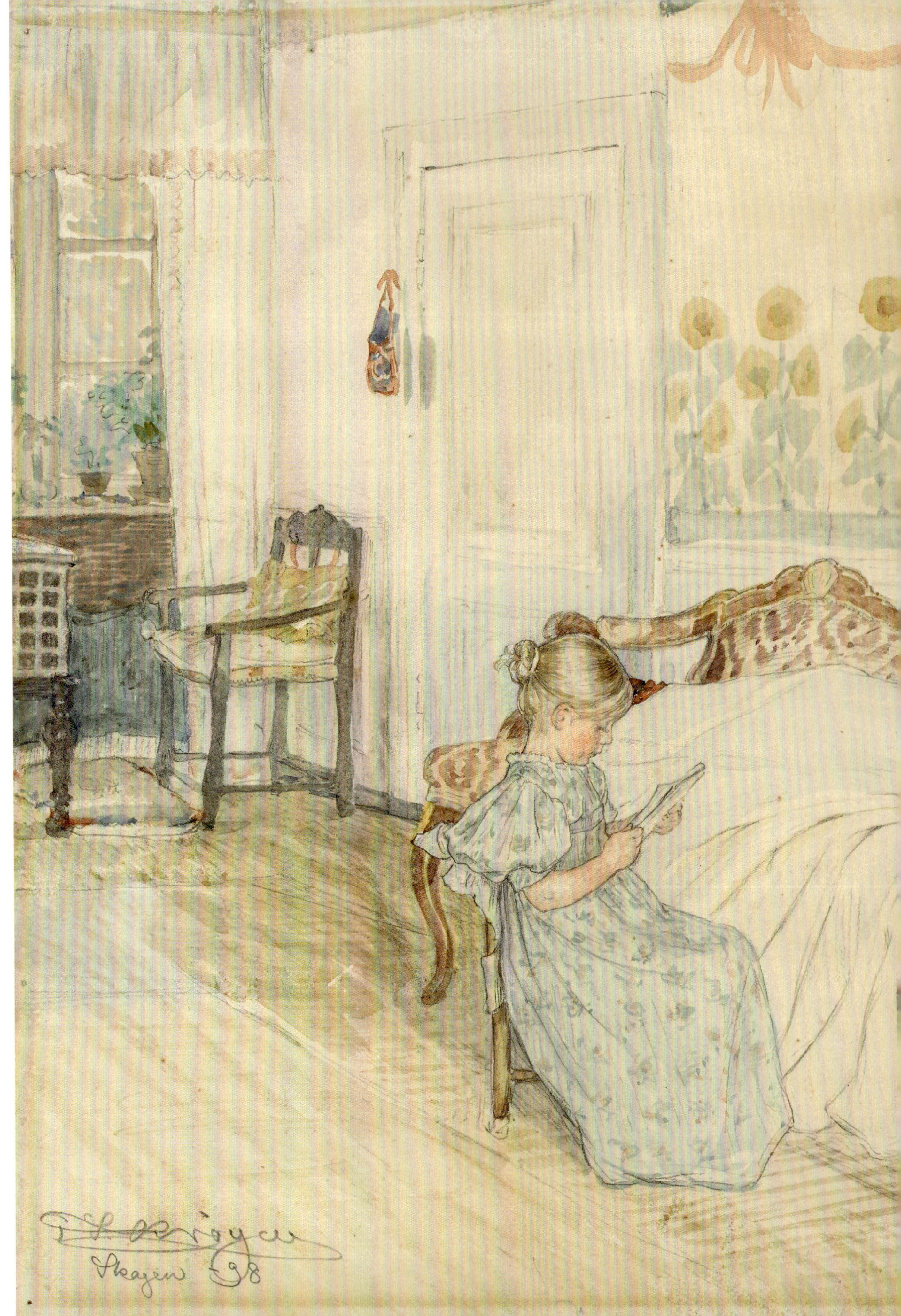
Skagen 98

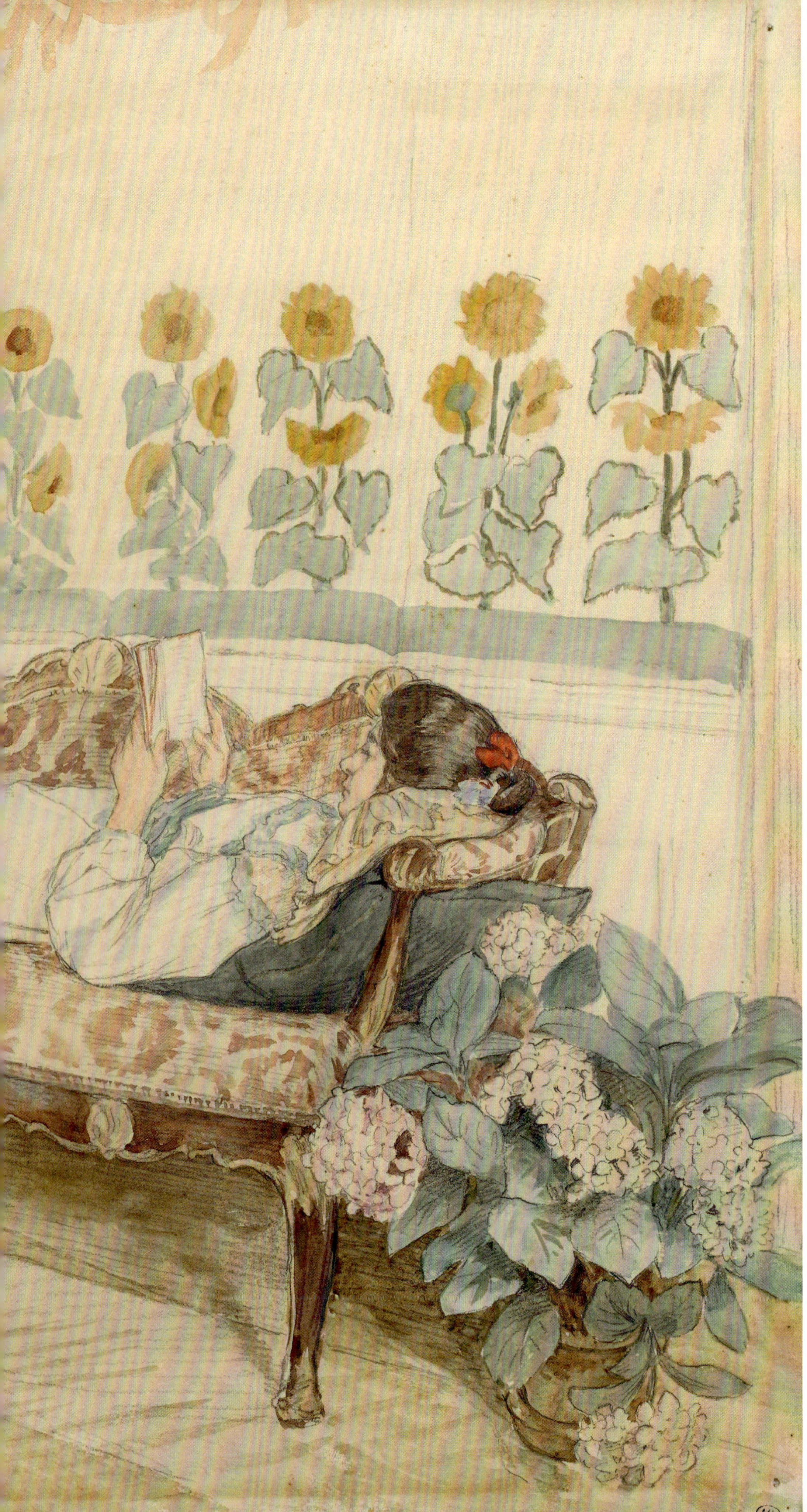

CAT. 55 Peder Severin Krøyer: *Marie and Vibeke reading at the home in Skagen*, 1898. Pencil and watercolours, 335×485 mm. Musée de Louvre, Paris, deposit from Musée d'Orsay. RF 2387

CAT. 56 OVER LEAF: Peder Severin Krøyer: *Summer Evening on Skagen Sønderstrand*, 1893. Oil on canvas, 100×150 cm. Skagens Kunstmuseer. SKM1288

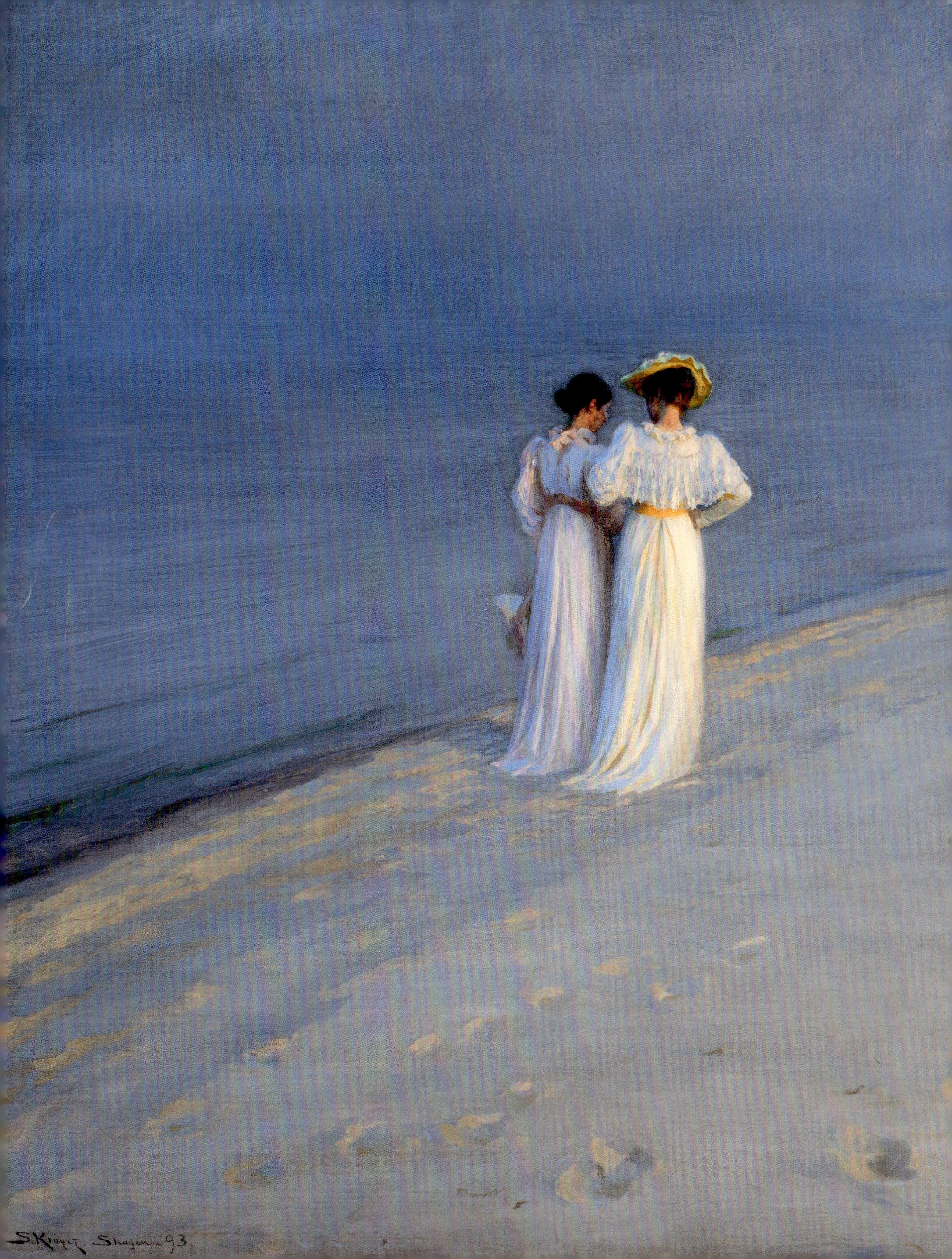
S.Krøyer. Skagen 93

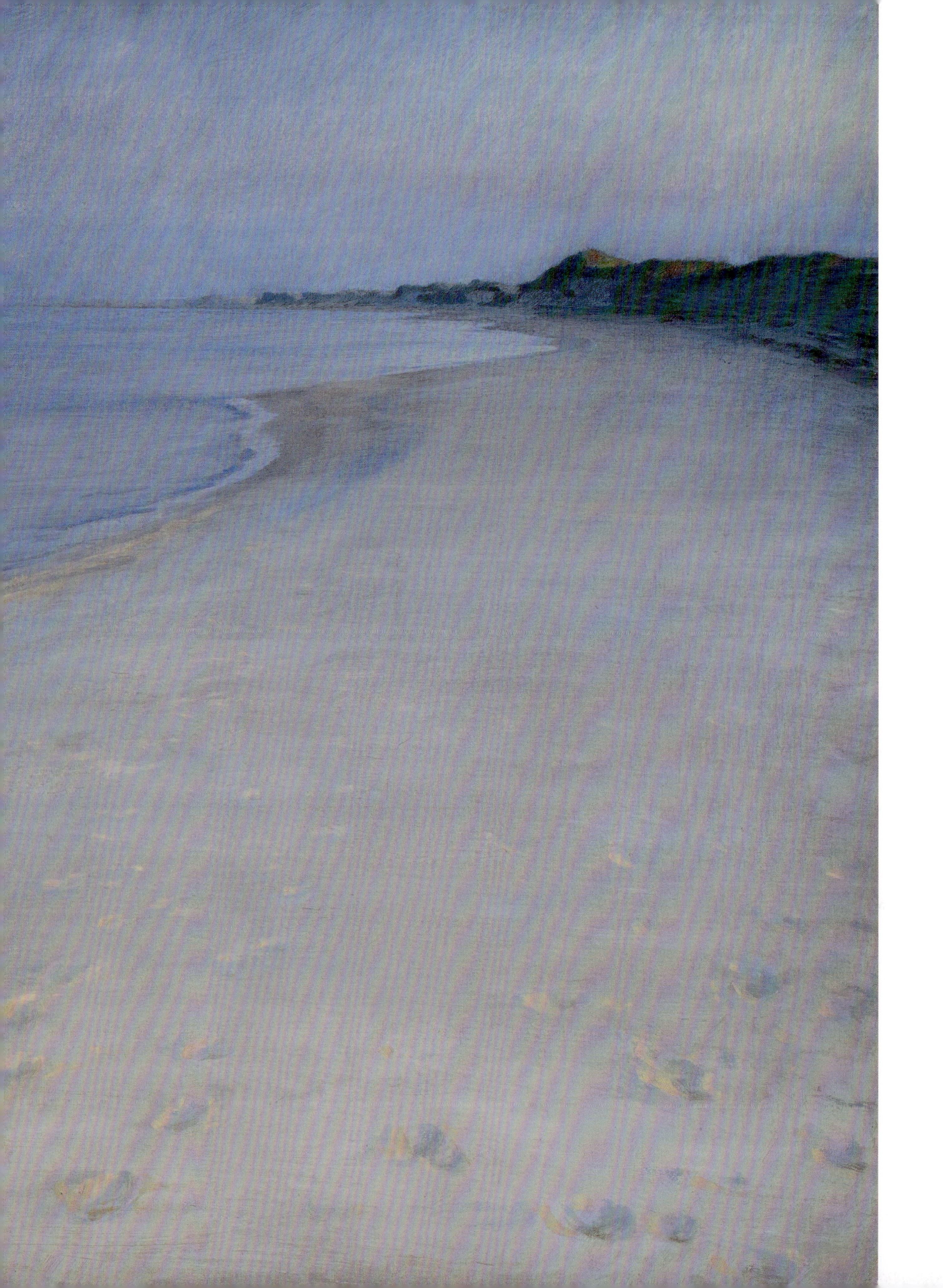

Impressionism

CAT. 57 Claude Monet
On the Beach at Trouville, 1870

CAT. 58 Claude Monet
Impression, Sunrise, 1872

CAT. 59 Claude Monet
The Train in the Snow. The Locomotive, 1875

CAT. 60 Claude Monet
Taking a Walk in Argenteuil, 1875

CAT. 61 Gustave Caillebotte
Paris Street. Rainy Day, 1877

CAT. 62 Claude Monet
Spring through the Branches, 1878

CAT. 63 Alfred Sisley
The Loing Canal in Spring, 1892

CAT. 64 Camille Pissarro
The Outer Boulevards, Snow Effect, 1879

CAT. 65 Alfred Sisley
Spring near Paris. Apple Trees in Blossom, 1879

CAT. 66 Berthe Morisot
Eugène Manet and His Daughter in the Garden at Bougival, 1881

Ten Impressionist masterpieces from Musée Marmottan Monet are part of the exhibition *Krøyer and Paris: French Connections and Nordic Colours*. They will enable us to complete our view of artistic life in Paris at the time when Peder Severin Krøyer was residing there. Before considering the paintings themselves, a few words are necessary in order to understand how this singular Paris institution is now able to lend such major works.

The history of the Musée Marmottan Monet began on 21 June 1934, the date when it opened its doors to the public. It was then that the recently deceased Paul Marmottan, who was responsible for its creation, gave the private mansion he had built to the Académie des Beaux-Arts, together with the collection – inherited from his father, Jules Marmottan – of paintings, sculpture, furniture, and *objets d'art* dating from the 18th century and the First Empire. It was a collection to which he added constantly throughout his life.

The attraction of the place and of the Académie des Beaux-Arts which administered it would soon lead to other gifts and legacies. In 1938, for example, the daughter of the painter William Adolphe Bouguereau, an eminent figure in academic art and an Academician, offered her father's drawings to the museum. Shortly afterwards, Émile Bastien-Lepage made the Académie his sole legatee and bequeathed paintings, drawings, and engravings by his brother, Jules, the high priest of Naturalism.

Several donations between 1940 and 1947 from Victorine Donop de Monchy, the daughter of Georges de Bellio, who was a collector of Impressionist paintings, and her husband Eugène brought the first Impressionist paintings into the collection. Donations of works by participants in the 1874 Boulevard des Capucines exhibition subsequently followed. The most important donations were those of 1966 from Michel Monet, the son of Claude Monet, and those from the Rouart family in 1993 and 1996, making the Musée Marmottan Monet the largest repository of works by their ancestor Berthe Morisot. Thanks to all this generosity, the museum, standing in the Jardin de la Muette, has become an essential place of pilgrimage for those wishing to expand their knowledge of Impressionism through its rich collection.

The oldest of the works presented here in Skagen was painted by Claude Monet in the summer of 1870, on the beach at Trouville. Fleeing from Paris during the war, the painter, his partner Camille Doncieux, and their son Jean took refuge in Normandy. Inspired by the beach scenes painted by Eugène Boudin, his early master, Monet produced several pictures in which Camille and her cousin are posing on the beach, as in the one exhibited, *On the Beach at Trouville* (CAT. 57) The composition is both skilful and dynamic, closely framing the two women in the foreground while the diagonal separating the water from the beach rises behind them, thus creating an effect of space and depth. The shapes are sketched out with little detail, as the painter's attention is focused more on the effects of light. The freedom of the brushwork and the rapid execution already illustrate the experimentation that is underway, and which will lead to Impressionism.

Although this term did not appear in art criticism before 1874, it was two years earlier, in November 1872, that Monet created the work that was emblematic of this new style of painting. It was during a stay in Le Havre that he painted *Impression, Sunrise* (CAT. 58) from the room in the Hôtel de l'Amirauté where he was lodging. His subject – a view of the outer harbour, from the southeast, in the early morning when the quaysides and docks, chimneys, and masts were bathed in the autumn morning mist – was treated with a rare freedom of technique which prompted Monet to title it *Impression*. Presented at the first Impressionist exhibition in 1874, and then several times after that, the work would become the symbol and icon of a movement without, however, establishing methods and forms.

Thus it was that the following year, he painted *Train in the Snow. The Locomotive* (CAT. 59), in memory of the snowy landscapes of winter 1874–1875; and, when spring returned, *Taking a Walk in Argenteuil* (CAT. 60) in which Camille and little Jean figure once again, together with an unknown person. The figures are not painted for their own sake but in order to animate the landscape with a play of new colours. This was clear proof of Monet's feeling for composition and his talents as a colourist, as his light palette and touches of pure colour were placed at the service of an idealised vision of nature.

The first Impressionist exhibition included most of the group's representatives, but it was not until 1876 that a newcomer, Gustave Caillebotte, appeared; he was heir to a traditional form of training acquired in the studio of Léon Bonnat. At this second Impressionist exhibition, as at the following one, in 1877, he attracted attention – enthusiastic or otherwise – with his views of contemporary Parisian life. He produced many pictures of interiors and their occupants, as well as images of those inhabiting the capital's new residential districts. Caillebotte came from a well-to-do background and would help out his Impressionist friends financially, as well as passing some of his pictures on to them. This was how Monet came to possess this sketch of *Paris Street. Rainy Day* (1877, The Art Institute of Chicago), which depicts the busy neighbourhood of the Place de l'Europe. The picture is cleverly constructed, with several vanishing points and division of the space into two sections by the central streetlamp, which rises to cover virtually the whole height of the canvas. The umbrellas, particularly those of the couple occupying the right-hand side of the picture, reflect the title of the work, as do the cold monochrome tones which dominate it.

Monet left Argenteuil in late 1877 and returned with his family to live in Paris – Camille then being pregnant with their second son, Michel. From there, he made several trips by train to the Île de la Grande Jatte, where he produced some original compositions of landscapes seen through a screen of trees. This series confirmed his interest in Japanese prints, which, like his fellow artists, he collected. Based on the reinvented memory of these 'images of a floating world' (the translation of the Japanese term *ukiyoe*), Monet applied his technique of dabbed brushstrokes, varying the sizes and contours, enabling him to achieve a momentum leading the eyes of the viewer towards the Seine and the still peaceful banks of the Paris suburbs. An echo of this creative process was to be found later, in 1892, in a painting by Alfred Sisley exhibited under the title *The Loing Canal in Spring* (CAT. 63).

The oldest of the Impressionist artists to have joined the group, in 1874, was Camille Pissarro, who was born in the then Danish colony of St. Thomas. By this date, he already had a long career behind him, as he first took part in the Salon in 1859 – with varying success, since in 1863, for example, he exhibited at the Salon des Refusés (rejected artist's exhibition). Considered to be a painter of rural landscapes, in 1879 he painted his first urban view, *The Outer Boulevards, Snow Effect* (CAT. 64), a prelude to the many series he would devote to the capital from 1893 onwards. The framing and the very slightly elevated viewpoint lead us to imagine that he is painting from the top of one of the succession of omnibuses that can be seen along the diagonal providing the structure of the composition. The work is not lacking in humour; it succeeds in evoking the difficulty of moving from place to place when it is snowing. Pissarro depicts the snow against the coloured ground by juxtaposing touches of white, yellow, blue, and brown, so as to represent the effects of snow rather than the snow itself.

Alfred Sisley was younger by almost ten years and he, too, began his Salon career in 1866, before becoming one of the early Impressionists in 1874. Throughout his career – a difficult one because it was not until the 1880s that he began to meet with real success – Sisley was mainly a landscape painter, a painter of the sky and of the seasons, whose movements can be easily followed in both France and Britain. In this 1879 picture, *Spring near Paris. Apple Trees in Blossom* (CAT. 65), he opts for a very sober composition, superposing planes considered *di sotto in su* (a perspective shown from below in extreme foreshortening), linking the trees with their white blossom rising from the foreground towards the sky. The work is remarkable for its colour range and chromatic daring, as well as for its varied brushwork, from the dynamic strokes in the foreground to the arabesques that cover the sky.

Several women joined the Impressionist group during the course of its existence. The earliest to do so – being present at the first Impressionist exhibition in 1874 – and the most loyal – since she figured in seven out of their eight exhibitions – was Berthe Morisot. She is present here with her portrait of Eugène Manet – her husband and the brother of Édouard Manet – accompanied by their daughter Julie Manet, in their garden at Bougival (CAT. 66). Praised by some of the critics for her participation in the first exhibition, to which she sent *The Cradle* (1872, Musée d'Orsay, Paris), she continued to be lauded for her evocations of private life and was again acclaimed in 1882, when she sent the picture seen here, of *Eugène Manet and his daughter in the garden of Bougival*, to the seventh Impressionist exhibition. In the garden at Bougival, in the Paris suburbs, where the family stayed regularly from 1881 to 1884, Julie is playing with a construction game that rests on her father's knees, as he sits on a bench. At the time, the critic Philippe Burty described it as 'Impressionism *par excellence*' for its clear, luminous palette and the rapid brushstrokes used by the artist to create her picture.

Dominique Lobstein

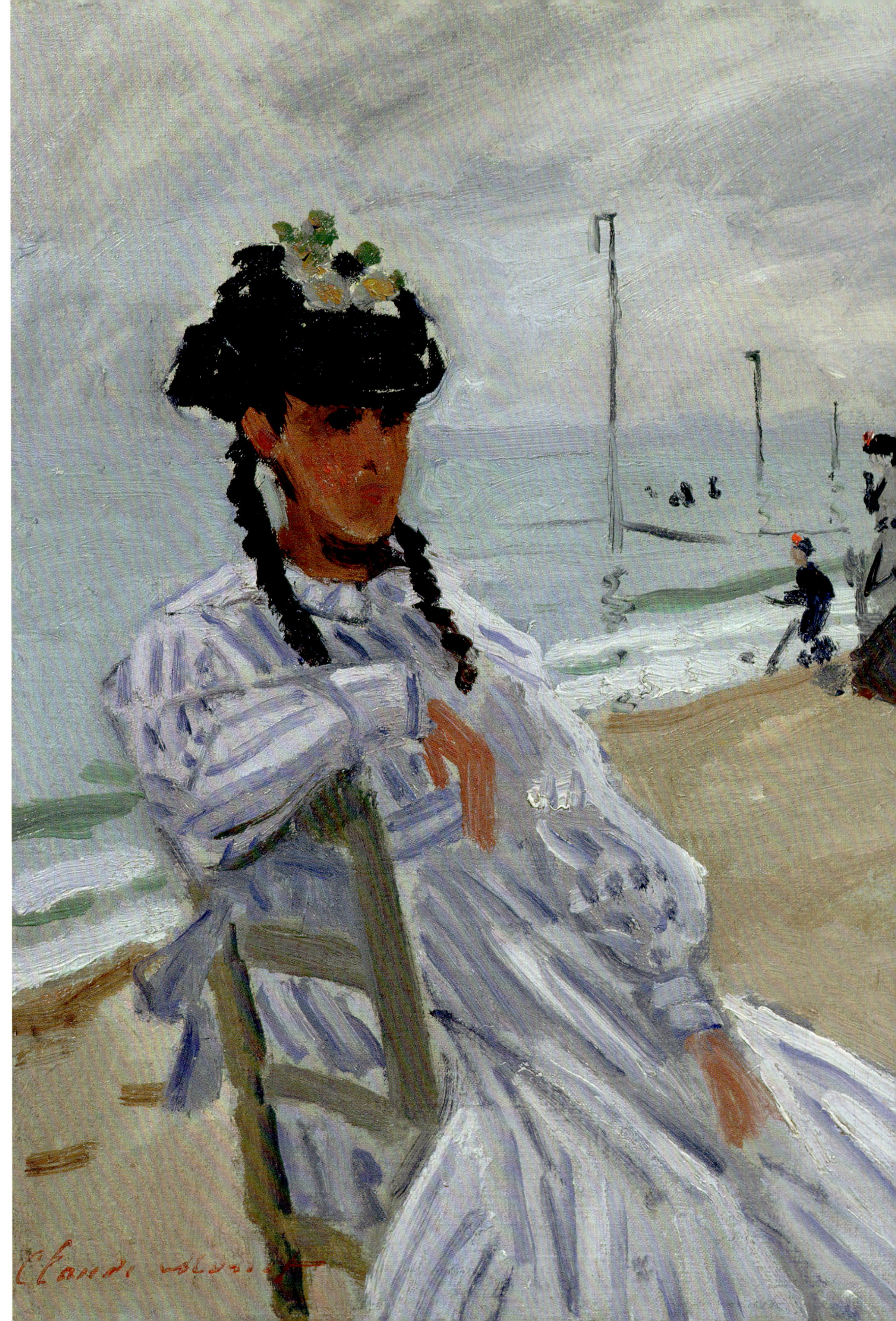

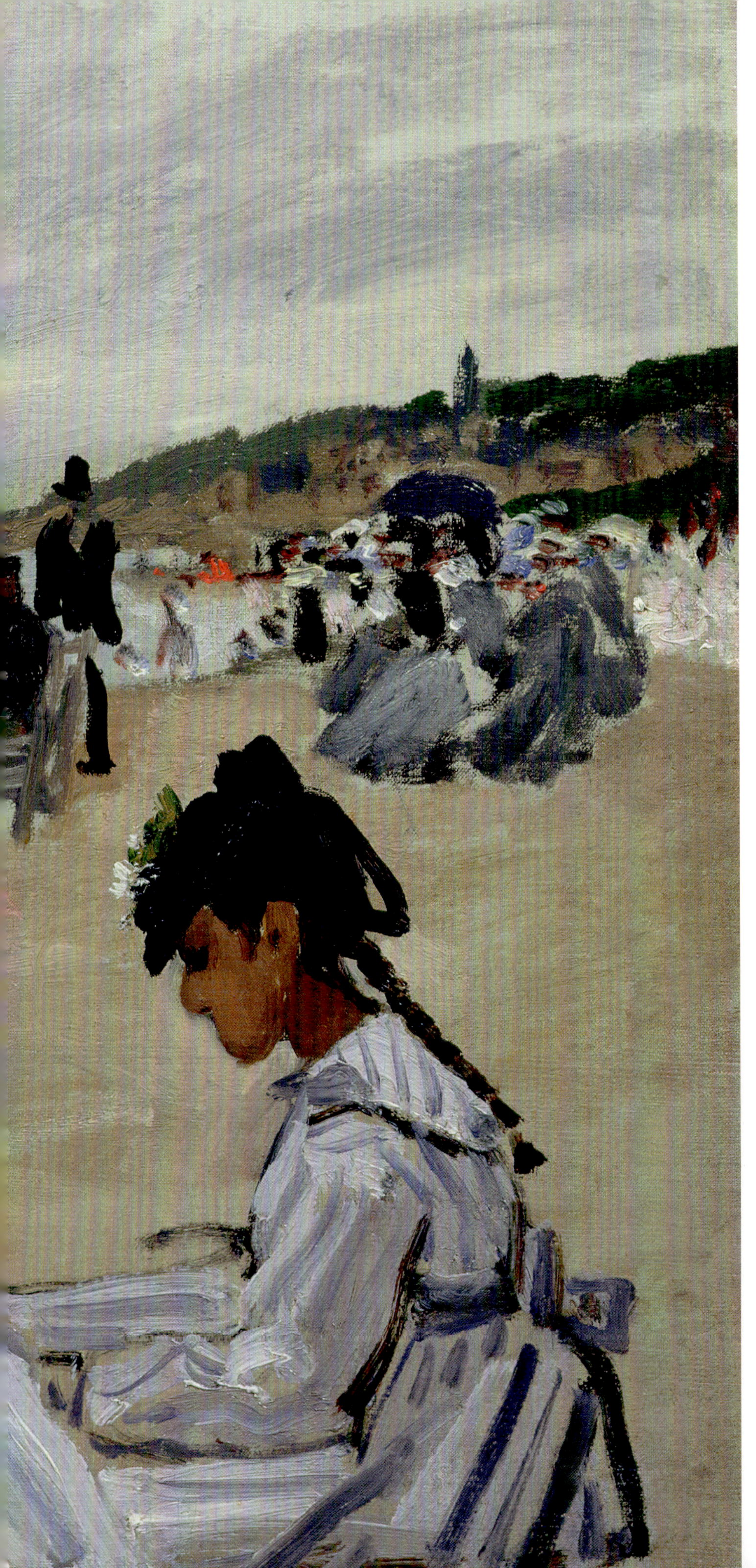

CAT. 57 Claude Monet: *On the Beach at Trouville*, 1870. Oil on canvas, 38 × 46 cm. Musée Marmottan Monet, Paris. 5016

CAT. 58 Claude Monet: *Impression, Sunrise*, 1872. Oil on canvas, 50 × 65 cm. Musée Marmottan Monet, Paris. 4014

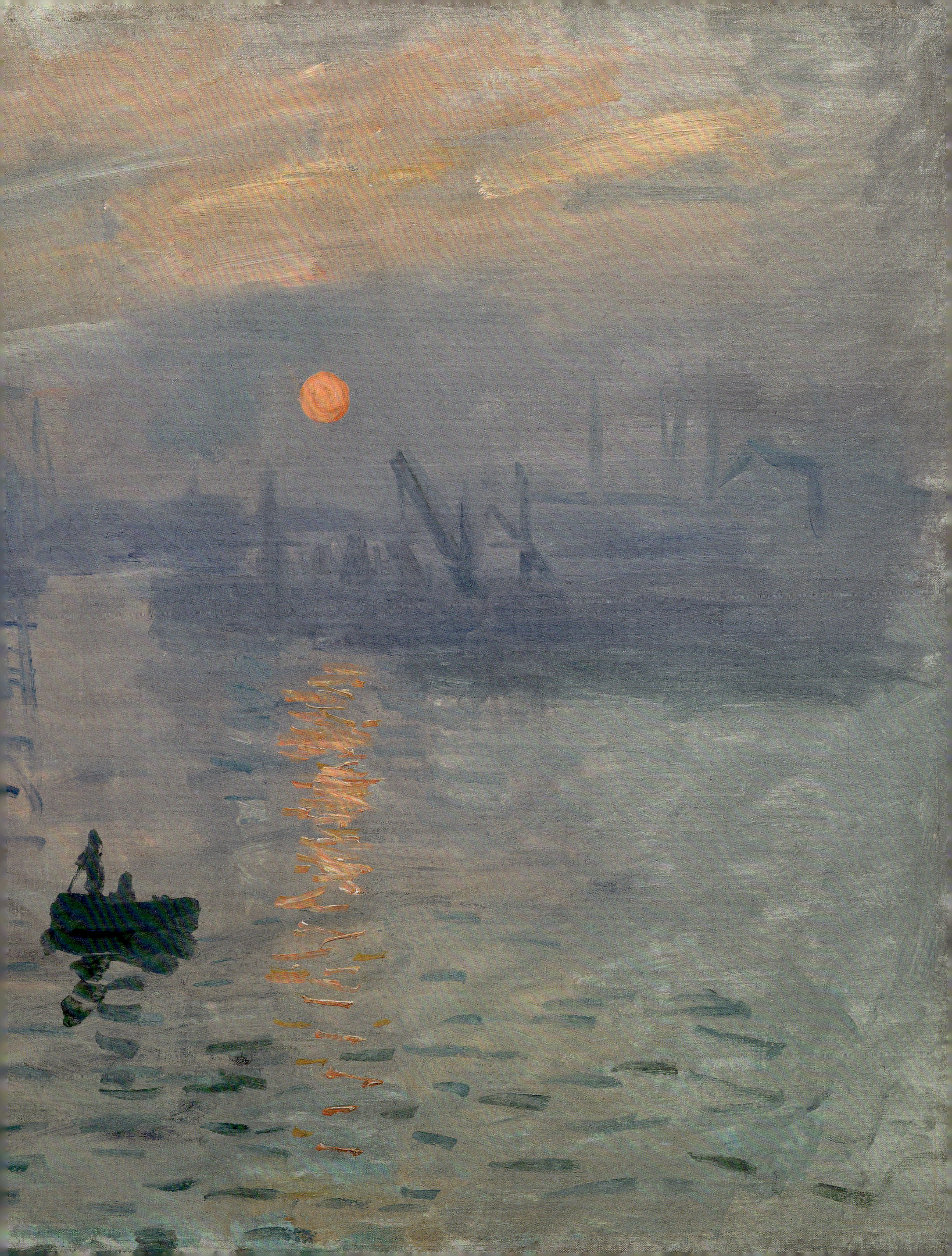

CAT. 59 Claude Monet:
The Train in the Snow. The Locomotive,
1875. Oil on canvas, 59×78 cm.
Musée Marmottan Monet, Paris. 4017

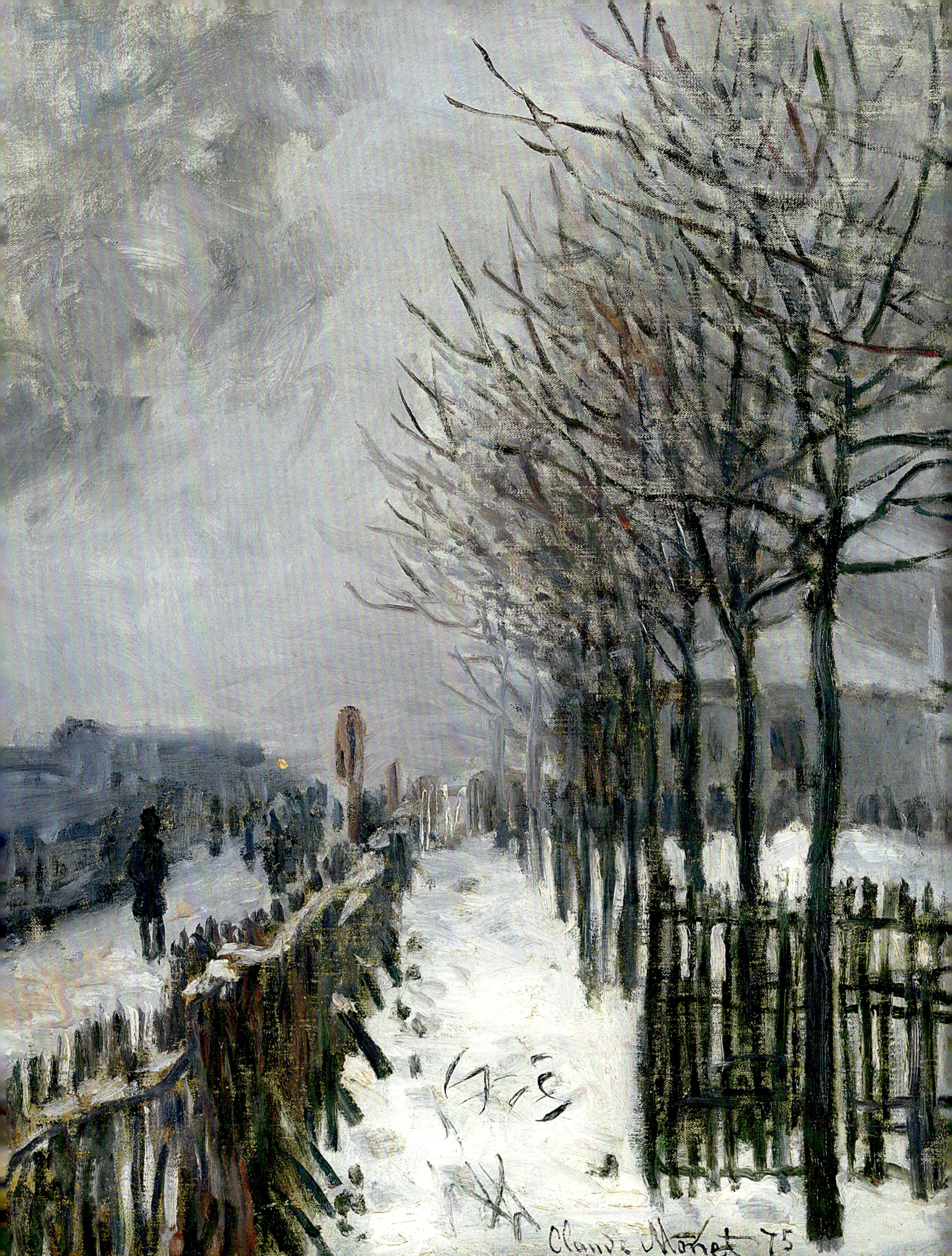
Claude Monet 75

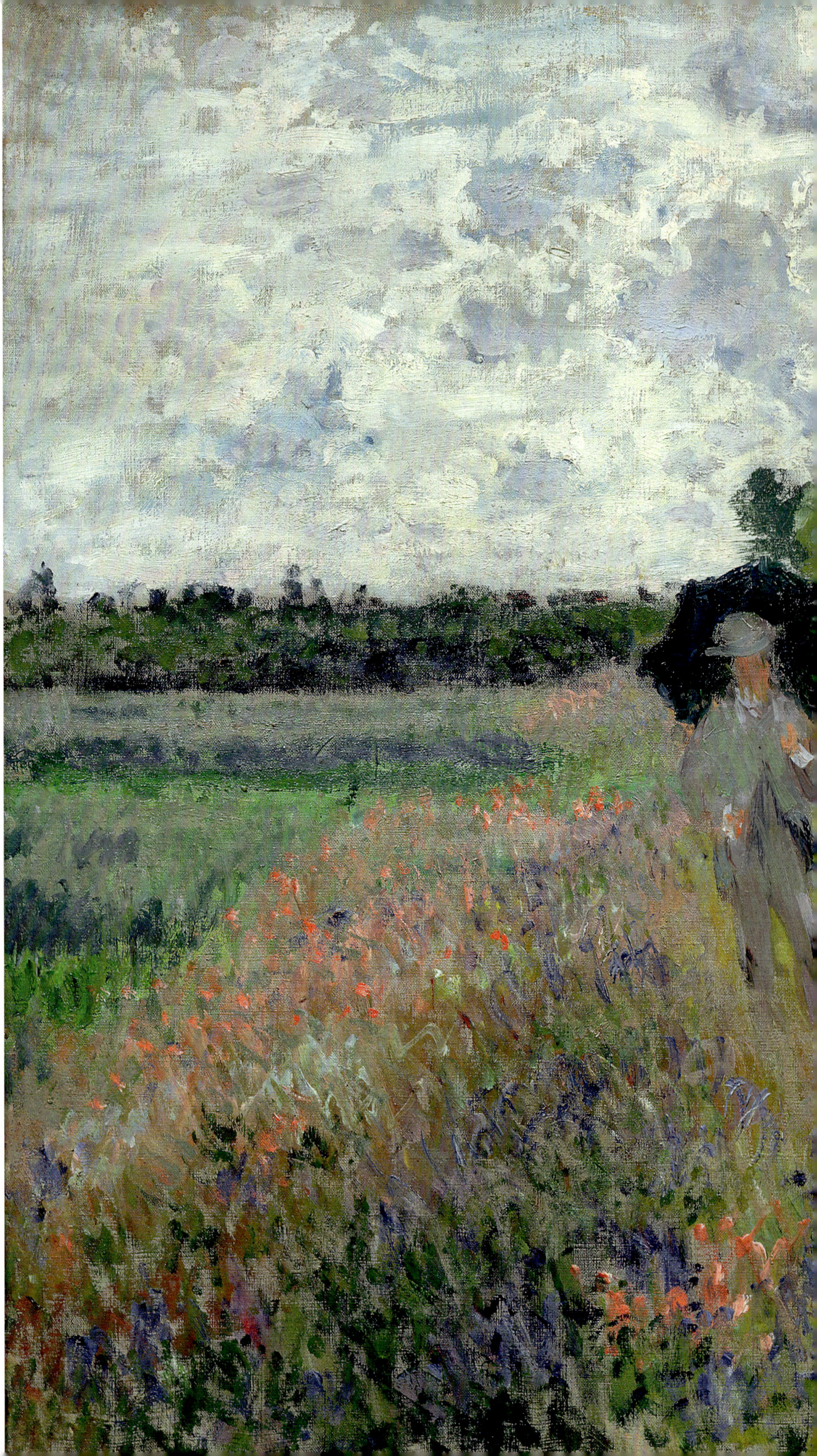

CAT. 60 Claude Monet: *Taking a Walk in Argenteuil*, 1875. Oil on canvas, 61×81.4 cm. Musée Marmottan Monet, Paris. 5332

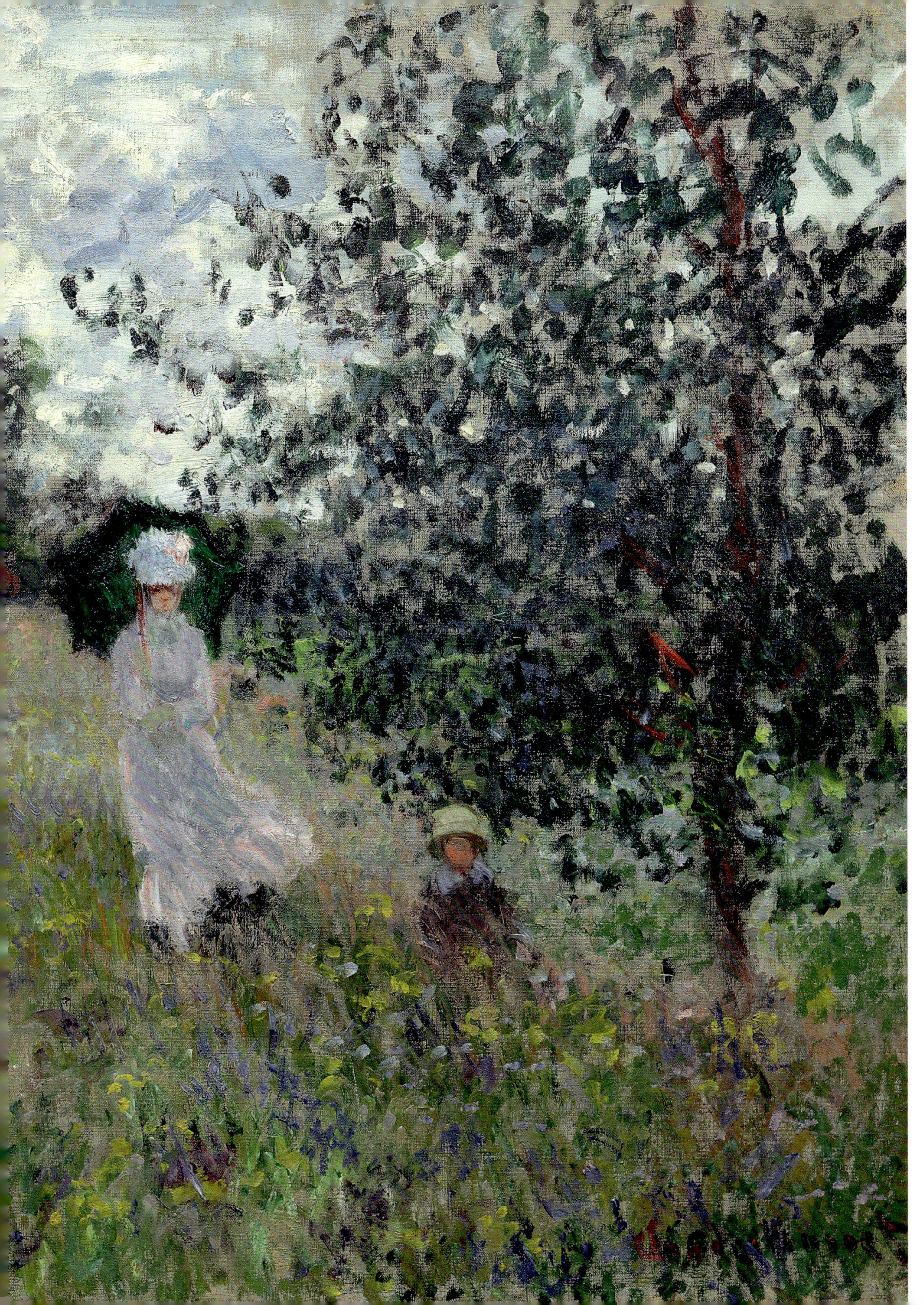

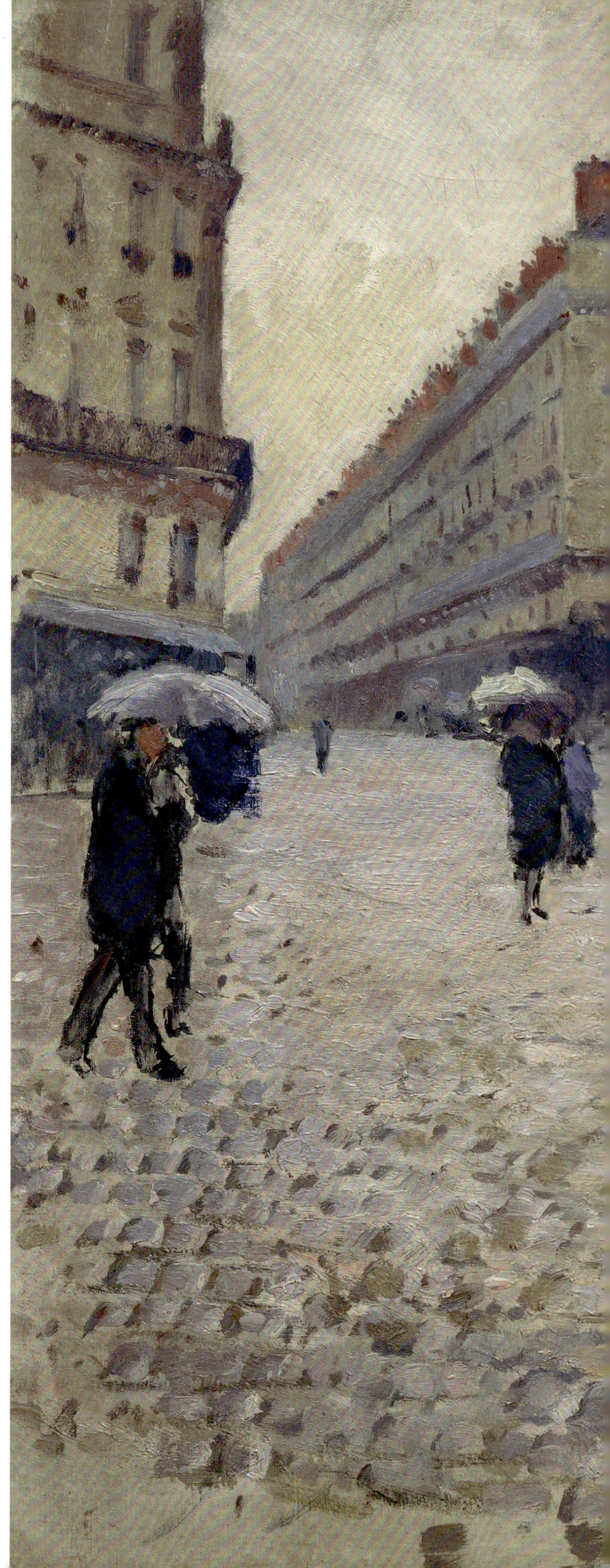

CAT. 61 Gustave Caillebotte: *Paris Street. Rainy Day*, 1877. Oil on canvas, 54×65 cm. Musée Marmottan Monet, Paris. 5062

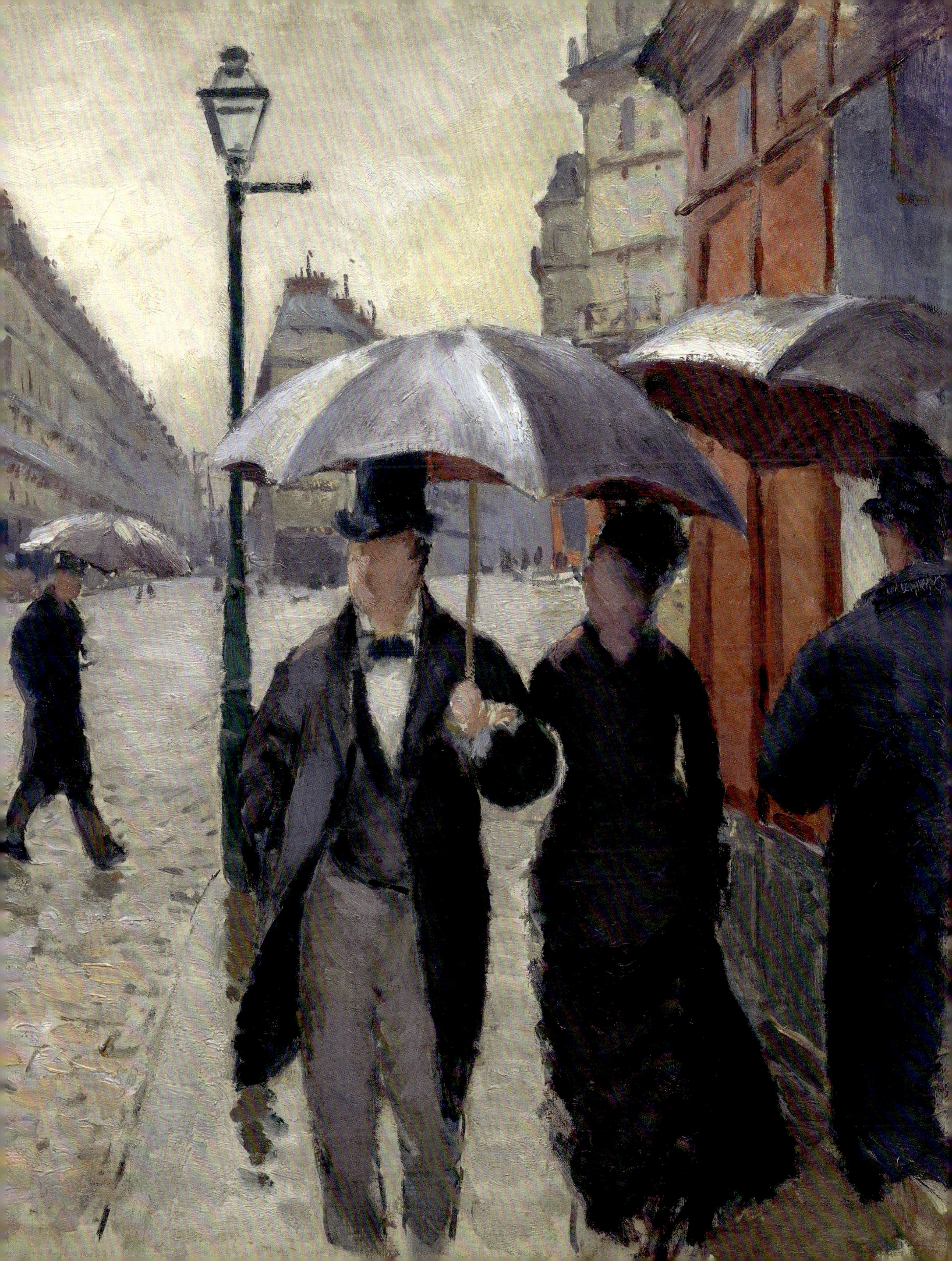

CAT. 62 Claude Monet: *Spring through the Branches*, 1878. Oil on canvas, 53.8 × 65.4 cm. Musée Marmottan Monet, Paris. 4018

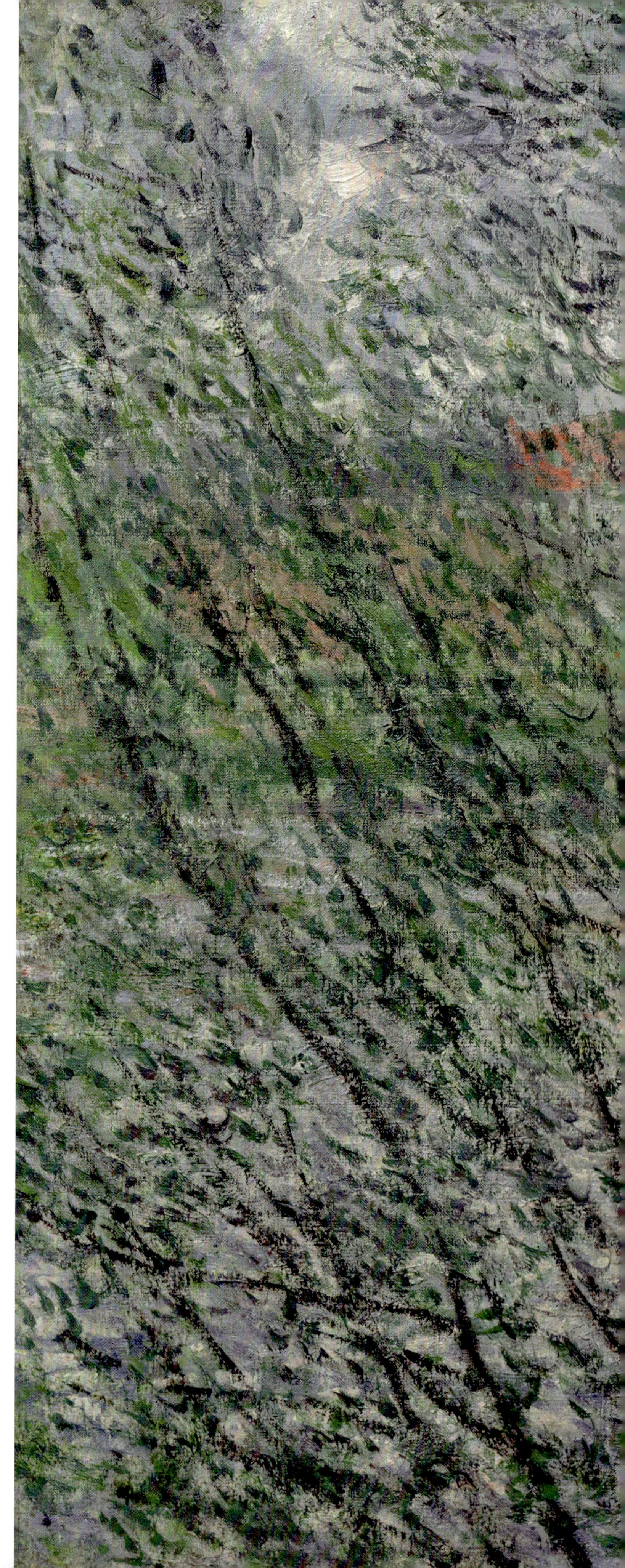

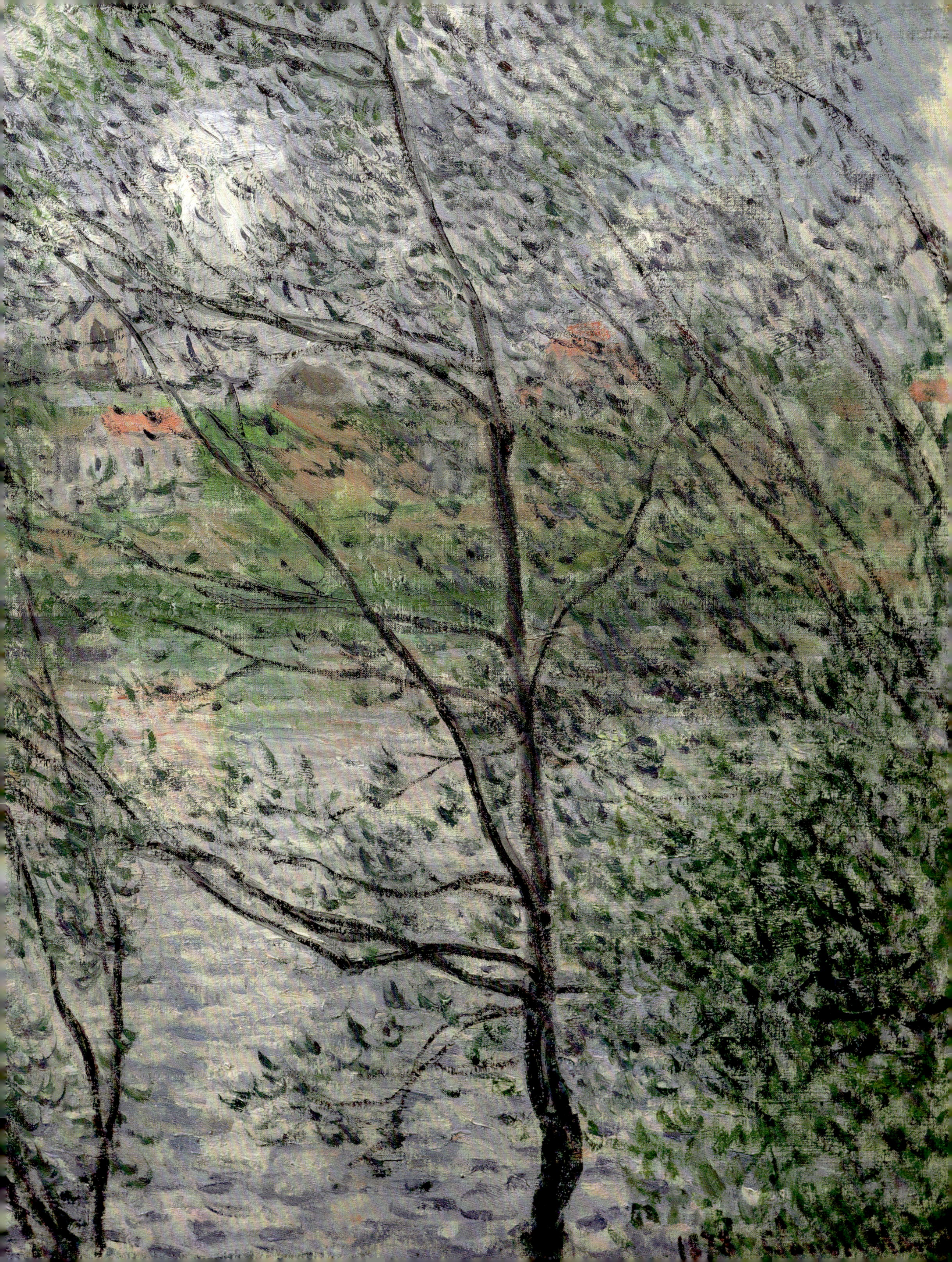

CAT. 63 Alfred Sisley: *The Loing Canal in Spring*, 1892. Oil on canvas, 54×66 cm. Musée Marmottan Monet, Paris. 5331

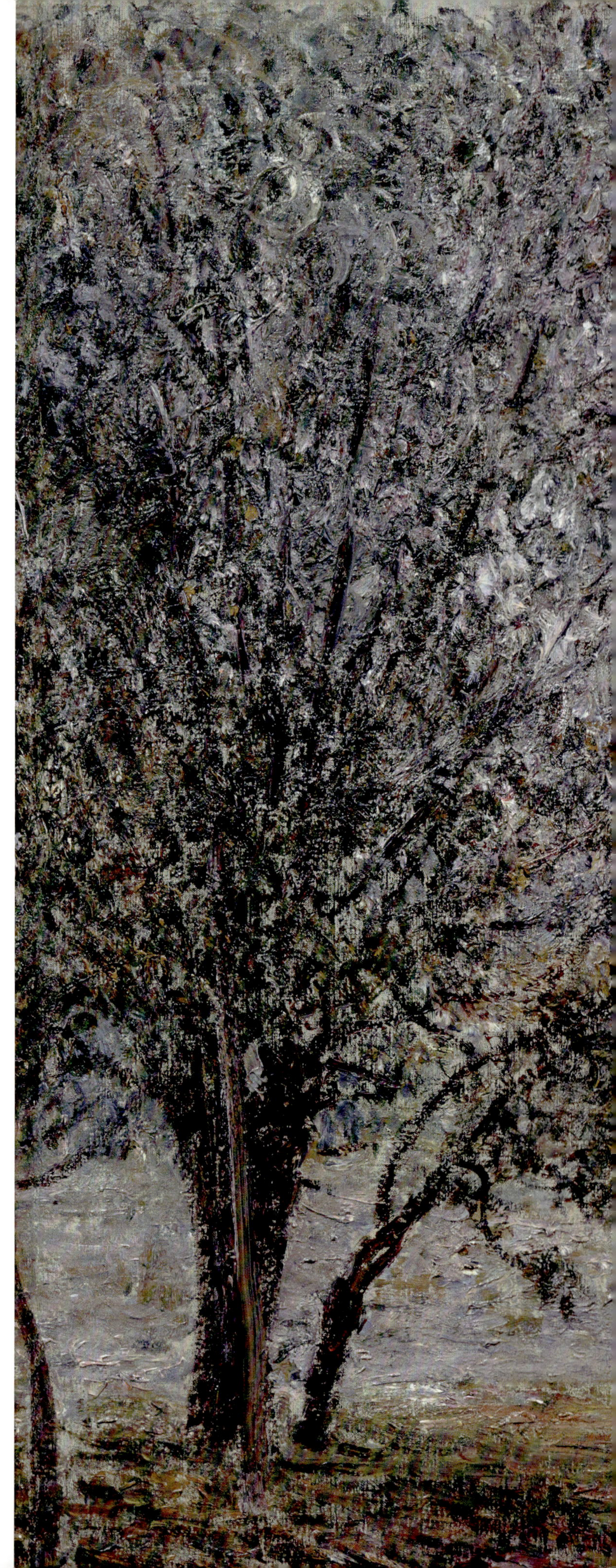

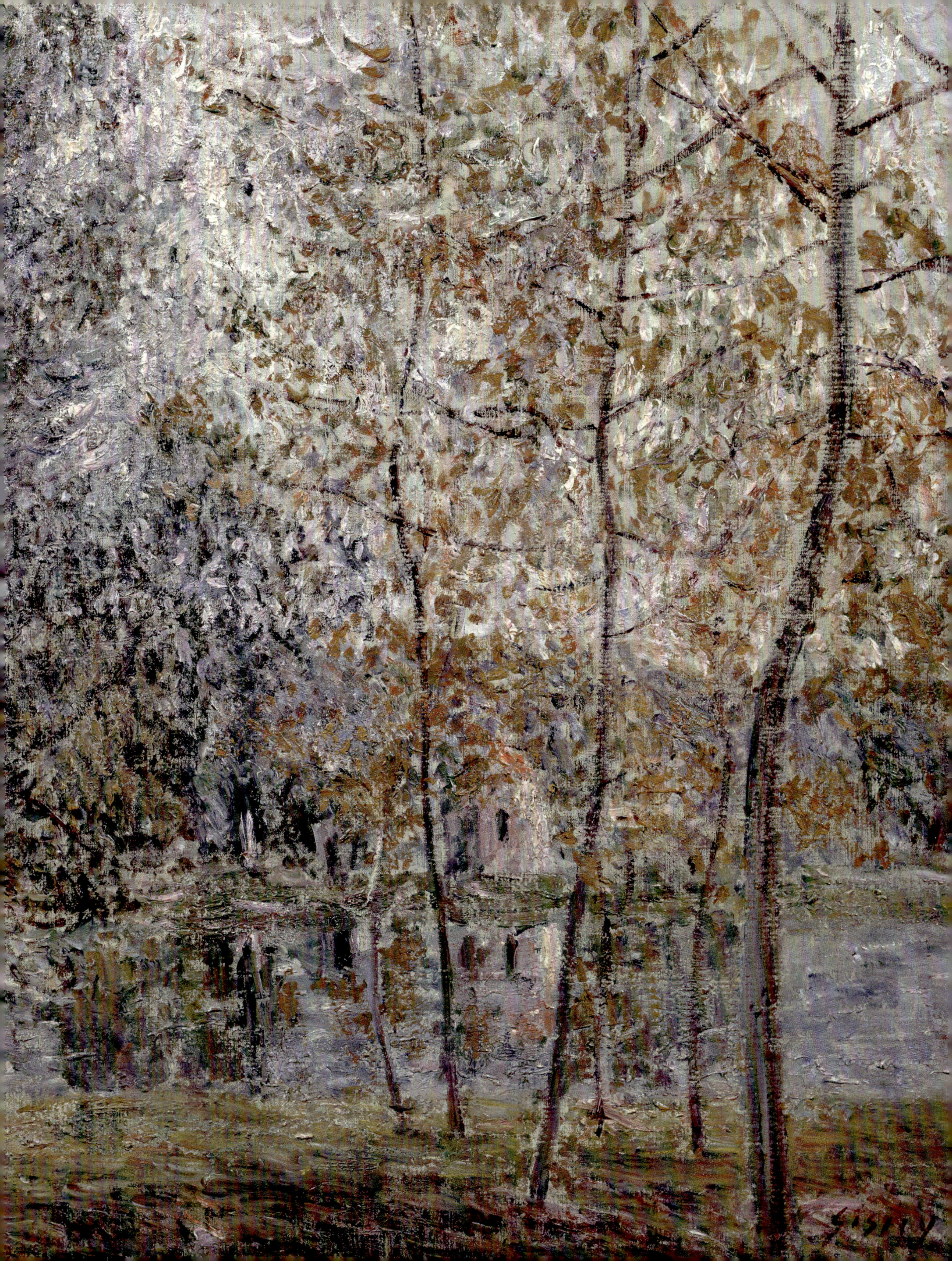

CAT. 64 Camille Pissarro: *The Outer Boulevards, Snow Effect*, 1879. Oil on canvas, 54×65 cm. Musée Marmottan Monet, Paris. 4021

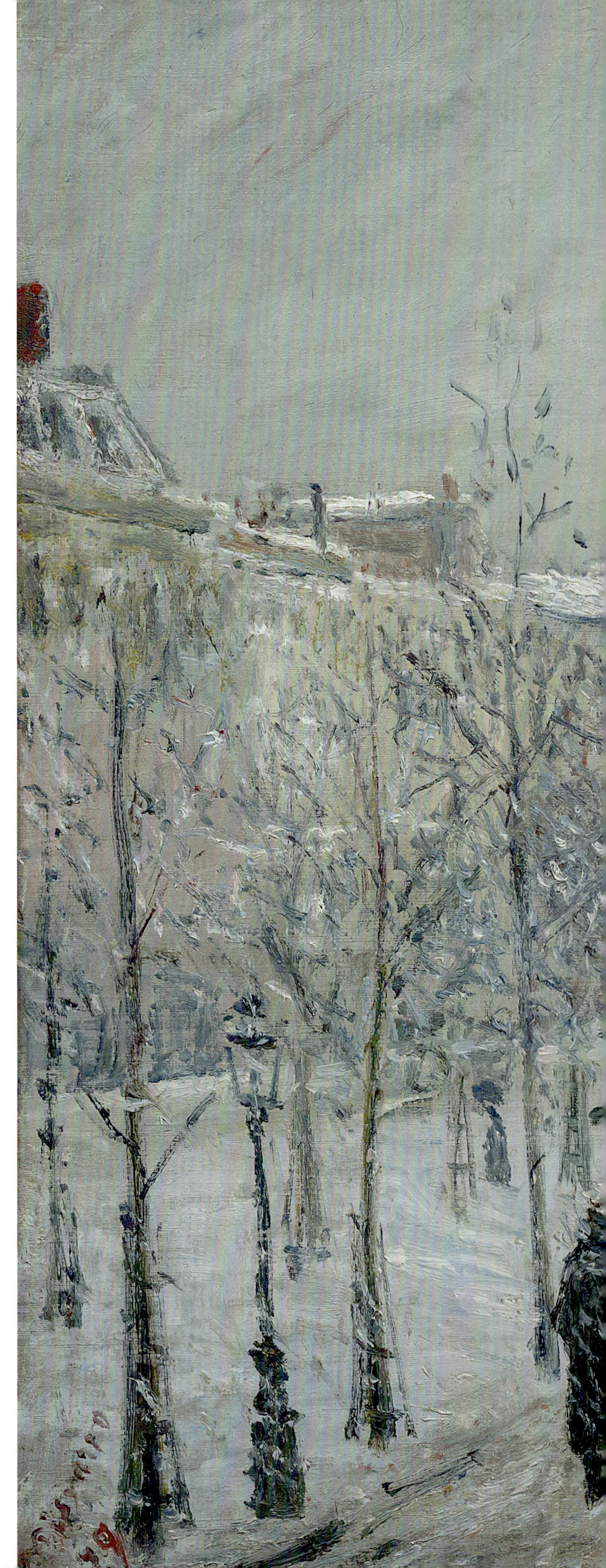

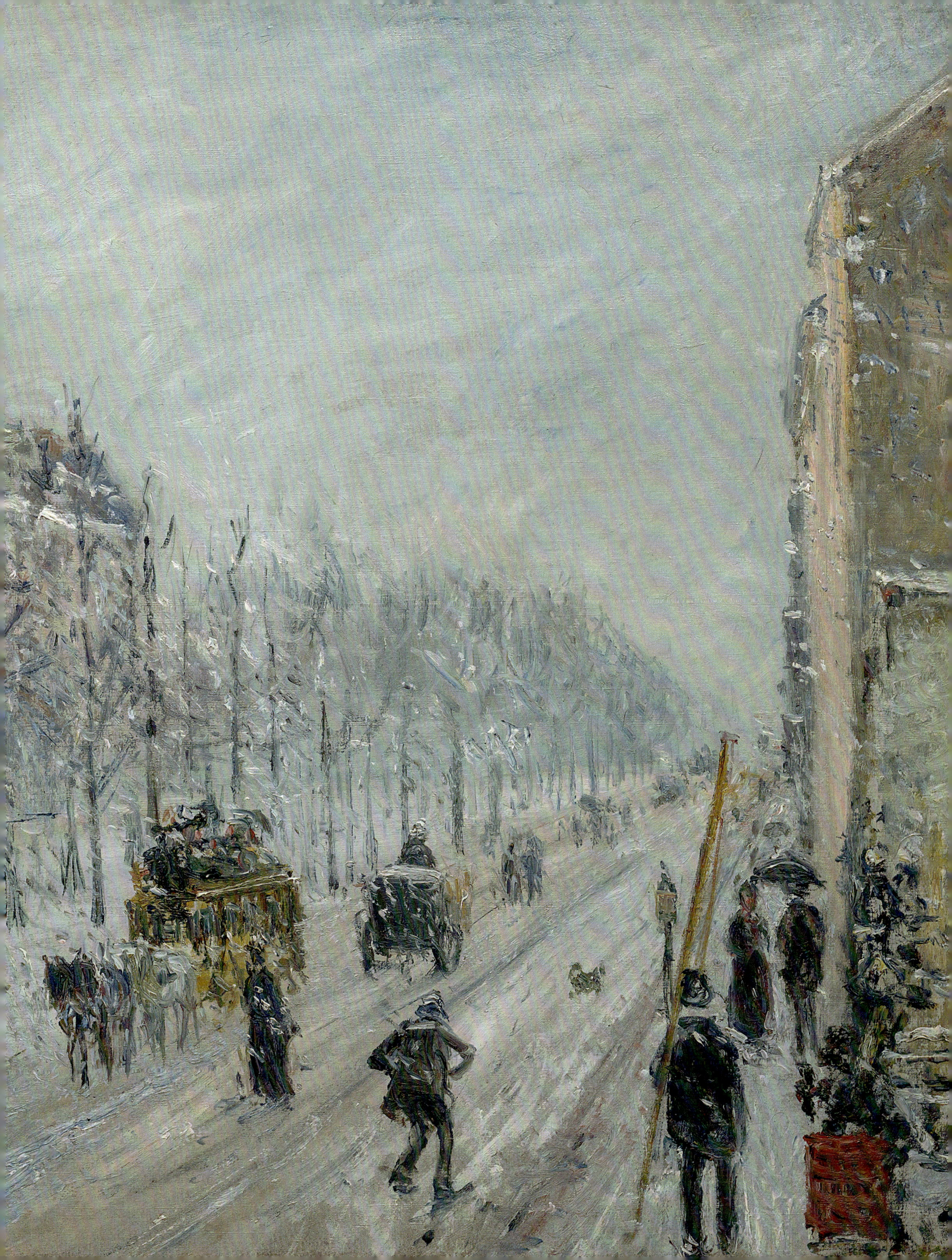

CAT. 65 Alfred Sisley: *Spring near Paris. Apple Trees in Blossom*, 1879. Oil on canvas, 47 × 62 cm. Musée Marmottan Monet, Paris. 4025

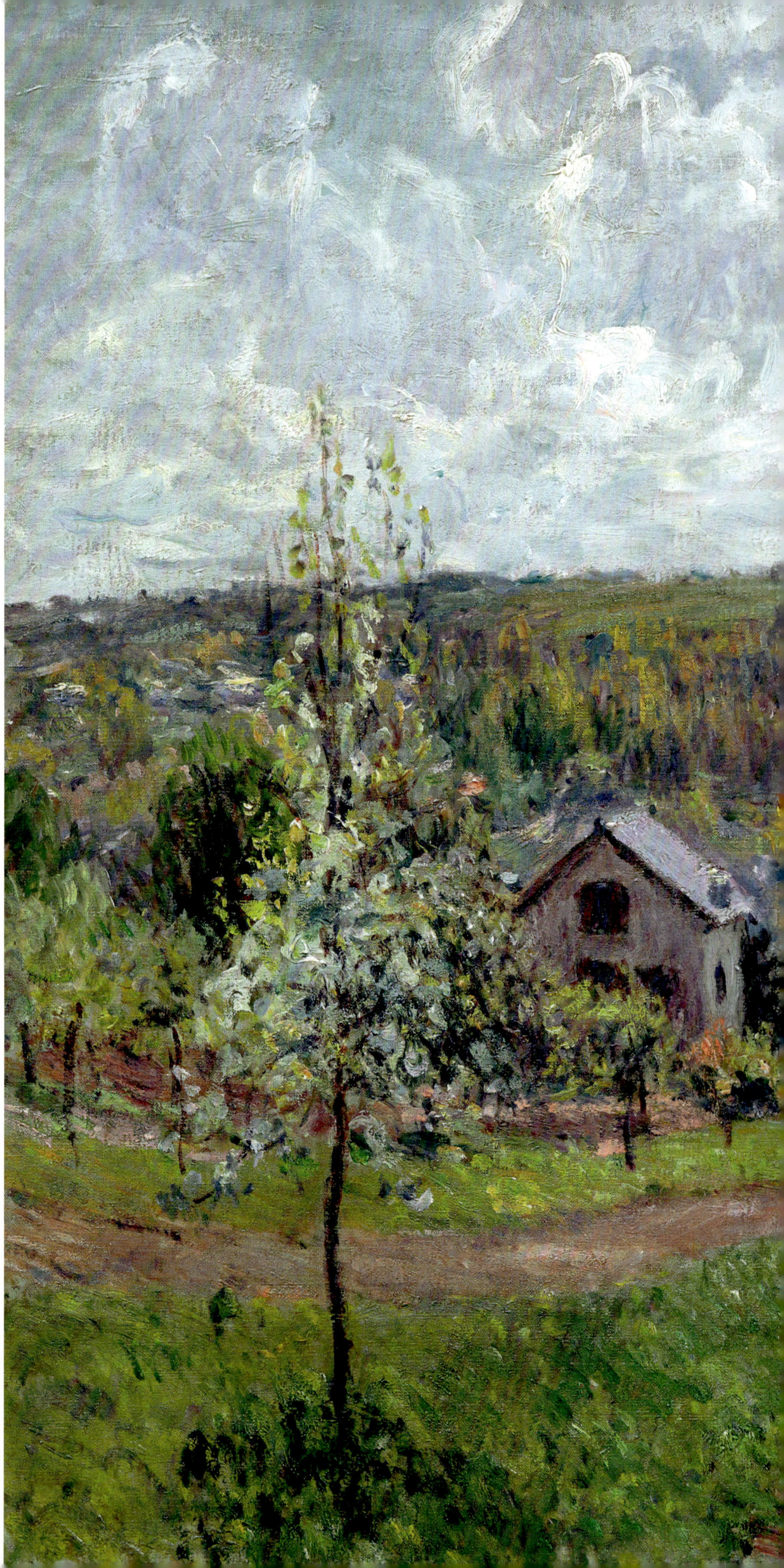

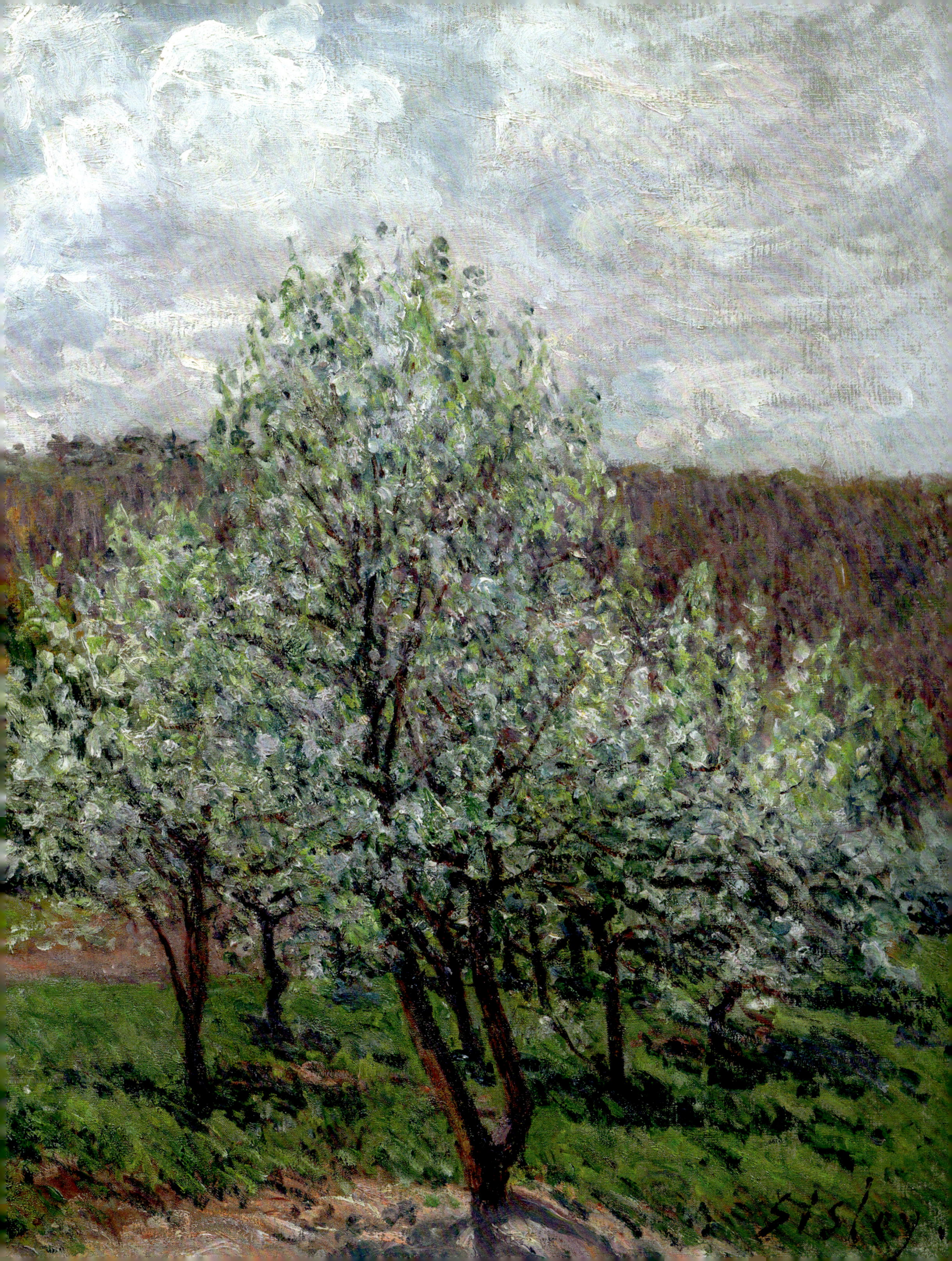
Sisley

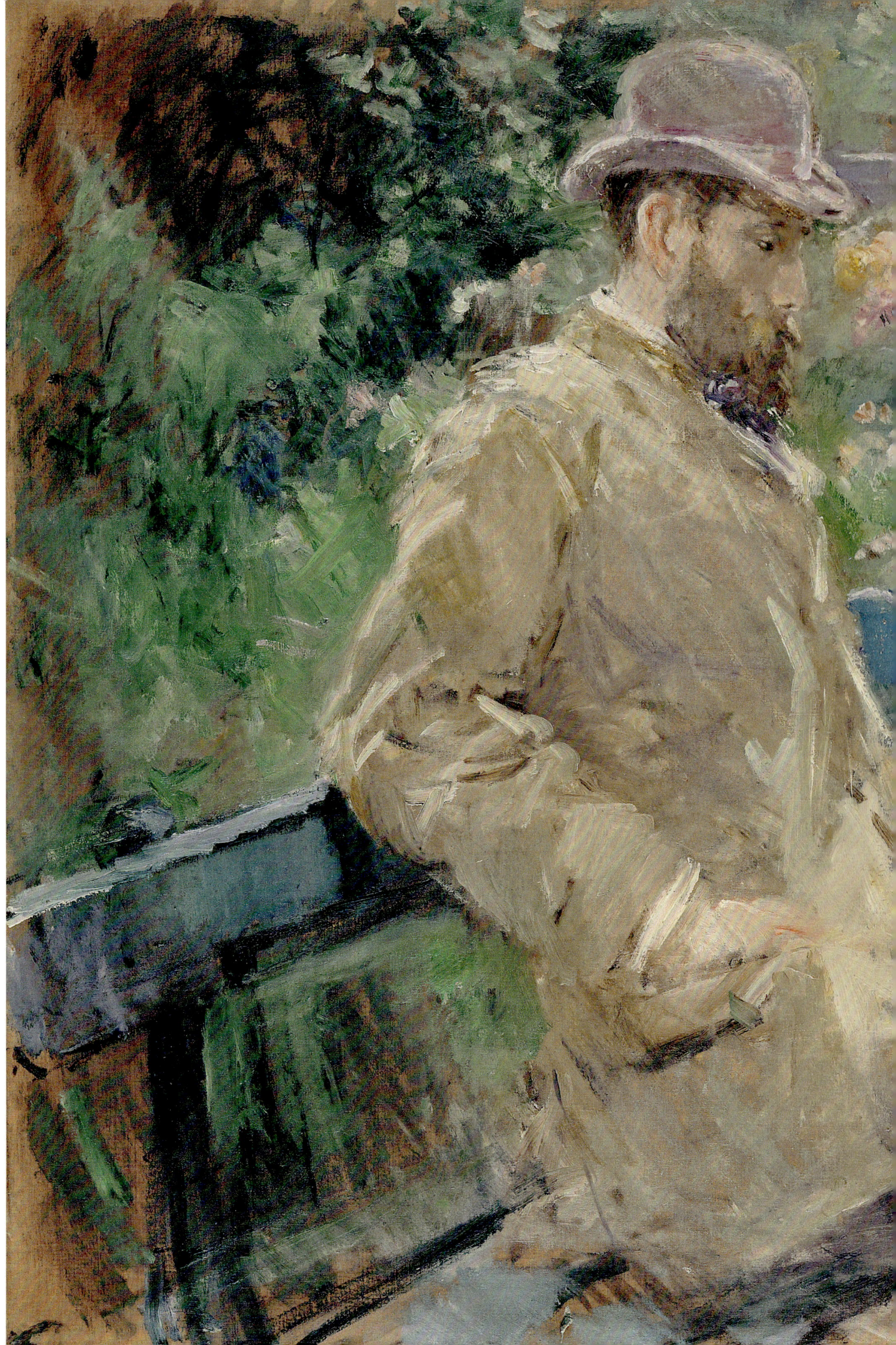

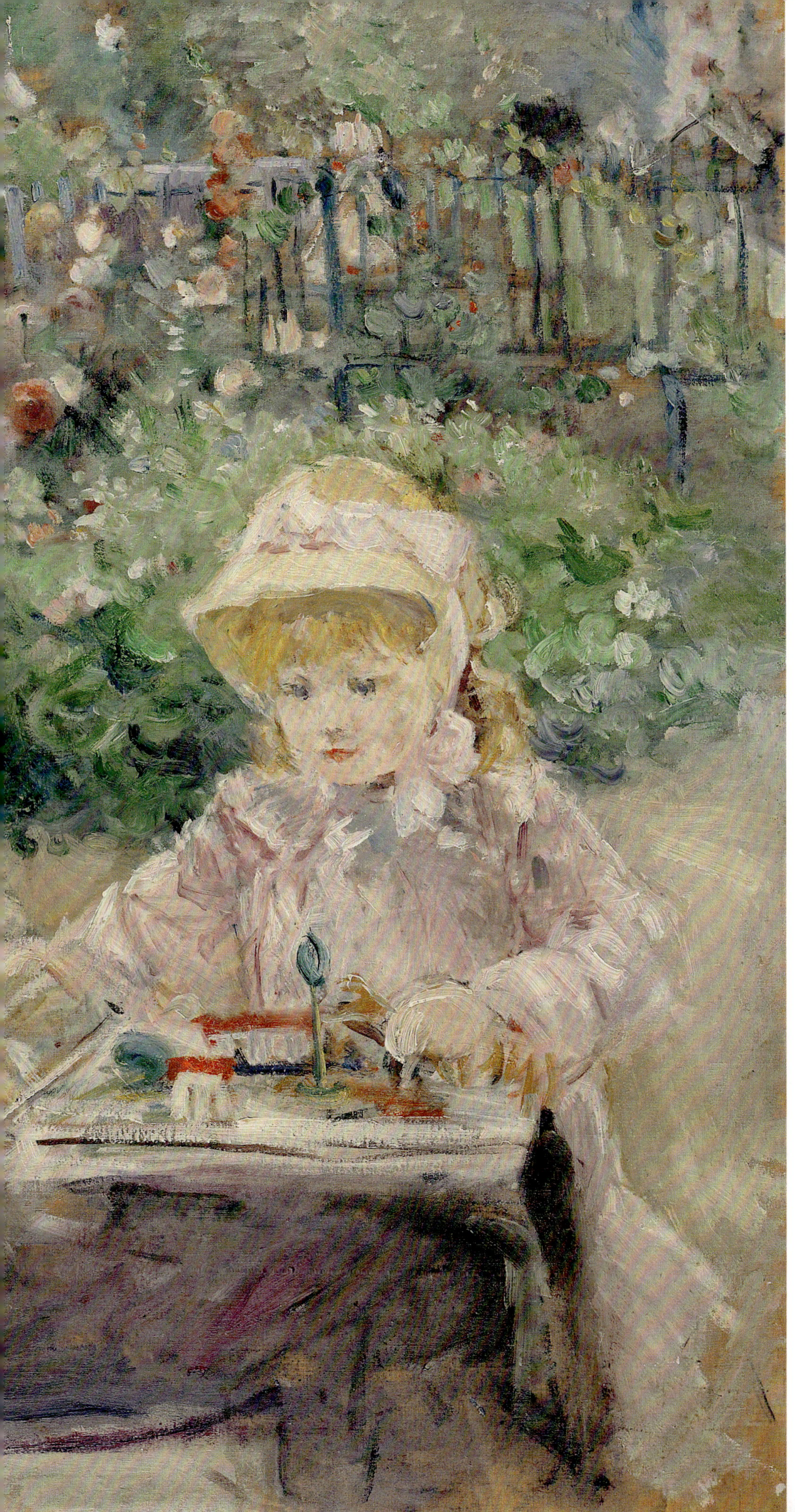

CAT. 66 Berthe Morisot: *Eugène Manet and His Daughter in the Garden at Bougival*, 1881. Oil on canvas, 73×92 cm. Musée Marmottan Monet, Paris. 6018

Bibliography

Abbreviations for the archives conserving the sources used:
KB: the Royal Library (Kgl. Bibliotek) of Denmark, Copenhagen
HH Archive: Heinrich Hirschsprung's archive of letters at Den Hirschsprungske Samling
PSK Archive: P.S. Krøyer's archive of letters at Den Hirschsprungske Samling

About, Edmond. 'Salon de 1877. IV. Les Peintres d'histoire'. *Le XIXe siècle* (14 June 1877).

Aicard, Jean. 'Salon de 1872'. *La Renaissance littéraire et artistique* (6 July 1872).

Ancher, Michael. *Notesbog 1879, 1880 og 1881.*

Ariste, 'Salon de 1874 à Paris'. *L'Indépendance belge* (13 June 1874).

Aubrun, Marie-Madeleine. *Jules Bastien-Lepage, 1848–1884: catalogue raisonné de l'oeuvre*. M. M. Aubrun, 1985.

'Au Salon. Les Deuxième Médailles de la Peinture'. *Le Matin* (25 May 1884).

Bergeron, Louis. 'Une France entre deux mondes', in *Des plaines à l'usine. Images du travail dans la peinture française de 1870 à 1914*. 16–25. Somogy, 2001.

Berman, Patricia G. *In Another Light. Danish Painting in the Nineteenth Century*. Thames & Hudson, 2007.

Blanc, Charles. *Les Beaux-Arts à l'Exposition Universelle de 1878*. H. Loones, 1878.

C., E. 'Chronique. Beaux-Arts. Exposition de peintures modernes'. *Revue de France* (1874).

Cardon, Émile. 'Avant le Salon'. *La Presse* (28 April 1874).

–. 'Avant le Salon: l'Exposition des Révoltés'. *La Presse* (29 April 1874).

Carjat, Etienne. 'L'Exposition du boulevard des Capucines'. *Le Patriote français* (17 April 1874).

Castagnary, Jules-Antoine. 'Exposition du boulevard des Capucines: Les Impressionnistes'. *Le Siècle* (29 April 1874).

–. *Salons (1872–1879)*. Charpentier et Fasquelle, 1892.

Challons-Lipton, Siulolovao. *The Scandinavian Pupils of the Atelier Bonnat, 1867–1894*. The Edwin Mellen Press, 2001.

Chatellier, Christian. *Impression, soleil levant: un autre regard*, edited by Dominique Lobstein and Marianne Mathieu. 194–201. Hazan, 2015.

Cherbuliez, Victor. 'La peinture à l'Exposition Universelle'. *Revue des deux mondes (1829–1971)*, vol. 28, no. 4 (1878).

Chesneau, Ernest. 'Au Salon: avertissement préalable'. *Paris-Journal* (9 May 1874).

–. 'A côté du Salon: II. Le Plein-air: Exposition du boulevard des Capucines'. *Paris-Journal* (7 May 1874).

Chevreul, Eugène. *De la loi du contraste simultané des couleurs et de l'assortiment des objets colorés considérés d'après cette loi dans ses rapports avec la peinture, les tapisseries des gobelins, les tapisseries de Beauvais pour meubles, les tapis, la mosaïque, les vitraux colores, l'impression des étoffes, l'imprimerie, l'enluminure, la decoration des édifices l'habillement et l'horticulture*. Pitois-Levrault, 1839.

Christensen, H. Chr. *P. S. Krøyer 23. juli 1851–20. november 1909 fortegnelse over hans Oliemalerier*. G. E. C. Gads Forlag, 1923.

Christiansen, Rasmus. 'Minder om Samvær og Samarbejde med Laurits Tuxen'. *Samleren*, vol. 5 (1928).

Christophe. 'Le Salon intime'. *Journal des artistes* (20 June 1886).

'Chronique'. *L'Univers*, no. 7480 (17 June 1888).

Claustrat, Frank. *La peinture nordique et ses maîtres modernes. Danemark, Finlande, Islande, Norvège, Suède (1800–1920)*. Le Faune éditeur, 2020.

Conférences de l'Académie royal de peinture et de sculpture pendant l'année 1667. Paris, chez Frédéric Léonard, 1668.

Dagbladet (28 April 1875).

Dalgaard, Knud. 'Arbejderklassens Økonomiske Kaar i Danmark i de sidste 50 Aar'. *Nationaløkonomisk Tidsskrift*, vol 3, row 34 (1926).

Dangeau. 'Nouvelles du jour. La ville'. *La Presse* (26 May 1884).

Dayot, Armand. 'Exposition Universelle de 1889. XXXIX. L'Exposition décennale étrangère (1878–1889)'. *Journal official de la République française* (17 September 1889).

de Mont, Elie [Elizé Louis de Montagnac] *Les Beaux-Arts au palais de l'Industrie. Exposition 1874*. Reims, Imprimerie Lagarde, 1874.

Descubes, A. 'Le Salon de 1877 (suite)'. *Gazette des lettres, des sciences & des arts* (20 May 1877).

Dictionnaire encyclopédique des amusemens des sciences mathématiques et physiques: des procédés curieux des arts, des tours récréatifs & subtils de la magie blanche, & des découvertes ingénieuses & variées de l'industrie. Recueil des planches du Dictionnaire encyclopédique des amusemens des sciences mathématiques et physiques. Panckoucke, 1792.

Drumont, Édouard. 'L'Exposition du boulevard des Capucines'. *Le Petit Journal* (19 April 1874).

E., A. 'Au Salon. Les tableaux de genre'. *La Lanterne* (20 May 1881).

Fabritius, Elisabeth. 'Tuxen og de frie studieskoler', in *Tuxen – farver, friluft og fyrster*, edited by Mette Bøgh Jensen and Gertrud Oelsner. 26–39. Systime, 2014.

–. *Michael Anchers ungdom 1865–1880*. Helga Anchers Fond og Poul Kristensens Forlag, 1992.

Fortegnelse over den af Kunstnernes Studieskole foranstaltede Udstilling af Arbejder i Udstillingsbygningen ved Charlottenborg. Thieles Bogtrykkeri, 1896.

Fouquier, Marcel. 'Le Salon du Champ de Mars'. *Le XIXe siècle*, no. 8504 (28 April 1895).

Frederiksen, Finn Terman. 'Kyhns mareridt', in *Vilhelm Kyhn & det danske landskabsmaleri*, edited by Gertrud Oelsner and Karina Lykke Grand. 37–63. Aarhus University Press, 2012.

Faaborg, Th. *Johan Frederik Nicolai Vermehren: 1823 – 12. Maj – 1923*. Foreningen for National Kunst. H. Hagerups Forlag, 1923.

Galschiøt, Martinus. 'Bastien-Lepage'. *Illustreret Tidende*, vol. 6, no. 14 (4 January 1885).

Gaudet, François-Charles. *La Bibliothèque des petits-maîtres ou Mémoires pour servir à l'histoire du bon ton et de l'extrêmement bonne compagnie*. Au Palais Royal, 1761.

'Gazette du jour'. *La Justice*, no. 3073 (13 June 1888).

Geffroy, Gustave. 'Salon de 1884. Portraits. II'. *La Justice* (11 June 1884).

Grand, Karina Lykke. 'Rejsebilleder – Turist i Arkadien?', in *Guld – skatte fra den danske guldalder*, edited by Karina Lykke Grand, Lise Pennington and Anne Mette Thomsen. 200–239. Systime, 2013.

Greaves, Kerry. 'Pedagogy, Provocation and Paradox: Denmark's Kunstnernes Studieskole'. *Studies in Ethnicity and Nationalism*, vol. 13, no. 3 (December 2013).

Groth, Vilhelm [En dansk kunstner]. *Dansk Kunst i Forhold til Udlandets*. Rudolph Klein, 1886.

Halkier, Katrine. 'The Studio at Bredgade 33', in *Krøyer. An international perspective*, edited by Marianne Saabye. 66–68. Den Hirschsprungske Samling and Skagens Museum, 2011.

Havard, Henri. 'Le Salon de 1880 (3e et dernier article)'. *Le Siècle* (1 June 1880).

Hervet, Emile. 'Le Salon. XI'. *Le Pays* (15 May 1886).

Hornung, Peter Michael. *Peder Severin Krøyer*. Forlaget Palle Fogtdal, 2005.

Illustreret katalog over udstillingen af franske kunstvaerker i Kjøbenhavn 1888. August Bangs Boghandels Forlag, 1888.

Illustreret Tidende. No. 1241 (8 July 1882).

'Impression', in Œuvres *de Denis Diderot. Dictionnaire encyclopédique*. Brière, 1821.

'Informations'. *Le Figaro* (18 June 1894).

Jensen, Mette Bøgh. *Brøndums spisesal. Til tak for glade dage*. Skagens Museum, 2011.

Johansen, Anette and Mette Bøgh Jensen, eds. *Zorn besøger Skagen*. Skagens Museum, 2006.

Købke, Peter. 'Breve fra Julius Lange'. Det nordiske Forlag, 1902.

Kyhn, Vilhelm. *Dansk Kunst og Kunstudstillingen på Charlottenborg. Nogle Betragtninger af Vilh. Kyhn, maler*. Karl Schønbergs Forlag, 1876.

–. *Dansk Kunst. Svar fra V. Kyhn til den 'danske Kunstner'*. Karl Schønbergs Forlag, 1877.

Labat-Poussin, Brigitte and Caroline Obert. *Archives de l'Ecole Nationale Supérieure des Beaux-Arts (AJ52 1 à 1415)*. Centre historique des Archives nationales, 1998.

Lange, Julius. *Vor Kunst og Udlandets. Et foredrag*. P.G. Phillipsens Forlag, 1879.

–. *Bastien Lepage og Andre Afhandlinger*. P.G. Philipsens Forlag, 1889.

Larsen, Peter Nørgaard. 'The transcendence of the spirit and immanence of the flesh. New and forgotten meaning in the major works of Frederik Vermehren'. *Journal / Statens Museum for Kunst*, vol. 1 (1997).

Le Masque de fer [The Iron Mask]. 'Echos de Paris'. *Le Figaro* (28 April 1874).

Lehmann, Mette Harbo. 'Skagensmaleren Johannes Wilhjelm', in *Johannes Wilhjelm – fra Italien til Skagen*, edited by Mette Harbo Lehmann and Tine Nielsen Fabienke. 66–91. Fulsang Kunstmuseum, Skagens Kunstmuseer and Ribe Kunstmuseum, 2018.

Leroy, Louis. 'L'Exposition des impressionnistes'. *Le Charivari* (25 April 1874).

'Les Modèles, la petite histoire'. *C'est la Vie! Image d'archives* (25 November 2017)

'L'Exposition de Copenhague (par service spécial)'. *Le Matin* (12 June 1888).

'L'Exposition scandinave'. *Le Temps*, no. 9923 (3 July 1888).

Lichtenberg, Hanne Honnens de. *Zahrtmanns skole*. Forum, 1979.

Lobstein, Dominique and Mette Harbo Lehmann. *The Blue Hour of Peder Severin Krøyer*. Hazan, 2020.

Lobstein, Dominique. 'Alexandre Cabanel au Salon, chronologie d'une activité exemplaire de juré' in *Alexandre Cabanel, la tradition du beau*, edited by Michel Hilaire. 53–65. Somogy Editions, 2010.

–. '"A Lover of Light" Under the Skies of Paris', in *The Blue Hour of Peder Severin Krøyer*, edited by Dominique Lobstein and Mette Harboe Lehmann. 49–63. Hazan, 2020.

–. 'Claude Monet et l'impressionnisme dans les critiques de l'exposition de 1874', in *Impression, soleil levant. L'histoire vraie du chef-d'oeuvre de Claude Monet*, edited by Dominique Lobstein and Marianne Mathieu. 106–115. Hazan, 2015.

–. 'Ernest Hoschedé et Impression, soleil levant', in *Impression, soleil levant. L'histoire vraie du chef-d'oeuvre de Claude Monet*, edited by Dominique Lobstein and Marianne Mathieu. 116–133. Hazan, 2016.

–. 'Jules Bastien-Lepage (1848–1884)', in *Jules Bastien-Lepage (1848–1884)*. 15–51. Éd. Nicolas Chaudun and Musée d'Orsay, 2007.

–. 'Jules Bastien-Lepage (Damvillers, 1848–Paris, 1884): une révision du catalogue raisonné'. *Le Pays Lorrain*, vol. 91, no. 1 (March 2010).

Locher, Carl. 'Fra Krøyers Ungdom'. *Illustreret Tidende*, vol. 51, no. 12 (4 December 1909).

Lostalot, Alfred de. 'Le Salon de 1886. La Peinture (1er article)'. *La Gazette des Beaux-Arts* (1 June 1886).

Lübbren, Nina. *Rural artists' colonies in Europe 1870–1910*. Manchester University Press, 2001.

M., Soph. 'Krøyer og Frits Thaulow paa Verdensudstillingen i Paris'. *Illustreret Tidende*, no. 39 (24 June 1900).

Madsen, Karl. *Japansk Malerkunst*. P.G. Philipsens Forlag, 1885.

–. 'Indtryk fra Verdensudstillingen. Fransk Malerkunst. II' in *Tilskueren*, vol 6. Gyldendalske Boghandel – Nordisk Forlag, 1889.
–. 'Krøyer'. *Gads Danske Magasin* (1910).
–. *Skagens Malere og Skagens Museum*. Gyldendalske Boghandel, Nordisk Forlag, 1929.
'Malerier + Antikviteter'. *Bruun Rasmussen auktionskatalog. Traditional auktion 895*. June 2020.
Mantz, Paul. 'Le Salon. IV'. *Le Temps* (27 May 1877).
–. 'Le Salon. VII'. *Le Temps*, no. 7001 (20 June 1880).
–. 'Le Salon. I'. *Le Temps* (11 May 1884).
–. 'Le Salon. IV'. *Le Temps* (30 May 1886).
Mauclair. Camille. *L'Impressionnisme. Son histoire. Son esthétique. Ses maîtres*. Librairie de l'Art ancien et moderne, 1904.
Mednick, Thor J. 'Danish Internationalism: Peder Severin Krøyer in Copenhagen and Paris'. *Nineteenth-Century Art Worldwide*, vol. 10, no. 1 (spring 2011).
Meldahl, Ferdinand and Peter Johansen. *Det Kongelige Akademi for de Skjønne Kunster 1700–1904*. H. Hagerups Boghandel, 1904.
Mentze, Ernst. *P.S. Krøyer. Kunstner af stort format – med brændte vinger*. Schønberg, 1969.
Merson, Olivier. 'Le Salon de 1874. XI'. *Le Monde illustré* (11 July 1874).
–. 'Salon of 1877. IV'. *Le Monde illustré* (26 May 1877).
–. 'Salon de 1880. VI'. *Le Monde illustré* (12 June 1880).
Méry, Gaston. 'Le Salon du Champs-de-Mars'. *La Libre Parole* (24 April 1895).
M., A. [André Michel]. 'Le Tour du Salon (Champ-de-Mars)'. *Journal des Débats politiques et littéraires* (24 April 1895).
Michel, André. 'Feuilleton du Journal des Débats of 29 August 1889. Les Beaux-Arts à l'Exposition universelle (1). Les écoles étrangères. Norvège – Suède – Danemark – Finlande'. *Journal des Débats politiques et littéraires* (29 August 1889).
–. 'Le Comité français à l'Exposition de Copenhague. Tableau de M. P.-S. Krøyer'. *Gazette des Beaux-Arts* (1 February 1890).
–. 'Feuilleton du *Journal des Débats* du vendredi soir 8 juin 1894. Les Salons de 1894. VI. De l'expression morale et du portrait'. *Journal des Débats politiques et littéraires* (8 June 1894).
–. 'Feuilleton du *Journal des Débats* du vendredi soir 24 mai 1895. Les Salons de 1895. V. L'exposition de Corot. – Quelques paysages'. *Journal des Débats politiques et littéraires* (24 May 1895).
Mitchi. 'Notes sur les Salons. Champ-de-Mars'. *La Vie parisienne* (27 April 1895).
Montaiglon, Anatole de. 'Le Salon de 1875. 1er article'. *La Gazette des Beaux-Arts* (1 June 1875).
Montifaud, Marc de. 'Exposition du boulevard des Capucines'. *L'Artiste* (1 May 1874).
'Mouvement des arts. Oeuvres de Bastien-Lepage', *La Chronique des arts et de la curiosité* (16 May 1885).
Müller, Sigurd. 'Peter Severin Krøyer'. *Illustreret Tidende*, no. 1145 (4 September 1881).
'Musée de la Chambre des Pairs. 3ième et dernier article'. *Le Moniteur universel* (7 June 1818).
'Nouvelles diverses'. *Journal des Débats politiques et littéraires* (29 May 1881).
'Nouvelles du jour. Les récompenses du Salon'. *Le Globe*, no. 752 (29 May 1881).
Oelsner, Gertrud and Karina Lykke Grand. 'Introduktion til Vilhelm Kyhn', in *Vilhelm Kyhn & det danske landskabsmaleri*, edited by Gertrud Oelsner and Karina Lykke Grand. 9–35. Aarhus University Press, 2012.
Ohlsen, Nils. 'Seks vigtige spørgsmål om Viggo Johansens akvareller', in *Skagensmaleren Viggo Johansen – Landskabernes tillokkende skønhed*, edited by Mette Harbo Lehmann and Niels H. Bünemann. 22–37. Skagens Kunstmuseer, 2019.
Olson, Donald W. 'La datation d'Impression soleil levant', in *Impression, soleil levant. L'histoire vraie du chef-d'oeuvre de Claude Monet*, edited by Dominique Lobstein and Marianne Mathieu. 80–105. Hazan, 2015.
Parkinson, Nicholas. 'Copenhagen 1888: The First Centennial of French Modern Art', unpublished.
Petersen, Carl V. (ed.). *Dansk Kunstnerliv i Firserne: i-IV: Breve til og fra P.S. Krøyer 1877–1879*. Copenhagen. Excerpt from *Tilskueren* 1925.
Polday, Henri. 'Les Intransigeants'. *La Renaissance littéraire et artistique* (3 May 1874).
Porsmose, Erland. *Johannes Larsen. Menneske, kunstner og naturoplevelser*. Gyldendal, 1999.
Pothey, Alexandre. 'Chronique'. *La Presse* (31 March 1876).
Proth, Mario. *Voyage au pays des peintres. Salon Universel de 1878*. Ludovic Baschet, 1879.
Rabelais, François. *The Complete Works of François Rabelais*, translated by Donald M. Frame, with a Foreword by Raymond C. La Charité. University of California Press, 1991.
République française. Ministère du Commerce et de l'Industrie. Exposition Universelle de Barcelone. Catalogue officiel de la section française. Ed. Monnier & Co, 1888.
Rewald, John. *The History of Impressionism*. The Museum of Modern Art, 1946.
Röstorp, Vibeke. *Le mythe du retour les artistes scandinaves en France de 1889 à 1908*. Stockholms Universitets Förlag, 2013.
–. *Zorn och Frankrike*. Mora, Zornmuseet, 2017.
–. 'Third Culture Artists: Scandinavians in Paris', in *Imagined Cosmopolis. Internationalism and Cultural Exchange, 1870–1920s*, edited by Grace Brockington et al. 165–183. Peter Lang Verlag, 2019.
Sanchez, Pierre. *Les expositions de la Galerie Georges Petit 1881–1934. Répertoire des artistes et liste de leurs oeuvres*. 4 vols. 1963 (2011). Dijon, Echelle de Jacob.
Scavenius, Bente. *Den frie Udstilling i 100 år*. Borgen, 1991
Seigneur, Maurice du. *L'Art et les artistes au Salon de 1880*. Paul Ollendorf, 1880.
Silvestre, Armand. 'Chronique des beaux-arts: Physiologie du refusé. – L'Exposition des révoltés'. *L'Opinion nationale* (22 April 1874).
Sizeranne, Robert de la. 'Les Portraits d'homme aux Salons de 1898'. *Revue des Deux Mondes* (1 June 1898).
Stop. 'Le Salon de 1872'. *Le Journal amusant* (1 June 1872).
Sureau, Jean-Yves. *Les rues de Reims: mémoire de la ville*. Reims, Ed. Sureau, 2002.

Svanholm, Lise (ed.). *Skagen Leksikon. Malerne, modellerne og stederne*. Gyldendal, 2003.

Svenningsen, Jesper. 'Chronology – Krøyer's life and movements', in *Krøyer. An International Perspective*, edited by Marianne Saabye. 328–333. The Hirschsprung Collection and Skagens Museum, 2011.

Saabye, Marianne. *Hirschsprung. Kunstsamler og mæcen*. Den Hirschsprungske Samling, 2002.

–. '1879 Cernay-la-Ville', in *Krøyer. An International Perspective*, edited by Marianne Saabye. 180–183. The Hirschsprung Collection and Skagens Museum, 2011.

–. '1880–81 Naples, Rome & Paris', in *Krøyer. An internationalt perspective*, edited by Marianne Saabye. 204–210. The Hirschsprung Collection and Skagens Museum, 2011.

–. 'Krøyer & Bastien-Lepage', in *Krøyer. An International Perspective*, edited by Marianne Saabye. 24–32. The Hirschsprung Collection and Skagens Museum, 2011.

–. 'Krøyer & Edelfelt', in *Krøyer. An International Perspective*, edited by Marianne Saabye. 84–90. Den Hirschsprungske Samling and Skagens Museum, 2011.

–. 'P.S. Krøyer, Pasquale Fosca and the Neapolitan art scene', in *Analecta Romana Instituti Danici*. 143–177. Accademia di Danimarca, 2019.

Saabye, Marianne (ed.). *Krøyer. An International Perspective*. The Hirschsprung Collection and Skagens Museum, 2011.

'The Copenhagen Exhibition (by special service)'. *Le Matin* (12 June 1888).

Thomson, Richard. *Art of the Actual: Naturalism and Style in Early Third Republic France, 1880–1900*. Yale University Press, 2012.

Thiébault-Sisson. 'Le Salon du Champ de Mars'. *Supplément au journal Le Temps*, no. 12383 (24 April 1895).

Tisserand, Louis Eugène. Études économiques sur le Holstein, le Slesvig [sic] *et le Danemark*. Masson, 1865.

Tuxen, Laurits. *En Malers Arbejde gennem tredsindstyve Aar fortalt af ham selv*. Jespersens and Pios Forlag, 1928.

Vachon, Marius. 'Le Salon de 1880. Section de peinture. VIII Les étrangers'. *La France* (4 June 1880).

–. 'Le Salon de 1881'. *La France* (1 May 1881).

Vad, Poul. *Hammershøi*. Gyldendal, 1988.

Vaisse, Pierre. *La Troisième République et les peintres*. Flammarion, 1995.

Van Gogh, Vincent. *The Letters*, vols. 4 and 5. Van Gogh Museum, 2009.

Véron, Pierre. 'Chronique parisienne. Le Salon de 1877'. *Le Journal amusant* (12 May 1877).

Véron, Théodore. *Dictionnaire Véron: ou mémorial de l'art et des artistes de mon temps*. Chez M. Bazin; Chez l'Auteur, 1827.

Voterro, M. '"Je leur donne le meilleur de mon âme et de ma vie". L'enseignement d'Alexandre Cabanel à l'Ecole des Beaux-Arts (1864–1889)', in *Alexandre Cabanel, la tradition du beau*, edited by Michel Hilaire. 414–429. Somogy Editions, 2010.

Weisberg, Gabriel. *Beyond Impressionism. The Naturalist impulse in European art 1860–1905*. Thames and Hudson, 1992.

Wellington, Hubert (ed.). *The Journal of Eugène Delacroix*, translated by Lucy Norton. Phaidon Press, 1995 (1951).

Willumsen, Jens Ferdinand. *Mine erindringer fortalt til Ernst Mentze*. Berlingske Forlag, 1953.

Wolff, Albert. 'Le Salon de 1873'. *Le Figaro* (10 May 1873).

–. 'Courrier de Paris'. *Le Figaro* (9 June 1988).

Wyzewa, T. de. 'Le Salon de 1894 (premier article)'. *Gazette des Beaux-Arts* (1 June 1894).

Zahrtmann, Kristian. 'Om Vilhelm Hammershøi'. *Berlingske Politiske og Avertissementstidende, Aften* (14 February 1916).

Zola, Émile. 'Le Naturalisme au Salon. III'. *Le Voltaire* (21 June 1880).

–. *Ecrits sur l'art, introduced and annotated by Jean-Pierre Leduc-Adine*. Gallimard, Collection Tel, 1991.

About the Authors

Mette Harbo Lehmann

Born 1976
Mag.art. (MA – research degree) in art history from Aarhus University, curator at the Art Museums of Skagen. Lehmann curates exhibitions, conducts research, and prepares learning and dissemination materials. Her endeavours have centred on the artists' colony in Skagen, with particular emphasis on Viggo Johansen, Holger Drachmann, and Peder Severin Krøyer.

Among other things, Lehmann's research activity has resulted in exhibitions about building customs and artists' studios in Skagen, Axel Locher's sculptures, Viggo Johansen's watercolours, and Johannes Wilhjelm's travels, as well as a retrospective on Holger Drachmann and his works. In 2020–2021, she was co-curator of *L'heure bleue de Peder Severin Krøyer* at the Musée Marmottan Monet in Paris.

Dominique Lobstein

Born 1953
After studying economics and art history, Dominique Lobstein entered the Musée d'Orsay's research department and subsequently became head of the museum library. Since 2013, he has continued to publish as an independent researcher, focusing mainly on academic painting and its collectors, as well as on the history of official art events. This has led him to study the work of various non-French artists, among them Joaquín Sorolla y Bastida (2011, Musée de l'Orangerie) and Peder Severin Krøyer (2021, Musée Marmottan Monet).

Lobstein's current research is on the painter Théodule Ribot, to whom he devoted a solo exhibition in 2018 at the Musée Roybet Fould in Courbevoie. In 2021–2022, he is also taking part in a travelling exhibition on this artist, to be held in Toulouse, Marseille, and Caen. In 2022 Lobstein will curate an exhibition on the portrayal of emotions from the Middle Ages to the 21st century, together with the historian Georges Vigarello.

Index of persons

Page numbers in **bold** refer to illustrations and captions.

Photographic Credits

© Beaux-Arts de Paris, Dist. RMN-Grand Palais / image Beaux-Arts de Paris 28
© RMN-Grand Palais (Musée d'Orsay) / Stéphane Maréchalle 29, 153, 172–173, 174, 181
Archives nationales, site de Pierrefitte-sur-Seine 31 top
© RMN-Grand Palais (Musée d'Orsay) / image RMN-GP 31 bottom
© RMN-Grand Palais (Musée d'Orsay) / Hervé Lewandowski 32, 38, 76, 79, 88–89, 102, 158, 163, 168–169, 170, 209, 230tv, 248, 266, 271, 290–291
© RMN-Grand Palais (Musée du Louvre) / René-Gabriel Ojeda 36
Skagens Kunstmuseer 40, 47, 53, 55, 56, 63, 68–69, 71, 106 top, 111, 112, 120–121, 125, 126, 144–145, 188, 191, 192, 217, 225, 246–247, 275, 278–280, 283
SMK Foto / Jakob Skou-Hansen 41, 50–51, 64, 67, 117, 134–135, 195, 214–215, 243, 282
Det Kgl. Bibliotek 43, 267
Stockholms Auktionsværk 60
© M.Petit / Ville de Verdun – Musée de la Princerie 74, 167
© Paris Musées / Petit Palais, Musée des Beaux-Arts de la Ville de Paris 80, 284–285
© RMN-Grand Palais (Musée du Louvre) / Philippe Fuzeau 84
© Musée Marmottan Monet, Académie des beaux-arts, Paris / Christian Baraja SLB 85, 237, 298–299, 304–305, 310–311
Städel Museum, Frankfurt am Main 86
© The Metropolitan Museum of Art, Dist. RMN-Grand Palais / image MMA 90, 151, 235
The Walters Art Museum, Baltimore 92
Ny Carlsberg Glyptotek, Copenhagen 257, 270
Ny Carlsberg Glyptotek, Copenhagen / Ole Haupt 94, 96, 264–265
© Artefact / Alamy Stock Photo 97
© RMN-Grand Palais (Musée d'Orsay) / Martine Beck-Coppola 98, 150, 246
© Artepics / Alamy Stock Photo 101
The J. Paul Getty Museum, Los Angeles 105
Bruun Rasmussen Kunstauktioner 106 bottom, 197

© Den Hirschsprungske Samling 115, 140–141, 205, 227, 250–251, 260–261
Gothenburg Museum of Art, Sweden 118, 154
Universitätsbibliothek Heidelberg, Digitale Bibliothek 123
Gallica Digital Library 129
The Walters Art Museum, Baltimore 133
Denis Vidalie © Musée des beaux-arts, monastère royal de Brou 136–137
Photograph © Museum of Fine Arts, Boston 138
Det Nationalhistoriske Museum på Frederiksborg Slot / Kit Weiss 142, 268
© Beaux-Arts de Paris, Dist. RMN-Grand Palais / image Beaux-Arts de Paris 147
© Mairie de Bordeaux / F. Deval 149
© Michel Petit / Collection du Musée Barrois, Bar-le-Duc (France) 152
© Musée de Picardie, Amiens / Irwin Leullier 156–157
© RMN-Grand Palais / René-Gabriel Ojeda 160
Arras, Musée des Beaux-Arts, Musée d'Orsay reserve collection 161
© Bibliothèque de l'Académie nationale de médecine (Paris) / Philippe Fuzeau 162
© RMN-Grand Palais (Château de Versailles) / Gérard Blot 164
© Bibliothèque de l'Académie nationale de médecine (Paris) / Philippe Fuzeau 165
Sammlung Emil Bührle, Dauerleihgabe im Kunsthaus Zürich 171
© Reims, Musée des Beaux-Arts / C. Devleeschauwer 176–177, 182–183
© Musée d'Orsay, Dist. RMN-Grand Palais / Patrice Schmidt 179
Musée de Saint-Maur, Villa Médicis / Thierry Ollivier 184–185
© RMN-Grand Palais / Benoît Touchard 187
National Gallery of Art, Washington 193
© Musée des Beaux-arts et de la Dentelle, Alençon (France) / David Commenchal 196
Ribe Kunstmuseum 200–201
Jack Varlet / Musée Charles de Bruyères, Remiremont 202–203

© RMN-Grand Palais / Thierry Ollivier 204
Georgi Iliev / Musée d'art et d'histoire de Saint-Brieuc 206, 224
Musée des Beaux-Arts, Quimper, France 207, 218th
© Y. Deslandes /Réunion des Musées Métropolitains Rouen Normandie 210–211
© Mairie de Bordeaux / F. Deval 212–213
Musée des Beaux-Arts, Dunkerque, France 218 left
Kunstmuseum Den Haag 219
© Evreux, Musée d'Art, Histoire et Archéologie 220–221
© Musée de Pont-Aven / Bernard Galéron 223
Collection of the Museum of Fine Arts, Tournai (Belgium) 229, 233
© RMN-Grand Palais (Musée du Louvre) – © Hervé Lewandowski 230 right
© MAD, Paris / Jean Tholance 234
© CSG CIC Glasgow Museums Collection 236 left
© National Galleries of Scotland, Dist. RMN-Grand Palais – © Scottish National Gallery Photographic Department 236 right
© RMN-Grand Palais – © Philipp Bernard 239
© Artefact / Alamy Stock Photo 240
Marc Jeanneteau / Musée de Picardie 241
© RMN-Grand Palais (Musée d'Orsay) – © Gérard Blot / Hervé Lewandowski 253, 254–255
National Gallery of Victoria, Melbourne 272
© Jacques Boulissière / Musée de La Roche-sur-Yon (France) 280–281
© RMN-Grand Palais (Musée d'Orsay) / Thierry Le Mage 288–289
© Musée Marmottan Monet, Académie des beaux-arts, Paris 294–295, 296–297, 300–301, 302–303, 306–307, 308–309, 312–313, 327–336

Krøyer and Paris. French Connections and Nordic Colours

Cover: Peder Severin Krøyer: *Fishermen Hauling a Seine Net at Skagen Nordstrand. Late Afternoon,* 1883 (detail). Skagens Kunstmuseer

Authors: Mette Harbo Lehmann and Dominique Lobstein
Editorial board: Mette Harbo Lehmann,
Dominique Lobstein, and Anne Walther
Publishing editor: Cecilie Harrits
Translation from French, including quotes from sources:
Avantigruppen
Translation from Danish, including quotes from sources:
René Lauritsen
Proofreading: Mia Gaudern
Design: Carl-H.K. Zakrisson

Typeset with Lyon and printed on Perigord 135 g
at Narayana Press, Gylling

Printed in Denmark 2022
ISBN 978 87 7219 896 5

Skagens Kunstmuseer
skagenskunstmuseer.dk

Aarhus University Press
unipress.dk

Musée Marmottan Monet
marmottan.fr

Published to coincide with the exhibition
Krøyer and Paris. French Connections and Nordic Colours
at Skagens Museum: 13 May – 18 September 2022

The introduction and chapters 1-7 are peer reviewed.

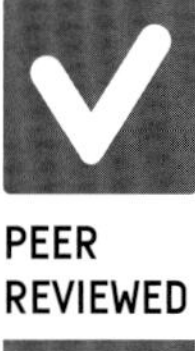

PEER
REVIEWED

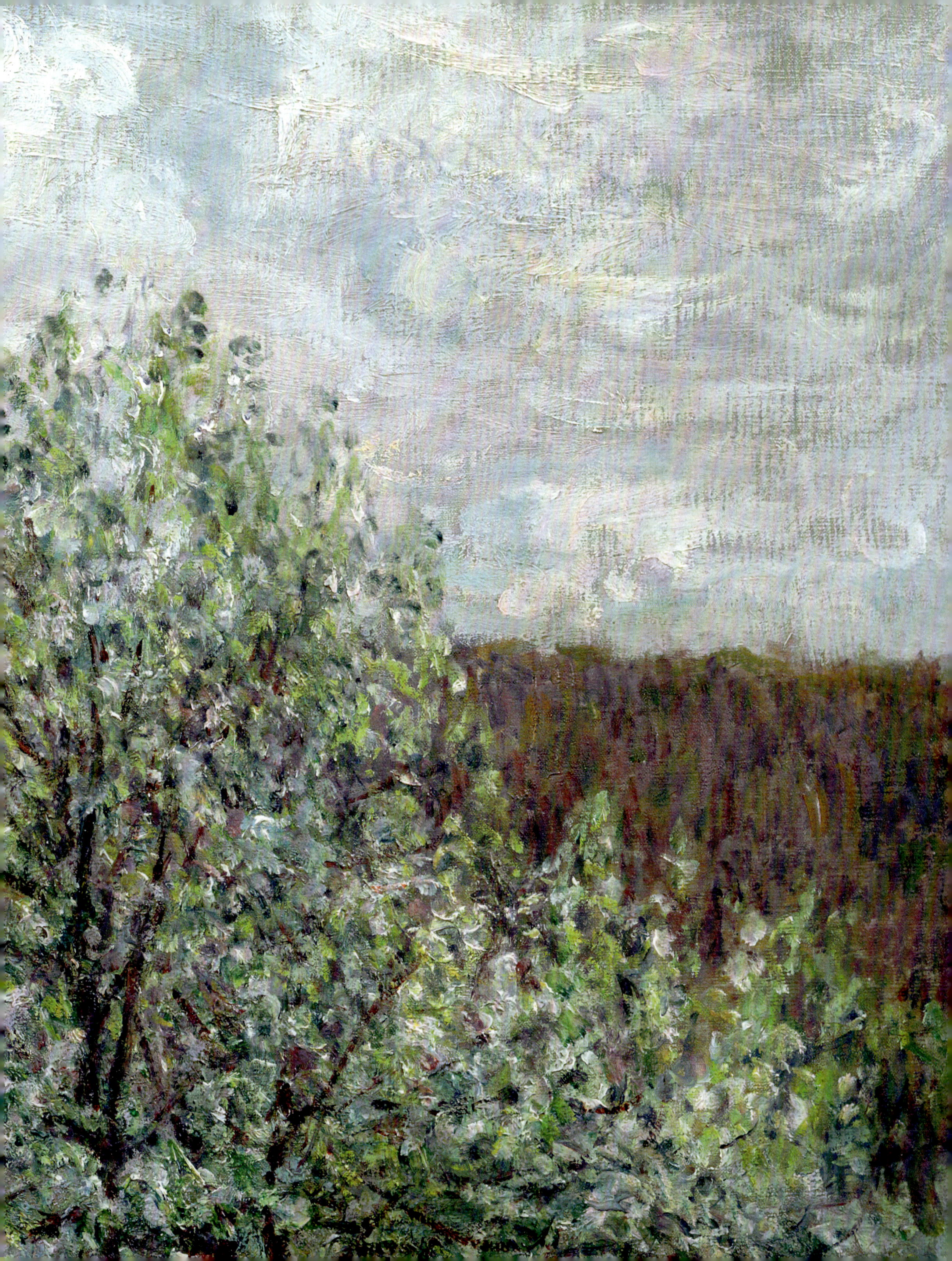

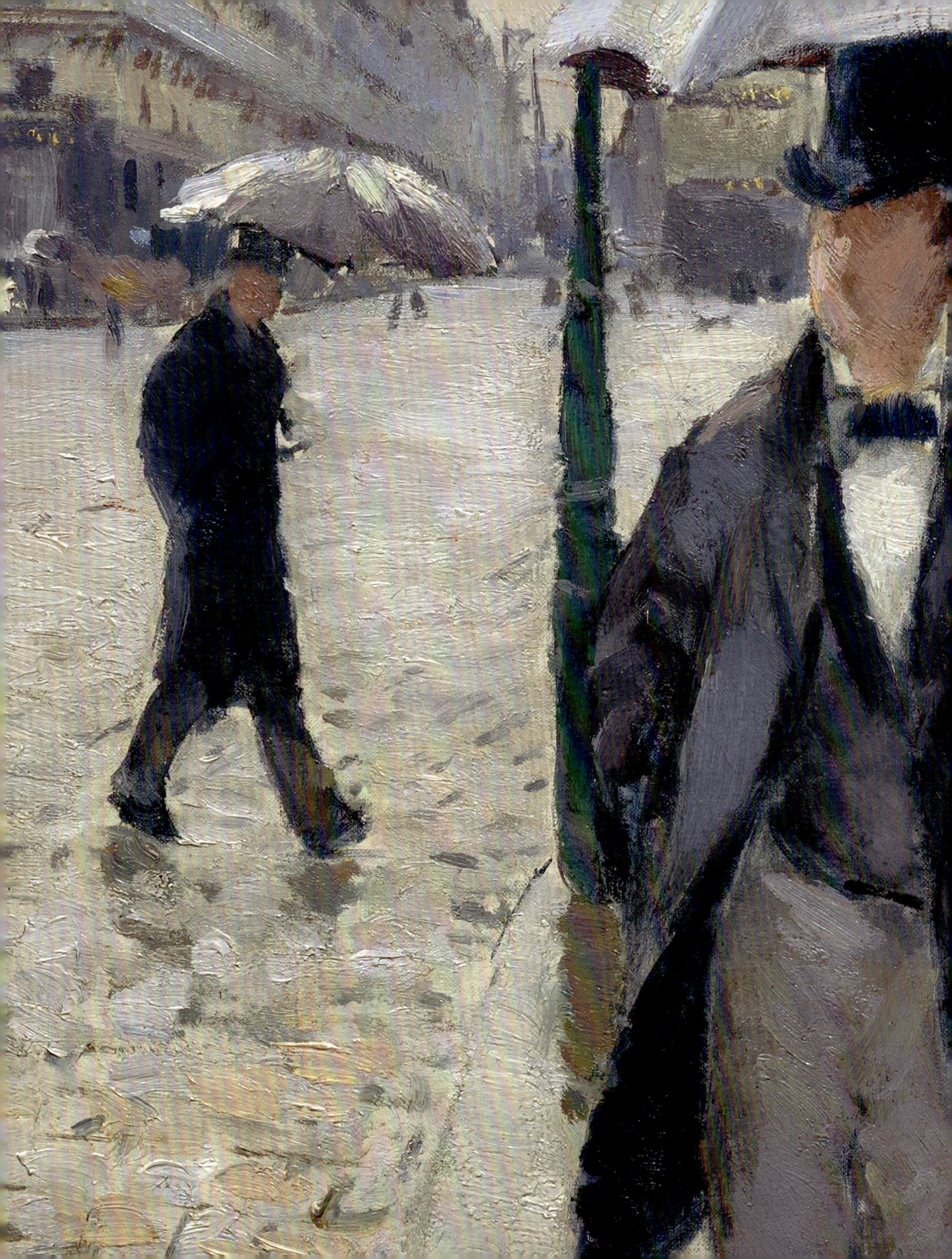

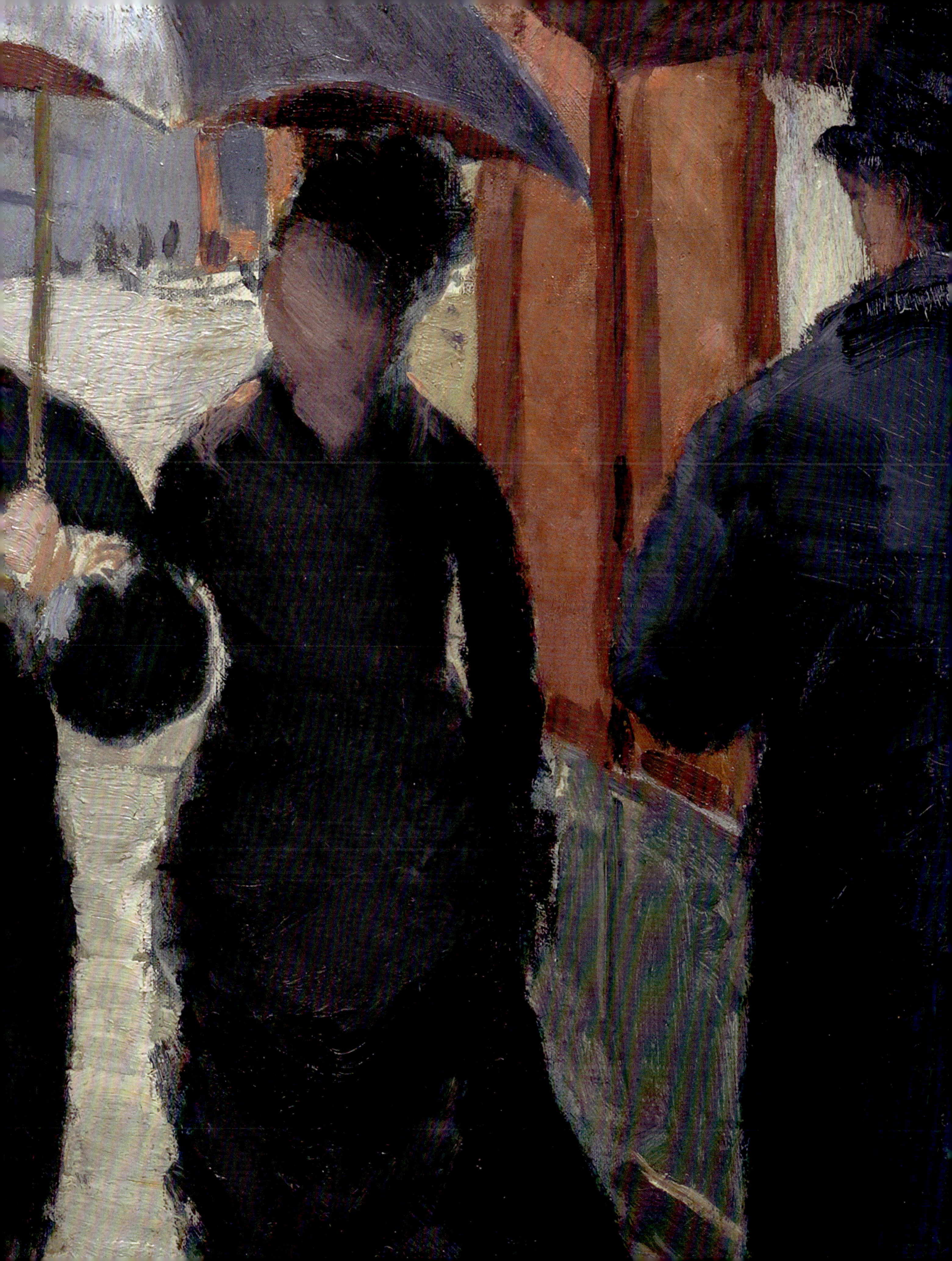

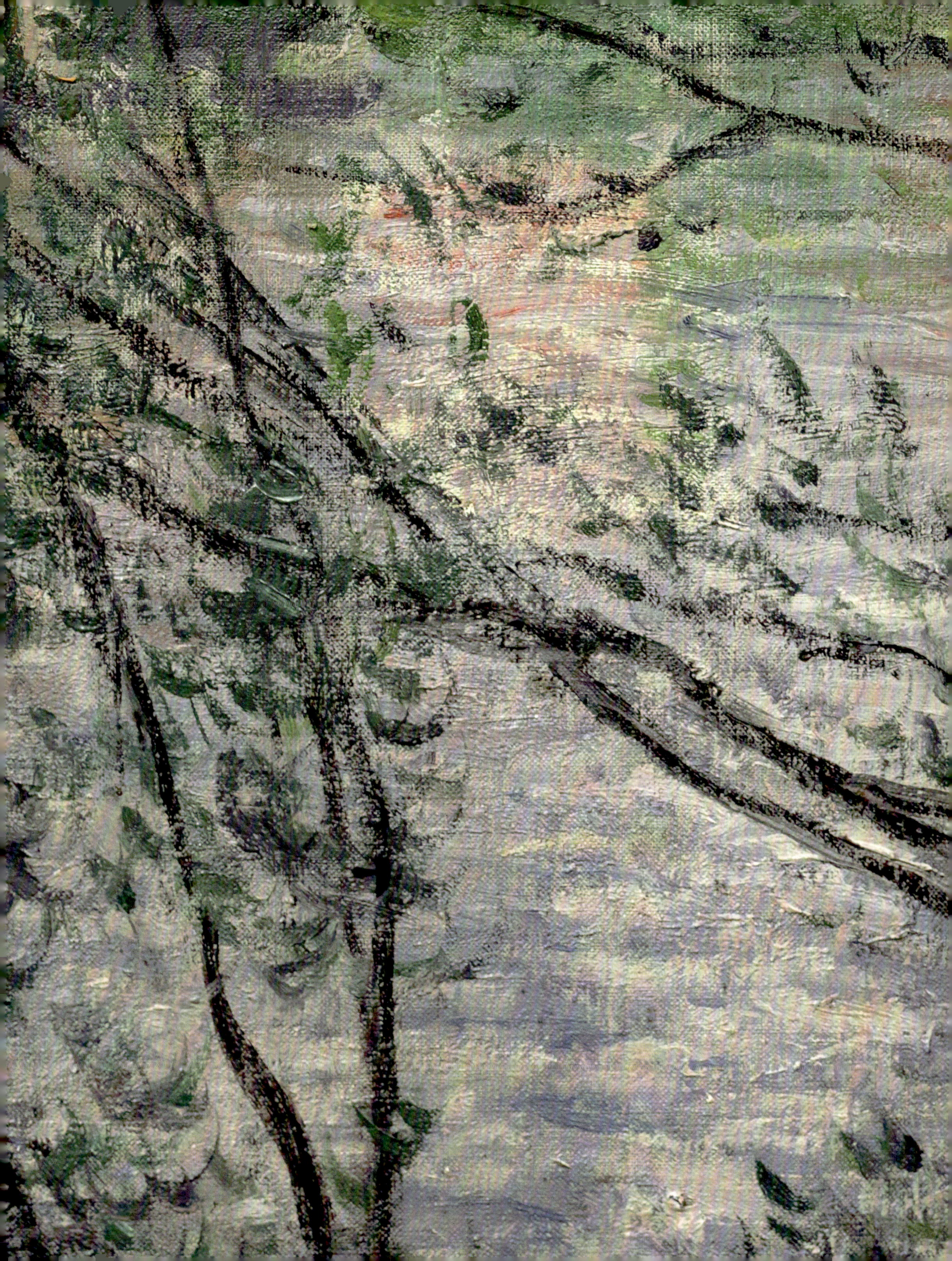

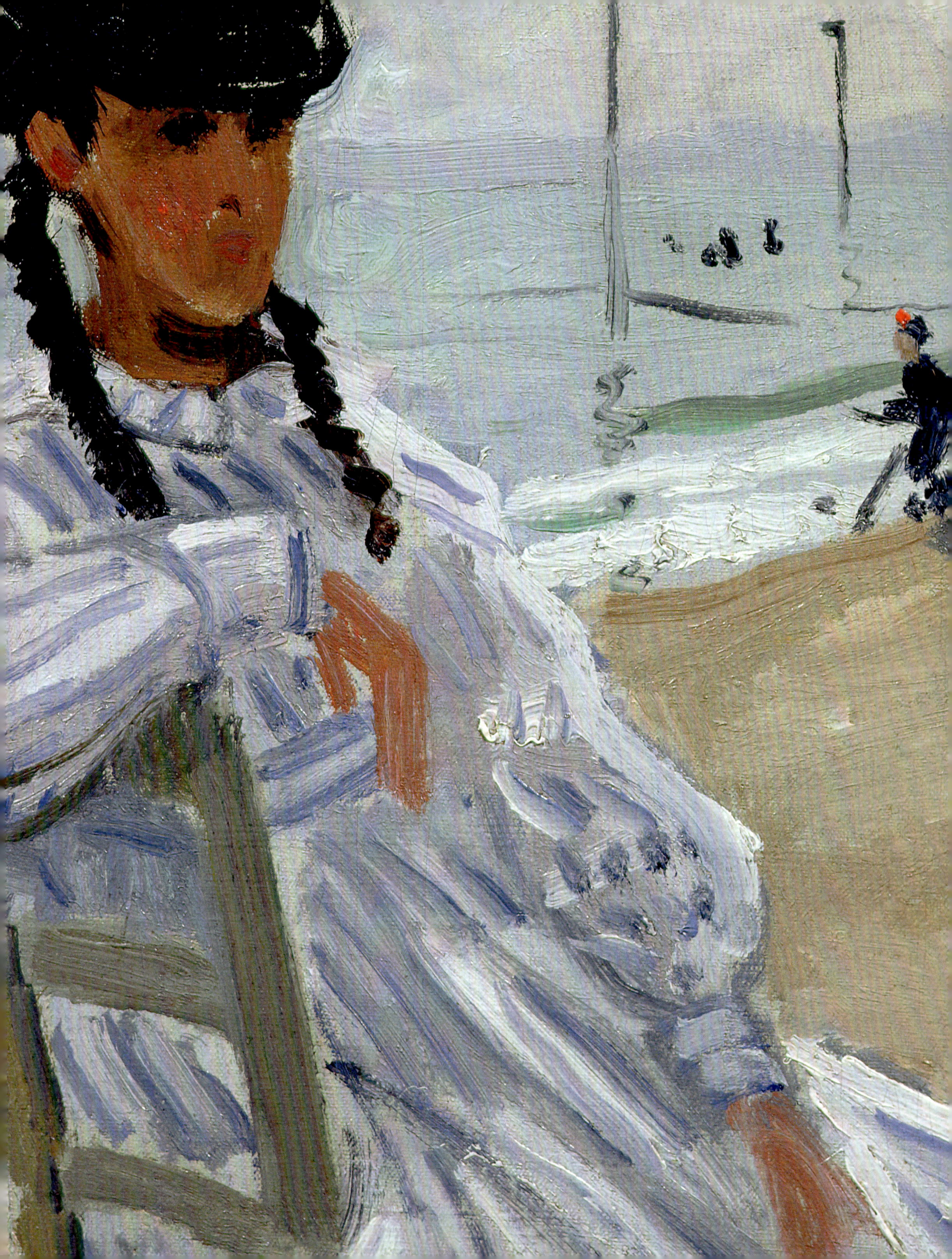

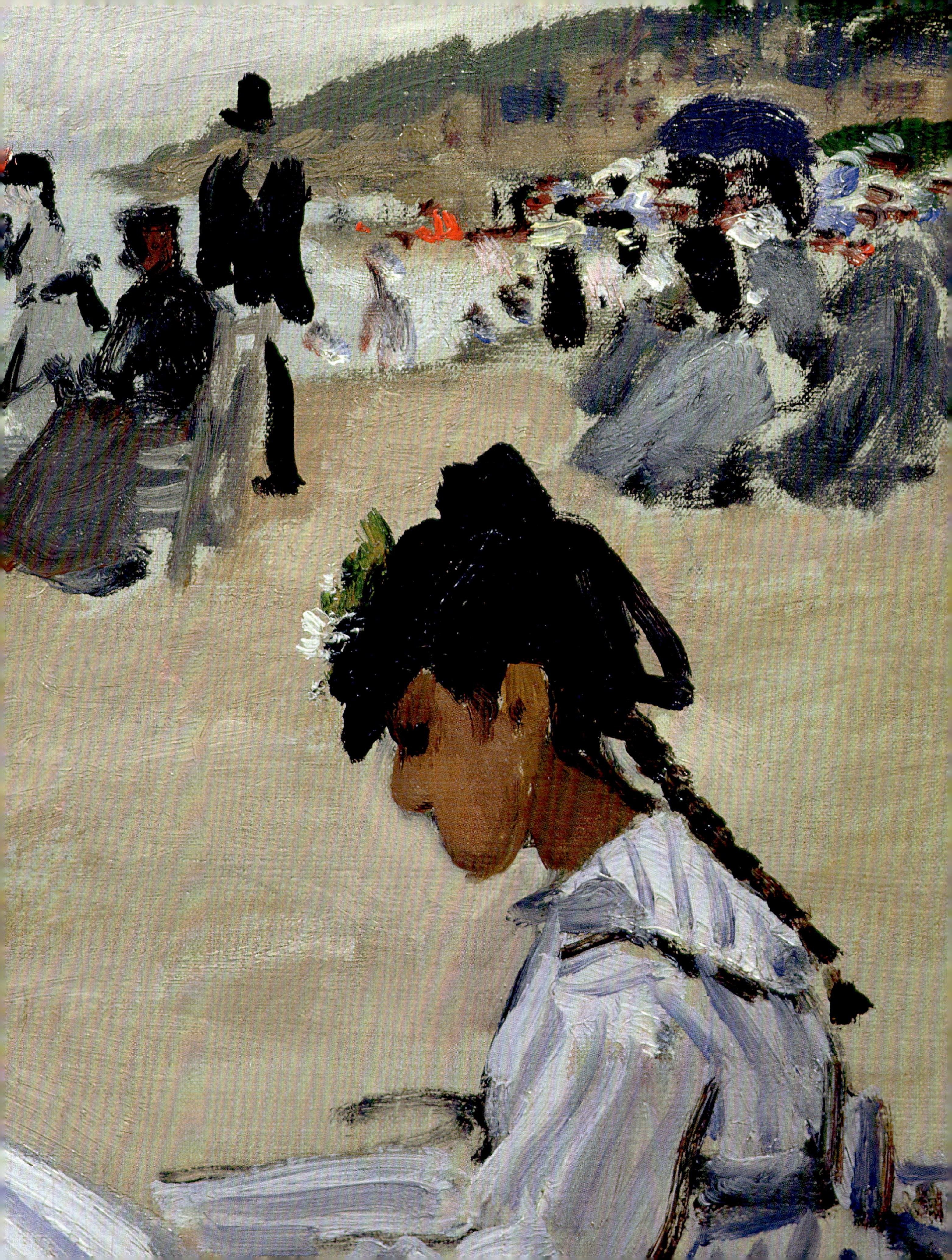

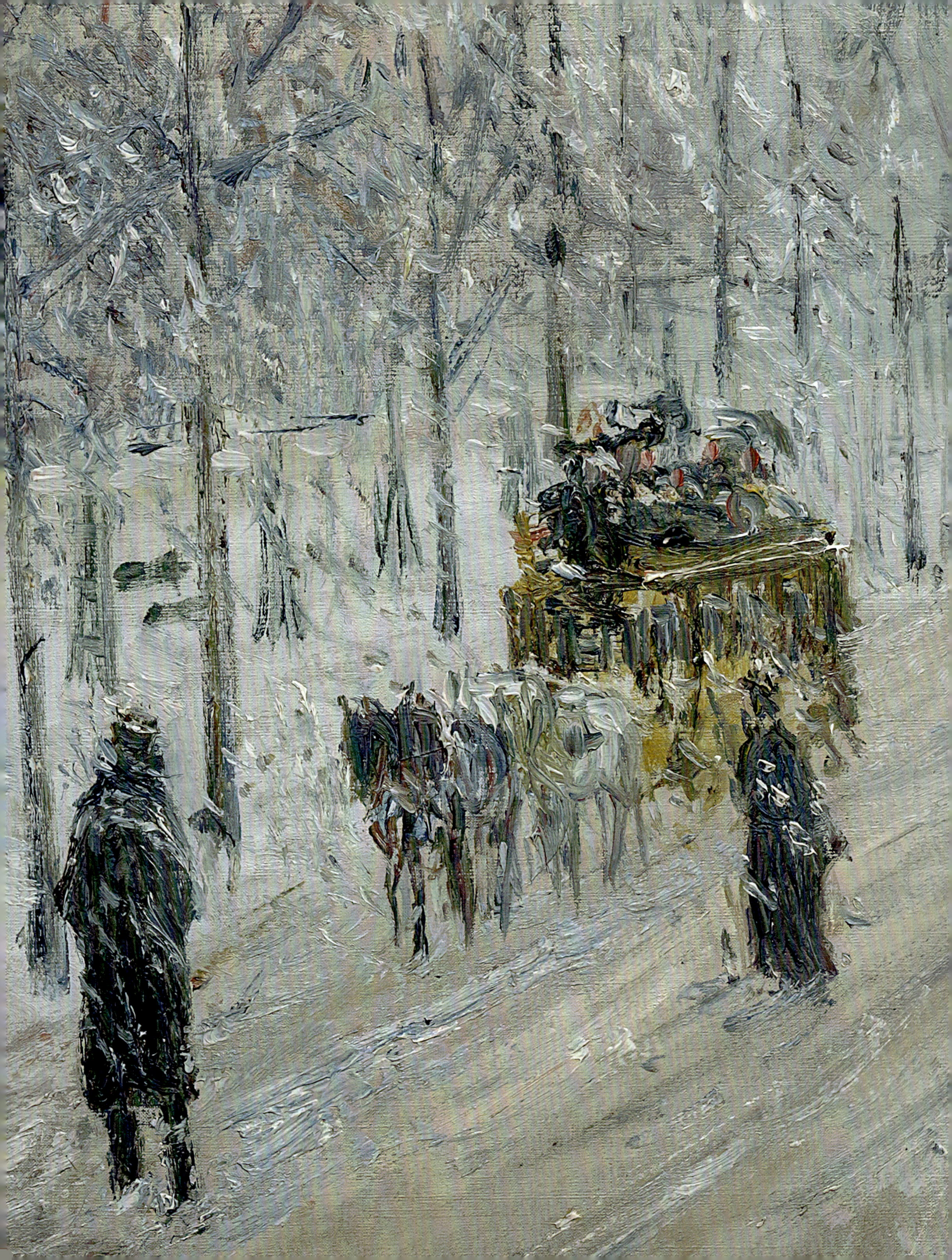

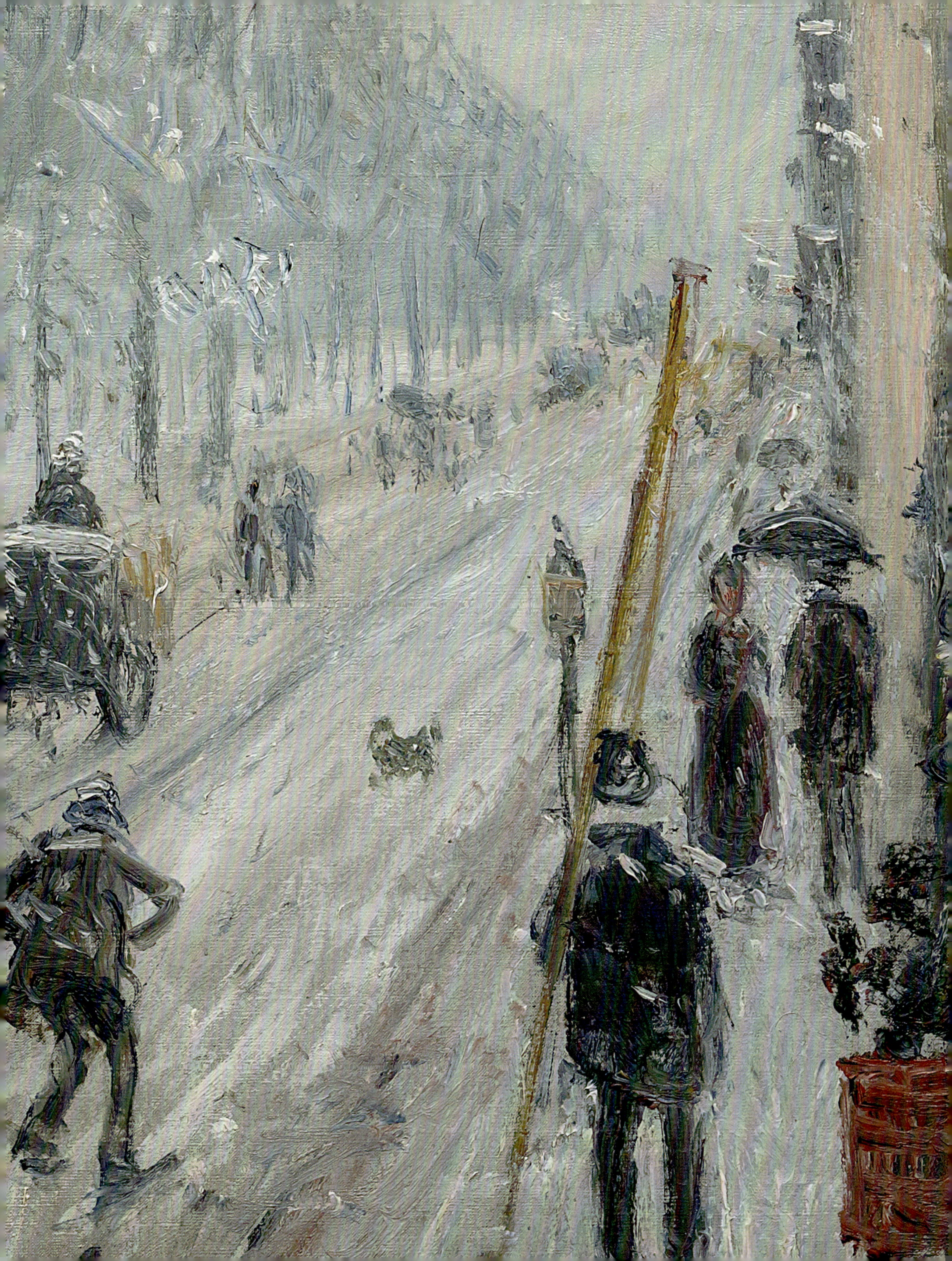

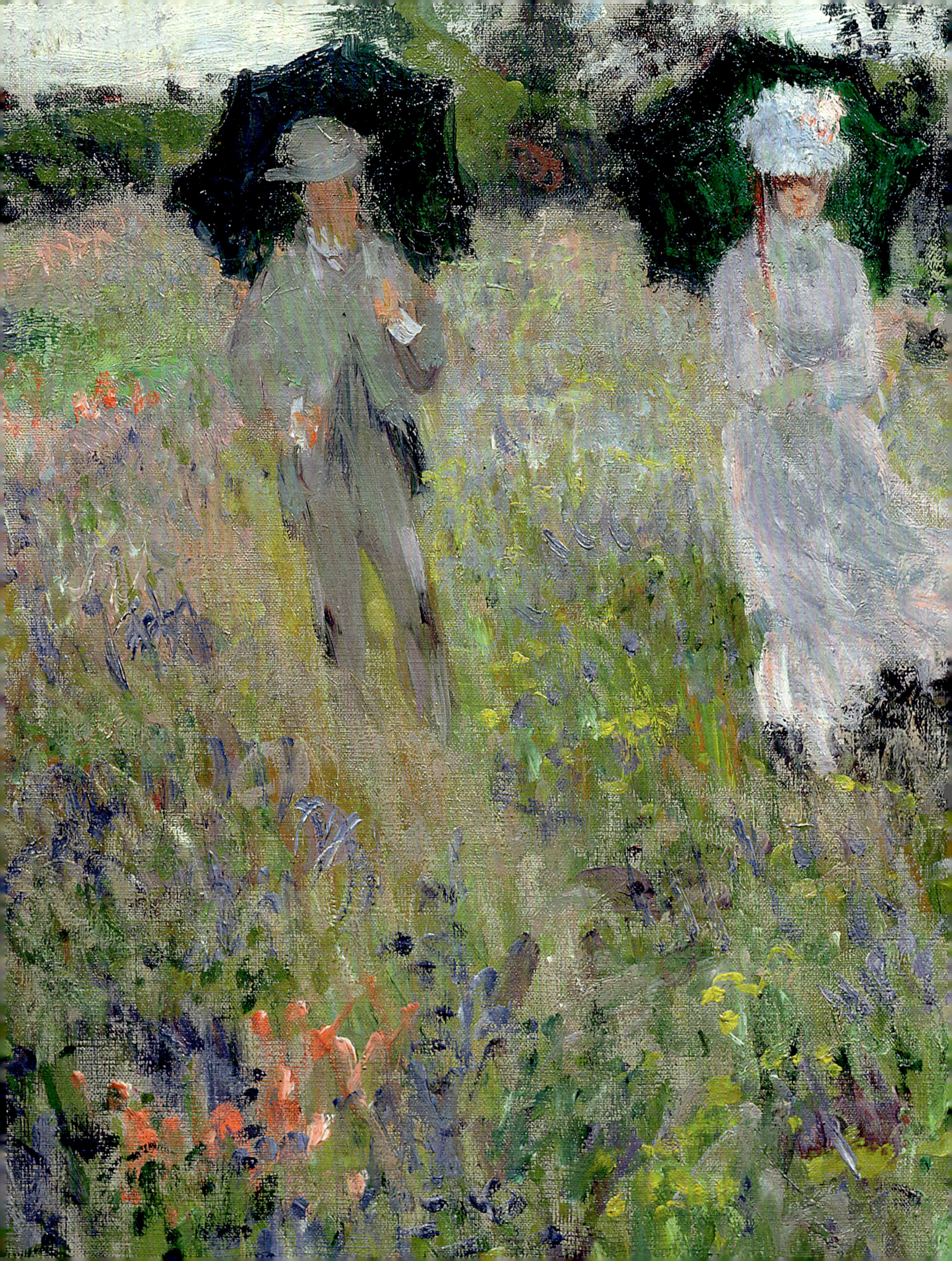

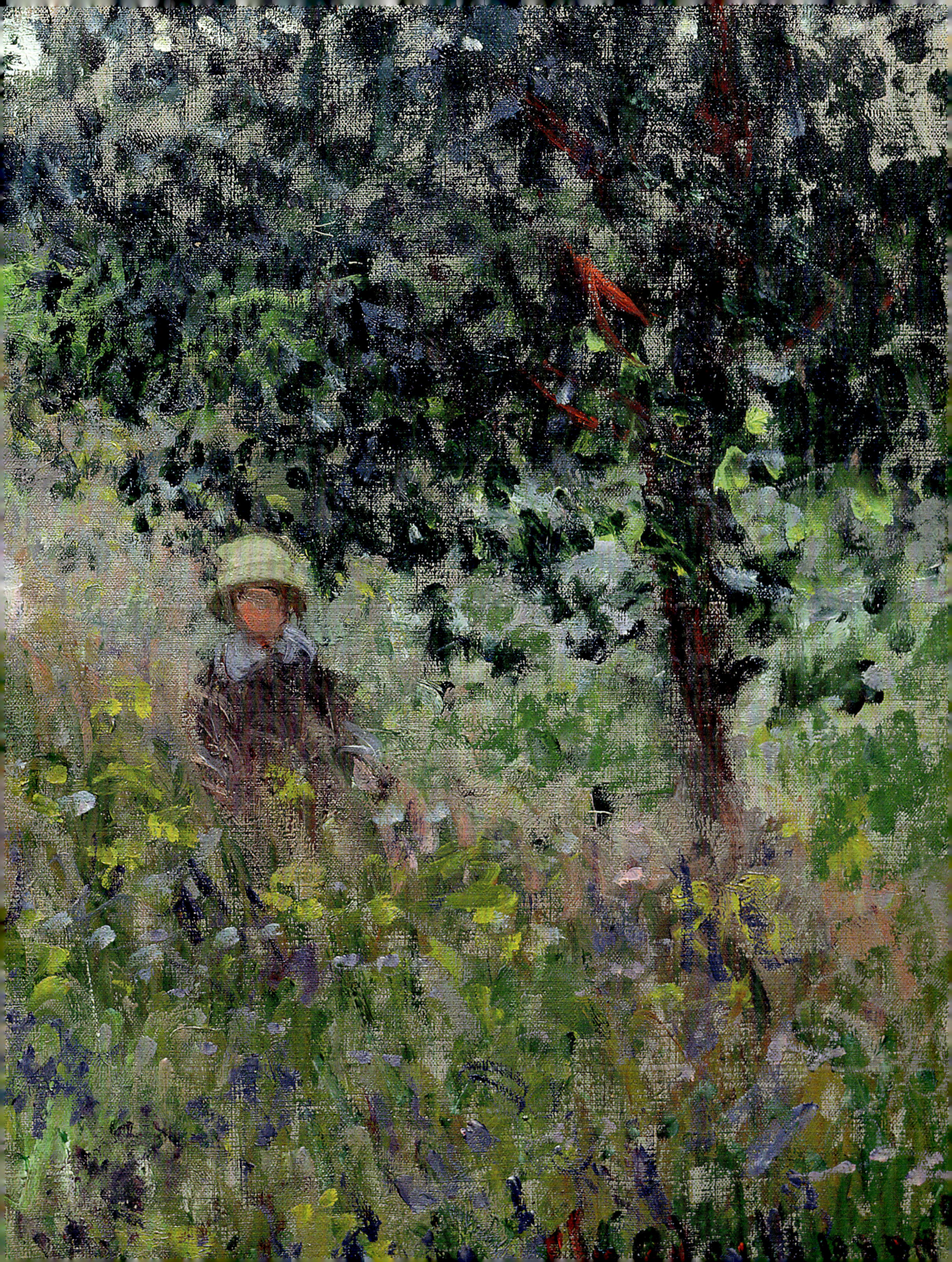

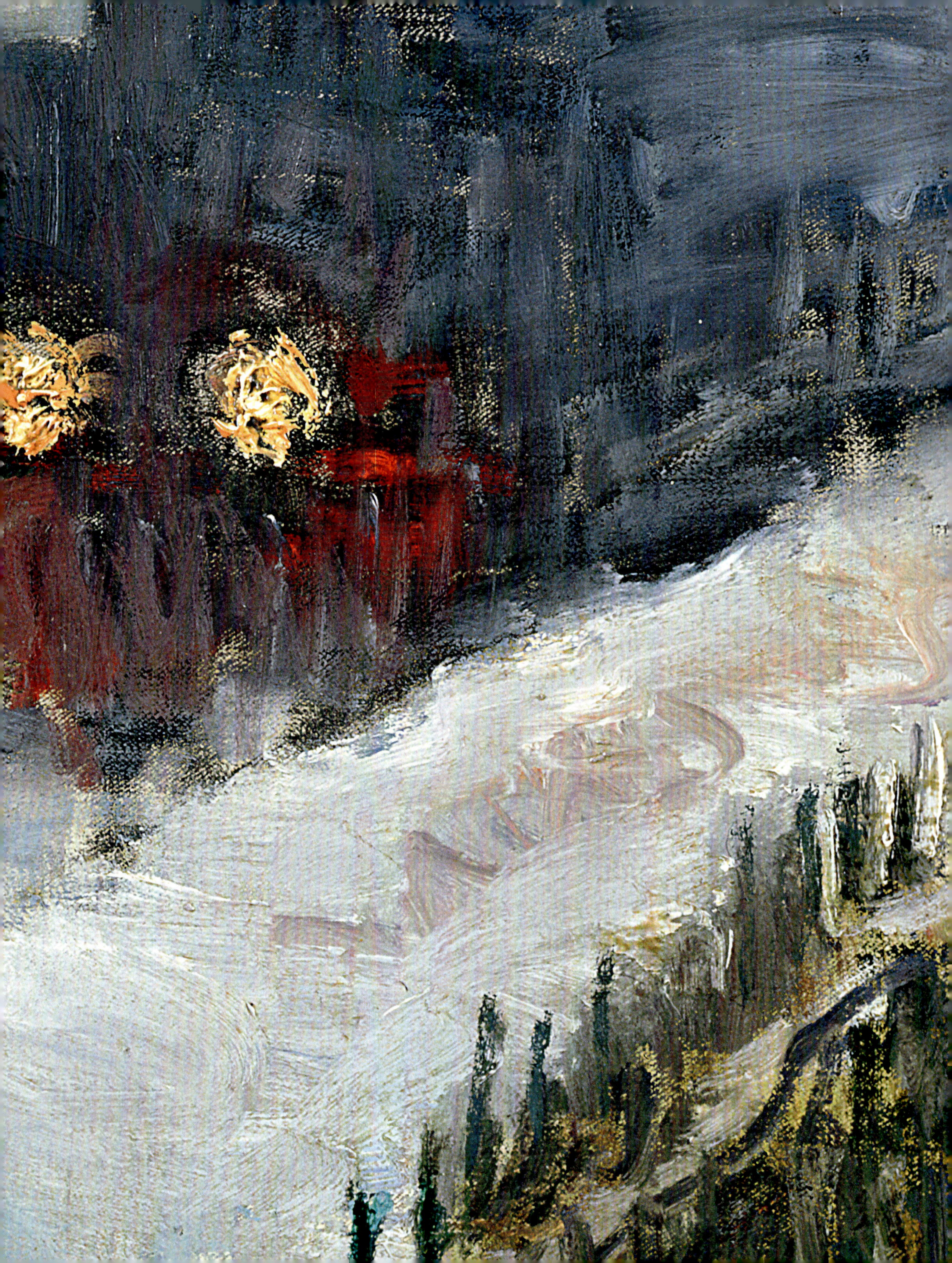